Children's
Literature
Review

Guide to Gale Literary Criticism Series

When you need to review criticism of literary works, these are the Gale series to use:

If the author's death date is: **You should turn to:**

After Dec. 31, 1959
(or author is still living)

CONTEMPORARY LITERARY CRITICISM

for example: Jorge Luis Borges, Anthony Burgess,
William Faulkner, Mary Gordon,
Ernest Hemingway, Iris Murdoch

1900 through 1959

TWENTIETH-CENTURY LITERARY CRITICISM

for example: Willa Cather, F. Scott Fitzgerald,
Henry James, Mark Twain, Virginia Woolf

1800 through 1899

NINETEENTH-CENTURY LITERATURE CRITICISM

for example: Fedor Dostoevski, Nathaniel Hawthorne,
George Sand, William Wordsworth

1400 through 1799

LITERATURE CRITICISM FROM 1400 TO 1800
(excluding Shakespeare)

for example: Anne Bradstreet, Daniel Defoe,
Alexander Pope, François Rabelais,
Jonathan Swift, Phillis Wheatley

SHAKESPEAREAN CRITICISM

Shakespeare's plays and poetry

Antiquity through 1399

CLASSICAL AND MEDIEVAL LITERATURE CRITICISM

for example: Dante, Homer, Plato, Sophocles, Vergil,
the Beowulf Poet

Gale also publishes related criticism series:

CHILDREN'S LITERATURE REVIEW

This series covers authors of all eras who have written for the
preschool through high school audience.

SHORT STORY CRITICISM

This series covers the major short fiction writers of all nationalities
and periods of literary history.

ISSN 0362-4145

volume 18

Children's Literature Review

Excerpts from Reviews,
Criticism, and Commentary
on Books for Children
and Young People

Gerard J. Senick
Editor

Sharon R. Gunton
Associate Editor

 *Gale Research Inc.*
Book Tower
Detroit, Michigan 48226

STAFF

Gerard J. Senick, *Editor*

Sharon R. Gunton, *Associate Editor*

Susan Miller Harig, Melissa Reiff Hug, Motoko Fujishiro Huthwaite, *Assistant Editors*

Jeanne A. Gough, *Permissions & Production Manager*
Linda M. Pugliese, *Production Supervisor*
Jennifer E. Gale, Maureen A. Puhl, Suzanne Powers, Lee Ann Welsh, *Editorial Associates*
Donna Craft, Christine A. Galbraith, David G. Oblender, Linda M. Ross, *Editorial Assistants*

Victoria B. Cariappa, *Research Supervisor*
Karen D. Kaus, Eric Priehs, Maureen R. Richards, Mary D. Wise, *Editorial Associates*
Rogene M. Fisher, Kevin B. Hillstrom, Filomena Sgambati, *Editorial Assistants*

Sandra C. Davis, *Permissions Supervisor (Text)*
H. Diane Cooper, Kathy Grell, Josephine M. Keene, Kimberly F. Smilay, *Permissions Associates*
Maria Franklin, Camille P. Robinson, Shalice Shah, Denise M. Singleton, Lisa M. Wimmer, *Permissions Assistants*

Patricia A. Seefelt, *Permissions Supervisor (Pictures)*
Margaret A. Chamberlain, *Permissions Associate*
Pamela A. Hayes, Lillian Quickly, *Permissions Assistants*

Mary Beth Trimper, *Production Manager*
Anthony J. Scolaro, *External Production Assistant*

Arthur Chartow, *Art Director*
C. J. Jonik, *Keyliner*

Laura Bryant, *Production Supervisor*
Louise Gagné, *Internal Production Associate*
Michelle M. Stepherson, *Data Entry Associate*
Shelly Andrews, *Internal Production Assistant*

Library of Congress Catalog Card Number 76-643301
ISBN 0-8103-2778-3
ISSN 0362-4145

Printed in the United States of America

CONTENTS

PREFACE

As children's literature has evolved into both a respected branch of creative writing and a successful industry, literary criticism has documented and influenced each stage of its growth. Critics have recorded the literary development of individual authors as well as the trends and controversies that resulted from changes in values and attitudes, especially as they concerned children. While defining a philosophy of children's literature, critics developed a scholarship that balances an appreciation of children and an awareness of their needs with standards for literary quality much like those required by critics of adult literature. *Children's Literature Review (CLR)* is designed to provide a permanent, accessible record of this ongoing scholarship. Those responsible for bringing children and books together can now make informed choices when selecting reading materials for the young.

Scope of the Series

Each volume of *CLR* contains excerpts from published criticism on the works of authors and illustrators who create books for children from preschool through high school. The author list for each volume is international in scope and represents the variety of genres covered by children's literature—picture books, fiction, folklore, nonfiction, poetry, and drama. The works of approximately twenty authors of all eras are represented in each volume. Although earlier volumes of *CLR* emphasized critical material published after 1960, successive volumes have expanded their coverage to encompass criticism written before 1960. Since many of the authors included in *CLR* are living and continue to write, it is necessary to update their entries periodically. Thus, future volumes will supplement the entries of selected authors covered in earlier volumes as well as include criticism on the works of authors new to the series.

Organization of the Book

An author section consists of the following elements: author heading, author portrait, author introduction, excerpts of criticism (each followed by a bibliographical citation), and illustrations, when available.

- The **author heading** consists of the author's full name followed by birth and death dates. The portion of the name outside the parentheses denotes the form under which the author is most frequently published. If the majority of the author's works for children were written under a pseudonym, the pseudonym will be listed in the author heading and the real name given on the first line of the author introduction. Also located at the beginning of the introduction are any other pseudonyms used by the author in writing for children and any name variations, including transliterated forms for authors whose languages use nonroman alphabets. Uncertainty as to a birth or death date is indicated by question marks.

- An **author portrait** is included when available.

- The **author introduction** contains information designed to introduce an author to *CLR* users by presenting an overview of the author's themes and styles, occasional biographical facts that relate to the author's literary career or critical responses to the author's works, and information about major awards and prizes the author has received. Where applicable, introductions conclude with references to additional entries in biographical and critical reference series published by Gale Research Inc. These sources include past volumes of *CLR* as well as *Authors & Artists for Young Adults, Contemporary Authors, Contemporary Literary Criticism, Dictionary of Literary Biography, Nineteenth-Century Literature Criticism, Short Story Criticism, Something about the Author, Something about the Author Autobiography Series, Twentieth-Century Literary Criticism,* and *Yesterday's Authors of Books for Children.*

- **Criticism** is located in three sections: **author's commentary** and **general commentary** (when available) and within individual **title entries,** which are preceded by **title entry headings.** Criticism is arranged chronologically within each section. Titles by authors being profiled are highlighted in boldface type within the text for easier access by readers.

The **author's commentary** presents background material written by the author or by an interviewer. This commentary may cover a specific work or several works. Author's commentary on more than one work appears after the author introduction, while commentary on an individual book follows the title entry heading.

The **general commentary** consists of critical excerpts that consider more than one work by the author being profiled. General commentary is preceded by the critic's name in boldface type or, in the case of unsigned criticism, by the title of the journal.

Title entry headings precede the criticism on a title and cite publication information on the work being reviewed. Title headings list the title of the work as it appeared in its country of origin; titles in languages using nonroman alphabets are transliterated. If the original title is in a language other than English, the title of the first English-language translation follows in brackets. The first available publication date of each work is listed in parentheses following the title. Differing U.S. and British titles of works originally published in English follow the publication date within the parentheses.

Title entries consist of critical excerpts on the author's individual works, arranged chronologically by publication date. The entries generally contain two to six reviews per title, depending on the stature of the book and the amount of criticism it has generated. The editors select titles that reflect the entire scope of the author's literary contribution, covering each genre and subject. An effort is made to reprint criticism that represents the full range of each title's reception—from the year of its initial publication to current assessments. Thus, the reader is provided with a record of the author's critical history. Publication information (such as publisher names and book prices) and parenthetical numerical references (such as footnotes or page and line references to specific editions of works) have been deleted at the editor's discretion to provide smoother reading of the text.

Entries on authors who are also illustrators will occasionally feature commentary on selected works illustrated but not written by the author being profiled. These works are strongly associated with the illustrator and have received critical acclaim for their art. By including critical comment on works of this type, the editors wish to provide a more complete representation of the author's total career. Criticism on these works has been chosen to stress artistic, rather than literary, contributions. Title entry headings for works illustrated by the author being profiled are arranged chronologically within the entry by date of publication and include notes identifying the author of the illustrated work. In order to provide easier access for users, all titles illustrated by the subject of the entry will be boldfaced.

CLR also includes entries on prominent illustrators who have contributed to the field of children's literature. These entries are designed to represent the development of the illustrator as an artist rather than as a literary stylist. The illustrator's section is organized like that of an author, with two exceptions: the introduction presents an overview of the illustrator's styles and techniques rather than outlining his or her literary background, and the commentary written by the illustrator on his or her works is called illustrator's commentary rather than author's commentary. Title entry headings are followed by explanatory notes identifying the author of the illustrated work. All titles of books containing illustrations by the artist being profiled as well as individual illustrations from these books are highlighted in boldface type.

• Selected excerpts are preceded by **explanatory notes,** which provide information on the critic or work of criticism to enhance the reader's understanding of the excerpt.

• A complete **bibliographical citation** designed to facilitate the location of the original book or article follows each piece of criticism.

• Numerous **illustrations** are featured in *CLR*. For entries on illustrators, an effort has been made to include illustrations that reflect the characteristics discussed in the criticism. Entries on major authors who do not illustrate their own works may also include photographs and other illustrative material pertinent to the authors' careers.

Other Features

• An **acknowledgments,** which immediately follows the preface, lists the sources from which material has been reprinted in the volume. It does not, however, list every book or periodical consulted for the volume.

• A list of **authors to appear in future volumes** follows the acknowledgments.

• The **cumulative index to authors** lists authors who have appeared in *CLR* and includes cross-references to *Authors & Artists for Young Adults, Contemporary Authors, Contemporary Literary Criticism, Dictionary of Literary Biography, Nineteenth-Century Literature Criticism, Short Story Criticism,*

Something about the Author, Something about the Author Autobiography Series, Twentieth-Century Literary Criticism, and *Yesterday's Authors of Books for Children.*

- The **cumulative nationality index** lists authors alphabetically under their respective nationalities. Author names are followed by the volume number(s) in which they appear. Authors who have changed citizenship or whose current citizenship is not reflected in biographical sources appear under both their original nationality and that of their current residence.

- The **cumulative title index** lists titles covered in *CLR* followed by the volume and page number where criticism begins.

Suggestions Are Welcome

In response to various suggestions, several features have been added to *CLR* since the series began, including author entries on retellers of traditional literature as well as those who have been the first to record oral tales and other folklore; entries on prominent illustrators featuring commentary on their styles and techniques; entries on authors whose works are considered controversial or have been challenged; occasional entries devoted to criticism on a single work by a major author; explanatory notes that provide information on the critic or work of criticism to enhance the usefulness of the excerpt; more extensive illustrative material, such as holographs of manuscript pages and photographs of people and places pertinent to the authors' careers; a cumulative nationality index for easy access to authors by nationality; and occasional guest essays written specifically for *CLR* by prominent critics on subjects of their choice.

Readers are cordially invited to write the editor with comments and suggestions for further enhancing the usefulness of the *CLR* series.

ACKNOWLEDGMENTS

The editors wish to thank the copyright holders of the excerpted criticism included in this volume, the permissions managers of many book and magazine publishing companies for assisting us in securing reprint rights, and Anthony Bogucki for assistance with copyright research. We are also grateful to the staffs of the Detroit Public Library, the Library of Congress, the University of Detroit Library, the University of Michigan Library, and Wayne State University Library for making their resources available to us. Following is a list of the copyright holders who have granted us permission to reprint material in this volume of *CLR*. Every effort has been made to trace copyright, but if omissions have been made, please let us know.

COPYRIGHTED EXCERPTS IN *CLR*, VOLUME 18, WERE REPRINTED FROM THE FOLLOWING PERIODICALS:

The Alan Review, v. 13, Fall, 1985 and Winter, 1986. Reprinted by permission of the publisher.—*America,* v. 104, January 7, 1961. © 1961. All rights reserved. Reprinted with permission of America Press, Inc., 106 West 56th Street, New York, NY 10019.—*American Artist,* v. 30, September, 1966. Copyright © 1966 by Billboard Publications, Inc. Reprinted by permission of the publishers. *(The McClurg Book News,* January, 1966 for an excerpt from "Why I Write About Colonial American Craftsman" by Leonard Everett Fisher. Reprinted by permission of the author.)—*American Speech,* v. XXXIV, October, 1959 for "The Language of 'The Catcher in the Rye'" by Donald P. Costello. Copyright 1959, renewed 1987 by Donald P. Costello. Reprinted by permission of the author.—*Best Sellers,* s.33, December 15, 1973. Copyright 1973, by the University of Scranton. Reprinted by permission of the publisher./ v. 41, November, 1981; v. 46, August, 1986. Copyright © 1981, 1986 Helen Dwight Reid Educational Foundation. Both reprinted by permission of the publisher.—*Book World—The Washington Post,* November 5, 1972; April 9, 1978; May 13, 1979; November 8, 1981; April 13, 1986; November 9, 1986; May 29, 1988. © 1972, 1978, 1979, 1981, 1986, 1988, *The Washington Post.* All reprinted by permission of the publisher.—*Booklist,* v. 73, May 15, 1977; v. 74, July 15, 1978; v. 75, April 15, 1979; v. 76, October 15, 1979; v. 76, May 15, 1980; v. 77, October 1, 1980; v. 77, January 1, 1981; v. 77, June 15, 1981; v. 79, January 1, 1983; v. 79, January 15, 1983; v, 80, September 1, 1983; v. 81, October 1, 1984; v. 81, November 1, 1984; v. 81, January 1, 1985; v. 81, February 1, 1985; v. 81, April 15, 1985; v. 82, September 1, 1985; v. 82, October 1, 1985; v. 82, December 15, 1985; v. 82, March 15, 1986; v. 82, April 1, 1986; v. 82, August, 1986; v. 83, March 15, 1987; v. 83, July, 1987; v. 84, September 1, 1987; v. 84, October 1, 1987; v. 84, October 15, 1987. Copyright © 1977, 1978, 1979, 1980, 1981, 1983, 1984, 1985, 1986, 1987 by the American Library Association. All reprinted by permission of the publisher.—The Booklist, v. 72, February 15, 1976. Copyright © 1976 by the American Library Association. Reprinted by permission of the publisher.—*Books,* New York, July 23, 1961. © 1961 I. H. T. Corporation. Reprinted by permission of the publisher.—*Books for Keeps,* n. 42, January, 1987; n. 52, September, 1988. © School Bookshop Association 1987, 1988. Both reprinted by permission of the publisher.—*Books for Young People,* v. 1, February, 1987. All rights reserved. Reprinted by permission of the publisher.—*Books for Your Children,* v. 12, Winter, 1976; v. 20, Spring, 1985; v. 21, Spring, 1986; v. 23, Summer, 1988. © *Books for Your Children* 1976, 1985, 1986, 1988. All reprinted by permission of the publisher.—*Bulletin of the Center for Children's Books,* v. XIV, May, 1961; v. XVIII, May, 1965; v. 19, November, 1965; v. 19, February, 1966; v. 24, June, 1971; v. 25, September, 1971; v. 25, June, 1972; v. 26, June, 1973; v. 27, July-August, 1974; v. 28, June, 1975; v. 29, September, 1975; v. 29, December, 1975; v. 29, July-August, 1976; v. 30, February, 1977; v. 31, September, 1977; v. 31, May, 1978; v. 34, September, 1980; v. 34, July-August, 1981; v. 35, September, 1981; v. 35, October, 1981; v. 35, December, 1981; v. 35, July-August, 1982; v. 37, April, 1984; v. 37, May, 1984; v. 38, September, 1984; v. 38, January, 1985; v. 40, October, 1986; v. 40, December, 1986; v. 40, May, 1987; v. 40, June, 1987; v. 41, October, 1987; v. 41, June, 1988. © 1961, 1965, 1966, 1971, 1972, 1973, 1974, 1975, 1976, 1977, 1978, 1980, 1981, 1982, 1984, 1985, 1986, 1987, 1988 by The University of Chicago. All reprinted by permission of The University of Chicago Press. *Business History Review,* v. LIV, Winter, 1980. © 1980 by The President and Fellows of Harvard College. All rights reserved. Reprinted by permission of Harvard Business School Publishing Division.—*Canadian Children's Literature,* n. 15-16, 1980; n. 20, 1980; n. 35- 36, 1984; n. 46, 1987. Copyright © 1980, 1984, 1987 Canadian Children's Press. All reprinted by permission the publisher.—*Canadian Library Journal,* v. 39, October, 1982 for "Book of the Year for Children Award" by Janet Lunn. © 1982 Janet Lunn. Reprinted by permission of the publisher and the author.—*Catholic Library World,* v. 58, March/April, 1987. Reprinted by permission of the publisher.—*Children's Book News,* London, v. 3, May-June, 1968. Copyright © 1968 by Baker Book Services Ltd. Reprinted by permission of the publisher.—*Children's Book Review,* v. II, April, 1972; v. II, October, 1972; v. III, December, 1973. © 1972, 1973 by Five Owls Press Ltd. All rights reserved. All reprinted by permission of the publisher.—*Children's Book Review Service,* v. 5, May, 1977; v. 6, Spring, 1978; v. 7, November, 1978; v. 8, May, 1980; v. 9, December, 1980. Copyright © 1977, 1978, 1980 Children's Book Review Service Inc. All reprinted by permission of the publisher.—*Children's Literature: Annual of the Modern Language Association Seminar on Children's Literature and The Children's Literature Association,* v. 10, 1982. © 1982 by Francelia Butler. All rights reserved. Reprinted by permission of Yale University Press.—*Children's Literature Association Quarterly,* v. 10, Spring, 1985. © 1985 Children's Literature Association. Reprinted by permission of the publisher.—*Children's literature in education,* n. 5, July, 1971 for "Warm Sun, Cold Wind: The Novels of Helen

COPYRIGHTED EXCERPTS IN *CLR*, VOLUME 18, WERE REPRINTED FROM THE FOLLOWING BOOKS:

Arbuthnot, May Hill. From *Children and Books.* Scott and Foresman, 1947. Copyright 1947, renewed 1974 by Scott, Foresman and Company. Reprinted by permission of the publisher.—Arbuthnot, May Hill and Zena Sutherland. From *Children and Books.* Fourth edition. Scott, Foresman, 1972. Copyright © 1972, 1964, 1957, 1947, by Scott, Foresman and Company. All rights reserved. Reprinted by permission of the publisher.—Ayres, Harry Morgan. From *Carroll's Alice.* Columbia University Press, 1936. Copyright 1936, renewed 1964 Columbia University Press. Used by permission of the publisher.—Baskin, Barbara H. and Karen H. Harris. From *Books for the Gifted Child.* Bowker, 1980. Copyright © 1980 by Xerox Corporation. All rights reserved. Reprinted with permission from R. R. Bowker, Division of Reed Publishing (USA) Inc.—Carpenter, Humphrey. From *Secret Gardens: A Study of the Golden Age of Children's Literature.* Houghton Mifflin, 1985, Unwin Hyman, 1985. Copyright © 1985 by Humphrey Carpenter. All rights reserved. Reprinted by permission of Houghton Mifflin Company. In Canada by Unwin Hyman Ltd.—Chambers, Aidan. From *Introducing Books to Children.* Second edition. The Horn Book, Inc., 1983. Copyright © 1973, 1983 by Aidan Chambers. All rights reserved. Reprinted by permission of the publisher.—Clark, Beverly Lyon. From "Lewis Carroll's Alice Books: The Wonder of Wonderland," in *Touchstones: Reflections on the Best in Children's Literature, Vol. l.* Edited by Perry Nodelman. Children's Literature Association, 1985. © 1985 ChLA Publishers. Reprinted by permission of the publisher.—Coveney, Peter. From *The Image of Childhood: The Individual and Society, a Study of the Theme in English Literature.* Revised edition. Penguin Books, 1967. Copyright © Peter Coveney, 1957, 1967. Reproduced by permission of Penguin Books Ltd.—Cresswell, Helen. From "Ancient and Modern and Incorrigibly Plural," in *The Thorny Paradise: Writers on Writing for Children.* Edited by Edward Blishen. Penguin Books, 1975. © 1975 by Helen Cresswell. All rights reserved. Reprinted by permission of the author.—Darton, F. J. Harvey. From *Children's Books in England: Five Centuries of Social Life.* Edited by Brian Alderson. Third edition. Cambridge University Press, 1982. Copyright © 1958, 1982, Cambridge University Press. Reprinted with permission of the publisher.—Davis, John. From an introduction to *The Illustrators of Alice in Wonderland and Through the Looking Glass.* Edited by Graham Ovenden. Academy Editions, 1972. © 1972 Academy Editions. All rights reserved. Reprinted by permission of the publisher.—Dessner, Lawrence Jay. From "The Salinger Story, or Have It Your Way," in Seasoned "Authors" for a New Season: The Search for Standards in Popular Writing. Edited by Louis Filler. Bowling Green University Popular Press, 1980. Copyright © 1980 Bowling Green State University Popular Press. Reprinted by permission of the publisher.—Donelson, Kenneth L., and Alleen Pace Nilsen. From *Literature for Today's Young Adults.* Scott, Foresman, 1980. Copyright © 1980 Scott, Foresman and Company. All rights reserved. Reprinted by permission of the publisher.—Dreyer, Sharon Spredemann. From *The Bookfinder: When Kids Need Books, Annotations of Books Published 1979 through 1982, Vol. 3.* American Guidance Service, 1985. © 1985 American Guidance Service, Inc. All rights reserved. Reprinted by permission of the publisher.—Faulkner, William. From *Faulkner in the University: Class Conferences at the University of Virginia 1957-l958.* Edited by Frederick L. Gwynn and Joseph L. Blotner. The University of Virginia Press, 1959. Copyright 1959, renewed 1987 by University of Virginia Press. Reprinted by permission of the publisher.—Fisher, Margery. From *Intent Upon Reading: A Critical Appraisal of Modern Fiction for Children.* Brockhampton Press, 1961. Copyright © 1961 by Margery Fisher. Reprinted by permission of Hodder & Stoughton Limited.—French, Warren. From "The Age of Salinger," in *The Fifties: Fiction, Poetry, Drama.* Edited by Warren French. Everett/Edwards, Inc. 1970. Copyright © 1970 by Warren French. All rights reserved. Reprinted by permission of the publisher.—Frey, Charles, and John Griffith. From *The Literary Heritage of Childhood: An Appraisal of Children's Classics in the Western Tradition.* Greenwood Press, 1987. Copyright © 1987 by Charles H. Frey and John W. Griffith. All rights reserved. Reprinted by permission of Greenwood Press, Inc., Westport, CT.—Gardner, Martin. From an introduction to *The Annotated Alice: Alice's Adventures in Wonderland & Through the Looking Glass.* By Lewis Carroll. Potter, 1960. Copyright © 1960 by Martin Gardner. All rights reserved. Reprinted by permission of Clarkson N. Potter, published by Crown Publishers, a Division of Random House, Inc.—Geismar, Maxwell. From *American Moderns: From Rebellion to Conformity.* Hill and Wang, 1958. Copyright © 1958 by Maxwell Geismar. Renewed 1986 by Anne Geismar. All rights reserved. Reprinted by permission of McIntosh and Otis, Inc.—Green, Roger Lancelyn. From *Lewis Carroll.* Bodley Head, 1960. © The Bodley Head Ltd. 1960. Reprinted by permission of the publisher.—Greenacre, Phyllis. From *Swift and Carroll: A Psychoanalytic Study of Two Lives.* International Universities Presses, 1955 Copyright 1955, International Universities Press, Inc. Renewed 1983 by Phyllis Greenacre. Reprinted by permission of the author.—Hancher, Michael. From *The Tenniel Illustrations to the "Alice" Books.* Ohio State University Press, 1985. © 1985 by the Ohio State University Press. All rights reserved. Reprinted with permission of the publisher.—Hassan, Ihab. From *Radical Innocence: Studies in the Contemporary American Novel.* Princeton University Press, 1961. Copyright © 1961 by Ihab Hassan. All rights reserved. Reprinted by permission of the author.—Hearn, Michael Patrick. From "Arthur Rackham's Adventures in Wonderland," in *Lewis Carroll Observed: A Collection of Unpublished Photographs, Drawings, Poetry, and New Essays.* Edited by Edward Guiliano. Potter, 1976. Copyright © 1976 by Edward Guiliano. All rights reserved. Reprinted by permission of Clarkson N. Potter, published by Crown Publishers, a Division of Random House, Inc.—Hodnett, Edward. From *Image and Text: Studies in the Illustration of English Literature.* Scolar Press, 1982. Copyright © Edward Hodnett, 1982. Reprinted by permission of the publisher.—Hürlimann, Bettina. From *Three Centuries of Children's Books in Europe.* Edited and translated by Brian W. Alderson. Oxford University Press, London, 1967. Reprinted by permission of the publisher.—Inglis, Fred. From *The Promise of Happiness: Value and Meaning in Children's Fiction.* Cambridge University Press, 1981. © Cambridge University Press 1981. Reprinted with the permission of the publisher and the author.—Jan, Isabelle. From *On Children's Literature.* Edited and translated by Catherine Storr. Allen Lane, 1973. Copyright © Allen Lane, 1973. Reproduced by permission of Penguin Books Ltd.—Landsberg, Michele. From *Michele Landsberg's Guide to Children's Books.* Penguin Books Canada Limited, 1986. Copyright © 1986 by Psammead

AUTHORS TO APPEAR IN FUTURE VOLUMES

Adams, Harriet S(tratemeyer)
    1893?-1982
Adams, Richard 1920-
Adler, Irving 1913-
Anderson, C(larence) W(illiam)
    1891-1971
Arrick, Fran
Arundel, Honor (Morfydd) 1919-1973
Asbjörnsen, Peter Christen 1812-1885
    and Jörgen Moe 1813?-1882
Asch, Frank 1946-
Atwater, Richard Tupper 1892-1948
    and Florence (Hasseltine Carroll)
Avery, Gillian 1926-
Avi 1937-
Aymé, Marcel 1902-1967
Bailey, Carolyn Sherwin 1875-1961
Ballantyne, R(obert) M(ichael)
    1825-1894
Banner, Angela 1923-
Bannerman, Helen 1863-1946
Barrett, Judi(th) 1941-
Baumann, Hans 1914-1985
Beatty, Patricia Robbins 1922-
    and John 1922-1975
Beckman, Gunnel 1910-
Behn, Harry 1898-1973
Belaney, Archibald
    Stansfeld 1888-1938
Belloc, Hilaire 1870-1953
Berenstain, Stan(ley) 1923- and
    Jan(ice) 1923-
Berger, Melvin H. 1927-
Berna, Paul 1910-
Bianco, Margery Williams 1881-1944
Bishop, Claire Huchet
Blake, Quentin 1932-
Blumberg, Rhoda 1917-
Blyton, Enid 1897-1968
Bodecker, N(iels) M(ogens) 1922-1988
Bødker, Cecil 1927-
Bonham, Frank 1914-
Boutet De Monvel, (Louis)
    M(aurice) 1850(?)-1913
Brancato, Robin F(idler) 1936-
Branscum, Robbie 1937-
Breinburg, Petronella 1927-
Bright, Robert 1902-1988
Brink, Carol Ryrie 1895-1981
Brinsmead, H(esba) F(ay) 1922-
Brooke, L(eonard) Leslie 1862-1940
Brooks, Bruce
Brown, Marc Tolon 1946-
Browne, Anthony (Edward Tudor)
    1946-
Buff, Mary 1890-1970 and Conrad
    1886-1975

Bulla, Clyde Robert 1914-
Burch, Robert (Joseph) 1925-
Burgess, Gelett 1866-1951
Burgess, Thornton W(aldo) 1874-1965
Burkert, Nancy Ekholm 1933-
Burnett, Frances Hodgson 1849-1924
Butterworth, Oliver 1915-
Caines, Jeannette (Franklin)
Carlson, Natalie Savage 1906-
Carrick, Carol 1935- and Donald 1929-
Chambers, Aidan 1934-
Chönz, Selina
Christopher, Matt(hew F.) 1917-
Ciardi, John (Anthony) 1916-1986
Clapp, Patricia 1912-
Clarke, Pauline 1921-
Cohen, Barbara 1932-
Colby, C(arroll) B(urleigh) 1904-1977
Colman, Hila
Colum, Padraic 1881-1972
Cone, Molly 1918-
Coolidge, Olivia E(nsor) 1908-
Coolidge, Susan 1835-1905
Cooney, Barbara 1917-
Corbett, W(illiam) J(esse) 1938-
Courlander, Harold 1908-
Cox, Palmer 1840-1924
Crane, Walter 1845-1915
Crompton, Richmal 1890-1969
Crutcher, Chris(topher C.) 1946-
Cunningham, Julia (Woolfolk) 1916-
Curry, Jane L(ouise) 1932-
Dalgliesh, Alice 1893-1979
Daly, Maureen 1921-
Danziger, Paula 1944-
Daugherty, James 1889-1974
D'Aulaire, Ingri 1904-1980 and Edgar
    Parin 1898-1986
DeClements, Barthe 1920-
De la Mare, Walter 1873-1956
De Regniers, Beatrice Schenk 1914-
Dickinson, Peter 1927-
Dillon, Eilís 1920-
Dillon, Leo 1933- and Diane 1933-
Dodge, Mary Mapes 1831-1905
Domanska, Janina
Drescher, Henrik
Duncan, Lois S(teinmetz) 1934-
Duvoisin, Roger 1904-1980
Eager, Edward 1911-1964
Edgeworth, Maria 1767-1849
Edmonds, Walter D(umaux) 1903-
Epstein, Sam(uel) 1909- and Beryl
    1910-
Ets, Marie Hall 1893-
Ewing, Juliana Horatia 1841-1885
Farber, Norma 1909-1984

Farjeon, Eleanor 1881-1965
Field, Eugene 1850-1895
Field, Rachel 1894-1942
Fisher, Dorothy Canfield 1879-1958
Flack, Marjorie 1897-1958
Forbes, Esther 1891-1967
Forman, James D(ouglas) 1932-
Freedman, Russell 1929-
Freeman, Don 1908-1978
Fujikawa, Gyo 1908-
Fyleman, Rose 1877-1957
Garfield, Leon 1921-
Garis, Howard R(oger) 1873-1962
Garner, Alan 1935-
Gates, Doris 1901-1988
Gerrard, Roy 1935-
Giblin, James Cross 1933-
Giff, Patricia Reilly 1935-
Ginsburg, Mirra 1919-
Goble, Paul 1933-
Godden, Rumer 1907-
Goodall, John S(trickland) 1908-
Goodrich, Samuel G(riswold)
    1793-1860
Gorey, Edward (St. John) 1925-
Gramatky, Hardie 1907-1979
Greene, Constance C(larke) 1924-
Grimm, Jacob 1785-1863 and Wilhelm
    1786-1859
Gruelle, Johnny 1880-1938
Guillot, René 1900-1969
Hader, Elmer 1889-1973 and Berta
    1891?-1976
Hague, Michael 1948-
Hale, Lucretia Peabody 1820-1900
Haley, Gail E(inhart) 1939-
Hall, Lynn 1937-
Harnett, Cynthia 1893-1981
Harris, Christie (Lucy Irwin) 1907-
Harris, Joel Chandler 1848-1908
Harris, Rosemary (Jeanne) 1923-
Hayes, Sheila 1937-
Haywood, Carolyn 1898-
Head, Ann 1915-
Heide, Florence Parry 1919-
Heinlein, Robert A(nson) 1907-1988
Henkes, Kevin 1960-
Hoberman, Mary Ann 1930-
Hoff, Syd(ney) 1912-
Hoffman, Heinrich 1809-1894
Holland, Isabelle 1920-
Holling, Holling C(lancy) 1900-1973
Hunter, Mollie 1922-
Hurd, Edith Thacher 1910-
    and Clement 1908-1988
Hutchins, Pat 1942-
Hyman, Trina Schart 1939-

xvii

Ipcar, Dahlov (Zorach) 1917-
Jackson, Jesse 1908-1983
Janosch 1931-
Johnson, Crockett 1906-1975
Johnson, James Weldon 1871-1938
Jones, Diana Wynne 1934-
Judson, Clara Ingram 1879-1960
Juster, Norton 1929-
Kelly, Eric P(hilbrook) 1884-1960
Kennedy, (Jerome) Richard 1932-
Kent, Jack 1920-1985
Kerr, (Anne-)Judith 1923-
Kerr, M. E. 1927-
Kettelkamp, Larry (Dale) 1933-
Kherdian, David 1931-
King, (David) Clive 1924-
Kipling, Rudyard 1865-1936
Kjelgaard, Jim 1910-1959
Klein, Robin 1936-
Kraus, Robert 1925-
Krauss, Ruth (Ida) 1911-
Krumgold, Joseph 1908-1980
La Fontaine, Jean de 1621-1695
Lang, Andrew 1844-1912
Langton, Jane (Gillson) 1922-
Latham, Jean Lee 1902-
Lattimore, Eleanor Frances 1904-1986
Lavine, Sigmund A(rnold) 1908-
Leaf, Munro 1905-1976
Lenski, Lois 1893-1974
Levy, Elizabeth 1942-
Lightner, A(lice) M. 1904-
Lindgren, Barbro 1937-
Lipsyte, Robert 1938-
Lofting, Hugh (John) 1866-1947
MacDonald, George 1824-1905
MacGregor, Ellen 1906-1954
Mann, Peggy
Marshall, James 1942-
Martin, Patricia Miles 1899-1986
Masefield, John 1878-1967
Mattingley, Christobel
   (Rosemary) 1931-
Mayer, Marianna 1945-
Mayne, William (James Carter) 1928-
Mazer, Norma Fox 1931-
McCaffrey, Anne (Inez) 1926-
McGovern, Ann
McKee, David (John)
McKillip, Patricia A(nne) 1948-
McNeer, May 1902-
Meader, Stephen W(arren) 1892-1977
Means, Florence Crannell 1891-1980
Meigs, Cornelia 1884-1973

Merrill, Jean (Fairbanks) 1923-
Miles, Betty 1928-
Milne, Lorus 1912- and Margery 1915-
Minarik, Else Holmelund 1920-
Mizumura, Kazue
Mohr, Nicholasa 1935-
Molesworth, Mary Louisa 1842-1921
Morey, Walt(er Nelson) 1907-
Mowat, Farley (McGill) 1921-
Munsch, Robert N. 1945-
Neufeld, John (Arthur) 1938-
Neville, Emily Cheney 1919-
Nic Leodhas, Sorche 1898-1969
North, Sterling 1906-1974
Norton, Andre 1912-
Ofek, Uriel 1926-
Ormerod, Jan(ette Louise) 1946-
Ormondroyd, Edward 1925-
Oxenbury, Helen 1938-
Parish, Peggy 1927-1988
Patent, Dorothy Hinshaw 1940-
Paulsen, Gary 1939-
Peck, Robert Newton 1928-
Perl, Lila
Perrault, Charles 1628-1703
Petersen, P(eter) J(ames) 1941-
Petersham, Maud 1890-1971 and
   Miska 1888-1960
Picard, Barbara Leonie 1917-
Pierce, Meredith Ann 1958-
Platt, Kin 1911-
Politi, Leo 1908-
Price, Christine 1928-1980
Pyle, Howard 1853-1911
Rackham, Arthur 1867-1939
Rawls, Wilson 1919-
Reiss, Johanna 1932-
Reeves, James 1909-1978
Richards, Laura E(lizabeth) 1850-1943
Richter, Hans Peter 1925-
Robertson, Keith (Carlton) 1914-
Rockwell, Anne 1934- and Harlow
   19??-1988
Rodgers, Mary 1931-
Rollins, Charlemae Hill 1897-1979
Ross, Tony 1938-
Rounds, Glen H(arold) 1906-
Sandburg, Carl 1878-1967
Sandoz, Mari 1896-1966
Sawyer, Ruth 1880-1970
Scarry, Huck 1953-
Scoppettone, Sandra 1936-
Scott, Jack Denton 1915-
Seton, Ernest Thompson 1860-1946

Sharmat, Marjorie Weinman 1928-
Sharp, Margery 1905-
Shepard, Ernest H(oward) 1879-1976
Shotwell, Louisa R(ossiter) 1902-
Sidney, Margaret 1844-1924
Silverstein, Alvin 1933- and Virginia
   B(arbara Opshelor) 1937-
Sinclair, Catherine 1800-1864
Skurzynski, Gloria (Joan) 1930-
Sleator, William (Warner) 1945-
Slobodkin, Louis 1903-1975
Smith, Jessie Willcox 1863-1935
Snyder, Zilpha Keatley 1927-
Spence, Eleanor (Rachel) 1928-
Sperry, Armstrong W. 1897-1976
Spykman, E(lizabeth) C. 1896-1965
Starbird, Kaye 1916-
Steele, William O(wen) 1917-1979
Stolz, Mary (Slattery) 1920-
Stratemeyer, Edward L. 1862-1930
Taylor, Sydney 1904?-1978
Taylor, Theodore 1924-
Thiele, Colin 1920-
Thomas, Joyce Carol 1938-
Thompson, Julian F(rancis) 1927-
Thompson, Kay 1912-
Titus, Eve 1922-
Tolkien, J(ohn) R(onald) R(euel)
   1892-1973
Trease, (Robert) Geoffrey 1909-
Tresselt, Alvin 1916-
Treviño, Elizabeth Borton de 1904-
Turkle, Brinton 1915-
Twain, Mark 1835-1910
Udry, Janice May 1928-
Unnerstad, Edith (Totterman) 1900-
Uttley, Alison 1884-1976
Vining, Elizabeth Gray 1902-
Waber, Bernard 1924-
Wahl, Jan 1933-
Ward, Lynd 1905-1985
White, T(erence) H(anbury) 1906-1964
Wiese, Kurt 1887-1974
Wilkinson, Brenda 1946-
Wood, Audrey and Don 1945-
Worth, Valerie 1933-
Wyeth, N(ewell) C(onvers) 1882-1945
Yates, Elizabeth 1905-
Yonge, Charlotte M(ary) 1823-1901
Yorinks, Arthur 1953-
Zelinsky, Paul O. 1953-
Zemach, Harve 1933-1974 and Margot
   1931-1989
Zion, Gene 1913-1975

Readers are cordially invited to suggest additional authors to the editors.

Children's Literature Review

Janet (Hall) Ahlberg
1944-
Allan Ahlberg
1938-

English authors and illustrators of picture books and fiction.

As the creators of immensely popular works for preschoolers and older reluctant readers which include contributions to such genres as the toy book, the fantasy, the informational book, and the nonsense story, the Ahlbergs demonstrate a vivacity and exuberance that is often lauded by critics. Although Janet is primarily the illustrator and Allan the author, they work together on all stages of book production and consider their work a joint effort; reviewers often comment on how well the Ahlbergs integrate their words and pictures. They are also frequently commended for their innovation as well as for their insightfulness about the very young and their world. Often written in verse, their works convey a clever sense of humor in both text and illustration that gives the books a special charm. The illustrations, done in pen-and-ink or watercolor, or both, are packed with details, offering children the opportunity to create small dramas out of the minutiae of the drawings.

From the beginning of their collaboration, the Ahlberg's objective was evident: to present their readers with entertaining stories, complete with morals and happy endings. They began their partnership with the "Brick Street Boys" series, five lively books done in comic-strip style which describe the adventures of a group of spirited multiracial street kids living in a working-class neighborhood characterized by its factories and alleyways. In subsequent books, the Ahlbergs often depict cluttered, cosy homes filled with warm-hearted family members. Several of the Ahlbergs's works feature fairy and nursery tale characters as well as figures from popular culture such as the cowboy. They have also created several joke books, filled with silly puns and riddles of the type that particularly appeals to small children. Other efforts to involve their audience in reading include slot books which allow youngsters to place paper objects in different slots on the pages, thus devising logical or completely nonsensical combinations. Likewise, in *Each Peach Pear Plum: An "I Spy" Story* (1978), the reader explores the illustrations for hidden characters; the winner of the Kate Greenaway Medal in 1979, *Each Peach Pear Plum* is often considered a contemporary classic. *The Jolly Postman or Other People's Letters* (1986) depicts a mailman on his daily rounds, while the audience is treated to an extremely inventive format: as the illustrations show the postman delivering correspondence to familiar nursery characters, the Ahlbergs alternate pages of verse with envelopes containing messages from other characters or from outside sources. While satirizing many social conventions such as business letters and invitations, the book also allows the reader the often-forbidden chance to read others' mail. Often called a work of genius, *The Jolly Postman* received a commendation from the Kate Greenaway Medal committee in 1986, an honor they also received for *Burglar Bill* in 1977 and for *The Baby's Catalogue* in 1982. Through their lighthearted and beguiling approach, the Ahlbergs have given interesting, intelligent books to young readers that clearly demonstrate the joy that can come from reading.

(See also *Something about the Author,* Vols. 32, 35; and *Contemporary Authors,* Vols. 111, 114.)

AUTHOR'S COMMENTARY

[*The following excerpt is from an interview by Victoria Neumark.*]

The first published Ahlberg books were the highly popular **"Brick Street Boys"** readers, published in 1975. They began "really as a spoof against the banality of Janet and John-style readers", and went on under the steam of "their own fun". Though they have an educational use, as readers for 10-11 year-olds with a reading age of six to seven, Allan Ahlberg conceives of them as "little lightweight farces for children".

The Ahlbergs view their work as a unity. Ideas are constantly being mooted, talked about, drawn and modified, always with the production of a book in mind. "The text is easy" says Allan Ahlberg. "It's very easy to write books in the plainest simplest words and put all the complicated narrative in the pictures. The tale is in the pictures — or, the tale is not in the typescript of the pictures but in the way the two go together.

Words and pictures appear together and have a rhythm, a marriage of words and pictures."

Of course, all the best children's literature from Beatrix Potter to Maurice Sendak has had this integrity. Sendak is greatly admired by both Ahlbergs — "you pick up a book and everything is right" as Janet Ahlberg says—and they see themselves as craftsmen who "make a printed bound object, a mixture of saying something and design". "We choose everything" explains Allan, leafing through *Each Peach Pear Plum,* "the size of the book, the typeface, the endpapers, what should go on the blurbs and the cover, so", he holds up a tomato cupped in his hand, "that's the book, like an egg or nut, we can get both hands round it." Such perfectionism is not quickly satisfied. The illustrations for *Each Peach Pear Plum* took four months to complete; *The Old Joke Book* with its complicated strip-cartoon format six months to illustrate and three months to write — Allan Ahlberg's research turning up 2,000 jokes from which to structure the book. Not that the jokes are going to be allowed to go to waste — another joke book is on the stocks.

Although Allan is the one to come up with ideas — "I say wouldn't it be nice if we wrote a book about this" — his part in direct authorship can be over very quickly. The text for *Each Peach* took only a day to write. But: "We work together, we discuss everything, every stage", both Ahlbergs emphasize. . . .

Both of them are unanimous in feeling that it is important to conceive the book first and only later think of its audience. They sense a "corrupting pressure" on authors to write for the book fair market and create the sort of "boneless characters" which will be blandly international.

Determined to resist this pressure which affects "not all, but some" children's writers, they regard each idea as "a seed, which grows into a book, which then becomes what it should be — for whatever age". Some books are more sophisticated than others — for instance the light-hearted medley of fairy-tale characters which constitutes *Jeremiah in the Dark Woods* solely because "we want to do them like that". "The thing which does drive us on" Janet explains "is an urge not to do the exact same thing again". Freshness of invention constantly vitalizes their work. . . .

The more serious implications of their work are not taken too solemnly by the Ahlbergs. . . . Allan Ahlberg is keen to stress "It's play, it's farce, it's the neatness of plot"; there are, as Janet adds, "no deep philosophies". They are unassuming. "We are very lucky, so lucky. It is enormous fun."

> Victoria Neumark, *"A Marriage of Words and Pictures,"* in The Times Educational Supplement, *No. 3340, June 20, 1980, p. 42.*

GENERAL COMMENTARY

AIDAN CHAMBERS

Janet and Allan Ahlberg say they regard themselves as picture-book makers rather than as an artist and a writer who happen to work together. And their books certainly possess that integrated relationship between words and pictures usually achieved only when writer and illustrator are the same — one person.

So in the Ahlbergs we have a two-in-one artistic as well as

personal marriage that has given birth to a family of books which in a very short time have made themselves extremely popular in England and which are also critically well regarded. The Ahlbergs are even known by their name as well as by their works. You only have to say, "The Ahlbergs," to a crowd of teachers and librarians and now of parents, too, to be rewarded with the kind of warm smile and immediate interest that flow from genuine pleasure and affection.

Just published is their latest picture book, *The Baby's Catalogue.* In nature and kind it makes a threesome with two others: the classic *Each Peach Pear Plum* . . . and *Peepo!* (p. 686)

Like its companions, *The Baby's Catalogue* takes a very simple idea, an everyday baby experience, and by inventive visual treatment and richness of detail, gives it a new life full of the personality of its makers. Who, at three and four and five, did not pore over (as well as paw) sales catalogs? Who did not go shopping in imagination and play with all the best things selected from those stacked-up pages of goodies? Who did not use sales catalogs as baby reference books, glowing with satisfaction at being able to name all the familiar objects, puzzling over the strange and wonderful gadgets that Mum or Dad or anyone had to tell you the names of? (pp. 686-87)

Properly enough, *The Baby's Catalogue* begins with "Babies": five pictures, framed in strip-cartoonlike manner, showing six babies belonging to five families (two of the babies are twins). You can play the game of tracking them all through the rest of the book, and no doubt many young catalogers will also want to tell themselves — and anyone else who will listen — stories about what is happening to the six characters and which objects belong to which child. (pp. 687-88)

Typical Ahlberg: warm-hearted, amusing, gentle, touchingly cozy and secure, and comfortably accomplished at including a baby's-eye-view of things while allying itself also with adults. Family literature with baby at the center. But although the surface appearance of the drawings is simple, even naïve, you soon see connections between the images that create second, third, fourth, and sometimes more stories within the simple one.

Here is a game of I Spy to be played, just as it was the starting point for *Each Peach Pear Plum.* And there is always more than one story going on at the same time in all three books. In fact, in all three you — the reader — have to make up the stories as you go along, using the carefully associated pictures to give you the clues you need. Plenty of indeterminacies for the reader to resolve, just as in all the best modern literature for grownups as well as children. Helping to make up the story has been elevated into a current fashion, among teenagers in my country, as it has I expect in yours, in what are being called story games supplied by magazines like *White Dwarf* and even by a brand new Puffin book, *The Warlock of Firetop Mountain* by Steve Jackson and Ian Livingstone, which the blurb says is "a fighting fantasy in which YOU become the hero!" and about which more another time.

Graduates of Ahlberg baby books will have no trouble cracking that one, although with any luck they will also regard "fighting fantasies" as unnecessary because the Ahlbergs (and others, too, like my ever-ready favorite Anthony Browne, not to mention — how could one not? — Maurice Sendak) will have shown them how much more interesting everyday living can be without fighting, whether fantastic or otherwise.

In fact, one of the best virtues of the Ahlbergs' work is that they treat plot — the eventful, what-happens-next, action part of a story — with the respect it deserves, which is to say not much. They give it an amused nod and occupy themselves and their baby readers with the real business of literature: creating and placing together images in words and pictures that spark off all kinds of diverse and often unexpected meanings and responses. The Ahlbergs make numerous meanings possible; they give pleasure and add interest in this way. Their books are dramatic, not because they pack them with thrills and spills or popeyed goings on but because they know how to select from life and make a pattern of what they select that changes every-dayness from dull routine to an excitement. (pp. 689-90)

> *Aidan Chambers, "Letter from England: Two-in-One," in* The Horn Book Magazine, *Vol. LVIII, No. 6, December, 1982, pp. 686-90.*

HERE ARE THE BRICK STREET BOYS; A PLACE TO PLAY; SAM THE REFEREE (1975)

All those people who worry about the hard-core non-reading boys (and girls too) in primary school ought to welcome *The Brick Street Boys,* a series [of three books: *Here Are the Brick Street Boys, A Place to Play,* and *Sam the Referee*]. . . . (p. 146)

Using the comic-strip style with less inhibition than most of the attempts by reputable trade and educational publishers so far, the books tell funny tales about the goings-on of the lads from Brick Street during their soccer-playing activities on the field and off. Not great art, not great literature, but certainly great in popular parlance: fun to look at, fun to read. The kind of thing that can help make readers. (pp. 146-47)

[Making] readers out of non-readers is now the most urgent educational need. Brick Street's creators, Allan and Janet Ahlberg, at least are approaching the problem with verve and lack of fussiness. (p. 147)

> *Pelorus, in a review of "Here Are the Brick Street Boys," "A Place to Play," and "Sam the Referee," in* Signal, *No. 18, September, 1975, pp. 146-47.*

With the minimum of fuss and polemic and the maximum of good humour the collaborators in these three books [*Here Are the Brick Street Boys, A Place to Play,* and *Sam the Referee*] (which, for their generous provision of illustrations could legitimately be called extended picture-books), have done what sociological critics are constantly pressing writers to do — and for the right reasons. They have described an urban back-street school, with children of mixed race, aptitude and temperament, exercising bodies and wits together in football games that make up in enthusiasm for what they lack in orthodoxy. A slight heightening of probability in the adventures of the busy boys and girls is echoed in the pictures, whose exuberant colour and slightly caricatured faces show as plainly as the texts with what undidactic good will author and artist have chosen this particular, neatly detailed and explicit slice of life. A real triumph, recommended for backward readers.

> *Margery Fisher, in a review of "Here Are the Brick Street Boys," "A Place to Play," and "Sam the Ref-*

eree," in Growing Point, *Vol. 14, No. 4, October, 1975, p. 2726.*

FRED'S DREAM; THE GREAT MARATHON FOOTBALL MATCH (1976)

Everything is zany, grotesque, rainbow-coloured, in two more instalments of the Brick Street Saga, *Fred's Dream* and *The Great Marathon Football Match.* When Fred falls asleep in Mrs. Orris's story-telling class the nightmare of pursuing Indians, endless ladders and the like culminates at Wembley where the small boy, popping out of a tunnel on to the pitch, scores a brilliant goal. In the second book he and his friends set about doing odd jobs to earn money for the new shirts and shorts the games-master says they must have to do the school justice, and the fund is swelled by the proceeds of a sponsored match that lasts through Saturday and:

> On Sunday everybody was very tired.
> Sam stayed in bed till three o'clock.
> Fred stayed in bed till four o'clock.
> Eric didn't get up till it was time to go to bed.
> Mr. Mott didn't get up at all.

On the facing page the artist has shown a procession of Dads, boys, Mums and sisters trudging home by moon and starlight. A short, snappy text well suited to early solo reading, illustrations, some in strip form, full of entrancingly comic detail — don't miss the expression on the face of the plaster gnome in Mrs. Green's garden after being tidied up by Stanley and Fred — these are books right on a young wave-length. (pp. 2888-89)

> *Margery Fisher, in a review of "Fred's Dream" and "The Great Marathon Football Match," in* Growing Point, *Vol. 15, No. 1, May, 1976, pp. 2888-89.*

THE OLD JOKE BOOK (1976)

This is an entirely successful production. Pictures are beguiling comic strips in full colour. It could become the old groan book in your household — it's full of every old playground joke you've ever heard. Buy it for any child but especially for those who need the colour and fun put back into books. It may not be literary but it's certainly irresistible.

> *A review of "The Old Joke Book," in* Books for Your Children, *Vol. 12, No. 1, Winter, 1976, p. 10.*

The presentation of a joke is, as every comedian knows, far more important than the joke itself and the best raconteur can raise a laugh from the worst material. *The Old Joke Book* is amply filled with jokes which one has heard before and would rather not have met again. Nevertheless, if they are to be suffered ad nauseam there could be no better way than through Janet and Allan Ahlberg's book which makes use of vivid and lively drawings to ensure a groan if not an actual chuckle from many old favourites. Some of the jokes are purely visual and put many newspaper cartoons to shame while others, of the knock, knock or waiter, waiter variety, gain immeasurably from the colourful caricatures and other irrelevances which decorate many of the pages and are frequently funnier than the jokes themselves. For anyone who can face such a barrage of humour this collection certainly gives a freshness to jokes which in any other form would be unbearable.

Christopher Williams, "Knock, Knock," in The Times Literary Supplement, *No. 3900, December 10, 1976, p. 1557.*

BURGLAR BILL   (1977)

Janet and Allan Ahlberg are now well known for their "Brick Street Boys" cartoon stories. In **Burglar Bill** they extend their considerable talents for off-beat humour in a picturebook with a long text that turns out to be as moral as it is entertaining. Burglar Bill steals a box with holes in it and discovers to his horror that he has also stolen a baby. By happy accident the baby's mother, a widow lady called Burglar Betty, burgles Burglar Bill. He catches her, in more senses than one. There is an Alf Doolittle ring to the dialogue; and the denouement, a series of pictures in which Bill and Betty return their ill-gotten gains to the rightful owners before starting a new life, is happy nonsense.

Elaine Moss, "Solace for Spring," in The Times Literary Supplement, *No. 3915, March 25, 1977, p. 355.*

The book has a modicum of humor in the hoist-by-his-own-petard plot, and there are amusing bits in the illustrations (a chamberpot marked "HMS Eagle," a portrait that shows full-face and profile shots, police style) but the gag seems over-extended, and the blithe disposition of the baby (Burglar Betty's reaction to the discovery of her lost child is, "Well blow me down, that baby's mine!") may amuse adults more than it does children.

Zena Sutherland, in a review of "Burglar Bill," in Bulletin of the Center for Children's Books, *Vol. 31, No. 1, September, 1977, p. 1.*

JEREMIAH IN THE DARK WOODS   (1977)

Janet and Allan Ahlberg follow their comic-style adventures of the Brick Street Boys with a fantasy that is a sort of nostalgia trip into storybook land. The epigraph from Krazy Kat Comic, "There are no days like the good old days", introduces the story of Jeremiah Obadiah Jackenory Jones, who sets out through the Dark Wood to find the no-good robber who has stolen his grandma's tarts, plate and all, from the windowsill of her gingerbread house.

On his quest he encounters three bears, a frog prince, the Mad Hatter, an insinuating crocodile that ticks, and several other characters including a dinosaur who speaks in accents strongly reminiscent of W. C. Fields, and five Runyonesque gorillas. His journey takes him through a delightful landscape, beyond the Dark Woods, over the river into an ornamental gardens, past the Brickworks and the old Botanical

From Each Peach Pear Plum: An "I Spy" Story, *written and illustrated by Janet and Allan Ahlberg.*

Gardens and "the place where giant beanstalks grow up into the sky". And finally the mystery is solved—even down to the question of what the robber did with the plate:

> "I kept it," Goldilocks said. "Only then I had to throw it at those bears—they were going to eat me!"
> "No, they only eat porridge," Jeremiah said.
> "Well, I was more or less full of porridge at the time," Goldilocks said.

Nowhere in this splendidly eclectic tale is there any sense of a forced inventiveness. Janet Ahlberg's cosy and colourful illustrations enrich the text without competing with it. This is a book by someone who has a story to tell and who clearly enjoys telling it.

> *Myra Barrs, "Comic Horrors," in* The Times Educational Supplement, *No. 3258, November 18, 1977, p. 32.*

I am not sure about this one. It is based on a good idea, but the treatment at times approaches archness; the reader may not quite be embarrassed, but the fear may put him off his enjoyment. . . . The narrative is competent, and so is the dovetailing of the various episodes, but the hero is not nearly as cute as the writer hopes.

This is a story with pictures rather than a picture-book. The drawing is accomplished, but as with the writing, there is just a hint of condescension. This, one feels, is what they think the kiddies will like, rather than what the makers believe.

> *M. Crouch, in a review of "Jeremiah in the Dark Woods," in* The Junior Bookshelf, *Vol. 42, No. 3, June, 1978, p. 133.*

THE VANISHMENT OF THOMAS TULL   (1977)

No Treehorn shrinking quietly away, Thomas Tull is the object of much concerned fuss and bother when he begins to dwindle. A chef is hired to encourage him to eat, three inept (and ineptly satirized) foreign doctors ply their cures, and an odd lot of crackpots have a go. But Mrs. Tull won't allow her son to smoke, and so it is not until after a series of adventures—stunt flying with the Baron von Bolivar, being stolen away by a gang of burglars, and escaping with a psychic called The Double-Sighted Youth—that the three-inch, five-and-a-half-ounce Tom finally puffs on the pipe of a retired Apache medicine man and begins to grow. The ending is a cliché, with family jubilation short-lived as Thomas continues now to grow excessively. Throughout, the Ahlbergs practice the same straight-faced presentation of the preposterous that they sometimes get away with in their picture books; but in this extended form it falls flat.

> *A review of "The Vanishment of Thomas Tull," in* Kirkus Reviews, *Vol. XLVII, No. 3, February 1, 1979, p. 124.*

This is a small tale, as opposed to a tall tale, but the amount of stretching is about the same. . . . The details of poor Thomas' dilemma are extremely silly: the family cat has to be removed from the premises; clothes and bed are a problem. . . . Pen-and-ink comic drawings pick up where the straightfaced text leaves off, with the result of a zany read-aloud well matched to the humor and exaggeration natural

to the intended age group, who will, hopefully, have already heard Paul Bunyan, etc.

> *Betsy Hearne, in a review of "The Vanishment of Thomas Tull," in* Booklist, *Vol. 75, No. 16, April 15, 1979, p. 1291.*

COPS AND ROBBERS   (1978)

This rollicking little Christmastime adventure in catchy rhyme has the humorous exaggeration and compelling rhythm of all good comic verse. The illustrations are packed with very funny detail beautifully thought-out, in particular the cut-away diagrams of the London police station, first on a working day, then in festive mood, and the smiling villainous masked robbers lurking in every conceivable nook and cranny of the street scenes. Officer Pugh, best at sports such as egg-and-spoon as well as on duty, foils the dastardly attempt to steal all the children's presents on Christmas Eve, though singlehanded and reduced to his underpants. A Santa-Claus copper returns them in the nick (pardon the expression!) of time, while the rest of the force goes after Grandma Swagg who, cleverer than her male accomplices, has got away.

> *M. Hobbs, in a review of "Cops and Robbers," in* The Junior Bookshelf, *Vol. 42, No. 6, December, 1978, p. 292.*

Who says crime doesn't pay? Well, as a matter of fact, the Ahlbergs do, in their latest picture book collaboration. However, that seems mere lip service on their part—a nod to conventional children's-lit morality in what is otherwise an all-in-fun ode to an odious gang of thieves.

No self-sacrificing Robin Hoods stealing for the poor, these unregenerate robbers are prompted by old-fashioned greed, and on Christmas Eve they tiptoe through London houses making off with all the toys that Santa has left. Of course, the police mean to stop "the scalliwag scum," but it takes all the cunning of one fair-haired boy in blue — "upstanding Officer Pugh" — to bring the gang to justice.

For his part, Allan Ahlberg pulls off the heist with nimble, if overly British verses that are aided by his wife's tidy watercolor cartoons. Janet Ahlberg's miniature drawings (there are sometimes as many as six to a small 6-by-8-inch page) reduce the crime to appropriately childlike proportions. And her rogue's gallery is most memorable, including such hardened criminals as bucktoothed, baby-faced Billy-the-Bag; an oily ladies' man named Fingers Maurice; and, bless her crooked little heart, Grandma Swagg, a bonneted British Ma Barker who manages to get away scot-free.

> *Jane O'Connor, in a review of "Cops and Robbers," in* The New York Times Book Review, *May 20, 1979, p. 38.*

EACH PEACH PEAR PLUM   (1978; U.S. edition as *Each Peach Pear Plum: An "I Spy" Story*)

Each Peach Pear Plum . . . is a rhyming and visual "I Spy" game for very young children: Nursery characters—Three Bears, Jack and Jill, Baby Bunting, Bo Peep, a Wicked Witch—are hiding in a pleasant, rural, watercolor world that's decorative but never precious or self-regarding. This is a lovely small book, well-conceived and very well drawn, gentle, humorous, unsentimental. Here the "I Spy" game at first supplies the narrative; but soon the pictures and characters interconnect to form a story, complete with a picnic everybody-all-together ending.

Harold C. K. Rice, in a review of "Each Peach Pear Plum," in The New York Times Book Review, *April 29, 1979, p. 46.*

This is a most inventive collection of familiar nursery characters — Cinderella, Jack and Jill, etc. — which as well as being deliciously decorative performs a valuable service for those guiding children in their first experiences of reading. If that sounds as though there is a plodding didactic note to be heard in its pages, let reassurance be given. The subtle text sequences, where the last words on each page are an echo of the next, and where each pastoral picture, full of romantic landscapes and cottage interiors, holds within it the answer to a variety of questions, are both imaginative and piquant. It is a book that will delight children's thirst for puzzles and make an ideal introduction for the pre-reader to what books are for and how to 'make reading work'. A word of gratitude must go to the publishers for the generous page size and clear typeface. Ideal for all nursery, infant and remedial collections.

Gabrielle Maunder, in a review of "Each Peach Pear Plum," in The School Librarian, *Vol. 27, No. 2, June, 1979, p. 127.*

[*Each Peach Pear Plum*] is fast becoming that often claimed cliché, the 'nursery classic'. But this is exactly what it is. In thirteen simple rhyming couplets, Allan Ahlberg leads us through a medley of well-known fairytale and nursery characters, thus:

> Each Peach Pear Plum
> I spy Tom Thumb
>
> Tom Thumb in the cupboard
> I spy Mother Hubbard
>
> Mother Hubbard down the cellar
> I spy Cinderella
>
> Cinderella on the stairs
> I spy the Three Bears

The satisfying unfolding of sequence, the neatness of the text and its clever accommodation of each new character contribute to the pleasure with which the reader is led round in a kind of literary loop to the gentle finale. By using a nursery-rhyme structure, Mr Ahlberg captures that elusive feeling of a rhyme like 'Sing a Song of Sixpence', where seemingly arbitrary sequences acquire the quality of a story in miniature. *Each Peach Pear Plum* has affection, humour, a perfect interweaving of words and pictures as simple as plaiting hair. It reverberates beyond what is actually in the book because it draws on and contributes back to a much larger tradition — the nursery rhyme — in a mutual enrichment.

The book is illustrated in a series of double spreads: each couplet is on the left-hand page with a vignette above (which is repeated in the jacket decorations) facing an illustration on the right-hand page which depicts the character named in the first line of the couplet, with the next character hidden somewhere in the picture for the reader to find. Janet Ahlberg uses a slightly wobbly line and watercolour, tentative yet with flourish; executed so simply that you can see the pen strokes and brush marks: you can see how it's done. Her shapes are enclosed in brown ink line, and hatched and shaded at the

edges to give them a half-rounded feeling. Perspectives are flattened in a slightly childlike way, and the picture depths are fairly shallow: characters are always in the foreground, and the backgrounds resemble painted backcloths hung just behind them. It's a device much used by Maurice Sendak, which I always attribute to his early work as a shop-window display artist. Mrs Ahlberg uses this shallow picture depth to give the viewer a feeling of intimacy with the picture, of being right up in front of it; the effect is like looking into a diarama or a shop window, or into one of those model-pictures which children make inside shoeboxes.

To my mind, this graphic treatment is at least partly an instinctive response to function, to the eventual use of the book being held close to the face by a young child in her mother's lap, probably. It is yet another instance of Janet Ahlberg's thoroughness of response to bookmaking, the light-hearted carefulness which makes her turn even the title page's panoramic landscape into a pictorial map containing all the locations of each event in the story — because of course, there *is* a story, just a small one, hinted at, shown in clues and details in every picture. So, each time the reader returns to the book, there is more to discover. When you consider that the picture-book age goes from maybe eighteen months to maybe seven or eight years, and when you consider how fast children develop and change during that time, a book which can be returned to over and over again for even a couple of those years is an extremely skilful creation. (pp. 155-57)

Celia Berridge, "Taking a Good Look at Picture Books," in Signal, *No. 36, September, 1981, pp. 152-58.*

Sometimes an author will deliberately play on previous reading knowledge in order to make a story. This happens in *Each Peach Pear Plum* . . . , in which nursery rhymes and stories are brought together to provide characters in a new book. At its simplest level, the Ahlbergs offer children a game of I Spy. If the child reader has had the misfortune to have lived for three or four years without having heard the stories of Tom Thumb or Cinderella or the three bears, the book can still be read, the game still played, because the characters who are obviously the ones named can be found hidden in the pictures. But the child who has the advantage of being brought up enriched by hearing stories and reading books will have the added and much greater pleasure of playing the game, airing his knowledge, re-experiencing the pleasure of the nursery stories, and finding a whole new story based on those familiar tales and verses. (p. 179)

Aidan Chambers, "A Critical Blueprint," in his Introducing Books to Children, *second edition, The Horn Book, Inc., 1983, pp. 174-93.*

SON OF A GUN (1979)

Son of a Gun proves yet again that the comic Western is our most durable art form. Alan Coren revived it for children some years back. This present volume takes on where he left off, and has a cast of cut-outs: a blundering, myopic sheriff, his Amazonian wife and pesky son, Amos, not to mention a pair of sidewinders called the Slocum brothers, and a traveller in patent medicines. The individual parts of this work are somehow indifferent: predictable plot; awful dialogue; deliberately atrocious grammar. Yet I'll be hornswoggled if the

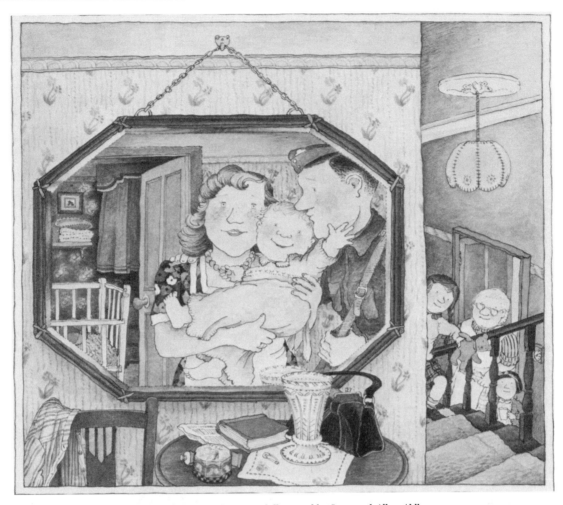

From Peek-a-Boo! *written and illustrated by Janet and Allan Ahlberg.*

whole darn thing ain't plumb deelightful. Dem Ahlbergs is sure one helluva pair.

John Naughton, "Pesky Parts," in The Listener, *Vol. 102, No. 2636, November 8, 1979, p. 644.*

All the stock characters of the Wild West romp through the pages of this witty and amusing spoof. . . .

Every now and again the authors provide a brief summary of the story so far in case the reader has got lost in the ramifications of the plot or just simply been laughing too much at the dialogue. It is the kind of book that can be read more than once and will induce companions to demand tetchily what it is that keeps the reader so continuously chuckling to himself. It should become a family favourite.

D. A. Young, in a review of "Son of a Gun," in The Junior Bookshelf, *Vol. 43, No. 6, December, 1979, p. 321.*

THE LITTLE WORM BOOK (1979)

Janet and Allan Ahlberg have scored yet again with a hilarious parody of a solemn information book. *The Little Worm Book* has sections on The Common Worm, Pet Worms, the History of Worms, Worms around the World and so on, get-ting funnier and funnier. The final word on this topic—and on many other topics that primary children are asked to mug up from scrappy disconnected fact books.

Virginia Makins, "A Laugh a Minute," in The Times Educational Supplement, *No. 3311, November 23, 1979, p. 30.*

The irrepressible Ahlbergs, husband and wife, have already witnessed the huge success of this tiny book in their native England. Readers from three through 93, it's reported, have created such a demand for the comic encyclopedia about worms that it keeps going back to press. No wonder. All the "facts" delivered are accompanied by skillful, insanely humorous pictures of the creepers who were on Earth before us and may inherit the world. Here are worms as pets, advice on purchasing healthy worms with examples of those to avoid (a worm with a squint, for one), cunning traps to catch worms, tips on caring for your worms (a converted glove, finger tips removed, makes a cozy home for five worms) plus data on such exotics as the vicious wild worm of the Pampas, the Borneo Dog Worm that barks, etc. Seldom does a mere three dollars buy so much amusement as this treasure.

A review of "The Little Worm Book," in Publishers

Weekly, *Vol. 217, No. 3, January 25, 1980, p. 340.*

TWO WHEELS, TWO HEADS; THE ONE AND ONLY TWO HEADS (1979)

The idea of a monster with two heads but one body, so that he washes his faces, refuses to tell himself secrets, quarrels, and calls himself rude names, can produce many imaginative possibilities for a series, especially when his friends are the Four Arms family. Although the language and actions are suitable for four- to six-year-olds, it is the older child or reluctant reader who will best appreciate the verbal play, cartoon asides and old jokes. These books fall between the vintage delicacy of **Each peach pear plum** for younger children and the garish exuberance of the **Brick Street boys,** but if they do not achieve their excellence, they will nevertheless be useful additions to many libraries, for as usual the illustrations not only complement but add to the text. (pp. 32-3)

> *Margaret Payne, in a review of "The One and Only Two Heads" and "Two Wheels Two Heads," in* The School Librarian, *Vol. 28, No. 1, March, 1980, pp. 32-3.*

Only a talented artist such as Janet Ahlberg could get away with a two-headed hippopotamus-like creature who actually looks cuddly and appealing.

> One morning Two Heads sits up in bed
> He is beside himself
> Half of him has a secret and
> will not tell the other half

Soon all is discovered – it is Two Heads' birthday, a party is planned and his friend Four Arms is invited. Big print will make this book and its companion volume **Two Wheels Two Heads** popular on the shelves of five and six year olds.

> *J. Russell, in a review of "The One and Only Two Heads," in* The Junior Bookshelf, *Vol. 44, No. 3, June, 1980, p. 114.*

FUNNYBONES (1980)

What happens in the story is of less importance than the basic situation and the way in which the story's told, in a book in comic strip format. It begins in proper ghost story style, with a dark dark town, and a dark dark street and a dark dark house with a dark dark cellar . . . where a big skeleton and a little skeleton and a dog skeleton live. They go out for some midnight fun on a playground and the zoo, and since they can't find anyone else to frighten, they have a high old time frightening each other. The Ahlbergs have fun with words and with the concept of skeletons at play, and their communicable zest precludes any note of the macabre.

> *Zena Sutherland, in a review of "Funnybones," in* Bulletin of the Center for Children's Books, *Vol. 34, No. 11, July-August, 1981, p. 205.*

I suppose this might be regarded as [Raymond Briggs's] *Fungus the Bogeyman* translated into less sophisticated form for younger children! There is a spice of delightful shiver-down-the-spine at the "dark, dark cellar" down the staircase in the house in the street in the town on the hill, all dark too, where a family of skeletons with smiling very human faces live with their dog, walk in the park, play games and live an entirely

normal life, except that it all occurs at night and even their Zoo animals are skeleton ones. . . . With the Ahlbergs, however, one expects surprises. This one happens to the tune of "Dem bones gonna rise again" (a pity that the tune is nowhere included with the adaptation of the words, for home readers!). The funny illustrations and familiar rhythms and repetitions take the sting out of the young reader's natural ghost fears. (pp. 142-43)

> *M. Hobbs, in a review of "Funnybones," in* The Junior Bookshelf, *Vol. 45, No. 4, August, 1981, pp. 142-43.*

PEEPO! (1981; U.S. edition as Peek-a-Boo!)

For young children, a book game of small revelations. On the left-hand page, a vignetted picture of the bouncy baby. Between that baby and the scene around him is a plain peekaboo page with a circle cut in the center; until this page is turned, most of the illustration beyond is concealed. The cycle of the day goes from waking to the kitchen at breakfast to the back yard, park, supper, bath and good night. The "reader" is invited to explore the lavishly detailed pictures with rhymed promptings: "Baby in the bath/PEEK-A-BOO!/ He can see a rubber duck/ Can you?" The setting is England in World War II, with the father home on leave; there is a coal grate, wooden ironing board, free-standing wardrobe, gothic radio. The interior views are disarmingly untidy, the colors soft and rather faded. For all its adult appeal, this demands quite a lot from young eyes; shapes and objects are neither large enough nor sharply enough defined for its intended audience. Children just at the prereading stage revel in this sort of illustration, but the text is young for them. A treat for the earliest reader, but otherwise a little off the mark.

> *Pamela Warren Stebbins, in a review of "Peek-a-Boo!" in* School Library Journal, *Vol. 28, No. 5, January, 1982, p. 58.*

In **Peepo!** which is made up in a series of four-page sequences, we see one day through the eyes of a baby in a forties wartime setting. Janet Ahlberg uses a similar illustrative style to that of **Each peach pear plum:** gentle watercolours outlined by dark brown pen and ink lines. The scenes she creates are littered with life's ephemera but great care and precision have given the scenes an air of busy domesticity. Other ingredients — shape and size, the paper used, the enchanting cover, the delicate pink endpapers, the peephole views on the title pages, the shaped frames with small items at the corners, and the final picture with its happily-sleeping infant and words which invite the reader to return immediately to the beginning of the book and relive the day — all contribute to the aesthetic quality of a book whose rhyming text is a pleasure to read aloud.

> *Jill Bennett, in a review of "Peepo!" in* The School Librarian, *Vol. 30, No. 3, September, 1982, p. 221.*

THE HA HA BONK BOOK (1982)

This small, cheerful book offers eleven chapters of jokes, dividing them into those suitable for Dad, Mum, Baby Brother, teacher, your Mother-in-Law . . . .

> "How do you start a jelly race?

Get set."
"How do you start a pudding race?
Sago!"

Even the authors admit that, if their audience is of an age to appreciate jokes like these, they are unlikely to be old enough to have mothers-in-law.

Every page carries a quick fire succession of four or five ancient, predictable but frequently still funny jokes and the effect is reminiscent of the traditional patter routines of pairs of stand up comedians. A new freshness is given to much of the humour by the tiny, spontaneous-seeming black and white sketches which Janet Ahlberg appears to have doodled in all available margins.

> *R. Baines, in a review of "The Ha Ha Bonk Book," in* The Junior Bookshelf, *Vol. 46, No. 4, August, 1982, p. 137.*

The Ahlbergs preface their dippy sections of gags, appropriate for various people, with notes more hilarious than the jokes themselves, although these are, with few exceptions, original and a cinch to tickle kids here as they have in the author-illustrators' native England. The only drawback is that some references are definitely British and probably incomprehensible to American boys and girls. Otherwise, the book abounds with merriment, illustrated by the Ahlbergs' inimitable ink drawings.

> *A review of "The Ha Ha Bonk Book," in* Publishers Weekly, *Vol. 222, No. 19, November 5, 1982, p. 71.*

THE BABY'S CATALOGUE (1982)

From the title you might assume that the book is no more than a picture dictionary of a series of unrelated items and incidents, but do not be misled. Its potential is enormous. In her inimitable style Janet Ahlberg illustrates twenty-four hours in the lives of five families and their babies. The pictures abound with closely observed and delightful touches: a dog clearing up the food spilt beneath a highchair, a sister sitting her brother on her lap and getting a wet knee for her pains. There are dozens of stories to be discovered and invented through its pages as well as jokes to enjoy, matching games, talking points and personal memories to recall.

> *Jill Bennett, in a review of "The Baby's Catalogue," in* The Signal Review of Children's Books, 1, *1982, p. 8.*

Given the appeal of commercial catalogs—adult- and child-oriented examples abound—an eventual baby-size version seems, in retrospect anyway, almost inevitable. That the Ahlbergs should undertake the task is merely good fortune. From teddy bears to high chairs, **The Baby's Catalogue** reveals a young child's reality, and though the paper-diapered offspring of the pampered '80s may not readily recognize the cloth versions drying on the line, most toddlers will find much that is familiar, and dear, to point at and ponder over (even an anatomically accurate baby boy in a bathtub). The tots are carefully balanced throughout—curly-haired and straight, dark-skinned and light, singles and twins—as are the families and life styles—bewhiskered as well as button-down dads, both career moms and stay-at-homes. Common to all, however, is the universal sense of caring; the inclusion of the child in the life of the family is everywhere apparent. As such, the catalogue becomes more than a mere display of the items, events and people that make up a baby's world; it is, in fact, a vision of where, and how, a child fits into life.

> *Kristi Thomas Beavin, in a review of "The Baby's Catalogue," in* School Library Journal, *Vol. 29, No. 8, April, 1983, p. 96.*

Served up in a clever new format for the familiar first picture book dictionary, this volume has an antipasto eye appeal: Page after page of intricate, colorful items are carefully arranged for visual consumption. But on closer inspection one loses appetite.

The delicate watercolor diaper pins, high chairs, buttocks and duckies are too pastel and cute. They do not invite conversation or even always illustrate the text. For instance, "Accidents," presumably a depiction of childhood mishaps, has a little girl quite deliberately feeding a fancy cake to her puppy and a baby boy putting blocks into a fishbowl. To call these "Mistakes" would be more accurate but would deprive the authors of a patronizing joke at the expense of their subjects.

> *Janice Prindle, in a review of "The Baby's Catalogue," in* The New York Times Book Review, *May 29, 1983, p. 18.*

PLAYMATES; YUM YUM (1984)

Janet and Allan Ahlberg's ingenious new books have pictures with small slots into which can be fitted a variety of cut-out objects—if the robot tires of his breakfast of old cans, pans, bolts and pins he can swop it for a boiled egg. The books work on the principle that such possibilities are endless and the great thrill (not merely for a child) is that there are no rules. To combine reading with game is a tricky business: a child can easily become suspicious and refuse to play. But when one is allowed to make up one's own rules, "reading" is less onerous; indeed it takes place almost unconsciously.

The figures in **Playmates** may be sited "correctly" (duck in bath, chicken in farmyard, baby in buggy) but if a fantasist chooses to sit the "sitting-room mouse" on the elephant's back or the hedgehog in the bath and use the cat as a ball for the monkey, the concepts "bath" and "ball" will still be absorbed. **Playmates** provides scope for a variety of activities, from swopping to tidying-up.

Yum Yum gives marginally greater pleasure, probably because it is always fun to play with one's food. There are enough moveable feasts for everyone on the party page to have a savoury course first, parents will be glad to know. The dog and cat can have the same bone and fish that they got on the "Feed the animals" pages. The witch tends to end up with the boiled egg, but if she is still hungry she can always have the baby's bottle too. (The slots are wide enough, and the slotters strong enough, for two or even three to be gathered together.) Take the sweets from the shop and with the puddings and cake the table will groan. Janet and Allan Ahlberg's earlier books, though always good, have sometimes dipped too deep into whimsy. In **Yum Yum** and **Playmates** the reader takes final responsibility for crazy or comic juxtapositions (even though these have only been made possible by the Ahlberg's inventiveness) and can impose his own pattern or disorder. Among the cast and slotters are some of their particular favourites: witches, bears, cats, frogs and babies.

These books are beautifully produced, tough enough to last

a long time and provided with complete sets of spare slotters. They are attractive, inventive and educational and, like most of the Ahlbergs' books, they are sure to have the popular success they deserve.

Paula Neuss, "Moveable Feasts," in The Times Literary Supplement, *No. 4261, November 30, 1984, p. 1380.*

Young children often incorporate familiar characters and story elements into their spontaneous play. [In *Playmates*] the Ahlbergs cater to that impulse, encouraging children to try out meanings with the book itself as a play area. An ingenious combination of toy and book, *Playmates* invites children to manipulate small cutout figures with tabs that fit into slots in the sturdy doublefold pages. . . . There is no story sequence except for the "tidy up" of the last page. The variations on the single theme of playing with toys make it similar to other concept books; a companion volume featuring real and imagined foods is called *Yum Yum.* Every toy's tab is labeled, and the words that caption the pages ("catch . . . the ball") are in oversize, eye-catching print. Yet the real language opportunities here are more for talk than for reading. Lots of conversation and ministries about the toy characters are likely to evolve if the book is shared one-on-one, as it probably should be. The inevitable question of durability is only partly answered by the provision of a punch-out sheet of playmate "spares" that comes with each book.

Janet Hickman, in a review of "Playmates," in Language Arts, *Vol. 62, No. 7, November, 1985, p. 788.*

THE JOLLY POSTMAN OR OTHER PEOPLE'S LETTERS (1986)

The contents of the letters which Postman Pat makes such efforts to deliver generally remain frustratingly unrevealed. Janet and Allan Ahlberg's splendidly inventive book, however, satisfies curiosity by allowing not just to read, but to open other people's mail.

The Postman's round is described in cheerful, but unremarkable rhymes, as he travels from one fairy-tale character to another, wobbling slightly from champagne as he cycles away from the celebrations at Cinderella's palace. The delight of the book lies in the envelopes which are interleaved with the pages of verse. Their exteriors release preliminary hints about the senders. Careful child's handwriting and a crookedly stuck-on stamp lead, when extracted and unfolded, to a prettily illustrated if badly spelt letter of apology to the Three Bears' household from Goldilocks: she offers amends with an invitation to Baby Bear to come to her party, promising "3 kinds of jelly and a conjoora". Any suspicion that all the correspondence will be from children of the reader's own age is quickly dispelled, however, by the circular which the Wicked Witch receives, second class, from Hobgoblin Supplies Ltd, offering, among other bargains aimed at the "modern witch", a new newt (buy four, and get one free), a non-stick Cauldron Set (with the bonus of a recipe for toad in the hole), and flying goggles for the cat. Unsurprisingly, the Postman is shown hiding behind the paper, as the Witch cackles through her mail, leaving his green tea on one side.

The Ahlbergs encourage the importance of looking carefully, and of making visual connections with already held fairy-tale and nursery-rhyme knowledge; not just by rustling through the contents of the Postman's sack, but by showing the countryside he works in, the interiors he visits. A cow jumps over the moon in the early evening sky as he cycles back from Goldilocks' party, having played — what else? — Postman's Knock. Among the guests there are Mr Jack, with sticking plaster on his broken crown; a rotund egg in braces, and, eating crisps, a small black sheep. Little Miss Muffet and Old King Cole find their way on to the pound note which Mrs Bunting and Baby are kind enough to enclose in their birthday card to Goldilocks; while on the holiday postcard that Jack sends Mr V. Bigg in Beanstalk Gardens, the old woman's shoe has been refurbished as a luxury hotel, with entertainment from the cat and the fiddle.

Additionally, full use is made of contemporary culture. Peter Piper has pleasure in sending a copy of his book for younger readers to Cinderella on the occasion of her marriage to H R H Prince Charming, reminding one, on the final page of his tiny souvenir, that the headlines had proclaimed "FAIRY-TALE PRINCESS". A less pleasant communication is sent to Mr Wolf, from Meeny, Miny, Mo & Co, Solicitors, requesting that he cease the harassment and impersonation of their client's grandmother. The Ahlbergs' book succeeds in making the familiar new, even surprising. In its inventiveness and immaculate execution, it is a delight to read.

Kate Flint, "Forms of Address," in The Times Literary Supplement, *No. 4365, November 28, 1986, p. 1345.*

Once in a while a picture-book arrives that's so brilliant, so broad in its appeal, it seems to be a summation of the state-of-the-art. For me, *The Jolly Postman* is just such a book. As a matching of word and image it's a virtuoso performance; as a feat of design it's without a flaw; as an instance of the sort of bliss only a book can confer it's equally alluring for child and adult; as a conspectus of Where It's At Right Now it gives the current latitude and longitude of the illustrated book for children with pinpoint accuracy. In short, Janet and Allan Ahlberg have come up with a Mistress-and-Masterpiece.

In my view, that is. But my view is certainly suspect for reasons shrewdly diagnosed by the former pupil who remarked 'we can always tell when you're keen on a book because you go all starry-eyed and get over-excited'. Beware, then. This appraisal of *The Jolly Postman* is offered in the spirit of celebrant rather than critic — my vision being cluttered and my emotions a-twang from sheer enthusiasm. Mind you, I'm in good company. When judging the 1986 Emil Award with Margaret Meek and Elaine Moss, I had an early and unsettling impression that this distinguished pair were holding back in much the way I was — like gamblers saving an ace for just the right moment. They were, too. Our admiration and pleasure at this year's offerings by Blake and Burningham and Foreman and Hutchins and Wilson was entirely shared but so, it turned out, was our preferred front-runner. (p. 4)

[What] lifts *The Jolly Postman* above even competition as classy as this is the sort of simple, bright idea that's obvious once someone has thought of it. After all, what's the most personal, most user-friendly mode of written communication — opted for by storytellers from the very start of sustained narrative? A letter, yes. Link this mode, deployed as correspondence in real envelopes between the most familiar and best-loved characters from nursery rhymes and tales, with an illustrated 'holding' text and what have we got? Well, a neat

So 'Grandma' read the letter
And poured the tea,
Which the not-so-Jolly Postman
Drank . . . nervously.

From The Jolly Postman or Other People's Letters, *written and illustrated by Janet and Allan Ahlberg.*

example of what scholars of a structuralist and semiotic disposition call intertext — a strategy we've encountered before in the Ahlberg opus with *Each Peach Pear Plum* and *Jeremiah in the Dark Woods.* It's a joke scene, . . . but also a very serious game for behind every text stand other texts, not just as references but as embeddings in our culture.

Hence our delight as differing registers, rhetorics and conventions are gloriously mocked by Goldilocks's letter of apology to the three bears (personal interaction), Jack's postcard to the giant (holiday brochure), a mail-shot to Hansel and Gretel's Witch (advertising), a solicitor's warning to the Big Bad Wolf (the law), a complimentary first-off-the-press marriage memento for Cinderella (publishing) and so on . . . a succession of send-ups woven together in a marvellous montage of writing and re-writing.

All of which, you may say, is very well for structuralists and semiologists but what about the kids? Will they be laughing? You bet, because, as always, Janet and Allan Ahlberg have their implied child-reader firmly in focus — any from top-infant on upwards who is ready to grin at stories partly outgrown but still recalled with affection. Indeed, my guess is that many youngsters will also spot the element of inter-pic in Janet Ahlberg's warm, witty illustrations — the stamps and postmarks and handwriting deftly parodied, the sly refer-

ence to other imagery by way of a Briggs giant or Pienkowski owl or Bestall bear.

Yes, *The Jolly Postman* is clever stuff — made cleverer still by the traditional virtues it's careful not to neglect. Author and illustrator play craftily off each other, for example:

> Once upon a bicycle
>   So they say,
> A Jolly Postman came one day
>   From over the hills
> And far away . . .

. . . so Janet teases Allan with a sign-post that reads *Faraway 4 miles* and offers an end-piece which has the hero reading his own letter. Both text and illustration, in fact, are as balanced and free-wheeling as the postman's progress through the book's pages which is, to say the least, fluid:

> So Cinders read her little book,
>   The Postman drank champagne
> Then wobbled off
>   On his round again
>   (and again and again — Oops!). . . .

Altogether, it's hard to imagine the book giving more pleasure — unless, perhaps, it just happens to miss a reader's favourite storybook set-up. In which case no more is required than a bit of *readerly* intervention. The book is envelope-sized, after all, so why not reach for pencils, paper and the family post-kit to continue the delivery? Not least of **The Jolly Postman**'s virtues is the bond it makes between reading and writing. It's an R.S.V.P. of a book which invites participation through an implicit post-or-inter script. There's been no better encouragement for epistolary enterprise since the invention of the pen-pal. Small wonder it gives me stellar-vision and hyper-activity: a condition, I fancy, we can predict for almost everyone on whom this postman calls. (pp. 4-5)

> *Chris Powling, "The Jolly Postman: Another Ahlberg Classic," in* Books for Keeps, *No. 42, January, 1987, pp. 4-5.*

The fame of this remarkable book will have far outrun anything which appears in this review. From time to time the sheer exuberant genius, which is the deep foundation of the appeal of children's books, defeats description. (p. 39)

As the postman cycles on his round, to the rhythm of a new nursery rhyme, we see the thoughtful brilliance of the detailed illustration on every page. The letters are miniatures of our social interaction, with lawyers, publicity, greetings cards and publishing (Cinderella's biography is actually *there*). The postmarks and handwriting are allusive, the tiny faces at a window, a duck, a sheep, a dish and spoon on the table at the party, the snatches of text, Cinderella reading the book we've got, all create a layered *polysemy* that adults sometimes fail to recognise in children's books. As far as the young reader (about eight?) is concerned, this is the joyful recognition of old friends, a mixture of the now and the then. Don't miss the Mirror Mirror, the interiors of the houses and . . . . Having been party to decisions which gave this book the Emil Award, I have had my say. A book in the great tradition. (p. 40)

> *Margaret Meek, in a review of "The Jolly Postman or Other People's Letters," in* The School Librarian, *Vol. 35, No. 1, February, 1987, pp. 39-40.*

If I had to pick just one book I couldn't be without from the past few years, it would have to be the Ahlbergs' **The Jolly Postman.** Initially this can be seen as just a novelty but it conveys a valuable message (and indeed one rarely found in books for younger readers): the envelopes and their contents delivered by that Jolly Postman, and an integral part of the story, powerfully demonstrate some of the varied purposes for writing. In addition, by their use of familiar fairy tale characters such as Goldilocks and Cinderella, the Ahlbergs reinforce and build on the literary knowledge of young readers. I've seen this book act as inspiration for many writers as well as readers.

> *Jill Bennett, in a review of "The Jolly Postman," in* Books for Keeps, *No. 52, September, 1988, p. 25.*

THE CINDERELLA SHOW (1986)

The Town End Primary School presents a play based on Cinderella, and readers are invited to watch the action onstage, backstage and in the audience. From the multiracial cast of kids who perform, to the ongoing comments of the watchful parents, this is quite a good first look at how plays happen, without ever losing track of the Cinderella storyline. While performers are onstage, some children are slipping into costume; others are quietly pushing scenery and props into

place. The funniest scenes in this hand-sized book are of the stepsisters bossing poor Cindy around, and the entire comic strip-like production, in black-and-white miniature drawings, is as informative as it is fun.

> *A review of "The Cinderella Show," in* Publishers Weekly, *Vol. 231, No. 8, March 13, 1987, p. 82.*

A charming book for one-on-one sharing, **The Cinderella Show** gives readers a front-row seat at Town End Primary School's Christmas play. Beginning with a title-page sketch of a bundled-up Cinderella walking through the starry night on her way to the performance, the small black-and-white drawings almost stand alone. The chaos in the dressing room gives way to two small actresses peeking through the curtain at the audience. The perspective shifts to the audience as the play begins. Then comes intermission, with the audience chatting over refreshments while the cast relaxes backstage. The play resumes and moves toward the Prince's proposal. Post-performance confusion ensues, and then audience and actors head for home through freshly-fallen snow. Scratchy cartoon-style pencil illustrations are cleverly laid out, giving the impression of a series of film segments. Full-page drawings and two-page spreads are used for wide angle scenes; a close-up effect is created by dividing the page into four sections bordered in white, à la comic strips. Humorous details abound. While the book's small size and dialogue preclude story hour use, this is a terrific lap book; older primary children could read it alone.

> *Lucy Young Clem, in a review of "The Cinderella Show," in* School Library Journal, *Vol. 33, No. 10, June-July, 1987, p. 75.*

THE CLOTHES HORSE AND OTHER STORIES (1987)

Each of the six shaggy-dog stories in this collection provides a literal interpretation of an everyday expression. . . . While the initial concept may appeal to the literal-mindedness of children and their fondness for wordplay, the stories themselves are somewhat disappointing. Their silliness seems strained and arbitrary rather than genuinely funny, with adult undertones instead of a truly childlike perspective; and the chatty narrative voice begins to seem intrusive, even fey. In format, the collection falls somewhere between picture book and middle-reader. Full-color pictures decorate, rather than illustrate, the text; but these contain all the charm, humor and liveliness for which this husband-and-wife team is renowned.

> *A review of "The Clothes Horse and Other Stories," in* Publishers Weekly, *Vol. 233, No. 4, January 29, 1988, p. 430.*

How do they do it? Last year, **The jolly postman;** now, the text and pictures that turn our common phrases into narrative japes and word-play and uncommon storytelling. It's such a game, but, goodness, so much more, and such skill. . . . In the *Tristram Shandy* tradition of (apparently) free (unpaid for) associations, the tales tumble out with the closeness of oral narrative, rich in asides, intertextual references, jolly jokes for those who choose to make a night of it (a riot for text critics). The exquisite pictures anchor the metaphors to the presentation of the giant, the train, the savings box, God reading, and so on. Only books and stories can make it happen, and here reading is the ordinary way of capturing the magic of demotic speech.

Margaret Meek, in a review of "The Clothes Horse and Other Stories," in The School Librarian, *Vol. 36, No. 1, February, 1988, p. 19.*

Joan W(insor) Blos

1928-

American author of fiction and picture books and critic.

A teacher and reviewer of children's literature as well as a student of psychology and child development, Blos is well known as the author of *A Gathering of Days: A New England Girl's Journal 1830-32* (1979), a work of historical fiction for middle graders which was awarded the Newbery Medal in 1980. This book, which was prompted when Blos researched the history of the New England summer home which belonged to her husband's family, tells of fourteen-year-old Catherine Cabot Hall and of the events in her life during the months documented in her journal. By using the journal format to reveal Catherine's innermost thoughts, Blos creates a character who is praised both for her striking realism and for transcending the differences between her time and ours. Catherine reaches maturity through confronting such situations as offering assistance to a member of another race, facing the intrusion of a stepparent, and agonizing through the death of a close friend. Lauded for its accurate representation of Catherine's emotions, *A Gathering of Days* is also considered a remarkable piece of documentation of everyday life in early nineteenth-century New Hampshire. Blos again turned to historical fiction with *Brothers of the Heart: A Story of the Old Northwest, 1837-1838* (1985), the portrayal of Shem, a crippled boy who learns to overcome his handicap largely through the sagacity of a native American woman who teaches him the meaning of self-worth. As with *A Gathering of Days,* Blos's depiction of frontier life is supplemented by her inclusion of excerpts from the diaries and letters of her characters, a feature celebrated for adding flavor to both works. Blos has also written picture books which promote such themes as the significance of imagination in childhood play and the need for compromise between extremely dissimilar types of people.

(See also *Something about the Author,* Vols. 27, 33; *Contemporary Authors,* Vol. 101; and *Contemporary Authors New Revision Series,* Vol. 21.)

"IT'S SPRING," SHE SAID (1968)

"After it had been cold for a long time a sweet warm wind came into the city." Coat buttons open, snow plows pack up their shovels, the ice cream man goes to his garage, the shoe store has a boot sale. "Too soon, too soon," says Mrs. Mundy, and she is right. Cold blasts return, and Matthew Peterson regrets his lost mittens. Mrs. Mundy again outguesses the vegetable man as warm south winds return to stay. By trying to maintain several scenes this diffuses very simple impressions. . . .

> *A review of " 'It's Spring,' She Said," in* Kirkus Service, *Vol. XXXVI, No. 4, February 15, 1968, p. 177.*

Low-keyed and elliptical in style, this book on spring will tickle early readers and listeners into comments on signs of spring in the city. Mr. Lynn checks over the ice cream truck, janitors put away their snow shovels, and Matthew looks for

his bat and his gray felt baseball hat. Only Mrs. Mundy knows that this is a false spring, but she also correctly predicts the real arrival of spring. A slight but satisfying and appealing seasonal story.

> *Peggy Sullivan, in a review of " 'It's Spring,' She Said," in* School Library Journal, *Vol. 14, No. 7, March, 1968, p. 127.*

A GATHERING OF DAYS: A NEW ENGLAND GIRL'S JOURNAL 1830-32 (1979)

AUTHOR'S COMMENTARY

[*The following excerpt is from a speech Blos delivered at the presentation of the Newbery Award in 1980.*]

It is an awesome thing to be told that you have made a distinguished contribution to children's literature.

I learned that I had won the Newbery Medal late in January. The actual moment of notification—suitably close to midnight—was an event of transformative proportions, having all the trappings of magic, and not to be believed. (p. 393)

As rational beings we have come to expect development through stages, or something like orderly growth: from football practice to victory and thus to cheering throngs. The rhyme we chanted as children taught that first comes love and then comes marriage and then comes whoever and the baby carriage. . . . When events defy our expectations and we cannot locate the causes of effects, we start to think of magic. However, as readers of fairy tales know, magic, however magical, doesn't begin from scratch. Magic is merely a method of change; the means by which something existing in state A is made to assume state B. Pumpkin to coach or prince to frog; Joan Blos to Newbery winner. But the prince was a prince before he was a frog and the pumpkin will soon be a pumpkin again. And I, most of all, am my everyday self, a teacher of children's literature. And I must ask your forgiveness if I sometimes sound like one!

I have long believed that children's books are best when they are the work of those who share the essential, ancient, and parental need to cherish and inform the young. This does not mean that the books which they write must all be serious! Our first delight in the infant is the smile, and language itself arises in pleasure, in the "aahs" and coos of the baby at rest; for anger, the scream suffices.

Be that as it may, *A Gathering of Days* began in facts which I had collected about a particular New Hampshire house, its region, and its past; for example, that in 1809, ten years prior to his marriage, the builder of the house had purchased the homestead from an elder brother. He died at the age of thirty-seven in 1825. The will he wrote commenced as follows: "I," and then his name was given, "being sound of mind but weak in boddy . . ." [sic]. The *Grafton Journal* is said to have published a notice of the death. Initially random, my set of notes began to suggest certain patterns and include more distant events. It was at this time that I first suspected that I might have a book on my hands. I determined that it would be nonfiction; perhaps I would call it something like "The New Hampshire Book." Time passed, and despite the oppressive title, the thought to write endured. Meanwhile, the book decided for itself that fiction would serve the content better than the document I had planned. "The wind roared up the hill," I wrote, "and flung itself at the white painted house—" *Was* it white then? Would it have been red? I soon discovered to my chagrin that I did not know the color of the house toward which the wind roared up the hill, and furthermore, did not care. As truth exists in different forms, it was not exterior coloration but life as human experience that mattered most to me. (p. 394)

Looking back, I can now discern at least three kinds of truthfulness with which I was concerned: the *social truthfulness* of the situation, the *psychological truthfulness* of the characters, and the *literary truthfulness* of the manner of telling. A three-year-old child I once heard about was delighted to have discovered that they call it *orange juice* because it is orange, and juice. I, with equal earnestness, had just reinvented historical fiction. The story is what resulted. "How much of it is true?" I am asked. "I tried to make it truthful," I reply, "but not much of it is true."

The story's characters are the people who stare and stare from New England portraits by artists who left no names. Its location is rural New Hampshire. It was therefore important that the tone be closer to *Leavitt's Almanac,* for farmers, than *Godey's Ladies' Book.* Both the form and style of my book were suggested by period writings. It therefore pleases me

very much when people comment on the book's resemblance to actual family journals, or offer to share them with me.

Contemporary literature—post-Freudian and post-Joycean—has come to rely on open introspection to chart the changes in characters who are gifted self-observers. Within the journal form I had chosen lay an unexpected problem: how to present psychological change in persons not psychologically minded in the modern sense. I had to make two assumptions: first, that any report of events is going to be selectively determined by the reporting person; second, that that selectiveness is itself determined by inner priorities and needs, and so can represent them. These were enabling insights for me; and thereafter much of the work became the arrangement, in sequence, of such events as my diarist might record. She could then reveal herself without violation or contradiction; as she changed, responsively it would show how she was changing. So it is that, early in the book, Catherine, the heroine, busily reports that:

> Only three more weeks remain until Thanksgiving Day! I must attach my new lace collar to my Sabbath dress. Also, it being snug for me, I must take up the patterned frock which I have given to Matty. She can use it nicely, I think, together with her new knit stockings and the red Morocco boots that were mine once also.

Domestic details preoccupy her. Catherine, although but a child herself, is full of motherly cluckings and concerns about the younger sister for whom she has been made responsible by their mother's death.

One year later, she writes of a friend:

> Sophy, once so flibbertigibbet, sends good earnings home. All of the mill girls protested their pay, and as 'tis known no girl in New-England would take a place till the issue's resolved, the owners knuckled under rather than stop the mill.

The larger world impinges on Catherine's, while, at home, her father's remarriage proves a circumstance of importance. Through the difficult accommodation, through challenge, loss, and learning to trust, Catherine is able to achieve more lasting and more genuine growth.

Will young readers be aware of such aspects of the story? I am less worried about reader awareness, in the sense of articulate response, than hopeful that the inner story will generate understanding of others and of the self. Will some find the book old-fashioned, and thus irrelevant? Circumstances explored by the book are pertinent today: sex, as well as its consequences, the challenge to children when respected adults hold conflicting opinions, the making of new families out of shattered parts, the personal responsibility that lies between the socially accepted and the morally right. All of these are as centrally placed in my historical fiction as in more topical novels for children and for young adults. In a sense, my book was made possible by the books which recently, cogently, and usefully have enlarged the realm of the permissible in children's literature. The freedom which their authors won benefits others as much as themselves. I needed and I used that freedom; I gladly acknowledge that debt. (pp. 395-96)

On hearing about the book's award, a friend asked one of our children, "Is it another story in which someone somewhere grows up? I always used to notice," he said, "that all the Newbery books I read turned out to be about that." Well, of course. For what other subject can, and will so lastingly, appeal to those who write for children out of their adult lives? As parent, teacher, yes, *and writer,* I can comprehend the bond which derives from the age-old wish to encourage, literally meaning *to fill with courage,* those who are still young. The medal, as at last I understand, exacts rededication even as it rewards. In that spirit, I accept it with pride, believing in its magic, persuaded that it is true. (p. 396)

Joan W. Blos, "1980 Newbery Acceptance Speech," in Top of the News, *Vol. 36, No. 4, Summer, 1980, pp. 393-96.*

Her 14th is a pivotal year for 19th-Century New Englander Catherine Cabot Hall—one of change, loss, and leave taking. It's allowed to unfold slowly, as it was lived, in spare, pithy journal entries. In the course of it, her widowed father weds; her bookish stepmother unbends; and Catherine lets down her own reserve, notch by reluctant notch. She secretly gives her late mother's quilt to a runaway slave and suffers a guilty conscience and a "sorely offended" friend before the truth outs and she's set the exacting task of hand sewing a replacement (Mariner's Compass, with a nod to the fugitive). A loved friend dies tragically young and by year's end Catherine is about to go out in the world. Blos adroitly sidesteps the worst sin historical fiction for this age is heir to: her characters are truly of their times, not 1970s sensibilities masquerading in 1830s homespun, and old-fashioned in the best sense of the word—principled. The "simple" life on the farm is not facilely idealized, the larger issues of the day are felt (the teacher's abolitionist leanings cause trouble with the board; a school mate is sent to work in the mills), but it is the small moments between parent and child, friend and friend that are at the fore, and the core, of this low-key, intense, and reflective book.

Pamela D. Pollack, in a review of "A Gathering of Days: A New England Girl's Journal," in School Library Journal, *Vol. 26, No. 3, November, 1979, p. 84.*

Of the myriad forms novel-writing can take, the diary demands least in return for its indisputable charms. The author of a fictional journal need not pay too close attention to plot, character or even pertinent incident, since the form is by nature episodic, self-centered and, more often than not, rambling. In addition to these open invitations to literary license, the diary has built-in assets as well. There is, for one, the seductive attraction of the illicit: We can peruse the privately recorded thoughts of another human being, real or invented.

These broad truths affirmed, what specifically can be said of Joan Blos's *A Gathering of Days?* The fictional diary (though the fact that it is fictional is obscured rather than clarified by the book's subtitle) of 13-year-old Catherine Cabot Hall during the years 1830-32, Mrs. Blos's novel relies heavily on actual events gleaned from early 19th-century books, journals and newspapers of the region around Meredith, N. H.—the work's locale. What story there is couched in the language of that distant time—or what Mrs. Blos perceives that language to have been. An involute collage of quaint locutions, her prose is likely to discourage all but the most devoted readers.

A typical entry (about a winter outing) reads:

When we girls grew weary of skating, the boys cut

branches of evergreens and quickly pronounced them royal sleighs. . . . How festively we laughed and called, pretending we were ermine'd queens, and leaning back against the boughs while, before us, the boys' long strokes carried us over the ice."

On another day, Catherine reports her stepmother's words:

You must learn to like the doing of that which we like you to do. Glad submission of the will is the obedience that proves control. I do not mean you merely to comply. Reflect, accept, obey!

Did ever flesh-and-blood mortals communicate thus?

We can, of course, take Mrs. Blos's word for it, but we could also look, for comparison, to the journal of a near contemporary of Catherine, the real-life New Englander Louisa May Alcott. Only 10 years later, she is telling her diary:

Life is pleasanter than it used to be, and I don't care about dying any more. . . . I wish we were rich . . . I don't see who is to clothe and feed us when we are so poor now.

Surely the confidential tone and naturalness are worlds apart from Mrs. Blos's ersatz post-Colonial English.

In order to supply a pinch of suspense, the author introduces a runaway slave who is secretly given an old quilt by the heroine. But their shadowy encounter, shrouded in melodrama, is neither memorable nor enlightening. Another incident, this one concerning a Jewish peddler, is distressingly ambiguous. . . .

What is Mrs. Blos's purpose in telling us many of the things she does? The book's contents are a crazy quilt of seemingly random authentic incidents and mostly banal fictional filler material. No grand pattern or purpose emerges. When all is said and done, the reader knows little not found in history books—that there were, then, more than 13 million people in 28 states; that young girls from poor families were often packed off to work in the textile mills of Lowell, Mass.; that life was hard and many died young. On a more workaday level, there is dry, textbook information about such subjects as stenciling, the camera obscura and itinerant weavers. One interesting item is a report of the heroine's family freezing soup in November to re-heat and eat during the long winter.

Mrs. Blos's book is informed both by painstaking research and diligent collation, but the reader is left neither with bona-fide history nor nourishing fiction.

Selma G. Lanes, in a review of "A Gathering of Days," in The New York Times Book Review, *March 23, 1980, p. 34.*

Joan Blos has been involved with words and books, with children and books for children, for much of her life. Having been an avid reader as a child, a writer in school and at work, a student of child development, and a parent, she rediscovered the world of children's books as a volunteer reviewer in 1954. (p. 374)

For most of her career she has thought of herself primarily as a teacher, and she is a good one. Her love of language, her knowledge of psychology and child development, her demanding standards, her humor and easy personal style make children's literature enjoyable and important for her students in education and—through them—for the children they will teach. She takes children and children's books seriously though never pretentiously—unlike the young student who applied for admission to her writing seminar some years ago. "Oh, Mrs. Blos," this untried writer exclaimed. "I've always wanted to write children's literature!"

Despite her amusement at the ingenuous remark, it is apparent that Joan Blos has, in fact, done just that; she has written children's literature. The field in which she has served as scholar, critic, and teacher is now enriched by her own contribution to its source. She thinks of her book [*A Gathering of Days*] as "one part of her life." Now this book—this gathering of days—will become, in turn, a part of the lives of many people. And her own regard for self-understanding, for empathy, and for realized growth, quietly stated in her nineteenth-century heroine's clear voice, will encourage and move young readers for many years to come. Tying together the past, the present, and the promise of the future in a tale that confirms human bonds—this is what Joan Blos, as a teacher, has always believed to be the role of literature. Her book is true to that belief and to her life.

Joan Blos has said that the nineteenth-century New England family imagined in *A Gathering of Days* represents "a borrowed past" for someone who, as a child, knew only two grandparents and who even now knows nothing of those who went before. That the Holocaust obliterated any chance to trace her own roots perhaps accounts for her deep interest in continuities and connections and in the relationship of apparently disparate people's lives to one's own.

"I see the writing of *A Gathering of Days* as an extension of the rest of my life," she says. "It's not something that makes it all worthwhile; not some culmination. It's one *part,* and I hope that new things are going to come from it."

New things *will* come of it; new things always come to Joan Blos. She invites them. (p. 375)

The precisely observed detail in *A Gathering of Days* is predictable from someone who cares, as she does, about the color of wooden beads against a dress or of a picnic cloth spread on meadow grass. On being asked to describe herself for young readers, Joan Blos says that she likes to take long walks with her husband, to knit, and to make soup and that she doesn't like mean jokes, scary movies, or blueberries cooked into muffins.

She says (and knowing her genuine modesty, I believe her) that she is absolutely astonished to have won the Newbery Medal. I say, with the pride and pleasure of long acquaintance, that it is an honor worthy of her. (p. 377)

> Betty Miles, *"Joan W. Blos,"* in The Horn Book Magazine, *Vol. LVI, No. 4, August, 1980, pp. 374-77.*

I have long supported a dichotomous way of understanding children's literature, one that is simplistic but helpful. Books reflect one of two basic views of the human experience: Awe and Wonder, the religious perspective, or Self-reliance and Rationalism, the humanist perspective. (p. 169)

Not surprisingly, last year's list of the most admired children's books is dominated by the humanist perspective. These books explicate modern life, offer models of growth, and confront a now-slim list of previously off-limit subjects. Some become so direct and precise in their problem-solving style that they edge perilously close to the realm of pamphlet or guidebook. However, five powerful books emerge whose

religious tendencies and artistic elegance make them what Stevens calls "ten-foot poets among inchlings." [These books include *A Gathering of Days* as well as *All Together Now* by Sue Ellen Bridgers, *How I Hunted the Little Fellows* by Boris Zhitknov, *Ladder of Angels* by Madeleine L'Engle, and *Words by Heart* by Ouida Sebestyen.] Each departs from the humanist commonalities and yet uniquely differentiates itself from the other four. (p. 170)

Joan Blos's award-winning *A Gathering of Days* is a book which is not wholly given to the religious perspective, but rather to a contest between that world-view and the humanist one, as they are reflected in the diary of young Catherine Hall, from a Sunday in October 1830, to a Tuesday in March 1832. We encounter in Catherine's spontaneous entries a nonintrusive narration of the struggle between her father's rougher, rural authority and God-ridden world and her Bostonian stepmother's more sophisticated, reason-centered view of life. We feel the authenticity of this struggle all the more because Blos skillfully approximates early American syntax through phrases such as "so busy were tongues and finger," "also were the jet buttons used," and "he cares for her not"; presents quaint local customs such as syrup gathering; prints rejected readings and arcane spelling; and refers to recognizable historical events. As the days are gathered from that first October Sabbath, Catherine tells of both the daily matter of her life and its signal moments: giving aid to a fugitive slave, adjusting to her father's new wife, and grieving at the death of her dearest friend, Cassie. All of these events and feelings, though set 150 years ago, call up issues which resonate across our age. Racial justice, communal authority, educational styles, women's roles, and other questions are woven into the fabric of the novel. We see the compliant but questioning Catherine scrutinizing all of these issues, wondering about the mores of the hardy back-country people: she decides, like Huck Finn, that kindness toward escaped slaves is better than legal compliance, although her father thinks otherwise; she challenges Teacher Holt's classroom authority in thinking he "believes that very much; and so do I, I think"; and she recognizes that only the boys are allowed to study higher math.

In a sense the religious view of her father and the humanist perspective of her stepmother stand on either side of all these issues. The acceptance of this central dimension of her father's world is complete at first and her distance from her stepmother is clear when the woman first arrives; but, as the days move on, she is more confused and divided. Early on she attends church twice on each Sabbath (even though she says that it is breathtakingly cold on winter days) and prays dutifully (though she recounts her desire to shorten vespers because of her cold floor). And when her new stepmother arrives from Boston, Catherine self-righteously notes the "open v's at Ann's throat and back and well shaped bodices," is conscious of Ann's overly rational approach to life, and refers to Ann only as "her" and "she." But when Catherine ends her petulance over this invasion of her world, she begins to see Ann in a new light, compares Ann's care for the youngest child with that given by her own mother, and begins to call Ann by the child's endearing name "Mammann."

This strong feeling for Ann precipitates a movement toward Ann's Boston world-view which is best expressed in Ann's response to the illness and death of Catherine's friend Cassie. The rural folk commit Cassie unflinchingly to the local doctor's care and to God's grace. Ann, however, clearly believes that a Boston physician can offer better help and when the local doctor's ineffectual work leads to Cassie's death, she writes to Boston to order a book to help in future cases. Out of her grief at the deaths of Cassie and of an entire family in a rock slide, Catherine wonders, "How can what we call *Providence* so oft, so cruelly, deprive." She begins to question Cassie's mother's report that her daughter died with a smile on her lips. Nevertheless, she seems uncertain about Ann's "faith in books" and the ability to "inform ourselves against another occasion," and concludes by brooding over the two world-views as she asks herself, "Whom shall I believe?" She ultimately answers her own question in part when she recognizes that Cassie has been "called on a greater journey, to rest on the opposite shore," that her recollection has been "a gathering of days wherein we learned . . . to accept," and that "for Cassie it is spring forever." Blos does not violate her young character by having her articulate her religious quandary; the final balance, however, seems to be tipped toward the religious perspective. (pp. 174-75)

> *Joseph O. Milner, "The Emergence of Awe in Recent Children's Literature," in* Children's Literature: Annual of the Modern Language Association Seminar on Children's Literature and The Children's Literature Association, *Vol. 10, 1982, pp. 169-77.*

MARTIN'S HATS (1984)

Bright paintings [by Marc Simont], realistically detailed and skillfully composed, illustrate a story that has variations on a theme rather than a plot. Martin, who has a collection of hats, wears some of them in turn as—in his imagination—he explores caves, drives a train, puts out a fire, cooks a meal, does farm work, etc. At the end of the book he finds a nightcap hanging on his bed and goes to sleep. Adequate, but not really substantial and rather static.

> *Zena Sutherland, in a review of "Martin's Hats," in* Bulletin of the Center for Children's Books, *Vol. 37, No. 9, May, 1984, p. 161.*

While all the action in this exquisitely illustrated book takes place within a small boy's imaginings as he sits in his bedroom, readers will find themselves eagerly joining in Martin's life-affirming spirit.

From his first adventure—when he dons a "real" explorer's cap—to his last, complete with snuggly wool nightcap, Martin wears as many as 10 different hats. Whether it's a wedding picnic, playing the role of a T-shirted conductor on an old-style locomotive, or welding a girder high among the skyscrapers, Martin's hats aren't so much playthings as invitations to explore a number of lives. The book is really a display of boyish imaginings, all hanging together somehow with remarkable cohesiveness—the hats being the "glue" of the myriad experiences.

It's not only himself whom Martin pictures wearing different hats. Most of the people he imagines throughout the book have *their* own favorite hats, too—all of which give, very cleverly, an inkling into each wearer's distinctive personality.

Martin's dreams are what a lot of children fantasize about: heroes saving the day! experts on the job! It's healthy, constructive musing which, in the case of this book, has the added virtue of illustrating a wide-ranging love of life, with

the effect of complementing, not risking, one's own individuality.

> *Darien Scott, "An Invitation to Explore Life," in* The Christian Science Monitor, *May 4, 1984, p. B5.*

BROTHERS OF THE HEART: A STORY OF THE OLD NORTHWEST, 1837-1838 (1985)

In 1837, Michigan *was* the Northwest frontier, where Blos sets her story about Shem, a crippled boy who comes to the small town of Millfield with his parents and younger sister, Annie. A deed misunderstood by his father causes Shem to run away from home; a job as an accounting clerk in Detroit leads to an offer with a trading party. His twisted foot proves too much an encumbrance in the wilderness, however, and when the winter weather sets in Shem is left behind to guard the cabin. Shem nearly dies; then Mary Goodhue, an elderly Indian woman comes into his life and teaches him survival skills but, more importantly, gives him a sense of self as well as a different outlook on life. In the spring after Mary's death, Shem returns home—a different person. Into this fairly simple plot, Blos, in a somewhat convoluted manner, interweaves the story of various family members and friends. She achieves a full, textured atmosphere using many devices found in adult novels, but her leisurely unfolding and complex structure demands readers willing to peruse every word. Though she writes as if actual letters and diaries from her characters existed, less sophisticated students may be confused. Still, the many-faceted characters are finely etched and her nicely turned phrases and interesting metaphors are thought-provoking. Not so much a survival story, but more a philosophical rite-of-passage novel set in historical trappings. (pp. 622-23)

> *Barbara Elleman, in a review of "Brothers of the Heart: A Story of the Old Northwest," in* Booklist, *Vol. 82, No. 8, December 15, 1985, pp. 622-23.*

There are many memorable scenes and fine characterizations in this story. Excerpts from letters and diary entries are liberally sprinkled throughout the text, giving a sense of authenticity and a documentary tone to the story; but too often the abrupt transitions and changes of perspective tend to interrupt the smooth flow of the narrative. The style, while true to the period, may prove slow going for most readers, but this certainly fills a need for good historical fiction of the early 19th Century.

> *Connie C. Rockman, in a review of "Brothers of the Heart: A Story of the Old Northwest," in* School Library Journal, *Vol. 32, No. 5, January, 1986, p. 72.*

Blos . . . has written a first-rate, powerful novel set in the 1830s in Michigan.

Brothers of the Heart succeeds on many levels: as convincing historical fiction, as a coming-of-age story, as a gripping adventure story, as an exceptional exploration of the relationship between young and old. The story is warm and moving but never sinks to sentimentality. The dialog rings true and the author's use of characters' letters and diaries helps set the novel in its historical context. Beautifully done.

> *Alice F. Stern, in a review of "Brothers of the Heart," in* Voice of Youth Advocates, *Vol. 9, No.*

1, April, 1986, p. 28.

OLD HENRY (1987)

By a Newbery winner, a rhymed picture-book about a non-conformist who moves into a derelict of a house and, to his tidy neighbors' consternation, doesn't improve it. Tired of their importunings and even of their kindness, Old Henry takes off for Dakota. But after a winter away, he misses their apple pies, if not the nagging, and is ready to compromise and come back. "If I mended the gate, and I shoveled the snow, would they not scold my birds? Could I let my grass grow?"

Using the rainbow colors of one of his Caldecott Honor books, *The Relatives Came,* [illustrator Stephen] Gammell depicts Old Henry's chaos with such gleeful enthusiasm that anyone would be on Henry's side. No matter that he spends his days reading, eating, and painting rather than doing something "useful." He exudes joy; and Gammell shows us not only Henry's gusto for life but also the delight of discovering beauty in any scene he depicts—not just the blooming garden but the gloomy sky; not just Henry's cheerful face, but his anxious, unfriendly neighbors in their dumpy clothes; not just the brilliant hues, but the warm mutations in winter grays and old, unpainted wood.

Gammell has turned Blos' rueful cautionary tale into a visual feast. (pp. 295-96)

A review of "Old Henry," in Kirkus Reviews, *Vol. LV, No. 4, February 15, 1987, pp. 295-96.*

An intriguing poem-portrait of an old man who offends the neighbors with his raggedy house and renegade ways. . . . The moral is explicit: "Maybe, some other time, we'd get along/ not thinking that somebody has to be wrong."/ "And we don't have to make such a terrible fuss/ because everyone isn't exactly like us." The illustrations are rich with lines that, when closely worked, create color-textured planes in sharp contrast with the linear detail of grasses and objects that are closer in perspective. Gammell's art, in fact, lends the verse an assymetry that keeps the rhymes from sounding too neat. An absorbing combination.

Betsy Hearne, in a review of "Old Henry," in Bulletin of the Center for Children's Books, *Vol. 40, No. 9, May, 1987, p. 162.*

The book ends on a suspenseful note, for Henry with his mailbox, a pail with a red *H* on it, is waiting for an answer to his letter to the mayor that expresses Henry's wish to return and a very mild offer to compromise. The drawings in colored pencil show Old Henry as a cheerful, almost childlike, but resolutely determined hermit and the neighbors as cold and grudging. The artist's ability to catch a character is particularly impressive, and the rainbow of color is lively and exhilarating. The text is written in loose and, on the whole, rather distracting rhyme, but accompanied by Stephen Gammell's splendid illustrations, which both enlarge and enrich the story, the book becomes an ode to nonconformity, both touching and humorous. (p. 328)

Ann A. Flowers, in a review of "Old Henry," in The Horn Book Magazine, *Vol. LXIII, No. 3, May/June, 1987, pp. 327-28.*

Sue Ellen Bridgers

1942-

American author of fiction.

Bridgers is acclaimed as one of the most skillful and perceptive writers of young adult literature. Drawing both from her roots and her current life as a small town Southener, she creates works which reveal her belief in the ability of family and place to bring self-awareness, comfort, and healing to adults as well as to young people. Her protagonists, adolescents of both sexes who come closer to maturity through positive relationships with their elders, are not the exclusive focus of Bridger's works. As her teenage characters become involved with the lives of the older members of rural communities, Bridgers interweaves their stories to provide her readers with a tapestry of human feelings and relationships. The situations which she describes in her books are starkly realistic; in *Notes for Another Life* (1981), for example, thirteen-year-old Wren struggles with the mental illness of both her father and her older brother, who tries to commit suicide. Through their experiences, Bridgers's characters learn about love, risk-taking, communicating with a variety of people, the meaning of loyalty and commitment, and the importance of family life, a theme which is central to all of her works. Often praised for the integrity, poignancy, and life-affirming quality of her books, Bridgers is considered an especially gifted literary stylist whose works are distinguished by the superiority of their characterizations. Bridgers received the ALAN Award from the Assembly on Literature for Adolescents of the National Council of Teachers of English in 1985 for her outstanding contributions to young adult literature.

(See also *Contemporary Literary Criticism,* Vol. 26; *Something about the Author,* Vol. 22; *Contemporary Authors New Revision Series,* Vol. 11; *Contemporary Authors,* Vols. 65-68; and *Dictionary of Literary Biography,* Vol. 52: *American Writers for Children Since 1960: Fiction.*)

AUTHOR'S COMMENTARY

In fiction, the writer pins down a place, identifies and defines it, gives the reader directions to it. For James Herriott, it is Yorkshire, for Eudora Welty, Mississippi, for Wilma Dykeman, it is western North Carolina and east Tennessee. For me, it is North Carolina.

That is not because what we know best is easiest to write about. To the contrary, the knowing makes it hard. That terrain that touches us deepest, that moves us most, is the most difficult to capture, but the most necessary. This is the map of my memory, the place I want to understand well and to illuminate completely. I want to show you my vision. I want to see it for myself. (p. 47)

· · · · ·

Time and place are joined to each other in a blood tie. The vital signs for a novel pulse there, at the "where" and "when". Once identified, they lack only the "who" because surely the "what" that follows will come naturally, the progression of events in time and place directed by a cast of char-

acters to whom things will happen. "And so" the writer scribbles, frequently with invisible ink — and goes ahead.

The longer I work with the characters who people my books, the less sure I am of where they come from and why. There are some like Maggie Grover in **Home Before Dark** who take on a life apart from my intention and thereby change the course of the story, and some like Mae Willis who are so unsure and desperate that they let me control their destinies. There is Hazard Whitaker in **All Together Now** who proposed to Pansy quite spontaneously and against my better judgment. There is Jane Flanagan who assumed with ease and validity the role I gave her. I give up trying to approach these people in an objective fashion. I will leave that to scholars and reviewers whose hapless job it is to study creative-after-the-fact.

Of course I wouldn't deny the technical aspects of fiction writing, for writing is more work than inspiration and more practiced than spontaneous. It's important to me that I know what I'm doing while I'm doing it, but generally I don't know it in a way that can be recounted later. Recalling what I am thinking while I'm writing would be as impossible as recalling the actual words spoken between my great-grandmother and her sister-in-law on [their] front porch in 1898.

And yet, I know what they were saying, not because I heard it then, but because I can imagine it now. Their voices come to me over the snap and rhythmic fall of beans into a tin pan, over the squeak of a chair and the swish of feet under the swing. They speak of a wedding, a dress cut from Aunt Clarsy's new pattern ordered by mail. They talk of the new teacher who is coming to board for the winter, the new books they will send for. Aunt Clarsy recounts in half whisper the gossip from town because she has recently been there. They worry over a summer cough that doesn't go away, that common dreadful sign of impending doom. They speak without guile, or pretense or conceit, binding the common wounds of their difficult lives with a language that is sincere and supportive.

I could put words in their mouths, punctuated with the scene around them — fading light through the trees, a lamp suddenly lit in the parlor, the soft throaty warble as one of the girls sits down at the piano to accompany herself. I could give them words and you would not object because fiction would make the words real. You would be willing to be there with them. Together, you and I would make it happen, whether it did or not.

What is real and what is not? What is truth and where is it separate from fiction? Eudora Welty says that "human life is fiction's only theme." And so there is a place beyond the physical location, the land, the home. There is the heart.

When I began writing my second book which became *All Together Now,* I knew the place and it was not a country homeplace like the one Stella had loved, but a town homeplace — a big house on a shady street with more rooms than it needed — a room for a granddaughter, a room for a traveling man. It was the kind of house my great-grandfather built at the turn of the century for families of comfortable means in eastern North Carolina towns. It was a grandmother's house. It had a sideporch off the kitchen with red geraniums in clay pots on the ledge, a front porch with a swing, a dining room of inherited china and bulky, substantial furniture with a place for everyone at the table.

If *Home Before Dark* is about the land, then *All Together Now* is about the heart. And it is a grandmother's heart. Readers are apt to tell me what they think of Casey and Dwayne, and of course, I hear about Pansy and Hazard because their affairs seem most poignant and were intended to be. And yet it is Jane Flanagan, the grandmother, who holds the story together. She is the reason for Casey's coming and for Hazard's, too. She is Ben's wife, Taylor's mother, Pansy's friend. She provides the sustenance of their lives and it is not just meals, clean clothes and dustless surfaces, but also comfort and courage and a stillness at the center of things. . . . She was like the women on the porch in 1898, but brought into 1950. Although she saw the world getting larger while her life stayed the same, she was proud of who she was. Beyond her identity as wife, mother, grandmother, she knew another one — a personal private sense of her womanhood itself. . . . She believed that the hand that rocked the cradle ruled the world. Her world was small until she lost brothers in one war and sons in another. While the starred flag hung in the shadow of her window, she planted a victory garden. She never failed to vote. She survived the Depression, supported the Red Cross and joined the Mother's March for the March of Dimes. Her faith in her own power was so unquestionable that she never even identified it as power. She was admired for her community service, her patience, her thriftiness, her cooking, her cunning, her grace. In 1950, this woman, herself in her fifties, was content in little towns and rural communities all across this country.

She is not so happy today. Young women around her are making choices that didn't exist when she was younger. They are questioning the validity of the "stay-at-home" life she accepted, of volunteerism, of commitments that now seem more supportive than active. . . . She's back in college herself. Her granddaughters have no intention of "coming out" or of marrying young, but they share expenses and apartments with their boyfriends. This grandmother has a job now outside the home or else there is something she "does."

In *Notes For Another Life,* the grandmother is a music teacher and a tennis player who cleans house because it is a necessary chore. She has taken in her grandchildren and also her son who is mentally ill and unable to function outside her care. She tries to understand her daughter-in-law who lives a life separate from her husband and children. She struggles to accept the fact that, just as she didn't make her son ill, she cannot make him well.

When this grandmother was young, she did not have options available to her daughter-in-law or her granddaughter. Perhaps she didn't even want them. Or perhaps she has regrets. Still she has accepted another woman's pursuit of a consuming, dynamic career and is supportive of her granddaughter's intention to become a concert pianist. But even with all the changes in the world that reflect on her life and values, this woman is still related to the women on the porch. The blood tie to place and family is still intact.

Because I feel this attachment keenly I write about life in families. I find that the lives that interest me most are not isolated ones but those involved daily in the complicated footwork of family living. People related by blood share, whether they want to or not, a past and prospect of a future as real and as important as their present. I believe that a nurturing figure, whether it be mother, father, grandparents or some other adult, is essential to family life but I realize, looking back on my accumulated efforts as a writer, that I do not have many successful mothers. Forced to face this subject, I have tread on the troubled waters of my own psyche to discover that for me, motherlessness provides the ultimate, the all-consuming conflict. No matter what the relationship is, close or distant, strained or loving, mothers are still our source. They are perhaps the most unique and certainly the most complex attachment we will ever have.

Surely Casey's summer would have happened with her mother there. Surely Stella could have found a place to be without her mother's death. I admit that Kevin and Wren could have had plenty of trouble dealing with their father's illness even if their mother had been available to them. But for me, the absence of these mothers makes every word more poignant, every step more stumbling, every question more difficult to answer.

So there is a personal reason for these motherless situations, but at the same time, I believe I write about people as I find them. Technically the characters always come first and then the kind of people they are dictates what they do, just as you and I are products of heredity and environment.

Every writer faces the dilemma of whether to write about life as it is or life as it should be. I have never found much to say about the best of all possible worlds because fiction is based on conflict, not perfection. If Kevin and Wren were perfectly adjusted to their mother's absence and their father's illness, there would be no story to tell about them. In the world as it should be, there would be no mental illness and the decisions Karen Jackson had to make would be non-existent. She would be free to do whatever was best for her, unhampered by misunderstandings or disapproval. But that isn't how the world is, although I believe that in *Notes For Another Life,* three women are working toward their individual best possible worlds, each in their own way and with their own set of values and commitments. Bliss the grandmother is making the best of what life has given her. Karen, the mother, has changed her life drastically, taking action to save herself. The daughter Wren who is reaching maturity in the 80s, has the possibility of everything: faithful inspired commitments to other people, work she loves to do, a sustaining sense of self-worth that is not based on nurturing someone else. What these three women share over three generations of experiences is the hard knowledge that love is not always enough. They are each living with loss, but they are surviving.

I celebrate their opportunities and their achievements. I approach them longing to understand, never to prosecute or defend. They are part of a widening circle of family that I embrace everyday: men and women, both blood relations and close friends, who take us in, lending their security to our panic, their hopefulness to our despair, offering their acceptance of us which is not unlike that of a mother who, knowing our dark places, loves us anyway.

In the making of a book there are the essentials I have spoken

of: time, place, the human element of character. But also commitment on the part of the writer to create this work she has envisioned, a world which contains the essentials in particular rather than general terms: a particular place, a certain time, human beings who are both singular and familiar. The writer must have an intention of some sort, a base of action. I see family life as the core of my writing. I have a personal past, a family history that, while providing me with fertile creative ground, also provides me with awesome responsibility. These people who remind me of the child in me, also remind me of the continuum. They show me that I am a link between the past and the future. In the present, I can explore a way of life that is the expectation of some and the memory of others.

We are all caught in our culture, searching for sense in the confusion, and no one is more trapped than the teenager. Faced with the problems of daily life — the tremendous freedom they have, the problems of ecology and economy, the real and oppressive fear of nuclear holocaust, they have more need for interdependence than ever before. They need to share their mutual concerns with adults. They need concrete goals. They need to know we are with them and that they have ideas and visions and love to share that we adults are in true need of. They need books that reflect both the confusion and the calm, books that speak to the basic human need for companionship, books that portray family life in such a way that young people see the possibility of commitments to it that can sustain rather than destroy them.

I hope that the characters in my books portray such a commitment. I believe they are responsive to the collective well-being as well as to their individual goals and accomplishments. They face their days knowing how often the rain will fall, how frail we all are and yet how resilient.

My great-grandmother Bett and my Aunt Clarsy knew that. They came together in the late afternoon on one porch or the other. They came loving each other, hearing in the silence between them as much as in the words they spoke, a history, a past woven into the present so that who could separate either of them from the future. They came knowing the world was changing. Already in cities electric lamps brightened the evening sky. There was a telephone in the house and a sewing machine that bore stitches quicker than the eye could see. There was money now to send the children to college and colleges to send them to. They knew their daughters and their sons — those survivors — would be different from them, would know more about the world away from Renston, would be better educated, lose fewer children, find better ways to preserve the land and harvest its yield. Between them, as always, there was common cause and therefore, common language. And so I know what they spoke of and so do you. It was of the earth and of life and death and always — of love. It was women's talk, the fabric of fiction. I can hear it now. (pp. 53-5, 61)

Bett Abbott Hunsucker with daughters Sandra and Sue Ellen in 1944.

Sue Ellen Bridgers, "Stories My Grandmother Told Me: Part One" and "Stories My Grandmother Told Me: Part Two," in The ALAN Review, Vol. 13, Nos. 1 and 2, Fall, 1985 and Winter, 1986, pp. 44-7; 53-5, 61.

GENERAL COMMENTARY

LINDA BACHELDER AND OTHERS

Writing in the tradition of O'Connor, McCullers, and Faulkner, Sue Ellen Bridgers, in her masterfully constructed novel, *Home Before Dark,* looked at the lives of migrant workers and at the need to settle and the need not to settle for failure and success. Flawlessly written and loaded, like the great Southern novels, with gothic humor and with fascinating characters, *Home Before Dark* is a likely candidate for the young adult novel teenagers and adults will read for years to come. In *All Together Now,* Bridgers wrote a glorious story of a young girl's summer of growth and insight as she played a strange kind of baseball with a retarded neighbor. In this novel, the full potential of the young adult novel was, for us, met. (p. 89)

> *Linda Bachelder and others, "Looking Backward: Trying to Find the Classic Young Adult Novel," in* English Journal, *Vol. 69, No. 6, September, 1980, pp. 86-9.*

HOME BEFORE DARK   (1976)

Reading a first novel is like meeting a stranger—one has no idea what to expect. We come prepared to accept the mildest of diversions, though we long for much more. We want to be stirred, involved and enlightened.

The home of the title is a tobacco farm in Montreet County, N.C., to which James Earl Willis returns after an absence of 16 years. Those years have given him a wife, four children and a life of endless wandering as a migrant worker. Acting from some dimly realized compulsion to return to the world of his childhood, he brings his family to live in an old cabin on the family property, which now belongs to his brother.

The homecoming is experienced by each member of the Willis family in a different way. For James Earl, it represents a chance for self-renewal; for his wife, the threat of exposure, inasmuch as "All her life Mae had wanted to hide, and her migrant experience had meant she could." For the children, it offers the chance to explore a world they've fleetingly glimpsed from the back seat of a car. And for 14-year-old Stella Willis it means everything: "A place to store the secret Stella and draw her longings out slowly, carefully, one by one, and keep them safe." . . .

[By] the time the book ends, she is well on her way to fulfillment. She has learned a little about love and friendship, about keeping and letting go—about growing up.

No summary can convey the tremendous integrity of a book like **Home Before Dark.** The author speaks with a voice that is intensely lyrical yet wholly un-selfconscious. Character and theme have been developed with such painstaking attention that each episode seems inevitable and right.

Try to find some thoughtful adolescent to share this book with you. Young adults needn't have all the fun.

> *Barbara Helfgott, in a review of "Home Before Dark," in* The New York Times Book Review, *November 14, 1976, p. 40.*

Although the nominal heroine is Stella, the 14-year-old daughter of a migrant farm worker, the plot centers more around the changes in the lives of her parents when her father decides to return to his childhood home and settle down. The adults in the story are almost painfully real, especially Stella's father as he tries to deal with his wife's alienation and death and rediscovers romance. Bridgers writes gracefully and well (albeit not for a wide teen audience) in this first novel that skillfully explores themes of growth and change and evokes life in the rural South.

> *Diane Haas, in a review of "Home Before Dark," in* School Library Journal, *Vol. 23, No. 5, January, 1977, p. 99.*

An outstanding first novel. . . . The events are engrossing, to be sure, but the plot is secondary to the style. [Stella's] unique insights are expressed in profound metaphors, and she creates haunting images. Stella sleeps on a fancy mattress that is bloodstained from the day her grandmother shot herself; her father gave it to her because Stella had " 'never seen a mattress with flowers on it.' " The character studies are thorough and concise; the author records equally well the emotions of a middle-aged man and a teen-aged girl, and she is able to explore the innermost thoughts of her characters within the confines of a few pages. Perceptive, masterful writing for mature readers. (pp. 165-66)

> *Sally Holmes Holtz, in a review of "Home Before Dark," in* The Horn Book Magazine, *Vol. LIII, No. 2, April, 1977, pp. 165-66.*

ALL TOGETHER NOW   (1979)

The summer twelve-year-old Casey Flanagan spends at her grandparents' — while her mother is working and her father is fighting in the Korean War — is a time of growing self-awareness. A shy, sensitive girl, she is at first apprehensive about the arrangement but cheers up when she meets Dwayne Pickens — a retarded man who was once a boyhood friend of her father's. Dwayne dislikes girls, but he easily mistakes Casey, with her short hair and jeans, for a boy. Anxious to have him as a friend, the girl convinces her family to keep her secret, and though she sometimes feels guilty about deceiving Dwayne, the two become inseparable. The narrative winds through a summer of family dinners, fishing trips, and outings to the track where Uncle Taylor races stock cars. Casey, living in her father's old room, is enfolded into the loving circle of family and friends, and in the course of the summer her refreshingly innocent personality touches them all. The thoughts and feelings of each character are revealed through shifting viewpoints as each in his own time learns that love must be based on truth and acceptance. And when Dwayne is threatened with institutionalization, Casey comes to understand that a commitment to another person cannot be passive. The characters — from good-natured, honest Dwayne to bumbling Hazard Whittaker — are remarkably individualized. The book is exceptional not only for its superb writing and skillful portrayal of human relationships but for its depiction of a small southern town, where everyone knows everyone and neighbors care enough to rally in times of trouble. (pp. 197-98)

> *Kate M. Flanagan, in a review of "All Together Now," in* The Horn Book Magazine, *Vol. LV, No. 2, April, 1979, pp. 197-98.*

The book starts with Casey's last summer as a child, yet it is not about emerging adolescence. Rather, it is, as the title suggests, a story of the members of an extended family reaching towards one another. It is a book about simple people learning how to love, and because love is a difficult task for the wisest of us, these simple people botch and bungle but never quite give up.

The book reminds me of a square dance with four couples: The various partners dance together and interact with the others in the square and then come home again. Jane and Ben Flanagan, Casey's paternal grandparents are the head couple. It is against the solid harmony of their relationship that the other three pairs counter and clash and finally resolve. Casey's partner is Dwayne Perkins, a man her father's age who has been suspended in childhood ever since a porch swing broke, driving him headfirst into a wall. Couple number three are Casey's Uncle Taylor, working in his father's lumberyard but living for Saturday and the stock-car races, and Gwen, scooping popcorn and candy-covered raisins at the dimestore and draping herself on a car hood to be watched at the races. Bridgers gently leads the reader from distaste to great concern for this five-and-dime romance between the peroxided clerk and the stock-car racer.

But the most fragile partnership, the one which makes the reader laugh and cry and wring her hands, is that of two friends of the Flanagan family. Bridgers' ability to create character is poignantly apparent in these two—the outwardly prim and meticulous Pansy, Jane's best friend from childhood, and the ex-travelling man and dancing waiter Hazard, who finally and disastrously dares to marry the doctor's aging daughter.

In order to propel the reader into the center of this complex square, Bridgers has made a risky technical decision. She tells the story from the point of view of all of these eight people, sometimes switching point of view more than once on a single page. The reader is being asked to follow the intricate steps of the dance, and he may not always understand the calls. There is also, perhaps because of the frequent shifts in point of view, a consciousness of a presence behind that of the characters—not an intrusive 19th-century author-observer, to be sure—but a presence all the same. According to Flannery O'Connor it is always wrong "to say that you can't do this or you can't do that in fiction. You can do anything you can get away with, but nobody has ever gotten away with much." I hesitate to say then that a writer can't change points of view so often or enter into her own story. Bridgers has, and if she has not gotten clean away with it, she has certainly written a lovely book—a book for all of us who crave a good story about people we will come to care about deeply. (pp. K1, K4)

Katherine Paterson, "Learning to Love," in Book World—The Washington Post, *May 13, 1979,* pp. K1, K4.

A superior novel about a twelve-year-old's summer friendship with a 33-year-old man whose mind is that of a boy of twelve. . .and about her allowing him to believe that she's a boy because she knows he can't stand girls? It sounds like another of those worthy and sensitive problem stories, with a neat moral dilemma worked in. But this is different from the start. Duane Pickins is a real person, someone you can love and laugh at. Casey, too, is a real person, who might make you think of yourself at twelve even if you weren't a bit like her. And the other characters are far more than a supporting cast, even though they do all come to Duane's support, preventing his proud, uptight brother from sending him away to a dismal institution. . . . [Assuredly,] this is a real novel, rec-

ognizably a juvenile for its general good feeling and individual happy endings, but remarkably full and genuinely empathic in its projection of the characters and their relationships.

A review of "All Together Now," in Kirkus Reviews, *Vol. XLVII, No. 10, May 15, 1979, p. 579.*

Sue Ellen Bridgers's **All Together Now** exudes a life and quality which are indisputedly rich. . . . It makes no overtly religious comment and centers on human relationships, yet something almost too delicate to articulate or measure suggests its ties with a religious world-view. It seems clearly out-of-step with most of the books of our day. The presence of the family, as it extends itself vertically and horizontally, and of the larger community run deep in the account of Casey's summer with her grandparents. In contrast, much of today's children's fiction reports the family as extinct or, if alive, merely meddling. As a part of this difference, Bridgers pays homage to powerful adults and attends to them sufficiently to allow her reader to feel both their silliness and their wisdom. Although she focuses on Casey and her relationship to the quick-spirited, but slow-minded, Dwayne Pickens, Bridgers's omniscient point of view carries her into the minds of folk who are placed all along the chronological path of life. She deftly slips into the thoughts of most of her characters and renders a less rarified, more complete assessment of life than is found in much of children's literature. Multiple interior responses to Dwayne's threatened institutionalization by his prideful brother Alva, to the misfire honeymoon and subsequent estrangement of the middle-aged Pansy and Hazard, to the quiet solidity of the elder Flanagan's relationship, and to the on-and-off courtship of Uncle Taylor and the candy-counter girl Gwyn, make the book less parochial and more

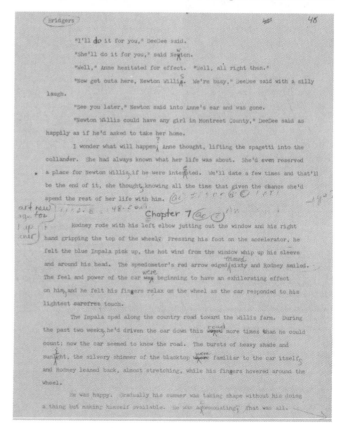

Corrected typescript page for Home Before Dark. *1976.*

real than the typical single-issue, youth ghetto books of our time. Furthermore, although Casey's summer includes a good bit of pain and foolishness, Bridgers persistently affirms life at its core; without being a Pollyanna she departs from the current norm of despair by championing brotherhood and love. Casey symbolically plays catch with Dwayne rather than have him continue to thump balls off the metal garbage cans. Even though this act and its articulation as love, "unencumbered by questions of degree or worth," can be seen as essentially the humanist goal, something gnaws at this assessment of her world-view. Perhaps it is the stated assumption that Dwayne's freedom is in God's hands, or the unpitying acceptance of his mental limitations or the admissions of Pansy, Dr. Kemble, and finally Casey herself that an individual ultimately is unable to control his destiny. Such is not the stuff of humanism. (pp. 176-77)

> *Joseph O. Milner, "The Emergence of Awe in Recent Children's Literature," in* Children's Literature: Annual of the Modern Language Association Seminar on Children's Literature and The Children's Literature Association, *Vol. 10, 1982, pp. 169-77.*

NOTES FOR ANOTHER LIFE (1981)

Home Before Dark and **All Together Now** quickly established Bridgers' reputation in the YA field and **Notes for Another Life** puts her at the head of the pack. In this latest novel, Bridgers introduces us to thirteen-year-old Wren and her older brother, Kevin. They live with their grandparents because their father is in and out of the state mental hospital. Their mother, after years of living with the ups and downs of a mentally ill husband, has chosen a career of high fashion and city life over Wren and Kevin.

Once again it is Bridgers' fine sense of characterization that makes her book work so well. The reader watches Kevin and Wren struggle with developmental tasks made more complicated by mental illness in the family and absent parents.

The author beautifully balances the father's retreat from reality with what appears to be a similar journey by Kevin. Kevin's moodiness, his lack of friends, and his perceived rejection by his mother and his girlfriend push him to a suicide attempt. The family comes together to help Kevin and to deal, this time successfully, with yet another tragedy.

Running through this finely crafted novel is the theme of the soothing power of music, which is an ointment to ease the pain, an escape, and an old friend to lean on for help and strength. It is music that provides notes for another life. Because **Notes** is not as demanding as *Ordinary People* nor as simplistic as *Lisa Bright and Dark*, this fine novel will get a bigger share of teenage readers.

> *Dick Abrahamson, "Old Friends with New Titles," in* English Journal, *Vol. 70, No. 5, September, 1981, pp. 75-7.*

The story is superbly written, with every word manipulated to count. Topics of contemporary interest—suicide, mental illness, divorce, living with loss—are placed in the context of family living so skillfully that they appear as universal rather than contemporary themes. There is genius in the development of so many rounded characters in a medium length novel. Sue Ellen Bridgers continues a pattern developed in

Home Before Dark and **All Together Now** of portraying incredibly strong women, young and old. Bliss is so in touch with her household that foreboding strikes her in the middle of the night and she is able to prevent impending disaster. Wren knows she cannot accept the comfort and confinement of Sam's simplistic view of the world—she aspires to more. Bridgers' objectivity is most noteworthy in the attitude toward Karen, who receives no blame except from her own needs and ambitions. Male characters, while less complex as a whole, are given individuality and effectiveness. Bill and Sam are sensitive and staunch support-givers; the minister is capable of understanding Kevin and leading him toward self insight. The novel's guardedly positive ending leaves one pondering and wanting to return to the book again. Its picture of an adolescent brother and sister deeply concerned for and never failing each other is hard to find in literature and is entirely believable. Definitely a candidate for YASD Best Books.

> *Joan L. Atkinson, in a review of "Notes for Another Life," in* Voice of Youth Advocates, *Vol. 4, No. 4, October, 1981, p. 20.*

The devastating impact of mental illness upon family relationships is intimately explored in this young adult novel. (p. 317)

In focusing intimately upon each family member's personal struggles with Tom's mental illness, the book moves away from the current spate of young adult novels which concentrate on the afflicted patient's inner struggles. It encompasses the lives and thoughts of one family so powerfully that readers are made aware of the special problems teenagers encounter when confronted with a family member's disability.

The author has succeeded in painting a portrait of mental illness that, for once, is not overburdened with melodrama and journalistic self-examination. It's intimate without being confessional, and it presents the points of view of each family member so successfully that, by the novel's conclusion, all characters are fully developed and easily understandable. No easy answers or conclusions are drawn—the book is just an excellent portrait of life's varied influences upon one family, among them mental illness. (pp. 317-18)

> *Diane C. Donovan, in a review of "Notes for Another Life," in* Best Sellers, *Vol. 41, No. 8, November, 1981, pp. 317-18.*

Unlike many who write for young adults, Sue Ellen Bridgers affirms the earned sweetness of life without ever pretending it has a cream center or sugar coating. Like her earlier prize-winning novels, **Home Before Dark** and **All Together Now, Notes for Another Life** acknowledges the high cost of growth in disenchantments and losses; yet the first and last chapters frame even madness and near-death in tough-minded earned joy, as the Jackson family drives both times toward a difficult visit at the state mental hospital, but "singing as they went." . . .

In all three of her novels, Sue Ellen Bridgers endorses the survival of family love and values, which nearly always are stronger in women than men. Grandfather Bill Jackson is a mere shadow here, and both tormented males lack the resonance of Bliss or Wren. Slowly and steadily the women teach the rest what has come naturally to them. At novel's end, hearing the women in song, Kevin "croaked out a little noise. . . . He doubted he would add much, a ragged note now and then, a jumble of words, but at least he would be with them."

Doris Betts, "Themes and Variations on Family Life," in Book World—The Washington Post, November 8, 1981, p. 17.

SARA WILL (1985)

[*First published as an adult novel,* Sara Will *was remarketed as a young adult novel in 1986.*]

In her fifties and never married, Sara Will has given up her dreams and hidden her emotions in the very core of her being, projecting the image of an unfeeling spinster. She has become comfortable with the minutiae of daily routine, opting for self-imposed isolation in the remote, aging house where her parents died and where she now lives with her widowed, high-spirited sister, who chafes at the lack of social contacts. The sisters' lives change suddenly and irrevocably when Fate Jessop (brother-in-law of the two women's dead sister), his unwed teenage niece Eva, and her baby—followed by Eva's ardent suitor—turn up in search of sanctuary. The narrative seesaws between past and present, filling in the backgrounds of these disparate people who eventually establish a three-generation family. The focus of the tale, however, remains on Sara Will and the process through which she overcomes her own fear of the messiness of love and the unreliability of commitment. A beautifully written, ultimately heartwarming

gem of a novel, with vital, memorable characterizations. (p. 602)

• • • • •

Older fiction-loving teens, particularly those familiar with Bridgers' teenage novels, will not only enjoy this affecting story but will also take its characters into their hearts. (p. 603)

Sally Estes, in a review of "Sara Will," in Booklist, Vol. 81, No. 9, January 1, 1985, pp. 602, 603.

In her finest novel, Bridgers tells the love story of Sara Will Birney, a spinster in her 50s, and Fate Jessup, her dead sister's brother-in-law. . . .

Like Bridgers' previous **All Together Now,** a young person provides the catalyst to begin the story, and in this case, an interesting subplot, as Eva falls in love (after the fact) with her baby's father. However, this novel cannot in any way be construed as YA. It is primarily an *adult* love story, and a very rare and satisfying adult story at that. **Sara Will** shows a mature, exceptionally good writer on a critical par with Gail Godwin and Lois Battle, but with a unique and lovely voice. A real pleasure to read but not YA in my judgment.

Mary K. Chelton, in a review of "Sara Will," in Voice of Youth Advocates, Vol. 8, No. 5, December, 1985, p. 318.

Sara Will . . . is a slow, every-day paced story of love at last.

The Bridgers Family Portrait. Clockwise: Sue Ellen, Elizabeth, Bennett, Ben, and Sean. Painting by Shirley Grant, 1980.

Sara Will is in her fifties, in a rut but in control. Her life is ordered and isolated. A white 1965 Mustang, her only acknowledgement of the outside world, is in the garage, unseen, unused, unchanged. Sara's struggles are all settled, all surprises subdued, all affections submerged. Then, Fate steps in. . . . Sue Ellen Bridgers has painstakingly and beautifully detailed the minutia and the manner of Sara's living. Light, sound, smell, memories, nuances, layer upon layer of fifty years of routine life are intimately rendered by the author. All the characters, in perfect proportion to Sara, are just as carefully and minutely etched. The interrelationships among all the characters are just as exquisitely pictured as the characters themselves. Sister to sister, girl to boy, man to woman, all ring painfully true. Fate, especially, is clearly and cleanly delineated — Fate, the obviously splintered, the outwardly handicapped expression of Sara's own invisible vulnerability. Though Fate, too, has been deluged by life, unlike Sara, he is still willing to struggle and to risk. It is the acceptability of taking risks that Sara must confront. It is between the struggle of loving and the ease of solitude that she must decide.

Bridgers makes wonderful use of symbolism in depicting Sara's growing need both to risk and to decide. Most significant, of course, is the symbol of the car. Well-served, untouched except by Sara, it waits. And like Sara, when touched by Fate, it suffers greatly before it comes to life.

Sara's story is a quiet one. It's appeal to the young adult reader is limited. Eva, the unwed niece and her boyfriend are the only young adults in the book. Even though Eva and her predicament are prime-time teen-age fare, the story is all Sara's, middle-aged, muffled, enmeshed in time. Nevertheless, it is a beautifully written story with wonderful characterizations, a slowly paced but engrossing plot and finely crafted descriptions and dialogue. *Sara Will* will never jump off the shelf. Sara Will never would. But her deeply moving story of feelings found just in time will enrich all who seek her out. (pp. 213-14)

> *JoJo Hilliard, "Travel Tips: Life Choices," in* Catholic Library World, *Vol. 58, No. 5, March/April, 1987, pp. 213-14.*

PERMANENT CONNECTIONS (1987)

Seventeen-year-old Rob Dickson is angry and resentful when he has to accompany his father to North Carolina to visit his uncle Fairlee in the hospital. Worse yet, Rob has to stay behind and live in the rickety old Dickson house while Fairlee recuperates. Life is very different for the privileged teenager from suburban New Jersey; Rob is caught in a morass of anger and self-pity. Although he is enamored of Ellery, another newcomer to the town, Rob is too self-destructive to be pleasant to her for very long. Rob remains in his shell until he almost causes his grandfather's death. Only then is he able to acknowledge his place in the family, and how much other people mean to him. This marvelous book movingly evokes the tortured feelings of young people, and the viewpoints of their elders, who are coping as best they can. Bridgers's latest work transcends the YA genre; readers of all ages will be moved by its rich characterizations and universal themes.

> *A review of "Permanent Connections," in* Publishers Weekly, *Vol. 231, No. 2, January 16, 1987, p. 75.*

With immediacy and candor, Sue Ellen Bridgers writes about rural North Carolina, where she has lived for most of her life. Like her four previous acclaimed young adult novels, *Permanent Connections* affirms the bonds of extended family and community, part of a general trend in adult and teen-age fiction that shows young people coming of age by finding roots and staying home. Not that home is the pre-60's haven with parents who are always wise and strong — adults and young people struggle together now. This new novel shows clearly not only the affection but also the meanness and defeat in a small Appalachian town. Much of the story takes place at night; the mood is caught in one character's quoting from the letters of Sylvia Plath: "You have seen me through that black night when the only word I knew was NO." . . .

When his uncle breaks his hip on the old Southern family farm and Rob is sent to help out for a few months, the resolution is predictable — the lost boy will find a place — but Ms. Bridgers avoids cheery folksiness. Rob's journey is dangerous and dark. . . .

He keeps himself apart from the relatives he barely knows, including querulous, half-senile Grandpa and agoraphobic Aunt Coralee, who hasn't left the farmhouse in three years. Unaware of their affection, he sees no connection between their anger and panic and his own. When he asks if Coralee's fears are imaginary, his gentle uncle replies: "Could be, but that's the worst kind of thing to be afraid of. Something in your head. Who can tell you it ain't there?"

Rob wants easy answers. Soon afterward he meets his bright classmate Ellery and they make love, tenderly and passionately, so he thinks their relationship will fill the void inside him. But Ms. Bridgers challenges the romantic formulas; it isn't enough that Rob and Ellery are in love. The scenes between them vibrate with passion. With their bodies and with words they grope for each other, come suddenly too close ("I can't breathe," she says when they dance), flare into a quarrel, and separate in pain. "You expect too much," she tells him, unable to cope with his desperate need. It's Ellery who quotes him Sylvia Plath.

Ellery has her own problems — hating herself, trying to forgive her mother Ginny's flight to these backwoods from a safe suburban marriage. Ginny remembers the suburbs as an outsider, with clichés of frenetic cocktail parties and shallow fashion, and the picture of her isolation in suburban affluence lacks the painful authenticity of Coralee's fear in the kitchen shadows. But Ginny's search for independence and friendship is wonderfully realized when she reaches out to help her neighbor Coralee move outside.

The sudden appearance of a wise priest-commentator is intrusive. The story and language woven from common experience suggest more complex truth. In the final crisis Rob and Grandpa part in rage and then search all night for each other in a storm; Rob saves the old man and finds the courage to uncover his own wounds and admit his guilt and love. And Rob's need brings his father back to some connection with the home he has long denied. Though "the words were hard to come by," what remains a powerful center is that sagging farmhouse in the mountains with the half-crippled family and a few neighbors trying to care for each other and make it through the night.

> *Hazel Rochman, in a review of "Permanent Connections," in* The New York Times Book Review, *July 26, 1987, p. 21.*

This [is an] excellent YA novel. . . . Essentially, it is a story of redemption. The main character, Rob, is a 17-year-old boy on the edge of real trouble—sullen, drinking and using drugs, not working in school, drifting. Rob and his father travel to North Carolina one summer when there is an accident in the family, and the decision is made that Rob will stay there in the country, helping out, at least for three months. So, in this way, Bridgers comes to the subjects she knows and loves: the rural South; a family situation in which there are difficult personalities to contend with; and a young person who is finally healed through a strong connection with a family and a place.

Bridgers is incredibly good when she describes feelings: Rob's love for Ellery, a girl recovering from her parents' divorce; his despair when she rejects him; his guilt and self-hatred when he gets arrested for possession of narcotics; and his contentment at the end when the healing begins. Fine characterization, realistic situations, and wonderful descriptions throughout make this one of Bridgers' best works, and it will appeal to many YA readers.

A review of "Permanent Connections," in Kliatt Young Adult Paperback Book Guide, *Vol. XXII, No. 4, May, 1988, p. 2.*

Ashley F. Bryan

1923-

Black American reteller and illustrator.

In an attempt to preserve African traditions, Bryan has collected several volumes of spirituals and has collected and retold numerous African and West Indian folktales. In his books of spirituals, which he produces to introduce children to the richness of this art form, Bryan uses black-and-white linoleum block print illustrations to simulate medieval religious books. He plans to reprint one hundred spirituals in all, a task already half completed. Bryan is well-known for his readings of poetry in which he utilizes the work of Paul Laurence Dunbar, Gwendolyn Brooks, and others to further an understanding of verse and its link with the oral tradition of literature. Acknowledging the influence of poetry on his writings, he models the rhythms of the prose in his folktales after poetic cadences. Often using close rhythms, rhyme, onomatopoeia, alliteration, and interior rhyme in his texts, Bryan forces the reader to consider the sound of the printed word. At the same time, Bryan has taken talking beast stories, pourquoi tales, and other standard folktale forms and, by his use of colloquialisms and rather loose adaptations, given them vitality and modernity. The tempera paintings, linocuts, and woodcuts which Bryan uses to illustrate his folktales are usually done in black and white, sometimes combined with rich colors like red and gold, and show the influences of African art and textiles. With *The Dancing Granny* (1977), however, he departed from his typical style. The story of a woman who outwits crafty Spider Ananse, the book is illustrated with pictures done in the style of Japanese brush paintings. Demonstrating a fluidity and vigor which echoes the liveliness of the tale, the illustrations are witness to Bryan's versatility and craftsmanship. In all of his works, Bryan manifests his goal as a reteller. Quoting a line written by Senegalese poet Leopold Sedar Senghor "un pont de douceur les relie" ("a tender bridge connects them"), Bryan has expressed the hope that his work will be "a tender bridge" that brings African traditions to present-day American children. Bryan has also illustrated books for children by other writers such as Susan Cooper. He won the Coretta Scott King Award in 1981 for *Beat the Story-Drum, Pum-Pum* and received honorable mention from the Coretta Scott King committee in 1983 for *I'm Going to Sing: Black American Spirituals, Volume Two* and in 1987 for *The Lion and the Ostrich Chicks.*

(See also *Something about the Author,* Vol. 31 and *Contemporary Authors,* Vol. 107.)

AUTHOR'S COMMENTARY

[The following excerpt is from an interview by Sylvia and Kenneth Marantz.]

[Marantz]: When do you create your books and how do you create your illustrations?

[Bryan]: I generally paint during the day, and in the evenings I work on other projects, books being one of them. My illustrations for the African tales *The Adventures of Aku, Beat*

the Story Drum, Pum-Pum, and *Lion and the Ostrich Chicks,* are often referred to as block prints or silk screens, but they are all painted. I paint them in this manner because I can get almost a one hundred per cent relation from my original to the reproduction in the books. . . . These illustrations are based on my study of African art; the sculpture, masks, and rock painting, and they are absorbed into the style that is my own. If reviewers ask, "Is that Masai?" they have missed the point, because I am not copying any specific group. Just as in my retelling of the African stories, I want something in my art that reflects African art without being necessarily authentic. In *Walk Together Children* and *I'm Going to Sing* the illustrations are block prints. I was inspired by the early religious block-printed books. The spirituals are religious songs, and over a thousand have been collected since the end of the Civil War. Since there were no books introducing these songs to young people, doing selections of them is one of my major projects. I'm planning to do a hundred songs in the style of the medieval religious books. Each of the two that I've done contains twenty-five songs, so I've two more to go! (pp. 175-76)

I do a lot of sketching. Many ideas for my illustrations come from my sketchbooks. For example, in my books of the spirituals you can see illustrations of my grandmother and the children I have drawn on a playground, adapted from my sketchbooks. I always have a sketchbook with me. (p. 176)

M: In *The Dancing Granny* how were the illustrations originally done?

B: That story from the Ashanti was collected in Antigua in the West Indies, on the island my parents came from. My grandmother stayed behind, but she finally came to visit after World War II, when she was past seventy. She picked up the latest dance steps from the great-grandchildren and outdanced them all! I drew upon that.

The illustrations for *The Dancing Granny* are brush paintings. Generally my illustrations are the same size as those in the book, but the Granny originals are a third larger. They were based on my study of Japanese brush painting. I particularly like the work of Hokusai — his sketchbooks of scenes from daily life. I have done a lot of drawing from dancers, and I really like to draw from life. I went to my sketchbooks for help. I did hundreds of brush paintings of the dancing figure and assembled them in the layout. I wanted the book to move in the rhythm of the figures dancing. When they were reproduced, the variation in dark and light in the brush strokes was, unfortunately, lost. But the spirit of the dancing figure is there, and the book remains popular.

M: How do you feel about encapsulating a story into this frozen form when folk tales generally change and evolve with the teller and the circumstances?

B: The oral tradition lives today, and it lives in books as well. The problem is how to give a written story that texture and vitality and drama — the back and forth play of teller and audience of the oral setting. I try things that will give a vitality of surface, a textural feeling, a possibility of vocal play to the prose of my stories. So I take risks in my books. I do a lot of things that people writing prose generally do not do: close rhythms, rhyme, onomatopoeia, alliteration, interior rhyme — the poet's tools, what you usually avoid when you write prose because it stops the story. But I want to stop readers to slow them down; I want readers to hear the sound of the printed word.

M: Do you try out your ideas on anyone before you publish them?

B: I read to friends and to children, sometimes in the little one-room schoolhouse on the island [Bryan refers to a small island off the coast of Maine where he has his studio]. I always read aloud to hear how my work sounds. If something is not clear or not rhythmically right, they help me. But I do a lot of revision through my own ear. It's very important to me that the sound and the play of the voice are meaningful and accurate in terms of the listener. (pp. 176-77)

M: Do you travel to collect the stories for your books?

B: No. My stories are mainly collected in libraries, because I'm working from hundreds of tribal languages. Much of the material that I work with was collected by missionaries and anthropologists in the late 1800s, often with the desire to get a written alphabet, and they used stories as a way of developing a vocabulary. The forms are generally very stilted in the direct English translations from which I work. Sometimes they use only four or five sentences to tell the story, but the story-motif is documented. I take off from there.

M: Why specifically do you go to Africa?

B: As a black American, I have African roots. Retelling and illustrating African tales has kept me close to African sources. So it's only natural that I'd want to visit Africa. Long before my first visit, I'd read African tales and studied African art and history. The visits were wonderful! I was in the African setting, observing and meeting Africans and drawing all the time. So the visits have deepened the commitment to my work.

The artist working today has the world cultures at hand. In my work as a black American artist, it is the African root that nourishes whatever other world culture I may draw upon. (p. 179)

Sylvia Marantz and Kenneth Marantz, "Interview with Ashley Bryan," in The Horn Book Magazine, *Vol. LXIV, No. 2, March-April, 1988, pp. 173-79.*

GENERAL COMMENTARY

KATHARYN F. CRABBE

[We] must consider what we want for children from folklore as literature as well as ethnology. Good folklore does not automatically yield good literature.

The renderings of folktales by editors, retellers, or adaptors are translations. They are efforts to make the imaginative constructs of one culture seem at home in, and accessible to, another. . . . As Edward Fenton wrote in *Horn Book* . . . , a translation is only truly successful if it has the qualities of "credibility, of inevitability, of authority." It has to give the impression of having been written originally in the language of the reader. And that is the impression a literal translation almost never gives. The problem may lie in the structure, or it may lie in the language.

Many of the most highly structured folktales for children are really fakelore. Writers often have a Pavlovian response to folk art, only the flowing juices are creative rather than digestive. . . .

As ethnologists, adaptors of folk material must come to terms with every nuance of a tale as it has been traditionally told. This may require leaving out episodes which cannot be woven into the main thread; or adding enough background information to let children understand motivation and behavior. (p. 42)

Preserving too many features of an unusual or difficult narrative structure may cause a tale to fail as children's literature, though it is a great success as folklore. The most common occasion for this difficulty is the trickster cycle. These stories often become a lengthy list of short, fragmentary episodes that leave readers with a sense of having heard a series of one-liners. . . . [The] stories, like many oral anecdotes, are strong on beginnings and middles, weak on ends. Some seem to conclude without accounting for all the strands or simply fail to conclude at all.

In addition to problems of structure, too much commitment to authenticity may cause problems of language for children. The best retellers are those who manage to convey a sense of the style of the original. . . .

Successful redactors then, must be dramatists as well as ethnologists. More than one student of folk cultures has noted that what happens in a storytelling session is more akin to theatrical than to narrative art. Storytellers give signals that express their own emotional and intellectual responses—in tone of voice, in posture, in expressions and gestures—and the audience responds. Their responses are important in forming the shape and style of the story as it travels. . . .

That our ideal teller's task is difficult seems self-evident: that it is not impossible is clearly shown in the number of fine retellings of folktales for children available. In addition to [Christie] Harris, [Frederic] Guirma, and [Verna] Aardema, I think of Ashley Bryan's *The Ox of the Wonderful Horns and Other African Folktales* which captures completely the cadences of an oral telling. Equally impressive is his retelling of an Antiguan tale, *The Dancing Granny,* in which the cultural context is depicted in swirling line drawings as well as in strongly rhythmic language. . . .

As artists, tellers of folktales must be capable of re-creating each story so that it seems to have grown naturally. The tale must reflect a wholeness of vision that will give it Fenton's qualities of credibility, inevitability, and authority. This non-negotiable requirement has several implications: It means that documentation and annotation must be unobtrusive, and it suggests that contextual information is best integrated into plot. Retellers must, indeed, be true to the world view of the original, but they must also make that view live for their own audiences. (p. 43)

> *Katharyn F. Crabbe, "Folk Over Fakelore—But Is It Art?" in* School Library Journal, *Vol. 26, No. 3, November, 1979, pp. 42-3.*

From The Dancing Granny, *retold and illustrated by Ashley Bryan.*

ALICE K. SWINGER

The scene is a school auditorium; the speaker is Ashley Bryan, artist, illustrator, singer of poetry, teller of tales. For more than an hour he has demonstrated, with the poems of Langston Hughes, Paul Laurence Dunbar, Gwendolyn Brooks, and Eloise Greenfield, how the rhythm and sound of poetry work together. Then, telling stories from his own book, *The Ox of the Wonderful Horns,* he emphasizes both rhythm and sound in his prose style. In this way, he seeks to recreate a sense of the oral tradition. In an oral African culture, song, drums, dance, and audience participation all enhance storytelling sessions. (p. 305)

Poetry and stories, he explains [to his audience], should be practiced, then read aloud, for the reader to understand the relationship between sound, spirit, and meaning. Then, when the materials are read silently, the reader will receive more benefit because the sound and the spirit will already have been felt in the muscles and heard in the ears. . . .

Bryan, seasoned teacher and experienced entertainer, begins to play softly "Swing Low, Sweet Chariot." Attention is riveted on him; the only sound in the vast room is the sweet melody of the recorder. . . .

Laying the recorder aside, Bryan speaks of the spiritual he has just played. "I've traveled in many countries and in each of them I have noticed that the folk songs, the songs of the people, are gathered into books. I discovered I could buy folk music books in varied presentations everywhere I traveled, but nowhere in the United States could I buy an introductory book of spirituals, the songs of American black people.

"When I realized this, I started work on my first book of spirituals, *Walk Together, Children.* I used block prints, reminiscent of the early block-printed religious books. Since the spirituals are religious songs, I wanted to make the visual connection to the early block-printed religious books. These songs celebrated the hopes, the spirit, of a people in slavery. The spirituals are a great gift to the world, a unique contribution to music. I decided to make selections from these hundreds of songs available in book form.

"I've just started the work," Bryan says, "and I hope other people will find their own ways to put the songs together in books, with their own designs and musical notations so that more of these great spirituals will become known."

A spiritual grows. In endless variations, it is recreated with each singing, each interpretation. Bryan's dream is that books of spirituals will be as profuse and as available to children as alphabet, counting, and nursery rhyme books. Many artists, he thinks, in their maturity, wish to create new images for what is already known and loved. It is for this reason new presentations of old favorites appear each year.

Thus, in Bryan's vision, boys and girls who experience spirituals during their growing years by singing them, hearing them sung, seeing them in books, may someday want to produce their own visual interpretations and collections. Bryan sees this as a tremendous cooperative effort, free from competition, joined for the common purpose of bringing a rich national resource into the world cultural mainstream. (p. 306)

Ashley Bryan's love of music is anchored in family experiences in childhood. His earliest recollections are of his mother singing and of his father making music with his boyhood friends. Like Bryan's parents, these friends had come from

Antigua in the West Indies after World War I. Living in New York, they kept alive their traditions and memories of the far-away home with their Sunday afternoon songfests.

Just as the love of music and appreciation of its patterns is rooted in childhood, Bryan's work with African folktales stems from an early life experience. He remembers that he loved reading folktales from all over the world. He found that the African folk stories were often poorly told. He also remembers that as a child he loved drawing and would illustrate many books that he read, creating the images from his own experiences. In this way, he illustrated Mother Goose, the songs he heard his mother singing, the folk and fairy tales he read, and the stories he wrote. Continuing in the tradition of illustrating, he embarked on a project of illustrating African folktales during his college art studies.

Bryan worked from primary sources: the transcriptions of anthropologists, missionaries, and linguists. He discovered that the folk stories were generally written, not to tell a story beautifully as a storyteller would, but to get a written transcription of the language. In many cases, the persons writing the story motifs were interested in vocabulary to translate the Bible into the tribal language. Anthologists, using these stories in collections of African tales, do not improvise, interpret, and polish these motifs into literary works.

Bryan realized that the stories should be restored to their full meaning, complete with storytellers' beautiful language, sense of sound, rhythm, and imagery. He began the restoration, working with sounds and rhythms in stories, as poets work with the sounds and rhythms in poems.

Bryan relates the work he is doing with African folk stories to the work of storytellers everywhere who seek to carry over the flavor of the oral tradition in their printed versions of folktales. Wilhelm and Jacob Grimm, for example, were linguists interested in identifying the phonology of the people of Germany when they recognized that the stories people told were a priceless treasure of the people.

The Brothers Grimm set about retelling the stories. They did it with such style and beauty that, to this day, German children read them as they were written at that time. In countries around the world, these stories have become so popular that each year new translations, with new illustrations, are published.

In reading the original sources of African folk stories, Bryan read texts with the African language on one column of the page and English on the other. He worked from the English translation, searching for a motif he liked. Finding one, he began to develop it, releasing the spirit of the story with imagery, sound, meaning, and rhythm.

Bryan believes that everyone, given a theme or motif of personal interest, could develop a story in a unique way, just as each storyteller in the oral tradition interprets stories in a personal way. A story can be developed from the writer's memory of the rhythms of language, of the sounds of people talking, of the melody of written works, of images of experiences. Bryan uses all of those sources, as well as research into the customs of the people who told the original story. He is not, however, confined to what has been written, or what has been heard. He is intent on creating a story in the spirit in which a storyteller in the oral tradition would create. Authenticity

of work is not the same for a storyteller as it is for an anthropologist or a linguist.

Every Bryan book has its own image. He begins with the basic motif, enriching it with words that have just the right sound, then expands with phrases to produce an appropriate rhythm. Finally, he provides a context for all of this with the illustrations.

The folktale books, *The Ox of the Wonderful Horns, The Adventure of Aku,* and *Beat the Story Drum, Pum Pum* are done with tempera paints. Black-and-white paintings are interspersed with those in red, black, and ochre. Endpapers are in one or the other of these colors, as are backings, giving the books warm earthtone unity. (pp. 307-09)

Two books illustrated for other writers employ different techniques to create the image that works best with the story lines. In Susan Cooper's *Jethro and the Jumbie,* a tale set in the Caribbean Isles, the pictures were drawn from life, during trips to Antigua, with form, thrust, and perspective that has been basic to drawing since the Renaissance. Bryan felt that this style and the light, silvery touch of pencil drawings would best illuminate the story of the little boy who became friends with the Jumbie, the Caribbean boogeyman.

Mari Evans' *Jim Flying High,* is in full color, painted with watercolor and touches of tempera. The shapes are separated by narrow, white channels which give a flat, patterned effect, reminiscent of Gothic stained glass.

Of special interest to Ashley Bryan is the poetry of Paul Laurence Dunbar. Although about two-thirds of Dunbar's poetry is in standard English, the dialect poems are better known. This was a disappointment to Dunbar during his life and a loss to the people who were not familiar with the larger body of his work. Bryan wrote the foreword and selected the poems in *I Greet the Dawn* to provide a representation of the artistry, range, and richness of Dunbar's language. About ninety percent of the poems in this volume are in standard English, the rest in dialect.

Bryan presents examples of modern black poets, as well as those from earlier years. All of these poems, literature meant primarily for the ear rather than the eye, support his effort to demonstrate to students and teachers the relationship between poetry and story, and the interplay between voice, meaning, sound, and rhythm. (p. 310)

What will we be seeing of Ashley Bryan in coming years? He continues to work with spirituals, gathering and preparing collections for people to savor and share. Thus he serves as a motivator for others to create collections of these beautiful songs. Always he works with traditional African tales, "getting way down in the music" of each one, to bring sound, rhythm, meaning, and motif together. He combines these elements in his printed versions of African tales to create a whole that might recapture the oral tradition of storytelling. (p. 311)

Alice K. Swinger, "Profile: Ashley Bryan," in Language Arts, *Vol. 61, No. 3, March, 1984, pp. 305-11.*

THE OX OF THE WONDERFUL HORNS AND OTHER AFRICAN FOLKTALES (1971)

Four short stories of animal fun and trickery, and a longer story about Mungalo—a chief's son constantly being tormented by his father's many wives. Ananse the spider is outwitted by Crow in a fishing deal; Frog Kumboto has a problem in the rainy season with his two wives, who get confused and call him to eat mush at the same time; Frog makes good his boast that Elephant is his horse; and Hare, "a born trickster," is outwitted by Tortoise in the sweet potato patch. Attractively printed and boldly interpreted in five large red, black, and tan woodcuts and several smaller black designs, the tellable tales will reach a wider audience of young readers than most of the other recent volumes containing African lore. The sources used were two late nineteenth-century and two early twentieth-century collections.

> *Virginia Haviland, in a review of "The Ox of the Wonderful Horns and Other African Folktales," in* The Horn Book Magazine, *Vol. XLVIII, No. 2, April, 1972, p. 141.*

Five stories are retold and are illustrated in woodcuts that are bold in design and color, stylized and effectively African in mood. Four of the tales are about animals and their trickery, one of them (**"Frog and His Two Wives"**) a "why" story; the title story is on the familiar theme of the outcast youth who, with the aid of magic, gains love and success. The stories have humor and action but the style of the retelling does not quite capture the flow and cadence of the oral tradition.

> *Zena Sutherland, in a review of "The Ox of the Wonderful Horns and Other African Folktales," in* Bulletin of the Center for Children's Books, *Vol. 25, No. 10, June, 1972, p. 152.*

WALK TOGETHER CHILDREN: BLACK AMERICAN SPIRITUALS (1974)

Walk Together Children is as sweet and varied a collection of black spirituals as one could hope to find for children. Out of the collected mass of spirituals, just 24 are presented here. These sweep the emotions from the majestic command of **"Go Down Moses"** to the mournful grandeur of **"Deep River."** (pp. 28-9)

Walk Together Children is a beginning statement, just as the body of spirituals is the total record, of the *Soul* of black slaves in America.

Slaves in America were the only creators of the spirituals. Endowed with a unique musical instinct and talent inherited from the motherland, they took into bondage with them their intricate African rhythms. They embraced the Christianity of the American masters when they could no longer bare the sorrow born of servitude. And combining their age-old rhythms with Biblical stories of hope and freedom, mainly from the Hebrew testament, blacks fused a profoundly harmonious, newly melodic, "spiritual" music.

The spirituals might have been lost forever if not for northern collectors who set down words and music in the first years after the Civil War. For the newly-emancipated wanted nothing, not even their moving melodies, to remind them of bondage. In 1871, the Jubilee Singers of Fisk University introduced the spirituals to the public and made them famous throughout the world. Since that time, each new generation of black Americans has joined its elders to sing these noble songs in church. Other peoples have sung them as well. With Ashley Bryan's collection, the tradition of preserving the spirituals through teaching the young is surely enriched. . . .

Mr. Bryan has graced *Walk Together Children* with bold, flowing woodcuts. Black and white contours of beasts and human beings complement simple lines of melody, along with their musical notations, and the texts. (p. 29)

> *Virginia Hamilton, in a review of "Walk Together Children: Black American Spirituals," in* The New York Times Book Review, *November 3, 1974, pp. 28-9.*

The Black American spirituals are songs through which the world was enriched by people who had nothing. *Walk Together Children* contains two dozen spirituals, including **"Little David," "Go Down, Moses," "Deep River," "Swing Low, Sweet Chariot"** — the old favorites plus some less familiar ones.

Among the great masterpieces of religious folk music, these were the brave and lovely cries of men and women forced to trust in heaven because they had no hope on earth.

Mr. Bryan's black-and-white illustrations surge with compassion and raw life.

From Beat the Story-Drum, Pum-Pum, *retold and illustrated by Ashley Bryan.*

For all ages, all races.

Neil Millar, "Songs of Lands and Seasons," in The Christian Science Monitor, *November 6, 1974, p. 14.*

THE ADVENTURES OF AKU: OR, HOW IT CAME ABOUT THAT WE SHALL ALWAYS SEE OKRA THE CAT LYING ON A VELVET CUSHION, WHILE OKRAMAN THE DOG SLEEPS AMONG THE ASHES (1976)

"Long ago," we are told in Ashley Bryan's fascinating recounting of an African tale, "Cat and Dog lived among people as brothers." It is a long, involved magic tale that has echoes of Aladdin's lamp and Jack and the Beanstalk to mention just two familiar stories with similar motifs. There is the stupid-but-good-hearted son, the long-suffering mother, the unfair trade, a transformed king, a magical ring that grants wishes, the traditional African trickster Ananse and, most important, the noble cat and the base dog.

Bryan, who has a growing reputation for retelling African stories and for the strong, primitive woodcuts that decorate his books, is most effective here when he tells his tale in prose. Then he is direct, colloquial, with a good rhythmic sense. But most folktales break into rhyme, into song in the form of magical charms, oracular wisdom or the naming of names. When Bryan tries verse, his ear fails, his tongue stumbles. Instead of a direct folk quality, what comes out is rhyme that is reminiscent of television commercials:

> The ring, the ring,
> What a wonderful thing!

goes one couplet. . . .

Still, the story is strong enough to hold until the end when Mr. Bryan writes in true folk style: "I've told the tale through. You may take some as true and go with it."

This reader, at least, would have been happier knowing what is *literally* true about the tale: which part of Africa or what tribe the story is from; an explanation or glossary for the many untranslated or untranslatable words. Mostly, I wanted a key to the artwork, for Bryan is a sophisticated professor of art and the handsome illustrations and striking designs are obviously modeled on tribal patterns and traditional motifs. But what tribe or tribes, what motifs, are left for the reader— less versed in African art than Mr. Bryan—to unriddle.

Jane Yolen, in a review of "The Adventures of Aku," in The New York Times Book Review, *October 10, 1976, p. 30.*

Illustrated with dramatic, stylized pictures in black and white or in black, red, and gold, this synthesis of African folktales into one story that contains other tales is smooth and effective. Basically it is a "why" story that explains the different ways people treat dogs and cats, but it also contains many familiar folklore patterns: the child who comes magically to a lonely, childless person; the dolt who forgets his errand; the crafty creature (Spider Ananse, in this case) who is outwitted; the kind deed rewarded, and others. Bryan's style is direct and colloquial in the best storytelling tradition.

Zena Sutherland, in a review of "The Adventures of Aku; or How It Came About That We Shall Always See Okra the Cat Lying on a Velvet Cushion, While Okraman the Dog Sleeps among the Ashes," in Bul-letin of the Center for Children's Books, *Vol. 30, No. 6, February, 1977, p. 87.*

THE DANCING GRANNY (1977)

Hard working and hard dancing Granny Anika is deceived four times by con artist Spider Ananse before she finally succeeds in transforming him into her best dancing partner ever. The telling of this West Indian folk tale is monotonous, and the line drawings, though lively, fail to convey the vitality of that culture. Moreover, both narrative and illustrations unwittingly tend to reinforce objectionable stereotypes, caricaturing those of African ancestry as having rhythm but not brains. The allure of the Spider character is still best captured in Gerald McDermott's picture book *Anansi the Spider* (1972). (pp. 59-60)

Allene Stuart Phy, in a review of "The Dancing Granny," in School Library Journal, *Vol. 23, No. 9, May, 1977, pp. 59-60.*

A touch of rhyming talk and the visual portrayal of Ananse as a slouch-hatted dude spice Bryan's exuberant, musical retelling of a trickster story from the Antilles. Both Granny Anika, the joyful, dancing old woman whose garden Spider repeatedly raids before he's tricked in return, and Ananse himself are heartily evoked in visual and verbal terms: freewheeling, loosely lined studies of Granny in motion novelly extend the story's powerful sense of life and movement, and the overall text with its song chants and snatches of dialogue is rich for reading aloud.

Denise M. Wilms, in a review of "The Dancing Granny," in Booklist, *Vol. 73, No. 18, May 15, 1977, p. 1418.*

BEAT THE STORY-DRUM, PUM-PUM (1980)

Five African folk tales for storytelling, humorous, informal and direct, with the rhythm and idiom of the African oral tradition. Integrated into the text are the appropriate actions, beats and chants and changing voices (even animal noises) for each character. Some of the stories are simple cumulative tales. The fun is often more in the telling (monkey forgets his important message to Head Chief and dances around chattering, "Hay baa ba ree bop, hay baa") than in the ending. As in the creation story, **"How the Animals Got Their Tales,"** the language is poetic ("He awoke and fleshed fish with scales to flash through the seas.") and wonderfully rhythmic ("Lion's first mane tripped him up, had to be shortened. Goat's first coat was too tight a fit, had to be loosened."), with much unforced use of rhyme. Beautifully illustrated with bold stylized woodcuts, some in black and white, some also with brick red and mustard yellow. For younger children, but also appropriate for any good folklore collection.

Hazel Rochman, in a review of "Beat the Story-Drum, Pum-Pum," in School Library Journal, *Vol. 27, No. 5, January, 1981, p. 47.*

These five Nigerian stories have all the wit and rhythm we have come to expect from African folktales. In addition, Bryan's retellings make graceful dips into modern slang, giving the stories a faint American bouquet without compromising their ethnicity. The stories are a little long for telling, but well worth the time; independent readers will enjoy them just as much as listeners. Like woodcuts, the author's many illustrations in black and white and color tell just enough to keep readers' imaginations working.

> *Judith Goldberger, in a review of "Beat the Story-Drum, Pum-Pum," in Booklist, Vol. 77, No. 9, January 1, 1981, p. 622.*

Five Nigerian folk tales retold in an infectious, rhythmic style and accompanied by strong, interpretive illustrations, chiefly in black and white with six full-page pictures in gold, black, and red. Even such prosaic information as publication data and the list of sources are integrated into the total elegant design through the judicious placement of illustrative material. The motifs and the story types — cumulative details and talking beast, droll, and *pourquoi* tales — are universal; the retellings make the stories unique, offering insight into the heart of a culture. And while the stories are linked by setting and format, each one has a style and a beat appropriate to the subject, the overall effect being one of a musical composition with dexterously designed variations and movements. Marvelous folk aphorisms are skillfully integrated into the narratives: For instance, the village elders — distraught by the constant destructive actions of the protagonists in **"Why Bush Cow and Elephant Are Bad Friends"** — cry out, " ' "When two big ones fight, it is the grass that suffers." ' " The use of repetition, rhyming phrases, and alliteration are but some of the poetic devices in a collection as pleasing to the eye as it is to the ear; the book is ideal for storytelling or reading aloud.

> *Mary M. Burns, in a review of "Beat the Story-Drum, Pum-Pum," in The Horn Book Magazine, Vol. LVII, No. 2, April, 1981, p. 200.*

I'M GOING TO SING: BLACK AMERICAN SPIRITUALS, VOLUME TWO (1982)

In this companion to **Walk Together Children,** Bryan presents 25 more spirituals, illustrating them with complex, striking woodcuts that dominate the open music-picture spreads. The author's introduction explains his early exposure to spirituals at family music fests and emphasizes their distinctive style as "unique among the folk songs of the world." He also takes note of their evolving forms, which is perhaps why it is only the melody lines, sans harmonies or interpretive markings, that appear in the specially designed musical notation. Not so much a functional music book as a striking artistic appreciation of the existence of this special genre of song. (pp. 677-78)

> *Denise M. Wilms, in a review of "I'm Going to Sing: Black American Spirituals, Vol. 2," in Booklist, Vol. 79, No. 10, January 15, 1983, pp. 677-78.*

A companion volume to **Walk Together Children,** the collection of twenty-five black American spirituals equals the first one in power of design and variety of selection. In the introduction the author-artist explores the sources of his inspiration, sets forth the reasons for his choices, and emphasizes the significance of spirituals in American history and in the development of American music. The words of Anton Dvořák are included as an indication of their global and their national importance:

> What songs, then, belong to the American? . . .
> The most potent, as well as the most beautiful among them, according to my estimation, are cer-

tain of the so-called plantation melodies and slave songs.

Cut in wood, the illustrations suggest the block-printed style of early religious books and reflect the emotions and fervor of the spirituals. The song titles and the musical notation, within the range of the soprano recorder, are executed in the same medium to afford visual unity and balance. For most of the selections — among them **"When the Saints," "Joshua Fit the Battle," "Gospel Train," "My Lord What a Morning,"** and **"Rise Up Shepherd and Follow"** — more than one verse is included. A substantial addition to available song books for young people, the book is also another handsome example of book design. (pp. 57-8)

> *Mary M. Burns, in a review of "I'm Going to Sing: Black American Spirituals, Volume Two," in The Horn Book Magazine, Vol. LIX, No. 1, February, 1983, pp. 57-8.*

THE CAT'S PURR (1985)

"Once upon a time, Cat and Rat were the best of friends," begins Bryan's briskly told tale—but no more. Not after Cat got a tiny "Cat family drum" from his old uncle, and Rat decided he just had to play it even though his friend Cat said no. Rat's trickery gives the story a nice bit of dramatic tension, and the notion of the tiny drum as the reason cats purr today will amuse young listeners or readers with its novelty. Bryan's text has a distinctive flavor that marks it as a capital read-aloud. Accompanying illustrations in sepia lines have an unfinished, sketchbook quality, but the lines are fluid and true in capturing postures and nuances of expression. The source for this retelling appears on the final page—a tight, dialect-flavored rendition by a Montserrat storyteller.

> *Denise M. Wilms, in a review of "The Cat's Purr," in Booklist, Vol. 81, No. 16, April 15, 1985, p. 1189.*

This version of a folktale from the Antilles . . . has a twist or two that goes beyond the original. However, the refrains, the expressive dialogue, and the inclusion of sound effects in the narrative voice make the text seem as if it had been lifted word for word from the oral tradition. Ashley Bryan is a master storyteller, in person and on paper, and those who have heard him perform will recognize the potential drama and musicality built into this brief story. It would lend itself well to retelling or reading with drum and other musical accompaniment. One of the pleasures of this small book is its pictures. Antic Rat and stolid Cat dress and live like humans in Bryan's entertaining sepia-tones sketches.

> *Janet Hickman, in a review of "The Cat's Purr," in Language Arts, Vol. 62, No. 6, October, 1985, p. 654.*

[One] way to keep folk literature from becoming stultified is in locating seldom-told tales. For example, Ashley Bryan's **The Cat's Purr** is an expanded version of a tale anthologized in 1936. . . .

Bryan illustrates this text with relaxed, easy line—with a casual quality that makes one think of an artist's sketch pad of personal jottings. In keeping with the Cat-Rat drama, he tenderly strokes objects into being with tentative little lines that suggest contour, as well as a third dimension. It looks as if he used conté crayon or conté pencil—that responsive brown drawing substance that is typically prized by art students, but

From I'm Going to Sing: Black American Spirituals, Volume Two, *selected and illustrated by Ashley Bryan.*

not much used in commercial work. It smudges a bit, but that very quality gives the edges of the drawing a soft, sketchy dimension. Accents can be created by simply pressing down a bit harder for a darker line. . . . The effect is an easily read, unpretentious drawing.

Folklore journals and old anthologies are a rich hunting ground for materials such as **The Cat's Purr,** for tales that offer an alternative to the plague of redundantly retold stories. When such fresh materials are more widely known, the flow of warmed-over (and frequently sexist) folk narratives may finally subside.

> *Donnarae MacCann and Olga Richard, in a review of "The Cat's Purr," in* Wilson Library Bulletin, *Vol. 60, No. 6, February, 1986, p. 45.*

LION AND THE OSTRICH CHICKS AND OTHER AFRICAN FOLK TALES (1986)

Bryan presents lively, tellable stories about animal and human characters. He includes extensive dialogue and numerous songs from four previously published collections of the folklore of the Masai, Bushmen, and Hausa, and from Angola. The stories give no evidence of their African origin, which is a result of three of the sources that Bryan used being

decontextualized, which was typical of African folklore collections at the turn of the century. The morals of these stories are universal in application. Bryan's lively illustrations focus on animals engaged in the action taking place in the stories, but without any context, thus reinforcing the generic content of the stories. The illustrations of people and houses from the stories about the Bushmen (who live in southern Africa) and Hausa (who live in northern Nigeria) are similar and misrepresent both the physical features of the people and their cultures. Although the stories can be enjoyed as narratives when read or told aloud, the collection reinforces the concept that Africa is a country, rather than a diverse continent with distinctively different cultures. The illustrations for most of Verna Aardema's recent retellings of African folklore more authentically represent distinctive features of the African cultures in which the narratives are told.

> *Nancy J. Schmidt, in a review of "Lion and the Ostrich Chicks and Other African Tales," in* School Library Journal, *Vol. 33, No. 5, January, 1987, p. 60.*

In the splendid format of his two previous collections — **The Ox of the Wonderful Horns** and **Beat the Story-Drum, Pum-Pum** — Ashley Bryan presents four stories representing various cultures of Africa, while his dynamic, somewhat stylized black-and-white drawings, augmented by five illustrations in red, black, and gold, add not only decorative designs but a handsome choreography of animated creatures. . . . Playing with the sounds as well as with the meanings of words, Ashley Bryan invites oral interpretation of the tales by his liberal use of onomatopoeic language, alliteration, interior rhymes, and repeated rhythmic chants. He indicates the source of each tale, although by his own admission he is more interested in approaching "the spirit of the Black oral tradition" than he is in "literal authenticity," and he once stated that his object is to build for children, both black and white, a "tender bridge between the African past and the American present."

Ethel L. Heins, in a review of "Lion and the Ostrich Chicks and Other African Folk Tales," in The Horn Book Magazine, *Vol. LXIII, No. 2, March-April, 1987, p. 227.*

Lewis Carroll

1832-1898

(Pseudonym of Charles Lutwidge Dodgson) English author of fiction and poet.)

The following entry presents criticism of *Alice's Adventures in Wonderland* and *Through the Looking-Glass, and What Alice Found There.*

Carroll is perhaps the foremost writer of fantasy in literary history. He is best known as the creator of *Alice's Adventures in Wonderland* (1865) and *Through the Looking-Glass* (1872), works which are usually considered the greatest and most influential children's books to have been written in English. Lauded as a genius who fused his eccentric personal characteristics and opinions about Victorian life with a genuine love of children and childhood, he is recognized for liberating juvenile literature from its history of didacticism and overt moralizing. With the *Alice* books, Carroll ushered in the Golden Age of children's literature, a period characterized by its imaginative and purely entertaining works for the young. The stories about Alice are often praised as the first children's books that could be read with equal pleasure by both children and adults; appeal to the latter group is so strong that the tales have transcended their status as books for children to become classics of the English language. Along with the Bible and the works of Shakespeare, the *Alice* books are noted for providing Western culture with its most consistent source of quotes. They are also considered the best examples of their author's literary output. Carroll is often acknowledged for creating a totally unique landscape, a fairyland without precedent, with his stories about Alice. These works, which are usually considered as a whole and are loosely based around a pack of cards and a game of chess, describe how a curious seven-year-old enters two dream worlds, one which she encounters by falling down a rabbit hole, and the other by passing through a mirror. Through her experiences, which are frustrating as well as wonderful, Alice meets a host of fascinating and unusual characters, both humans and anthropomorphic animals. Many of these figures are accepted as universal symbols, among them the White Rabbit, the Cheshire Cat, Tweedledum and Tweedledee, the Red Queen, and the Mad Hatter; two of them, the Dodo in *Alice's Adventures* and the White Knight in *Looking-Glass,* are considered Carroll's self-portraits. As Alice meets these creatures, who are often thought to be Carroll's satire of adults, she is drawn into totally unfamiliar societies which challenge her knowledge and beliefs. Alice becomes involved in a series of amusing yet often disagreeable events which test her perceptions of time, space, form, and sense. Surprising and terrifying, yet with their own inherent logic, the characteristics of the worlds in which Alice finds herself are revealed through her reactions to them. Each book concludes with Alice ending her dream after becoming disgusted with the insanity, selfishness, and cruelty of the inhabitants of her unconscious regions. Most contemporary observers conclude that Alice's maturation is at the core of each story. By enduring her often negative experiences with resilience, intelligence, and courte-

sy, Alice becomes wiser and more self-assured and is therefore able to leave behind the childish aspects of herself.

A clergyman, mathematician, and logician who was a also humorist, poet, and philosopher, Carroll is usually considered, in critic Peter Coveney's words, "the casebook maladjusted neurotic." Most of his contemporary biographers affirm that he was probably in love with Alice Liddell, the small daughter of the Dean of Christ Church, Oxford, where Carroll was a lecturer in mathematics. Alice Liddell was the model for the protagonist of his most famous works, which began as an extemporaneous story which Carroll told to entertain Alice and her two sisters on a boating trip in 1862. When Alice pressed Carroll to write down his tale for her, he transcribed and illustrated it as *Alice's Adventures Under Ground* and presented her with a personal copy. He later expanded his text to form *Alice's Adventures in Wonderland,* and arranged for Sir John Tenniel, a popular artist who was the political cartoonist for the magazine *Punch,* to illustrate it. [See entry on Tenniel beginning on page 201 of this volume.] The success of *Alice's Adventures in Wonderland* prompted its sequel, *Through the Looking-Glass,* which Tenniel also illustrated. It is generally agreed that in these books Carroll joined the dual elements of his nature with his affection for Alice Liddell to transcend convention and repression through his art. By discovering an outlet for his feelings, Carroll was able to escape his own situation while providing Alice Liddell, and all children, with a vital and ultimately positive view of life. Reviews of the books during Carroll's lifetime most often concentrated on their magnificent invention and Carroll's skill as a linguist, parodist, and literary stylist. After his death, critics began to analyze the stories in a variety of interpretations—including political, philosophical, metaphysical, and psychoanalytic—which often evaluated the tales as products of Carroll's neuroses and as reactions to Victorian culture. Because of the nightmarish qualities of Alice's adventures and their violent, even sadistic, elements, the *Alice* books are sometimes considered inappropriate for children; due to their classic status and Alice's occasional priggishness, the stories are not always enjoyed by the audience for whom they were intended. However, Carroll is consistently applauded as the world's best writer of nonsense, an author who successfully combined the logical with the illogical in two timeless novels which capture the essence of the child mind and are unequalled in their originality.

(See also *CLR*, Vol. 2; *Nineteenth-Century Literature Criticism*, Vol. 2; *Yesterday's Authors of Books for Children*, Vol. 2; and *Dictionary of Literary Biography*, Vol. 18: *Victorian Novelists After 1885*.)

AUTHOR'S COMMENTARY

Many a day had we rowed together on that quiet stream—the three little maidens and I—and many a fairy-tale had been extemporised for their benefit—whether it were at times when the narrator was 'i' the vein,' and fancies unsought came crowding thick upon him; or at times when the jaded Muse had to be goaded into action, and plodded meekly on, more because she had to say something than that she had something to say—yet none of those many tales got written down: they lived and died, like summer midges, each in its own 'golden afternoon,' until there came a day when, as it chanced, one of my little listeners petitioned that the tale might be written out for her. That was many a year ago, but I distinctly remember, now as I write, how, in a desperate attempt to strike out some new line of fairy-lore, I had sent my heroine straight down a rabbit-hole, to begin with, without the least idea what was to happen afterwards. And so, to please a child I loved (I don't remember having any other motive), I printed in manuscript, and illustrated with my own crude designs—designs that rebelled against every law of Anatomy or Art (for I had never had a lesson in drawing)—the book which I have just had reproduced in facsimile [*Alice's Adventures Under Ground* was published in 1886]. In writing it out, I added many fresh ideas, which seemed to grow of themselves upon the original stock; and many more added themselves when, years afterwards, I wrote it all over again for publication: but (this may perhaps interest some readers of *Alice* to know) every such idea, and nearly every word of the dialogue, *came of itself*. Sometimes an idea comes at night, when I have had to get up and strike a light to note it down—sometimes when out on a lonely winter walk, when I have had to stop, and with half-frozen fingers jot down a few words which should keep the new-born idea from perishing—but, whenever or however it comes, *it comes of itself*. I cannot set invention going like a clock, by any voluntary winding-up: nor do I believe that any *original* writing (and what other writing is worth preserving?) was ever so produced. If you sit down, unimpassioned and uninspired, and

tell yourself to write for so many hours, you will merely produce (at least I am sure *I* should merely produce) some of that article which fills, so far as I can judge, two-thirds of most magazines—most easy to write, most weary to read—men call it 'padding,' and it is, to my mind, one of the most detestable things in modern literature. *Alice* and the *Looking-Glass* are made up almost wholly of bits and scraps, single ideas which came of themselves. Poor they may have been; but at least they were the best I had to offer: and I can desire no higher praise to be written of me than the words of a Poet, written of a Poet,

> He gave the people of his best:
> The worst he kept, the best he gave.
>
>   (pp. 179-80)

Stand forth, then, from the shadowy past, *Alice,* the child of my dreams! Full many a year has slipped away, since that 'golden afternoon' that gave thee birth, but I can call it up almost as clearly as if it were yesterday—the cloudless blue above, the watery mirror below, the boat drifting idly on its way, the tinkle of the drops that fell from the oars, as they waved so sleepily to and fro, and (the one bright gleam of life in all this slumberous scene) the three eager faces, hungry for news of fairy-land, and who would not be said 'nay' to: from whose lips "tell us a story, please," had all the stern immutability of Fate!

What wert thou, dream-Alice, in thy foster-father's eyes? How shall he picture thee? Loving, first, loving and gentle: loving as a dog (forgive the prosaic simile, but I know of no earthly love so pure and perfect), and gentle as a fawn: then courteous—courteous to *all*, high or low, grand or grotesque, King or Caterpillar, even as though she were herself a King's daughter, and her clothing of wrought gold: then trustful, ready to accept the wildest impossibilities with all that utter trust that only dreamers know; and lastly, curious—wildly curious, and with the eager enjoyment of Life that comes only in the happy hours of childhood, when all is new and fair, and when Sin and Sorrow are but names—empty words, signifying nothing!

And the White Rabbit, what of *him?* Was *he* framed on the *Alice* lines, or meant as a contrast? As a contrast, distinctly. For *her* 'youth,' 'audacity,' 'vigour,' and 'swift directness of purpose,' read 'elderly,' 'timid,' 'feeble,' and 'nervously shilly-shallying,' and you will get *something* of what I meant him to be. I *think* the White Rabbit should wear spectacles. I am sure his voice should quaver, and his knees quiver, and his whole air suggest a total inability to say 'Bo!' to a goose!

But I cannot hope to be allowed . . . half the space I should need (even if my *reader's* patience would hold out) to discuss each of my puppets one by one. Let me cull from the two books a Royal Trio—the Queen of Hearts, the Red Queen, and the White Queen. It was certainly hard on my Muse, to expect her to sing of *three* Queens, within such brief compass, and yet to give to each her own distinct individuality. Each, of course, had to preserve, through all her eccentricities, a certain queenly *dignity*. *That* was essential. And, for distinguishing traits, I pictured to myself the Queen of Hearts as a sort of embodiment of ungovernable passion—a blind and aimless Fury. The Red Queen I pictured also as a Fury, but of another type; *her* passion must be cold and calm; she must be formal and strict, yet not unkindly; pedantic to the tenth degree, the concentrated essence of all governesses! Lastly, the White Queen seemed, to my dreaming fancy, gentle, stupid, fat and pale; helpless as an infant; and with a slow, maundering, bewildered air about her, just *suggesting* imbecility, but never quite passing into it; *that* would be, I think, fatal to any comic effect she might otherwise produce. There is a character strangely like her in Mr. Wilkie Collins' novel 'No Name:' by two different yet converging paths we have somehow reached the same ideal, and Mrs. Wragg and the White Queen might have been twin-sisters. (pp. 181-82)

> Lewis Carroll, " 'Alice' on the Stage," in The Theatre, n.s. Vol. IX, No. 52, April 1, 1887, pp. 179-84.

THE ATHENAEUM

[*Alice's Adventures in Wonderland*] is a dream-story; but who can, in cold blood, manufacture a dream, with all its loops and ties, and loose threads, and entanglements, and inconsistencies, and passages which lead to nothing, at the end of which Sleep's most diligent pilgrim never arrives? Mr. Carroll has laboured hard to heap together strange adventures, and heterogeneous combinations; and we acknowledge the hard labour. . . . We fancy that any real child might be more puzzled than enchanted by this stiff, over-wrought story.

> A review of "Alice's Adventures in Wonderland," in The Athenaeum, No. 1990, December 16, 1865, p. 844.

THE LONDON REVIEW

Alice's Adventures in Wonderland is a delightful book for children—or, for the matter of that, for grown-up people, provided they have wisdom and sympathy enough to enjoy a piece of downright hearty drollery and fanciful humour. Alice is a little girl who falls down a rabbit-hole into some strange subterranean region, where she meets all kinds of odd people and things, and goes through a world of marvellous adventures. The style in which these things are related is admirable for its appearance of wondering belief, as if the mind of the child were somehow transfused into the narrative; and the book, small as it is, is crammed full of curious invention.

> A review of "Alice's Adventures in Wonderland," in The London Review of Politics, Society, Literature, Art, & Science, Vol. XI, No. 286, December 23, 1865, p. 675.

THE SPECTATOR

[*Alice's Adventures in Wonderland* is a] book for little folks, and big folks who take it home to their little folks will find themselves reading more than they intended, and laughing more than they had any right to expect. Alice is a charming little girl . . . with a delicious style of conversation. . . . Mr. Carroll's story is very funny, but we wish that he had left out the hatter. . . . (pp. 1441-42)

> A review of "Alice's Adventures in Wonderland," in The Spectator, Vol. 38, No. 1956, December 23, 1865, pp. 1441-42.

MARGARET GATTY

[*The following excerpt is from the first number of* Aunt Judy's Magazine for Young People, *an English periodical established by Mrs. Gatty in 1866 as a place in which to publish the stories of her daughter Juliana Horatia Gatty (nicknamed Judy), who* became a popular author for children under the name Mrs. Ewing. Carroll later became a contributor to the magazine.]

[*Alice's Adventures in Wonderland* has an] exquisitely wild, fantastic, impossible, yet most natural history. . . . [Mr. Lewis Carroll] has a secret, and he has managed his secret so much better than any author who ever "tried on" a secret of the same sort before, that we would not for the world let it out. No; the young folks for whom this charming account is written must go on and on and on till they find out the secret for themselves; and then they will agree with us that never was the mystery made to feel so beautifully natural before. . . .

The above hints will probably make "parents and guardians" aware that they must not look to *Alice's Adventures* for knowledge in disguise.

> Margaret Gatty, in a review of "Alice's Adventures in Wonderland," in Children and Literature: Views and Reviews, edited by Virginia Haviland, Scott, Foresman and Company, 1973, p. 20.

THE SPECTATOR

Alice in Wonderland is, beyond question, supreme among modern books for children. We do not forget the *Water-Babies,* but we exclude it from competition, as being not simply a child's book, but something more. Not that we would gainsay any one who should discover treasures of hidden wisdom in *Alice's Adventures.* Indeed, we have reason to believe that nothing has prevented them from being adopted as a text-book at Cambridge, but the insuperable jealousy of Oxford mathematics which notoriously prevails at that university. . . . We find, then, that Alice, having already made all English-speaking children her subjects, is about to extend her dominion to the nurseries of France and Germany. We confess that our first hasty impulse was to exclaim, "Translate *Alice?* Impossible!" But we were straightway rebuked by the philosophic rejoinder of the caterpillar, "Why not?" And presently reason added, when the shock of surprise had passed off, "Not only it may be, but it must be." For what are in fact the qualities which are the marks of a really good child's book? Imprimis, it must amuse children; item, it must have no obvious moral; but this is not enough. The best children's tales, the tales which have really lived among the people, address themselves to all ages; witness the treasures preserved for us by the Brothers Grimm. . . . But farther, not only is the true child-mind of no age in particular; it is also cosmopolitan. There is no delight in local colouring for its own sake, and we seldom find more of it than is unavoidably imposed by the limits of the story-teller's experience. In the fairy world there are no foreign parts, and in the centre of the earth or on the other side of the moon we are as much at home as on the Thames or the Weser. It follows that a child's book of genuine worth ought to suffer less by translation than any other kind of book; and the volumes now before us may to that extent be considered a farther test of the excellence of the original. If any person objects to any part of the foregoing argument on the score of paradox or otherwise, we are willing to refer the dispute to the Cheshire cat. (p. 933)

It is natural to suppose that *Alice,* having now become trilingual, may be called in to assist in teaching languages in families. We hardly know whether to recommend such a course as humane or to denounce it as barbarous. Will lessons become amusing by association with *Alice,* or will even *Alice* become hateful by being regarded as a lesson-book? The experiment is a hazardous one, and will demand no small skill and tact on the part of the operator. And the moral of that is—we have forgot to mention the crowning merit of the work. Notwithstanding any remarks of the Duchess, *Alice* has no moral. (p. 934)

> *"Alice Translated," in* The Spectator, *Vol. 42, No. 2145, August 7, 1869, pp. 933-34.*

THE ATHENAEUM

It is with no mere book that we have to deal here [in *Through the Looking-Glass, and What Alice Found There*] . . . , but with the potentiality of happiness for countless thousands of children of all ages; for it would be difficult to over-estimate the value of the store of hearty and healthy fun laid up for whole generations of young people by Mr. Lewis Carroll and Mr. John Tenniel in the two books which they have united to produce. In the first volume, Alice won the affections of a whole child-world as she wandered through Wonderland; in the second, that now before us, she will be sure to add fresh troops to the number of her unknown friends, besides retaining her place in the hearts of her old admirers.

Before many days have elapsed thousands of bright eyes will be watching her as she glides through the drawing-room looking-glass, which suddenly softens before her, and passes into the land of reflections which lies on the other side, where animated chessmen are walking and talking cheerily, and finds herself as a White Queen's Pawn playing across a chess-board earth, and striving to arrive at Queendom at its farther end. Many a little head will puzzle itself—children like to be puzzled—over the people who thought in chorus; and the wood in which names got lost; and the Red King's dream of which Alice was told she was a mere feature, her existence being absolutely subjective; and the land in which events took place backwards, like a sentence in Hungarian, so that a criminal was sentenced first, and tried afterwards, for a crime he was going to commit. Much young blood will run cold with fright—children dearly love to be frightened—at the awe-inspiring portrait of the Apollyon-like Jabberwocky. . . . And many a heart both old and young will be stirred with wholesome laughter at the quarrel of Tweedledum with Tweedledee, the arithmetical genius of Humpty Dumpty, the vagaries of that King's Messenger who was as mad as a Hatta, and the metamorphosis of the Red Queen into a kitten, which synchronizes with Alice's own return from her eighth-square queendom into her old life on this side of the looking-glass.

Even the face of a reviewer, of one whose heart has been rendered heavy within him by the involuntary study of our comic literature, may be dimpled by a smile of admiration as he watches the skill with which both the author and the illustrator have worked in the difficult atmosphere of nonsense. . . .

[Bands] of children will deservedly feel personally grateful to both author and illustrator. . . . (p. 787)

> *A review of "Through the Looking-Glass, and What Alice Found There," in* The Athenaeum, *No. 2303, December 16, 1871, pp. 787-88.*

THE EXAMINER

Mr. Lewis Carroll's *Through the Looking-Glass, and What Alice Found There* is a sort of sequel to *Alice's Adventures in Wonderland* and, though hardly as good as that altogether delightful book, is quite good enough to delight every sensible reader of any age. It tells, with wit and humour that all children can appreciate, and grown folks ought as thoroughly to enjoy, how Alice—in a dream as she afterwards found out—broke through the drawing-room looking-glass to look at the furniture that was the reverse of all that was around her, and then entered upon a series of wonderful adventures among Red Kings and White Queens and all the people of the chess-board, saw funny things without number, met with Humpty Dumpty and other wonderful people, and heard, and herself sang, queer songs of all sorts. And the best of all is that the book has no moral, and is nothing but a capital jumble of fun.

> *A review of "Through the Looking-Glass, and What Alice Found There," in* The Examiner, *No. 3333, December 16, 1871, p. 1250.*

THE SPECTATOR

Looking-Glass House is a very pretty place, and Alice was quite the right person to go and see what was in it [in *Through the Looking-Glass*]. Of course everybody knows who Alice is. Does any one say no? Perhaps there may be an excuse for you, good reader. At the time of her Adventures in Wonderland you may have been in the Mountains of the Moon, in search of your own adventures—perhaps not more true than hers, and certainly not so good—or ice-bound in the North Polar Seas, or not old enough to read, or in a passing fit of common sense thinking yourself too old to read children's books. If so, you must go and get Alice to tell you what she did in Wonderland, or you will not be able to understand her new story. What happened to the three little sisters who lived in a well? why are whitings' tails in their mouths? and what are tarts made of? Those who can answer these questions off-hand will follow us. We will run a caucus-race with them till you are ready, and then we will all go on together. (pp. 1607-08)

[Alice goes through the looking glass] almost before she knows it . . . with the heroic simplicity that beseems a child loved of the fairies. The glass becomes a silvery mist for her, and she stands in the other room where the clock makes faces at you, and the words in all the books run the wrong way. . . .

[The] Red Queen is of a dry, snappish character; the White Queen is desultory, disorderly, and helpless. Her oddities are partly accounted for by her habit of living backwards. The idea, so far as we know, is quite novel: it suggests frightful metaphysical puzzles, but it is touched here with a light hand, and we accept it quite comfortably:—

> 'What sort of things do *you* remember best?' Alice ventured to ask.—'Oh, things that happened the week after next,' the Queen replied, in a careless tone. 'For instance, now,' she went on, sticking a large piece of plaster on her finger as she spoke, 'there's the King's Messenger. He's in prison now, being punished, and the trial doesn't even begin till next Wednesday, and of course the crime comes last of all.'

The plaster is the shadow of coming events. In due time the Queen begins to scream, and finally she pricks her finger,—after which we cannot presume to doubt her word when she says she has sometimes believed as many as six impossible things before breakfast. There is something very fascinating in her faculty of reversing the engine of time, but she turns abruptly into a sheep, and we hear no more of it. After all, it would not do to have people living backwards all through a book. We should run against them too often in reading forwards.

This episode of the White Queen shows the shade of difference between the humours of Wonderland and those of Looking-glass House. The creations of Alice's second fairyland have a comparatively mature air. Without being a bit more like the outer world than before, they have an increased element of inner congruity in their nonsense. They seem this time to work by some obscure law,—a law of nonsense, of course, but discoverable by the corresponding faculty. . . . Perhaps this is why Alice's new story is so much more like a real dream than the other. So it is, at all events. Quite early in her travels Alice floats in the air down the stairs of Looking-glass House with just the tips of her fingers on the handrail, a mode of locomotion long familiar to the dreams of the present writer. Then the changes of scene, wholly unaccounted for, and yet carrying on some thread of grotesque resemblance, are exactly such as take place in a series of efforts to wake. Above all, have we not all held with ourselves conversations very like [the one] which Alice held with Tweedledum and Tweedledee when they found the Red King asleep? (p. 1608)

Humpty Dumpty's talk with Alice is in the author's best manner. It recalls the Gryphon and the Mock-Turtle. His retort to Alice's objection that one can't help growing older,— "*One* can't, perhaps, but *two* can. With proper assistance you might have left off at seven," is unsurpassed by any saying in the original *Wonderland.* And his un-birthday presents will be allowed even by alarmed parents to be a brilliant invention.

Then the vagaries of the White Knight must not be forgotten. . . . [We] hope that not many children will try to make the pudding invented by him which was never cooked, founded on blotting-paper, and improved by sealing-wax and gunpowder. . . .

One or two matters remain obscure to us. The March Hare and the Hatter reappear in slightly changed forms, but not the Dormouse. Why did he not come to Alice's dinner when she became a Queen? His beloved treacle was there—"treacle and ink, or anything else that is pleasant to drink;" at least it was promised. And what is a Bandersnatch? (pp. 1608-09)

A review of "Through the Looking-Glass, and What Alice Found There," in The Spectator, *Vol. 44, No. 2270, December 30, 1871, pp. 1607-09.*

EDWARD SALMON

Though *Alice's Adventures in Wonderland* and *Through the Looking-Glass* are, of course, undeniably clever and possess many charms exclusively their own, there is nothing extraordinarily original about either, and certainly the former cannot fairly be called, as it once was, the most remarkable book for children of recent times. Both these records of Alice's adventures would be but half as attractive as they are without Mr. John Tenniel's illustrations. . . . In *Alice in Wonderland* the funniest idea is the little heroine's telescopic physique. Mr. Carroll's style is as simple as his ideas are extravagant. This probably accounts for the fascination which these stories of a child 'moving under skies never seen by human

eyes' have had over the minds of so many thousands of children and parents. (pp. 571-72)

Edward Salmon, "Literature for the Little Ones," in The Nineteenth Century, *Vol. XXII, No. CXXVIII, October, 1887, pp. 563-80.*

THE ACADEMY

The world can show few writers who from first to last have used their talents so joyously, diligently, and to such kindly purpose as Lewis Carroll.

Lewis Carroll's best period lasted, roughly, from his thirtieth to his forty-fifth year. . . . Indeed, he never again quite caught the simplicity of his first book. *Alice in Wonderland* is an outpouring of inspired nonsense which flowed forth without hindrance and without perceptible impulse. But in *Through the Looking-Glass* we now and then hear the pump at work. The quality of the nonsense is no whit the worse; but simplicity is endangered. In *Through the Looking-Glass,* for example, there is the White Queen's exposition of living backwards, and the theory advanced by Tweedledum and Tweedledee that Alice and themselves had no existence apart from the Red King's dream—a perilous approach to metaphysics. Moreover, *Through the Looking-Glass* is a game of chess, which is the sheer superfluity of cleverness. But *Through the Looking-Glass* is only a shade less admirable than its companion. . . .

We may, indeed, feel quite certain of the longevity of the Alice books. They belong to no one period, but to all. They touch nothing actual but human nature, and human nature is continuous and unchanging. Alice is a matter-of-fact, simple-minded child, and the world is full of Alices, and always will be. Hence the assured popularity of her history. Again, in the manner there is no sense of antiquity, although some thirty years have rolled by, each bringing its modification to literary style. Lewis Carroll wrote as plainly and luminously as he could; and we read and read and can think of no emendation whatever. The words are the best words in the best order. Of hardly any other humorist can it be said that in no instance do we ever wish his manner of narration altered. But Lewis Carroll was a merciless critic of himself and a tireless elaborator of his work, and he sent nothing forth until it was perfect.

By his art *Wonderland* is made not less conceivable than *Fairy Land.* It is almost impossible to believe that there is not somewhere such a region, where dwell for ever the Cheshire Cat and the Mock Turtle, the Gryphon and Humpty Dumpty, the Red Knight and the Duchess. They have each and all an individuality; and they are at once so mad and so reasonable: as real and recognisable as the people in Dickens. Partly it is Lewis Carroll's favourite trick of finding fun in pedantic literalness that persuades us. Again, the illusion is assisted by the abruptness with which the stories open. *Alice in Wonderland* has no preamble, there is no laboured description, we are in Wonderland in a moment, before there is time to think about the pinch of salt with which to season the exaggeration. . . .

[It] may be said of Lewis Carroll that, above all men, he had the art of dreaming with a pen. His great colleague as a nonsense maker—Edward Lear—could be foolish enough, but always with direction and with responsibility. Lewis Carroll, as does the mind when asleep, took the line of least resistance. (p. 98)

Lewis Carroll has had many imitators—some quite shameless, and none worthy to stand beside him. They were, of course, doomed to failure, since they had neither his temperament nor his motive. Lewis Carroll, whose attitude to children was more devotion than mere affection, approaching even to adoration, was not a professional author: he was a kindly playmate of little people, and he wrote *Alice in Wonderland* to give pleasure to two friends. . . . It was published that others might share that pleasure. Of not many of the diligent writers who have attempted to reap in the same field can it be said that their stories proceeded from a similar impulse. Indeed, the failure of the many imitations of *Alice* is another proof that good work must come from within, must be born of the author's own individuality. There has been, and can be, but one Lewis Carroll. To borrow his formulae is not to reconstruct himself. (p. 99)

> *"Lewis Carroll," in* The Academy, *n.s. Vol. 53, No. 1342, January 22, 1898, pp. 98-9.*

THE SATURDAY REVIEW, LONDON

More than any other English writer Carroll has attracted to himself with equal force the crabbed age and the youth of his generation. For that, mere cleverness cannot account: to have taken such root, to have become so naturalised, his work must have struck a note of peculiar appropriateness to his day: it was as it were a microbe that fell upon a constitution happily prepared for its inroads. Yet his rendering of fairy-tale was a departure from tradition.

Of all true fairy-tale this may be said: it has never been "written down" to the intelligence of childish readers: rather it has been the meeting-point of interests, the medium through which the child can experience the thrill of big-hearted adventure, and the grown man the romantic sense and undisturbed belief in poetic justice which are the birthright of childhood. For centuries the child has warmed its imagination upon the folk-tales which once gave contentment to its less simple-minded elders, and do still have an interest for them more or less vague. But up to the latter half of this century the workings of a child's mind were of little interest to its elders. Now, however, an astonishing change has come over the dream of mankind; and to-day the child is the grown-up man's fairy-book. Almost by instinct a wise mind stoops to look into that under-world so close at hand, so stored, perhaps, with the wisdom of the ancients; and so a new ground for fairyland has been reclaimed from the prose of existence. To minds still sensitive to chivalry and romance, the old fairy-tale remains true; but a far larger world of believers has been gathered to the imaginative world of childhood, and arrested, almost studiously, to a contemplation of its laws.

It was through this change of outlook, and as almost its first portent, that Lewis Carroll's fairy-books struck the light. Without condescension, without any "putting back of bright intelligence," rather with all the resources of wit and humour, and a sub-pathetic sense of the ridiculous, Carroll, a man of grave reserve and fine intelligence, turned round upon all tradition to find a new fairyland ready-made, fresh-sprung from humanity's new interest in the things of childhood.

The seriousness of his work, and its safety, come from the fact that it is as much fairy-tale for elders as for children; and the highest interest of these two time-divided classes is the interest they have in common. Lewis Carroll's ability to evoke this common interest was the measure of his success; the material for it was his great discovery. This tendency to bring grown-up minds where a little child shall lead them showed a further advance twenty years after *Alice in Wonderland* had appeared, in Stevenson's *Child's Garden of Verses,* where, almost too much, it is the elder's mind that is appealed to, and the youngster stands somewhat out of it through being analysed to excess. Yet even that charming failure at combined interests indicates the road along which men's absorption in youth has progressed since then.

It may seem strained, in the face of the mirth-moving spirit of the *Wonderland* and *Looking-glass* tales, to claim for them so much purpose and seriousness; but few can feel that their quaint wit and baffling logic were but the outcome of a mere sense of fun. Wherever there is beauty in human things there must also be pathos, something intent if not wistful: and in many of Carroll's tender extravagances there is beauty of a high order. Take, as an instance, the Fawn that has forgotten its name and accompanies Alice fearlessly till the wood is cleared; then, crying, "I am a fawn, and you—you are a human child!" springs startled away. So, also, the whole episode of the White Knight, of so much wisdom gone foolishly astray, has about it almost the same charm as Millais' "Sir Isumbras," now delighting all who make Burlington House their mild wintry resort. There is satire, too, light and stingless, but satire none the less, conveyed under a cajoling disguise, of parody; and some may be able to see in the "aged, aged man a-sitting on a gate" a not distant reference to Wordsworth's "leach-gatherer," and in the figure of the White Knight, with his horse-like face, some likeness to the poet himself.

Lewis Carroll was too much a scholar and a recluse in temperament not to find many things contrary to his taste in the world from which, almost with acerbity, he guarded his private personality; its slipshod speech and illogical ways of thought received many a passing rap from his wit; and the desire for interrogation and argument which his heroine Alice, charming type of her age, carries to the length of foolishness, gets resolutely put down with a finality which leaves the incorrigible little offender breathless. (pp. 102-03)

Alice, indeed, moves through her wonder-world with much of the modern spirit, which has now and then to be wholesomely repressed. This also is noticeable, that in *Wonderland* to her alone come magic attributes making her alternate from gigantic to microscopic proportions. And, as giant, she fares badly, in the good old way, at the hands of the natives. They, on the other hand, behave like ordinary unreasonable human beings: the positions, therefore, of the traditional fairy-tale are reversed. But even against her might the moral order of Wonderland stands; and she gets expelled for bad behaviour.

If Wonderland was her school, the Looking-glass world was her college. She enters as a freshman, having learned by now to do without unreasonable habits of growth; but her inquisitiveness is unabated, and her moralisings have positively increased. And so in the end she gets sent down for her moralisings, when she takes the law, and the august person of the Red Queen, into her own hands. And because of her importunacy in the ways of Providence we shall never know what would have happened at that gorgeous feast where the can-

Carroll's first attempt at writing "Jabberwocky" (1855).

dles went up like sky-rockets, and the guests and the viands changed places.

Is not all this a warning against that spirit of the age which will ask too many meanings, and try to import too much reason into the Edens still marvellously left to us? It seems as if Lewis Carroll was sent to poke fun with unexampled urbanity at the new age which has sprung upon us, and yet, from many grave and tender reasons, to welcome it. (p. 103)

"Lewis Carroll," in The Saturday Review, *London, Vol. 85, No. 2204, January 22, 1898, pp. 102-03.*

STUART DODGSON COLLINGWOOD

[*With* The Life and Letters of Lewis Carroll, *Collingwood— Carroll's nephew—wrote what is considered the standard biography of the author. However, the work has also become controversial among twentieth-century critics, some of whom claim that Collingwood, as official family biographer, conspired with his uncle to suppress the fact that he was in love with Alice Liddell as well as any facts which could give offence to people living at the time of the biography's publication.*]

On July 4, 1862, there is a very important entry [in Mr. Dodgson's diary]: "I made an expedition *up* the river to God-

stow with the three Liddells; we had tea on the bank there, and did not reach Christ Church till half-past eight."

On the opposite page he added, somewhat later, "On which occasion I told them the fairy-tale of *Alice's Adventures Underground,* which I undertook to write out for Alice." (pp. 93-4)

Alice's Adventures Underground was the original name of the story; later on it became *Alice's Hour in Elfland.* It was not until June 18, 1864, that he finally decided upon *Alice's Adventures in Wonderland.* (p. 96)

On July 4, 1865, exactly three years after the memorable row up the river, Miss Alice Liddell received the first presentation copy of *Alice's Adventures in Wonderland;* the second was sent to Princess Beatrice.

The first edition, which consisted of two thousand copies, was condemned by both author and illustrator, for the pictures did not come out well. All purchasers were accordingly asked to return their copies, and to send their names and addresses; a new edition was prepared, and distributed to those who had sent back their old copies, which the author gave away to various homes and hospitals. The substituted edition was a complete success, "a perfect piece of artistic printing," as Mr. Dodgson called it. He hardly dared to hope that more than two thousand copies would be sold, and anticipated a considerable loss over the book. His surprise was great when edition after edition was demanded, and when he found that *Alice,* far from being a monetary failure, was bringing him in a very considerable income every year.

A rough comparison between *Alice's Adventures Underground* and the book in its completed form, shows how slight were the alterations that Lewis Carroll thought it necessary to make.

The *Wonderland* is somewhat longer, but the general plan of the book, and the simplicity of diction, which is one of its principal charms, are unchanged. His memory was so good that I believe the story as he wrote it down was almost word for word the same that he had told in the boat. The whole idea came like an inspiration into his mind, and that sort of inspiration does not often come more than once in a lifetime. Nothing which he wrote afterwards had anything like the same amount of freshness, of wit, of real genius. The *Looking-Glass* most closely approached it in these qualities, but then it was only the following out of the same idea. (pp. 104-06)

> *Stuart Dodgson Collingwood, in his* The Life and Letters of Lewis Carroll, *The Century Co., 1899, 448 p.*

MAX BEERBOHM

[The following excerpt was originally published in 1900.]

Between us [adults] and children—even the least "reserved" children—there is always a certain veil of mystery. It is not safe to dogmatise about their tastes by reference to what *we* should have liked at their age; for children are probably as different as are adults in different generations. The punning of which Lewis Carroll was too prodigal, and which delighted us as children, may, for aught I know, bore children nowadays as greatly as it bores us. Their ringing peals may be a mere affectation. Again, do they, I wonder, really share our delight in Carroll's philosophic *aperçus?* We laugh long when someone, to whom Alice has declared that she likes the Carpenter better than the Walrus "because *he* was just a little bit sorry for the poor oysters," replies "Yes, but he ate more of them;" we find in that reply a more deliciously just indictment of sentimentalism than ever was made, even by Mr. Meredith. The children laugh, too; but their laughter may be hollow mimicry of ours. Through the veil of mystery, we can but make wild shots at their true tastes. My own personal shot is that they do really like *Alice,* as a story, by reason of its perfect blend of fantasy with moral edification. I believe the love of these two separate things to be implanted in the child for all time, and I believe that Carroll's inimitable conjunction of them keeps, and will keep, *Alice* really popular in nurseries. Behind Lewis Carroll, the weaver of fantastic dreams, the delighter in little children, there was always Mr. Dodgson, the ascetic clergyman, the devoted scholar in mathematics. And the former had to pay constant toll to the latter—to report himself, as it were, at very brief intervals. It was as though the writer never could quite approve of his deviations into the sunny path that he loved best. When he was not infusing mathematics into his humour, he was stiffening out his fantasy with edification. In his later books, mathematics and morals triumphed. . . . In him the fair luxuriance of a Pagan fancy was gradually overcome by the sense of duty to his cloth, and by the tyranny of an exact science. In the two books about Alice, however, you have a per-

fect fusion of the two opposing elements in his nature. In them the morality is no more than implicit, and the mathematics are not thrust on you. Though modern adults are apt to resent even implicit morality in a book for children, children delight in it. They delight in feeling that, in some way or other, Alice is being "improved" by her adventures. Orally, she seems to be an awful prig, but various internal evidence makes them suspect her of having "a past"—of having been naughty; and they feel that, somehow or other, the Caterpillar and the Red Queen and all the rest of them are working out her redemption. (pp. 111-12)

> *Max Beerbohm, "'Alice' Again Awakened," in his* Around Theatres, *revised edition, Rupert Hart-Davis, 1953, pp. 109-12.*

ARCHIBALD MacMECHAN

Exactly forty-nine years ago, a little book was published in London, called *Alice's Adventures in Wonderland* which almost at once became a nursery classic. (p. 235)

Nor is it a favourite in the nursery alone; it has penetrated into almost every department of English thought. The periodical press of the last twenty years teems with allusions to this curious production. A quotation from it is almost as readily understood as a tag from *Hamlet;* and the little heroine herself has joined that undying band of shadows, who live only in books and are yet so much more real to us than nine-tenths of the men and women we pass every day upon the street. . . . [Alice] has invaded the classroom of the college; and the ordinary course in metaphysics is rather incomplete without her. The prim textbook even admits her within its bounds and is brighter for her presence. (pp. 236-37)

The question naturally arises, What is the cause of this widespread popularity? What is there in the little book to make it a favourite not only with children everywhere, but with learned professors, busy journalists, men of the world? The book consists of less than two hundred loosely printed pages, and nearly fifty pictures encroach seriously upon the letterpress. Any one can run through it in an hour. Clearly, then, it is not imposing size and solidity which have made it famous. Still less is its theme of a kind to attract general attention. What is it about? To do more than allude to the main outlines of such a classic tale is surely unnecessary, in any English-speaking audience. Every one knows how Alice sat beside her sister on that memorable summer's afternoon when the White Rabbit ran by, looking at his watch; and how she followed him down the rabbit hole, falling and falling, until she landed at last safely in the land of wonders. . . . A writer is, of course, a privileged person, but there are limits to the liberties he may take, and to assume that to *you,* Gentle Reader, the Mad Tea-Party, the Queen's croquet-ground, the Mock-Turtle's story, the Lobster Quadrille, the trial of the Knave of Hearts are names and nothing more is like insinuating your ignorance of the multiplication-table.

Why the book finds favour with the little ones is no mystery. They have all Alice's preference for a book with pictures and conversation: and here they find both in plenty. The story is a real story. There are no digressions, no repelling paragraphs of solid information, no morals except the delightful aphorisms of the Duchess. Something is continually happening; and that something is always marvellous. Children are the fairest and frankest critics in the world. . . . To have won their suffrages by a brand-new fairy-tale is an achievement of which any man might be proud. Most nursery legends are seemingly as old as the race and made according to a few well-worn patterns. It is only at the rarest intervals that any addition is made to the small stock of world-wide fable.

The charm which **Alice** possesses for children of a larger growth is more manifold, but still easy to trace out. There are happily many who never quite lose the heart of the child in the grown man or woman, who never grow old, whose souls remain fresh and unhardened after half a century of rough contact with this work-a-day world. (pp. 238-40)

Over a child's story-book, they can dream themselves back again into their childhood as Chamisso says, and be all the better for it. Again, **Alice's Adventures** reveals a quite unusual aptitude for being read a second time, and a third, and so on indefinitely. This is not the result of chance. This artlessly artful narrative is the outcome of much thought and labour on the part of the writer; but, as Thoreau says of Carlyle, the filings and sweepings and tools are hidden far away in the workshop and the finished, polished product is all we are permitted to see. Considered merely as a piece of clear, straightforward, idiomatic English, this little book is not unworthy to rank with such masterpieces as *Robinson Crusoe* and *The Pilgrim's Progress*. The story runs on so smoothly, the marvels dawn upon us so clearly and succeed one another so swiftly, the interest is so absorbing, that it is only by a strong effort that we can wrench our attention away from the illusion to consider the means by which the illusion is produced. Such books are not made every day. As Sheridan said, "Easy reading is extremely hard writing"; only he employed a more energetic adverb than is agreeable to ears polite. It is, therefore, not surprising to learn that the present story represents what German critics call an Überarbeitung, or working over of previous material, and that the book begun in 1862 was not really finished until three years later.

Apart from its fascination as a story and the artistic pleasure arising from the contemplation of skilful workmanship, there are other reasons why grown-up readers find their account in a child's story-book. For one thing, it possesses humour. I do not mean to say that young readers are entirely unaware of its presence in the book. On the contrary, though I speak under correction as one who is not a psychologist, I hold that one of the first faculties the infant mind develops is a sense of humour. (pp. 241-42)

Forty-nine years is really a very respectable span of life for a book. It has outlasted a whole generation of mankind, and seen many revolutions in the world of thought and outward human activity. Three more decades of such swift and sweeping changes, and the book will need footnotes and explanations. Who knows but some day a Doctor of Philosophy may edit it with various Prolegomena and complete *apparatus criticus;* or some Oxford man get his research degree by a thesis on it. (p. 249)

[Flashes] of fun do not by themselves make up the book. Apart from veiled and gentle satire, there is another humorous element which can be enjoyed by young and old alike,—I am speaking of English stock. This is the incongruous in words, the absurd, or nonsense. This is language where faint, illusory mirages of meaning vanish, language which triumphantly resists all efforts at logical analysis and sometimes even parsing. For three centuries it has formed part of our intellectual bill-of-fare. (p. 254)

There is wisdom as well as wit in this nursery classic. Indeed, it was a professor of metaphysics who described it as "a wise little book." The Duchess, as we know, is very fond of finding morals in everything; sometimes she evolves mere incongruities, but sometimes she hits the mark with a maxim of universal importance. (pp. 255-56)

In truth, underneath all this surface sparkle of wit, and fun, grotesque, and incongruity flows a deep serene current of true wisdom. Without the second, the first is impossible. "It takes a wise man to play the fool."

From still another point of view, this child's storybook has what may without exaggeration be called a scientific importance. A German psychologist might call it "Ein beitrag zur Psychologie des Traümens," or a contribution to our knowledge of the phenomena of dreaming. Perhaps the most widely observed and most puzzling of all mental phenomena are the phenomena of dreaming. All peoples, all literatures have noted and recorded them. Except in rare instances they are the most difficult to recall or to fix. . . . Dreams are vivid enough; but how hard to recall them when our senses are completely alert. Sometimes we can re-tell these strange freaks of subconsciousness; but this is not the rule, rather the exception. The main outlines we may retrace; but the details, the attending circumstances, the atmosphere of reality in which the marvels took place, escape us altogether. How can we make words give back impressions so vivid, so confused, so seeming real at the time, so unreal afterwards? Yet this most difficult literary feat is accomplished by this child's storybook. The child does not perceive this, is not, in fact, meant to perceive this; but even a hasty analysis will make the author's intention clear.

In the first place, the border-line between consciousness and unconsciousness is very faint and hard to define. The process of transition from the one estate to the other is gradual. In the book, the illusion is produced by the closest mimicry of reality. A tired little girl, on a hot summer's afternoon, is resting on a bank beside her sister, when she sees a white rabbit run by. The scene is in England where the "bunnies" range freely through the fields. There is nothing more common than the sight. Alice is still awake; but when she sees the creature take his watch out of his waistcoat pocket, the line between asleep and awake has been crossed. The dreaming has begun, but it is only in the last chapter when her sister speaks to Alice that we are actually told that this is a dream, "a most rare vision." True to experience also is the sensation of falling which so soon follows: this is produced, observers say, by the stretching of the foot an inch or two. In dreams we always fall slowly, and feel that we can control the motion. In falling down the rabbit-hole, Alice has time to take jam-pots out of cupboards, to replace them in other cupboards farther down, and even to curtsy as she descends. Admirably accurate also is the short cross-current of thought, where the remembrance of Dinah, her cat, diverts the progress of the main dream.

Once Alice is fairly afoot in Wonderland, marvels thicken. A whole pack of cards take part in the story. Gryphons and Mock-Turtles dance the lobster quadrille. Croquet is played with live flamingoes for mallets, and live hedgehogs for balls. In the mind of Alice, two feelings alternate,—calm acceptance of the marvellous as perfectly natural, and the faint protest of reason against the strange happenings, or, perhaps I should say, the attempt to rationalize them. Sudden appearances or unexplained disappearances, events however strange, do not surprise us in the world of dreams, but generally the mind makes an effort to relate them to ordinary experience. When the White Rabbit mistakes Alice for the housemaid, and sends her off for his gloves, she obeys, but is not surprised. Only by degrees does the oddity of the situation dawn upon her. (pp. 256-59)

Another constant phenomenon of dream life, which is most vividly portrayed, is the inexplicable way images present themselves, and then fade into nothingness. Alice is going to play croquet; she finds a live flamingo in her hands; a little later, the game is over, and no more mention is made of it. Neither its coming nor its going is explained. Nor is there felt to be any need of explanation. Everything happens in accordance with a new set of laws, which govern this strange mental state in which the absurd is accepted as the real. The most famous instance is the Cheshire Cat, whose grin appeared long before the rest of the animal, and remained when all else of it had vanished. And our author follows his own maxim, "Adventures first; explanations take such a dreadful time."

Another well-known sensation of dreaming is the wilful opposition, the malicious contrariety of things. For instance, you dream that you are going on a journey; you get to the station or the steamer and find that your luggage has not come; or you get into the wrong train, or (my own favourite nightmare) you haven't money enough to buy your ticket. So Alice is ordered about by the animals, made to repeat lessons and verses, snubbed by the Caterpillar, bored by the Duchess. Allied to this, or another phase of it, is what may be called reaching out after the unattainable. You wish to go somewhere, or to do something, and find yourself perpetually balked and disappointed. Alice sees, through the little door, the beautiful garden, with its fountains and flowers; but she is too large to squeeze through, and when she is small enough, the key that will admit her is on the glass table out of her reach. It is a pleasure to the reader, when, after many mischances, she at last finds her way into that Enchanted Ground.

Interesting, too, and true to fact, is the concrete way in which the return to consciousness is pictured. There is first the return of courage, and then, of reason half alert and working drowsily. Poor Alice has been tremendously bullied and made to feel literally very small; but at last she feels herself regaining her natural size. Then the formalities of the courtroom, the fury of the Queen have no terrors for her.

> "Hold your tongue!" said the Queen, turning purple.
>
> "I won't," said Alice.
>
> "Off with her head!" the Queen shouted at the top of her voice. Nobody moved.
>
> "Who cares for *you?*" said Alice (for she had grown to her full size by this time). "You're nothing but a pack of cards!"
>
> At this, the whole pack rose up into the air, and came flying down upon her; she gave a little scream, half of fright and half of anger, and tried to beat them off, and found herself lying on the bank, with her head in the lap of her sister, who was gently brushing away some dead leaves that had fluttered down from the trees upon her face.

This is as faithfully observed as it is admirably worded. Every one knows how a noise or slight accident has the power to suggest, in some cases, an entire dream. Here the falling of the leaves on the child's face suggests the assault of the cards; and the trifling fright and effort to defend herself effectually

arouse her. Of course, to describe the fairy-tale as a scientific treatise would be to do it an injury; but that the fairy-tale has this solid framework of sound observation it is impossible to deny.

What has been said will go far to account for *Alice*'s great and ever-increasing popularity. There is a very great difference between careful and flimsy work; and in order to value the *Alice* books rightly, it is only necessary to examine any one of the hundred melancholy imitations of them; for there is a definite type or fashion of child's story brought into existence by their originality and freshness. Photographers have so perfected their art that the different motions of a bird on the wing, of a horse in full gallop, of a bullet from the muzzle of a rifle, are caught and fixed to the most minute detail. Our author has triumphed over difficulties almost as great. He has made words, simple words that children understand and delight in, do the work of the sensitive plates. They have caught and they hold in cold print those fleeting impressions of an experience, which though universal is the hardest to make comprehensible. The process of dreaming is, as it were, arrested at various stages, and we have time to examine each of them as clearly as we care to. Under correction, be it stated, nothing better in this kind exists. (pp. 260-63)

A living book is a great power. Ruskin says that the imagination in its play is either mournful or mischievous; and that it is a most difficult thing to invent a fairy-tale which is neither the one nor the other. But this, Lewis Carroll has done. His book has influenced and will influence hundreds and thousands of children; and that influence can only be for good. His own attitude toward the work of his hand is most significant. Tiny and humble as the book may seem, almost unimportant, it manifests the spirit of a very wise Teacher, who spoke many weighty words, but kept his tenderest for the little children. (p. 272)

Archibald MacMechan, "Everybody's Alice," in his
The Life of a Little College and Other Papers,
Houghton Mifflin Company, 1914, pp. 233-72.

JOHN COWPER POWYS

Alice is after all as much of a classic now and by the same right, the right of a universal appeal, to every type of child, as Mother Goose of the Nursery Rhymes. She had only to appear—this slender-legged, straight-haired, Early-Victorian little prude, to enter at once the inmost arcana of the temple of art. The book is a singular evidence of what the power of a desperate devotion can do—a devotion like this of Mr. Dodgson to all little girls—when a certain whimsical genius belongs to the possessed by it.

The creator of Alice has really done nothing but permit his absorbing worship of many demure little maids to focus and concentrate itself into an almost incredible transformation of what was the intrinsic nature of the writer into what was the intrinsic nature of the "written-about."

The author of this book has indeed, so to speak, eluded the limitations of his own skin, and by the magic of his love for little girls has passed—carrying his grown-up cleverness with him—actually into the little girl's inmost consciousness. The book might be quite as witty as it is and quite as amusing but it would not carry for us that peculiar "perfume in the mention," that provocative enchantment, if it were not much more—Oh, so much more—than merely amusing. The thousand and one reactions, impressions, intimations, of a little girl's consciousness, are reproduced here with a faithfulness that is absolutely startling. What really makes the transformation complete is the absence in *Alice* of that half-comic sententious priggishness which, as soon as we have ceased to be children, we find so curiously irritating in Kingsley's *Water Babies.* (pp. 60-2)

> *John Cowper Powys, in a review of "Alice in Wonderland," in his* One Hundred Best Books, *G. Arnold Shaw, 1916, pp. 60-2.*

G. K. CHESTERTON

[*The following excerpt was originally published in the* New York Times *in 1932.*]

Any educated Englishman, and especially any educational Englishman (which is worse), will tell you with a certain gravity that *Alice in Wonderland* is a classic. Such is indeed the horrid truth. The original hilarity that was born on that summer afternoon among the children, in the mind of a mathematician on a holiday, has itself hardened into something almost as cold and conscientious as a holiday task. That logician's light inversion of all the standards of logic has itself, I shudder to say, stiffened into a standard work. It is a classic; that is, people praise it who have never read it. It has a secure position side by side with the works of Milton and Dryden. It is a book without which no gentleman's library is complete, and which the gentleman therefore never presumes to take out of his library. I am sorry to say it, but the soap-bubble which poor old Dodgson blew from the pipe of poetry, in a lucid interval of lunacy, and sent floating into the sky, has been robbed by educationists of much of the lightness of the bubble, and retained only the horrible healthiness of the soap.

This is not the fault of Lewis Carroll, but it is in one sense the fault of Charles Dodgson; at least the fault of the world which he inhabited and incorporated and to some extent encouraged and carried forward. His nonsense is a part of the peculiar genius of the English; but a part also of the elusive paradox of the English. None but they could have produced such nonsense; but none but they, having produced such nonsense, would ever have attempted to take it seriously. There is, by this time, a sort of implication of national loyalty about the thing; against which I for one would mildly protest. It is a moral duty to listen to reason, but it is not a moral duty to listen to unreason. It is only a lark, and no admirer of Lewis Carroll can outstrip me in liking it as a lark. As I shall suggest later, many of its really original merits as a fantasia have been missed by this heavy-handed applause; applause of work that should be criticised as it was created, with a light touch. Men may be told to listen, and in a sense even made to listen, when a man of adequate authority is talking sense. But we cannot be made to listen to a man who is talking nonsense; it sins against the whole spirit and atmosphere of the occasion, which is a holiday. Yet I have a dreadful fear that the works of Lewis Carroll are now a part of education, which in these liberal modern days means compulsory education. I once lectured before a congress of elementary schoolmasters, trying to persuade them to tolerate anything so human as Penny Dreadfuls or Dime Novels about Dick Turpin and Buffalo Bill. And I remember that the Chairman, with a refined and pained expression said, "I do not think Mr. Chesterton's brilliant paradoxes have persuaded us to put away our *Alice in Wonderland* and our"—something else, possibly *The Vicar of Wakefield* or *Pilgrim's Progress.* It never struck him that

the nonsense tale is as much an escape from educational earnestness as the gallop after Buffalo Bill. For him it was simply a classic, and it went along with the other classics. And I thought to myself, with a sinking heart, "Poor, poor little Alice! She has not only been caught and made to do lessons; she has been forced to inflict lessons on others. Alice is now not only a schoolgirl but a schoolmistress. The holiday is over and Dodgson is again a don. There will be lots and lots of examination papers, with questions like: (1) What do you know of the following; mime, mimble, haddock's eyes, treacle-wells, beautiful soup? (2) Record all the moves in the chess game in *Alice Through the Looking-Glass,* and give diagram. (3) Outline the practical policy of the White Knight for dealing with the social problem of green whiskers. (4) Distinguish between Tweedledum and Tweedledee.

I will give only one deadly and devastating fact, to show how Nonsense, in the case of Alice's story, has been allowed to become cold and monumental like a classic tomb. It has been parodied. People sit down solemnly to burlesque this burlesque. They imagine they can make it funny, or at least make it funnier, by twisting its features into paltry political caricatures. They think they can give a twist, to that which has no imaginable purpose except to be twisted, by wreathing it into emblems of everyday comedy and commonplace farce. Now that is a thing that nobody would dream of doing with anything he really thought *funny.* It is only serious, and even solemn things, that can be made funny. It may be said that Sheridan burlesqued Shakespeare; at least he burlesqued the sham Shakespearean historical drama in *The Critic.* But nobody could burlesque *The Critic.* . . . We have had Comic Histories of England and Comic Latin Grammars, because there remains a tradition that there is something serious, and even sacred, about the story of the English nation and the strong tongue of Rome. But even those who can enjoy, more than I can, what is now called a Comic Strip, would not think it a promising venture to bring out a Comic Comic Strip.

But, in the case of *Alice in Wonderland,* so strangely solid was this impression that the thing was a national institution, an educational classic, a well of English undefiled, a historic heritage like *Othello* or the *Samson Agonistes,* that satirists set seriously to work on it to make it amusing. Political parodists actually thought it a sort of improvement to give all that pure and happy pointlessness a point. They even felt, I think, a tingle of timid daring, in taking liberties with this monumental Victorian volume. (pp. 113-16)

It is a delightful but difficult enterprise to liberate Lewis Carroll from the custody of Charles Dodgson. It is a hard though happy task to try to recapture the first fresh careless rapture of the days when Nonsense was new. We have to put ourselves in an utterly different attitude from that of the admirers who have come after the achievement, and feel something of the first stir and movement that went before it. In the eyes of a number of those admirers our attitude will seem like an antic, and they will be far too serious to see that it is like the original antics of Lewis Carroll. To appreciate it we must appreciate more deeply the paradox of the whole people and its literature, and the really comic contrast between its responsible and its irresponsible moods. There were a great many things that Charles Dodgson took only too seriously; but the things which his devotees have taken seriously were the things which he took lightly.

Everybody knows, I imagine, that the Rev. Charles Lutwidge Dodgson was a Fellow of Christ Church College, . . . and

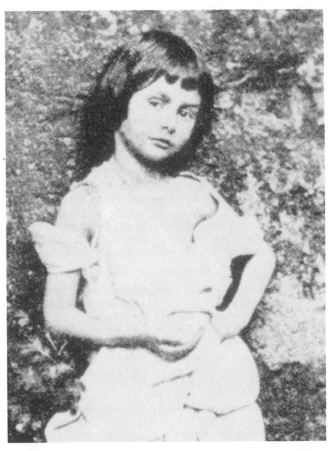

Alice Liddell. Photograph by Lewis Carroll.

was a successful and even distinguished Professor of Mathematics and Logic. Superficially speaking, the most curious thing about him was that it was only through these iron gates of reason that he entered his own private paradise of unreason. All that part of the man that might have been, and in a literary man often has been, loose or light or irresponsible, was in his case particularly prim and respectable and responsible. It was only his intellect that took a holiday; his emotions never took a holiday; and certainly his conscience never took a holiday. It was perhaps a rather conventional conscience; but his moral views were quite incapable, I will not say of wavering, but even of moving or stirring; whether we class them as conventions or convictions. He had no outlet, even of imagination, on the moral or social or philosophical side: he had it only on the mathematical side. Though a conscientious mathematical teacher, he could imagine something that made plus equal to minus. But though a conscientious Christian, he could not really imagine anything that made the first last and the last first; that put down the mighty from their seat or exalted the humble and the poor. . . . He was, in the ordinary sense, limited everywhere by convention; and yet it was he who with one wild leap burst the very limits of reason. It was this stodgy and stuffy Victorian parson, who followed the wild vision of utter unreason further than it was ever pursued by any wild poet working without a conscience or an aim; by any wild painter when he dips his brush in hues of earthquake and eclipse.

The liveliest thing about him, no doubt, on the purely human side, was a real affection for children; especially for certain children. But though this was doubtless the motive that made him tell the children a story, it was not this, or anything like this, that made the story. It is a story for children, but it is not a story about children, in the same sense as the majority of children's stories. The natural extension of his imagination was all in the direction of the inverted ideas of the intellect. He could see the logical world upside down; he could not see any other kind of world even right side up. He took his triangles and turned them into toys for a favourite little girl; he took his logarithms and syllogisms and twisted them into nonsense. But, in a rather special sense, there is nothing but nonsense in his nonsense. There is no sense in his nonsense; as there is in the more human nonsense of Rabelais or the more bitter nonsense of Swift. If he had been suggesting any moral or metaphysical ideas, they would never have been so deep or grand as those of Rabelais or Swift. But he was only playing The Game of Logic; and it is his glory that it was a new game, and a nonsensical game, and one of the best games in the world.

Nevertheless, in a certain subconscious world of the English spirit, of his whole home and tradition and ancestry, there is something rather deeper than this. There was something that a man must perhaps be an Englishman to understand; something perhaps that he must even have been a Victorian to understand; something, after all, that he must perhaps reconcile himself to enjoy and not understand. It works back to that word "holiday", that I have used several times in this connection, and which is really the key of the problem. There is a sense in which a man like Rabelais was not really on a holiday. He really was building The Abbey of Theleme, however fantastically and with whatever wild gargoyles or toppling spires. In every sense we may say that Mr. Lemuel Gulliver, when he went on his travels, was not going merely on his holidays. These writers had a purpose, and it was, whatever its defects, very largely the serious intellectual purpose of their lives. But the strange nation of the English, in their strange phase of Victorianism, had something much more subtle about their ideas of business and pleasure; and the pure nonsense they invented really was a holiday of the mind. I have said that it was an original thing, and it was; one of the few things, like Gothic architecture, that had really never been done before. It was something to invent a happy nightmare; it was something more to create a thing that was at once lawless and innocent. It was a sort of dream-life, lived by the nineteenth-century Englishman parallel to his rather too realistic real life. It had something of Dual Personality, though without any savour of diabolic possession. It had a suggestion of living a double life; though without anything of the mortal moral issue of Jekyll and Hyde. Dr. Jekyll tried to perform a surgical operation to remove his conscience; Mr. Dodgson only amputated his common sense. It was his head, and not his heart, that he detached and sent adrift like a bubble in a world of merely abstract anarchy. And in this he discovered some secret in the mind of the modern Englishman, which has given the story and the style a secure position; even, as has been hinted, a position almost too secure. It was the avowal of a sport or enjoyment to which the whole mind of the people must have been already tending. Perhaps it was not for nothing that one of the comic artists of *Punch* wrote a serious novel, about a man who lived a continuous dreaming life, side by side with his waking life. The Victorian Englishman walked the world in broad daylight, a proverbially solid figure, with his chimney-pot hat and his mutton-chop whiskers, with his business bag and his business-like umbrella. But something happened to him at night; some wind of nightmare blowing through his soul and his subconsciousness dragged him out of bed and whirled him out of the window, where he rose into a world of wind and moonshine; his chimney-pot hat sailing high above the chimneys and his umbrella bellying like a balloon or bearing him upwards like a witch's broom; with his whiskers waving like wings. (pp. 116-19)

> *G. K. Chesterton, "Lewis Carroll," in his* A Handful of Authors: Essays on Books & Writers, *edited by Dorothy Collins, Sheed and Ward, 1953, pp. 112-19.*

WALTER DE LA MARE

[Alice] with her familiar little toss of the head, with her serene mobile face, courteous, amiable, except when she *must* speak up for herself, easily reconciled, inclined to tears, but tears how swiftly dashed away; with her dignity, her matter-of-factness, her conscientiousness, her courage (even in the most outlandish of circumstances) never to submit or yield; and with one of the most useful of all social resources, the art of changing a conversation—what a tribute she is not only to her author but to Victorian childhood! Capable, modest, demure, sedate, they are words a little out of fashion nowadays; but Alice alone would redeem them all. And even if now and then she is a trifle superior, a trifle *too* demure, must not even the most delicate of simple and arduous little samplers have its wrong side? (p. 54)

[*The* sovereign element in the *Alices*] consists in the presentation of what is often perfectly rational, practical, logical, and, maybe, mathematical, what is terse, abrupt and pointed, in a state and under conditions of life to which we most of us win admittance only when we are blessedly asleep. To every man his own dreams, to every man his own day-dreams. And as with sense, nonsense and un-sense; as with me, you and a sort of us-ishness; as with past, future and the all-and-almost-nothing in between; so with Greenwich time, time and *dream* time; with good motives, bad motives, and dream motives; self, better self and dream self. Dreaming is another state of being, with laws as stringent *and* as elastic as those of the world of Nonsense. And what dream in literature has more blissfully refreshed a prose-ridden world than the dream which gently welled into Dodgson's mind that summer afternoon, nearly seventy years ago, when, sculls in hand and eyes fixed on little Alice Liddell's round-orbed countenance, the Lewis Carroll in him slipped off into Wonderland?

Who can say what influences one silent consciousness may have upon another? May it not be to some magical suffusion and blending of these two, the mathematician's and the child's, that we owe the *Alices?* Even the technical triumph of the two books consists in having made what is finally declared to be a dream actually and always *seem* to be a dream. Open either of them at random; ask yourself any one of the questions on the page exposed; endeavour to find an answer not merely as apt and pungent as are most answers of the *Alice* order, but one that will at the same time fret by not so much as a hair's breadth the story's dream-like crystalline tissue: and then turn back to the book for *Carroll's* answer. That alone, though a trivial one, will be proof enough of the quality of his genius. (pp. 60-2)

> *Walter De La Mare, in his* Lewis Carroll, *Faber & Faber Limited, 1932, 67 p.*

EDMUND WILSON

[*The following excerpt was originally published in 1932.*]

If the Lewis Carroll centenary has produced anything of special interest, I have failed to see it. C. L. Dodgson was a most interesting man and deserves better of his admirers, who revel in his delightfulness and cuteness but do not give him any serious attention. (p. 540)

The truth is that, if Dodgson and his work were shown as an organic whole, his "nonsense" would not seem the anomaly which it is usually represented as being. It is true that on one of his sides he was a pompous and priggish don. . . . But even this side of Dodgson should not be kept out of the picture: the *Alice in Wonderland* side has an intimate relation with it. Under the crust of the pious professor was a mind both rebellious and skeptical. The mathematician who invented Alice was one of those semi-monastic types—like Walter Pater and A. E. Housman—that the English universities breed: vowed to an academic discipline but cherishing an intense originality, painfully repressed and incomplete but in the narrow field of their art somehow both sound and bold. (p. 541)

It is curious what ordination as a clergyman of the Church of England can do to an original mind. The case of Dodgson is somewhat similar to those of Donne and Swift—though Dodgson was shy and stammered and never took priest's orders; and he was closer, perhaps, to Swift and Donne than to the merely whimsical writer like Barrie or A. A. Milne, for Dodgson had a first-rate mind of a very unusual sort: he was a logician who was also a poet. (p. 542)

Dodgson, in terms of his age and place, was remarkably "well-adjusted." His enjoyment of the Oxford "Studentship," with its relatively agreeable work and exceptionally comfortable quarters, which he won on his graduation was dependent on his acceptance of celibacy; and there is nothing to show that this irked him much. His admiration and affection for his father seem to have been complete; the rectory in which he grew up was obviously as little as possible like that described by Samuel Butler in *The Way of All Flesh;* and with the Dodgsons the church tradition was strong. . . . There is mockery of course in Alice, who finds herself at odds with the "creatures"; there are . . . outbreaks of contemptuous violence at the ends of the *Alice* books and *Sylvie and Bruno;* but the forces of benevolence and common sense always triumph in what is not merely the conventional Victorian happy ending, as they certainly did in Dodgson's life. The conditions of teaching in an English university in the middle of the nineteenth century may seem to us today unnatural, but all social and professional situations involve their special disabilities, and in the position that Dodgson had chosen he seems to have functioned well. If a part of his intelligence lived underground, if a part of his personality was screened, it is plain that . . . Alice would never have gone down the rabbit-hole, would never have walked through the mirror, if this had not been the case. (pp. 547-48)

> *Edmund Wilson, "C. L. Dodgson: The Poet Logician," in his* The Shores of Light: A Literary Chronicle of the Twenties and Thirties, *Farrar, Straus and Giroux, 1952, pp. 540-50.*

HARRY MORGAN AYRES

[*The following excerpt is from an essay originally delivered as a lecture on 4 May 1932 at Columbia University. A professor of English at Columbia, Ayres delivered his lecture to honor Alice Liddell Hargreaves, who was made a Doctor of Letters as part of the university's celebration of the centenary of the birth of Lewis Carroll.*]

Our present purpose . . . is unashamedly festive. . . . You ask me to rejoice with you that in our youth a couple of little books fell in our way, books that turned the world inside out and stood it on its head that we might learn to laugh at it and love it, furnished us with sharp turns of language that brightened the rather drab pattern of everyday discourse and gave us a whole new and friendly mythology, figures that stand closer to us and in no less number than the divine imaginings of alien and older ages. Our proper business then is to ask what sort of appearance this benefactor of ours made in his world and how he compounded the simple gifts that have so enriched us. (pp. 4-5)

[Alice is] a child who is anxious to please, thrust forth from the nursery into a world with which she is obviously ill prepared to cope. On all sides she is betrayed. The geography that unrolls and dissolves before her is not the geography of the schoolroom. Her sums will not come right. The verses she has learned insist on saying themselves in exasperatingly erratic fashion. Space and time lose their homelike dependability—she finds herself moving downwards or backwards, time moving backwards or standing still in an eternity of tea, relative magnitudes suddenly and disconcertingly altering; now she is larger and now she is smaller than she has hitherto regarded herself to be with respect to the familiar surroundings of the nursery. Sometimes it almost seems like a dream, the way things shift about and babies merge into pigs and White Queens become sheep, but it is a highly intellectualized dream; its events are not merely entertainingly successive, they are disciplined; and demand, and in some measure bestow, discipline. For poor little Alice does not do very well when she tries to work it out for herself. When she has the golden key in her hand, the door is too small for her to squeeze through; when she is sufficiently diminished to enter, she has left the key out of reach on the glass table; then when ("curiouser and curiouser") she is tall again, she waxes sentimental about her distantly retreating feet, is diverted by the appearance of the White Rabbit, speculates on her own identity, and then grows small again without ever having thought of the key. Clearly Alice has much to learn, and what she has been taught in her schoolroom is of precious little use to her. . . . But after she has learned something of the world, come to know the Caterpillar and the Duchess and the Cheshire Cat, and, at the Mad Tea Party, learned to ask questions and speak up a bit for herself, she lays hold of the key and without difficulty enters the alluring little garden of further adventures.

At the outset Carroll places himself squarely in a great literary tradition . . . by setting forth the society through which Alice takes her way, whose qualities she is instrumental in revealing, whose lesson she learns, in the guise of animals and of mythologic and symbolic *creatures* (Alice's own word). The first group that crowd around her, the Dodo, the Lory, and the rest, are all confessedly symbolically representative of the members of the boating party—she carries earth with her, that is, for a time into her dream and only by a gradual transition passes to the more abstract and instructive creations of the pure intellect. They are a little snappish with each other—these animals. . . . They only contrive to pass the time in a grotesque and inexplicable kind of social ceremonial—it is called a Caucus Race but it gets nowhere. What Alice discovers is that almost every word she utters gives of-

fence. Her store of affection and pleasure that centers round Dinah, the cat, is wholly unacceptable to the gloomily and aimlessly active society on which she seeks to bestow it. The Mouse's tail wriggles from view in a high dudgeon, and the birds agitatedly move off. Alice's first efforts at social adjustment are a dismal failure.

But she is not left long alone to meditate on this desolating fact in quivering self-distrust. "How the creatures order one about!" she has to remark on a good many occasions. The White Rabbit begins it, and they keep it up, all of them, till a matured, a discerning, a self-reliant Alice finds herself growing up and denounces them all for a pack of cards, or, herself a crowned queen, takes in hand the Red Queen, no less formidable a personage than that, and gives her a good shaking. . . .

It is plain, I think, that Carroll recollected childhood, for one thing, as environed by loud voices, shouted snatches, difficult to piece together into a trustworthy pattern, but falling like blows that left a bruise on the memory. (pp. 22-7)

To him . . . the child is encompassed by a din of speech, afloat on a roaring sea of language, lapped as in an element of it which takes to itself fantastic, puzzling, and indeed dangerously misleading shapes; and worse than that, it is something not merely outside of you but something that goes a way of its own inside you, and there are the most complicated and sometimes disastrous results from the contact of the two—the great big buzz outside and the smaller buzz inside. You are misled, tripped up, exasperatingly betrayed. (p. 30)

[It] is full of pitfalls, this business of language—"beating time," "murdering the time," "every *other* day" (with its painful deficiency of jam), "flower *beds*," "answer the door" (What's it been asking of?), "catch a crab," "feather, feather," "I beg your pardon" (It isn't respectable to beg)—they seem, these expressions, to want to go two ways at once and either way you follow them you are likely to be wrong. And the odd snatches of verse, . . . or proverbial phrases like, "A cat may look at a king," "mad as a March hare," "mad as a hatter," "grinning like a Cheshire cat." What would happen if we suddenly let them, as the mathematician says, mean something; if indeed, as with a child such as Carroll appears to have been and in a sense remained, they insisted on meaning something? "*That* would never do!" What wouldn't do what? Suppose songs like "Twinkle, Twinkle, Little Star" or "How Doth the Little Busy Bee" or "Star of the Evening,"—suppose they began to sing themselves of their own accord with new words? Whether all children are stimulated and perplexed after this fashion—by verbal identities called puns. . . . Or by verbal resemblances like "Reeling and Writhing," "Mystery," "Drawling, Stretching and Fainting in Coils," or "Tortoise" and "taught us," or by such tricks of negation as "un-birthday present," Carroll evidently remembered *his* childhood as so linguistically distracted, and in a way delighted, for he at least loved puzzles and adored precision. And what would happen again if these troublesome words lost all their many meanings? Alice and the fawn got on beautifully together until *it* remembers that it *is* a fawn and *she* a human child.

And are they not silly things, these words? A *butterfly* does not tell by its name the shape it is, but a *bread-and-butter-fly*, now, reveals its whole physical structure and habit. A *horse-fly* is an incredible monster, but a *rocking-horse-fly* is a complete and intelligible proposition. Pushing beyond such verbal prestidigitation, Carroll contrives finally and credibly to deliver, if you will read attentively the episode of the Lion and the Unicorn, his opinion that the one "fabulous monster" in all creation, the one thing that *nobody* (with one reservation which I will explain later) will accept as a fact and treat helpfully and affectionately, is a human child. And what the human child has to learn in self-defence, if it is going to secure any credence for itself, is the lesson which Humpty Dumpty (in the story I mean, not the professor of whom he is a caricature) has to teach it, namely, to become lord of words and their meanings, and not their servant.

A third assumption that Carroll makes with respect to childhood . . . is that the adult world, as viewed by the child, is full of indifferent, worried, busy, incompetent, meddlesome, and distinctly disagreeable people. Alice frequently has to comment on that. It should be a great lesson to all grown-ups, and Carroll meant it to be. (pp. 33-6)

I have a trick of my own which I learned from Professor Humpty Dumpty—I like to place in my students' hands a great and ancient tome called the *Ship of Fools* and say, "Here, make the acquaintance of some of your friends, possibly for the first time." Now the literary method of the *Ship of Fools* and the whole related body of "character writings" and of "humours," the presentation of a person by means of some exaggerated trait (two eyes on one side of the nose, for example), is, as Professor Humpty Dumpty insisted, the literary method of Carroll, who often, too, after the fashion of these books—and the Duchess herself—points out the moral. Viewed in this light we have a whole portrait gallery—and Alice thus comes to know her world of grown-up people. (p. 38)

[The] Cheshire Cat [lets] her into a secret. "We are all mad here." And the moral of that is, What is there left but a smile? And so Alice wholesomely begins to suspect that the Mad Tea Party is no more madly inconsequential than all tea parties and the Croquet Game no more languidly incomprehensible than all games of which it is the enduring symbol. She learns from the Walrus and the Carpenter that tears seemingly born of compassion may seek to cover only a ruthless intention to exploit. Such discoveries mark the beginning of wisdom. (pp. 39-40)

[That the White Knight is Carroll himself] is plausible, because the White Knight is the one "creature" in all the two books that shows a touch of human affection for the little girl. With his odd little inventions for making life more convenient and entertaining (" 'You see, it's as well to be provided for *everything.*' "—and didn't Dodgson carry a store of safety pins at the seashore to aid little girls who might venture in wading?), surely this is Carroll's satire upon himself, explaining, as he falls from his horse, that the great art of riding is to keep your balance properly. And his place in the structure of the story is pivotal—it is from the White Knight that Alice learns what the hard, worldly lessons of the other creatures had not taught her—the lesson of affection—and it is from his hands that she passes on to be crowned a queen. Crowned and mitred over herself, she has in the White Knight for a brief moment her Virgil, her Beatrice, and her St. Bernard. (pp. 44-5)

Alice [comes] through arduous adventures to the brink of wisdom. She becomes convinced of what at various points she had begun to suspect (intellectually to understand, I mean, not as a mere pert bit of self-confidence) namely, that these

elders who are so short with one aren't themselves so very wise after all; and just as she had seen quite through the pretentious ritual of the trial scene to the flat pasteboard fatuity of it all, so turning from the retreating figure of the White Knight, her bestower of wisdom, she puts the Red Queen and the White through *their* examination until they both fall into the sleep of exhausted incompetence. She is nearly ready to wake up. She has only to penetrate now the hollow ceremonial of her own coronation banquet, with its "Alice-Mutton: Mutton-Alice," and Alice's adventures in education are completed. (p. 52)

You will admit it is hard for me to believe in the *impromptu* of that July day on the Thames in 1862. It is no child's tale that was there begun, it is a *summa* of human experience in its disillusioning quest for wisdom; it is a plea for the child in a day when the child needed a friend. It was all thought out *in* him if not *by* him, though it was the chief of his many child-friends that drew it out of him and insisted on its preservation. If you insist that the ***Alice*** books are children's books, then I can only say, so are Homer and Shakespeare and every great book that a child is willing to sit down with. (pp. 53-4)

> *Harry Morgan Ayres, in his* Carroll's Alice, *Columbia University Press, 1936, 98 p.*

WILLIAM EMPSON

[The following excerpt by Empson, a distinguished English poet and critic, is from his essay "Alice in Wonderland: The Child as Swain," which is generally considered the most important example of twentieth-century Carroll scholarship. In 1978, critic Roger Sale called it "still the best essay ever written about (Carroll)."]

It must seem a curious thing that there has been so little serious criticism of the Alices, and that so many critics, with so militant and eager an air of good taste, have explained that they would not think of attempting it. . . . There seems to be a feeling that real criticism would involve psychoanalysis, and that the results would be so improper as to destroy the atmosphere of the books altogether. Dodgson was too conscious a writer to be caught out so easily. . . . The books are so frankly about growing up that there is no great discovery in translating them into Freudian terms; it seems only the proper exegesis of a classic even where it would be a shock to the author. On the whole the results of the analysis, when put into drawing-room language, are his conscious opinions; and if there was no other satisfactory outlet for his feelings but the special one fixed in his books the same is true in a degree of any original artist. I shall use psycho-analysis where it seems relevant, and feel I had better begin by saying what use it is supposed to be. Its business here is not to discover a neurosis peculiar to Dodgson. The essential idea behind the books is a shift onto the child, which Dodgson did not invent, of the obscure tradition of pastoral. The formula is now 'child-become-judge,' and if Dodgson identifies himself with the child so does the writer of the primary sort of pastoral with his magnified version of the swain. (pp. 253-54)

Pope engraved a couplet 'on the collar of a dog which I gave to His Royal Highness'—a friendly act as from one gentleman to another resident in the neighborhood.

> I am his Highness' dog at Kew.
> Pray tell me, sir, whose dog are you?

Presumably Frederick himself would be the first to read it. The joke carries a certain praise for the underdog; the point is not that men are slaves but that they find it suits them and remain good-humoured. The dog is proud of being the prince's dog and expects no one to take offence at the question. There is also a hearty independence in its lack of respect for the inquirer. Pope took this from Sir William Temple, where it is said by a fool: 'I am the Lord Chamberlain's fool. And whose are you?' was his answer to the nobleman. It is a neat case of the slow shift of this sentiment from fool to rogue to child.

Alice, I think, is more of a 'little rogue' than it is usual to say, or than Dodgson himself thought in later years:

> loving as a dog . . . and gentle as a fawn; then courteous,—courteous to *all*, high or low, grand or grotesque, King or Caterpillar . . . trustful, with an absolute trust. . . .

and so on. It depends what you expect of a child of seven.

> . . . she had quite a long argument with the Lory, who at last turned sulky, and would only say, 'I am older than you, and must know better'; and this Alice would not allow without knowing how old it was, and as the Lory positively refused to tell its age, there was no more to be said.

Alice had to be made to speak up to bring out the points— here the point is a sense of the fundamental oddity of life given by the fact that different animals become grown-up at different ages; but still if you accept the Lory as a grown-up this is rather a pert child. She is often the underdog speaking up for itself.

A quite separate feeling about children . . . may be seen in its clearest form in Wordsworth and Coleridge; it is the whole point of the *Ode to Intimations* and even of *We are Seven*. The child has not yet been put wrong by civilisation, and all grown-ups have been. It may well be true that Dodgson envied the child because it was sexless, and Wordsworth because he knew that he was destroying his native poetry by the smugness of his life, but neither theory explains why this feeling about children arose when it did and became so general. . . . It depends on a feeling, whatever may have caused that in its turn, that no way of building up character, no intellectual system, can bring out all that is inherent in the human spirit, and therefore that there is more in the child than any man has been able to keep. (The child is a microcosm like Donne's world, and Alice too is a stoic.) This runs through all Victorian and Romantic literature; the world of the adult made it hard to be an artist, and they kept a sort of tap-root going down to their experience as children. Artists like Wordsworth and Coleridge, who accepted this fact and used it, naturally come to seem the most interesting and in a way the most sincere writers of the period. Their idea of the child, that it is in the right relation to Nature, not dividing what should be unified, that its intuitive judgment contains what poetry and philosophy must spend their time labouring to recover, was accepted by Dodgson and a main part of his feeling. He quotes Wordsworth on this point in the 'Easter Greeting'—the child feels its life in every limb; Dodgson advises it, with an infelicitous memory of the original poem, to give its attention to death from time to time. That the dream books are

> Like Pilgrim's withered wreaths of flowers
> Plucked in a far-off land

is a fine expression of Wordsworth's sense both of the poetry of childhood and of his advancing sterility. (pp. 259-61)

Dodgson will only go half-way with the sentiment of the child's unity with nature, and has another purpose for his heroine; she is the free and independent mind. Not that this is contradictory; because she is right about life she is independent from all the other characters who are wrong. But it is important to him because it enables him to clash the Wordsworth sentiments with the other main tradition about children derived from rogue-sentiment. (p. 262)

One might say that the Alices differ from other versions of pastoral in lacking the sense of glory. Normally the idea of including all sorts of men in yourself brings in an idea of reconciling yourself with nature and therefore gaining power over it. The Alices are more self-protective; the dream cuts out the real world and the delicacy of the mood is felt to cut out the lower classes. This is true enough, but when Humpty Dumpty says that glory means a nice knock-down argument he is not far from the central feeling of the book. There is a real feeling of isolation and yet just that is taken as the source of power. (pp. 262-63)

The talking animal convention and the changes of relative size appear in so different a children's book as *Gulliver;* they evidently make some direct appeal to the child whatever more sophisticated ideas are piled onto them. Children feel at home with animals conceived as human; the animal can be made affectionate without its making serious emotional demands on them, does not want to educate them, is at least unconventional in the sense that it does not impose its conventions, and does not make a secret of the processes of nature. So the talking animals here are a child-world; the rule about them is that they are always friendly though childishly frank to Alice while she is small, and when she is big (suggesting grown-up) always opposed to her, or by her, or both. But talking animals in children's books had been turned to didactic purposes ever since Aesop; the schoolmastering tone in which the animals talk nonsense to Alice is partly a parody of this—they are really childish but try not to look it. On the other hand, this tone is so supported by the way they can order her about, the firm and surprising way their minds work, the abstract topics they work on, the useless rules they accept with so much conviction, that we take them as real grown-ups contrasted with unsophisticated childhood.'The grown-up world is as odd as the child-world, and both are a dream.' This ambivalence seems to correspond to Dodgson's own attitude to children; he, like Alice, wanted to get the advantages of being childish and grown-up at once. . . . He made a success of the process, and it seems clear that it did none of the little girls any harm, but one cannot help cocking one's eye at it as a way of life. (pp. 265-66)

The changes of size are more complex. In *Gulliver* they are the impersonal eye; to change size and nothing else makes you feel 'this makes one see things as they are in themselves.' It excites Wonder but of a scientific sort. Swift used it for satire on science or from a horrified interest in it, and to give a sort of scientific authority to his deductions, that men seen as small are spiritually petty and seen as large physically loathsome. And it is the small observer, like the child, who does least to alter what he sees and therefore sees most truly. . . . Children like to think of being so small that they could hide from grown-ups and so big that they could control them, and to do this dramatises the great topic of growing up, which both Alices keep to consistently. In the same way the charm of Jabberwocky is that it is a code language, the language with which grown-ups hide things from children or children from grown-ups. Also the words are such good tongue-gestures, in Sir Richard Paget's phrase, that they seem to carry their own meaning; this carries a hint of the paradox that the conventions are natural.

Both books also keep to the topic of death—the first two jokes about death in *Wonderland* come on pages 3 and 4—and for the child this may be a natural connection; I remember believing I should have to die before I grew up, and thinking the prospect very disagreeable. There seems to be a connection in Dodgson's mind between the death of childhood and the development of sex, which might be pursued into many of the details of the books. Alice will die if the Red King wakes up, partly because she is a dream-product of the author and partly because the pawn is put back in its box at the end of the game. He is the absent husband of the Red Queen who is a governess, and the end of the book comes when Alice defeats the Red Queen and 'mates' the King. Everything seems to break up because she arrives at a piece of *knowledge,* that all the poems are about fish. I should say the idea was somehow at work at the end of *Wonderland* too. The trial is meant to be a mystery; Alice is told to leave the court, as if a child ought not to hear the evidence, and yet they expect her to give evidence herself. . . . I think Dodgson felt it was important that Alice should be innocent of all knowledge of what the Knave of Hearts . . . is likely to have been doing, and also important that she should not be told she is innocent. That is why the king, always a well-intentioned man, is embarrassed. At the same time Dodgson feels that Alice is right in thinking 'it doesn't matter a bit' which word the jury write down; she is too stable in her detachment to be embarrassed, these things will not interest her, and in a way she includes them all in herself. And it is the refusal to let her stay that makes her revolt and break the dream. It is tempting to read an example of this idea into the poem that introduces the *Looking-Glass.*

> Come, hearken then, ere voice of dread,
>   With bitter summons laden,
> Shall summon to unwelcome bed
>   A melancholy maiden.

After all the marriage-bed was more likely to be the end of the maiden than the grave, and the metaphor firmly implied treats them as identical.

The last example is obviously more a joke against Dodgson than anything else, and though the connection between death and the development of sex is I think at work it is not the main point of the conflict about growing up. Alice is given a magical control over her growth by the traditionally symbolic caterpillar, a creature which has to go through a sort of death to become grown-up, and then seems a more spiritual creature. It refuses to agree with Alice that this process is at all peculiar, and clearly her own life will be somehow like it, but the main idea is not its development of sex. The butterfly implied may be the girl when she is 'out' or her soul when in heaven, to which she is now nearer than she will be when she is 'out'; she must walk to it by walking away from it. Alice knows several reasons why she should object to growing up, and does not at all like being an obvious angel, a head out of contact with its body that has to come down from the sky, and gets mistaken for the Paradisal serpent of the knowledge of good and evil, and by the pigeon of the Annunciation, too. But she only makes herself smaller for reasons of tact or pro-

portion; the triumphant close of *Wonderland* is that she has outgrown her fancies and can afford to wake and despise them. The *Looking-Glass* is less of a dream-product, less concentrated on the child's situation, and (once started) less full of changes of size; but it has the same end; the governess shrinks to a kitten when Alice has grown from a pawn to a queen, and can shake her. Both these clearly stand for becoming grown-up and yet in part are a revolt against grown-up behaviour; there is the same ambivalence as about the talking animals. Whether children often find this symbolism as interesting as Carroll did is another thing; there are recorded cases of tears at such a betrayal of the reality of the story. I remember feeling that the ends of the books were a sort of necessary assertion that the grown-up world was after all the proper one; one did not object to that in principle, but would no more turn to those parts from preference than to the 'Easter Greeting to Every Child that Loves Alice' (Gothic type).

To make the dream-story from which *Wonderland* was elaborated seem Freudian one has only to tell it. A fall through a deep hole into the secrets of Mother Earth produces a new enclosed soul wondering who it is, what will be its position in the world, and how it can get out. It is in a long low hall, part of the palace of the Queen of Hearts (a neat touch), from which it can only get out to the fresh air and the fountains through a hole frighteningly too small. Strange changes, caused by the way it is nourished there, happen to it in this place, but always when it is big it cannot get out and when it is small it is not allowed to; for one thing, being a little girl, it has no key. The nightmare theme of the birth-trauma, that she grows too big for the room and is almost crushed by it, is not only used here but repeated more painfully after she seems to have got out; the rabbit sends her sternly into its house and some food there makes her grow again. In Dodgson's own drawing of Alice when cramped into the room with one foot up the chimney, kicking out the hateful thing that tries to come down (she takes away its pencil when it is a juror), she is much more obviously in the foetus position than in Tenniel's. The White Rabbit is Mr. Spooner to whom the spoonerisms happened, an undergraduate in 1862, but its business here is as a pet for children which they may be allowed to breed. Not that the clearness of the framework makes the interpretation simple; Alice peering through the hole into the garden may be wanting a return to the womb as well as an escape from it; she is fond, we are told, of taking both sides of an argument when talking to herself, and the whole book balances between the luscious nonsense-world of fantasy and the ironic nonsense-world of fact.

I said that the sea of tears she swims in was the amniotic fluid, which is much too simple. You may take it as Lethe in which the souls were bathed before re-birth (and it is their own tears; they forget, as we forget our childhood, through the repression of pain) or as the 'solution' of an intellectual contradiction through Intuition and a return to the Unconscious. Anyway it is a sordid image made pretty; one need not read Dodgson's satirical verses against babies to see how much he would dislike a child wallowing in its tears in real life. (pp. 267-72)

The symbolic completeness of Alice's experience is I think important. She runs the whole gamut; she is a father in getting down the hole, a foetus at the bottom, and can only be born by becoming a mother and producing her own amniotic fluid. Whether his mind played the trick of putting this into the story or not he has the feelings that would correspond to

Photograph of Edith, Lorina, and Alice Liddell by Lewis Carroll.

it. A desire to include all sexuality in the girl child, the least obviously sexed of human creatures, the one that keeps its sex in the safest place, was an important part of their fascination for him. He is partly imagining himself as the girl-child (with these comforting characteristics) partly as its father (these together make *it* a father) partly as its lover—so it might be a mother—but then of course it is clever and detached enough to do everything for itself. . . . So far from its dependence, the child's independence is the important thing, and the theme behind that is the self-centred emotional life imposed by the detached intelligence. (pp. 272-73)

The Gnat gives a . . . touching picture of Dodgson; he treats nowhere more directly of his actual relations with the child. He feels he is liable to nag at it, as a gnat would, and the gnat turns out, as he is, to be alarmingly big as a friend for the child, but at first it sounds tiny because he means so little to her. It tries to amuse her by rather frightening accounts of other dangerous insects, other grown-ups. It is reduced to tears by the melancholy of its own jokes, which it usually can't bear to finish; only if Alice had made them, as it keeps egging her on to do, would they be at all interesting. That at least would show the child had paid some sort of attention, and he could go away and repeat them to other people. The desire to have jokes made all the time, he feels, is a painful and obvious confession of spiritual discomfort, and the freedom of Alice from such a feeling makes her unapproachable. . . . He is afraid that even so innocent a love as his, like all love, may be cruel, and yet it is she who is able to hurt him, if only through his vanity. The implica-

tions of these few pages are so painful that the ironical calm of the close, when she kills it, seems delightfully gay and strong. The Gnat is suggesting to her that she would like to remain purely a creature of Nature and stay in the wood where there are no names.

> '. . . That's a joke. I wish *you* had made it.'
>
> 'Why do you wish *I* had made it?' Alice asked. 'It's a very bad one.'
>
> But the Gnat only sighed deeply, while two large tears came rolling down its cheeks.
>
> 'You shouldn't make jokes,' Alice said, 'if it makes you so unhappy.'
>
> Then came another of those melancholy little sighs, and this time the poor Gnat really seemed to have sighed itself away, for, when Alice looked up, there was nothing whatever to be seen on the twig, and, as she was getting quite chilly with sitting so long, she got up and walked on.

The overpunctuation and the flat assonance of 'long—on' add to the effect. There is something charmingly prim and well-meaning about the way she sweeps aside the feelings that she can't deal with. One need not suppose that Dodgson ever performed this scene, which he can imagine so clearly, but there is too much self-knowledge here to make the game of psychoanalysis seem merely good fun.

The scene in which the Duchess has become friendly to Alice at the garden-party shows Alice no longer separate from her creator; it is clear that Dodgson would be as irritated as she is by the incident, and is putting himself in her place. The obvious way to read it is as the middle-aged woman trying to flirt with the chaste young man. . . . [The] Duchess seems to take the view of the political economists, that the greatest public good is produced by the greatest private selfishness. All this talk about 'morals' makes Alice suspicious; also she is carrying a flamingo, a pink bird with a long neck. 'The chief difficulty Alice found at first was in managing her flamingo . . . it *would* twist itself round and look up in her face.'

> 'I dare say you're wondering why I don't put my arm round your waist,' the Duchess said after a pause: 'the reason is, that I'm doubtful about the temper of your flamingo. Shall I try the experiment?'
>
> 'He might bite,' Alice cautiously replied, not feeling at all anxious to have the experiment tried.
>
> 'Very true,' said the Duchess: 'flamingoes and mustard both bite. And the moral of that is—"Birds of a feather flock together." '

Mustard may be classed with the pepper that made her 'ill-tempered' when she had so much of it in the soup, so that flamingoes and mustard become the desires of the two sexes. No doubt Dodgson would be indignant at having this meaning read into his symbols, but the meaning itself, if he had been intending to talk about the matter, is just what he would have wished to say. (pp. 274-77)

This sort of 'analysis' is a peep at machinery; the question for criticism is what is done with the machine. The purpose of a dream on the Freudian theory is simply to keep you in an undisturbed state so that you can go on sleeping; in the course of this practical work you may produce something of more general value, but not only of one sort. Alice has, I understand, become a patron saint of the Surrealists, but they do not go in for Comic Primness, a sort of reserve of force, which is her chief charm. Wyndham Lewis avoided putting her beside Proust and Lorelei to be danced on as a debilitating child-cult (though she is a bit of pragmatist too); the present-day reader is more likely to complain of her complacence. In this sort of child-cult the child, though a means of imaginative escape, becomes the critic; Alice is the most reasonable and responsible person in the book. This is meant as charmingly pathetic about her as well as satire about her elders, and there is some implication that the sane man can take no other view of the world, even for controlling it, than the child does; but this is kept a good distance from sentimental infantilism. There is always some doubt about the meaning of a man who says he wants to be like a child, because he may want to be like it in having fresh and vivid feelings and senses, in not knowing, expecting, or desiring evil, in not having an analytical mind, in having no sexual desires recognisable as such, or out of a desire to be mothered and evade responsibility. He is usually mixing them up—Christ's praise of children, given perhaps for reasons I have failed to list, has made it a respected thing to say, and it has been said often and loosely—but he can make his own mixture; Lewis's invective hardly shows which he is attacking. The praise of the child in the Alices mainly depends on a distaste not only for sexuality but for all the distortions of vision that go with a rich emotional life; the opposite idea needs to be set against this, that you can only understand people or even things by having such a life in yourself to be their mirror; but the idea itself is very respect-

able. So far as it is typical of the scientist the books are an expression of the scientific attitude (*e.g.* the bread-and-butter fly) or a sort of satire on it that treats it as inevitable.

The most obvious aspect of the complacence is the snobbery. It is clear that Alice is not only a very well-brought-up but a very well-to-do little girl; if she has grown into Mabel, so that she will have to go and live in that poky little house and have next to no toys to play with, she will refuse to come out of her rabbit-hole at all. One is only surprised that she is allowed to meet Mabel. All through the books odd objects of luxury are viewed rather as Wordsworth viewed mountains; meaningless, but grand and irremovable; objects of myth. The whiting, the talking leg of mutton, the soup-tureen, the tea-tray in the sky, are obvious examples. The shift from the idea of the child's unity with nature is amusingly complete; a mere change in the objects viewed makes it at one with the conventions. But this is still not far from Wordsworth, who made his mountains into symbols of the stable and moral society living among them. In part the joke of this stands for the sincerity of the child that criticises the folly of convention, but Alice is very respectful to conventions and interested to learn new ones; indeed the discussions about the rules of the game of conversation, those stern comments on the isolation of humanity, put the tone so strongly in favour of the conventions that one feels there is nothing else in the world. . . . Dodgson was always shocked to find that his little girls had appetites, because it made them seem less pure. The passage about the bread-and-butter fly brings this out more frankly, with something of the wilful grimness of Webster. It was a creature of such high refinement that it could only live on weak tea with cream in it (tea being the caller's meal, sacred to the fair, with nothing gross about it).

A new difficulty came into Alice's head.

> 'Supposing it couldn't find any?' she suggested.
>
> 'Then it would die, of course.'
>
> 'But that must happen very often,' Alice remarked thoughtfully.
>
> 'It always happens,' said the Gnat.
>
> After this, Alice was silent for a minute or two, pondering.

There need be no gloating over the child's innocence here, as in Barrie; anybody might ponder. Alice has just suggested that flies burn themselves to death in candles out of a martyr's ambition to become Snapdragon flies. The talk goes on to losing one's name, which is the next stage on her journey, and brings freedom but is like death; the girl may lose her personality by growing up into the life of convention, and her virginity (like her surname) by marriage; or she may lose her 'good name' when she loses the conventions 'in the woods'— the animals, etc., there have no names because they are out of reach of the controlling reason; or when she develops sex she must neither understand nor name her feelings. The Gnat is weeping and Alice is afraid of the wood but determined to go on. 'It always dies of thirst' or 'it always dies in the end, as do we all'; 'the life of highest refinement is the most deathly, yet what else is one to aim at when life is so brief, and when there is so little in it of any value.' A certain ghoulishness in the atmosphere of this, of which the tight-lacing may have been a product or partial cause, comes out very strongly in Henry James; the decadents pounced on it for their own purposes but could not put more death-wishes into it than these respectables had done already.

The blend of child-cult and snobbery that Alice shares with Oscar Wilde is indeed much more bouncing and cheerful; the theme here is that it is proper for the well-meaning and innocent girl to be worldly, because she, like the world, should know the value of her condition. 'When we were girls we were brought up to know nothing, and very interesting it was'; 'mamma, whose ideas on education are remarkably strict, has brought me up to be extremely short-sighted; so do you mind my looking at you through my glasses?' This joke seems to have come in after the Restoration dramatists as innocence recovered its social value; there are touches in Farquhar and it is strong in the *Beggar's Opera*. . . . [Even] **Wonderland** contains straight satire. The Mock Turtle was taught at school

> Reeling and Writhing, of course, to begin with, and then the different branches of Arithmetic— Ambition, Distraction, Uglification, and Derision . . . Mystery, ancient and modern, with Seaography; then Drawling—the Drawling-master used to come once a week; *he* taught us Drawling, Stretching, and Fainting in Coils.

Children are to enjoy the jokes as against education, grown-ups as against a smart and too expensive education. Alice was not one of the climbers taught like this, and remarks firmly elsewhere that manners are not learnt from lessons. But she willingly receives social advice like 'curtsey while you're thinking what to say, it saves time,' and the doctrine that you must walk away from a queen if you really want to meet her has more point when said of the greed of the climber than of the unselfseeking curiosity of the small girl. Or it applies to both, and allows the climber a sense of purity and simplicity; I think this was a source of charm whether Dodgson meant it or not. Alice's own social assumptions are more subtle and all-pervading; she always seems to raise the tone of the company she enters, and to find this all the easier because the creatures are so rude to her. A central idea here is that the perfect lady can gain all the advantages of contempt without soiling herself by expressing or even feeling it. (pp. 277-83)

[Alice] is almost too sure that she is good and right. The grown-up is egged on to imitate her not as a privileged decadent but as a privileged eccentric, a Victorian figure that we must be sorry to lose. The eccentric though kind and noble would be alarming from the strength of his virtues if he were less funny. . . . (pp. 284-85)

The qualities held in so subtle a suspension in Alice are shown in full blast in the two queens. It is clear that this sort of moral superiority involves a painful isolation, similar to those involved in the intellectual way of life and the life of chastity, which are here associated with it. (p. 285)

Death is never far out of sight in the books. (p. 287)

Once at least in each book a cry of loneliness goes up from Alice at the oddity beyond sympathy or communication of the world she has entered—whether that in which the child is shut by weakness, or the adult by the renunciations necessary both for the ideal and the worldly way of life (the strength of the snobbery is to imply that these are the same). (p. 290)

[About] all the rationalism of Alice and her acquaintants there hangs a suggestion that there are after all questions of pure thought, academic thought whose altruism is recognised and paid for, thought meant only for the upper classes to whom the conventions are in any case natural habit; like that suggestion that the scientist is sure to be a gentleman and has plenty of space which is the fascination of Kew Gardens. (p. 291)

The Queen is a very inclusive figure. 'Looking before and after' with the plaintive tone of universal altruism she lives chiefly backwards, in history; the necessary darkness of growth, the mysteries of self-knowledge, the self-contradictions of the will, the antinomies of philosophy, the very Looking-Glass itself, impose this; nor is it mere weakness to attempt to resolve them only in the direct impulse of the child. Gathering the more dream-rushes her love for man becomes the more universal, herself the more like a porcupine. Knitting with more and more needles she tries to control life by a more and more complex intellectual apparatus— the 'progress' of Herbert Spencer; any one shelf of the shop is empty, but there is always something very interesting—the 'atmosphere' of the place is so interesting—which moves up as you look at it from shelf to shelf; there is jam only in the future and our traditional past, and the test made by Alice, who sent value through the ceiling as if it were quite used to it, shows that progress can never reach value, because its habitation and name is heaven. The Queen's scheme of social reform, which is to punish those who are not respectable before their crimes are committed, seems to be another of these jokes about progress:

> 'But if you *hadn't* done them,' the Queen said, 'that would have been better still; better, and better, and better!' Her voice went higher with each 'better' till it got to quite a squeak at last.

There is a similar attack in the Walrus and the Carpenter, who are depressed by the spectacle of unimproved nature and engage in charitable work among oysters. The Carpenter is a Castle and the Walrus, who could eat so many more because he was crying behind his handkerchief, was a Bishop, in the scheme at the beginning of the book. But in saying so one must be struck by the depth at which the satire is hidden; the queerness of the incident and the characters takes on a Wordsworthian grandeur and aridity, and the landscape defined by the tricks of facetiousness takes on the remote and staring beauty of the ideas of the insane. It is odd to find that Tenniel went on to illustrate Poe in the same manner; Dodgson is often doing what Poe wanted to do, and can do it the more easily because he can safely introduce the absurd. The Idiot Boy of Wordsworth is too milky a moonlit creature to be at home with Nature as she was deplored by the Carpenter, and much of the technique of the rudeness of the Mad Hatter has been learned from Hamlet. It is the ground-bass of this kinship with insanity, I think, that makes it so clear that the books are not trifling, and the cool courage with which Alice accepts madmen that gives them their strength.

This talk about the snobbery of the Alices may seem a mere attack, but a little acid may help to remove the slime with which they have been encrusted. The two main ideas behind the snobbery, that virtue and intelligence are alike lonely, and that good manners are therefore important though an absurd confession of human limitations, do not depend on a local class system; they would be recognised in a degree by any tolerable society. And if in a degree their opposites must also be recognised, so they are here; there are solid enough statements of the shams of altruism and convention and their horrors when genuine; it is the forces of this conflict that make a clash violent enough to end both the dreams. In **Wonderland** this is mysteriously mixed up with the trial of the Knave of Hearts, the thief of love, but at the end of the second book the symbolism is franker and more simple. She is a grown queen and has acquired the conventional dignities of her insane world; suddenly she admits their insanity, refuses to be a grown queen, and destroys them.

> 'I can't stand this any longer!' she cried, as she seized the table-cloth in both hands: one good pull, and plates, dishes, guests, and candles came crashing down together in a heap on the floor.

The guests are inanimate and the crawling self-stultifying machinery of luxury has taken on a hideous life of its own. It is the High Table of Christ Church that we must think of here. The gentleman is not the slave of his conventions because at need he could destroy them; and yet, even if he did this, and all the more because he does not, he must adopt while despising it the attitude to them of the child. (pp. 292-94)

> William Empson, "Alice in Wonderland: The Child as Swain," in his Some Versions of Pastoral, Chatto & Windus, 1935, pp. 253-94.

VIRGINIA WOOLF

[*The following excerpt was originally published in 1939.*]

[The] Rev. C. L. Dodgson had no life. He passed through the world so lightly that he left no print. He melted so passively into Oxford that he is invisible. He accepted every convention; he was prudish, pernickety, pious, and jocose. If Oxford dons in the nineteenth century had an essence he was that essence. He was so good that his sisters worshipped him; so pure that his nephew has nothing to say about him. It is just possible, he hints, that "a shadow of disappointment lay over Lewis Carroll's life". Mr. Dodgson at once denies the shadow. "My life", he says, "is free from all trial and trouble." But this untinted jelly contained within it a perfectly hard crystal. It contained childhood. And this is very strange, for childhood normally fades slowly. Wisps of childhood persist when the boy or girl is a grown man or woman. Childhood returns sometimes by day, more often by night. But it was not so with Lewis Carroll. For some reason, we know not what, his childhood was sharply severed. It lodged in him whole and entire. He could not disperse it. And therefore as he grew older this impediment in the centre of his being, this hard block of pure childhood, starved the mature man of nourishment. He slipped through the grown-up world like a shadow, solidifying only on the beach at Eastbourne, with little girls whose frocks he pinned up with safety pins. But since childhood remained in him entire, he could do what no one else has ever been able to do—he could return to that world; he could re-create it, so that we too become children again.

In order to make us into children, he first makes us asleep. "Down, down, down, would the fall *never* come to an end?" Down, down, down we fall into that terrifying, wildly inconsequent, yet perfectly logical world where time races, then stands still; where space stretches, then contracts. It is the world of sleep; it is also the world of dreams. Without any conscious effort dreams come; the white rabbit, the walrus, and the carpenter, one after another, turning and changing one into the other, they come skipping and leaping across the mind. it is for this reason that the two Alices are not books for children; they are the only books in which we become

children. President Wilson, Queen Victoria, *The Times* leader writer, the late Lord Salisbury—it does not matter how old, how important, or how insignificant you are, you become a child again. To become a child is to be very literal; to find everything so strange that nothing is surprising; to be heartless, to be ruthless, yet to be so passionate that a snub or a shadow drapes the world in gloom. It is to be Alice in Wonderland.

It is also to be Alice Through the Looking Glass. It is to see the world upside down. Many great satirists and moralists have shown us the world upside down, and have made us see it, as grown-up people see it, savagely. Only Lewis Carroll has shown us the world upside down as a child sees it, and has made us laugh as children laugh, irresponsibly. Down the groves of pure nonsense we whirl laughing, laughing—

> They sought it with thimbles, they sought it with care;
> They pursued it with forks and hope . . .

And then we wake. None of the transitions in Alice in Wonderland is quite so queer. For we wake to find—is it the Rev. C. L. Dodgson? Is it Lewis Carroll? Or is it both combined? (pp. 81-3)

> Virginia Woolf, "Lewis Carroll," in her The Moment and Other Essays, 1947. Reprint by Harcourt Brace Jovanovich, Inc., 1948, pp. 81-3.

FLORENCE BECKER LENNON

Charles, trapped in the cave of his period, was the laughing philosopher who could show others the way out. He spoke the language and played the rôle of Ariel—the mantle of Prospero ill became him, though he fancied it. His proper medium was the looking-glass, in which he caught a sunbeam and flashed it in the eyes of a solemnity, or held a child's laughing face, or cast weird shadows from his cave upon the world outside. The Mad Hatter and the Duchess, the Mock Turtle and the Jabberwock, are as real and as enduring as Punch or Falstaff. Charles tried to carve heavier figures too, but they fell with a dull thud and are heard no more.

Moving to an unseen pattern of wish and will, of fear and courage, he grew in creative power. He outgrew the tiny rectangular box he spent his life trying to re-enter, and the chessboard where Alice saw the game of life being played was too simple to compass his thinking. It is true that no one finds room for complete expansion and expression, but here was a particularly big person who spent his life fitting himself, with infinite art and patience, and even, as if it were one of his own puzzle games, with a certain amusement, into a particularly small and exactly delimited box. It is like the genie trying to climb back into the bottle or like the human brain making more and more convolutions to squeeze itself into that tiny box, the skull. The brain could almost symbolize Charles—almost. But the affectionate soul also demands its due, and likewise the animal soul, though the families of Christian clergymen in Charles's youth (overtly) rejected the tenth talent, while welcoming the eleventh child. The subsidiary souls, excluded from the drawing-room, weep outside, like the Mock Turtle, the Walrus, and all the other sad animals whose whimsical, melancholy expression greatly resembles Carroll's own.

The freshness and newness of his symbols, their applicability to his own era, or to any era when people stupidly interfere with one another and lay down needless rules, gave his best writings their indubitable vitality. "Vitality" is a suitably perverse word to associate with the old-maidish don he became, with his professorial habits and accuracies, his uncertain gait, his stammering, his air of Don Quixote rather than of Don Juan. But the man had a mind, and the mind had almost an independent life of its own, so that when he tired of the game of chess that was his daily life, he could summon a gryphon and fly away to Wonderland.

So one summer afternoon, when he was rowing on the Isis with Canon Duckworth (the Duck in the Caucus-race) and the three entrancing daughters of Dean Liddell, he began putting his escapes into an art form. Some nine years later he deliberately tapped the same vein that had opened spontaneously before, and found his other world again, in that always exciting moment when Alice, who has been hankering to see beyond that tantalizing glimpse into the passage, suddenly finds herself on the mantelshelf with the glass melting, and jumps down into Looking-Glass House.

Later he just as deliberately abandoned that form because of the hordes of imitators, and tried to devise new ways out of the intolerable cramping of his box. The queer animals of the empire, of the university, and of his own inner life, continued to plague him, like Adam in the garden, with demands for names and classifications. In return, he expected the creatures to serve as symbols and carry him on flights.

Perhaps because he was squeezed so tight, and because he was really a genius, he wrung out of himself a complete bible of folklore, poetry, mythology, and humor. Theology was his weak point and must be discounted. He was religious in the sense that he cared truly for the growth of the spirit, but, since he never found Ariadne's thread and would not use an ax, his religion belongs under "Box" rather than "Escape." Wherever he let himself go, however, he helped to smash the box for his contemporaries, and for their children and ours. (pp. 7-9)

Many persons who have read **Wonderland** at least once a year since they could read, fail to notice the plot. The story revolves about the golden key to the enchanted garden and Alice's endless frustrations and wanderings in bypaths until she enters at last, to find the flowers really beautiful, though some of them need painting—but the place is populated by disagreeable persons attempting to play croquet under trying circumstances. Then comes a Last Judgment with the entire cast—and an anti-climax.

The garden is an equally rich symbol if we call it adult life viewed by a child, or vice versa. The protean Alice with her formulas for growing and shrinking and cutting back and forth across the borders of childhood and maturity, yet remaining always a wise child, is of course Dodgson himself—or herself. It is hard, studying some of his portraits and reading some of his works, to realize that he was a man indeed. It is still harder to find any evidence that he himself realized it. He seems increasingly like a maiden aunt with the heart of a girl, even with all the satires on his fellow dons and the refined cruelties of his verse. (p. 120)

[It is] the blend of logical with dream material that gives Carroll's works their distinct and inimitable flavor. The fall down the Rabbit hole, for instance, is a birth dream indeed—and what a symbol—the Rabbit for fertility! The motif is always cropping out; when Alice is in the long hall, later the Hall of Tears, she finds the key to the little door, that "led into a small passage, not much larger than a rat-hole: she knelt

down and looked along the passage . . . but she could not even get her head through the doorway." Later she slips into the pool of tears and swims about easily. Then, in the Rabbit's house, she starts to grow uncomfortably large and threatens to burst the house. When Bill the Lizard comes down the chimney after her, she makes a final effort and succeeds in retracting one leg far enough to kick him back up.

Birth dreams are universal, but since we are born without language, they use visual and muscular imagery; whatever reminds us of birth retains a mysterious fascination, unaccountable till this great discovery of Dr. Rank's. **Wonderland** contains all the elements—the comfortable swimming about in the water, the doubt of being able to get her head through the narrow passage, the constriction of the small room, increasing threateningly as she grows; the attempt to kick out in a narrow space. To name and classify a dream element is merely to recognize the unconscious. But these birth images must have had a meaning to their inventor; a spiritual rebirth, perhaps—for Carroll was just over the hill from one of his major crises. He had been looking down into the Deanery garden from the library window for seven years, he was thirty years old, and he had taken holy orders six months before. And perhaps that was it.

Acceptance of ordination after so many doubts and such a long postponement—he had been eligible for six years—must have required a new synthesis. The scene in the Hall of Tears, where Alice gives herself good advice, the one where "Once she remembered trying to box her own ears for having cheated herself in a game of croquet, for this curious child was very fond of pretending to be two people," and other hints, suggest Dodgson may have had fleeting doubts of his own identity, no doubt intensified since his ordination. For it was not Alice Liddell who pretended to be two people. Some sort of rebirth was in order. (pp. 122-23)

[Dodgson] resigned himself—on the surface—to being the Reverend Charles Dodgson; but, as the outer bonds gripped tighter, the inner self soared more and more. For such a nature, actually, "stone walls do not a prison make," since the space inside a spirit of genius is infinite.

The **Alice** books are frankly dream stories; both have an elaborate and rather orgiastic nightmarish awakening, though only in the first one does the dreamer direct the dream. Both use the materials of the universal dream or folk tale; their prime value lies in this articulation of the inarticulate impressions of childhood and in their multiple use on several planes simultaneously, which make them interesting to all ages and cultural levels. (pp. 123-24)

[In some way the very sacrifice it cost Charles] to take orders seems to have fired him to the highest point of his career. **Alice in Wonderland** is the choice flower of his genius. **Through the Looking-Glass** is witty, inventive, quaint, what you will; but the shadow of the Red Queen of Logic and the mysterious threat of the Red King hang over it; the dreamer who may own not only the dream but even the characters in it, keeps it from being an unclouded childish story. The little girl who said she liked both stories, but thought **Through the Looking-Glass** was "stupider" than **Wonderland,** conveys the same idea. Nothing in **Wonderland** parallels the complete severance of the Reds and Whites in **Through the Looking-Glass.** In **Sylvie and Bruno,** author and story have begun to disintegrate. The archness and sweetness of parts, the utter

Illustration by Lewis Carroll from Alice's Adventures Under Ground.

cruelty and loathsomeness of others, predict literal decomposition into his elements.

Wonderland has none of that. In it Carroll wields a nimble shuttle, weaving disparate threads into a unified and perfect textile, of the pattern of the search for the golden fleece, or the golden apples, or the fountain of youth, or the pot of gold at the rainbow's end; the search for the universal treasure, that mankind recognizes with a joyful stirring. It is the plot of our life here on earth, and any honest story that conforms to it, adds to it, find new forms and characters for it, even for the thousandth telling, will move us. It is not even a special result of civilization that finding the treasure does not bring happiness—what of the fisherman whose wife would be pope, or the one whose wife won three wishes and had to use the third to get the sausage off her husband's nose? The wish can be fulfilled only in a dream, and the happy ending is—to awaken and find one is still oneself, and can trace some of the dream elements, as Alice did, to familiar sights and sounds. As Carroll's fellow-mathematician and Yankee contemporary, Willard Gibbs, remarked, "The whole is simpler than its parts."

Here sits Mr. Dodgson, then, in the tightest kind of box—Christ Church Don by his own exertions, Student by the grace of Dr. Pusey, Deacon of the Church of England by the hand of Bishop Wilberforce; with his thoughts and actions prescribed by medieval tradition, by the prejudices of Prince Albert, by the governing body of Oxford University, by his father the Archdeacon and his old schoolmaster the Archbishop of Canterbury, by the whole hierarchy through Oliver Cromwell clear up to God, not to mention the Reverend Charles Dodgson himself, one of the strictest of the lot. Tighter and tighter, oh Lord! The only escape is down the rabbit hole and into the beautiful garden.

And like Carl Sandburg's *Gimme the Ax,* "when he gets to

the moon he will find everything the same as it always was." (pp. 125-26)

Looking-Glass is a masterpiece—only a shade less than *Wonderland*—but it already exudes the ripe flavor of approaching decay and disintegration into the cruel (on paper) and unusual Mr. Dodgson and the sentimental-religious Louisa Caroline, as one of the Oxford parodists signed "The Vulture and the Husbandman."

A certain grimness and harshness of *Through the Looking-Glass* derive from the Red Queen and her consort. The plot is Berkeleyan and horrible—"Who dreamed it?" If Alice dreamed it, then the Red Queen was really one of Dinah's kittens, and the Red King merely a chess piece—but suppose it was the Red King's dream?

The chess game, instead of Reds and Whites, might be divided into Lefts and Rights, with Carroll on the Left side. The Red King, Queen, and Knight, are all strong and disagreeable characters; the White royalty, weak and ridiculous, but amiable. Was Archdeacon Dodgson—as the righteous representative of established order—strong, unreasonable perhaps, though hardly disagreeable? The Red Queen's rules of behavior are the rules of a right-handed world interpreted by a left-handed child, who feels he is asked to do everything backwards. Hence the idea of going the other way to reach the top of the hill, and of running hard without getting anywhere. If the dream is the Red King's, the world belongs to father—if it is Alice's dream, little Charles has a place in the world. Every child has such fantasies—the wonder is to have remembered them in the twilight state before sleep, and to have been able to write them down before they faded.

This chess game, so much—perhaps so consciously—like Life (as Carroll would write it), is played on several planes, has several interpretations, and no definitive triumph. Although Carroll claims it is a complete game, Mr. Madan says "it is not up to chess standard, and had no normal checkmate." The White Knight does win permission to escort Alice to the last brook. Does this mean "Carroll's Alice-self finds that the left way is the right way"? Professor Harry Morgan Ayres, who recognizes the White Knight as Carroll's spokesman, finds it significant that he is the only one with the courtesy and wit to help a lost child—"the one 'creature' in all the two books that shows a touch of human affection for the little girl."

The book has one grim defeat in the trappings of victory. Humpty Dumpty demonstrates *Looking-Glass* methods by analyzing "Jabberwocky." The youth slays the Jabberwock—is the author trying to tell himself, by writing the poem backwards, that this is a disastrous victory? What drove Charles back into himself and his childish memories? Was it not his acceptance of ordination without resolving his doubts? For him, taking orders was, implicitly, giving in to his father. No one, reading the elder Dodgson's letter, would say he exercised no tyranny over his son.

The letter shows how stern the Archdeacon was under his gentleness. His grandniece, who recalled little else about him, said that he had "decided ideas" about his children's character development. A mere lifted eyebrow, in a home keyed to sensitive response, is more urgent than infinite beatings in a more happy-go-lucky environment. How could anyone revolt against the Canon, with his charm, his faultless altruism, his perfect fatherhood?

Even less could Charles revolt against his mother, the vague, the gentle, the good, with the soft voice that was never raised. Charles was the eldest son, the eldest child, probably the favorite. He had the energy to attempt revolt, but loyalty blocked him. His loved ones and the whole social system were against him. He has left brave and heartening documents of his struggle against distortion, locked in the velvet-lined iron maiden of his period, and his caricatures of that iron maiden helped later generations to master her. Nobody knows how many middle and late Victorians found life more bearable because of the *Alice* books, or how often Carroll's gallows humor helped other sensitives to bear the cross, or even to wriggle out from under it in a good-natured way. Yet the timeless quality of *Looking-Glass,* as of *Wonderland,* rests not on the neurosis of a man or of an age, but on the genius that illuminates our essential nature.

An admirer gushed, "Mr. Dodgson is broad—as broad as Christ." He shared other characteristics with Christ too; at least the Christ of the nineteenth century stained-glass attitudes. One interpretation of the Christ story is that he crucified his infantile jealousy of his father and love of his mother by renunciation (Hamlet, Oedipus). Carrying the renunciation to its logical end, he gave up everything, including life. Whether that was the historic Christ is not the question here. But for millions of persons, for two thousand years, the cross has symbolized this very renunciation of jealousy and power, and the crucifixion of the animal natural man, beginning with his infant desire to supplant his father.

Charles too left his father enthroned. In *Sylvie and Bruno* it was as true king of Elfland. In *Through the Looking-Glass* the Red King's dream may be considered as abject submission to the father, the potent king who could annihilate the other characters simply by awakening. Charles surrenders everything—except his sense of humor. The unpleasantness

of the Red King in no way represents the charming Canon Dodgson, but may show how Charles felt in his early childhood about his father's power. The conflict in his nature comes out all through the chess games, with the characters split into Reds and Whites. The Reds are fierce and irritable, the Whites gentle and sheepish—literally sheepish in the White Queen's metamorphosis. In the attempt to separate out pure forms, the opposites always encroach. An artist who travels too far toward "purity" always produces horrors too, and whoever, dissatisfied with the rainbow scheme of nature, tries to achieve whiteness, is startled to see black shadows at his heels.

The attempt to curb his youthful revolt also did strange things to Charles. The younger generation, knocking at the door, is not usually too disturbed at the older generation's shudders (or bluster). But Charles, who describes the proper feeling for God (perhaps for his earthly father too) as a sort of dread—not fear, but respect and love tempered with reverence—lacked the courage to make the final thrust and dethrone his father. "Jabberwocky" is not so much a parodied epic as an epic in reverse. The hero does slay the monster, but not with the ring of the true victor—and he is welcomed by his parent, instead of by a beautiful maiden. To such a pass is Beowulf-Siegfried fallen. (pp. 173-76)

It has been hinted that [Charles's] sex symbolism, and therefore presumably his sex life (in the mind—for no one claims he had any other sort), remained on an immature level. But it seems that he made at least one attempt to escape from celibacy into matrimony. If there was such an attempt, it was frustrated, and must have left him permanently discouraged; there is no intimation of a second. That the attempt, or the falling in love, occurred between the telling of the first *Alice* story in 1862 and the printing of the second late in 1871, is suggested by the increased sentimentality and the increased shadow in the latter. His first defeat was his acceptance of ordination; his second, less certainly documented as to names, dates, and reasons, was surely his failure to achieve a satisfactory adult love-relationship. The second defeat shows in a certain asperity of the *Looking-Glass* creatures—those that are not on the "sweet" side.

Several signposts point to disintegration; moments when the author steps out of character and reminds the reader that it is a dream, as in the boat ride, when the rushes fade so quickly, and he announces that, being dream-rushes, they must fade even faster than real ones. In transcribing *Alice's Adventures Underground* into the published version, he carefully deleted all such passages. In fact, therein lies his invention of a whole new genus of literature, in which "psychological facts" are treated as objective fact—in which coexistence in the mind implies ability to coexist objectively. The dead, the unborn, the non-existent, talking animals, humans in impossible situations—all are taken for granted, and the dream is not disturbed. (p. 177)

Through the Looking-Glass, like *Wonderland,* is an infinite onion, with many other leaves. After all, Carroll was a philosopher, which means he transmuted his experiences into something beyond life. . . . As a mathematician he was a great poet. Under the guise of nonsense he shows the ephemerality and unimportance of our most cherished categories, including time and space, and his social criticism is present by implication. The pacifists of 1914 might have described the soldiers fraternizing in the trenches in terms of the wood where things have no names. The stern categories called them back to the logical-nonsensical business of murdering one another as the fawn that trustfully allowed Alice to put her arms around its neck inside the wood, emerged suddenly exclaiming, "Why—I'm a fawn—and you're a human child!"

Space is annihilated in the garden of talking flowers. Alice and the Red Queen were "running hand in hand, and the Queen went so fast that it was all she could do to keep up with her: and still the Queen kept crying 'Faster! Faster!' but Alice felt she *could not* go faster, though she had no breath left to say so.

"The most curious part of the thing was, that the trees and other things round them never changed their places at all: however fast they went, they never seemed to pass anything. 'I wonder if all the things move along with us?' thought poor puzzled Alice. And the Queen seemed to guess her thought, for she cried 'Faster! Don't try to talk!' "

The Queen continues to hurry her along. " 'Are we nearly there?' Alice managed to pant out at last.

" 'Nearly there!' the Queen repeated. 'Why, we passed it ten minutes ago! Faster!' "

When they stop, Alice leans against a tree, which to her surprise is the tree they had stood under before they started running.

" 'Well, in *our* country,' said Alice, still panting a little, 'you'd generally get to somewhere else—if you ran very fast for a long time as we've been doing.'

" 'A slow sort of country!' said the Queen. 'Now, *here,* you see, it takes all the running *you* can do, to keep in the same place. If you want to get somewhere else, you must run twice as fast as that!' " . . . (pp. 178-79)

This is a wholly original sort of thinking, now made familiar by Einstein, but in the nineteenth century just coming slowly to birth, here and there, in the minds of scattered philosophers. Carroll upsets everything, tests everything, and does not hesitate to change the frames of reference. (pp. 179-80)

The White Knight is the gem of *Through the Looking-Glass.* He is the only character in the book with any sweetness of temper; although he falls off his horse and makes the ridiculous upside-down inventions of a left-handed person trying to live right-handed, he shows Alice-Charles the way out of the wood, which none of the others had the sense or the courtesy to do.

The book ends with the coronation and banquet. The awakenings in the dream books grow more nightmarish each time, from the first Alice mildly brushing the leaves off her face, through *Looking-Glass* Alice shaking the Red Queen into a kitten after the dreadful banquet, to a still more dreadful one in *Sylvie and Bruno Concluded,* where everything shakes and changes, ending with Prince Uggug's transmogrification into a porcupine.

The dream did not belong to the Red King, because the Red Queen becomes a kitten; the kindly old bumble-headed Don Quixote, the White Knight, shows Alice out of the wood—she is crowned and becomes a Queen herself. The story has a happy ending, but it is hardly a happy story. The black shadow of Jabberwock hangs over it from the earliest pages; Jabberwock, standing for failure, in the sense of burying and betraying some at least of the ten talents. Escape is no longer so complete or so satisfying as in *Wonderland,* though the

moment when Alice steps through the gauzy looking-glass never loses its thrill. (pp. 184-85)

The essence of Carroll is the extreme refinement—one might almost say Christianization—to which he brought the humor of cruelty. A lifelong process of refinement in himself produced the perfection of the *Alice* books. It is possible to trace the crude beginnings and shameless primitive forms of the motifs in his youthful writings, the fusion of opposites in his middle years, and the desiccated sweetness of *Sylvie and Bruno,* no longer blended, but alternated with a cruelty and ugliness that almost return to his early forms.

While his powers were at their apogee, he maintained the proper tension between sadism and sentimentality, giving his writings a subtlety, a delicacy, an extra twist of perversity, an incomparable flavor. (p. 216)

While not everyone who met him was alive to his genius, his writings cannot be denied universal validity. It may well be a comment on some sort of dullness in them for any of his acquaintances to have missed his fire, or perhaps he carried a dark lantern, and hid his light on occasion. But why was he forever fretting about the "child of the pure unclouded brow," implying that his own brow was in some way shadowed? How does a man of blameless life get the horrors? His very blamelessness may produce them. Creative (other than procreative) impulses, or altruistic or other respectable and elevated desires may also suffer repression. All was not so quiet as it seemed that afternoon when Mr. Dodgson and Mr. Duckworth took the three enchanting daughters of Dean Liddell rowing on the placid Isis. (pp. 217-18)

[What was Carroll, and Carroll alone,] was his flavor. It was more than flavor, it was taste—his exquisite taste, his perfect delicacy of feeling, his considerateness, his accurate balance.

What Carroll lacked was what all England lacked—abandon. . . . Carroll may not have succeeded in his task of spiritualizing the pig-child, but he did make friends in adult life with symbolic crocodiles and fabulous monsters, as in his childhood he played with actual frogs and worms. In Looking-Glass land all this is sensible, nor is there anything odd about a draftsman whose best drawings were made with an old box camera, a dramatist whose only operetta was written by someone else, or an immortal poet whose greatest poetry was in prose form. (p. 269)

[Carroll's] best writing was his simplest, and though all his critics deplore his arabesques, yet he wrings flowery tributes from the sternest stylists. The *Alice* books are inexhaustible, like the *Fifth Symphony,* or Botticelli's "Primavera"—the pattern, the rhythm, the flow, the color, the relation of parts to each other and to the whole, are at the same time so basic and yet so subtly woven that the eye, the ear, the soul never tire of contemplating them. There is also a fruitful joy in returning to them after absence, for each new contemplation yields new beauties, new infinities, strengths, and subtleties, and—in the single case of *Alice*—new humor. (p. 335)

Behold the poet who was no prosodist, the artist who could not draw, the actor who stuttered, the preacher who could barely believe his own doctrine, the dramatist who could not write plays, the instructor of geometry who bored his students, the inventor of games and gadgets, the champion doodler of Christ Church, the Curator of the clubrooms—dull, conscientious, kindly, awkward, and lonely. But stutter as he did, irregular as his gait was, left-handed as his approach to a carving knife may have been, in the presence of a basic issue he was fundamentally sound—not only sound, but accurate as a surgeon who makes no unnecessary scars. He carries the imbecilities of the creatures up to a certain point, and then with a sure stroke puts an end to them.

" 'What's your name, child?'

" 'My name is Alice, so please your Majesty,' said Alice very politely; but she added, to herself, 'Why, they're only a pack of cards, after all. I needn't be afraid of them.'

" 'And who are *these?*' said the Queen, pointing to the three gardeners who were lying round the rose-tree. . . .

" 'How should *I* know?' said Alice, surprised at her own courage. 'It's no business of *mine.*'

"The Queen turned crimson with fury, and, after glaring at her for a moment like a wild beast, began screaming 'Off with her head! Off with—'

" 'Nonsense!' said Alice very loudly and decidedly, and the Queen was silent."

For the master of nonsense knew when fun was fun, and when it was necessary to be loud and decided about it. Without solving all his own life problems, or making full use of the science of his own day, he still broke ground that has proved endlessly fertile for his inheritors. (pp. 336-37)

> *Florence Becker Lennon, in her* Victoria through the Looking-Glass: The Life of Lewis Carroll, *Simon and Schuster, 1945, 387 p.*

ALEXANDER L. TAYLOR

It would, in my opinion, be quite wrong to regard **Alice's Adventures in Wonderland** as an allegory or a satire. It is equally wrong to insist, as so many children of uncertain age have insisted, that it is a story for children of all ages. Certainly it began as a story for children, the three Liddell children, though even then two out of the five persons in the boat were adults. Next it became a private and personal matter between Dodgson and Alice Liddell, and for inspiration he drew on his mathematics and anything else that would yield this fascinating new amalgam or distillation which he called nonsense. Lastly he rewrote the story for a public which was to consist, like Kingsley's, of 'children and grown folks'. The mathematician and the statesman quote from Alice every time they open their mouths in public or try to explain to us the latest theory of space and time. In the dug-outs of the First World War ('How doth the little crocodile' in *Journey's End*) or the Anderson shelters of the Second ('remembering her own child-life, and the happy summer days' in *Mrs Miniver*) it became the symbol of normality and sanity, good days gone by and better days, we hoped, ahead.

To call it a minor triumph or a 'tiny little masterpiece' is intolerable condescension. It will be read, and not by children only, when all its critics and commentators, their comments and criticisms, are dust. (pp. 62-3)

[Regarding **Through the Looking-Glass,** it] seems quite clear to me through all the nonsense that the White Knight is Pure Science and the Aged, Aged Man is Applied Science.

The book, so far from having no moral, is thus a new kind of Morality. The characters are all abstractions and we are prevented from realizing this only by sheer verbal sleight-of-hand. The symbols are deceptively simple—but so are the

properties of a great conjuror. It is the second-rate magician who requires elaborate scaffoldings of chromium-plated tubes and other complicated apparatus. Give Dodgson a ball of wool, a kitten, some chess-men, a looking-glass and a little girl out of the audience—and watch carefully. (p. 116)

[In] his serious verse Dodgson was a minor nineteenth-century romantic, but in his prose he was the latest, and greatest, of the metaphysical poets. [**Through the Looking-Glass**] is not so much an allegory as a kind of plastic fable or parable, the same symbols, even Alice, being used in different ways at different times in the way that a phrase is used in music or an expression in algebra. (p. 137)

How can such work be assessed? Resemblances to different branches of art and literature have been noted. It is a form of caricature, containing satire and burlesque, wisdom and speculation and mischief. In some ways it resembles *Gulliver's Travels* or *Erewhon,* in others the fables of Aesop or the parables of Jesus. It is the nothing that is more than matter on the lips of distracted Ophelia, the assumed madness of Hamlet or Edgar, the professional madness of the court fool. It is entirely unlike the contemporary nonsense of Edward Lear; nor is it in the least Gilbertian. It has more in common with the theories of non-Euclidean geometry or with the poetry of Donne or Blake.

But in the aggregate it is unlike anything else, a separate and distinct form of art. It is not mere ingenuity, for of that we would tire, and we never tire of it. It is as 'full of quotations' as Hamlet or the Bible. Familiarity with its symbols is expected of educated people, though the literary convention is to misapply and the parliamentary tradition to misquote. It has provided countless books with titles and illumined the profundities of modern physics at least for those who write them. One meets Alice wandering, puzzled but not downhearted, through sermons, treatises on relativity or psychology, examination papers—and invariably one experiences a sudden lifting of the load as at the sight of a known face in a strange city, 'a white sail on a windy sea, a green tree in a solitary place'. (pp. 144-45)

Dodgson was for much of his life a very eligible bachelor; he remained unmarried from choice, not because he could not fall in love but because he had fallen in love once and finally—

> But either it was different in blood . . .
> Or else misgraffèd in respect of years . . .
> Or else it stood upon the choice of friends—

or else Alice simply preferred Reginald Hargreaves.

Dodgson started off his relationship with Alice as adopted uncle to adopted niece at a time when he felt repugnance towards the physical aspect of love, probably due to fear and inexperience. (His very sheltered upbringing, preoccupation with independence and cloistered life at Oxford must be remembered.) There was a time when that relationship might have developed into the kind of love which leads to marriage, but at that critical time something happened which threw him back upon his loneliness. Perhaps he was waiting until Alice was old enough to be capable of choosing for herself, as a man twenty years her senior was bound in honour to do, but by the time she was old enough to choose she had met Reginald Hargreaves; her parents approved of him and disapproved of Dodgson. The older man accepted the loser's part without putting the matter to the test and his loneliness was permanent. Then, like Arthur in *Sylvie and Bruno,* he determined that the secret should die with him, except that he told Collingwood, who respected his confidence and left it out of his biography.

There was once a slave who whispered a secret to the earth, and when he passed again, the reeds were telling it.

The importance of Alice is that she acted upon Dodgson as a powerful stimulus and catalyst. She made him put forth all his powers at once in her service, and rewarded him with a smile. Their love was an irrelevance in both their lives, yet its by-products were two masterpieces. (pp. 198-99)

> *Alexander L. Taylor, in his* The White Knight: A Study of C. L. Dodgson (Lewis Carroll), *Oliver & Boyd, 1952, 209 p.*

DEREK HUDSON

> *[Hudson is generally considered Carroll's best contemporary biographer; critic Richard Kelly calls Hudson "perhaps the most sensible writer on Carroll."]*

Alice in Wonderland owes its unique place in our literature to the fact that it was the work of a unique genius, that of a mathematician and logician who was also a humorist and a poet. It broke new ground because it was in no sense a goody-goody book but handled childhood freshly and without sententiousness. If we must look, in the **Alice** books, for any didactic Victorian message, perhaps we may find in them, as Peter Alexander has suggested, some such general warning as: "Pay attention to the language you use but not too much attention. Remember that words were invented to refer to things." The nearest parallel to the humorous method of Lewis Carroll is probably that of the Marx Brothers, whose dialogue not only has many verbal similarities with his, but who also, like him, assert one grand false proposition at the outset and so persuade their audiences to accept anything as possible. It is as foolish to look for sustained satire in the one as in the other. Both have been based largely on a play with words, mixed with judicious slapstick, and set within the framework of an idiosyncratic view of the human situation; their purpose is entertainment. Lewis Carroll has one transcendent advantage—with his limpid prose he paints the colours of poetry.

The Freudian or psycho-analytical interpretation remains. For those who accept it, who see Charles Dodgson—with some justice—as a strongly repressed individual, and who apply the doctrine not with prurience but with love and understanding, it may have its uses. It cannot touch the merit or detract from the achievement of **Alice.** Indeed, Sir Herbert Read believes that "such significance only adds to the value of such literature. . . . From our point of view, Lear is a better poet than Tennyson, Lewis Carroll has affinities with Shakespeare."

Alice, the Victorian child, still walks modestly forward with her patrician dignity and courage—through her own dream-adventures, through the applause, through the controversy: herself the simple answer, as she was the inspiration, for it all. (pp. 146-47)

The most remarkable thing about **Alice** is that, though it springs from the very heart of the Victorian period, it is timeless in its appeal. This is a characteristic that it shares with other classics—a small band—that have similarly conquered the world. We best understand the importance of this factor

when we compare **Alice** with Kingsley's *The Water Babies,* which is cluttered up with Victoriana of all kinds and, even after rigorous pruning, can never be emancipated from the 'sixties.

But, though **Alice** cannot "date", its author is held fast in his period. The more paradoxical and irresponsible his humour, the more does it emphasise the earnestness of the shy Victorian clergyman whose frigidity could repel those who did not know him well and whose eccentricity grew with the success of his book. (p. 151)

[With *Through the Looking-Glass,*] literature was enriched by another children's classic, and . . . henceforth **Alice** would sparkle as a double-star. *Through the Looking-Glass* has never caught up the lead in sales and popularity that **Alice in Wonderland** had already won, but it is doubtful whether children or grown-ups make any marked distinction between the two books, considering them rather as two parts of the same story. Indeed, if it is a question of a comparison of characters, the Looking-Glass team, with the White Knight (capt.), Tweedledum and Tweedledee, the Walrus and the Carpenter, the Jabberwock, Humpty Dumpty and the Red and White Queens might conceivably outplay Father William (capt.), the White Rabbit, the Duchess, the Cheshire Cat, the Mad Hatter, the March Hare, the Dormouse and the Mock Turtle, who would be among those selected to represent Wonderland. Alice remains the essential common factor. . . . (pp. 181-82)

It is not often that an author produces such a successful sequel to a best-seller as Lewis Carroll did; there is no better method, however, of proving that success is not a flash in the pan. (p. 182)

Through the Looking-Glass, being based informally on a game of chess and "hammered-out" as an intellectual process more than **Alice in Wonderland,** lends itself much less to Freudian theorising. The Freudians, indeed, derive their conclusions mainly from the early spontaneous chapters of **Wonderland.** But some of the characters in Tenniel's drawings, especially in the **Looking-Glass,** have suggested political caricature . . . , and there have been many other conjectures.

It is not surprising that such an unusual *tour de force* as the **Alice** books should have aroused enormous curiosity and stimulated a minute examination of the text, an occupation harmless enough so long as it was treated humorously and taken not too seriously—as in the parallel case of Sherlock Holmes. "Nonsense" lends itself particularly to an endless search for hidden meanings. But when we are told, as we have been told in *The White Knight* by Alexander L. Taylor, that the books are laced throughout with intentional references to religious and academic controversy, the joke has gone too far. One might as well carry the search for direct meanings and allusions into the charmingly nonsensical letters that Dodgson wrote to his child-friends.

The **Alice** books are adequately explained as the original work of a mathematician and logician, interested in the precise meaning of words, who was at the same time a genius of invention and poetic imagination with a love for children and a gift for entertaining them. There are, certainly, a few passing references to contemporary Oxford matters that might have amused the young Liddells, but such satire as there is in the books is based mainly on a general observation of human nature rather than on the exploitation of actual circumstances. Inspiration came in bits and pieces. . . . That Dodgson did have a lot of contemporary controversy whirling in his mind while he wrote the *Alice* books is undeniable; and Mr Taylor has indicated some of the embittered circumstances of the time. But they remained in the background, were assimilated by the mind of an artist, and transmuted unconsciously into a work of genius. (pp. 183-84)

Dodgson's character was exceedingly complex. He had disciplined himself so thoroughly and cultivated his self-control so successfully that he might well have been mistaken by those who met him for a person of great steadiness with a restricted inner life. In fact, however, this surface control disguised a precarious balance and much inner tension, which showed itself in occasional outbursts of irritability. He was one of those perplexing beings who are at once self-centred and unselfish, richly endowed emotionally but at the same time emotionally immature. A paradox himself, it is not surprising that the strange dichotomy of his character should have revealed itself (in his writing) in subtle changes of significance, and in statements no sooner made than they were abruptly reversed.

He was a man who carried his childhood with him; the love that he understood and longed for was a protective love. He had a deep instinctive admiration for women, yearning for their sympathy and often finding it. But it is probable that he could not reconcile in himself love and desire, and likely that he avoided problems of adult love and intimacy in his own life because he knew that he was pulled in two different ways (ambivalence is the modern term), and that in any close relationship something compelled him to seek distance and detachment.

To live such a lonely life—although he came to recognise, probably rightly, that it was the best life for him—must have required great courage. Dodgson was indeed a very brave man. (p. 188)

It was not [Lewis Carroll] who introduced nonsense to nineteenth-century English literature—that honour belongs to Sydney Smith—and to weigh Lewis Carroll in the scales against the delightful Edward Lear would be an invidious task where both are indispensable. Yet it was Lewis Carroll, with his logician's equipment and his rare understanding of the mind of childhood, who really won us our freedom of the world of nonsense (a freedom that, like most freedoms, has been abused) and it is the purity of his art—"almost unique", as Edmund Wilson has said, "in a period so cluttered and cumbered"—that has ensured his survival.

For this we have honoured him excessively and thus unkindly, Chesterton thought, by turning *Alice* into a "national institution, an educational classic". There is a degree of truth, and some danger, here. "This day ye shall remember before God all those His servants"—thus runs a prayer read in Liverpool Cathedral in 1932—"who write what many read, especially His servant, Charles Lutwidge Dodgson, sometime deacon in the church of God, through whom the healing power of mirth has been vouchsafed; and ye shall bless the name of the Lord Most High for every delight of the imagination which makes us friends of God in this world of wonder." Lewis Carroll would have been embarrassed, no doubt, by this and other signs of our respect. It is not his fault if *Alice* is now "a part of education". We have, perhaps, made rather too much of him, humour being important to the English;

foreigners will forgive us, however, because Lewis Carroll has enriched their imagination as well as ours. (pp. 235-36)

In the long run, the polished writer of humorous verse takes his place in the English tradition; the nonsense-poet who made his own rules remains always fresh. That achievement of Lewis Carroll's is distinct and unchallengeable. (p. 236)

We who have followed Lewis Carroll's life know that all sweeping judgements must be put aside; that for each moment of brusqueness there was a touch of kindness, that always beside the pedant stood the generous, imaginative friend. The sensitive boy from the Rectory, with his genius and his principles, was allotted no easy task in life. More than once the balance had trembled; he had found the courage to keep it true.

Above all, he had kept faith with the children, the Alices, the Ellens and all the rest. He had loved them as children, had hopelessly longed for them as women; but in the final test it was love that conquered; he had not failed his own early vision in the garden. He had passed on to children the special gift that only he could give; he had created a whole new mythology for the world; and for his reward he had been loved more than most men, and is still loved. (p. 311)

Derek Hudson, in his Lewis Carroll, *Constable, 1954, 354 p.*

PHYLLIS GREENACRE

As [Charles] grew up, he established an extraordinary self-discipline and iron control. He obviously had a horror of little boys and would have preferred to be a little girl. The sadistic impression of sex and of birth which—in the days of home deliveries—confronted him four times by the time he was six and as many times again between six and fifteen, left a paralyzing impression. Masturbation, sexual union, birth—such glimpses as he had of them—left a terrified fascination in their wake, and caused a retreat from an ideal of sexual love, to one of brotherly-sisterly universal love. . . . He seems to have almost abolished any sexual wishes in himself and to have attempted to live in his mind alone—by reason, learning, imagination, and looking.

The mind (in which vision played so important a part) then became his important vital source both of pleasure and acquisitiveness. And it was injury to the mind that he feared most, by loss of consciousness, of memory or of reality sense. He made mnemonic devices for himself, catalogued and recorded endlessly, built up in fact extensive projections of his disciplined mind in the order and thoroughness of his records. But he was unnerved by seeing fainting, convulsions and idiocy, which seemed to provoke fear of similar reactions in himself. He may even have feared the loss of control inherent in sleep.

His sensitivity to excitement from whatever stimulations increased his fears and may have given him in childhood those very sensations which alarmed him most—feelings of alienation from himself, of "losing the head," of being beside himself. Even pleasurable excitement may be intolerably intense to a sensitive child, as Bruno well knew and explained to the Other Professor [in *Sylvie and Bruno*] that when he was too happy he was uncomfortable and needed to be a little miserable, and so would set himself straight again by getting Sylvie to give him lessons. (pp. 244-45)

Carroll's compulsiveness was both symptomatically and

Carroll's sitting room at Christ Church, Oxford, where he wrote Alice's Adventures in Wonderland.

structurally . . . complex, widespread and massive. The enormous number of ritualized activities, suggesting both an effort to keep things under total and reasonable control and a reliance on irrational magic in the doing, have already been described. These rituals were like an extensive web of steel filaments which looked like gossamer threads but bound him firmly. That it was not so much the hostile aggressions of the anal period and the stress of too strong or too early toilet training belonging to the mastery of the bowel functioning, but a more primitive oral cannibalistic aggression which was feared, is obvious in the **Alice** books. More than this even he seemed to fear a general muscular explosiveness which might bring total destruction to himself and all others. Against this he wove endless intertwining defenses in which he had himself so encased that there were few peepholes of relief and release. There is indication that he may have had some infantile struggles of urinary control which left a symptomatic imprint in his fantasy life. . . . It is possible that the infant Charles Dodgson suffered early and severe rages of a shattering nature, which were followed by so perfect a control as to permit him no overt expressions of hostility. This we cannot know as a certainty. It is clear, however, that whether or not such explosive feelings within himself ever culminated in recognizable temper outbursts, he did very early react strongly to muscular aggression, sensed as dangerously near convulsive death in others. What general hostility he inevitably felt, was early grounded in fantasy and the very control of muscle aggression became a shield of muscular tension and physical rigidity. Even the fantasies must have been sensed as extremely dangerous, for he made an idol of reasonableness and factuality, and had difficulty in sleeping, probably out of fear of relaxing conscious control of his thinking. Only when his irrational fantasy escaped in his humorous stories to little girls

and won great recognition for him could he find the way to an acceptance of unreason. . . . The gratification of looking which is such a peculiarly dexterous combination of activity and passivity, and so close to fantasy, was his other big sensory gratification, and was made official through his photography. (pp. 254-56)

Carroll's defenses . . . controlled a disturbance, so basic and primitive as to be closer to the psychotic. His outer life seems to have been impoverished in emotional attachments and in achievements, and his reality sense cramped and invaded by the prohibitions invoked against his hostile fantasies which terrified him, until they became masked in humor. He then, even in official life, became more and more two men, Lewis Carroll and Charles Dodgson, sometimes with an imperative need to keep them apart. In the content of his writing his confusions of identity were manifold, bizarre and almost kaleidoscopic, involving not only individuals but time, space, and inanimate objects. That one man could have held in check so vast a Hitlerian fantasy as is expressed in the **Alice** books and that he should finally have expressed this in a form which touches and bemuses people in the psychotic part of Everyman's soul which is generally disclaimed, is not only a colossal personal achievement but represents the birth of a unique form of literary art which has not been equalled.

This, I believe, is the basis of the peculiar cultish attitude of the admirers of the **Alice** books. Just as the mystic union with the breast, dating from the earliest weeks of infancy, is the basis of the oceanic religious feeling of union with God and the Universe, so the terrible cannibalistic rage which sometimes follows this is held in check by inner defensive maneuvers which, when externalized and organized in religious rituals, involve the turning of the oral rage into a nondestructive re-incorporation and assimilation of the inner and outer worlds, symbolized in the Christian religion by the communion service. In those individuals in whom these early months and years are particularly tormented ones, the vulnerability is greater and the work of restraint more intense. But some nucleus of this primitive infantile struggle persists in everyone. It is Carroll's supreme art that he furnishes an unconscious outlet through humor for exactly these primary destructive pressures without a provocation to action. Readers are charmed and comforted rather than stimulated by the fantastic adventures which he conjures up. It is a mistake, however, to consider that *Alice's Adventures in Wonderland* appeals equally positively to all children. There are many children who recoil from or are frightened by the story, probably because they are themselves in a stage of development in which such primitive urges have—for one reason or another—been rearoused and only barely mastered again. They can ill-afford the danger of another arousal. Such children will turn away from the story as silly, boring, or cruel. But in general, the sadism of the *Adventures* is so outspoken and so grotesque a caricature that it protects rather than stimulates. There is a quaint Victorian expression of this in Carroll's preface to the *Nursery Alice,* in which he states that it is his ambition to have this book, in the nursery form, read by children aged from naught to five, and adds, "Nay, not so. Say rather to be thumbed, to be cooed over, to be dog-eared, to be rumpled, to be kissed by the illiterate, ungrammatical, dimpled Darlings. . . ." He proceeds then to the anecdote of the child so admonished against greediness and told never to expect more than *one* of anything, that on awakening from sleep she was puzzled at possessing two feet. It seems that Carroll would like the illiterate darling of naught to five to eat up the book, and that kissing, like the communion service, may have been a personal way of counteracting the destructive devouring urges. (pp. 256-58)

[We would say that Alice] is both a pleasantly feminine and yet essentially neutral figure, a just and questioning, as well as stoical observer of the turmoils of life, appropriately guileless, to wear the cloak of judgment. It is our belief that a peculiar condensation of stresses in Dodgson's own life created this figure in unusually pure form . . . , which fit then so extraordinarily as a collective symbolic figure of the time. The books in their entirety contain, however, so much that is true in general, regardless of era and place, that the appeal is as universal as that of fairy tales of obscure origin. (p. 260)

Carroll wrote with gentle gruesomeness, but always under the umbrella of nonsense. (p. 261)

> *Phyllis Greenacre, "Lewis Carroll," and "Certain Comparisons between Swift and Carroll," in her* Swift and Carroll: A Psychoanalytic Study of Two Lives, *International Universities Press, 1955, pp. 117-46, 247-61.*

MARTIN GARDNER

The fact is that Carroll's nonsense is not nearly as random and pointless as it seems to a modern American child who tries to read the *Alice* books. One says "tries" because the time is past when a child under fifteen, even in England, can read *Alice* with the same delight as gained from, say, *The Wind in the Willows* or *The Wizard of Oz.* Children today are bewildered and sometimes frightened by the nightmarish atmosphere of Alice's dreams. It is only because adults—scientists and mathematicians in particular—continue to rel-

ish the *Alice* books that they are assured of immortality. (pp. 7-8)

Like Homer, the Bible, and all other great works of fantasy, the *Alice* books lend themselves readily to any type of symbolic interpretation—political, metaphysical, or Freudian. (p. 8)

In recent years the trend has naturally been toward psychoanalytic interpretations. Alexander Woollcott once expressed relief that the Freudians had left Alice's dreams unexplored; but that was twenty years ago and now, alas, we are all amateur head-shrinkers. We do not have to be told what it means to tumble down a rabbit hole or curl up inside a tiny house with one foot up the chimney. The rub is that any work of nonsense abounds with so many inviting symbols that you can start with any assumption you please about the author and easily build up an impressive case for it. Consider, for example, the scene in which Alice seizes the end of the White King's pencil and begins scribbling for him. In five minutes one can invent six different interpretations. Whether Carroll's unconscious had any of them in mind, however, is an altogether dubious matter. More pertinent is the fact that Carroll was interested in psychic phenomena and automatic writing, and the hypothesis must not be ruled out that it is only by accident that a pencil in this scene is shaped the way it is.

We must remember also that many characters and episodes in *Alice* are a direct result of puns and other linguistic jokes, and would have taken quite different forms if Carroll had been writing, say, in French. One does not need to look for an involved explanation of the Mock Turtle; his melancholy presence is quite adequately explained by mock-turtle soup. Are the many references to eating in *Alice* a sign of Carroll's "oral aggression," or did Carroll recognize that small children are obsessed by eating and like to read about it in their books? A similar question mark applies to the sadistic elements in *Alice,* which are quite mild compared with those of animated cartoons for the past thirty years. It seems unreasonable to suppose that all the makers of animated cartoons are sado-masochists; more reasonable to assume that they all made the same discovery about what children like to see on the screen. Carroll was a skillful storyteller, and we should give him credit for the ability to make a similar discovery. The point here is not that Carroll was not neurotic (we all know he was), but that books of nonsense fantasy for children are not such fruitful sources of psychoanalytic insight as one might suppose them to be. They are much too rich in symbols. The symbols have too many explanations. (pp. 8-9)

It is easy to say that Carroll found an outlet for his repressions in the unrestrained, whimsically violent visions of his *Alice* books. Victorian children no doubt enjoyed similar release. They were delighted to have at last some books without a pious moral, but Carroll grew more and more restive with the thought that he had not yet written a book for youngsters that would convey some sort of evangelistic Christian message. His effort in this direction was *Sylvie and Bruno,* a long, fantastic novel that appeared in two separately published parts. (p. 14)

Ironically, it is Carroll's earlier and pagan nonsense that has, at least for a few modern readers, a more effective religious message than *Sylvie and Bruno.* For nonsense, as Chesterton liked to tell us, is a way of looking at existence that is akin to religious humility and wonder. The Unicorn thought Alice a fabulous monster. It is part of the philosophic dullness of our time that there are millions of rational monsters walking about on their hind legs, observing the world through pairs of flexible little lenses, periodically supplying themselves with energy by pushing organic substances through holes in their faces, who see nothing fabulous whatever about themselves. Occasionally the noses of these creatures are shaken by momentary paroxysms. Kierkegaard once imagined a philosopher sneezing while recording one of his profound sentences. How could such a man, Kierkegaard wondered, take his metaphysics seriously?

The last level of metaphor in the *Alice* books is this: that life, viewed rationally and without illusion, appears to be a nonsense tale told by an idiot mathematician. At the heart of things science finds only a mad, never-ending quadrille of Mock Turtle Waves and Gryphon Particles. For a moment the waves and particles dance in grotesque, inconceivably complex patterns capable of reflecting on their own absurdity. We all live slapstick lives, under an inexplicable sentence of death, and when we try to find out what the Castle authorities want us to do, we are shifted from one bumbling bureaucrat to another. We are not even sure that Count West-West, the owner of the Castle, really exists. More than one critic has commented on the similarities between Kafka's *Trial* and the trial of the Jack of Hearts; between Kafka's *Castle* and a chess game in which living pieces are ignorant of the game's plan and cannot tell if they move of their own wills or are being pushed by invisible fingers.

This vision of the monstrous mindlessness of the cosmos ("Off with its head!") can be grim and disturbing, as it is in Kafka and the Book of Job, or lighthearted comedy, as in *Alice* or Chesterton's *The Man Who Was Thursday*. When Sunday, the symbol of God in Chesterton's metaphysical nightmare, flings little messages to his pursuers, they turn out to be nonsense messages. One of them is even signed Snowdrop, the name of Alice's White Kitten. It is a vision that can lead to despair and suicide, to the laughter that closes Jean Paul Sartre's story "The Wall," to the humanist's resolve to carry on bravely in the face of ultimate darkness. Curiously, it can also suggest the wild hypothesis that there may be a light behind the darkness.

Laughter, declares Reinhold Niebuhr in one of his finest sermons, is a kind of no man's land between faith and despair. We preserve our sanity by laughing at life's surface absurdities, but the laughter turns to bitterness and derision if directed toward the deeper irrationalities of evil and death. "That is why," he concludes, "there is laughter in the vestibule of the temple, the echo of laughter in the temple itself, but only faith and prayer, and no laughter, in the holy of holies."

Lord Dunsany said the same thing this way in *The Gods of Pagana*. The speaker is Limpang-Tung, the god of mirth and melodious minstrels.

> I will send jests into the world and a little mirth. And while Death seems to thee as far away as the purple rim of hills, or sorrow as far off as rain in the blue days of summer, then pray to Limpang-Tung. But when thou growest old, or ere thou diest, pray not to Limpang-Tung, for thou becomest part of a scheme that he doth not understand.
> "Go out into the starry night, and Limpang-Tung will dance with thee . . . Or offer up a jest to Limpang-Tung; only pray not in thy sorrow to Lim-

pang-Tung, for he saith of sorrow: 'It may be very clever of the gods, but he doth not understand.'

Alice's Adventures in Wonderland and *Through the Looking-Glass* are two incomparable jests that the Reverend C. L. Dodgson, on a mental holiday from Christ Church chores, once offered up to Limpang-Tung. (pp. 14-16)

> *Martin Gardner, in an introduction to* The Annotated Alice: Alice's Adventures in Wonderland & Through the Looking Glass *by Lewis Carroll, Clarkson N. Potter, Inc., 1960, pp. 7-16.*

ROGER LANCELYN GREEN

[Both of the *Alice* books are] original with the absolute originality of sheer genius. (p. 50)

[Consciously] and for several skins at least of that fascinating onion the Subconscious—Dodgson told stories to children, following whatever development came into his logical mind, whatever new twist was given by some sudden question or misunderstanding from his audience, or whatever path a conscious or unconscious literary, dramatic or visual recollection might lead him—transmuted by the act of creation. (p. 51)

Those who have told impromptu stories to children know how easy and natural it is to weave such fantasies as Dodgson wove, and by what means they are born and grow and suffer sudden and unexpected changes and developments; only our stories are but clay models, and into his the genius of Lewis Carroll breathed the breath of life.

Also we, like all subsequent writers, are under his influence. Lewis Carroll has so permeated our thoughts—subconsciously and unknowingly far more than consciously—that we can seldom do more than imitate. *Alice* is so much a part of the cultural heritage of the western world that it is hard to realise its uniqueness or to see how startlingly new it was. (pp. 51-2)

The revolutionary nature of 'Lewis Carroll's' achievement cannot be exaggerated. Alice was a genuine child who, instead of tripping her demure way round the parish with the Mays in *The Daisy Chain* or emulating Mary Charlesworth's *Ministering Children,* danced joyously into Wonderland, turning all Miss Prickett's teachings topsy-turvy, joking with the Duchess about the necessity for there being a moral in every story, and came home to her Victorian nursery without a spot on her character—or a suspicion of having learnt anything more serious than the rules of a Caucus Race or the way to cut Looking-Glass cake. (p. 53)

[*Alice* has] been accepted officially as a classic for the adult—for without question the reader of mature age gets much out of it that is lost upon the child, or perceived in a different way. It is partly as an excuse for this new attitude that critics have tried so hard to prove that Dodgson meant very much more by his two stories than mere lighthearted amusement for children.

With those who believe that an extremely careful and detailed religious, political or mathematical allegory is intended, it seems hardly necessary to deal. Except in an odd momentary flash such double meanings are not the work of the subconscious mind—and Dodgson's conscious intentions seem hardly open to doubt. The subconscious as explored by the psycho-analysts such as Professor Empson or Dr Greenacre may yield a few clues as to Dodgson's character and suggest a few possible twists or preoccupations which could have produced certain incidents in *Alice;* but they *were* subconscious and have no direct bearing on the stories. If, however, the adult reader sees them as composed of Freudian symbols, there may be some reluctance in giving them to a child to read; the modern preoccupation with the new and only half-understood science of psychology sometimes tends to see *Alice* as full of horrors, from Alice's fear of going out like a candle to the Queen's decapitation complex.

It seems unlikely that more than one child in a million will see anything but amusement in *Alice*—and it is impossible to predict the odd child, who might equally have been frightened by the most unexpected thing elsewhere. Tenniel's drawing of Alice with the long neck has been found frightening, and Dodgson himself hesitated over the possible terrors of the Jabberwock. But it might be the White King's threat to Haigha; 'If you do that again, I'll have you buttered'— which to one child was the funniest line in either book; just as (to take an actual case) a mother discussing what books frightened children confessed that *Peter Pan* was the terror of her childhood—not because of any of the doings of Captain Hook, but because Mr Darling lived for a while in the dog kennel!

Setting aside this possibility, it seems only fair to point out that decapitation, change of size, the Dormouse in the teapot, or the Red Knight falling into his own helmet are quite unreal to children, and a part of their natural imagination which can invent for itself, and acclaim as riotously funny 'horrific' ideas which far outdo the experiences of Red Riding Hood's grandmother or the Myth of Cronos.

That a number of modern children find little enjoyment in *Alice* is not a sign of a more fastidious and humanitarian mind, but of lesser powers of imagination. The modern accent is once again upon the inculcation of facts, as it was in the days before Catherine Sinclair registered the first effective protest against 'the reading which might be a relaxation from study becoming a study in itself'. The willing suspension of disbelief becomes harder to achieve, and the attempt to do so has become far less common or necessary since there are so many more books—and other occupations—from which today's children may choose.

Alice, moreover, was at its most popular among children when reading aloud was still customary. The ideal age is from four till eight, and often by the time it can be read easily the perfect moment is passed, for—to generalise—the only decade in life during which *Alice* does not appeal is from eight to eighteen. Sophistication has lowered the age-limit which would probably have been at twelve in Dodgson's day; the appeal to the 'eighteen-plus' group is by no means new—*Alice* was the rage among undergraduates by the mid seventies, and the language of 'Jabberwocky' became current in public schools at much the same time. (pp. 54-6)

Roger Lancelyn Green, in his Lewis Carroll, *The Bodley Head, 1960, 83 p.*

MARGERY FISHER

To both [Lewis Carroll and Edward Lear], nonsense provided an escape, a world of fantasy in which they could forget that they were not entirely at ease in their own world. . . . [If Lewis Carroll was trying in *Alice in Wonderland* and *Through the Looking-Glass*] to satisfy a child's curiosity and spontaneous love of life, he put into them, too, his own

doubts, his fears and nightmares, and something of the barbarity of childhood as it survived in himself. (p. 163)

Obviously, these are books which have a special meaning for different ages. Alice's character, which young people take for granted, can seem, when they are older, rather tiresome and priggish; and perhaps she is never (except for Carroll himself) more to anyone than a centre round which the delightful and peculiar creatures can revolve. . . . Anyone can make jokes, but nobody can write another *Alice in Wonderland.* (p. 164)

[Ultimately] anyone who tries to imitate Carroll has to reckon with his style, and this is inimitable. His is the tongue of the university man, scholarly, urbane, a little diffident, absolutely uncondescending but conscious of superiority, repressed but generous. It belongs to the Establishment, to a particular way of life which is now part of history.

In some ways it is a bad thing that these two books have the air of the Establishment round them. Not that we would want to do without the gravity and stylishness of *Alice* simply because people nowadays do not live as the author had lived; but because the fact of their special flavour has given rise to an absurd amount of snobbery about the books. They are spoken of with reverence; two words quoted from them, by a dignitary of the church or state, bring roars of sycophantic laughter; they may not be criticized. All this is absurd. No book is as good as this. And the result of this persistent adulation is that children nowadays either read *Alice* in the potted form in which she appears in comic papers, or they read her with the adjurations of their parents ringing in their ears and feel let down when they have finished (if, indeed, they ever do finish). In many middle-class circles it is as important to know *Alice* as it is to use the word napkin and not the word serviette; but this intellectual snobbery cuts the ground from under Carroll's feet, for it makes the books tiresome and gives them an artificial importance. Let us take *Alice* down and dust her off and consider her critically and then give her to our children without any sermons. Let us not tell them they will be amused, or that this is a book they must like or be for ever beyond the pale. Let them discover it for themselves. They will discover it, in their own time, and re-discover it many times in the rest of their lives. (pp. 167-68)

Margery Fisher, "Climates of Humour," in her Intent Upon Reading: A Critical Appraisal of Modern Fiction for Children, *Brockhampton Press, 1961, pp. 153-69.*

PETER COVENEY

Everything for Carroll pointed to disaster in his personal life. He was almost the case-book maladjusted neurotic. The tale of the stammering, awkward, spinsterish don, imprisoned within Christ Church, Oxford, from the age of nineteen till his death, has been often enough told, with its dinner-parties in college rooms for little girls, with his obsessive interest in that most nostalgic of all arts, photography. Children were, he confessed, three-fourths of his life. . . . He led perhaps as uneventful a life as anyone possibly could. Everything led to his withdrawal.

As a young man of twenty-one he wrote:

> I'd give all wealth that years have piled,
> The slow result of life's decay,
> To be once more a little child
> For one bright summer-day.

At twenty-three, on seeing a performance of *Henry VIII,* he wrote: 'It was like a delicious reverie, or the most beautiful poetry. This is the true end and object of acting—to raise the mind above itself, and out of its petty cares.' The 'one bright summer-day' became the fixated symbol of Dodgson's living fantasy, with its escape from 'life's decay' and the 'petty cares' of his mind.

The 'cares' were, we suspect, not merely 'petty'. . . . In the Introduction to *Sylvie and Bruno* he declared his ambition to write a children's Bible, to compile a selection of Biblical quotations for children, and a selection of moralizing passages from other religious works: 'These . . . will help to keep at bay many anxious thoughts, worrying thoughts, uncharitable thoughts, unholy thoughts.'

This sense of sin recurs in his reminiscing account of what he had intended by the creation of Alice. She should have: 'the eager enjoyment of Life that comes only in the happy hours of childhood, when all is new and fair, and when sin and sorrow are but names—empty words signifying nothing.' Alice was then the expression of the romantic pastoral child, the symbol of Blake's innocent Life, but also the expression of Dodgson's frustrated exclusion from Life, the means through which his sense of guilt and sorrow could become for him 'empty words signifying nothing'.

The fusion of the romantic tradition with his own personal nostalgia is so poignantly displayed in that *Easter Greeting* he composed in 1876 to 'Every Child who Loves Alice'. It is as sad an expression of a deeply troubled psyche as one could ever not wish to read. (pp. 242-44)

The implied commentary on the Victorian Sabbatarians, the reminiscence of Blake's *Innocence,* the evocation of the romantic symbol of 'life' in childhood, merge into Dodgson's own subjective regret. To grow up is no more than to become 'feeble and gray-headed, creeping wearily'. The 'fresh' innocence of the child is not something, as it was for Wordsworth and Coleridge, to conserve, in order to nourish the fulfilment of the adult; its evocation merely serves to create a sense of poignant contrast. There is no plea for continuity; but an insurmountable barrier of nostalgic regret for the 'eager enjoyment of Life that comes only in the happy hours of childhood', and the forlorn emphasis lies on that one word 'only'.

It was extraordinary that the artist, Carroll, could distinguish from all this, from the 'delicious dreamy feeling', from this 'shame and sorrow', from this self-apologia, the valid emotions which went to the creation of the *Alice* books. Every factor which made for weakness became focused into the astringent and intelligent art of *Alice in Wonderland,* so that, in a strange way indeed, the 'dream', the reverie in Dodgson, becomes in *Alice in Wonderland* the means of setting the reader's senses more fully awake. Lewis Carroll is in fact one of the few cases where Lawrence's famous dictum of trusting the art and not the artist happens to be absolutely true. The *Easter Greeting* with its embarrassing sentimentalities reveals painfully enough all the weakness which the romantic child was heir to, if it subserved a personal regret. The image of the romantic child could become a currency only too easily seized by the writer who had every good reason to seek its comfort in face of a sense of personal failure and shame.

The remarkable fact about Dodgson is that by using the very means of his weakness, by succumbing to his dream and fantasy, he should become so intelligently awake. *Alice in Wonderland* releases the vitality of an intelligent and sensitive

commentary on life. It is precisely the opposite of withdrawn. The innocence of Alice casts its incisive, but delicately subtle intelligence upon Victorian society and upon life. But it is not simply that. It is not *simply* anything. Even in this first and greatest work, there is a content not far removed from nightmare. *Alice in Wonderland* has the claustrophobic atmosphere of a children's Kafka. It is the frustrated 'quest' for the 'Garden' which in the event is peopled with such unpleasant creatures. In those poignant lines of Alice's awakening, we feel the work turn towards unfulfilment, and very obviously towards death:

> At this the whole pack rose up into the air, and came flying down upon her: she gave a little scream, half of fright and half of anger, and tried to beat them off, and found herself lying on the bank, with her head in the lap of her sister, who was gently brushing away some dead leaves that had fluttered down from the trees upon her face. . . .

The juxtaposition of waking and the image of the dead leaves is no casual coincidence. Carroll's art was too carefully organized for it not to have some special reference of feeling. It has all the force of a poetic continuity, a felt development. With all the vitality and intelligence released within the dream, Carroll becomes very much Dodgson when he wakes. One feels a sense of shock at this sudden, waking reality, of the face of the girl's innocent life blighted with the 'dead leaves'. The whole tone of the work changes from this point. Alice's sister dreams:

> First, she dreamed of little Alice herself, and once again the tiny hands were clasped upon her knee, and the bright eager eyes were looking up into hers. . . . Lastly, she pictured to herself how this same little sister of hers would, in the after-time, be herself a grown woman; and how she would keep, through all her riper years, the simple and loving heart of her childhood; and how she would gather about her other little children . . . remembering her own child-life, and the happy summer days.

This idealization introduces a note alien to the work as a whole. The Alice of the ending of the book is in fact not Carroll's Alice, in Wonderland, but Dodgson's Alice Liddell. Already in 1862 we are approaching the world of the *Easter Greeting* of 1876.

Returning to the fantasy of Alice seven years later, Carroll almost achieved the artistic triumph again. But the emotional pressures of seven years' further deterioration had their unmistakable effects. The mood of *Through the Looking Glass* is ominously set by the introductory poem. . . . (pp. 245-46)

Through the Looking Glass is held between this and the dreaming denial of the reality of life of the final poem. . . . (p. 247)

Held within this frame, the book retains the intelligence of the *Adventures in Wonderland.* Alice remains the vehicle for Carroll's sensitive commentary. But the tone is perceptibly sharper. The humour is more sardonic. There is more merciless, embittered ridicule. The dream takes on a quality of horror. (p. 248)

It is as if Carroll in a more self-conscious way than ever in *Wonderland* turns aside from his own fantasy; as if he remains regretfully and painfully awake in his own dream. This may perhaps account for the savagery of so much of the humour. . . . Alice is subjected to a type of subtle cruelty in

PIG AND PEPPER.   91

"Well then," the Cat went on, "you see a dog growls when it's angry, and wags its tail when it's pleased. Now I growl when I'm pleased, and wag my tail when I'm angry. Therefore I'm mad."

"I call it purring, not growling," said Alice.

"Call it what you like," said the Cat. "Do you play croquet with the Queen to-day?"

Page 91 of the first edition of Alice's Adventures in Wonderland. *Illustration by Sir John Tenniel.*

a way quite alien to the earlier book. The episode in the railway carriage has all the horror of a sadistic nightmare. If life for Carroll was indeed a 'dream', the dream is evidently only too often in **Through the Looking Glass** Dodgson's own personal nightmare. With only the slightest susceptibility to the analysis of literature in psychological terms, it would be difficult not to see both works as psychological fantasies. They are clearly the works of neurotic genius. The initial rabbit-hole seems to serve as either a birth or copulative symbol. Dodgson's obsession with little girls was both sexual and sexually morbid. His own insistence on the purity of his interest has perhaps a telling, even a morbid undertone. But with Carroll's art, the neurosis is the irrelevance. Even in the clear references one feels to the neurosis, especially in **Through the Looking Glass,** one senses the extraordinary power of artistic sublimation that Carroll brought to the achievement of the two books. (pp. 248-49)

> *Peter Coveney, "Escape," in his* The Image of Childhood: The Individual and Society, a Study of the Theme in English Literature, *revised edition, Penguin Books, 1967, pp. 240-79.*

ISABELLE JAN

The special circumstances in which British children grew up

favoured the notion of a separate world, completely self-contained, and where strange, improbable or even impossible things might happen. In the nursery, the dormitory or the classroom, once the door was shut, children were free to perform all kinds of mysterious rituals and to conjure up wonders and monsters in their game. Adults were excluded from this world and knew nothing of what went on. Only a children's writer or a poet could discover these mysteries and that is what Lewis Carroll managed to do. (p. 60)

[**Alice**] is probably one of the first books for children to have been made up for and with a child, with no other object than to entertain and to appeal directly to the imagination. It is also one of the first literary explorations—at least where children's literature is concerned—of that fundamental human feeling, anxiety. The anxiety of **Alice in Wonderland** is typically that of a child: it pervades the book from the very first pages, investing every improbable encounter and each hilarious adventure. We find a child's anxiety at not growing up fast enough, perhaps never growing up, allied to a refusal to grow up; the traumatic experience of seeing one's own body in strange, incomprehensible metamorphoses that often seem shameful or even monstrous. A child frequently finds his body a source of embarrassment which, at certain stages in his development, can become almost painfully acute and these incommunicable sensations of bewilderment and disorientation—often translated into compensatory attitudes of braggadocio—have nowhere been better expressed than in Alice's adventures. Carroll also explores minutely all the degrees of inhibition a child can feel in the presence of adults. Alice is tongue-tied and incapable of finding answers to the questions that are put to her; she is stupefied by the clamour of incomprehensible conversations and she cannot make herself heard—or when she does, her words are distorted or dismissed in summary fashion. The March Hare's tea-party is perhaps the best illustration of the intractability and inadequacy of language as experienced by a child in adult company but there are examples in every chapter of both the **Alice** books. The child's loneliness and inability to merge with the adult world give him a distorted vision of reality. It is not so much that words do not mean anything: on the contrary, their significance is preserved too literally—so that language becomes impenetrable. When words are taken literally we are the prisoners of language and of the insuperable barriers of its logic. (pp. 61-2)

[Although] words are forever fixed in their literal meanings, objects and people keep on turning into something else. The visible world is blurred and evasive, or undergoes sudden preposterous mutations: babies become pigs and old women sheep, the Cheshire Cat vanishes leaving behind only its grin and at the end Alice finds herself in a land inhabited by monsters. These monsters are either the denizens of the nursery-rhyme world like the Knave of Hearts, Tweedledum and Tweedledee, Humpty Dumpty etc., or they are the products of everyday sayings and are absurd because they are the logical interpretations of the words. The British do say 'as mad as a hatter' and the mock turtle is drawn as a turtle with a calf's head because there is a soup made from a calf's head called 'mock turtle soup'.

Words create creatures and objects and permit weird associations; words also create their own causality: because the snark was a boojum the baker's death was inevitable—

whence the poem . . . and Lewis Carroll himself gives us the recipe.

> For first you write a sentence,
> And then you chop it small;
> Then mix the bits, and sort them out
> Just as they chance to fall:
> The order of the phrases makes
> No difference at all.

Lewis Carroll's creations are very much alive; some, like the caterpillar or the white rabbit, have haunting personalities. Others, like the mock turtle, owe their oddity to a linguistic peculiarity and thus strike the English-speaking child as old acquaintances, more comic than disturbing, but for the foreign reader, they are totally irrational and therefore the more disturbing. (pp. 62-4)

Alice's Adventures in Wonderland is really a national book with its roots firmly embedded in the English childhood lore.

Lewis Carroll did not fully realize the forces he had unleashed. After his two masterpieces *Alice's Adventures in Wonderland* and *Alice through the Looking Glass* and some nonsense poems, he decided to write a book for good children: *Sylvie and Bruno* was a patchy, inconsistent book, sometimes brilliant in its manically repetitive style, but, on balance, can only be considered a failure. Alice remains unique, but she had blazed the trail. (p. 64)

> Isabelle Jan, "Through the Looking Glass," in her
> On Children's Literature, edited and translated by
> Catherine Storr, 1973, Reprint by Schocken Books,
> 1974, pp. 56-78.

ROGER SALE

There is nothing odder in the annals of children's literature than the position occupied by the *Alice* books. They are the irreplaceable classics that everyone is supposed to know, and yet few people, so far as I can tell, sit down of their own volition to read them, or are unhappy when an episode or a book is over. . . . Yet there is barely a passage in the book that does not ring a bell for an educated reader, and at the level of word and phrase Lewis Carroll is the most memorable author of children's books who ever lived, and one of the most memorable of any kind. . . . (p. 101)

There is nothing contradictory in the fact that these classics, filled with memorable phrases and incidents, are not read or reread with much genuine enthusiasm. . . . What we remember most clearly is what we should remember, bits and pieces, and we do not have to reread either book all the way through to go back and pick these up. This means, however, something that those who write about Lewis Carroll seldom wish to admit: the generalizations one wants to make about him tend not to hold. Alice, for instance, does not "grow up," or grow in stature in either book. The events in neither book are consistently narrated as if taking place in a dream. Time, space, and chess are not consistently handled in *Through the Looking-Glass.* What Alice meets is not always fantastic, topsy-turvy, frightening, or nonsense. The two books are different from each other, but some episodes in each could safely be moved into the other book. Alice is not always priggish, or concerned with rules and manners, or a symbol or a type of anything or anyone. "Dodgson," asked the Canon Duckworth as he chaperoned the Liddell children and Dodgson up the Thames, "is this an extempore romance of yours?" "Yes," Dodgson replied, "I'm inventing as we go along."

Which is precisely what we would have surmised had we not been told. As a consequence of this "inventing as we go along" the books don't make very satisfactory or interesting wholes, but they do contain a great many memorable individual phrases and episodes. (p. 102)

The task with the *Alice* books, as with most children's literature, is to stick to the surface of what is presented to us and to read that surface hard. A writer whose "bits and scraps" "came of themselves" [as Carroll wrote in an essay about the *Alice* books] is willing to acknowledge mystery in what he did, but the mystery is in the writing, in the special unyielding quality of the *Alice* books. "Words mean more than we mean to express when we use them; so a whole book ought to mean a good deal more than the writer meant." Lewis Carroll said that, not, presumably, in order to give his readers full license to read his books any way they wished, but in acknowledgment that what we find and what he meant might well be very different. (p. 106)

Dodgson seems really to have been the person he presented himself as being, which is a fact many psychologists find difficult to live with. (p. 107)

His passion for girls is the most famous fact about him and probably the most important fact as well, and it is certainly the one people find hardest to accept at face value. What he wanted from his relations with girls he almost certainly got: their attention and companionship, their willingness to pose for his camera, their responsiveness to his kisses and to his black box of puzzles and games, which he used to introduce himself to girls he met on trains or in parks. Gradually he accustomed himself to the fact that girls become, about the age of fourteen, young women, and except near the end of his life he wanted no more to do with young women than with boys or with adults of either sex. His diary reveals no sign of sexual torment in him, and his letters to girls and to their mothers show nothing hidden or forbidden in what he sought. . . . In religious matters he was inclined to be reticent and slightly priggish; with girls he was open, direct, playful, frequently sentimental and mawkish.

It is hard, as William Empson has said in what is still the best essay ever written about him, not to cock one's eye at Dodgson's way of living, and we must wonder why someone wanted what he wanted. He was so active and diligent in pursuing his pleasures with girls, however, that it seems unwise to begin by seeing him as someone fearfully repressed, constantly "driven back into his childish thoughts." He never grew up and was surely blocked or retarded in important ways, but he lived with himself remarkably well after he came to understand the essential configurations of his life, desires, and possibilities. I don't mean to say he was happy, and one quality that emerges very strongly in his writing is a cruel desire for revenge that the surface of his life would seem to deny. He found life difficult and found himself unfit to live as many or most others seemed to live. His equipoise was sporadic, bits and pieces like everything else, so that his attitude toward living was essentially defensive. Everything was unstable, and if he strikes one note repeatedly it is that rules, orders, courtesies, and generalizations all break down under the pressure of selfishness, cruelty, idiocy, pedantry, shortsightedness, passion, and even, occasionally, decency. Dodgson adored Alice, but Lewis Carroll was merciless toward her, exposing her to everything he had himself suffered: teachers who made him reel and writhe, governesses who resembled the Red Queen and dowagers who resembled the Duchess, robust boys who acted like Tweedledum and Tweedledee, Humpty-Dumptys who stayed too long on their walls, footmen who wanted to know if he was to be allowed in at all. Yet, if Alice's defenses against these onslaughts were generally inadequate, Dodgson's own seem gradually to have become successful, perhaps because he was so very good at showing in his writing all that he feared and disliked.

The one thing that Dodgson was not is paranoiac. He imagined no conspiracy, no sense that anything in the world connected coherently enough for that. So we are forced back on to the bits and scraps. (pp. 107-08)

Lewis Carroll, for all that he adored Alice Liddell, for all that he idealizes his own Alice, treats his heroine mercilessly. She is idealized because she is free of the passions that rage in many of the other characters, but this does not keep her from rebuke and ridicule, and all she can do is to escape from each situation. She is never able to connect with anyone, never gives, never takes, so that she seems odd, alone, as much unyielding as brave. (p. 112)

Charles Dodgson himself had certain things on which he could rely, such as his station in life, his position at Oxford and in the church, his trust in God. But he denied himself all these in his transformation into Lewis Carroll, who had, also, no tradition or inherited form or direction. Lewis Carroll had only his native wits, his loneliness, his intense alertness, his passion for girls. Reading "Pig and Pepper," "A Mad Tea-Party," and the second scene with Alice and the Duchess in "The Mock Turtle's Story," I sense not so much a desire to expose or excoriate Alice as released anger and hatred—of domineering duchesses, squalling babies, insolent servants, and cavalierly rude people in general. Other things equal, Lewis Carroll in *Wonderland* always works to protect Alice, to make even her folly and pettishness seem more decent than anything she confronts. But other things are not always equal, and when a scene, coming and taking shape of itself, began to appeal strongly to Lewis Carroll's desire for revenge, then even Alice could be left in the wake of the waves.

There is much less of this in *Through the Looking-Glass,* which is altogether a softer and sadder book than *Wonderland.* Some of its episodes, we know, were written in at least some form before *Wonderland* was published— "Jabberwocky," the scene with the live flowers, and Tweedledum and Tweedledee are at least likely candidates—but there were nine years between the July 4 boat ride to Godstow in 1862, after which *Wonderland* began to take form as a book, and the publication of *Through the Looking-Glass* in 1871. If, in those nine years, the shapes of Dodgson's life became clearer to him, some of those shapes were signs of defeat, signs that, for all the great popularity of *Alice in Wonderland,* little was ever going to change for its author. The sharp, jabbing, nasty quality of much of *Wonderland* is almost gone, to be replaced by obscure battles and by three figures, two of which are versions of Lewis Carroll, who are fully grown, defeated, and pathetic: the Gnat, the White Queen, and the White Knight. Lewis Carroll had lost all touch with Alice Liddell, and he wanted, he said openly, to try to recapture whatever remained of the golden afternoon of their relation. (pp. 115-16)

[As] the opening of "Wool and Water" makes amply clear, in "the Looking-Glass country," time does *not* run back-

wards, and, apparently, not even the White Queen thinks it does:

> "I don't know what's the matter with it!" the Queen said, in a melancholy voice. "It's out of temper, I think. I've pinned it here, and I've pinned it there, but there's no pleasing it!"

> "It *can't* go straight, you know, if you pin it all on one side," Alice said, as she gently put it right for her; "and, dear me, what a state your hair is in!"

> "The brush has got entangled in it!" the Queen said with a sigh. "And I lost the comb yesterday."

If one loses one comb yesterday, and entangles one's brush in one's hair as well, then by today one's hair may well be in a state. Everything here is in perfect temporal order, or at least normal temporal order. But the White Queen needs a rule to explain why things are in such a mess: "jam tomorrow and jam yesterday—but never jam to-day." . . . Whatever the reasons for "no jam," her explanation has nothing to do with living backward or forward, since today "isn't any *other* day" regardless of whether it is preceded or followed by tomorrow. What the White Queen and Alice agree upon is that there ought to be rules for things. What the White Queen also knows is what Alice has persistently refused to learn in spite of all the evidence: things never go right, rules don't hold, explanations confuse as much as they explain, and there is never any jam.

The idea of living backward, as we approach it, thus, is not an idea offered by Lewis Carroll. It is the White Queen's effort to explain the mess that is her life:

> "What sort of things do *you* remember best?" Alice ventured to ask.

> "Oh, things that happened the week after next," the Queen replied in a careless tone. "For instance, now," she went on, sticking a large piece of plaster on her finger as she spoke, "there's the King's Messenger. He's in prison now, being punished; and the trial doesn't even begin until next Wednesday; and of course the crime comes last of all."

In *Wonderland* the Knave of Hearts is on trial for having already stolen the tarts, but it is also true that the Queen of Hearts does a good deal of sentencing before there has been either a crime or a trial. That is not a matter of time but of royal caprice, and here the White Queen seems to want to devise rules that will reverse crime and punishment. Still, if we just once imagine that the King's Messenger is in fact currently in jail, being punished for a crime not yet committed, then it will be tyranny we will be led toward. Certainly what Alice finds hard is not a matter of time running this way or that, but of justice:

> "Suppose he never commits the crime?" asked Alice.

> "That would be all the better, wouldn't it?" the Queen said, as she bound the plaster round her finger with a bit of ribbon.

> Alice felt there was no denying *that.* "Of course it would be all the better," she said, "but it wouldn't be all the better his being punished."

If it would be better for the Messenger never to commit the crime, the reason must be simply so that fewer crimes will be committed. Since the White Queen is imagining that it might be possible for the Messenger to break what seems an irreversible chain of events (punishment-trial-crime), then, if it can be broken by his choice, why not break it earlier, with the King's choice to punish him?

> "You're wrong *there,* at any rate," said the Queen. "Were *you* ever punished?"
>
> "Only for faults," said Alice.
>
> "And you were all the better for it, I know!" the Queen said triumphantly.
>
> "Yes, but then I *had* done the things I was punished for," said Alice: "That makes all the difference."
>
> "But if you *hadn't* done them," the Queen said, "that would have been better still; better, and better, and better!" Her voice went higher with each "better," till it got quite to a squeak at last.

[Critic] Roger Holmes cannot imagine that anything is happening here other than a philosophical puzzle, and even he must admit that as a puzzle it seems to make little sense. . . .

To say the White Queen does not make sense is to fail to consider the kind of sense she might be making. Elsewhere in either of the **Alice** books, an explanation is usually the act of a tyrant trying to make Alice into a victim. In this scene, we may want to assume, as Roger Holmes does, that the White Queen is trying to justify the intolerable, as if she were master of the world and as if the rules were her own invention. She is in fact inventing the rules, rather as the White Knight invents anklets for warding off sharks, because she is not at all the tyrant in her world, but the victim. The first rule is that there will be punishments; that goes along with "never jam today." If she were interested in puzzles, then time might be the subject, and Holmes would be right to say she makes no sense. But suppose the facts of life are the subject. The White Queen, Alice, and all the rest of us have been told, as if it were a fact of life, that punishments make one better. Having endured the punishment, having been "improved," the White Queen assumes she still can choose whether or not to commit the crime. The point at issue is not the way time runs, but how to respond to punishments for crimes one has not, or not yet, committed. Alice, like Roger Holmes, thinks it would be better if the White Queen, and the King's Messenger, would only be punished for crimes they have committed. The White Queen might like that arrangement better too, but she doesn't live in a world where that happens. The beauty of the White Queen is that, living in a tyranny as she does, where punishments often or even always precede crimes, she still imagines moral autonomy for individuals. In a world beyond politics, revolutions, or justice, people must still run their own lives, and therefore it would be better not to commit the faults one is going to be accused of anyway. Not because God is watching, because Lewis Carroll knows no God. Not because it makes one feel better, since the White Queen is clearly unhappy. But, as we say, just because. Of course, as Alice says, "there must be a mistake somewhere," but the White Queen knows she can do nothing about that.

Defeated and helpless the White Queen is, but imbecilic or stupid she is not. If her explanation for the world is that time runs backward, she is quite right to believe it, because she will prick her finger, after all, and there is much to gain by screaming first:

> "I haven't pricked it *yet,*" the Queen said, "but I soon shall—oh, oh, oh!"
>
> "When do you expect to do it?" Alice asked, feeling very much inclined to laugh.
>
> "When I fasten my shawl again," the poor Queen groaned out: "the brooch will come undone directly. Oh, oh!" As she said the words the brooch flew open, and the Queen clutched wildly at it, and tried to clasp it again.

So she cuts herself, and when Alice asks why she doesn't scream now, she answers cheerfully that she has done the screaming already. One deadens the pain of punishment by not committing crimes, one kills pain by anticipating it, one keeps from crying, as she goes on to tell Alice, by considering things.

Roger Holmes's comment on this grand moment glimpses some of this, but almost by accident, since what he is considering is not the White Queen, but whether or not she could exist:

> One *might* live in a world in which the screams and the pain came before the pin prick. Here is reversible time, the time Mechanists insist on, strange only because misunderstood. Within this temporal frame one must eliminate purposeful significances, such as catching at a brooch *in order* to pin it. But such a world is possible: certain philosophers from Democritus through Spinoza to the present have recommended it.

Holmes's knowledge is all drawing-board knowledge, what might be possible in theory, so he cannot imagine that Lewis Carroll is using reversible time and causation in order to reveal the White Queen's way of living in her intolerable world, in which of course there is injustice and of course time runs forward only. Holmes makes his own units, his own frames of reference, and cuts out much smaller bits and scraps than Lewis Carroll's and examines them in isolation from each other, so that the White Queen on justice is considered as a totally separate subject from the White Queen on brooches and screams, and the question of why the White Queen should want to apply the plaster before pricking her finger is never raised.

This conversation with the White Queen is so dazzling in its implications, it seems to me, that it is not surprising that Holmes is far from the only one who does not want to imagine them to exist. To think of a world in which the punishments come first is frightening, and most of us have too strong a sense of fairness not to protest bodily when confronted with such a world. It is easier just to think of the White Queen as daft, and she herself wishes she could remember the rule for being glad. When we think about a world in which there is jam, but never jam today, we usually are more comfortable doing so with a totally different part of our minds from the part we use to devise rules for explaining and accepting the painful and hateful. One could not develop such a beautiful, if despairing and deadening, view of life as the White Queen's either easily or willingly, and it is one of Lewis Carroll's most brilliant insights to sense that, after the scene is over, we might want to know how old she is. It is the only time in either book that it could matter. "Now I'll give *you* something to believe," the White Queen says, "I'm just one hundred and one, five months and a day." Alice says she cannot believe that, but I can. Time does run one way only, after all, and one would have to go back at least a century to find the White Queen starting out on her lonely life. She knows what she has learned and what she has endured. We that are young can see that this is Lewis Carroll's saddest, wisest, best moment. (pp. 117-23)

But, like everything else in the **Alice** books, "Wool and Water" is only a bit or a scrap, so that just as the horrors of "Pig and Pepper" pass, so too does the sweet and defeated beauty of the White Queen. "Wool and Water" gives way to Humpty-Dumpty and, once put in its place, becomes no more animate or useful, especially for children like Alice and Lewis Carroll, than a piece in a jigsaw puzzle or a square on a chess-board. There is nothing structural in any large sense about Lewis Carroll's imagination, nothing that accretes, gives from one moment to help the next. Within the episodes, . . . there is a good deal more that is coherent and resonant than most people, and especially the Humpty-Dumpty critics [defined by Sale as a group which "accepts and even delights in the fragmentary nature of the books because, like Humpty Dumpty, their pleasure comes from picking up brilliant bits and scraps and writing as though the others did not exist"] have cared to realize. These episodes are the crucial units; often they are not as long as a chapter, or a page or two, but, knowing what we know of Lewis Carroll's methods of composition, it should not be surprising that within these units much is going together, building up and breaking down, that only frequent careful rereading can show.

As long as we bear this in mind, there surely is no harm done if we say that Lewis Carroll's fragmentary view of life is a child's view; one suspects that children are more often forced to accept life as bits and scraps than are adults. This hardly means that the **Alice** books are, or ever really were, popular among children; the evidence is that some children like Carroll very much, as do some adults. His great appeal is to those people, who can be any age at all, who happen to find life as stern, sad, and intractable as he found it; who feel that what we need most in order to live are good defenses; who know that what schools teach is Ambition, Distraction, Uglification, and Derision; who know, concerning words, that the question is not whether one can make words mean different things, but who is to be master; who know that at the end of the mouse's tail, or tale, we all stand condemned to death. Such people find in Lewis Carroll not only the great quotable things anyone can find, but strength, courage, and consolation, because his great talent was for putting awful truths in ways that did not crush. If Alice learns little from what happens to her, she keeps up her end of the bargain and remains undefeated. (pp. 123-24)

Roger Sale, "Lewis Carroll," in his Fairy Tales and After: From Snow White to E. B. White, *Cambridge, Mass.: Harvard University Press, 1978, pp. 101-25.*

FRED INGLIS

Alice's Adventures in Wonderland speak up for Alice's unquenchable spirit against the arbitrary conditions, the vanity and cruelty of so many adults, their feebleness masked by their tart and punitive rituals for the scrutiny of children, their craziness and hypocrisy. In the name of the comedy of things, Lewis Carroll told children how childish adults were, how accurate a picture of the world children could make by imagining their elders in a bestiary. (pp. 95-6)

It really doesn't matter whether you classify [**Alice's Adven-** *tures in Wonderland*] as a children's or an adults' novel. Much more use is C. S. Lewis's much-quoted and attractively warm-hearted remark: 'No book is really worth reading at the age of ten which is not equally (and often far more) worth reading at the age of 50.' **Alice** is a great work; I read it with greater pleasure and understanding now than ever I did as a child, but I press it into my child's hands.

We may argue as to whether it really initiates the main line of children's fiction. There is nothing else in literature like it, and yet it is profoundly influential. (p. 102)

[Lewis Carroll] transpires from the Victorian culture and the family life which was made by the bourgeoisie from the materials to hand—their Christianity, their capital, their nursery. . . . [He] doesn't simply *reflect* that life; he criticizes it in the name of the greater freedom he saw as being due to children, and visible within their best representatives. He brought to life, as great writers will, the best tendencies of the children of the age, their dauntlessness, their confident selfhood, their sharp, bright vision of the cowardliness and bullying of their elders. Inasmuch as Alice is Victorian, and intent on seeing and judging quite artlessly the overdone respectabilities and deadly formulae of the times, she speaks for values and victories which are distinct from the present. To that extent, we read her historically, to enlarge and deepen our present by seeing it in that longer perspective. Inasmuch as Alice is timeless, it is because the vast energy of human pretentiousness is also timeless, and the deceits and small cruelties practised by adults on children, and by men on men, vary only in degree and not in kind. To see, with Lewis Carroll, that this energy is both perverse and overwhelmingly funny is to give children a great moral truth: that if you find the world comic you will not fear it. And although fear in itself is not vicious, you may as well reserve it for what is fearful. (p. 103)

Alice's combination of gravity and pertness, radical innocence and virtuous intelligence, courage and courtesy, makes her, as indeed she was, the best child of the Dean of Christ Church, both Queen of Oxford high society, and its subversive judge, especially at the end of *The Looking-Glass*. . . . (pp. 103-04)

Alice herself is changeless. Her maturity, at seven years six months, is that of the perfectly achieved little girl—perfect not in the governess's book, but in Lewis Carroll's. Thus, in the extremely subtle scene with the Gnat in *The Looking-Glass,* what comes out most strongly is her fear of inadvertently hurting so dreadfully sensitive and tender a creature. At the same time, she *will* speak the truth quite candidly and without trouble, because not hurting people's feelings is a negative virtue, and judging rightfully is a human duty. (p. 104)

In **Alice,** and perhaps in life, well-bred little girls are perfect and complete. The shift from latency to puberty is, on this view, so drastic as to constitute the advent of a new self. Certainly, it is easy for the adult to see the sexual symbolisms in those extraordinary and powerful dreams told, as they are, with a glassy calm which keeps terror at bay just as long as you stay within Carroll's tone of voice, and don't imagine too keenly what the language says. So the frightful images of tumescence in Alice's swelling to a monstrous size and as quickly diminishing, especially when we see her neck grossly extended in Tenniel's drawing, or see her crammed into the shrinking room, don't need any sexual interpretation for us to remember the horrible nightmares which are common to us all. We can manage them, as children can, because they are so calmly told. But they appear so abruptly and in such an *uncaused* way as to make it impossible to forget more elemental and life-shaking possibilities in the most social and conventional of encounters in this dense, Oxonian world. (pp. 104-05)

It is an amazingly packed novel. Whichever page you turn to is rich in its implication, familiar and fresh. . . . [Of] the many strengths of Carroll's masterpieces, it is enough for my purposes to note three. (p. 107)

The first is that, for all their brevity, the two *Alice* books are packed with *characters*. The busy world of the Victorian novel and the Victorian market place fills the rooms and gardens with social meeting. Whatever the peculiarities and crippled places of the White Knight, the Red Queen, the Gryphon, Gnat, Mouse, Duchess, and Hatter, they are unmistakably *there* (perhaps even most memorably there when, like the Cheshire Cat, they keep disappearing). The novels, like bourgeois social life at the time, occupy a peopled landscape, and it is supremely Carroll's intention, as it is Dickens's, to present 'the arrogant and the froward and the vain' as they 'fretted, and chafed, and made their usual uproar' (the last line of *Little Dorrit*). Christ Church and Oxford were Carroll's subject-matter, and in 1865, these places were sufficiently near the centre of things for them to prefigure the essence of Victorian bourgeois life.

Against this teeming and always located social life, Carroll's second strength is to counterpose this ideal little girl. The peculiar vantage point of this eccentric, original mathematician-logician, placed by his gifts and his bachelor solitude in that wide margin of history, gave him the ideal instrument with which to praise and blame his society. As I said, Alice is the best daughter imaginable—best, that is, not to a governess, not even to a Dean of an Oxford college, but to her author, able to see what Victorian manners and morality could do if they really set themselves to bring up a morally excellent daughter, a calm and pure centre of consciousness. If you celebrate courtesy *and* courage, calm good sense *and* dauntlessness, grace *and* candour, you can hardly do better than Alice. The theory of education and childhood development which the Romantics put into circulation has Alice as its first, best triumph. To say so is not to slur over her priggishness nor her wholesome self-centredness, for it is part of the greatness of what Carroll has done to make these qualities essential to her charm.

The third strength is implied both by the busyness of the world of *Alice* and by the solid presence of the heroine. It is that Carroll criticizes the society he pictures in the name of that society's best self. Like Huck Finn, Alice is innocent and right. The world is experienced (though it doesn't learn from experience, but dodges its lessons as hard as it can) and wrong, either confidently (the Duchess) or timorously (the White Knight). Either way, Carroll will leave none of the conventions undisturbed. He upturns pictures of the self (the Duchess says: 'Never imagine yourself not to be otherwise than what it might appear to others that what you were or might have been was not otherwise than what you had been would have appeared to them to be otherwise'), of sex (the Knave of Hearts, the rosebushes and Tiger-lily), of language and reality (the woods of namelessness where the pretty doe

118   HUMPTY DUMPTY.

fell off the wall in doing so) and offered Alice his hand. She watched him a little anxiously as she took it. " If he smiled much more, the ends of his mouth might meet behind," she thought : " and then I don't know what would happen to his head ! I'm afraid it would come off ! "

" Yes, all his horses and all his men," Humpty

Page 118 of the first edition of Through the Looking-Glass. *Illustration by Sir John Tenniel.*

comes, the nastier riddling of Humpty-Dumpty), of death, everywhere. . . . (pp. 107-08)

Fred Inglis, "The History of Children: Little Innocents and Limbs of Satan" and "The Lesser Great Tradition," in his The Promise of Happiness: Value and Meaning in Children's Fiction, Cambridge University Press, 1981, pp. 70-97, 101-23.

BEVERLY LYON CLARK

Carroll's 1865 volume ushered in what is generally considered the Golden Age of children's literature in English. (p. 44)

[Before] Carroll there had been some imaginative, nondidactic literature for children and somewhat realistic portraits of children. But not many. And no writer before Carroll had put the two together so effectively. (p. 45)

Carroll entered the mind of the child to an extraordinary degree. Not for him was the moralizing that metastasized in other nineteenth-century children's literature. . . . Carroll simply aimed to delight the child. . . .

Furthermore, Carroll portrays a believable Alice, neither a paragon nor a terror. She is sensible, courageous, dignified, thoughtful, imaginative; yet she is hardly perfect. She may try to be polite, but somehow she can't stop mentioning the predatory virtues of her cat in front of a mouse and some birds, and the verse she tries to recite comes out sounding rather bloodthirsty. Carroll's portrait of Alice in *Wonderland* and *Looking-Glass* is remarkably refreshing, not only by comparison with the way other nineteenth-century authors portrayed children but also with the way Carroll portrayed children in his verse and later fiction. (p. 46)

How did Carroll manage to avoid . . . saccharine excesses in the Alice books? How did he manage to write such a great work of children's literature? For one thing, he was inspired by his affection for a particular child, to whom he told the tales that he later incorporated into *Wonderland* and *Looking-Glass*. . . . Carroll's literature for children always evolved from his oral story-telling, and his best works grew out of tales told to a particularly inspiring child.

Another reason for Carroll's success is that he was at heart a nineteenth-century scientist, a keen observer. And he keenly observed the ways of children. Certainly, as a photographer, he needed to learn what puzzles, games—and especially stories—could mesmerize a wriggling child for the minute or more that it took to record her image.

Finally, Carroll managed to trick himself into believing that his excursions into Wonderland and Looking-glass world were simply temporary escapes from the serious business of life. The adventures were mere diversions from the "real" world, where the books begin and end, Alice eventually waking up from her dream. And because he considered his imaginative fantasies ultimately unimportant, Carroll could permit himself anything in them. At other times he lived a pious upright life and diligently plodded at his mathematics; in this realm he needed to be serious. But in his fantasies he could escape seriousness, foregoing the somewhat ponderous and exacting pedanticism of the rest of his life. Fantasy was, for him, profoundly liberating; he could give his imagination free reign, whether inventing flamingo mallets in an absurd croquet game or, in the person of the White Knight, horse anklets to ward off shark bites. He may try to undermine Wonderland and Looking-glass world by declaring that the adventures were just a dream, but this afterthought does not negate the liberating vitality of the tales.

Thus Carroll essentially considered his works amusing diversions. He was not using them to teach "real"-world precepts. They were not the vehicles of allegories. There is no one-to-one correspondence between the creatures and events in his stories and the creatures and events in some other realm. The books are too richly evocative to be reduced to a single meaning, and that is another facet of their greatness. (pp. 46-8)

[The] fact that the Alice books attract so much attention testifies to their continuing vitality. And, indeed, the books are not utterly divorced from Victorian "reality." The least heavy-handed of the Freudians, William Empson, acknowledges ambiguity and recognizes, for instance, that Carroll's portrait of Alice derives in part from Romantic notions of the child's unity with nature but also from what he calls roguesentiment, from the child as representing freedom and independence. Or a non-Freudian like Roger Henkle explores how the Alice books become a vehicle for expressing veiled criticism of and ambivalence about such Victorian attitudes

as belief in progress. Thus Carroll reflects Victorian attitudes, though complexly and indirectly.

The books do, further, contain some satire of things Victorian. The trial at the end of *Wonderland,* for example, satirizes the legal system. . . .

Carroll also satirizes the educational system to which Victorian children were subjected. He recognized, for instance, how tiresome children found it to memorize edifying poems. So when Alice tries to recite some of this improving verse in Wonderland, somehow it "all comes different." Isaac Watts' enormously popular "Against Idleness and Michief," which extols the little busy bee for improving each shining hour—for gathering honey, skillfully building cells, neatly spreading wax—is transformed into an absurd celebration of the hypocrisy and guile of the crocodile. (p. 49)

Carroll did not want to undermine the virtues of hard work—that's not what such a conscientious Protestant would satirize. But he did satirize inflicting such poems on children to teach moral precepts, once again showing sympathy for the child's point of view. And perhaps Carroll's satire of the didacticism of previous children's literature cleared a niche for the new kind of children's literature that he wanted to write. Much as Alice tries to define herself by attempting to recite familiar verse like that by Watts, Carroll seems, intentionally or not, to be defining his fiction through Alice's mangling of traditional children's literature.

Even now, more than a century later, this niche that Carroll created in children's literature seems new. For his work is startlingly modern and adult. Some twentieth-century commentators, such as Virginia Woolf and Martin Gardner, even argue that the Alice books are more appropriate for adults than for children. True, an occasional child may find some aspect of the tales distressing, just as an occasional child may be overwhelmed by Sendak's Wild Things in *Where the Wild Things Are* or the death of White's Charlotte in *Charlotte's Web.* But most children do not. Most find the plot and events engaging, even if they do not understand all the play with words and logic. Children can still enjoy the nonsense of the books, even if adults feel that full comprehension requires an adult intelligence.

What is becoming increasingly clear, however, is that the Alice books are for both children and adults. On the one hand, there's the philosophical *Alice,* for those who delight in logical play. . . . (pp. 49-50)

Then there's the literary *Alice,* for those who delight in modernism and postmodernism. . . . *Wonderland*'s modernity includes its associative, non-sequential plotting, anticipating the thematic structuring of works like *Ulysses* or *Mrs. Dalloway.* That of *Looking-Glass* includes its verse. . . . Carroll's parodies here are not true parodies; instead, they play against the scaffolding of pre-existing poems—like some of Yeats' poetry, which draws upon the imagery in *A Vision* yet does not require that structure in order to be appreciated. Carroll's verse too can stand alone, divorced from its sources. Not, though, from the narrative—and this integration of verse and narrative also seems modern. Recent works like Nabokov's *Pale Fire* incorporate verse yet subvert strict boundaries between poem and prose, the plot of the novel growing out of footnotes presumably annotating a poem.

Carroll anticipates twentieth-century adult fiction by defying other boundaries also. His Alice books are incipiently self-conscious. That is, they remind us that we are in fact reading a book. When, for instance, Alice thinks, "There ought to be a book written about me", she indirectly reminds us that we are indeed reading a book about her. Both books tend toward self-consciousness, *Looking-Glass* more radically than *Wonderland.* When Alice notes that the *Wonderland* Mouse has reached the fifth bend of his tail-shaped tale, she is being self-conscious about his tale, but only about his tale, not about the creatures she encounters nor about her own adventures. Her comment underscores the differences between the Mouse's tale and the rest of the narrative, which thus seems more "real." In *Looking-Glass,* though, she self-consciously wonders if she is part of the Red King's dream. She is wondering whether the entire narrative and all the characters, including herself, are fictional. Such self-consciousness can at first remind the reader of the boundaries between fiction and reality, since the fiction stresses its fictionality. Yet the self-consciousness also hints that what appears tangible in *Looking-Glass* may be only a dream, that presumed realities are really fantasies, that reality is subjective. The poem that concludes the book even ends with "Life, what is it but a dream?". *Looking-Glass* may not be as self-conscious as more recent works, but it does begin to confound reality and fiction. And thus it anticipates trends in contemporary adult fiction.

Carroll created great children's books by portraying a realistic child in imaginative, non-didactic works for children, works that continue to attract the attentions of commentators of all persuasions. But the Alice books resist commentary. And therein perhaps lies the root of their greatness. (pp. 50-1)

> Beverly Lyon Clark, "Lewis Carroll's Alice Books: The Wonder of Wonderland," in Touchstones: Reflections on the Best in Children's Literature, Vol. 1, edited by Perry Nodelman, Children's Literature Association, 1985, pp. 44-52.

CHARLES FREY AND JOHN GRIFFITH

Alice's Adventures in Wonderland constitutes a perennial enigma for all readers. Is it primarily funny or primarily frightening? Is Alice to be thought of as little, overpolite, easily cowed, too focused on manners, snobbish, often bored, often in tears? Or is she to be thought of as courageous, in love with adventure and fun, indomitably seeking self-understanding and her own maturity? The creatures Alice meets are mostly "mad," yes, but by *mad,* does Carroll mean senseless or angry? What is he saying about the nature of language and logic, reality, and growth and time? In *Alice* what are rules, manners, and social conventions for? What makes the creatures of Wonderland so original and so fascinating? Does Carroll make a case for linking creativity and perverseness? What is the basic human image that emerges from the book? To these and related questions readers will frame divers answers, but there will always be agreement on the central fact: the astounding brilliance of Carroll's tragicomedy.

No parent, teacher, or critic can really "do justice" to *Alice in Wonderland.* The work is far too dense and multivalent to be explicated and interpreted at all satisfactorily, and the work now has become surrounded by so much mystification and hoopla that interested readers must pick their way carefully through a mass of theories and countertheories about Carroll and *Alice* if they wish to guide themselves or any children to sensible understanding and judgment of the work.

It may be best to begin by attempting a "naive" reading of the text. One might usefully chart for oneself what happens in the twelve mock-epic chapters, keeping special track of Alice's changes in size. It is an open question whether the basic sequence of adventures suggests a progression in knowledge and mood. Alice might be seen as moving from a kind of birth trauma—falling down the tunnel, the long low hall, the amniotic pool—through meeting little animals (mouse, rabbit, lizard, caterpillar, pigeon) to meeting larger animals and adult humans. Her adventures intensify in the sense that the Duchess and plight of the baby seem more powerful and threatening than the Caucus Race or Caterpillar, and the tea party picks up the pace of madness while the Queen of Hearts and the Mock-Turtle adventures introduce increased fear and nostalgia ("off with her head," songs of voracious shark and panther). Then comes the final trial, a full social event in which Alice reaches the limit of her frustration and anger, asserts herself aggressively, yet wakes to "dead leaves" and "dull reality." Alice is in one sense "socialized" but with decidedly mixed results (just as in *Through the Looking-Glass* she becomes Queen all right yet finds it is not all "feasting and fun").

Another way to approach the same sequence of adventures is to note that Alice is engaged in a romance quest for her own identity and growth, for some understanding of logic, rules, the games people play, authority, time, and death. How each adventure contributes to or deepens the multiple quest is something each reader may answer variously, yet each time with keen connection to the work. Certainly as children's literature, the adventures are entertaining, but within the playfulness lies another dimension in which Alice repeatedly cries, is treated rudely, fears for her safety or life, and becomes genuinely angry. The book would not have fascinated millions if it were superficial fantasy. When the Caterpillar asks Alice, " 'Who are *you,*' " and Alice can barely stammer out a reply, " 'I—hardly know,' " then Carroll is exposing the quintessential vulnerability of the child whose growth and knowledge of self and the world vary so greatly from day to day that a sense of answerable identity becomes highly precarious if not evanescent.

An obvious and crucial feature of Alice's meetings with the animals is that she, unlike the heroes in tales of the Brothers Grimm or Hans Christian Andersen, is rarely aided by the creatures she meets. Whereas in a tale of Grimms or Andersen or John Ruskin, the protagonist's meeting with a helpful bird or beast would signal his or her charity toward the world or nature, and signal a concomitant abandoning of pure self-interest or pride (often represented in greedy siblings), in the *Alice* story, the animals do not represent nature responsive to innocence, good will, and charity, but rather they are masks for roles and attitudes of humans in a society based upon competitiveness and pride. Alice does not go out into nature but down into dreams and the sub- or un-conscious. No wind, wave, or mountain appears in Wonderland to provide a breath of feeling tone or a sense of living nature. The focus is relentlessly closed, societal, and sophisticated. The animals are chosen largely for incidental associations (mouse with long tail/tale, grinning Cheshire cat, crazy March hare, etc.) that allow for puns or eccentric personalities and behavior. Alice enters a world of intensely insecure but aggressively defensive adults whose narrowness of outlook expresses itself continually in attacks upon the reality or propriety of Alice in her appearance and behavior. Alice's consequent bewilderment is the subject of much mirth, but always ambivalence abounds because of the grotesque disparity in power and politeness between Alice and those she meets. (pp. 116-17)

At the heart of *Alice* may be a simultaneous defense of the dream of childhood's spontaneous, gentle, innocent beauty assailed by adult stuffiness and pride and also a wistful recognition of the imperious nature of the child who demands growth and accepted entry into that very adulthood which will eclipse childish innocence.

Some readers will resist seeing *Alice* not just as silly happy fantasy adventures but also as satire, sometimes hard-driving satire, directed at unruly egos everywhere, at adult attitudes toward children, at the foibles of various social classes, at our pretensions to logic and to manners, and at the child's absorption in self and in the gyrations of its developing personality. Certainly in the very first chapter we are asked to be amused at Alice's opinions and behavior. . . . In the second chapter she mocks "Mabel's" lack of knowledge and her "poky little house" and her few toys in a way that obviously leaves Alice the target of our amusement. But then when she begins meeting the generally rude and eccentric creatures in Wonderland, the equation of satire shifts from bemusement at Alice's ignorant innocence (her unintended insults to the mouse, for example) toward a special combination of laughter at antics of the brusque, logic-chopping creatures and sympathy for the plight of Alice who is forever fearful lest one of the creatures be offended in some way. (p. 118)

Once we recognize that Alice is easily and often dispirited, we may see better the significance of the fact that she is also very resilient and re-buoyant. She consistently comes back for more. In this portrayal of her endurance and comic bounce of spirit, Carroll sides with many writers of children's classics such as Andersen in "The Snow Queen" or Ruskin in *The King of the Golden River* or Robert Louis Stevenson in *Treasure Island,* all of whom reveal youth's incredible capacity to endure the shocks of local defeat and yet keep coming on for final gain. Children's literature in this sense becomes a recognition that *life is on their side,* and the literature also becomes a celebration of that fact.

One source of Alice's lively resiliency is her curiosity. We are told in the third paragraph of the book that Alice follows the rabbit because she is "burning with curiosity." Soon she finds things becoming "curiouser and curiouser." In Carroll's world, curiosity leads toward that which is curious, and the curious borders on the very strange, and the very strange borders on the mad ("we're all mad here"), and the mad borders on the angry. There is a surprising amount of violence, real and threatened, in *Alice,* and readers owe it to themselves to note its occurrences and to reach some conclusions as to its meanings. Does it appeal to children (who often experience violent emotions and behavior as part of daily life)? Or does it frighten them? Or both? We know from amusement parks that fun and fear are sometimes compatible for children. When is Alice said to be frightened? How does she respond to her fear? How often is she delighted? When does she laugh? Does she ever give in to the nonsense and argument? Enjoy it? " 'It's really dreadful,' she muttered to herself, 'the way all creatures argue. It's enough to drive one crazy!' " The violence of the cook and Duchess produces "an agony of terror" in Alice, but how seriously does she take her own suffering? How seriously do we? Notice how often Alice faces a fear of death, such as by shrinking away to nothing or in threats of headchopping or just growing ever older. There are implicit connections in *Alice* among youth, curiosity, and

time. Alice's curiosity is allied to her desire to learn to grow. In *Through the Looking-Glass,* she wants to become and does become a Queen. In *Alice,* she asserts her larger being at the end. But the way of curiosity or growth leads also to eventual extinction, and much of the nonsense seems designed to baffle curiosity and stop time, as if to provide an antidote to death. . . . (p. 119)

Certainly *Alice in Wonderland* fairly bristles with odd characters and conversation fit to fascinate anyone from eight to eighty. The varieties of fascination can be understood partly in terms of the kinds of wit, play, amusement, and nonsense present in the book. Selected examples of puns, parodies, and put-downs should be readily recognizable, such as *non sequiturs* like "It was the *best* butter, you know," and perverse literalisms, such as the Hatter's about "beating time," and capital rude remarks such as the Gryphon's about "uglifying." Then there are the gnomic tags such as the Duchess's "morals," the riddles, and the sheerly inventive wordplay as in the Mock Turtle's account of his school subjects. Once the variety and detail of Carroll's "nonsense" are noted, one is in a much better position to discuss some of the implications of the kaleidoscopic wordplay. Is Carroll reminding us that language, knowledge, and communication are not the clear, pragmatic, purposeful tools we generally assume? Is he drawing connections between game and bafflement or between play and non-purposiveness? Is he exposing his and our delight in using language to confuse and ridicule others? Is he suggesting that sense is balanced precariously close to nonsense in a highly volatile or "reversible" world of double-meanings and looking-glass effects? Undoubtedly many readers will want to extend such questionings in directions of their own choosing. (p. 120)

Carroll wrote an epilogue poem to *Through the Looking-Glass* and ended it with the lines: "Life, what is it but a dream?" In *Alice,* life is both a dream and a joke. We need, perhaps, to "get" and enjoy the joke but also to realize that Carroll is saying the joke of life is on us (though still funny), just as the joke most of the time is on Alice. Alice offers to readers who are relatively new at the serious study of literature a splendid opportunity to learn respect instead of suspicion for one of the great modes of literature, satire. Satire seems duplicitous and overly sophisticated to some readers who are easily put off by it. But *Alice* provides such genuine delight as well as mystification that such readers may be willing to work with their distrust and modify it. . . .

After being considered "for itself," *Alice* should be brought back into contexts of genre and of historical development in children's literature. Carroll mocks the conventions of quest stories such as the Grimms' tales in which the hero or heroine penetrates strange lands to win a consummate reward. Carroll mocks, furthermore, the tradition of didactic literature for children as in his parodies of supposedly edifying poems. He attacks also the vein of Romantic and Victorian sentimentalism that sees the child as savior of society and nature, Ruskin's Gluck pushed to the extreme. At the end of *Alice,* Alice shouts: "Who cares for you? . . . You're nothing but a pack of cards!" Allowing for a lurking pun in "cards," this finale may sum up part of Carroll's attitude to social organization and "fellowship." A sometimes reclusive bachelor who never married or formed much in the way of close and lasting friendship, Carroll's motto would hardly have been "only connect." Whom should Alice care for and why are questions the book may be asking. It comes up somewhat empty-handed. This is the world of Victorian doubt and isolation in which the little lame Prince must bear his own sufferings in a lonely tower. The fatuous Duchess remarks:

> " 'Oh, 'tis love, 'tis love, that makes the world go round!' "

> "Somebody said," Alice whispered, "that it's done by everybody minding their own business!"

> "Ah well! It means much the same thing," said the Duchess.

Love, then, becomes a matter of minding your own business, a kind of self-love. Alice's adventures tell us why. Yet we may be thankful that Carroll so honestly portrays our universal, if laughable, insistence upon minding each other's business. (p. 121)

> *Charles Frey and John Griffith, "Lewis Carroll: Alice's Adventures in Wonderland," in their* The Literary Heritage of Childhood: An Appraisal of Children's Classics in the Western Tradition, *Greenwood Press, 1987, pp. 115-22.*

Brock Cole

1938-

American author and illustrator of picture books and fiction.

Cole wrote and illustrated several winsome picture books for early primary-grade readers before he turned to his first book of fiction for a middle-to upper-grade audience. Many of his picture books have an aura of past ages and bear traditional morals and themes. *The King at the Door* (1979) tells of a chore-boy who is rewarded for his wisdom in recognizing the king despite his beggar's clothes; in *The Winter Wren* (1984), the protagonist goes out in search of the frightfully late Spring, who is asleep on Winter's farm, and frees his bewitched sister from Winter's spell. But some of Cole's books are sheer fun: *No More Baths* (1980), for example, simply relates a small girl's attempts to get clean like the animals do rather than consent to a hated bath. For his picture books, Cole has created lively, richly-colored illustrations of pen and ink and watercolor which have been praised for their spiritedness and wealth of expression and detail. When Cole wrote *The Goats* (1987), however, he attempted an entirely new genre with remarkable success. The story tells of two unpopular thirteen-year-olds, Howie and Laura, who are left unclothed on a small island by mean-spirited peers at summer camp. Beginning as a prank, the situation becomes a struggle for survival and Howie and Laura attain mutual respect, self-respect, and maturation. Critics have expressed surprise and admiration for Cole's first effort at fiction and note that his unpretentious style, believable characters, and compelling drama have made *The Goats* a heroic story of the human spirit in victory over degradation. Through *The Goats* as well as his picture books, Cole has offered young readers entertaining and stimulating works enriched by skillful, engaging illustrations.

THE KING AT THE DOOR   (1979)

The pictures are Rowlandson via Zemach, and the yarn might be termed School of Zemach—but it's a good yarn, and the pictures play effectively to it. "Master! Master!" cries chore-boy Little Baggit to the Pickwickian innkeeper. "The King is at the door!" But, on rushing to the window, all that the innkeeper sees is "an old man in a patched shirt"—so he sloughs off each of the stranger's requests. Instead of a glass of wine ("He's been walking over his roads all day counting his milestones," says Little Baggit, "and he's thirsty"), the innkeeper proffers a mug of dishwater; for dinner, the dog's scraps; and so on. But each time Little Baggit makes good his master's deficiency—with his own ale, his own bread, etc. And each time the innkeeper sardonically commends him: "Little Baggit, you're brighter than a burnt match," or such. As children will quickly guess, the last laugh is on the innkeeper—for doesn't the King come back to fetch Little Baggit "first thing tomorrow in his royal coach," just as he's said he will! Crisply told, energetically pictured, and unmistakably amusing.

A review of "The King at the Door," in Kirkus Re-

views, *Vol. XLVII, No. 18, September 15, 1979, p. 1063.*

The story's fun is strongly present in the illustrations—pen drawings that alternate with watercolor spreads. Relaxed but well-directed lines fashion a motley cast and pithy background details, all intermittently highlighted in colors that have Margot Zemach's kind of abandon. There's zest enough to make this wear quite well. (pp. 348, 350)

Denise M. Wilms, in a review of "The King at the Door," in Booklist, *Vol. 76, No. 4, October 15, 1979, pp. 348, 350.*

Cole makes an impressive debut with his spiffy illustrations of a questing monarch's experiences and their meaning to Little Baggit, slavey to a cold innkeeper. . . . It's no great surprise when the king rewards the boy handsomely and the innkeeper loses a good worker. Still, Cole proves that familiar plots can be fashioned into new, refreshing and mighty diverting tales by a gifted craftsman.

A review of "The King at the Door," in Publishers Weekly, *Vol. 216, No. 18, October 29, 1979, p. 82.*

NO MORE BATHS   (1980)

When Jessie McWhistle's unreasonable family tries to make her have a bath *in the middle of the day,* the outrage is too much, and she decides to leave home. She tries being a chicken "frazzling" in the sand but it makes her feel gritty. Next she tries copying her cat, licking her paws and smoothing her hair; that doesn't work either. So she attempts to follow the example of the happy pig in her deep, oozy wallow, with predictably uncomfortable results. At last, Jessie gives up the unequal struggle, marches home, and surrenders to the hot bath, the shampoo, the towel. . . . She may be clean, she may smell a whole lot better, but she doesn't LIKE it. Youngsters of the "I hate baths" age will enjoy Jessie's gallant blow for freedom from cleanliness. It's a funny story, with jolly, bright illustrations, that should be a favored read-aloud.

> Joan McGrath, in a review of "No More Baths," in School Library Journal, Vol. 26, No. 9, May, 1980, p. 52.

The author-artist tells a fresh, funny story with a clear text, well-paced for reading aloud. Stubborn, feisty Jessie is an appealing heroine, for what could be more vicariously thrilling to young children than a rebellious girl who gets dirtier and dirtier, finally even plunging right into the mud? The watercolor illustrations add detail and humor and help create a lively sense of farm life. Like Brock Cole's first book, **The King at the Door,** the book's impact is unfortunately limited by less than adequate production; his work deserves better packaging. (p. 394)

> Christine McDonnell, in a review of "No More Baths," in The Horn Book Magazine, Vol. LVI, No. 4, August, 1980, pp. 393-94.

Annoyed because her parents and her older brother tease her about being dirty, and more annoyed because her mother says she has to take a bath in the middle of the day, Jessie decides to decamp. . . . [After trying various alternatives], Jessie goes home and has a bath. Wrapped in a towel and cuddled on her mother's lap, Jessie is hugged. "There now," her mother says, "There are worse things than taking a bath, aren't there?" And Jessie answers, "Nope." Children should enjoy that ending as well as the situation, and readers-aloud should enjoy the lightness and humor of the writing; for example, when Jessie makes her poor try at frazzling, Mrs. Chicken says, "Not just anybody can be a chicken. Why, frazzling is child's play compared to laying eggs!" The illustrations, watercolors that have a light touch and intriguing detail that is reminiscent of Peter Spier's style, are engaging in detail and attractive in composition.

> Zena Sutherland, in a review of "No More Baths," in Bulletin of the Center for Children's Books, Vol. 34, No. 1, September, 1980, p. 5.

NOTHING BUT A PIG   (1981)

There is a short, frowsy dog whose tail never stops wagging in Brock Cole's **Nothing but a Pig.** This is just one of the many witty details enlivening this story of friendship between a poor, good-hearted man and his socially ambitious pig. Although the pig plays the prig for a while, and the man misses his companion, fine fellow feelings finally take the day. Mr. Cole accomplishes all this deftly. Animating his pleasantly moral tale are illustrations of country village life, looking quite English, filled with color and clutter and always on the verge of coming apart at the picturesque seams. (p. 57)

> Karla Kuskin, "The Art of Picture Books," in The New York Times Book Review, November 15, 1981, pp. 57, 60.

Ink and watercolor, Brock's illustrations have a vernal, pastel look that is alleviated by the humorous details and expressive faces of his characters. They are considerably more effective than the story, in which a conceited pig thinks he's better than the owner who's loved him as a friend, and leaves him to go off with a more impressive looking man, Mr. Grabble. The pig gets into Grabble's house, puts on a suit of his clothes, is mistaken for an uncle due to arrive for a visit on the following day, goes to the bank (he also plays the harmonium) and is in the office when his original owner comes in to say he'd made a mistake. The pig gives Grabble money out of his (Grabble's) pocket to redeem himself and goes happily off with the man who is his true friend. (Grabble had planned on butchering the pig.) The fact that the pig is taken for Grabble's uncle by everyone is not convincing; the writing style is amicably fluffy, but the fantasy doesn't quite come off.

> Zena Sutherland, in a review of "Nothing but a Pig," in Bulletin of the Center for Children's Books, Vol. 35, No. 4, December, 1981, p. 66.

The exceptionally colorful and detailed illustrations capture both the warmth and humor of the story. Facial expressions are vividly depicted, enabling Preston to emerge as an individual and not merely as another storybook pig. The illustrations also portray details of a turn-of-the-century setting, which should be an additional source of pleasure and interest to children. (p. 51)

> Anita C. Wilson, in a review of "Nothing but a Pig," in School Library Journal, Vol. 28, No. 4, December, 1981, pp. 50-1.

THE WINTER WREN   (1984)

Barren, windswept, old-country landscapes, and gaunt figures, give a certain severity, and semblance of weight, to the tale of simple-seeming Simon who heads off, with little sister Meg, to wake Spring at Winter's farm. (He overheard two ravens speaking figuratively.) As soon as grim, sepulchral Winter hears their mission, he pelts them with ice—turning Meg into a tiny brown wren . . . who then tells Simon how to put Winter to rout. Where Winter sows sleet, Simon spreads meal—and up spring stalks of wheat. Where Winter prunes buds, Simon throws an apple—and up springs a blossoming tree. And when Simon makes his way into the house, asking for "a princess in green and gold" (his mother's jesting description), a fair-haired, green-robed girl directs him up to a bedroom where Meg awakens—to look out with him over an expanse of green and gold. As a simpleton story, it has no particular punch. As an allegory, it's strained, overextended, overexplained. But Simon's battle with Winter is dramatically staged and briefly compelling.

> A review of "The Winter Wren," in Kirkus Reviews, Juvenile Issue, Vol. LII, Nos. 10-17, September 1, 1984, p. J-59.

The shading of hues and delicate airiness afforded by watercolors are fully realized in Cole's artistic evocation of this original story. Told in well-turned phrases ("The new wheat turned yellow and rotted in the furrows, and in the air was a taste of iron"), the tale concerns young Simon, called a "sweet befuddling fool" by his mother, and his sister Meg's search for spring. . . . Though the literal-minded may find the conclusion troublesome (Is Meg Spring or is Spring the girl Simon finds in Winter's kitchen?), others will use the ambiguity as a springboard to discuss the tale's transformation and renewal theme, the general elusiveness of spring, or children's own various interpretations. The art also deserves attention. Strikingly composed double-page spreads flow gracefully across the pages, with emphasis points carefully placed not to fall in inner margins. Soft colors, a few fine lines to delineate character, and an Old World, peasant-style ambience come together in a thoughtfully orchestrated harmony that enriches the tale.

> *Barbara Elleman, in a review of "The Winter Wren," in* Booklist, *Vol. 81, No. 5, November 1, 1984, p. 366.*

Magnificent watercolor landscapes in muted tones and Winter as a menacing, almost ghost-like old man are the strengths of this book, for the text is disjointed and hard to follow. Young readers may not understand who the child that Simon meets is, or how Meg got into that bed. Since Simon literally awakened Spring at Winter's farm, they will not understand why the villagers laugh at him, either. This theme of renewal and transformation is a satisfying one, but as a whole, the story lacks continuity. (pp. 68-9)

> *Joyce B. Hewitt, in a review of "The Winter Wren," in* School Library Journal, *Vol. 31, No. 4, December, 1984, pp. 68-9.*

THE GIANT'S TOE (1986)

In a whimsical tangent on "Jack and the Beanstalk," a bumbling giant cuts off his toe while hoeing cabbages; the toe becomes an elf-like, naked mite with a genius for survival.

"The toe" eats the giant's pie; the giant, annoyed, tries to put him in a pie, in a scene in a gloriously cluttered kitchen; but the toe climbs out and substitutes the resident hen. The pie is shared—though when the giant realizes he has eaten the hen that lays the golden eggs, he tries again to get rid of the toe. This time, still "trying to help," the toe disposes of the giant's harp, so that when Jack turns up there are no treasures to steal. Jack goes off disgusted; toe and giant live happily ever after.

This engaging diversion is much enhanced by Cole's bright watercolors, beautifully painted and full of funny details, like Jack armed with a wooden sword and garbage-can lid, and lovely vistas, like the frontispiece of the giant's home floating in ethereal clouds above the serene world below. The wry humor will be enjoyed by beginning readers, but would also be fun to share with younger children. (pp. 929-30)

> *A review of "The Giant's Toe," in* Kirkus Reviews, *Vol. LIV, No. 12, June 15, 1986, pp. 929-30.*

Children who like authors such as Roald Dahl and their quirkier perspectives on life will appreciate this revisionist version of "Jack and the Beanstalk." . . . This blithely told tale features Cole's lively, well-composed watercolors, which adroitly combine reality and whimsy. Fun for individuals and groups (though the little fellow's nonexplicit nudity might set off some giggles).

> *Ilene Cooper, in a review of "The Giant's Toe," in* Booklist, *Vol. 82, No. 22, August, 1986, p. 1686.*

An original, rather odd, tale of an elderly, dull-witted giant and his "toe." . . . The colorful watercolor illustrations are evocative and great fun. The delightful use of language makes this a super read-aloud choice for children old enough to appreciate the humor. Cole's best effort to date.

From The Winter Wren, *written and illustrated by Brock Cole.*

Luann Toth, in a review of "The Giant's Toe," in School Library Journal, *Vol. 33, No. 2, October, 1986, p. 158.*

THE GOATS (1987)

Brock Cole's picture books have hinted at his writing talents, but here is proof of an unusual capacity for sustaining fiction. Two outcasts, a boy and a girl, are left by their fellow campers on an island with no food or clothes. In a much larger sense, these two are social misfits, already marooned from their families and peers. They know it and, in an urgent but steadily credible story, they create a relationship that is unique, yet puts them back in touch with the rest of the world. There are many levels here. The action of survival and evasion of authorities when the children run away will hold readers on a plot basis. The main characters' vulnerability, desperate connection, and eventual expansion into trust of some black, inner-city, fresh-air camp kids create a different kind of suspense which is climaxed by a triumphant commitment after their success almost tears them apart. Their progress is marked by the emergence of each from an almost nameless anonymity to comfortable familiarity with each other and themselves. The style does not miss a beat, either in narrative or dialogue, asserting itself without ostentation. Brock hints at sacrificial myth in the boy's story of a haunting experience in a Greek cave, supposedly inhabited by a god to whom worshippers sacrificed goats. Yet the symbolic allusions here and elsewhere reflect rather than obtrude, even when reinforced by references such as a deputy Sheriff's trapping them in his goat-farm jeepster. Several complicated thematic questions of social cruelty and moral obligation arise subtly, through concrete development. This is an unflinching book, and there is a quality of raw emotion that may score some discomfort among adults. Such a first novel restores faith in the cultivation of children's literature. The bookmaking, including Cole's watercolor cover and pen-and-ink chapter heading sketches, is meticulous.

Betsy Hearne, in a review of "The Goats," in Bulletin of the Center for Children's Books, *Vol. 41, No. 2, October, 1987, p. 24.*

According to the oily and simpering director of the Tall Pine summer camp, "goats" are "boys and girls who are a bit, well, judgmental about their fellows. And some of the other campers might decide, mistakenly, that things could be improved if a boy and girl were put in a situation where they might realize that we are all just people. That there's nothing wrong, for example, in a healthy interest in members of the opposite sex."

One of the principal ironies of *The Goats,* Brock Cole's masterly first novel, is that the cruel practical joke that is intended to quicken the boy's and girl's interest in the opposite sex accomplishes just that, but in the right way of a profound sympathy and admiration, not the wrong way of simple lust.

The boy is Howie Mitchell, the quiet, slight, intelligent son of archeologists who are currently on a dig in Turkey. The girl is Laura Golden, a practical, physical, independent loner in rebellion against a mother who's been co-opted by her corporate job. In their own ways, they are, indeed, "judgmental about their fellows" and contemporary society, and so they're stripped and marooned on Goat Island with the hope that the

bullying, worldly campers can sneak back that night and catch them in compromising positions.

Instead Laura and Howie escape from Goat Island and the campgrounds, and in the few days they're on the run together acquire years of learning about cooperation and respect and the sort of intimate friendship and devotion that the happily married depend upon. "The girl was drifting into sleep beside him, leaning against his shoulder. He turned his head carefully and smelled her hair. He could smell the lake and something spicy and private underneath.

> " 'What are you doing?' she said.
> " 'Smelling you.'
> " 'Boy, you're gross,' she said comfortably, not taking her head away."

Brock Cole has written and illustrated *The Giant's Toe* and *The Winter Wren* and other picture books for children, and his experience shows, for Mr. Cole has resisted the temptation to make his story overly heartwarming or his Howie and Laura overly precious. We like them for their imperfections and insecurities, their inarticulate yearnings and insubordinate passions. Without clothing or housing or food, the pre-teen-age couple feel compelled to lie and steal and trespass over and over again, but there is a rightness and authenticity to that, and they make a rigorous accounting of "things they would have to come back and pay for" and "things they had borrowed without asking."

Laura snatches coins from inside a truck to make a telephone call, scrounges shoes and clothes for them at a municipal beach, schemes to get a room key so she and Howie can sleep overnight in the Starlight Motel, steals a Jeepster from a deputy sheriff who's trying to arrest them. Each scam and undertaking is intriguingly original and thrillingly presented in prose that is attentive and modest and quietly evocative.

At one point Laura comes upon the boy sitting alone and slightly apart from some campers at breakfast and she notices Howie "ate very neatly, like a cat. She felt a sudden raging tenderness toward him. She was so glad he was there. She wanted to roughhouse; to throw her arms around him and wrestle him to the ground."

Brock Cole has achieved just that with this good and thoughtful book. His "goats" are a boy and girl we want to throw our arms around because Mr. Cole has created them with such raging tenderness.

Ron Hansen, "Discovering the Opposite Sex," in The New York Times Book Review, *November 8, 1987, p. 31.*

Brock Cole has built an extraordinary first novel, *The Goats,* around classic adolescent group rejection. . . .

How the two fugitives use their wits to find clothes and food, how they manage to elude capture for days, how they are briefly taken in by a busful of black kids who understand only too well what it means to be outsiders, and how they grow in resourcefulness and find that the two of them can stand together against all the "others" of the world—all this makes an entrancing tale, beautifully told. From the first sentence the novel is utterly engrossing, with a satisfying rightness of phrase and event, an inevitability of character and action, and yet a constant tension of suspense. The style is deceptively simple and straightforward, completely free of sentimentality. The boy and the girl are funny and touching and quite real, but without the false smart-aleck sophistication that is the trademark of many young adult novelists. The effect is reminiscent of the film *Stand by Me* in its tender but clear-eyed evocation of the last days of innocence. The word "luminous" comes inevitably to mind in trying to capture the quality of this lovely story: its simple events shimmer with their own rainbow light.

Unfortunately, this is not going to be a book that teenagers will embrace at first glance. It needs introduction, as we say too often. The protagonists are barely thirteen, and our rule of thumb has always been that teens don't want to read about anyone younger than themselves. And the publisher has not helped matters with the format. The large typeface, the heavy paper, and the woodcuts at the head of each chapter, while handsome, make the book look like a juvenile title. Yet this story is meant to be read by those who look back and remember what it was like. The details of the marooned pair's nakedness, the innocence of their not-quite-sexual explorations, the mystery of the girl's menstrual period—all this is inappropriate for sixth graders who have no perspective yet about these things.

The literary structure, too, is sophisticated beyond the simplicity of the surface. Brock Cole plays with the idea of "goats" and their symbolism as the creatures of Pan. The boy remembers a strange time in Greece with his archaeologist parents when he strayed into a cave "that belonged to an old god" and had a fleeting but overwhelming encounter with something unseen. This same presence was half-glimpsed in the woods one memorable day when he and his father walked from Delphi to the sea, he tells the girl. "Weird!" she marvels. Strangest of all, when the girl is captured by an indignant chambermaid in a motel, the boy terrifies the woman by peering at her strangely through the window with vines and leaves twined in his hair. "Wild things!" she cries, sinking onto a couch, while the girl walks casually out the door and escapes. The boy's dream, hidden from the girl until the last, is that he and she should live always deep in the forest in sylvan innocence, away from the corruptions and complexities of civilization and adulthood. A remarkable book to enjoy first and ponder later, and one that deserves to become a YA classic.

Patty Campbell, in a review of "The Goats," in Wilson Library Bulletin, *Vol. 62, No. 5, January, 1988, p. 75.*

Because at The Horn Book we are always searching for such works, I was thrilled this fall to read an extraordinary first novel, *The Goats* by Brock Cole. . . . *The Goats* reaffirms my belief that children's literature is alive and thriving. Recently in *The New York Times Book Review*, critic Charles Newman talked about the plight of current adult literature: "The fact of the matter is that a sense of diminishing control, loss of individual autonomy and generalized helplessness has never been so instantly recognizable in our literature—the flattest possible characters in the flattest possible landscape rendered in the flattest possible diction." But like many of the fine children's novels published today, *The Goats* does not succumb to any of these problems.

Like all powerful books, *The Goats* will repel some readers and attract others. Critics of the book are concerned with the absence of positive adult characters—as was the case with *Harriet the Spy*—and the change in the young protagonists from innocents to thieves. And all adult readers, I think, are disturbed by the raw emotion in the book—and the feelings brought forth from the reader. Because we have all, at some time in our existence, been the outcasts—the goats—whether as children or adults, we know what it means to feel severe alienation from life and one's peers. On a philosophic level *The Goats* explores that great human struggle when we are betrayed, isolated, pushed aside by society and people. Yet to be healed and to become whole again, humans must be able to reach out to others—to trust again even when betrayed. In this novel that deals with man's inhumanity to man, those outcasts become the heroes and heroines—because they are able to reach out and embrace each other.

It is wonderful to see a children's book that affirms the individual and yet speaks of togetherness and bonding. It is exciting to find a book of this quality which makes us think and argue and debate again about what makes a good children's book. The publication of a novel like *The Goats* signifies that we are still creating children's books that affirm the human spirit and the ability of the individual to rise above adversity.

Anita Silvey, "The Goats," in The Horn Book Magazine, *Vol. LXIV, No. 1, January-February, 1988, p. 23.*

Pam(ela Stampf) Conrad

1947-

American author of fiction.

Considered one of the most talented authors of recent children's literature, Conrad is a prolific writer who has published six books within five years for elementary and upper-grade readers. In each of her works for older readers, Conrad typically presents a familiar situation, but elevates it with what critics deem particularly sensitive characterizations and a masterful prose style. *Prairie Songs* (1985), for example, introduces a fragile doctor's wife, Emmeline Berryman, who predictably crumbles under the strain of the austere pioneer life. Conrad enhances her novel with her depiction of young Louisa Downing, whose views of Emmeline show Louisa's romanticism and immaturity and her growth of awareness. Through this portrayal and her poetic descriptions of the prairie, Conrad lifts the plot from the obvious to tell a touching and tragic story. Writing other young adult fiction of common yet disconcerting contemporary problems such as divorce and substance abuse, Conrad has shown the ability to truly understand her teenage characters and to portray their lives with tenderness and perceptiveness. She has also written two books for early elementary-grade readers which recount humorous situations in the life of an eight-year-old female protagonist. *Prairie Songs* was awarded the International Reading Association Children's Book Award in 1986; it was also selected as a Golden Kite Honor Book and a *Boston Globe-Horn Book* Honor Book in the same year.

(See also *Something about the Author,* Vol. 49 and *Contemporary Authors,* Vol. 121.)

I DON'T LIVE HERE! (1984)

Nicki is absolutely sure she'll never like the old house into which they've just moved, and she won't even unpack, because her plan is to secretly escape and go back with her best friend Lisa when Lisa comes to visit. Nicki even enlists the help of her new friend Jeffrey, who promises to create a diversion that will facilitate the escape. However, in the fortnight between moving and Lisa's visit, Nicki has begun to feel more at home in the new house, more at ease with her new friends, and less comfortable with Lisa. She decides she'll stay. This is a familiar situation and a fairly conventional development of that situation, but it's realistic and the writing style is quite commendable for a first book.

> *Zena Sutherland, in a review of "I Don't Live Here!" in* Bulletin of the Center for Children's Books, *Vol. 38, No. 5, January, 1985, p. 81.*

This is a pleasant story that is adequately written. Nicki is the only character who is fully developed, but there is enough development of the other characters to give the story balance. Readers know that Nicki comes from a warm, loving family and that she has found a good friend in Jeffrey. This may be just the story for readers ready for their first chapter book.

> *Karen Stanley, in a review of "I Don't Live Here!"*

in School Library Journal, *Vol. 31, No. 6, February, 1985, p. 72.*

While the story line is predictable, Conrad's characters have a nice reality to them. Nicki's change of heart develops credibly after a sequence of positive exchanges with neighborhood residents, and there is some humor in the telling. . . . [This] is a relatively smooth first novel for an age level where good reading is hard to find.

> *Denise M. Wilms, in a review of "I Don't Live Here!" in* Booklist, *Vol. 81, No. 11, February 1, 1985, p. 786.*

PRAIRIE SONGS (1985)

Louisa loves the solitude of the wide Nebraskan prairie and feels secure in her isolated soddy house with her loving pioneer family. Her younger brother Lester is less confident, fearful and withdrawn since the death of their baby sister. Louisa idealizes the beautiful, cultured, doctor's wife, Emmeline, who comes from New York City, shares her books with Louisa, and teaches her to love poetry. But Emmeline cannot adjust to the harsh pioneer life, especially to the loneliness. Through her pregnancy she becomes increasingly fragile and uncontrolled; and, when her baby dies in a long, excruciating childbirth, she goes mad. Louisa's first-person narrative is spare and lyrical, evoking both the daily rounds and the elemental struggles of prairie living. When Louisa's mother comes home after the baby's death, the family holds each other "slowly in big rocking movements, back and forth, as vast as the Milky Way, as wide and as far as the prairie." The characters are not explained but perceived by Louisa as complex and mysterious. The doctor appears insufficiently supportive, yet it is clear that he loves his wife and feels her suffering. Emmeline is whining and snobbish, but also sensitive, sad, and passionate. Momentarily, Louisa glimpses even her strong mother's loneliness, and that Louisa herself harries Lester in much the same way as the doctor urges his wife to "get on with life, and not give in so easily." Though Conrad tries to portray the native Americans objectively, librarians may want to discuss with children the fact that the pioneers' view of Indians as unwashed savages is as false a stereotype as Emmeline's clouded perception of the uncivilized pioneers.

> *Hazel Rochman, in a review of "Prairie Songs," in* Booklist, *Vol. 82, No. 1, September 1, 1985, p. 56.*

It is unusual for a children's book to have such a memorably imperfect adult character as Emmeline Berryman (her husband calls her a "hothouse flower") in a central role. This is a good opportunity for older children to discuss characterization in more than the usual depth: Was she simply a victim of circumstances? What were her strengths and weaknesses? How was she different from Louisa's mother? And Louisa is an uncommonly good first-person narrator, compassionate and articulate without seeming overschooled for the time and place. This is a satisfying book and a promising new author. (pp. 85-6)

> *Janet Hickman, in a review of "Prairie Songs," in* Language Arts, *Vol. 63, No. 1, January, 1986, pp. 85-6.*

Narrated by Louisa, this beautifully written first novel presents a fictionalized story that highlights a chapter in American history. . . . The story is as quiet as life in the Nebraska town; even the arrival of two Indians at their sod house is a brief, tense moment, like a flash of lightning against the vast prairie sky. But the feeling for and love of the land and the emotional relationships between characters are magnificently created. Like Patricia MacLachlan's *Sarah, Plain and Tall*, **Prairie Songs** is a quiet, gentle, yet moving recreation of another period and another way of life.

> *Anita Silvey, in a review of "Prairie Songs," in* The Horn Book Magazine, *Vol. LXII, No. 1, January-February, 1986, p. 57.*

Even the Indians are here in this *Little House on the Prairie* revisited. . . .

The quieter elements in the story are the most convincing, particularly Louise's slowly developing acceptance of her painfully shy younger brother. However, the story lacks the convincing detail of the Wilder book, and so fails to hold the reader.

> *Jo Goodman, in a review of "Prairie Songs," in* Magpies, *Vol. 3, No. 1, March, 1988, p. 30.*

HOLDING ME HERE (1986)

Conrad's second novel is set in the suburbs, far from the rural Nebraska of her much-praised *Prairie Songs.* Robin Lewis, 14, seems to have adjusted to life with her divorced parents, shuttling between her mother's and father's separate households. Then Mary Walker, a boarder, arrives and awakens a sadness in Robin. She pries into Mary's life, and tries to reunite her with the children and husband she's left behind. But Mary's past (which readers will figure out, even if Robin can't) is that of a battered wife; reconciliation with her husband means more abuse. Robin's interference brings disastrous results. A problem here is that Robin, who narrates the story, seems normal—there is no underlying sense that she is troubled. When she snoops it is an ugly act, but the reader never has a clear idea of what motivates Robin. And the final chapter seems tacked on and false. So do Mary's reasons for leaving her children with her husband, with his record for violence. But Conrad's writing is strong and clear, and draws one into the story.

> *A review of "Holding Me Here," in* Publishers Weekly, *Vol. 229, No. 26, June 27, 1986, p. 95.*

One sure test of good literature for children is whether or not an adult can read the book, relate to it, and enjoy it. Does it speak to the child in us? *Everyday Friends,* by Lucy Diggs, and **Holding Me Here,** by Pam Conrad, meet the test in full measure. Both deal with the universal problem of being thirteen, "Lonely and Furious," as Marcy describes herself in *Everyday Friends;* and both address some of the problems unique to being thirteen in 1986: divorce, single parenthood, and domestic violence. They succeed as good reading because they tell a believable story well and introduce us to characters familiar enough to recognize, attractive enough to want to know better. And withal, there is a sense of humor. These two books seem in tune with a new kind of teenage movie which has proven very popular with young audiences. My daughter and I enjoyed "Pretty in Pink" because Molly Ringwald and her father really liked each other, and could say so without sounding corny; because they never pretended their unhappy family life had to have a happy ending; and because Molly's relationship with the "boy-friend-next-door" was deep enough to accept Molly's first real romance. Even the high school principal was a nice guy without being phoney. This kind of sophistication acknowledges the maturity of adolescents while accepting their limited life experience. It is the appeal of *Everyday Friends* and **Holding Me Here** as well. . . .

[**Holding Me Here**] deals with self-discovery . . . Robin has been keeping a terrible secret from herself. On the surface she has "coped" with her parents' divorce: she is happy living at home with her mother, and she enjoys the week-end visits with her father, secure in their love. It takes a dangerous indiscretion on her part to force the truth that she was desperately hurt by the dissolution of her family life, by the fragmentation of her parents' love for her. It was a costly lesson for both Robin and the innocent people who precipitated the crisis, but it was, Robin knew, an inevitable confrontation which was necessary for her growing up.

Like Molly, Marcy and Robin are "pretty in pink," the way thirteen and fourteen are supposed to be, but they are also vulnerable, intelligent, and brave, and that makes the prospects for the years ahead promising and challenging, the way growing up is supposed to be.

> *Carolyn S. Lembeck, in a review of "Holding Me*

Here," in Best Sellers, *Vol. 46, No. 5, August, 1986, p. 196.*

This is a sophisticated story in its setting, dialogue and allusions. In it, children turn for their poetry to the TV screen, old films and airliners streaking the sky. Without wounds, they still suffer grievously; the more they imagine, the more they open themselves to that suffering. The narrative is true to its urban scene, the feelings of an uncertain girl, and the devious situations that families can find themselves in. It is also an exciting story, with sharply-outlined home and street scenes and a wit that persists even in the saddest moments.

Dorothy Atkinson, in a review of "Holding Me Here," in The School Librarian, *Vol. 36, No. 1, February, 1988, p. 26.*

WHAT I DID FOR ROMAN   (1987; British edition as *A Seal upon My Heart*)

While her mother travels in Europe on her honeymoon, 16-year-old Darcie McAllistair stays with her aunt and uncle, who operate a zoo restaurant. She has never known her father, and, after seeing pictures of him in a family photo album, she becomes obsessed with the idea of finding him and learning why he deserted her when she was a baby. In spite of her aunt's silence about the past and her uncle's antagonism toward Darcie, her mother, and the mystery surrounding her father's desertion, Darcie is determined to learn the truth. It is at the zoo that Darcie meets handsome Roman Sandman, the seal and bird keeper. Roman is sometimes protective, sometimes romantic, but he frightens Darcie when he speaks in riddles about death. It is her naivete that finally leads her into a life-threatening situation with Roman. Conrad has written a readable story with interesting characters in an unusual setting. The theme of a missing parent will appeal to the needs of those young adults searching for an absent parent. Short letters from Darcie's mother to introduce each chapter keep the absent mother in readers' minds as the plot develops. However, the theme and plot seem contrived and hardly believable, and the profanity is often unnecessary.

Judy Butler, in a review of "What I Did for Roman," in School Library Journal, *Vol. 33, No. 7, March, 1987, p. 169.*

The author has made the most of the raw and powerful ingredients of the story to explore the feelings of rejection by the daughter of a father who has gone unaccountably missing. The behaviour of her Uncle George and her relationship with Roman do little to improve her understanding of the opposite sex. She is as much of a mixed-up kid at the end of the tale as when it began.

If you are tired of the cream cake and roses school of romantic stories for teenagers this bitter brush with reality will provide a more than adequate antidote. Few authors can have dealt their heroines so rough a hand of cards to play in life's game.

D. A. Young, in a review of "A Seal upon My Heart," in The Junior Bookshelf, *Vol. 52, No. 3, June, 1988, p. 156.*

Pam Conrad writes with an enviable combination of narrative drive and sensitivity, and handles the cliched theme of an adolescent's search for identity with welcome insight.

This, her third novel, confirms that she is one of the brightest talents to emerge in the last few years.

Steven Lillington, in a review of "A Seal upon My Heart," in Books for Your Children, *Vol. 23, No. 2, Summer, 1988, p. 19.*

SEVEN SILLY CIRCLES   (1987)

In this sequel to *I Don't Live Here!,* Nicki, the young heroine, is upset to find that the circles she made on her face (by licking a rubber arrow tip and repeatedly suctioning) are not going away. Not wanting to face humiliating questions, she decides she will stay in her room until they fade. Fortunately, she has made a pet of the miller moth that's the last vestige of summer, but even a pet moth is not much consolation when Nicki realizes she will have to hide in her room during the family's leaf-raking party. The story is slight and some obvious solutions to Nicki's problem are overlooked. (Why not put cover-up makeup on the red circles?) Still, Nicki is an engaging heroine and Conrad's enticing way with words makes up for plotting deficiencies.

Ilene Cooper, in a review of "Seven Silly Circles," in Booklist, *Vol. 84, No. 1, September 1, 1987, p. 61.*

Nicki, of *I Don't Live Here!,* returns in another amusing examination of suburban minutia.

Having absent-mindedly licked the inside of a rubber-tipped arrow, then pressed it on her face to see how long she could get it to stay there, Nicki now has several red blotches on her face that refuse to go away. So she hides out in her room, a decision that acquaints her with a moth for which she develops a great fondness, but which disrupts her human friendships. Her parents' annual leaf-raking party provides the denouement. Lured outside by the fun and by the proposal of her friend Jeffrey that they wear masks, she loses her embarrassment in enjoying the day and in the excitement when her father gets a fly stuck in his ear (a vividly described incident). In the end, her friends decide that they wouldn't mind having the same marks on *their* faces.

Some adults may not be fond of either the arrow or the fly incident, but the events are true-to-life and depicted from a child's point of view in a wonderfully concrete manner. This has virtually no plot, but its atmosphere is convincing. Conrad respects the priorities of her readers; they will reward her by looking forward to more adventures about Nicki and her friends.

A review of "Seven Silly Circles," in Kirkus Reviews, *Vol. LV, No. 18, September 15, 1987, p. 1390.*

Poignancy underscores this sweetly humorous story. Conrad allows readers to understand both Nicki's initial chagrin and her quiet maturing. The potential for melodrama is here, but the author never falters or overstates her case; her touch is light and sure. (p. 71)

A review of "Seven Silly Circles," in Publishers Weekly, *Vol. 232, No. 20, November 13, 1987, pp. 70-1.*

TAKING THE FERRY HOME (1988)

Although she has been prolific as a new author, Pam Conrad has certainly not been repetitive, and her latest novel is entirely unlike others she has written. Alternating chapters between the first-person voices of two sixteen-year-old girls, Ali and Simone, the novel tells of their meeting in an island resort community, their developing friendship, and ultimately the tragic occurrences that touch their lives. Although on the surface Ali and Simone seem utterly unlike each other—Simone is wealthy, beautiful, "reigning princess of Dune Island"; Ali, middle-class, sensitive, and insecure—their outward appearances prove to be quite deceiving. In the course of the narrative the reader grows to understand that Ali is the loved, cared for, and understood child in the home of a recovering alcoholic father, and Simone is a tormented, lonely, insecure child in an active alcoholic family. Not only the more likable, Ali also is the more fully developed of the two personalities; Simone—and even her suicide attempt—seems not completely believable. But the two families and two lifestyles are contrasted with great skill, and rarely have the disease of alcoholism and its effect on families been so well drawn in a book for young readers. Because of Pam Conrad's skill as a storyteller, the compelling and absorbing narrative keeps the reader interested, and the book never degenerates into being focused on an issue. In a society that is becoming increasingly aware of the hideous effects of alcohol and drugs, the book realistically portrays what recovery from addiction can mean—both to the person and his or her family. (pp. 356-57)

Anita Silvey, in a review of "Taking the Ferry Home," in The Horn Book Magazine, *Vol. LXIV, No. 3, May-June, 1988, pp. 356-57.*

As she did in ***Prairie Songs*** and ***What I Did for Roman,*** Conrad deals again with a character who is finally revealed to be profoundly disturbed; here, however, by using Simone as one of two narrators, she takes the reader within the troubled psyche, creating an enriched, more thought-provoking personality. . . .

Although there is much more here that has been well worked over in other YA novels, Conrad's well-rounded characters and skillful style lend fresh insight to the story, which is moving and memorable.

A review of "Taking the Ferry Home," in Kirkus Reviews, *Vol. LVI, No. 11, June 1, 1988, p. 825.*

Conrad transforms a YA stereotype—the nasty, beautiful rich girl—into a multifaceted character worthy of understanding and sympathy. . . . A romantic betrayal, a fiery accident involving cocaine free-basing and a near tragedy at the site of the earlier drowning unwind with precision and a feeling of inevitability, as if these two friends have been set on a fateful course from the first moment they met. Conrad's story resonates with truth and caring; she poetically elevates friendship to a state in which redemption is possible.

A review of "Taking the Ferry Home," in Publishers Weekly, *Vol. 233, No. 23, June 10, 1988, p. 84.*

Helen Cresswell (Rowe)

1934-

English author of fiction and picture books, reteller, and scriptwriter.

Cresswell is a prolific author whose career is marked by extraordinary diversity. Although she is best known for her fiction, her varied works for children from preschool to the middle grades include fairy tales, picture books, and stories for beginning and reluctant readers. She is considered a most original writer who has established herself as a superior contributor to the genres of fantasy and high comedy; she is also acclaimed for creating first readers which are surprisingly interesting and enjoyable due to her deft use of a limited vocabulary. From the beginning of her career, Cresswell has dealt with themes that recur in later titles. The "Jumbo Spencer" series, comic stories about an appealing young gang leader which began in 1963, demonstrate her fascination with individuals who defy social norms; in *The White Sea Horse* (1964), she introduces characters who fight for the right of existence to which all living things are entitled. These concerns figure prominently in her subsequent works. For example, in *The Night-Watchmen* (1969), a young boy befriends two vagabonds and helps them escape their fantastic nemesis, while in *The Bongleweed* (1973), a young girl struggles to save a magnificent plant which others fear as a threat. In these and other books Cresswell shows sentimentalism toward both the English countryside and times past, and her evocative prose has led critics to praise her increasing mastery of words.

Cresswell has been quoted as saying that her books are about life's journeys—not reaching the destination, but the road that leads there. She says, "[The] meaning of the journey lies in the making of it. In a sense, the moment one sets out, one is there." As this quote attests, Cresswell's fiction is not simplistic; she sometimes asks her readers to believe in the supernatural, and acquaints them with eccentrics and fabulous occurences by using a combination of fantasy and humor. This characteristic was first evident in *The Piemakers* (1967), a book which marked a definite change in the direction of Cresswell's writing. The story of a gigantic, exquisite pie which the Roller family bakes for the king of Danby Dale in Yorkshire, the story pays tribute to the pride of the craftsman while using comical, exaggerated descriptions. With *The Piemakers,* Cresswell moved toward expanding the boundaries of the fantasy genre; in later books, she continues to balance her humor with explorations of the darker side of humanity and the unknown. Cresswell's unique sense of humor manifests itself most sensationally in her "Bagthorpe Saga," six books that tell of an odd, outrageously funny family and their outlandish escapades. Applauded for their strong characterizations, the Bagthorpe books—the first of which was published in 1977—are recognized as English cult favorites. Cresswell is also the author of *At the Stroke of Midnight* (1971), a collection of classic nursery tales retold for younger children; in addition, she has adapted several of her works for British television. Throughout her career, Cresswell has given her readers insightful books buoyed with optimism which reflect her broad range of subjects, ability to probe the deeper issues of life and to shun complacency, and her mar-

velous wit. Cresswell has been the runner-up for the Carnegie Medal on four occasions: for *The Piemakers* in 1968, for *The Night-Watchmen* in 1970, for *Up the Pier* in 1972; and for *The Bongleweed* in 1974. She has also been the runner-up for several other prominent British awards.

(See also *Something about the Author,* Vols. 1, 48; *Contemporary Authors,* Vols. 17-20, rev. ed.; and *Contemporary Authors New Revision Series,* Vol. 8.)

AUTHOR'S COMMENTARY

Whenever I am called upon to write or talk about why and how I write, I usually find myself using not my own, but other people's words. I quote endlessly—Gide, Russell, Blake, Lichtenberg, Manley Hopkins, Goethe, MacNeice . . . I have even had it recently suggested to me that I should publish a *Helen Cresswell Commonplace Book,* so it now looks as if people are beginning to notice. In fact it was this suggestion that made *me* notice, and having noticed, think about it.

I think there is more than one reason why I always quote other people about the writing process. Firstly, it is because

I have an instinctive fear of meddling with my own inner mechanisms. (p. 108)

Secondly, having all my life been a solitary and dedicated thinker, a muser, an amateur philosopher, I am always delighted whenever I come across an endorsement of my own beliefs from a superior mind. I then quote to give them added weight for myself, as well as for others.

But the third, and I suspect the real reason, is that whatever I have to say that is of any value whatever, is contained in my work itself. If I could say what I have to say in any other form, then I would do so. And in any case, I do not usually know what I *do* think until I have said it. *The Nightwatchmen* is, quite simply, the book of that title, every single word of it (hopefully). I could add that it is a book about individual freedom and, in particular, freedom of the imagination. I could describe how months after the book was published I suddenly recalled a recurrent childhood nightmare, the climax of which was my finding myself enclosed in an underground cavern and seeing, there in the gloom, a pair of green eyes. This certainly explains why I should have chosen Greeneyes as a symbol of threat, rather than giants or phantoms or blind men. It also throws a light on the part played in fantasy by the subconscious. But it does not really add anything at all to the *book*. *The Nightwatchmen* is *The Nightwatchmen* is *The Nightwatchmen.*

I do not make a habit of thinking about why I write for children. Any thoughts I have had at all on the matter have been a result of a direct question put to me by someone else. The last time I had to give an answer to it in print, this is what I wrote:

> If you are going to use words (and I have no choice) you have to say something, and gradually you come to find that when you are saying what you really mean you tend to use words best of all, and so it is worth while finding out what you really mean. I am still working on this. With any luck, I shall *never* really be quite sure what I mean, and so I will never have to stop using words in order to find out. I think that may be one reason why my books are for children. They never know for sure what they mean, either. Most adults do. Most adults manage to find an attitude, and when they have found it, it takes them over, and fixes them like a fly in aspic (or whatever the expression is—I'm sure that's not it. Wasp in alabaster? Bee in marble? Fly in ointment. . . ? Drop it . . .)

Last night in bed I was reading Keats' letters for the first time for years. Just before I went to sleep I came across the letter in which he talks about 'negative capability'. This is a phrase indelibly fixed in my mind (like a fly in clover?) from school days, but I had quite forgotten what it meant. (If, indeed, I ever knew.) A week ago, if you had offered me a five pound note to tell you what 'negative capability' meant, I could not have told you. Which is extraordinary. Because it is exactly what *I* mean, exactly how I feel, exactly how I am as certain as so uncertain a person can be I shall always feel. It is:

> '. . . when a man is capable of being in uncertainties, mysteries, doubts, without any irritable reaching after facts and reason.'

I might have known it meant that, or something

like it. Keats was never the man to confuse truth with fact.

This still stands, as it has always stood, ever since I began writing as a child. And it leads on to other thoughts I have had about my own work, again prompted by others, not myself. I am by now used to reading, every so often, that my work is 'old-fashioned', that its action takes place in an 'idealized rural England of the past', that it is not, in a word, contemporary.

This is the first time I have publicly challenged this view of what I write, and I do so now not in self defence (because I am not even sure whether this is meant as a charge) but in the interests of truthfulness.

I am amazed, even astounded, that my work does not seem modern to some people, because since I have given this matter any thought at all, it seems to me that it is not only contemporary in outlook but positively *avant garde.* So much so, that half the time people do not know what I am getting at. (pp. 109-10)

I find the present technocracy alien and humanly barren, and I do not believe in the one-sided development of rationality at the expense of every other aspect of human experience. I look for balance to the shadow side of the psyche, the subjective reality of the individual, the power of the creative imagination. I believe (and I *will* quote Blake):

> The imagination is the only real and eternal world,
> of which our vegetable world is but a pale shadow.
>
> (p. 110)

On the title-page of *The Bongleweed* (true to form) I quote Turgenev:

> Whatever man prays for, he prays for a miracle.
> Every prayer reduces itself to this: 'Great God,
> grant that twice two be not four.'

Now I did not come across this statement and then write a book about it. I found it while the book was already with the printers, and had it inserted. Because by then, about a year after *The Bongleweed* was finished, I was fairly sure what it was about. I did not know when I started it. I never do. Pinned on the wall before me as I sit here now are some words of Leo Rosten: 'When you don't know where a road leads, it sure as hell will take you there.'

And these words say practically everything there is to be said about my writing processes. My books are roads, journeys, explorations. I do not know where I am going until I arrive there. I simply set out. I write at the top of a blank sheet the title I have given myself, and set out.

This is not properly expressed, and I never can find the right words to say it (probably because I do not really wish to.) When I was trying to say it recently to someone who was asking me questions, she said, 'You mean that your books are riddles that you set yourself, and you write them in order to solve them.' Which is more or less right, and here I am quoting other people's words again.

The Bongleweed probably comes as near to being a credo as anything I have yet written, though, of course, it is only my *latest* credo, as *The Nightwatchmen, The Beachcombers* and so on were in their turn. Each book simply rounds another bend in the road. And the more I read of writers like Jung,

Koestler, Roszak, Wilson, Laing and Lyall Watson, the more I see that the road I am travelling is not one that has already been mapped, because it is one for which each traveller must make his *own* map. It is not a wistful, nostalgic tour with an already certain destination, but a *real* one, being travelled here and now by countless thousands of others (most of them young) and with no fixed point of arrival. There never can be a final destination because the meaning of the journey lies in the making of it. In a sense, the moment one sets out, one is there.

The Outlanders do not wear modern dress, but the journey they make from the safe confines of the familiar and definable to the uncharted places of the Outlands, is an inner one which people always have made and are still making. (pp. 111-12)

The Beachcombers, on the other hand, is a kind of balancing act between the two worlds of Blake—the pale 'vegetable world' of the Scavengers, and the 'real and eternal' one of the Beachcombers. The reason why this book has no ending, is because there *is* no ending—not a truthful one, at any rate. We are all of us caught in the tension between these two worlds. It is the very essence of the human condition, and the dilemma is one that is never ending, it lasts a whole life long. (p. 112)

The kinds of meanings I have been talking about are really a substructure, underpinnings to what is on the surface a story. But I believe it is these underlying meanings that give the story power, even if not the faintest hint of them is consciously apparent to the reader. Much of the strength of a book, much of its real essence, is subliminal. The words are merely the tip of an iceberg. And if I anticipate another question, 'Do children really understand all this, does any of it come through to them?' my answer is an unequivocal 'Yes'.

I have a strong feeling now, as an adult, that I am practically a result of what I read as a child, and yet I am sure that I did not 'understand', in the sense of being able to formulate as an idea, even a fraction of what I read. But in reading, as in life, ninety per cent of what we experience, we experience as it were through the pores, and it comes to us directly without our translating it at all. We do not go through life constantly saying to ourselves 'I am now looking at the grass' or 'I can now feel a draught blowing on my neck', but these kinds of things are happening the whole time and are present to us in some way. The whole time things are filtering through direct, as it were, by-passing our conscious awareness. Paradoxically, then, one almost reads the real substance between the lines of a book.

I have said that I write partly in order to find out, and in a sense I do not know what I mean until I have said it. And in the same way as I am operating on this level as a writer, so the reader too is experiencing things which he recognizes but has no words for. This is partly what any kind of reading does. It makes accessible all kinds of floating feelings and attitudes and ideas which probably have never been crystallized before.

Now I have said some things to explain what I think certain of my books are about—it is, after all, my privilege, since I wrote them. But at the same time I think there is a very real danger in people taking books apart in this way. They should rest content with experiencing the book. That is all that is required in the way of response. I do not work out my books consciously, and so for someone to go about analysing them

consciously is an irrelevant if not actually damaging process. (pp. 113-14)

I gave this piece its title because I think much of what I write is ancient, in the sense that there is nothing new under the sun, but modern in that it embodies the attitudes not of the present establishment of technology, reason and materialism, but of the underground resistance to it. If the Bongleweed were a political party, I would vote for it. And this is where we come to the 'incorrigibly plural': 'The Bongleweed was a sign that all things are possible.'

If there is one phrase that has recurred over and over again in my work and thinking right from adolescence, when I first used it, that phrase is 'infinite possibility'. And I think I was trying to personify this in *The Bongleweed* by making the weed the hero of the book. I have been reliably informed by an unimpeachable psychological authority that the Bongleweed is a symbol of the creative imagination, and am happy to say that by the time I was told this I had already worked it out for myself.

The children in the story, and the Finches, who are themselves intuitive and childlike, love the Bongleweed at sight. . . .

But to the establishment, to Dr Harper with his scientific hubris, with his insistence on facts, with his strong urge to categorize—'It was all so *unbotanical!*'—the Bongleweed is a threat, with its 'careless lack of consideration for walls, boundaries, rules—even for the laws of nature'. The reaction of the typical adult is either to ignore it in the hope that it will go away, or failing that to chop—destroy. The experts do not like to be confronted by the inexplicable (an expert, as I define him, being a man who holds the subjective belief that we must all be objective). But children do, because they have not yet been fixed into conventional stances, because they have not yet been forced to make false boundaries and divisions, because they are still aware that life *is* 'incorrigibly plural' and glory in the knowledge, instead of forcing it away as an unpalatable truth.

The Bongleweed comes into the world as a figment of Becky's imagination, but is able to convert only the already converted. (p. 115)

The Bongleweed is not merely something in its own right, but also a *sign* of something. And so when it dies, as it naturally must, Becky knows that this is not really the end, nor anything like it:

> In a world where once a Bongleweed has sprung, anything would be possible, from now on. Perhaps *another* Bongleweed, clinging tenaciously to life down among the frosted roots, ready to wax again in the warmth and showers of April. Or perhaps it would be something quite different—out of the blue—desperate, beautiful, reckless—*anything!*
>
> She opened her eyes and glared fiercely down at the innocent, melting garden where the white was almost visibly yielding now to the green.
>
> 'You wait!' she thought exultantly. 'Just you wait!'
>
> Becky opened the window and felt her skin shrivel. She leaned right out above the blackened branches of the Bongleweed and drew in the heady smell of frost and was at once certain, in her very bones, that the world itself was both alert and mysterious

as those foxes' heads had been. The world had gone once and forever wild on her very doorstep.

And here I rest my case. (p. 116)

> *Helen Cresswell, "Ancient and Modern and Incorrigibly Plural," in* The Thorny Paradise: Writers on Writing for Children, *edited by Edward Blishen, Penguin Books, 1975, pp. 108-16.*

GENERAL COMMENTARY

MARCUS CROUCH

Miss Cresswell is a craftsman. . . . The slightest of her books—and she is wise enough not to work always at full stretch—is distinguished from those of her contemporaries by a singular purity of style. No writer today uses words with greater respect or deeper relish; none is more free of clichés. She comes to language freshly as if she had discovered it all by herself. And if the result of this discovery is a series of gay stories, fantasies light as air, comedies bubbling with fun, who is to say that she is misusing her rare powers? She feeds two of the child's most precious appetites, the hunger for laughter and the thirst for wonder. (p. 136)

[Miss Cresswell's] reputation is enhanced and transformed beyond measure by the three (soon to be four) major comic fantasies published by Faber. I call them fantasies because there is a larger-than-life quality in all of them, although the purely fantastic, that is the extension of the normal laws of nature, is an element in only two of them. *The Piemakers* and *The Signposters* are comedies of character and situation, triumphantly successful essays in a form which is almost the rarest in children's literature. *The Signposters* was published second, but bears all the signs of being written first, exploring just a little tentatively some of the themes developed fully in *The Piemakers.* Both books are kept on the ground by a pseudo-historical framework, so well contrived that at least one reader has been conned into acceptance of their historical authenticity. Both books explore in some depth the characters they present, but they are also, and perhaps primarily, as good novels must be, interpretations of society. In *The Signposters* it is the society of the road and of the great family of the Flockshire Smiths; in *The Piemakers* the society of Danby Dale. The books can be taken entirely seriously as contributions to the Novel for Children; thank goodness they can also be accepted as very good fun. The critical reader can surrender totally to the deep pleasure of writing so exquisitely right that it passes almost unnoticed, of ideas genuinely original and developed with satisfying logic, and of a truly comic view of life.

For me *The Piemakers* is Miss Cresswell's most delightful book, the one in which she blends most successfully her creative imagination and her acute observation. But Miss Cresswell is both an outstandingly successful writer and a young one. She is still experimenting, still developing. Some of the experiments, like *The Outlanders* . . . are disconcerting and may not please all her admirers, just as the brilliantly imagined and original *The Night-Watchmen*, with its mature explorations of character, distressed some. To these Miss Cresswell might reply, like an American film-actor, 'You ain't seen nuthin' yet!' This young writer who has already given us one of the best comic novels of the century, disconcertingly intelligent, restless, richly inventive, stands at a major cross-roads of her career. What comes next is anyone's guess. We may be assured that it will be brilliantly original and richly creative. (pp. 138-39)

> *Marcus Crouch, "Helen Cresswell—Craftsman," in* The Junior Bookshelf, *Vol. 34, No. 3, June, 1970, pp. 135-39.*

MARGARET GREAVES

Our golden age of children's literature is becoming a modern cliche: but there is a heavy vein of lead amid the gold. English Puritanism, driven out of the adult novel, is taking refuge in children's books under the name of realism. Many writers, as convinced as Mr Fairbrother that life is real and life is earnest, feel that it is their duty to help the young grow up and face it. Do not mistake me: one is grateful for literature in which the widest range of human feeling is opened to children. But looking along the junior library shelves at some of the most distinguished books of the last ten years or so, one sometimes feels a danger that the half truth of the toughness of experience can be as dangerous as the half truth of an eternal happy ever after. . . . [To] paint the shadows more than the sunlight is to present a view of life as falsely sentimental in its own way as the world of Little Lord Fauntleroy.

Not until I first met the work of Helen Cresswell did I realize that we are perhaps in some danger of dimming the sunlight too much. The joyful gratitude with which one recognized in her the essential quality of a normal happy childhood made one realize that this is a voice one has largely missed in recent years. Her approach is intuitive rather than intellectual. She is that rare person, the mature adult who still inhabits the world of childhood rather than merely remembering it. She writes not from recall or external observation but from immediate knowledge of a way of living that many have forgotten.

Helen Cresswell's books are largely concerned with three of the major experiences of childhood—the awareness of family, of miracle and of ceremony.

None of the books is 'family stories' in the librarian's sense; but (with one significant exception to which I will return) family is the very air the characters breathe. The comfort and dependability of its encircling relationships are established in the very first page. Molly Flower watches for the return of her father's boat; Harriet Garter awakes to the sounds of her parents getting up; Gravella is summoned at once to the family kitchen; Piers listens to his father's voice saluting the morning. The home relationship matters far more than the individuality of the parents. Indeed, all the older women are very much alike. Sometimes one would like them developed further; yet our view of them is after all one most natural to a child, who philosophically accepts the existence of adults without attempting to analyze character or motive. To a child a mother is often less a person than a quality or way of life. She is Jem of *The Piemakers* for whom cookery is the work of an artist; she is Fancy Garter, 'slamming the shutters back more to make sure everybody else woke up than for any other reason'; she is Hetty Signposter who 'treated each stopping place as if it were to be their home for ever'; tart of speech, warm of heart, houseproud, energetic, providing food and fire and commonsense while others provide dreams. Their virtues often exasperate, inconvenience or frustrate their families, as the necessary Marthas so often seem to jar upon the world of children and dreamers. . . . But secretly we admit that they are often right!

Fathers and uncles are more clearly distinguished; yet even

here after a lapse of time we remember them more by the visions they follow than by their own idiosyncracies. But they too are the incarnation of 'family', the closeness, the sense of belonging despite all disagreements, which *The Signposters* celebrates so splendidly. (pp. 51-2)

The children themselves are the storyteller's eyes. Because she sees and feels through them we have no need of specific definition or analysis. What we are most aware of in them is the sensitivity and subtlety of children towards adults. They are infinitely tolerant of the foibles of their parents, their uncles and aunts, though they see them with a sharply observant eye. (p. 53)

There is sometimes a touching delicacy in their understanding and respect for the unarmoured places in an adult's life. Piers, knowing his father's longing to be a Rhymer as all his family have been, keeps secret his own emerging power lest Tam should be saddened; and when the gift first comes to Tam Piers shelters its fragility.

> Piers, watching him, felt an emormous surge of pride. His father was a rhymer now, even though he did not know it. His dearest wish had been fulfilled, and he himself none the wiser.
>
> For a moment Piers was tempted to blurt out the lines himself and then confess the whole story, from beginning to end [of how he had already overheard his father's unconscious rhyming]. But he did not. Tam's rhyming was coming slowly, it was unfurling. And you could not tear a flower from a bud with your fingers. You had to wait for the sun.

Helen Cresswell has no need to get adults out of the children's way in chapter one. Adults and children are most richly themselves in relation to each other. 'Home' is so central that it is taken for granted. It consists of certain simple well defined experiences—people, objects, sounds—'familiar morning noises, the rattle of the latch, the working of the old iron pump, the clatter of pots and pans'. It is so complete a part of 'family' that it can be moved entire whenever its members move. People pack up their goods, abandon their houses, return to them again, with an easy nonchalance which is perfectly logical to children. After all a good many adult activities come upon children so suddenly that they must seem wholly unpredictable.

Perhaps this unpredictability encourages the second quality that one finds so strongly in Helen Cresswell's work—the sense of imminent miracle. Anything can happen, and does. It is both enormously exciting and perfectly natural. She still shares with children that freshness of vision which makes all things possible. The physical world itself promises wonders; magic fulfils it rather than confutes it. (pp. 54-5)

A child's very inexperience of limits and boundaries makes magic wholly natural. There is no essential contradiction between the 'curtained windows and sodium lights' of Henry's home and the 'There' of Josh and Caleb. But Henry himself hardly knows where one ends and the other begins. This same sense of the novelty and oddness of the world creates the vein of gloriously exaggerated comedy. It is the eternal children's joke of the little spunky wren in the ballad, that needed a horse and cart to drag it. All the zestful things are even larger than life in these books; the huge pie of the Danby Rollers and Dyke's vast family party are only more overt celebrations of the same delight. This is a world in which you can't have too much of a good thing. Helen Cresswell's language, with

its vivid sensory experience of the ordinary, is a part of this enormous vitality. There is no striving for literary effect, but the words have the crisp satisfying quality of crusty new bread. They keep us wakeful and alive like 'the day-long flapping of the wind about the ears' of Emily and Piers. The images come as in poetry 'as easily as leaves to the tree'. (p. 55)

A child's world, pivoting between the safe, ordered structure of familiar things and the continuous expectation of possible miracle, has—by its very nature a sense of ceremony—the marriage of custom with festival. Helen Cresswell's feasts and gatherings and journeys are 'solempne' in the true medieval sense, combining dignity, decorum, joyfulness and comedy. Physical experiences are so whole and satisfying, times and seasons so orderly and characteristic in their progression, that they take on an almost sacramental quality—a recognition of the essential goodness of such things. There is a sense of occasion in Uncle Pen's welcome to the Signposters just as much as in the opening of the great pie before the king. The year turns, the seasons pass, with the same processional decorum. (pp. 55-6)

She convinces us of the rightness of things, just as we are convinced of another profound and almost primitive magic—the rightness of names. To know the name of one of her characters is to know something quite essential about the person—Fancy Garter, Josh and Caleb, Uncle Crispin, Dyke, Ponder, Clemary. The loss of such names as these would be the diminishing of personality itself.

But if this were all, this splendid celebration of family and miracle and ceremony (and how grudging to say of such riches 'if this were all'!) Helen Cresswell's books might be thought merely escapist. (Again why should one say 'merely'?) But the other side of reality is there too, fully recognized—the greed of those who would imprison the little sea horse to bring them luck, the treachery of Uncle Crispin in *The Piemakers,* Kit's estrangement from his family in *The Signposters.* These are hints, reminders of the cold wind through the cracks of the house door. The two latest books have been a much fuller exploration of these things.

The Night Watchmen is unusual among Helen Cresswell's books in that Henry's adventures occur in a world outside the limits of home and family. Looked at in one way, home is a refuge from fear and danger; looked at in another, it is a prison that bars us from freedom and adventure. We are made to realize this double vision in the very first moment of Henry's meeting with Josh. 'Wild, wicked and impossible he loomed among the clipped, self-respecting laurels.'

There is much of the tramp in nearly every reader as there is in Henry too—'natural, born, do-as-you-pleasers', as Josh calls them. The night watchmen are so exciting, so provocative, that home becomes a mere impediment to freedom.

> Already his acquaintance with Josh and Caleb was having a very strange effect on his perspectives. His home, for instance, simply did not seem like home any more. In the space of two days it had become merely a place where he unfortunately had to put in an appearance from time to time in between visits to the place where he felt he *really* belonged— with Josh and Caleb.

But from the very beginning Henry's feelings towards them are ambivalent. 'He was not yet certain that he approved of them himself.' They are potentially dangerous. Caleb, 'small and neat as a weasel, lard-faced and slippery-looking', is hostile and suspicious. The weasel image occurs more than once. Yet the life of go as you please arouses the passionate yearning of those who see its poetry and the jealous resentment of the Green Eyes who envy it without the capacity to enjoy it. Henry is on the side of the dreamers and will be richer for it all his life. But dreams may carry us, like the Ancient Mariner, into unchartered seas beyond the world of men. If the human voices fade too far, the dream may become nightmare. Henry longs for the mysterious night train. But the very moment that he boards it becomes the moment of decision against it. He belongs Here, not There. The train sets him down before it thunders on into the dark. But it will never be forgotten. Henry, as much as Piers, will know for the rest of his life that the familiar exists on the very verge of miracle.

The Night Watchmen challenges the apparent safety of existence, and gives conditional release to the lawlessness deep within each of us. Push aside the 'clipped, self-respecting laurels' and you find the mysterious and rather frightening barrows of the tramps. Home is not the whole centre of the world; wind and darkness can be felt through the cracks in the door. But in *The Outlanders* the cold wind blows the door wide open. Piers knows from the beginning about the There that lies beyond Here. (pp. 56-7)

The comfortable town of Bray, where 'you can't go opening doors and letting fairies in' is warm and happy and sheltered. But its comfort is selfish and timid; at times we glimpse it, like Olemary herself, 'shrunk like a nut in a kernel, with walls all about'.

At the first touch of magic the folk of Bray are outraged; they meet it with fear and anger and torches. Anything beyond their experience must be undesirable as well as alarming. Even Sary is astonished when she first sees that the Midlanders live not in fog and bleakness but in a spring even brighter than their own. (pp. 57-8)

But beyond the Mid-lands lie the Outlands. Each has his own secret and unspoken vision of their fearful possibilities. Piers' dreams are haunted by wolves. He thinks of them as a threat from without, lurking beyond the bright ring of fire made by companionship and home. Only at the unexpected, unrecognized moment of testing does he find the enemy to be within, encountering his own cowardice and self-desertion, 'left cold and shamed, faced by his own worst fears come true'. In the sheltering circle he can neither escape nor forget it. Only in the cold grey bleakness of the Outlands can he meet his own wolf face to face, acknowledge it and tame it. Here and There must both be experienced, to make existence whole. The wolves will always prowl like the cold wind at the corner of the street; but human warmth and caring and courage prove stronger than the dark. Helen Cresswell is still a young writer. It is already a long step from *The White Sea Horse,* charming though this is, to the subtlety and excitement, the potential menace, of *The Night Watchmen* and *The Outlanders.* One looks for more complex and exciting things to come. Meanwhile we may be thankful for so joyful a writer to correct our perspectives when we have read too many sagas of the toughness of the world. (pp. 58-9)

Margaret Greaves, "Warm Sun, Cold Wind: The Novels of Helen Cresswell," in Children's literature in education, *No. 5, July, 1971, pp. 51-9.*

JOHN ROWE TOWNSEND

Helen Cresswell is a young and prolific writer who, beginning in 1960, produced at least twenty books in her first ten years as a published author. There is nothing wrong with being prolific. Some writers are, some are not. Probably there is no relationship, either direct or inverse, between productivity and literary merit. But there seems to be a limit to the number of books of distinction that one person can write over a given period; and prolific authors generally turn out a proportion of secondary work. Miss Cresswell has written several books that are slight, and some that are inferior. But her best is very good, and her slighter books have often shown true quality.

There are two main strands in her work: poetic fantasy and humour. The gift for fantasy was there from the beginning, but has strengthened and deepened in later books. The humour, often hackneyed and obvious at first, has developed even more strikingly into the comic richness which accompanied the fantasy of *The Piemakers* and *The Night-Watchmen.*

Where fantasy and humour lay side by side in an early book, the fantasy was clearly of a different quality from the humour. The difference can be seen in *The White Sea Horse:* the story of the small, magical horse that Molly's fisherman father found in his nets. . . . [The] book is marred by the crudity of its comic element, involving the stock figure of the pompous Mayor, Mr Winkle. . . . Mr Winkle could come from any of a thousand third-rate stories. He is not in the same imaginative world as the improbable tramp Josh, with the wild grey tufts of eyebrows and the voice 'rich and with built-in echoes as if it were in church', who suddenly appears in *The Night-Watchmen* five years later:

> Sun struck the dew that glinted on his hair and beard. Wild, wicked and impossible he loomed among the clipped, self-respecting laurels.

Stock figures on the level of Mr Winkle also populate the 'Jumbo' books, of which the first, *Jumbo Spencer,* was published in 1963, and which were the main channel for Helen Cresswell's humour at that time. These were strongly reminiscent of Richmal Crompton's 'William' books. Jumbo, like William, is a small boy who is the unquestioned leader of his gang of four, imaginative in a naive way, forever organizing clubs and exhibitions and absurdly ambitious projects. Unlike William, Jumbo also impresses the adult population with his abilities, and can call meetings which the whole of his village attends. He is successful on a big scale, starring in TV programmes, putting the village on the map, establishing legends, starting a dig that leads to real Anglo-Saxon treasures, getting a village hall built. He represents the wildest wish-fulfilment of the small boy as a member of his society. I find him, like William, engaging; but I would never have expected the creator of Jumbo to be also the creator of *The Piemakers.*

This was the book with which Miss Cresswell came into her own. It has all the qualities which should enable a children's book to last. The story it tells is memorable, funny, and unlike any other; it is dateless—being set in the past indefinite of rural England—and it has an equal appeal to child and adult, so that grown-ups can remember it with pleasure and share it with their own children and the child within. For adults there is the bonus of seeing more than the child can be expected to do: the accuracy of the family relationships, the mock-heroic nature of the whole story.

It is about the Rollers of Danby Dale—Arthy, Jem and Gravella—and the enormous pie they bake when the King, 'being desirous of supping on a pie of the Dales', offers a prize of 100 guineas and the honour of royal appointment to 'the Piemaker of the Dales who shall by the third day of June make a pie the biggest and best by common consent'. Backed by the people of Danby Dale, Arthy bakes a pie for two thousand: the biggest pie in the history of the world, involving strict security precautions and the manufacture by the blacksmith at Wedbury of a pie-dish so huge that it has to be floated down the river like a boat.

A pie of epic grandeur is a comic paradox in itself, and the author has developed it to the utmost. . . . [The] crew which brought the pie-dish down the river stood watching it 'as it lay rocking gently at its moorings. The reddish gleam of the setting sun lit the polished metal to splendour, and Gravella thought there could never have been a more noble vessel.' And finally there is Arthy's triumph:

> Delicately the King's eyebrows arched and the doors of the barn opened slowly on great groaning hinges. There was sudden silence. Out from the shadows came the huge pie-dish, wheeled by twenty men with straining shoulders. The sun fell for the first time on to that glorious crust, perfectly smooth and brown, gleaming faintly. It was impossible, a miracle under that blue sky, standing among the grass and clover like some enormous fruit . . . For a full minute the pie stood there and more than three thousand people stood and stared in silence, made into statues by their disbelief. Then the roar that broke out sent the skylarks somersaulting skyward and the din broke in deafening fragments and Arthy was borne up into the air and shouldered to the King.

In this moment of wide-eyed wonder, humour and fantasy blend. The piemakers' achievement is absurd but it is marvellous; and the author is perfectly, properly, almost poetically serious about it.

Among the ingredients of *The Piemakers* is nostalgia: a gentle, pleasing nostalgia for an innocent age of rural craftsmanship that probably never was. This nostalgia has increased in subsequent fantasies, and along with it has gone a preoccupation with the figure of the wandering artist whose freedom is threatened by an unsympathetic society. Only occasionally has there been the same sense of sheer delight. One hesitates to suggest, on slight evidence over a fairly short period, that it is a case of cause and effect, but it is possible to feel that the author has indulged her nostalgia too much and allowed this particular preoccupation to go too far. Certainly the three major books which up to the time of writing have followed *The Piemakers* have been less successful.

The Signposters is set in an England small and white and clean, an England of blue remembered hills, an England suspiciously close to being Merrie. Dyke Signposter's job of pacing out distances and painting signs allows him to be both artist and wanderer; his wife Hetty and daughter Barley go with him in the wagon drawn by the dawdling horse Cornish from Whipple to Plumtree, Plumtree to Makewith, Makewith to Haze. Complications arising from Dyke's ambition to bring about a great family reunion fill the long summer days of the story. The book is unfortunately placed in Helen Cresswell's work. Coming before *The Piemakers* it would have seemed to lead up to it; coming afterwards it is a slight disappointment, because it does a similar thing, and does it, though pleasantly enough, without quite the same joyous humour. *The Piemakers* is indeed the kind of book that an author cannot fruitfully aim to repeat, because it goes right to the end

of its line; after it, the way ahead must be to do something different.

The Signposters and its successors *The Night-Watchmen* and *The Outlanders* seem increasingly to be expressing an attitude to life: a belief that spontaneity, individualism, creative artistry or craftsmanship, a readiness to move on and to take what life offers are virtues to be prized; rigidity and stuffiness are sins against the human spirit. The one unlikeable character in *The Signposters* is Uncle Wick, the candlemaker, whose candles were every one the same, except that some were short and fat and dull and others were long and thin and dull'; and even Uncle Wick comes good in the end and starts making his candles curled and coloured and all different.

The Night-Watchmen has a darker streak. Two tramps Josh and Caleb, who are comic eccentrics but are also artist-wanderers—for Josh is a would-be writer and Caleb an imaginative cook—are driven by the jealous Greeneyes from their camp beside a hole in the road; and it appears that this is continually happening to them. Is, then, the freedom of the artist a fugitive thing: is he always to be the victim of jealous pursuit? The author has said that she did not know the Greeneyes were going to move in, and that she would have put up a fight against them if she had realized what a misery they were going to be. She has also said that 'you don't choose symbols—they choose you'. *The Night-Watchmen* is something of a mystery, for the story is told from over the shoulder of a boy who is convalescing from illness, and at the end he is not sure whether Josh and Caleb and the Greeneyes ever existed; but whether it all 'really' happened or whether it is an externalization of something in the boy's mind does not greatly affect the issue. The implications are pessimistic; art and imagination are defeated.

In *The Outlanders* we are back in the indefinite past; the theme is the traditional one of the Quest. The Rhymers—a family threesome like the Piemakers and the Signposters—set out from the lumpish town of Bray in search of a Boy of unearthly radiance who has briefly stayed with them and who, they know, can grant their dearest wish. This quest is successful; *The Outlanders* is a more positive, a more hopeful book than *The Night-Watchmen.* But *The Night-Watchmen* seems to me more interesting; it seeks to combine comedy and fantasy in a way quite different from that of *The Piemakers.* The two tramps are rich, larger-than-life characters, encountered in what at least appears to be the here-and-now; the Greeneyes are a menacing intrusion from a fantasy world which is elsewhere. Comedy shot through with dark fantasy: I cannot readily think of anything *like* this in children's literature. Yet the book cannot be called satisfactory; too much is vague or flimsy or unresolved; one feels that the author has not grappled hard enough with her material. *The Outlanders* has an occasional dreamlike beauty of its own, but to my mind lacks substance; the blood is drained out of it by a numinous mysticism and a feeling that the whole story is allegorical and nothing is really happening at all.

It is difficult to say where Helen Cresswell is going at present. Her progress has been hit-and-miss; her best book, *The Piemakers,* came almost unpredictably out of the blue. She is clearly capable of doing something just as unpredictable and successful at any time. Possibly the prolific writer is in greater need of self-discipline than others whose progress is more painful, and occasionally I suspect that Miss Cresswell's facility has been her undoing and she has been satisfied too easily with her work. But she is a young writer with a strong creative flow who can afford to make a few false moves. These are early days in her career. Her development will be clearer in five or ten years' time; and it may well be impressive. (pp. 57-63)

John Rowe Townsend, "Helen Cresswell," in his A Sense of Story: Essays on Contemporary Writers for Children, J. B. Lippincott Company, 1971, pp. 57-67.

DAVID BENNETT

Helen Cresswell creates stories from what surrounds her. 'Everything that I collect is a symbol of something in my interior world . . . Everything is to reinforce and help me keep a grip on things.' Conversation is frequently punctuated by a sudden ferret through a drawer to produce a photo that inspired; Lewis Bear, hero of a forthcoming set of picture books, sits on a chair not far from the Polly Flint doll, and books that are from both Helen's childhood and her mother's are drawn from the shelves to verify a reference or show an early childhood manuscript.

The house, its contents and people are only part of the inspiration. Helen's timeless rural fantasies, like *The Piemaker, The Signposters, The Bongleweed,* are set in the landscapes where Helen walks [her dog] Boz near her home; *The Secret World of Polly Flint* lies in nearby Rufford Country Park. Here also she finds echoes which spark her imagination. Helen Cresswell is very receptive to these echoes and to the coincidences that seem to over-run her life. (p. 12)

The recent writing of *Moondial,* a ghostly fantasy centred on another real location, Belton House near Newark, has had its elements of slightly more than mere coincidence. A photograph of the gnarled, sculptured Belton House sundial which started the story in motion sits on Helen's desk for inspiration. Putting it into a story seems at times to have had almost the quality of a psychic experience.

Like *Polly Flint,* and *Lizzie Dripping* ten years ago, *Moondial* was a double task; the TV version and the novel were written more or less simultaneously. But the *Moondial* project is a source of pride since Helen set up the whole thing herself. She hopes that it will be filmed at the exact location and do for Belton House what *Polly Flint* has done for Rufford Country Park, where a 'Polly Flint Tour' seems to have been instituted by local schools. (pp. 12-13)

Visiting schools and taking part in the 'Polly Flint Tours' delight Helen. She tries hard not to say no to school visits—'If you didn't do it you'd lose all touch with reality . . . When you go into a school it reminds you that that's where the world is.' Her mission is to encourage the children to appreciate their gift of imagination; boring adults get like that when their imaginations dry up. 'Imagination' is one of Helen's oft-used words. She says of her work that she is 'trying to pass on to children a dimension that I feel is there; I'm partly doing it for myself because it's real to me . . . the world of Polly Flint is more real than what's going on in Nottingham at this moment . . . it's the truth of the imagination. To me that's what really counts. The rest of it doesn't matter very much . . . The only way to involve children is through the imagination.' . . .

Helen is emphatic that she doesn't have any specific children in mind when she writes. However, like many writers for children, she has a strong remembrance of her own childhood, and in her published work she can point in retrospect to as-

pects of stories, plays and poems she wrote as a child and which are readily to hand. She identifies strongly with children, diagnosing herself as a case of arrested development—'I just think I've got a childish streak in me. I adore writing books like *Polly Flint* and *The Piemakers.* I love it. I absolutely live them . . . When I'm writing those books I am completely lost in them and that is my world and I actually prefer it to my daily life.'

One of her stories, something of a 'maverick' book in what Helen was once amused to overhear described as 'The Cresswell Canon' has produced a flood of moving letters from children. **Dear Shrink,** the story of three children thrown most unexpectedly into foster care, was a painful one for Helen to write and owes some of its origins to the experience of fostering a young girl one summer many years ago. But as a child Helen too suffered a similar experience—the kitchen reeking of rotting vegetables and ironing, where a mangy budgie moped, was once her lot.

The pain for the characters themselves is all the more emphasised by the suddenness of their predicament and the difficulty for three middle-class children of coming to terms with a drastic change of environment and values. Helen contends that this isn't a book that she intended for a teenage audience; for her it is just a book like her others, for real kids who 'still have a schoolbag stuffed with felt-tip pens, usually fluorescent colours with the lids off, and who still half believe in werewolves.'

'Time' is another of Helen's words. She writes with sepia brown ink on cream paper which 'has a timeless feel'. She confesses the ability to breathe the kiss of death into watches, which is a standing joke amongst her friends. She's convinced that watches know that she doesn't really believe in them. She has twenty or so that 'go sometimes and not others' and seldom bothers to wind the two clocks in the house, which she bought only for their aesthetic qualities anyway. She firmly contends that she'll become an eccentric old lady like Aunt Lucy in the Bagthorpes, who disregards time utterly. As a child she never had any sense of there being a future—'I never ever saw myself as an adult. I foresaw no future for myself whatsoever'—and supposes that her love of de la Mare's poetry is because he too seems to expound that 'what we know as linear time is really not very relevant'. *Moondial* measures Moontime, 'which is the *real* time of hearts and lives.'

She was made very conscious of this timeless quality in her fantasies, during the filming of *Polly Flint,* when the costume department couldn't find a period in the text from which to work. . . .

On the walls at [her home] Old Church Farm hang paintings, bought over several years. Since writing *Polly Flint* Helen Cresswell has realised that in one way or another they all contain arches, semi-circular shapes, bending trees within which the space recedes to invisible depths. For the time tunnel in *Polly Flint* she chose the arch of the bridge on Rufford Lake but subconsciously it seems she had been collecting time tunnels for a long time.

Their echoes have entered the books of a writer who believes firmly that 'a children's book isn't a watered-down adult book. It's generically different.' A difference which can make children call 'Hello, Aunt Em' to the owner of the cottage in Wellow with the tiny eaves window which they *know* is Polly Flint's. The same children who put their ears to the grass and 'definitely' hear the bells of Grimstone, timeless sounds from a story that has penetrated deep into their imaginations. So powerfully does the Cresswell magic work that one seven-year-old 'heard children counting down below'. Polly Flint's world had become a part of her own experience; she had been transported through the time tunnel, out of the web of time. Which is just as Helen Cresswell would have it. (p. 13)

> *David Bennett, "Authorgraph No. 42: Helen Cresswell," in* Books for Keeps, *No. 42, January, 1987, pp. 12-13.*

JUMBO SPENCER (1963)

Jumbo Spencer . . . [is] brimful of ideas and crackling with energy. This is really a farce—an action story of great pace with a setting and characters just a little larger than life; but at bottom here are real boys . . . , busy with their own plans, with a delirious sense of their own importance and a superb disregard for orthodox behaviour. To fulfil his ambition to be a leader of men, Jumbo resolves to reform the village, and unfolds to his admiring friends a plan to earn money for a swimming pool and club house. True, rich Mr. Bennet is to be asked for a large proportion of the necessary funds, but Jumbo sets no limit to what he can earn by himself in his Village Festival, and nobody, certainly no young reader, will be surprised to see him end on the television screen. Pace and a light hand with humour make this a splendid tale.

> *Margery Fisher, in a review of "Jumbo Spencer," in* Growing Point, *Vol. 2, No. 6, December, 1963, p. 245.*

Jumbo is a boy who resolves to spend his vacation as a great reformer and leader of men and announces to his gang they are going to improve their village single handed. Some reviewers have been amused by the schemes, devices, and plans that beautify the town, change the traffic lanes, and build a recreation center. However, the humor completely misfires with me. The boy is thoroughly obnoxious and I'm sure in a red-blooded American town would have received his proper come-uppance. This is a very disappointing book from the author of *The White Sea Horse.*

> *Anne Izard, in a review of "Jumbo Spencer," in* School Library Journal, *Vol. 13, February, 1967, p. 63.*

THE WHITE SEA HORSE (1964)

It's a slight, delicate, feminine fantasy about a sea horse caught in a fisherman's net—an eohippus-sized horse, pure white with yellow eyes and golden hooves. The daughter of the fisherman tends it, but soon the villagers learn about it and the mayor demands that the horse be caged as a gift for the King and Queen. Then the donkeys run into the sea, the villagers regret that they had imprisoned the horse, and let it free. The story is frail, and rather contrived, but an aura of mysticism has been achieved and some of the descriptions will please the quiet reader.

> *A review of "The White Sea Horse," in* Virginia Kirkus' Service, *Vol. XXIII, No. 17, September 1, 1965, p. 904.*

Whimsey is extravagantly thick in this tale about a miniature horse's spell over a quaint fishing village. . . .

The mood is romantic, the imagery graceful, but this modest fantasy wearies rather than enchants. Capricious and contrived events happen at the convenience of the storytelling and a magical horse that remains so docile and physically powerless in a cage is hardly credible.

> *Margaret F. O'Connell, in a review of "The White Sea Horse," in* The New York Times Book Review, *January 2, 1966, p. 18.*

THE PIEMAKERS (1967)

Helen Cresswell has found the perfect medium for the kind of humour which lifted Jumbo Spencer sometimes a little far off the ground in her stories about him. In fantasy, a touch of eccentricity is quite in order, and *The Piemakers* is very good fantasy. Arthy and Jem and their daughter Gravella are not 'real' people any more than the Danby Chronicles are real history (though as I read they seemed a good deal more so than some of the negative folk of my acquaintance). Violet Drummond, in her illustrations, helps to give them the special rustic solidity of Simple Simon or Miss Muffet. In fact the whole book has the neat, inconsequent humour of nursery rhyme. There is the King who rides in, 'neck arched, red comb of hair flaming', to taste the pies in the famous contest; there is the King's Recipe and the mystery of the extra pepper; there is the tremendous secret of the gigantic pie-dish (two-thousand-size), secretly made because of Uncle Crispin's rivalry and floated downstream disguised as a barge. Everywhere there is the circumstantial detail and the releasing humour of nursery-rhyme. (pp. 882-83)

This book is clean and crisp as a pie-crust and it has the power—again, a nursery-rhyme power—to embrace within comic fantasy an evanescent, elusive beauty of mood and scene. There can be few children who will not be captivated by the adventures of the Piemakers. (p. 883)

> *Margery Fisher, in a review of "The Piemakers," in* Growing Point, *Vol. 5, No. 9, April, 1967, pp. 882-83.*

Here is treasure. Helen Cresswell's story of the piemakers of Danby Dale is extremely funny—a rare enough quality in a book for children—and equally serious. It has the kind of authenticity which distinguishes Mary Norton's work, and a similar unobtrusively perfect style. These may seem large claims for a little book, but creative writing of this quality must be judged by the very highest standards, and by these *The Piemakers* is triumphantly successful. . . .

This book sets a testing standard for 1967. With three-quarters of the year still to go, it seems safe to bet that this will be among the year's best. Brilliantly original in conception, flawless in development, keeping the balance between character and caricature in its portraits, fusing all its qualities into one deeply pleasing whole, this is one of those rare books which makes an immediate impression and confirms it with each re-reading.

> *A review of "The Piemakers," in* The Junior Bookshelf, *Vol. 31, No. 2, April, 1967, p. 111.*

[There] is a special pleasure in the unexpected, in the discovery of a brand-new talent or the full flowering of an ascending writer. So it is with *The Piemakers.* Helen Cresswell has in a few years established herself quietly as a sensitive and imaginative writer. Even those who were most impressed with her 'prentice work could scarcely have expected her to achieve so quickly the maturity of this remarkable book.

In even the most prolific of writers there is latent one special book, a book which derives not from thought and patience and careful research—though all these come into it—but from the writer's heart's-blood. Often the book never gets written; somehow in a long lifetime the right button is never pressed. But if, by chance or circumstance or flash of light, the book comes into being, it is a book better than the author's best. Such a book is *The Piemakers.*

So portentous an introduction may seem, not least to Miss Cresswell, a heavy sledgehammer to crack so small and appetizing a nut. *The Piemakers* is a little book. It is also gay and sparkling. It is nevertheless so singularly flawless and so firmly based in truth that it commands critical approbation. It is a funny book. It is also, in the literal as well as the colloquial sense, a good book.

We are in Danby Dale, home of the master-piemakers. The Rollers of Danby Dale have made pies for generations beyond numbering, and Arthy currently holds the key to the mystery. There are Rollers too in Gorby Dale, and when Arthy receives a commission to make a pie quite literally fit for the King family loyalty outweighs discretion and he involves Uncle Crispin in the operation. Crispin is not a nice man. "As he walked his head always seemed to be several paces ahead of his legs." Just the man, in fact, to sabotage the Royal pie, and so he does. Arthy saves the family reputation only by burning the pie and the bakehouse in a disastrous and calculated accident. A second chance comes, and Arthy redeems the honour of the Rollers and of Danby Dale with a pie of stupendous magnificence.

Arthy is the dedicated craftsman, a man humbly aware that he was born to make pies. It is a clever device of the author's to show him through the eyes of a reluctant piemaker. The chorus of this high drama is played by Arthy's daughter Gravella. (When most disgusted with her name she finds comfort in her sex; had she been a boy she would have been christened Gravy.) Gravella has aspirations towards the stage and wants to hate pies, but her Roller blood will out. "Whenever another pie was on the go she could hear her own heart treacherously thudding." The splendour of Arthy's achievements seem all the more splendid when he wins his daughter's unwilling praise. . . . The Rollers discussing the technique of piemaking remind one of Pod and Homily talking about the finer points of Borrowing. There is the same practical approach touched with reverence. This is only one of the ways in which Miss Cresswell's writing resembles Mrs. Norton's. Not that it is in any way derivative. Both writers draw on a common fount of the framework of their inventions as if they were masters of the Dutch school. These are, one feels, not happily fantastic imaginings but studies from the life. Above all, both command a deceptively simple prose inspiration. Both treat an essentially comic (or impossible) idea with complete seriousness. Both are consistent in the use of detail, filling in style, writing with that perfection which is so good as to pass unnoticed.

One ventures at one's peril to make such comparisons between an established and unassailable master and a young newcomer, but the risk is worth taking. There is a warmth,

a richness of humour, an inner truthfulness in *The Piemakers* which puts this apparently slight tale in the select company of books which make nonsense credible, which make the reader laugh and cry and glow warm with delight in a job exceedingly well done. If Helen Cresswell is to be judged, it must be by her peers, by Mary Norton, Eleanor Estes and a very few others who, like her, speak the authentic language of childhood.

"Piemakers of Danby Dale," in The Times Literary Supplement, *No. 3404, May 25, 1967, p. 445.*

THE SIGNPOSTERS (1968)

[Helen Cresswell's] last book, the delicious *Piemakers,* was runner-up for the Library Association's accolade, the Carnegie Medal, and the *Times Literary Supplement* spoke of 'a major talent in the making'. Unfortunately *The Signposters,* although definitely in the same territory, is not in the same class. Perhaps painting signs is just not as inspiring an occupation as making pies. Certainly Dyke, Hetty and Barley don't care about signs in the way the Rollers of Danby Dale cared about pies. If your child has not yet discovered *The Piemakers,* that is the one to go for. The new book lacks the splendid simplicity of plot and obsession that marked the other. (p. 696)

Ann Thwaite, "Baiting the Hook," in New Statesman, *Vol. 75, No. 1941, May 24, 1968, pp. 695-96.*

Those who enjoyed *The Piemakers* (and is there anyone who didn't?) will find themselves on familiar territory in Helen Cresswell's new book. *The Signposters* is set in the same mould as its predecessor—humorous fantasy in an idealized rural never-never land—but it marks, in many ways, a step forward for this writer. The story and the writing are less broadly comic, but humour is still there, combined now with more subtle characterization and a skilful evocation of landscape.

We are familiar with the Danby Rollers and the saga of the Great Pie of Danby Dale. The obsession of Dyke Signposter is less grandiose, perhaps, but its realization presents as many hazards and meets as much opposition as did Arthy Roller's pie. Dyke had always been obsessed by his family, and his position as official Flockshire signpost-painter and distance-pacer made him a natural link between its many scattered members. *The Signposters* tells of his plan for a Grand Reunion of all the Flockshire Smiths and how this extraordinary event was accomplished with the aid of his wife, Hetty, and daughter, Barley. There is much humour in the telling, and a great deal of beauty, too; but Flockshire itself and its crisply delineated inhabitants are the triumphs of this book. The author has given us a masterly, nostalgic evocation of an undefined rural England and painted in sparkling prose its atmosphere and moods. Its people are all the idealized inhabitants of a bucolic wonderland. *The Signposters* is a haunting and captivating book; essential reading for children of nine and over.

L. E. Salway, in a review of "The Signposters," in Children's Book News, *London, Vol. 3, No. 3, May-June, 1968, p. 143.*

THE BARGE CHILDREN (1968)

It is not often that one hears of men from the Education Department having to round up children who are getting no schooling in these days. Helen Cresswell, in this story, has such a man who insists that Betsy and Bill should leave the barge on which they have lived all their lives and go to school. He does not even suggest the special barge school which exists for this sort of child, and for some reason, which is not clear, neither do the parents. The children stay with their Aunt Meg and go to a day school returning to the barge at weekends. The author seems to have her focus somewhat blurred being unable to decide whether she is dealing with the adjustment of barge children to life ashore, or whether she is writing about the life of such children on board. As it is the book is cut in half when the change takes place and from being an interesting story, full of fascinating background detail, becomes an ordinary, rather dull, school story.

> *A review of "The Barge Children," in* The Junior Bookshelf, *Vol. 32, No. 5, October, 1968, p. 295.*

Helen Cresswell is a very versatile writer. This present novel is more in the mould of stories for the six-plus who have just started to read. . . . I suppose if this is the first book a child has read it will all be new to him. My complaint is that it is a 'pot boiler', a competent one at that. Nevertheless if the author put her mind to it she could produce something of a much higher standard. Only the very best should be offered to these young readers.

> *Joan Murphy, in a review of "The Barge Children," in* The School Librarian and School Library Review, *Vol. 16, No. 3, December, 1968, p. 376.*

THE NIGHT-WATCHMEN (1969)

Unlike many of the talents which burst prematurely into flower, Helen Cresswell shows no signs of settling down into a sturdy and reliable mediocrity. Her major work—she writes also a great many slighter books distinguished from others of their kind by sound craftsmanship and an individual turn of phrase—refuses to conform to any of the recognized types of children's literature. *The Piemakers* has been called a fantasy, but while this enchanting tale strains credulity in the pleasantest fashion there is nothing in it which breaches the ordinary laws of nature; Arthy's magic is that of the inspired artist, albeit working in pie-crust instead of paint, not that of the warlock. In the open-air sunshine and showers of *The Signposters* there is not the least hint of unearthliness. Miss Cresswell is indeed no fantasist but that rarest of children's writers, a master of high comedy. As in the best comedy, too, there is in these books a hint of sadness and a vein of genuine poetry.

After a pause—for *The Signposters* represented not so much an advance as a variation on *The Piemakers*—Miss Cresswell now takes a commanding stride forward with *The Night-watchmen.* Not for the first time this year the reader is reminded that literature does not submit to classification into neat, mutually exclusive parcels or to the arbitrary tyranny of "age-groups". This hilarious, disturbing, sometimes frightening excursion to the borderline of reality is no more "for children" than the bitter irony of *Gulliver* is for adults; both are for people, people who are found worthy of them.

The Night-watchmen starts quietly enough. Not now the timelessness and the almost-never land of Danby Dale and Flockshire. We are firmly in the present and in Mandover, an English provincial town . . . which affords only the commonplaces of park and canal and crowded streets. Here lives Henry, impatiently convalescent after a bout of illness in which he had wrestled with "dragons with fiery tongues". Even the holidays which his sickness has won pall, the weeks stretching "empty and grey as the asphalt pavement". This is before he meets Josh and Caleb. These are the night-watchmen, tramps who shelter from inquisitive public and constantly-moving-on policemen behind a "Danger-Men-at-Work" sign. A hole in the ground—and Josh and Caleb are connoisseurs of holes—is their camouflage and their home, a home moreover where they live in style on chicken and mushrooms cooked with a touch of genius. For Caleb is Miss Cresswell's favourite being, an artist. "Takes his cooking to heart, Caleb does", says Josh. "He really threw himself into that stew."

Josh and Caleb are night-watchmen—among other things. The exploration of those "other things" takes Henry into enchanted country, in which he sees his shabby home town through the eyes of Josh, who is the author of an interminable book about places—interminable because "places is one thing you can never run out of". He accepts too the "do-as-you-please" philosophy of the tramps, and shares with them the pleasures of ticking—"sniffing at a place, getting the scent of it"—and the terror of *them,* the furtive green-eyed men who drive the night-watchmen to abandon their hole and take the night-train. And when they have gone, thundering through the dark with Caleb driving the train with his artists' hands, "as if he were playing an organ", Henry is left behind among the streets and the houses of Mandover. What he has gained from the wild and crazy and beautiful adventure is heightened sensitivity. He will never take a tree or a tramp or a lemon-meringue pie for granted again.

The Night-watchmen treads delicately on the brink of wonderland, yet it is planted in reality, in a close and affectionate observation of the ordinariness of back streets and holes in the ground and of the extraordinariness of human beings. Opinions may vary about the success of Miss Cresswell's fantasy; the green-eyed men are not quite as terrifying as they need to be. Of the richness of her central creation, as funny as it is beautiful, there can be no question. This is original invention, matched with an exquisite rightness of phrase. The scale is smaller than in her other books—there are only three considerable characters to set against the Flockshire Smiths and the pie-making Rollers of Danby—but in her ear for dialogue, her feeling for place, and her delight in the craft of living, Miss Cresswell is here the unquestionable master of her fine and characteristic art. *The Night-watchmen* adds inches to her already dominant height.

> *"Danger—Men at Work," in* The Times Literary Supplement, *No. 3513, June 26, 1969, p. 687.*

This strange and lovely book concerns two tramps who drift into an English village and are befriended by a child named Henry. As one might expect, the boy is attracted to the vagrants and yearns to share their life. Here, however, all resemblance to other stories in this subgenre fades—for Josh and Caleb are untraditional hobos. Meticulously organized, they investigate the town, create a bogus excavation, pose as night watchmen guarding it, and set up light housekeeping.

Their dialogue is complicated and romantic; a dark past is hinted at, escapes, enemies, journeys.

Eventually, Josh turns out to be a writer composing a book about places—and, while this alleviates Henry's curiosity to some degree, a greater mystery remains. Running through the tramps' conversation like a leitmotif is the "night train": a gorgeous, imaginary vehicle that speeds them from town to town and symbolizes their utter freedom in a world of conformity. We are rather stunned, at the end of the book, to discover that this train—as well as the tramps' enemies—is real. Indeed, as it thunders away, carrying Josh and Caleb into the future, the adult reader suddenly feels like a child. Something beautiful and brief has happened that will not come again.

> *Barbara Wersba, in a review of "The Night-Watchmen," in* The New York Times Book Review, *Part II, November 8, 1970, p. 26.*

The Nightwatchmen is a delicately imagined story set in an everyday contemporary town. The writing is limpid and humorous, the main characters well defined without being caricatured. (p. 21)

The mystery unfolds quietly, like a flower opening, moving from a small question such as 'What is "ticking"?' to the larger ones of 'Who are Josh and Caleb?', 'What is the mysterious Night Train?' and 'Who and what are Green Eyes?' The world of *The Nightwatchmen* is just out of sight of this one, a world round the corner of observed reality, recognizable, yet new and strange. Josh and Caleb travel by Night Train from Here to There 'park-sleeping', observing the 'ticking' of towns, digging holes so that they can, without suspicion, erect the hut that is their home. The Night Train travels only for them and comes to their whistle. By day it is an unused steam train buried in an overgrown siding. Josh is writing an undefined book, which is not *for* any purpose but just 'is' and is the apparent 'raison d'être' of both himself and Caleb. The world of Josh and Caleb is a mirror world. The fantasy is always contained in the reality, and at the end of the book Henry has no proof of the tramps' existence except that for him none of the things associated with them will ever be quite the same again.

The Nightwatchmen has its own inner logic, which by association seems perfectly acceptable. The jealous Green Eyes can see only at night: light blinds them. It is by this device that Henry, using a torch, rescues Josh and Caleb and the Night Train at the end of the story. The whole way of life of Josh and Caleb is based on a similar logic. For instance, they must camp near a railway and know the times of actual trains in order to know when they can safely whistle up the Night Train. The real world is shown some of its strange inner possibilities. Having read it, I wonder if one could ever see a workman's hut erected near a hole in the ground without just wondering, or notice people wearing sunglasses on a dull day, without a slight quiver. In just the same way that Helen Cresswell gives an unexpected twist to familiar reality in order to reveal the inner fantasy, or world of imagination, she also twists familiar figures of speech in order to reveal new aspects of them, vivid and humorous. Indeed, one of the great skills of the book is that its language, character and plot are so closely interfused. Looked at in one way, the whole idea of the book is an unfolding of possibilities in certain key associative words: 'ticking', 'Night Train', 'Here' and 'There'. Josh and Caleb *are* the language they speak. . . . Common figures of speech gain new life by the twist they are given, cli-

chés reborn and useful *because* they are clichés—the alteration makes us sit up and take notice: 'A rose by any other name might not be a rose at all' or ' "You've got Here," explained Josh . . . "and you've got There. We're from There;" ' or there is the Night Train going 'up dale and down river'. Apart from this, Helen Cresswell uses descriptive language sparingly but quite effectively, one word expressing the quality of something with great force. She describes the road beside the canal as 'the blankest road in England' and pictures for us the Night Train in Josh's words thus:

> . . . then shining rails come feeding up out of the dark and her breath goes up like the smoke was turned to silver and the wind over the top comes rushing into your mouth like jugfuls of cold water.

The whole book is a subtle weave of humour, mystery, reality and fantasy, leaving one enriched by its vision, with words and phrases caught in the memory. It is not fairytale fantasy completely divorced from life but the revelation of imaginative possibilities which exist in the ordinary and not quite ordinary things that lie around us. It invests the day-to-day realities with the kind of powers and potentialities that children themselves often give to them. (pp. 22-5)

The Nightwatchmen is unsuitable for children under the age of nine, but why is it that children of that age and older do not seem to take to it? The vocabulary is not difficult and the story has as its hero a boy of about their own age, which is a good start. There are 'interesting' characters and there is humour, all of which would seem to be the recipe for a book to appeal to children. Perhaps at the most superficial level the story is too subtle. The adventure gets off to a slow, rather reflective start, the characters develop quietly, without the aid of caricature, and the mystery is understated rather than overstated. The story's environment approaches a child's everyday environment, and this is where we come to the deeper difficulty. That Helen Cresswell's book draws very closely from a child's own experiences is, from an adult point of view, one of its strengths. We can look back, remember and recognize its truth. Children themselves are too close to it, too involved in this imaginative vision of the world about them to be able to stand back and observe it with interest. To them, 'nothing happens, there is nothing in it'. The same applies to the language. Most children are not aware enough of language for its own sake to appreciate Helen Cresswell's delicate and humourous use of it. It is all too pale, too ordinary, and much of it passes them by.

Another factor is also at the heart of the difficulty. I entirely discount the current idea that children only understand what shares with them a common class background. In fact that might well be a recipe for failure on the grounds already examined: something too close and ordinary to be felt to have any interest. But I do see that *The Nightwatchmen* springs very clearly from certain middle-class assumptions and as such is totally meaningless to children from the working class. The emphasis on creativity, on 'being' as opposed to 'doing', on tidiness and care for the environment (Josh and Caleb plant a tree after filling in their hole), on a certain nostalgia (steam trains), on free relationships between adults and children, and above all, perhaps, on the quality of food is something quite alien to very many children. This is vividly illustrated in Caleb's insistence on fresh, not frozen, chicken for his haute cuisine cooking. To children normally fed on fish and chips and baked beans this is quite outside their understanding. It underlines the whole tone of the book and is part of the reason that it fails to interest them sufficiently. (pp. 28-9)

Anne Merrick, " 'The Nightwatchmen' and 'Charlie and the Chocolate Factory' as Books to Be Read to Children," in Children's literature in education, *No. 16, Spring, 1975, pp. 21-30.*

A GAME OF CATCH   (1969)

[This] is a book in which a great many adult and child readers will meet on equal terms. Two children, on a winter holiday in the country, visit a castle at a shilling a head and become involved with children of a former century. The theme is commonplace, the treatment entirely individual. By Miss Cresswell's standards this is a slight book, but it displays all her finest qualities in miniature; a clearly identified setting, exquisitely drawn characters revealed through dialogue and action, a style, so unobtrusively right that it passes unnoticed, which evokes the wraith-thin atmosphere which is the key to the story.

It is appropriate that so haunted a story should also haunt the reader. There is something obsessive about the quiet, bittersweet tale, its sadness captured in lovely words. From the moment that the children's echoed shouts startle rooks out of the sky "like great black gloves" the reader is at Miss Cresswell's mercy, his nerve-strings played on with precise artistry. . . . Miss Cresswell's trifles are apt to look like other writers' masterpieces.

"Trifles Light as Air," in The Times Literary Supplement, *No. 3536, December 4, 1969, p. 1388.*

A game of catch is short and simple but, like a lyric poem, it has unexpected and entrancing subtleties in it. Phrases echo phrases and objects match objects. Words carry dual meanings; "catch" means chasing and also throwing a ball. Jigsaw puzzles in boxes become a simile as well as a piece of plot: the whole story is a jigsaw puzzle and the missing piece is only fitted in at the last moment. Few writers are as adept as Helen Cresswell in the kind of verbal counterpoint which is a spell in itself, preserving the unity (in this brief tale) between time present and time past. . . . The fantasy develops, as Helen Cresswell's stories so often do, from place—from a world immediately and meticulously imagined. The grey of stone and sky, the black of rooks in the cold sky, the white of frost on the stubble, the sudden crimson of the stitched velvet ball, form a second picture, more fluid than the stiff portrait of the children which a coincidence of name has drawn momentarily from the past. This beautiful piece of writing can stand beside the best of Helen Cresswell's fantasies. (pp. 1483-84)

Margery Fisher, in a review of "A Game of Catch," in Growing Point, *Vol. 8, No. 8, March, 1970, pp. 1483-84.*

THE OUTLANDERS   (1970)

Helen Cresswell grows with every book, not always in the way her admirers would like—but that is her affair. Like all the best artists she follows her own line, and we trail after her as best we can. In *The Outlanders* she steps boldly into the land of fantasy on whose borders she has been hovering for some time. It is not a land of escape; in the outlands men face

their problems squarely, perhaps for the first time, and some, like Piers, find no easy solutions.

This is a serious and difficult book. Children who cannot follow the author easily all the way will nevertheless find the journey enlivened, as always, by exquisite and revealing writing, and they will have for company a characteristic collection of Cresswell people: Tam who is a professional rhymer but can't rhyme, Emily who cheers a life over-full of soapsuds with fantasies of grandeur, and a marvelous old witch called Olemary. A rich, disturbing, wise book.

A review of "The Outlanders," in The Junior Bookshelf, *Vol. 34, No. 6, December, 1970, p. 367.*

The Rhymer family, Tam, Sary and son Piers, live in the town of Bray and like all the other inhabitants fear the Outlands that lie far beyond it. Until the arrival of the silent, mysterious Boy, Tam never possessed the family ability to make rhymes, so when the townsfolk accuse him of harbouring a fairy and Boy goes away, Tam knows he and his family must follow him even if their adventures lead them to the bleak and terrifying Outlands, from which few people return unchanged.

The book begins with the down-to-earth description and humour of *The Piemakers,* but ends with the mysticism of *The Nightwatchmen.* Although one is carried along by the quality and exuberance of the writing, re-reading shows many unsatisfactory non-sequiturs of characters and events. At times one gets the impression that the book has run away with the author, particularly when the meaning and purpose of the journey changes from one important to Tam to what happens to Piers. For those children who have yet to make the acquaintance of Miss Cresswell's books, *The Piemakers* remains the best introduction, but many eight- to eleven-year-olds will enjoy this story too.

Margaret Payne, in a review of "The Outlanders," in The School Librarian, *Vol. 18, No. 4, December, 1970, p. 480.*

[Some fantasies] are neither set entirely in the primary world, where the marvellous occurs exceptionally, nor are they set, entirely or completely, in a totally conceived secondary world, with all the imaginative complexity which that entails. They belong, rather, to an intermediate area of imaginative experience, where an often precarious balance must be maintained between two distinct worlds, and where the awareness of one world is constantly coloured by awareness of the other. Such fantasies involve the movement of characters in and out of some form of secondary world, but the perception of this world is often indistinct and dreamlike. . . . While perception of the secondary worlds may be dreamlike, movement from world to world and the constant cross-reference between them creates a sense of parallelism between the two. Their structures are inevitably thrown into sharp juxtaposition, while action in the secondary world may parallel hidden tensions and desires in the primary world.

One distinct type of secondary world in such fantasies of double experience is the world of time displacement. Such a secondary world is itself a true realization of the primary world, but with the additional disturbing perspective of a disruption in the normal perception of the time dimension. The parallels established are thus between different eras of the same physical world. On the other hand, the secondary world may indeed be a separate world, but when such dual worlds occur an apparently independent secondary world tends often to be a mirror of the inner mind. It may become an arena of intense experience for one central character, or for a group of characters linked by some close relationship. It may also present a visionary world of metaphysical reality. (pp. 44-5)

[The] visionary world . . . , as a literary form, has close links with the traditional form of the dream vision. Unlike [works of fantasy] . . . where parallels between the two worlds arise mainly from a subconscious level of the mind, the vision is at least a partly conscious realization of a paradisal or eternal world. In relation to this eternal world the primary world must seem either an imperfect copy, or else the anteroom of a much vaster and more complex palace of existence. Occasionally the visionary world may also be a symbolic representation of what is attainable at a mental or spiritual level in this life. Two notable post-war examples of this visionary quality in the fantasy of parallel worlds are Theresa Whistler's *The River Boy* and Helen Cresswell's *The Outlanders.* (p. 71)

The River Boy presents what is essentially a vision of a world of ideals. *The Outlanders,* on the other hand, is concerned more with achievements within this world. Strictly speaking, the initial setting of *The Outlanders* is not, in any case, the normal primary world. All of Helen Cresswell's books have this suggestive, secondary world atmosphere, even when her characters have such apparently mundane occupations as that of master pie-maker. In *The Outlanders* the different qualities of existence overlap; there is no sharp transition from primary to secondary world—the worlds ripple outwards from each other like the concentric circles of waves on a pond. At the centre is Bray, the smug, comfortable, narrow-minded town where Tam Rhymer lives with his family. Bray is the symbol of limited primary world awareness, rather than the primary world itself. Its inhabitants, with few exceptions, fear the world beyond, and hear a wolf in every wind which blows from outside. As with many puritanical and unimaginative people, their sense of security is only a thin veneer, and when life is disturbed by unknown forces they turn, as other similar societies have done, to witch-hunting. Bray is encircled by mountains and then by the Mid-lands, believed to be wild, savage country, but in fact prosperous farming land. Beyond this lie the outlands, which fill Tam's son Piers with terror whenever he wanders to the edge of the town 'where the cobbles yielded to the greedy grasses, whose seeds invisibly invaded the town whenever the wind blew from the hills'.

The grasses which blow into the town from the lands beyond are the key to the outlands. There are indeed wolves to be found there, but, as Piers discovers when he has to face them during one long night alone, they are not as frightening as his own irrational fears. The outlands are also the source of all that raises life above the mere humdrum existence of Bray. The seeds of more than grass are to be found there. The book is a quest by Tam, his wife Sary, his son Piers, and Emily, the indomitable daughter of the town washerwoman, in following a changeling fairy boy to the outlands. At the end they are joined by Olemary, Emily's half-mad grandmother, who wears sprigged muslin and ribbons so that the townsfolk will not suspect her of being a witch, and yet is too afraid of death by burning to realize her innate magical powers. The quest is one for artistic and individual freedom, an escape from the stultifying existence in a cramped and small-minded society. Tam Rhymer is a hereditary poet who cannot rhyme, although his son Piers finds to his distress that the Rhymer tal-

ent is beginning to appear in himself instead of his father. With the arrival of the fairy boy, Tam begins, apparently unconsciously, to compose rhymes.

The conventional world of Bray cannot tolerate an incursion from the outlands, however, and when the boy disappears from Bray, after the superstitious townspeople have attacked the Rhymers' house, Tam knows he must follow, even if it means searching for the rest of his life. For Tam the goal is clear-cut, and Sary, who believes in her husband's innate poetic gifts, swallows down her element of Bray common-sense and goes with him. Emily also has a passionate faith that life must hold something for her beyond the washtubs, while Olemary, half fascinated and half terrified, follows the boy until she achieves in the outlands the power to be herself, to cast off her madness and her fears, and use her magic at last. For Piers the quest is very different. His vivid imagination is possessed by fear, and he is largely responsible for the difficulties and delays which endanger the quest. At last, however, in facing the wolves and so bringing his hidden terrors out into the open, Piers unexpectedly achieves his own goal.

The world of the outlands, its shores washed by the sea, with its promise of even wider horizons beyond, is used by Helen Cresswell as a vision of personal and artistic freedom. Bray embodies the narrow limitations of most lives in the primary world. Only by climbing the surrounding mountains and facing both the mysteries and the fears of the outlands can one achieve one's true potential.

The Outlanders is particularly successful in combining its visionary world with a quality which is noticeably lacking in many of the books [of this type] . . . : a rich sense of humour. Olemary is a tragi-comic figure, but the inhabitants of Bray, with their confused prejudices and their hackneyed proverbs, are a comic interpretation of the blindness of the majority to the artistic gifts of the few. Where Russell Hoban, in *The Mouse and His Child,* attacks the cramping conventions of the materialist society with savage satire, Helen Cresswell makes many of the same points with a light-hearted mockery. (pp. 72-4)

> Ann Swinfen, *"Worlds in Parallel,"* in her In Defence of Fantasy: A Study of the Genre in English and American Literature since 1945, *Routledge & Kegan Paul, 1984, pp. 44-74.*

RAINBOW PAVEMENT (1970)

Helen Cresswell is perhaps the most brilliant of the talented team who make Benn's "Beginning-to-Read" books. She turns a "supplementary reader" into a work of art, handling her tiny vocabulary with great rhythmic resourcefulness and showing too, quite unobtrusively, real understanding of child and adult behaviour. The homely theme, with its poetic overtones, is ready made for [illustrator] Shirley Hughes, who captures nicely the tough tenderness of the story.

> *A review of "Rainbow Pavement," in* The Junior Bookshelf," *Vol. 34, No. 5, October, 1970, p. 288.*

AT THE STROKE OF MIDNIGHT: TRADITIONAL FAIRY TALES RETOLD (1971)

Helen Cresswell has rewritten the classic nursery tales in a style which she feels a 4-year-old will readily listen to; her voice is heard unmistakeably in domestic chat (godmother talking to Cinderella, stepmother snapping at Hansel and Gretel, Puss advising the Marquis of Carabas), while she adds an occasional visual detail to a well-worn moment of action. I feel she was unwise to include Hans Andersen in her selection. The salty talk of barnyard fowls in **"The ugly duckling"** is far better in one of the accepted translations than in her abbreviations and she loses much of the gravely beautiful description which can be a notable experience to a listening child of four or five. . . . On the whole, a good collection for very young listeners.

> *Margery Fisher, in a review of "At the Stroke of Midnight," in* Growing Point, *Vol. 10, No. 6, December, 1971, p. 1852.*

Although Cresswell states, in a prefatory note, that her adaptations of familiar fairy and folk tales are intended for reading aloud to children of four to six, the book seems—even with its limitations—more suitable for the independent reader, with reading aloud to younger children as a secondary use. The language is simplified, the violence in some stories abridged (Snow White's stepmother's heart breaks of passion, dancing in red-hot shoes being omitted; the wolf in **"Little Red Riding Hood"** is killed by the Green Archer's arrow as he springs malevolently out of bed—and there's a little lecture on disobedient girls that causes L. R. R. to blush). This doesn't really seem much more suitable for very young children than the standard versions, it's just a little easier to read. (pp. 159-60)

> *Zena Sutherland, in a review of "At the Stroke of Midnight," in* Bulletin of the Center for Children's Books, *Vol. 28, No. 10, June, 1975, pp. 159-60.*

UP THE PIER   (1971)

The mastery of Helen Cresswell's pen has brilliantly evoked the atmosphere of a seaside town in winter with its deserted promenade and pier and its shuttered boarding houses. As in some of her previous works such as **The Piemakers** and **The Nightwatchmen** characters and their states have a timeless quality about them. (p. 39)

Although Helen Cresswell says she prefers 'to let things happen as far as possible' in her stories, it does sometimes result in a certain looseness of plot. However, the fantasy element itself is well handled in a very matter-of-fact way. In this novel, she continues to explore a theme started with **The Wilkses,** developing it and giving it a greater depth. The characters have a certain deliberate shadowy quality which strengthens the timelessness.

Altogether a novel which will stand alongside some of her best works. I feel this is an author who has reached great peaks in her career, but who has yet to attain the greatness of which she is capable. (p. 40)

> *Vivien Jennings, in a review of "Up the Pier," in* Children's Book Review, *Vol. II, No. 2, April, 1972, pp. 39-40.*

A fantasy set along a bleak pier in Wales, past shabby, deserted kiosks, under leaden skies, where the gulls screech. Young Carrie chances upon the Pontifexes, an odd lot whom a magic spell has brought forward in time from 1921 to 1971. Is the author's wish to convey the struggle between man's *desiderata* and harsh reality? Or is her aim to entertain via the

antics of Welsh magical tradition in its cheerless modern-day degeneracy? She fails in either case; for the ethical crux remains buried under a farrago of contrived characterizations and the plot fizzles out despite its original promise of succulent mysteries.

> *Daisy Kouzel, in a review of "Up the Pier," in* The New York Times Book Review, *June 18, 1972, p. 8.*

BLUE BIRDS OVER PIT ROW; ROOF FALL!   (1972)

Much has been written recently about the problem of young people leaving school 'illiterate', or at least with a reading age far below their chronological age. One of the problems is the paucity of teachers outside the infant school with the technical skill to teach children to read, and another is the lack of suitable material available. As most children's readers are geared to children at infant or lower-junior level, many are dismissed by those in the upper junior or secondary schools as too babyish for them to bother with and consequently with this prime motivation missing, the incentive to read is often lost. The two new stories in this remarkable series should help to overcome the difficulty considerably as, although they have the usual short sentences and well structured phrases, they also have a story content for a higher age-group. Both stories are set in a small mining village, **Roof Fall** gives a vivid account of a mining disaster and [**Blue Birds over Pit Row**] is a humorous tale about a fanatical bird fancier who is looking for someone to look after his doves while he is on holiday. Both stories are well-written and show a warm concern for the characters in the story.

> *Pat Garrett, in a review of "Blue Birds over Pit Row" and "Roof Fall!" in* Children's Book Review, *Vol. II, No. 5, October, 1972, p. 149.*

It is a toss-up whether Miss Cresswell is writing the stories of this series in free verse or in a kind of rhythmic prose modelled on the new translations of the Psalms, but at least her style commands attention. **Blue Birds Over Pit Row** is a simple story of an absentee miner who dotes on his doves to such an extent that he is prepared to cancel his week's holiday because his usual stand-in with the birds has booked the same week. The substitute eventually commissioned proves an unhappy choice in the neighbours' view, and some practical joker takes a poetic revenge. (pp. 326-27)

> *A. R. Williams, in a review of "Blue Birds over Pit Row," in* The Junior Bookshelf, *Vol. 36, No. 5, October, 1972, pp. 326-27.*

In contrast to **Blue Birds Over Pit Row, Roof Fall** deals in a similar style with the saddest event that befalls any mining community. Miss Cresswell's treatment of the emotion and activity generated by a mining accident of any sort is honest and restrained. She does, in passing, administer, through one of her characters, a sharp slap on the hand to the impertinent Press. There is not much in the account that might not crop up in any other but the author's economy makes a fine impression on the reader. . . .

> *A. R. Williams, in a review of "Roof Fall," in* The Junior Bookshelf, *Vol. 36, No. 5, October, 1972, p. 327.*

THE BEACHCOMBERS (1972)

Two worlds—"the certain, workaday town filled with ticking clocks and people talking about the weather that scarcely touched them under their safe red tiles" and the sea "harnessed not to clocks but to the moon and winds, making its own rhythm, carrying the weather on its back." Two sets of people—the Pickerings in their basement, scratching through their junky furniture, and the Dallakers, free and alert on their three-master on the shore, waiting for the one tide that will bring inshore their lost family log in its brass-bound box and enough treasure to refit their ancient craft. Two sets of values—the greed of the Scavengers and the discrimination and generosity of the true Beachcombers. From the easily circumstantial opening ("It was Ned who wrote this story, of course") to the tantalising open ending, the story moves unerringly through scene after scene in which young Ned, uneasy guest of the Pickerings, discovers where his loyalty lies. Seaside smells and sounds, the idiom of generous and of mean people, suspense as Ned knocks at the door of the strange lodger's room and open joy as he first steps on to the *Sea Queen*—not a word wasted, not a word but carries its quirky, significant point. I would say without hesitation that this is Helen Cresswell's most impressive book so far—and, after all, there is a great deal to choose from. (pp. 2038-39)

> *Margery Fisher, in a review of "The Beachcombers,"* in Growing Point, *Vol. 11, No. 5, November, 1972, pp. 2038-39.*

Helen Cresswell continues her exploration of the strange recesses of the imagination. She is now, after some excursions into wonderland, back in the everyday world of overworked mums, cheap out-season holidays and cheaper food, but the ordinariness of this setting is a delusion. Just beyond the dreary two-up-and-a-basement houses of Bakers Road is a beach blown clean by the icy wind where the beachcombers collect jetsam and wait for treasure to come in on the tide. As always with this most intriguing of writers, who grows with every book, commonplace becomes mystery by the finest and most delicate of distortions of perspective, and the family feuds of beachcombers and scavengers take on almost cosmic significance as the tale, exciting, disturbing, often very funny, moves to a haunting and inconclusive close. Persistently Miss Cresswell declines to conform to classifications, and her new book stands aside from the main highways of modern children's literature and shares with her other work only one characteristic—extreme originality. (pp. 397-98)

> *M. Crouch, in a review of "The Beachcombers," in* The Junior Bookshelf, *Vol. 36, No. 6, December, 1972, pp. 397-98.*

The author of **The Night Watchmen** has woven another fantasy whose elusive threads of meaning form a spider web of substance depending on the sophistication and imagination of the reader himself. . . . The actual details of the story are relatively unimportant; the author has created a mood picture and has left it up to the reader to find his own treasure in the work. The Scavengers pat, ferret, knock, and sort. The Beachcombers dream, reap, and explore. Many readers will feel confused and short-changed at the rather abrupt conclusion, as though another chapter had been meant and then been mistakenly left out. Others will be satisfied with completing the fantasy themselves. The author is setting foot where no other fantasy writer has ever quite set foot before.

> *Sheryl B. Andrews, in a review of "The Beachcomb-*

ers," in The Horn Book Magazine, *Vol. XLIX, No. 1, February, 1973, p. 52.*

LIZZIE DRIPPING (1973)

Lizzie Dripping is dreamy, imaginative and very seldom practical. Her father understands her, her capable mother is often impatient with her, but there is no lack of affection in the little family.

The story is in five episodes, in each of which Lizzie's dreaminess involves her in trouble, mostly of a homely kind. One would like to see more of the witch in the churchyard who is busy knitting sooty black baby's clothes, but she only appears occasionally. For Lizzie Dripping, as for many children, the boundary between fantasy and reality is thin.

These episodes have been adapted from a very different medium, television, always a risk because the technique for writing for the two media is so different. Helen Cresswell has made the transition with her usual skill, but the visual impact with its convincing setting undoubtedly enhanced the individuality of the varied characters. (pp. 253-54)

> *E. Colwell, in a review of "Lizzie Dripping," in* The Junior Bookshelf, *Vol. 37, No. 4, August, 1973, pp. 253-54.*

Lizzie Dripping has already achieved the status of folk heroine through the television; you can tell by the way her song has been sung over and garbled in the playgrounds with the magically rude word 'pants' interpolated. This is a collection of stories about her, distinguished by vivid dialogue and Helen Cresswell's particular talent for creating a world full of adults seen from a child's vantage point but living in their own right. Patty, Lizzie's mother, loses her temper when things get broken, is too busy to listen and does not understand, but we feel her warmth all the same; Lizzie's father, a plumber, grows leeks in a taciturn way, and her Aunt Blodwen rattles on in a Welsh accent.

It is the words that do the magic. Lizzie is supported on a ground-swell of realistic chat and she herself has a fine line in subversive interior monologue. (pp. 275-76)

> *Dorothy Nimmo, in a review of "Lizzie Dripping," in* The School Librarian, *Vol. 21, No. 3, September, 1973, pp. 275-76.*

THE BONGLEWEED (1973)

Helen Cresswell's novels deserve to be judged by the highest standards—**The Piemakers, The Signposters, The Nightwatchmen** and **The Outlanders** rank with the finest examples of fantasy written in recent years. There is an unmistakably individual voice to her prose with its beautiful imagery and musical cadences, and the stories, however strange they seem on the surface, have at their best the ability to touch on the most profound aspects of human experience. Although they appear to be set in an idealized past, and move within the secure confines of tightly-knit families, they are never cosy or escapist, but deal with the problems of moral choice and the darker sides of ourselves.

It is a pity to have to say that **The Bongleweed** does not altogether measure up to these high standards. The story is concerned with a mysterious plant which grows at an extraordinary speed, several feet in one day, and which is in danger of over-running large areas of the countryside. Cut it down, says Authority (the vicar, the doctor, Mrs Harper, in whose garden the plant first grows: all insensitive, selfish people); preserve it, say the head gardener, his wife and their daughter, Becky. For the plant is intensely attractive; its leaves, buds and flowers fill the beholder who cares to look with an astonishing sense of the nature and mystery of creation. These opposing forces are finely balanced, but, unfortunately, the final solution does not come from inside the characters, or from their reaction to one another, but from an unsatisfactory *deus ex machina,* an unseasonable late frost which kills the plant.

Becky, the central character, is a person the author does not seem to have made up her mind about; she is on the side of the plant but she is spiteful, and fond of spying through a hole in the wall on her neighbours; it is through her selfishness that the seeds of the bongleweed are planted in the first place. But these aspects of her personality are forgotten in the last chapters of the book—at no point is she asked to undo the mischief she has created. Also forgotten to some extent is the boy next door, Jason, who is initially more interesting than Becky, and who seems as if he is to play a major role in the plot; but, having produced him, the author does not quite know what to do with him. And a final grumble: Mr and Mrs Finch and Becky are so like Mum, Dad, and the only child in many other books of Helen Cresswell's (and very like Pod, Homily, and Arrietty in *The Borrowers*) that the author is in real danger of repeating herself. This vein of fantasy is probably by now fully worked out.

"Exotic Flora and Fauna," in The Times Literary Supplement, *No. 3742, November 23, 1973, p. 1428.*

One clue to the theme of **The Bongleweed** may lie in Becky Finch's favourite exclamation—"Sweet mystery of life"—not totally meaningful to the ten-year-old, perhaps, but certainly significant to us, as we read how the child sows, tends and even masters the mysterious weed which she has christened at random. . . . The weed comes from an envelope of seeds given to Finch at a conference; it has no known origin and no explanation is offered for the sudden, explosive growth that threatens to engulf houses, church, gardens and who knows what else. What Helen Cresswell gives us instead of an explanation (which would, of course, have ruined the story and our pleasure in it) is an impression of its power, *as a weed,* to impress not only Else Finch (who cherishes weeds in her own kitchen plot), not only Jason, a Harper relative on a recuperative visit who is shaken out of his schoolboy calm, but even Finch himself, for whom weeds are naturally enemies. The tendrils and the astonishing orange and apricot flowers, the accelerated growth of the Bongleweed, are described with a mixture of humour and poetry very characteristic of Helen Cresswell:

The scene before them was changed, translated as it might be by frost or snow. Becky blinked to see a kind of fire let loose among sternly towering saints and stone angels with uplifted eyes and praying palms. The green had gently and inexorably parcelled headstones and bound the granite crosses with living rope, imprisoned them. Each sign of death was made null and cancelled out by the unmistakeable print of life. Not a slab or a tomb was left to read—not even the great monument of Sir William Crane (Peace Perfect Peace) and his wife Elizabeth (Come unto Me All Ye That Labour).

All through the book, as it dances its way along with chatter and musing and laughter and plain domestic veracity, there is what amounts to a hymn in praise of the odd, the unheralded, the wayward, the unnecessary but essential elements of life. Like all Helen Cresswell's books, this one gives the impression that its form has been dictated and shaped by an idea that could not possibly take any other form than that of a fantasy for the young.

Margery Fisher, in a review of "The Bongleweed," in Growing Point, *Vol. 12, No. 7, January, 1974, p. 2318.*

In **The Bongleweed,** we first see Becky in the potting sheds at Pew Gardens with her father, Finch, the head gardener, and in three quick lines of dialogue, their characters and their companionable relationship are established. " 'Oh Dad,' said Becky. 'Polishing spades again!' 'A good workman,' he began, not even lifting his head. 'Oh I know,' she said quickly, 'Don't tell me again. I believe you.' "

Becky loves the garden, perhaps more fiercely than her father does, but she is restlessly poised on the hinge of adolescence: Finch reproaches her for not having enough respect "for the things that really matter." True enough, Becky distrusts the scientific botanical mania shared by Finch and his boss Dr. Harper. Impatient, scornful but curious, she spies on the adult world through a peephole into the dining room of the Harpers' grand house, separated from the Finches' own little house by one thin wall.

In a moment of petulance—annoyed, too, because she is expected to entertain twelve-year-old Jason, a brainy but sickly boy who has come to visit the Harpers—Becky plants a mysterious seed, prized by Dr. Harper, in her mother's kitchen garden. That night, she hears a strange whispering noise under her window—"a hissing like wind in poplars, a conspiracy of leaves . . . bless, bless, bless . . . or was it wish, wish . . . or again us, us . . ."

It is the bongleweed growing, growing phenomenally, magically, and soon the giant plants are rioting in growth, springing to fifteen feet tall overnight, smothering the cemetery next door in a twining, leaping jungle of greenery. While Finch and his sturdy wife Else are badly rattled by the bongleweed (and their working-class pragmatism, touched with endearing eccentricity, makes them a marvelous creation), Becky and Jason are drawn into the conspiracy of uncontrollable life. (pp. 172-73)

Becky and Jason are like a prelapsarian Adam and Eve, sitting under the apple tree lost in wonder at the lush beauty of the bongleweed: When it flowers, the blossoms are apricot colored, of extraordinary sheen and delicacy, like silk umbrellas. This is, however, no passive flower; it has the strength and wiliness of a panther, a lion; its rush to growth is unstoppable, like Becky's own. And Becky learns that she has power over the weed. She created it, she named it, and, at last, she can command it to draw back and make a passage for her through its densest thickets.

The whole of this adventure is written with the most engaging poetic exuberance, always balanced by the gruff realism of Finch and the believably acerbic sparring of Becky and Jason. The bongleweed must die, of course, and it dies not by the hand of the scheming undergardener, but by "nature taking its course"—a spring frost. But Becky has changed. She has experienced not only the exultation of adolescence with its sudden burst of joy when it realizes its own surging power but also "a complicated sadness" at the opening of a subtle gap between her and her parents. But she is most definitely not sorry for having planted that seed. And when the bongleweed dies ("wish . . . loss . . . miss . . ." are the last evocative whispers Becky hears from it) she consoles the grieving Jason. She knows that now there has been one bongleweed, anything—anything desperate, beautiful, and reckless—is possible.

Not one youngster in a thousand may explicitly recognize the images of puberty, the echoes of the Garden of Eden, in this lovely and funny story, but many will respond to its energy without knowing why. (pp. 173-74)

> *Michele Landsberg, "Fantasy," in her* Reading for the Love of It: Best Books for Young Readers, *Prentice Hall Press, 1987, pp. 157-82.*

THE KEY (1973); THE TRAP (1974)

Backward readers in the early 'teens don't always need violent exaggerated plots to lure them towards the printed word, nor are they necessarily half-witted because they are bad readers. Helen Cresswell is among the few writers willing to give full measure of wit and precision within the limits of the difficult kind of writing required for this type of reader. Her two new books in the "Inner Ring" series depend on everyday situations in an urban lower-middle-class setting, but each of the situations is developed with humour and with effective indications of character. Nobody who has suffered from an overbearing, dictatorial, unattractive relative can fail to be riveted by the moods of old Aunt Ada or to sympathise with Mike's drastic device for driving her away; while in *The key* his mother's accident and his unwitting part in it are neatly true to life. With Helen Cresswell's limpid words, so carefully selected that they hardly seem the mono- or duo-syllables they mostly are, and with Richard Kennedy's enormously active drawings, these two books should do their job supremely well. (pp. 2371-72)

> *Margery Fisher, in a review of "The Key" and "The Trap," in* Growing Point, *Vol. 12, No. 9, April, 1974, pp. 2371-72.*

TWO HOOTS (1974); TWO HOOTS GO TO THE SEA (1974); TWO HOOTS AND THE BIG BAD BIRD (1975); TWO HOOTS PLAY HIDE-AND-SEEK (1977)

In the first of four books for beginning independent readers, Cresswell introduces two owls, Big Hoot and Little Hoot, who belie the vaunted wisdom of the species.

They're both silly, but it's Little Owl who decides he wants to fly about during the day; he can't really see, so he comes home happily carrying a stone that he's convinced is a mouse he can have for his next meal. The same pattern is followed in the other books, *Two Hoots Play Hide-and-Seek* (actually, only one does), *Two Hoots Go to the Sea,* and *Two Hoots and the Big Bad Bird.* Pleasantly foolish, but rather insubstantial . . . ; the large print and the small amount of text on each page make the series useful for its intended purpose, but each book has a gag situation rather than a story line. (pp. 139-40)

> *Zena Sutherland, in a review of "Two Hoots," in*

Bulletin of the Center for Children's Books, *Vol. 31, No. 9, May, 1978, pp. 139-40.*

[Despite] the deliberately simple plots and texts, an appropriate audience for these titles is hard to envision. . . . Besides the obvious inability of pre-schoolers to read, many may be unfamiliar with the concepts on which the humor depends (e.g., that owls are nocturnal creatures, that mice don't live near the sea). Children who know how to read would be bored with these, though some might derive a sense of one up-manship.

> *A review of "Two Hoots" and others, in* School Library Journal, *Vol. 24, No. 9, May, 1978, p. 80.*

THE WINTER OF THE BIRDS (1975)

[If this] book seems to reach a philosophical conclusion about life and death, it reaches it through close attention to individuals. The story is told partly in orthodox style, partly through extracts from "The Chronicles of Edward Flack", written "for posterity". Edward lives with his foster-parents, who keep a shop in a run-down district of a city. Bookish and imaginative, he sets himself to train as a hero, and to this end he dares himself to call upon the reclusive Mr. Rudge. Mr. Rudge confides in him his belief that the district, and perhaps the world, is threatened by steel birds attacking the roof-tops; at the same time two men visit the conventional Flack home—Mrs. Flack's brother Alfred, who has been fished out of the river, and the ebullient red-haired Patrick Finn who has convinced him after the unwelcome rescue that suicide is not the best way to defeat monotony and inertia. Finn becomes Edward's chief hero, more than matching Hercules or Odysseus; his unpredictable behaviour shakes Mrs. Flack from her normal matter-of-fact attitudes; with his various ingenious schemes to outwit the menacing birds, assuming that they exist, he brings the whole neighbourhood into an unlooked-for friendliness, besides helping Edward to form a new conception of what being a hero really means. All this is contrived in a narrative that flits from one style to another, from sub-ironic comment on how easily people misunderstand one another to the prim, homebound letters Mrs. Flack sends to the local paper about the nightmarish rumours, or the mixture of literary panache (with words like "girding on his sword" or "a feast fit for heroes") and clerkly cliché ("a true and faithful report", "I lift my pen") with which Edward presents his own account of the strange events. The lad is never in any doubt that "it is really a battle between day and night and between good and evil" and he believes "The dark will never vanquish the light", even though St. Saviour's is to be pulled down for a supermarket site and he has actually heard a hissing as of steel on Mr. Rudge's roof. On the other hand, he has his own sturdy way of equating reality and dream. In bed with 'flu, he reflects that heroes are not usually ill; "they went in more for being sorely wounded or swallowing fiery draughts':

> 'I feel sorely wounded,' he thought. 'All over'.
>
> In the end he decided that if an emergency should arise—such as a python emerging from the goat-skins or a deadly foe entering with lifted sword—then a wounded hero would deal with it at once. In the meantime, he would just lie there and read and doze like any other ordinary mortal who was sick.
>
> 'That's all right, then', he decided, secure in the

knowledge that neither python nor deadly foe was likely to appear at a moment's notice at Number 47 St. Saviour's Street.

Like the boys in **The Night Watchmen** and **The Beachcombers,** Edward finally changes one kind of imagination for another and is all the wiser for the change. In this intriguing, witty, wayward yet common-sensical piece of mystery, Helen Cresswell shows how each and every one of us has to look for a personal and private truth while still keeping the lines of communication open between us. (pp. 2772-73)

> *Margery Fisher, in a review of "The Winter of the Birds," in* Growing Point, *Vol. 14, No. 6, December, 1975, pp. 2772-73.*

Helen Cresswell continually pushes out the boundaries of her imagination, moving from the tender humour and gaiety of her first books to the realms of terror and the unknown. Happily, in pursuing new objectives, she has not lost her concern for the oddities of real human beings. **The Winter of the Birds** may deal with steel birds traversing the night sky on flightpaths of wire, but the world which they threaten is one inhabited by Mrs. Flack, grocer and hen-pecker, and the awful MacKays. It is this contrast between the ordinary and the horrific which keeps the momentum of the story and gives it its sharp reality. Not an easy book to read or to rationalise, but in its presentation of character in depth and in an almost tangible atmosphere it represents a long stride forward by this most remarkable and unpredictable of writers.

> *M. Crouch, in a review of "The Winter of the Birds," in* The Junior Bookshelf, *Vol. 40, No. 2, April, 1976, p. 101.*

TWO HOOTS IN THE SNOW (1975); TWO HOOTS AND THE KING (1977)

Cresswell has shaped up her Two Hoots formula since the foolish owls' first appearance . . . ; here the patronizing postscripts ("but *you* know better, don't you?") are gone, and the stories, though no more than simple kindergarten jokes, are at least that. In [**Two Hoots and the King**], the Hoots mistake a yellow bird for "the king of the sun" (because the sun is yellow too and is "king of the day") and ask him to make them wiser; so he tells them that he is a canary, not the king of the sun—"and now you are a little wiser than you were." In [**Two Hoots in the Snow**], Little Hoot mistakes falling snowflakes for the Moon Bird's feathers, and Big Hoot insists that they are white leaves. "What's it for?" they ask when told that what they see is snow. "Silly birds. Snow is snow and that is all there is to it." With Martine Blanc's blobby cartoons unchanged, it's still not much.

> *A review of "Two Hoots and the King," in* Kirkus Reviews, *Vol. XLVI, No. 21, November 1, 1978, p. 1187.*

These two Helen Cresswell books in the Early Reader series continue the saga of the dumb owls. This time they mistake a yellow bird for the sun king in **Two Hoots and the King** and the moon for a white bird and snow for white feathers or leaves in **Two Hoots in the Snow.** After six books based on similar mistakes, the underlying concept and resultant humor are beginning to pall.

> *A review of "Two Hoots and the King" and "Two*

Hoots in the Snow," in School Library Journal, *Vol. 25, No. 4, December, 1978, p. 66.*

ORDINARY JACK: BEING THE FIRST PART OF THE BAGTHORPE SAGA (1977)

After many excursions into the realms of fantasy Helen Cresswell has returned with a bang to her early mood of high comedy. Much as we have enjoyed her fruitful experiments we must give three or four very hearty cheers. There is too little sheer fun in children's books today. Here is a book crammed full of good belly laughs, laughs springing from incongruity, caricature and the humour of character and language.

Jack was born into the wrong family. All the rest of the dreadful Bagthorpes were geniuses. Not just specialists, either. Tess, at thirteen, reads Voltaire in the original for pleasure and is a Black Belt at Judo; she plays oboe and piano too. The horrible Rosie, at eight, swims like a fish, plays the violin and paints portraits. They don't boast, just take pride in their achievements. Jack does nothing well. His balmy Uncle Parker decides to give him a new image, and the book is devoted to the attempts to present him as a soothsayer. He gazes into space, murmuring (or shouting, to make himself heard above the usual Bagthorpe hubbub) "I see a Lavender Man who Bears Tidings". Uncle Parker not only supplies the idiotic ideas but makes sure that they materialise. Other actors in the dotty drama are Daisy who is four and a pyromaniac, Grandma, perpetually lamenting the timely death of her cat, and Grandpa, who practises S.D. (Selective Deafness). Given the existence of such a family, the events recorded by Miss Cresswell have the inevitability of the best Greek tragedy.

We already know that Miss Cresswell can transmute "what children like" into pure gold. She has done it again, and made sure that the grownups will like it too. Definitely a book for all the family to share.

> *M. Crouch, in a review of "Ordinary Jack," in* The Junior Bookshelf, *Vol. 42, No. 1, February, 1978, p. 36.*

The first novel of the Bagthorpe series introduces the irrepressible, eccentric characters in this unlikely family. Although Cresswell's plot is unique and wildly imaginative, her real forte lies in characterization, language, and exploitation of the humorous possibilities in situations. Characters typically violate standard role expectations. Rather than being a sweet, docile, affectionate woman, Jack's grandmother is a vain, obstinate, and unforgiving manipulator. The father, instead of providing a moderating, steady influence, is erratic, unreasonable, and competitive with his own children. He personifies, like the rest of his kin, the incongruity between self-perception and actuality. Totally committed in his view of himself as an unappreciated creative artist, the father is, in reality, a television script writer. Jack's mother writes an advice column for a newspaper and consequently sees herself as a perceptive, insightful counselor-therapist par excellence. She is, however, oblivious to the blatant and unceasing machinations of her own family, blithely unaware of the perpetual tides of crisis swirling around her.

Not only does the author contrast the self-perceptions of the characters with their actual behavior, but she creates multifaceted characters who are perceived differently, sometimes in quite opposite ways, by other members of the cast. Jack's totally undisciplined cousin is seen as a free spirit by her mother, as a destructive terror by Jack's father, as a potential ally and coconspirator by the grandmother, as a moldable moppet by Jack's sister, and as an adorable innocent by Uncle Parker. The various facets of each character's personality are selectively perceived by other Bagthorpes as these collide with their own eccentric needs. Despite the pomposity, humbug, egocentricity, and other such unadmirable attributes, the Bagthorpes are inevitably regarded with affection by the reader.

Cresswell is able to maintain character integrity during her deftly staged chaotic confrontations. Even in situations of unbounded confusion, their quirky personalities and idiosyncratic speech persist. Her images are vivid and highly visual; Zero, "the pudding-footed dog," is memorable. The dialogue is harmonious with the advanced interests and general brightness of the juvenile characters. In family encounters, language is a principal weapon, as figurative remarks are taken literally or an unintended meaning of a word is seized upon and exploited. With a caustic and frenzied wit reminiscent of Groucho Marx, the story sweeps along, gathering momentum, as one absurd vignette gives way to the next. While Jack may be ordinary, the novel is anything but. (pp. 117-18)

> *Barbara H. Baskin and Karen H. Harris, in a review of "Ordinary Jack," in their* Books for the Gifted Child, *R.R. Bowker Company, 1980, pp. 117-18.*

ABSOLUTE ZERO: BEING THE SECOND PART OF THE BAGTHORPE SAGA (1978)

Watching the March snowfall, my mood matched the patches of greyish ice which had lain for months under the azalea bushes. I began to read a book which the flap copy was recklessly trumpeting as a "side-splitting romp." Knowing the fragility of humor, I was quite aware that it was the wrong moment for such a book, but there was no help for it. Through clenched teeth, I dared the author to split my sides, and began.

Absolute Zero, as I was soon forced to admit, begins well. Uncle Parker, related only by marriage to the multitalented and poli-eccentric Bagthorpes, has won a slogan contest for "Sugar Coated Puffballs" which entitles him and his wife Celia (who writes poetry and pots) to a cruise in the Caribbean. By the end of chapter one, the fiercely jealous clan are feverishly entering every competition in the British Isles. Before long the prizes, some rather more welcome than others, begin pouring in.

The plot of this book, even more than that of the first volume in the saga, *Ordinary Jack,* defies description. I would sound like one of my children relating a Marx brothers movie. But the plot is not by any means the only thing that makes this a very funny book. Yes, funny, even hilarious. For there I sat, laughing out loud in my cold, dark, empty house, while the giant snowflakes falling outside my window not only continued but clung glumly to the wet ground.

The characters are marvelous, from Grandma Bag, who cannot bear to lose at anything, even if the result is a Bingo Hall riot, to four-year-old Daisy, a reformed pyromaniac. It is, however, a good thing that we met the family in *Ordinary Jack,* for in this volume no one stands around long enough to be introduced. Except perhaps Zero, Jack's pudding-footed, mutton-headed mongrel, who has only been known

to move rapidly on those several occasions when the house has caught fire. In this book, incidentally, Zero becomes the most celebrated and photographed dog in all of England.

Now a wild plot peopled by a family more harebrained than the Vanderhofs of *You Can't Take It With You* ought to be enough of a romp for any reader young or old, but the quality in Helen Cresswell's books which will charm a laugh out from between clenched teeth is her mastery of language. She has that Thurberlike ability to harness words and syntax for a fully satisfying comic effect.

The proper thing for a reviewer to do at this point is to quote a line or two to prove the point. Sorry, but it can't be done. Cresswell's books don't cut up into neat quotable snippets. A part of what makes them funny is the cumulative effect, not only of several pages, or chapters, but of the two books, read in sequence. And one reason *Absolute Zero* may seem funnier than *Ordinary Jack* is this great snowballing of humorous events and phrases through the course of both volumes. At this rate, volume three will do us all in. . . .

But, you ask, how many American children will understand, much less appreciate Cresswell's very British brand of humor? Isn't humor the most fragile of literary commodities, the one most likely to perish in transition? Anticipating this question, I asked my 13-year-old to read the books. I can report that at least one All-American Boy found himself laughing out loud at *Ordinary Jack*. . . . His report on *Absolute Zero* confirms my own opinion that it is even funnier. When I asked him how old a person would have to be to enjoy the books, he said that he thought children younger than himself might have trouble catching on.

My feeling is that the plot and characters are strong enough to delight younger children who might not, as John suggests, catch on to the batting about of literary allusions, but there is plenty of humor for all. It would be a great series of books to read aloud. And as for catching on to all the jokes—I found myself, magnifying glass in hand, poring over the small print of my compact edition of the *Oxford English Dictionary* to find the definition of "absolute zero." I suspect Cresswell's tucked another joke in there, and I hate to miss even one.

> *Katherine Paterson, "Not for Children Only," in* Book World—The Washington Post, *April 9, 1978, p. E4.*

Join the Bagthorpe Fan Club! The only qualification is a taste for, and if possible a share of, battiness.

Do I detect a small diminution of idiocy? Probably not. The pressure is so great in *Absolute Zero* that an ageing reader may be forced to retire exhausted before the end. Not so the young readers to whom the exquisitely zany book speaks so directly. For once a really funny book for children is for them, not about them for grown ups. . . .

Miss Cresswell's crazy world is just enough like reality to give an edge to her fun, so that the reader, instead of laughing himself sick, laughs always with an appetite for more, and, generous as she is, more Miss Cresswell gives him.

> *M. Crouch, in a review of "Absolute Zero," in* The Junior Bookshelf, *Vol. 42, No. 3, June, 1978, p. 151.*

BAGTHORPES UNLIMITED: BEING THE THIRD PART OF THE BAGTHORPE SAGA (1978)

In spite of some heavy-handedness, there are those who will welcome this latest part of the Bagthorpe Saga with open arms. This time, old Grandma Bags is robbed of her precious memorabilia which the thieves treat as rubbish and leave in the street. To make her feel better, a family reunion takes place bringing together, in fateful combination, the most eccentric group of people since the Marx Brothers and the Peterkins. The get-together proves to be a series of exploding dominoes, each event precipitating a disaster bigger than the first. Hysteria prevails as the housekeeper leaves in terror, Aunts become unhinged, Mother wrings her hands, Dad bellows acerbic comments, the house is virtually destroyed, cars are smashed, and Zero the dog wanders forlornly through it all. Even with all the silliness, much manages to get said about family relationships, and there is a particularly British respect for individuality.

> *Marjorie Lewis, in a review of "Bagthorpes Unlimited," in* School Library Journal, *Vol. 25, No. 1, September, 1978, p. 134.*

Domestic comedy for children has entered a new phase. It is no longer sufficient to trot out a succession of snobbish, absent-minded or sprightly old relatives and call them eccentric. Eccentricity now flourishes on an altogether more dramatic scale, although it is possible that Helen Cresswell's fictional family has taken this tendency to its limit. The even tenor of the usual day is a quality unknown to the Bagthorpes who are subject to recurrent catastrophe in the home. Mr Bagthorpe fears his family is the laughing stock of England, and who can blame him? The causes of his distraught state are recounted with gusto in the latest contribution to the Bagthorpe saga, where the narrative pursues a lively course between surrealism and farce. Only an excessively studious eleven-year-old, like the Bagthorpes' horrid cousin Luke, will fail to find this story amusing.

> *Patricia Craig, "Laughing Stock," in* The Times Literary Supplement, *No. 4000, December 1, 1978, p. 1398.*

BAGTHORPES V. THE WORLD: BEING THE FOURTH PART OF THE BAGTHORPE SAGA (1979)

The fourth part of the Bagthorpe saga is as good a place as any to make the acquaintance of a family whose antecedents are, strictly speaking, literary. Hilaire Belloc might have known them; the *Three men in a boat* could claim them as direct descendants. As characters they are at once entirely believable and wholly fictive, and the result is hugely comic. In this episode the Bagthorpes, whose Strings to their Bows make them a Top Family, are outdone. A cousin becomes Junior Brain of Britain; Aunt Lucy, on whom their financial hopes are pinned (despite her belief that time does not exist) comes to visit; Daisy has recurrent funerary passions; and Mr Bagthorpe fears bankruptcy and orders subsistence gardening. The combination of massive egotism, slapstick incidents involving a goat, a cat and a pekinese, and the wit which triumphs in situations which, in lesser mortals would provoke despair, all make this book a distinctive literary experience where the reader and the author are in such cahoots that it's the best in-joke in children's books for ages. The reader learns to share fun with the writer. But I guess that's only possible if there is enough space in your life to let you take disaster

lightly and to understand the nature of the comic that derives from excess.

> *Margaret Meek, in a review of "Bagthorpes v. the World," in* The School Librarian, *Vol. 27, No. 4, December, 1979, p. 391.*

Enjoyable as these frolics are, Miss Cresswell would be well advised to rest the Bagthorpes in 1980. They show signs of becoming an obsession with her, and she is far too important a writer to be side-tracked into Marx-Brother-like knock-about, however funny. There are deeper levels of humour awaiting her exploration and veins of poetic fantasy which she, better than anyone else, knows how to exploit. I yield to no one in my enthusiasm for the Bagthorpe saga, but I am prepared to forego them for a year and hope that their creator will do the same, for her own and her readers' good.

> *M. Crouch, in a review of "Bagthorpes v. the World," in* The Junior Bookshelf, *Vol. 44, No. 3, June, 1980, p. 141.*

DEAR SHRINK (1982)

The narrative convention of the young author writing for his (or her) peers takes a new turn in this book. But it cannot avoid the sometimes precious self-consciousness, the psychology of the individual responding to feelings and events. When the cliché of adolescent fiction is used skilfully to point up the clichés of adolescent fiction, as here, the results are significant. The events and the way they are 'seen' by the narrator are embedded in implicit social consciousness that carries the value system of the author.

Oliver Saxon introduces his middle-class family: 'One thing I will mention and then pass over quickly is that we had quite a lot of money compared with most people . . . if there is one thing I hate it is people who think that just because they've got a Jaguar car (which we had not, I hasten to add) . . . this is some kind of a big deal.' Lucy, Oliver's younger sister, 'is really something'. Then Oliver says that 'if you have read *Oliver Twist* or *Roots* it might give you some idea of what is to come'. His parents depart to South America to botanise (the traditional casting off of adults is explained by the son rather than seen as fortuitous), and what comes is serious enough: the children become 'minors in care'.

Three layers of the book merit close examination. First, the narrative conventions, traditional ones in children's fiction, are used here with great skill. The effect is downbeat, 'laid back', good humoured. The web of the text is derived from adolescent language registers and imitations of schoolboy reading. The effect is Bagthorpe serious. Miss Cresswell is a writer of great skill who runs the full scale of narrative invention on behalf of readers who are discovering writerly text. For example, the reader discovers the difference between the immediate past of Oliver's epistolary writing to Carl Jung, and the narrative past of the unfolding of the tale. There are serious commitments here to writing to extend the expectations of young readers.

Secondly, the author shows us a young adolescent relating his book experience, the literary way of construing events, to the 'facts' of the 'real' world. This is imaginatively powerful, and worth detailed scrutiny.

It is difficult to do a short analysis of the third focus. The characters who enter the lives of the Saxon children as the result of their changed circumstances are not liked by them for what must be described as cultural reasons. The elderly housekeeper watches *Crossroads* and eats biscuits. Her daughter looked to Oliver 'as if she was togged up for a Glamorous Mother of Two contest'. The first foster mother gives the children sardines; what Lucy calls 'the loo' is 'the toilet'. The Saxons are accused of lying—the greatest of all insults. A boy in the children's home vandalises the Saxons' house after they take him there on a visit. Now, for every event in the book there is a referential situation in the 'real' world, and the young are notoriously crude in some things they say when they are in fact responding sensitively. But it is not simply that Oliver, as narrator, is awakening to the lives of others in a sphere different from his own. He is bound to 'see' the ideological stereotypes of his creator. The particular details of the story are class related in a way that I find disturbing. In this novel are all the things that make children's literature important and criticism equally so. (pp. 250, 253)

> *Margaret Meek, in a review of "Dear Shrink," in* The School Librarian, *Vol. 30, No. 3, September, 1982, pp. 250, 253.*

Readers of the new book will look in vain for the subtlety and imagination of **The Winter of the Birds** and **Up the Pier,** for the vigorous tall-tale originality of **The Piemakers,** or for the comic spirit of the Bagthorpe chronicles. Reflective of current social realism is the story of three children—aged seven to fifteen—who are left in the charge of an elderly housekeeper, Mrs. Bartle, while their parents are away for six months studying plant life in the Amazon jungle. . . . After various harrowing experiences with some supremely nasty adults, the unhappy young people concoct an elaborate scheme to run away and spend Christmas in the family's summer cottage. But their plans go awry, and the three rush headlong into a disastrous situation—only to be rescued at the last moment by the melodramatic, and far from credible, arrival of their parents. Often the first-person narrator seems to run away with the story, which becomes talky and digressive. The author, however, maintains her sense of the ludicrous, and the most effective parts of the book are the tense individual scenes and Oliver's spontaneous portrayals of both child and adult characters, all done with perception and sardonic humor.

> *Ethel L. Heins, in a review of "Dear Shrink," in* The Horn Book Magazine, *Vol. LIX, No. 1, February, 1983, p. 51.*

THE SECRET WORLD OF POLLY FLINT   (1982)

The trouble with fantasy is that it requires extraordinary delicacy of touch. One false move and the reader is out there raising a curmudgeonly eyebrow. There is no reason why we should believe a word of it; suspend my disbelief, we mutter, and you'd better do it well.

Helen Cresswell, in **The Secret World of Polly Flint,** does it by way of that agreeably eccentric removal from a recognizable world that is her trademark. Her families never really do occupy the present as we know it; they are already shunted sideways, as it were, set in special suspended landscapes of their own. Polly Flint's father is a miner; he keeps pigeons and the household is normal enough in terms of amenities: nevertheless, there is the inimitable Cresswell touch in archaisms of speech and oddities of attitude to make the slide from reality to otherness, when it comes, both acceptable and in

a way natural. Polly, left to stay with an aunt while her father is treated in hospital for injuries received in a pit accident, is taken up by a family of Time Gypsies, frenetic waifs who have slipped the net of time. There is a lake with a time tunnel, a dog who may or may not be a real dog, and Polly herself, a lass with a mind of her own able to take on such disorienting manifestations with as much aplomb as she copes with her pathologically house-proud aunt. A whiff of sentiment here and there, maybe, but dialogue and pace that are models of how it can be done in the right hands.

> *Penelope Lively, "Time Slips," in* The Times Educational Supplement, *No. 3464, November 19, 1982, p. 34.*

Much as I enjoyed **The Secret World of Polly Flint,** I felt that it fell below [Helen Cresswell's] best in genuine creativity. Polly Flint, like Lizzie Dripping, sees things that less privileged, or imaginative, people do not see. . . . Polly goes to stay with Aunt Em at Wellow, where a maypole stands on the green. . . . [Below] the modern face of Wellow there is an older lost village called Grimstone, and . . . there is a passage between that village and time and this. It is a typical Cresswell idea, full of promise, and in the working out there are some characteristic inventions, notably Granny Porter, who comes out of the past 'dressed in stitched tatters of a thousand mucky rags'. The consequent dilemmas are worked out in a satisfactory manner and there are some exciting moments, but one misses the sheer fun of, for example, **The Piemakers.** Polly's poetic dad—such a typical Cresswell creation—hardly comes to life at all, and even Granny Porter is less than fully three-dimensional. With good actors to help the TV version will, I do not doubt, be first-class, but in cold print some of Miss Cresswell's exuberance and delight in her own imaginings are lacking. **The Secret World of Polly Flint** is well to the fore among recent fantasies, but from this writer we expect much more than other people's best.

> *M. Crouch, in a review of "The Secret World of Polly Flint," in* The Junior Bookshelf, *Vol. 47, No. 1, February, 1983, p. 21.*

ELLIE AND THE HAGWITCH   (1984)

Helen Cresswell, the queen of British fantasy, has already written better books than **Ellie and the Hagwitch.** This is of course a competent story, in the rather overworked vein of "the dark" versus "the light", with goodies and baddies already drawn up and defined before the book opens. We are told that one character, Digby, "like everyone else in the world", is part good and part bad but there is no evidence of this truism in the plot. Ellie has psychic powers but uses them for good. The Hagwitch is the Enemy.

There is a build up of menace and a final confrontation after which the Hagwitch's captives, including Ellie's mother, father and brother, are released. But you don't find out until page 16 that all the mysterious goings-on are in an imaginary country called Ramazin. Until then I rather thought it was Wales—it often is in fantasies. This is much less precise than Cresswell's usual work—rich as ever in the How, but lacking in the Why and Wherefore, without which fantasy becomes an insubstantial pleasure.

> *Mary Hoffman, "Talking Tomato and Wise-Guy*

Mice," in The Times Educational Supplement, *No. 3545, June 8, 1984, p. 49.*

Helen Cresswell returns to an earlier manner, but with more seriousness and barely a hint of humour. Ellie, who draws upon her latent supernatural powers to defeat the horrible hagwitch, is a distant cousin of Lizzie Dripping, but we miss the homely modern setting which made that young woman's adventures so acceptable. (p. 206)

Not even Miss Cresswell has served up such an odd helping of curious characters before, and her highly atmospheric writing and a certain waywardness of construction keeps the reader mystified, if not downright confused, right to the end. This is in fact a private kind of book, and not every reader will be admitted into its closed circle. But it is full of characteristic Cresswell touches: the colloquial shorthand of some of its dialogue, the invention of minor characters, notably a conceited talking raven, above all the delicate precision with which she uses words, her loving regard for their sounds and shapes. Even in her slighter works Miss Cresswell is a major writer, and this book is slight only in length. Its implications are very great. (p. 207)

M. Crouch, in a review of "Ellie and the Hagwitch," in The Junior Bookshelf, *Vol. 48, No. 5, October, 1984, pp. 206-07.*

BAGTHORPES ABROAD: BEING THE FIFTH PART OF THE BAGTHORPE SAGA (1984)

[Helen Cresswell] is a master-storyteller, in total control of her characters and plot. Her language is uncompromising, subtle and very funny. In this fifth title in the Bagthorpe saga, "sensitive, artistic" (or so he thinks) author, Mr Bagthorpe, having had a manuscript rejected, decides to take his amazingly gifted family abroad on holiday in a rented cottage, selected in the interests of his research into the supernatural. Helen Cresswell continues the saga without any falling-off in quality, inventiveness commitment. The family are as odd as ever and the pleasure and anticipation of disasters is increased by previous involvement with the family. This can be highly recommended for the committed, able reader.

Judith Elkin, "Spinning It Out," in The Times Literary Supplement, *No. 4261, November 30, 1984, p. 1377.*

The Bagthorpes are back! Oh, joy; oh, rapture; oh, dear! In this, the fifth installment of the continuing misadventures of the most wildly eccentric fictional family since the Peterkins peddled their papers, the Bagthorpes decide to go abroad. . . . Suffice to say that Cresswell continues to entertain with her patented combination of slapstick situations and sophisticated wit, that the characters are eccentric—and occasionally splenetic—as ever, that readers will find laughs on every page, and that the cinematic freeze-frame conclusion promises further adventures ahead.

Michael Cart, in a review of "Bagthorpes Abroad: Being the Fifth Part of the Bagthorpe Saga," in School Library Journal, *Vol. 31, No. 5, January, 1985, p. 84.*

BAGTHORPES HAUNTED: BEING THE SIXTH PART OF THE BAGTHORPE SAGA (1985)

This picks up exactly where **Bagthorpes Abroad** left off, with the full clan trying to cope with the underequipped house they've taken for a six-week stint in Wales. . . . The mayhem here strongly resembles that in the previous installment. Daisy and Billy Goat Gruff continue to wreak havoc, bringing consternation not only to the Bagthorpes but to the nearby village as well. There are more police cars wrecked, and Mr. Bagthorpe manages to unwittingly purchase a lot of junky goods at a house auction. Unfortunately, however, this time Cresswell seems to have run out of steam. While there are some laughs to be had, the caliber of humor is not up to previous books in the series. Action supersedes characterization and the slapstick nature of much of it becomes monotonous. Even when she's not at her best, Cresswell is still quite readable, and fans of the series will want to digest this latest development despite its weaker fiber.

Denise M. Wilms, in a review of "Bagthorpes Haunted: Being the Sixth Part of the Bagthorpe Saga," in Booklist, *Vol. 82, No. 3, October 1, 1985, p. 219.*

Not a frenzied beat is skipped between the ending of the fifth saga and the start of the sixth as this newest takes up the very next day, the third, of the Bagthorpes' holiday abroad in a "haunted" Welsh house. . . . The pace never falters with new twists and chuckles around every bend. There's no sagging in the series continuity or flagging of the individuality of each family "character." The preposterousness is maintained with freshness as the Bagthorpe tradition of mayhem and mirth is continued. Their ill-fated venture abroad is hauntingly funny.

Julie Cummins, in a review of "Bagthorpes Haunted: Being the Sixth Part of the Bagthorpe Saga," in School Library Journal, *Vol. 32, No. 3, November, 1985, p. 82.*

WHODUNNIT? (1986)

At first glance, this appears to be a picture book for the very young, with its cast of English animal characters. The only human character is the princess, a blonde little girl. However, as the title implies, it is more than that. It embodies neat little tests in visual discrimination which will engage the attention of six to eight year olds. . . .

Despite its Englishness, Helen Cresswell's text, presented in large type, makes the key issues of the story available to children. She addresses herself directly to the reader in a nicely conspiratorial way. The text reads aloud well and makes few concessions in vocabulary or sentence structure. . . .

An appealing book with the bonus of a visual literacy exercise built in.

Joan Zahnleiter, in a review of "Whodunnit?" in Magpies, *Vol. 2, No. 5, November, 1987, p. 21.*

MOONDIAL (1987)

"Even before she came to Belton, Minty Kane had known that she was a witch, or something very like it." With that enticing beginning, Cresswell launches her delicately wrought fantasy about a modern-day girl who travels backward in time to save the unfortunate spirits of a trio of abused children. Minty is staying in Belton for the summer holidays while her widowed mother works. "I always thought of Belton as a . . . *happening* sort of place," muses her mother, and Minty soon knows why. Spirits are there; after exploratory ventures around the grounds of a nearby estate, Minty senses something strange. Pockets of icy cold and strange intimations hint at a mystery that's confirmed by an elderly local known as World. He informs her that it is her task to set free the children that he's heard crying for more than 60 years. Little by little Minty figures out how to go about this mission; when success finally comes, there is a welcome feeling of relief, for the time-worn victims are heart wrenching. The story has some potent scenes that display the cruelty endured by Tom, a servant boy who yearns to be a footman, and Sarah, a wealthy child shut away and dreadfully tormented because of a birthmark on her face. Tom's sister Dorrie, beset with illness because of her gutter-picking work, is another haunting presence whose ill fortune drives home the distressing view of children in an age of no childhood. In addition to Cresswell's stellar plot is the virtuosity of her prose; she's a masterful engineer of mood and setting, both of which enhance the effect of her characters' fortunes. Another first-rate piece of storytelling from this amazingly versatile writer. (pp. 317-18)

Denise M. Wilms, in a review of "Moondial," in

Booklist, *Vol. 84, No. 3, October 1, 1987, pp. 317-18.*

It is some time since Helen Cresswell last wrote with such depth of feeling, such confidence in her rare powers. She is a writer who, in terms of the big Awards, has had less than justice done to her. Those who have charge of these prestigious offerings will ignore this book at their peril. (p. 43)

There is nothing specially original about the idea. Miss Cresswell puts her own highly individual imprint on the story, partly by brilliant use of an actual setting, partly by use of a most evocative and atmospheric style. She has not before, I think, written so sensitively, carrying the reader with her by sheer power of words. She paints the most vivid of pictures. Here is Minty going out early on a chilly morning: 'The street was thinly washed with gold and the shadows were icy. A cockerel crowed from the farm beyond the church, tearing the dawn hush. The graveyard was drenched with dew and littered with cats, strayed from the night.'

The writer has created a courageous and vulnerable heroine in Minty and a frightening villain in Miss Raven the ghost-hunter, who is also the horrible Miss Vole, tormentor of little Sarah in centuries past. The resolution of the mystery and the freeing of the troubled spirits is most moving in its simplicity. Altogether a most successful essay in the ghost story. (p. 44)

M. Crouch, in a review of "Moondial," in The Junior Bookshelf, *Vol. 52, No. 1, February, 1988, pp. 43-4.*

Thomas M(ichael) Disch

1940-

American author of fiction and poet.

A respected author of science fiction, short stories, and poetry for adults, Disch is best known in the field of children's literature for his fantasies *The Brave Little Toaster* (1981) and *The Brave Little Toaster Goes to Mars* (1988), works for middle graders which describe the adventures of a group of anthropomorphic appliances and are sprinkled with tongue-in-cheek morals, irony, satire, and puns. Initially an award-winning short story which Disch based around his two-slice Sunbeam, *The Brave Little Toaster* is about five household items—a Hoover vacuum cleaner, an electric blanket, a desk lamp, a clock radio, and the toaster—who leave a summer cottage and head toward Winnipeg, Canada in search of their missing owner. The appliances overcome a variety of dangers as they travel from the country to their owner's new apartment in the city. Compared to such works as *The Wizard of Oz* and *The Velveteen Rabbit*, *The Brave Little Toaster* is often considered a contemporary classic and has been made into a film by Walt Disney Productions. In *The Brave Little Toaster Goes to Mars,* the toaster and its companions—which now include a ceiling fan and a hearing aid made by Albert Einstein—travel to outer space to stop an invasion of the earth by warlike household machinery. The *Toaster* books are considered original, imaginative, and sophisticated works which both embrace and poke fun at the genres of epic fantasy and science fiction. Disch is also the author of *The Tale of Dan De Lion* (1986), an egalitarian fable written in couplets which describes the victory of a dandelion over the rose breeder who wants him destroyed.

(See also *Contemporary Literary Criticism,* Vols. 7, 36; *Contemporary Authors Autobiography Series,* Vol. 4; *Contemporary Authors New Revision Series,* Vol. 17; *Contemporary Authors,* Vols. 21-24 rev. ed.; *Dictionary of Literary Biography,* Vol. 8: *Twentieth-Century American Science-Fiction Writers, Part I.*)

THE BRAVE LITTLE TOASTER: A BEDTIME STORY FOR SMALL APPLIANCES (1986)

In this fairy tale . . . a vacuum cleaner, electric blanket, clock radio, tensor lamp, and Sunbeam toaster undertake an epic journey in search of the beloved master who has, shudder, forgotten them. Together they fashion a means of transport (a chair with wheels, power from a car battery), pass through a dark forest, are befriended by simple woodland creatures, cross over water, suffer capture by a kind of ogre, and more; indeed Disch touches on nearly every element of the classic fairy story. One can readily understand why Disney studios pounced on this book for an animated feature.

But adults will note that Disch gently mocks the tradition he employs. Throughout there are authorial interventions drawing tongue-in-cheek lessons, making didactic points; the narrative tone possesses an ironic edge that keeps the reader aware that this is both a scary adventure story and a playful science-fictional conceit. . . .

Though kids will get a real charge out of the story as such, the adult reader's joy will be more literary: admiration for the sustained tone, for the imaginative leaps into the very quiddity of what a toaster must feel, why an electric blanket would hate an air conditioner, how a tensor lamp might envy fixtures with 100-watt bulbs. Like Randall Jarrell's similar (but much more sentimental) *The Animal Family,* Disch's **The Brave Little Toaster** may prove a modern classic.

> *Michael Dirda, in a review of "The Brave Little Toaster," in* Book World—The Washington Post, *April 13, 1986, p. 11.*

If you love the concept, you will love Thomas Disch's book. Quite simply, it is the story of five small appliances, living in a summer cottage, who set off to find their missing owner. It either tickles you or it doesn't.

The toaster, whose idea of a good time is to daydream about making English muffins, leads a Tensor lamp, an electric blanket, a radio and a vacuum cleaner on their search. The blanket is a bit of a hysteric and threatens to go to bed when upset; the radio plays easy-listening music and quotes Karl

Marx . . . ; the vacuum cleaner pulls them all along on an office chair, using power from a car battery.

That mode of transportation is accompanied by a strong disclaimer.

> But before any of the small appliances who may be listening to this tale should begin to think that they might do the same thing, let them be warned: ELECTRICITY IS VERY DANGEROUS. *Never* play with old batteries! *Never* put your plug in a strange socket! And if you are in doubt about the voltage of the current where you are living, *ask a major appliance.* . . .

While the appliances find their master, this book may be looking for an audience. It is much too long and too sophisticated for preschoolers, and perhaps a little too fantastic and subtle for some older children. The publisher optimistically says "for both children and adults," but what would the average 10-year-old make of the information that flowers can speak only in verse and that "daisies, being among the simpler flowers, characteristically employ a rough sort of octosyllabic doggerel, but more evolved species, especially those in the tropics, can produce sestinas, rondeaux, and villanelles of the highest order"? Besides, most of the jokes are too good for children. Like C. S. Lewis's Narnia chronicles or *The Phantom Tollbooth* by Norton Juster, **The Brave Little Toaster** is a wonderful book for a certain sort of eccentric adult. You know who you are. Buy it for your children; read it yourself.

> *Anna Quindlen, in a review of "The Brave Little Toaster," in* The New York Times Book Review, *April 20, 1986, p. 29.*

In this book, household appliances come to life when humans aren't around. If readers like that idea, and can get past the suspicion that the author might be cloaking some complex parable in fairy tale terms, then they'll probably read on. The brave toaster and his four traveling companions—a Tensor lamp, a Hoover vacuum cleaner, an electric blanket and a clock radio (AM only)—leave home to find their owner. The journey owes much of its odd appeal to the matter-of-fact way the group goes forth. And puns? Disch is relentless as he describes an encounter between an amorous daisy and the toaster, who tries to keep his coils cool. . . . The human vulnerability of the hero and his friends—well-captured by [Karen Lee] Schmidt's drawings—and Disch's love for his subjects, will make this book (for some) a *Velveteen Rabbit* with extension cords.

> *A review of "The Brave Little Toaster," in* Publishers Weekly, *Vol. 229, No. 22, May 30, 1986, p. 68.*

At what point can the pathetic fallacy become lamentable idiocy? When electric household utensils not only speak but take to the open road, when this mechanomorphism is combined with anthropomorphism and when people are run by appliances. A vacuum cleaner, an electric blanket, a lamp and a clock-radio, rallied by the pop-up of the title, leave a vacation cottage unvisited by their owner for over two years to find him in Winnipeg, Canada. On the way they meet a talking squirrel and a villainous recluse who almost junks them in the city dump. Without much strain, they elude this perfectly reasonable end and find their owner's new apartment, settle in with his newer gadgets and arrange to be swapped to (who else?) a decrepit ballerina who loves them for their special purposes. Disch writes gracefully (well above the vo-

cabulary level indicated by the format), lacking only a believable concept or the power to impose internal logic on the unbelievable. . . . Fantasy overload.

> *Lillian N. Gerhardt, in a review of "The Brave Little Toaster: A Bedtime Story for Small Appliances," in* School Library Journal, *Vol. 32, No. 10, August, 1986, p. 91.*

THE TALE OF DAN DE LION (1986)

The Tale of Dan de Lion is a horse of a different color, with its murderously chic line-drawings of roses on crutches and turbid weeds that match to a "t" Thomas Disch's crisp little couplets gleefully celebrating the victory of the dandelions over the garden. It is a small book, an extended joke; it would make an unusually delectable Christmas card. It is not a book ostensibly written for children but winking over its shoulder at passing adults, enticing them to joys a child is too dull to savor; rather it is the other way around, an entirely adult production that a child, were he or she to stumble over it, might like a lot. It can be read aloud without embarrassment, repeated without weariness. (p. 14)

> *Angela Carter, "The Complex Pleasures of Picture Books," in* Book World—The Washington Post, *November 9, 1986, pp. 13-14.*

Disch's most recent book for young readers was that witty technological tall tale, **The Brave Little Toaster,** this new story is probably limited to fans of his adult SF writings—who may find it too didactic. Dan De Lion is a dandelion who believes that "all beings sown in mud/. . . Enjoy a simple natural right/To the rain that falls and to air and light." Belinda Buttertoast, who owns the garden and breeds roses, disagrees with Dan and has him sprayed. But soon he is reborn en masse—and the gardener decides his spraying days are over. Cynical black-and-white pictures [by Rhonda McClun] show cigar-smoking dandelions and roses on crutches—suitable for such a hard-edged story, which is more of a novelty than a work for children. Even making an ideological point doesn't require this heavy-handed approach.

> *A review of "A Tale of Dan De Lion," in* Publishers Weekly, *Vol. 231, No. 3, January, 1987, p. 72.*

The jacket blurb calls the book a "fable of the ordinary man confronting power and ruthlessness," told with "humor and philosophical insight." It is really too slight, however, to deliver any deep messages. A major problem is that we don't get involved enough with Dan De Lion and his weedy family. He is not well-defined as a character, so that when he struggles for survival we do not really root for him (so to speak). . . .

I don't think that **The Tale of Dan De Lion** will capture a cult audience as did *Jonathan Livingston Seagull* or even **The Brave Little Toaster.** For all its shortcomings, though, it might make a nice little gift for a friend. The book would have been much improved by some more depth, however.

> *Laurel Anderson Tryforos, "Weed Out 'Dan De Lion'," in* Fantasy Review, *Vol. 10, No. 2, March, 1987, p. 46.*

THE BRAVE LITTLE TOASTER GOES TO MARS (1988)

Readers may have believed that all that could be said about a band of loyal appliances was stated with electrifying eloquence in *The Brave Little Toaster.* But there is new territory to cover with old friends—like the AM radio—and new: a ceiling fan, an electric blanket and a microwave among them, as well as a hearing aid handmade by Albert Einstein. They all head to Mars after learning that there resides a force of warring appliances with plans to invade Earth. The toaster simply and persuasively speaks of peace to the planet's inhabitants and is elected president (a reign which lasts only until he returns to Earth). What is Disch talking about? Perhaps it doesn't matter, for while he seems to be amusing himself, much of what he writes will entertain readers, too. The epic elements will more than appease those awaiting this sequel, but the most exuberantly funny scenes are those in which the appliances while away the time with their distinctive brand of gossip.

> *A review of "The Brave Little Toaster Goes to Mars," in* Publishers Weekly, *Vol. 233, No. 20, May 20, 1988, p. 93.*

When Thomas M. Disch's *The Brave Little Toaster* was published two years ago, it was quite explicitly marketed as a children's book. With the sequel, *The Brave Little Toaster Goes to Mars,* the publisher seems to be leaning the other way. Gone are the illustrations, the printed plastic covers, the ivy borders surrounding each page of text. The first tale was subtitled *A Bedtime Story for Small Appliances;* this one seems directed more at owners and parents.

The Brave Little Toaster Goes to Mars . . . is less important as thriller than as meditation on the cosmos as seen from the viewpoint of an ordinary household object. Disch . . . has a tremendous amount of affection and sympathy for his subjects.

What keeps all this from becoming impossibly cute is the same mechanism that allows any piece of fiction to function: attention to detail. The invasion-defeating allies include the radio, which knows all about New Jersey because that's "where Bruce Springsteen comes from"; the toaster, which has trouble with English muffins and can't find its prepared speech ("I thought I put my notes in my crumb tray," it explains); and the Hoover, which is not only losing its suction but refuses to go to Mars: "I understand the place is *covered* with red dust. Imagine having to clean an entire planet. I couldn't cope."

After the toaster, which finds itself running for the presidency of Mars, is told its speech was "very interesting," it reflects: "Interesting! Not stirring, not powerful, not ringing: interesting! It hadn't felt so despondent since it had set the English muffin on fire."

The Brave Little Toaster Goes to Mars suffers the similar fate of being "very interesting." It tries to do only one thing, even if it does that thing quite well indeed. But within its self-appointed limits, it's entertaining and amusing. You'll never look at toast in the same way again.

> David Streitfeld, *"Rites of Passage," in* Book World—The Washington Post, *May 29, 1988, p. 8.*

This sequel takes its appliance protagonists to outer space—which, unfortunately, is not far enough away to avoid its predecessor's stylistic problems. (p. 825)

In his clumsy style, Disch packs a lot of moderately funny and interesting ideas into a plot that plods rather than builds. His talking appliances, however, are not believable even in the context of the book, existing only as mouthpieces for his whimsies. The talking-appliance genre may have been appropriated by Mr. Disch but, as yet, it eludes his mastery. (p. 826)

> *A review of "The Brave Little Toaster Goes to Mars," in* Kirkus Reviews, *Vol. LVI, No. 11, June 1, 1988, pp. 825-26.*

Leonard Everett Fisher

1924-

American author and illustrator of nonfiction, fiction, and picture books.

Fisher is distinguished as the creator of works which provide young readers with thoughtful, accurate treatments of unusual subjects and often reflect his interest in American and world history. Diverse and prolific, he has written and illustrated over fifty books for readers from preschool to high school. Fisher is also the illustrator of over one hundred and fifty books books for children by such authors as Washington Irving, Isaac Bashevis Singer, Madeleine L'Engle, Henry Wadsworth Longfellow, and Milton Meltzer; recognized as especially notable are his vibrant paintings for several books of poems by Myra Cohn Livingston, compositions lauded as the perfect complement to her evocative verse. In his works of nonfiction, Fisher offers concise, informative books to readers in the elementary and middle grades which demonstrate careful research and clear-cut exposition; his fiction for the same audience is considered dramatic, suspenseful, and humorous. In all of his books, Fisher has included impressive, carefully crafted pictures which handsomely and powerfully enhance the texts. His virtuosity as an illustrator is evident in his wide range of styles, from realistic to abstract, and his use of media from pen-and-ink to acrylics. Fisher is often applauded for the technical brilliance of the extremely intricate British scratchboard drawings with which he decorates many of his books.

Fisher's reputation as a writer and illustrator for children was firmly established with the publication of his "Colonial Americans" series (1964-76), nearly twenty titles which explicate and pay tribute to the crafts, trades, and occupations of that era. In these books, which explain both the history of each trade or job as well as the techniques employed, Fisher strives to teach children about the great technical and artistic skill used in the manufacture of everyday items of colonial times; he considers this knowledge a precious gift in an age of mass production. Fisher has also written and illustrated seven books on nineteenth-century American industry and culture as well as four books—*Alphabet Art: Thirteen ABCs from around the World* (1978); *Number Art: Thirteen 123s from around the World* (1982); *Symbol Art: Thirteen Squares, Circles, Triangles from around the World* (1985); and *Calendar Art: Thirteen Days, Weeks, Months, and Years from around the World* (1987)—which trace the development of each art form through time and across the globe and are praised for their uniqueness and beauty. Among other varied nonfiction books, Fisher has published several significant works on historical occurences, places, and monuments.

As with his nonfiction, Fisher likewise gives great import to historical atmosphere in his works of fiction. In *Across the Sea from Galway* (1975), *Letters from Italy* (1977), and *A Russian Farewell* (1980), he realistically and graphically depicts the perils and trials of the immigrants who came to America and honors their heroic struggle for survival. From *The Warlock of Westfall* (1974), which concerns the hysteria and tragedy of a witchhunt, to *Noonan: A Novel about Baseball, ESP, and*

Time Warps (1978), a comic story of psychokineticism and time travel, Fisher has created imaginative, stimulating works of fiction which often have a historical setting. Fisher is also the creator of numerous critically-acclaimed picture books, several of which draw on history and mythology for their subjects. Also a professional painter, he has written books for adults on the art of painting. Fisher has won several important awards, including the Joseph Pulitzer Painting Fellowship in 1950, the American Institute of Graphic Arts award for outstanding textbooks in 1958 and for outstanding children's books in 1963, the New York Library Association/School Library Media Section Award for Outstanding Contributions in the Fields of Art and Literature in 1979, and the University of Southern Mississippi Medallion in 1979.

(See also *Something about the Author*, Vol. 34; *Something about the Author Autobiography Series*, Vol. 1; *Contemporary Authors*, Vols. 1-4, rev. ed.; *Contemporary Authors New Revision Series*, Vol. 2; and *Dictionary of Literary Biography*, Vol. 61: *American Writers for Children since 1960: Poets, Illustrators, and Nonfiction Authors*.)

AUTHOR'S COMMENTARY

I've always been a book person. Someone recently asked me

what I thought motivates children to read. I know what motivated me. My father was a reader; so was my mother. There were always books around. . . .

As a youngster, I was affected by many illustrators: Howard Pyle, Arthur Rackham, Edmund Dulac, and N. C. Wyeth—particularly the monumentality of figure and composition of Wyeth's "Old John Silver," (i.e. *Treasure Island*). His whole presentation went far beyond the book. I think he had more soul than either his son or his grandson. Wyeth's pictures were engaging, and they were more than illustrations. He was a great artist, and he brought the painter's intellect and knowledge to those books. (p. 315)

By the time I was eight years old, I was in art school—the Heckscher Foundation. My mother took me there religiously, every Saturday morning for about a year. After class she would take me over to the Museum of Natural History, across the street, to see films. She would read to me from *Compton's Encyclopedia* at bedtime, so that I would wake up the next day a little smarter than I was when I went to sleep. Even during the Depression my mother had a subscription to the Civic Repertory Theatre, down on 14th Street. I saw Eva Le Gallienne in *Peter Pan* and *Babes in Toyland.* So even as a child I was being culturally programmed. (pp. 315-16)

Being an artist even dictated my life in the army, because I became a map-maker involved in highly sensitive work—such as the invasion of Southern France and, later, Japan. (p. 316)

After the war, I went to the art school at Yale, the first university art school founded in this country. I was educated there before the abstract expressionists changed the program and before Joseph Albers came in 1950. I never took a course in children's books. There were none. I was being trained to think pictorially and to do larger works. When I graduated from Yale, I went to Europe, and when I returned, I was broke. I got a job with a muralist and was fired at the end of a week. . . . I was painting the sky and fixing it up here and there. By the time Friday came I was fired, because I painted my sky not the boss's sky. When I was fired, there was a telephone call from New Haven asking me if I would be Dean of the Whitney School of Art.

After being at Whitney for a few years I resigned. I didn't know what I was going to do with my life. I had just gotten married; my wife, Margery, and I were about to have a family; and someone suggested that I talk to Oscar Ogg of the Book of the Month Club, and Alex Ross, a magazine illustrator. Ogg suggested that I speak to Warren Chappell, an illustrator. When Chappell looked at my drawings, he said, "You'll never make it in the children's book business. The drawings are not appropriate."

So I went back to Oscar Ogg, who said, "I'll write a letter to Louise Bonino at Random House, the juvenile editor, and you go up to see her." I decided not to take the things I had shown Chappell. All I wanted to show Miss Bonino was that I could draw. I brought photos of paintings and ten life drawings, nudes, with me. Louise Bonino was sitting behind her desk, very well turned out, tough as nails. Her piercing eyes were very amused when she saw the drawings. She sat there, very properly, behind her desk and said to me, "You know, anybody who has the gall to bring these drawings to the children's department should not walk out of here without a book to do." I came out with a book, *The Exploits of Xenophon,* a rewrite of a classic about the retreat of a Greek army

before the Persians. . . . I researched the book to such a point that I did a rotten job on it. It was all research, and the art was terrible. When that book came out, I was horrified that I hadn't been able to translate what I was doing in painting into illustration. I was so upset at myself that I decided I was going to take another try at illustrating.

I got another book to do, this time from Holiday House. It dealt with Central America and Columbus. . . . At that time, all my paintings were fantasy, but I never translated the fantasy into books. I'd go home and paint large, dreamlike paintings in egg temperas. I kept this kind of schizophrenic split-personality creativity going until 1960, when I did my first picture book for Holt. After a while I became bothered by straight, visually dull nonfiction, because I knew I was capable of other kinds of work. But I never showed my paintings, and no one in the children's book field even knew I was making them. Now I'm getting a chance to work on a larger scale, in full color, and present a bit of both fantasy and realism.

After those first two books I was driven to do the perfect book. I had become interested in solving a problem. I knew a great deal about printing because of my map experiences in the army. I realized, eventually, that I could produce art in books and not just pedestrian or comfortable illustrations. Today what interests me in nonfiction is giving youngsters a visual memory of a fact rather than just the fact. I am trying to present a factual mood. The Tower of London, for instance, is a creepy place, and if I can establish the creepiness of the place so that the youngster gets an unsettled feeling about the tower, then that child is going to have more of an understanding of history than just learning a date. I'm trying to create the emotion of the history, the dynamics of history, together with the fact of history. I'm trying to communicate what events in history felt like. These feelings will bring children back to reading information to find out the facts—back to reality! I want to give a sense of history, created by the fallible, mortal human beings who made it.

I considered many of my early books to be a learning laboratory; I experimented a great deal. I was interested in history, but I never thought there was any difference between graphically presenting a picture book of history or of fairy tales. As long as I could draw, design, paint, and create visual images, it didn't matter to me what it was called. Whether it's fiction or nonfiction in terms of pictorial matter, art is art. Even if people look at fiction as the more imaginative part of the creative process, the artist responds with just as much of an aesthetic concept to nonfiction as to fiction. I'm talking now about art, not about packaging. I come to illustration as a painter, not as a graphic designer or an entertainer. I'm not dealing solely in presentation. I'm trying to get readers to think about something humanistically. I present form, and I design according to the idea. I want to present art in nonfiction—to have people look at the power and dynamics of art regardless of the subject matter. Once they do that, I believe, they will have a memory of what they are reading in terms of the facts. If you are going to make a picture of a battle, you have to present it in such a way that a child never wants to be in one. If you are doing a picture of the ocean, I think it's important to evoke a sense of the smell and movement of that ocean. I come to these drawings with a great deal of instinct, more now than I did at the beginning. I have also become more romantic.

You could call Michelangelo an illustrator, because he took

a literary idea, a story, and translated it visually, making it memorable along the way. But what he created was a thunderclap on that ceiling, to such an extent that it invaded our senses. I'm trying for the same effect in books. The French painter, David, in illustrating his time, created universals; when you look at Marat in the bathtub or the crowning of Napoleon, or at Gericault's *The Raft of Medusa,* these pictures have nothing to do with that time anymore. They transcend their time. Someone like Norman Rockwell never transcends his time. The nostalgia becomes pervasive. That is often the problem with American illustration; it doesn't transcend the time.

I have traveled this world from Portugal to China. I'm not a preacher, but there is much that continues to be worthwhile in our world. I feel that I have to create dynamic and powerful images of this world, not some other world, that will permeate a child's consciousness. I am of an age where I really want to say something that is less escapist than the majority of offerings. I only know how to say it in my art. My art changes rapidly; it has all my life. People are unable to peg what I do. My themes are getting larger and larger. My feeling, however, is also that childhood has changed—children have no attention span; they travel; they are street-wise too early; they are bored a great deal. I'm trying to get children to contemplate a fact—a simple fact.

But even though I may have produced different images over the years, there are still connecting links in those images. After all is said and done, mine is the work of one individual. We live in a transitional period of time, and I think my artistic modus operandi reflects that transition. (pp. 316-22)

My ideas never begin as of the moment—they are always rattling around. I had thought about the Great Wall of China for years. . . . [I] went to China, and took a large number of photographs, although I never used any of them. If I had used the photographs, I would have been locked into a configuration around Beijing, where we saw the wall, and not let my imagination roam around the territory—like the Mongolians leaping over the wall. I studied it enough to know how they built it. I don't start on a book until I understand how something was made. Therefore, I can paint without too much reference, because a reference becomes a crutch. Basically I want to produce atmosphere; so I decided on a gray book. The whole country is gray. We didn't realize there is no color until we came out of China and crossed the border at Hong Kong, and all the neon lights jumped out. Had I not been in China, it never would have struck me that the book should be gray. I also noted how hard it was to walk up the wall, a real struggle. Because I had tried to climb the wall, I knew to make it difficult looking in the book. That is not to say you always have to be on the site. . . . I could have done the book without having gone to China, but it helped create a mood about the place.

When I went to the Tower of London, what I saw was another historical mood piece, very unhappy people who hadn't had the murder bred out of them yet. The Tower of London became another gray book. Once I had a sense of the place, I did take photographs to get accuracy of the buildings. When I work, I do very few sketches. I prepare a thumbnail sketch and do all of my final drawing on the illustration board. Once the final drawing is done, I start painting over it. If I were to make a lot of sketches, I would exhaust myself so much on the sketches that by the time I came to the painting, it would be flat, tired, and dried out. I try to keep the en-

ergy of an early stage of the drawing and preserve it. I do my painting in acrylics right on the illustration board and change things as I go along. I work background to foreground, northwest to southeast. Even if the composition doesn't turn out as I thought it should have, I leave it if it has energy and will only do it over if the energy is gone. Too often early on, I caught things very well in a sketch and the finished painting died. If I'm doing scratchboards, there are no sketches.

We have a tendency in children's nonfiction to respond only to the desires of curriculum and educators and to ignore the other needs. We just give the facts or what we think are the facts; or what someone wants as fact. The qualities of high art are hardly ever a factor for the judgment of nonfiction. What is important about me is the quality of my thinking, what drives me to do what I am doing: not the facts of my life—but the creative impulse behind that life. I am trying to make an artistic statement logically, and a logical statement to children artistically. I think the time has come for a stronger and more artistically expansive view of nonfiction. (pp. 322-23)

> *Leonard Everett Fisher, "The Artist at Work: Creating Nonfiction," in* The Horn Book Magazine, *Vol. LXIV, No. 3, May-June, 1988, pp. 315-23.*

GENERAL COMMENTARY

RODERICK NORDELL

[Leonard Everett Fisher] has come to an interesting conclusion about American art in the light of history.

> Our unique contribution may be in children's books. . . . This, I think, is our baby. . . . I'm a great nationalist when it comes to art—national, not nationalistic. . . . When a style is really national then it transcends it and becomes universal. . . .
>
> I look on art in children's books not as illustration—books stay on shelves, like works of art. I think it's a fine art.

A glance at the paintings on Mr. Fisher's walls confirms his classic, sculptured approach to anatomy, for example. He looks back to the great artists of the past in discussing the present.

> They didn't cry on everybody's shoulder. They just let the emotion seep through. Now [in much contemporary painting] there is so much emotion that once you get it, it exhausts itself more quickly. . . . I believe in discipline.

The discipline involves both knowledge and muscles. The hands must be disciplined to connect with the ideas.

"Non-fuzzy drawing leads to non-fuzzy thinking and non-fuzzy thought leads to more non-fuzzy thinking."

Mr. Fisher pointed to some of his framed works.

> I made the paper and colored the paper myself. It's made exactly as in the 15th century. . . . I'm not ready to give up this kind of knowledge just because I'm doing a children's book. . . . There's nothing wrong with using all the knowledge of 2,000 years in a children's book.

But what about the limitations in a book, the restrictions on size, color, process, subject matter?

> That's why I like books. . . . Imposing limitations—that's what the church did in the 15th century. . . . It's up to us to work within them and yet transcend them at the same time. This becomes quite a challenge. . . . Who selects the subjects doesn't matter.

Then he thought a moment, and smiled. "Maybe this is a rationalization." But anyway there was more to be said.

"It isn't enough when drawing for children to make childlike drawings that you think children draw. Children don't have the co-ordination of eyes and brains and hands. . . .

"We like naïveté, because we like to go back to childhood." But is this what children like?

"I didn't know what I was doing until I went to some book fairs, and I got talking to kids." To Mr. Fisher it seemed that children wanted not abstraction, but realistic intensity. "I'm a fairly intense person myself, so it's fairly easy to do it." To some parents, less intense, it has seemed that Mr. Fisher sometimes goes too far in depicting conflict and violence.

Authenticity is important. But to him this is a matter of impression and impact rather than minute detail. He showed one of his drawings for the First Book Edition of *The Man Without a Country.* The flag had the proper number of stars to indicate the period, but Mr. Fisher was not slavish in reproducing such things as uniforms. "This man's face is more important than his buttons."

> *Roderick Nordell, " 'Non-Fuzzy Drawing Leads to Non-Fuzzy Thinking," in* The Christian Science Monitor, *May 3, 1962, p. C7.*

JOAN HESS MICHEL

For the past two years, Fisher has devoted his time and creative energies to an unusual and important project—The Colonial Craftsmen Series, a group of books published by Franklin Watts, which he has conceived, written, designed, and illustrated. These handsome books present the story of various Colonial crafts, some no longer practiced, in clear and understandable terms intended for fifth-grade-level students (although adults will find them fascinating, too). . . . Fisher believes that there will be a minimum of twenty titles in the entire series—enough to keep him busy writing and illustrating for the next five years. These books are unique for several reasons—first, because of Fisher's tripartite function as author, illustrator, and designer. By his own admission, he is neither a collector nor an antiquarian. However, he has always been interested in the "how" of the arts. He has a deep respect for the technical skills which were employed in the Colonial era in the creation of the everyday necessities of life—necessities so finely wrought that some of them achieved beauty and artistic quality. The basic task of research for The Craftsmen Series is a weighty one, for these books must be historically accurate and authentic as well as readable and attractive. In an article written for *The McClurg Book News,* January 1966, Fisher explained why he had chosen to explore the field of American craftsmanship:

> I felt compelled to tell my children that no great society, however artistically conscious and intellectually literate, can remain great with a proliferation of artistically clumsy hands; that they must begin

to educate and use their hands as well as their heads with consummate skill and selectivity to produce an art that will be articulate and which will endure. This requires hard work. It is not easy for those whose wealth and liberty would be unfathomable to past civilizations.

> I decided to try and convey all this in a group of books concerning the colonial American craftsman. He was the embodiment of pride and purpose, both in himself and in the unwavering belief in a scheme of life. His pride and purpose had built-in goals of such high order that improvement of his singular abilities and product was the only way to reach them. Also, I felt that I had to convey the idea that freedom of expression is meaningless unless you know what "freedom" is; and that artistic freedom is not necessarily individuality devoid of obligation, but the expression of independent intellect molded by conscience and made communicable by disciplined manual skill. This is a fundamental matter. It was as true for the early American craftsman as it was for the fifth-century B.C. Greek sculptor; the Byzantine calligrapher; the fifteenth-century Siennese painter; and the nineteenth-century French Impressionist.

> The material for the project was everywhere—in museums, homes, restorations, and libraries. Also, I have gathered information, over the years, illustrating books about America. Surprisingly, some materials and tools originating in medieval Europe and used by Colonial craftsmen, have been employed in our modern era. I am acquainted with the form, properties, and use of these materials. I use them in the course of my work—albeit with different purpose and effect.

> In any event, I chose the colonial period to make my point because I am concerned with America. It was the only time in our history when national intent was clearly expressed via remarkable craftsmanship, despite inconceivable hardship. Such desire for perfection not only necessitated a proud passion to give one's best, but to recognize the best when confronted with it and to demand it always. This is what gives excellence to art and to the society that nourishes it. This is what I want my children to understand.

Fisher's black-and-white scratchboard illustrations for The Craftsmen Series have drama, vitality, a fine painterly quality, and are historically correct.

Fisher explains his basic approach to the scratchboard technique and his working procedure. Since he is also the author of The Craftsmen Series, he has a natural "feeling" for the illustrable sections of each book. Fisher plans the entire format of each book, noting where illustrations will fall in the text. He makes preliminary pencil sketches on tracing paper—general, roughly blocked-out drawings, not too detailed. For the actual, final illustration, Fisher uses English scraper board mounted on chip board, which he covers with a coating of India ink. . . . He then proceeds to trace the basic outline of his illustration (guided by his rough) on the blackened surface. Employing only two tools, a needle and a knife, he cuts and scrapes the ink away until he achieves the desired effect. The resultant illustrations are strong and effective, possessing a dramatic quality, as well as explaining and illuminating the text. His touch is sure and precise, carefully delineating even complicated equipment used by the Colonial craftsmen—looms, presses, tools. In all his scratchboard work, Fisher says, he is attempting to "express drama and form", and he believes this is close to the feeling he achieves in his more serious painting. (pp. 46-7, 67-8)

Fisher's paintings and illustrations reflect his strong, positive approach. They are commanding and intense, drawing the viewer to long and close study. One cannot easily turn aside, for they cry out to be seen, to have their message understood.

He is sincerely interested in the progress of his Craftsmen Series of books, anxious for their success and happily occupied daily with their preparation. In giving expression to his talent, Leonard Everett Fisher has found creative happiness and artistic exhilaration. (p. 70)

> *Joan Hess Michel, "Leonard Everett Fisher: Illustrator & Painter," in* American Artist, *Vol. 30, No. 7, September, 1966, pp. 42-7, 67-70.*

MAY HILL ARBUTHNOT AND ZENA SUTHERLAND

The Glassmakers was the beginning of a distinguished set of books by Leonard Everett Fisher on "Colonial Americans and Colonial American Craftsmen," a series admired as much for the excellence in its design, illustrations, and format as for its content. Long a subject studied in schools and of interest to young persons, colonial people had not been dealt with in single volumes in quite this fashion, and the books were welcomed, for they filled a great need. They are designed so that a full-page picture on the right faces three quarters of a page of text on the left, with an occasional double-spread picture. The illustrations, drawn with vigor, picture costume details and daily customs. There are many small, accurate drawings of the tools of each trade, and each drawing is carefully labelled and described. (pp. 595-96)

> *May Hill Arbuthnot and Zena Sutherland, in an excerpt in their* Children and Books, *fourth edition, Scott Foresman and Company, 1972, pp. 595-96.*

PUMPERS, BOILERS, HOOKS, AND LADDERS: A BOOK OF FIRE ENGINES (1961)

A book that covers the history of fire-fighting equipment in cursory fashion, with startling illustrations in red, massive and almost overpowering. Each illustration is on a double-page spread, with a few lines of text on one of the pages. Some of the writing is pedestrian: "Nearly everybody became a little sad when the Gasoline engine replaced the horse."—most of the text is however, factual if dry in style. For the young child who is very interested in fire engines, a variety in illustration or some added detail would make the book more useful. *The Big Fire* by Olds (1945) covers much of the same material and gives additional information in text and illustration.

> *Zena Sutherland, in a review of "Pumpers, Boilers, Hooks and Ladders," in* Bulletin of the Center for Children's Books, *Vol. XIV, No. 9, May, 1961, p. 142.*

With a fine blast of red and his usual decorative strength in the black outlines and shadows, Leonard Everett Fisher has made a series of wide double-page spreads of fire engines from the first pumpers to modern speeding giants. His text wisely confines itself to simple descriptions of the changes, and is attractively arranged on the pages of this low, wide picture book with a nice touch of the Victorian in the design of the capital letters. We can just see small boys eagerly noticing how the hats of the fire-fighters change with their changing engines, from tricorne to high hat and from helmets of various sorts to trim soldierly affairs. This is less detailed, but along the same lines as the splendid book that has been popular for many years. Elizabeth Olds' *Big Fire*, and, like it, has less simplified writing in it than the useful practice reader, *The True Book of Policemen and Firemen*, by Opal Miner.

> *Margaret Sherwood Libby, in a review of "Pumpers, Boilers, Hooks and Ladders," in* Books, *New York, July 23, 1961, p. 12.*

A HEAD FULL OF HATS (1962)

The comic-cartoon illustrations are the better half of this tale. In appearance Alfie Oliver is a Gay Nineties charmer with a bush-thick moustache, surprised eyes, and a closet full of derbies. Mr. Fisher uses Alfie's hat-collecting instincts to preach a sermon about Being Yourself. Adults may think along these moral-extracting lines, but they seem a little too pat for children, or, one would guess, Alfie Oliver.

> *Melvin Maddocks, "I Never Saw a Purple Quetzal," in* The Christian Science Monitor, *May 10, 1962, p. B3.*

Leonard Everett Fisher can be seen at his most robust and whimsical in the illustrations for his book *A Head Full of Hats.* There is a grand, old-fashioned comic strength to his pages that show a mustached man trying on a variety of headpieces, from an admiral's hat to an Indian chief's war bonnet. However, the story of Alfie Oliver's discovery that the hat does not make the man, is not memorable.

> *George A. Woods, "For Fun, Frolic, Wisdom and Wonder," in* The New York Times Book Review, *Part II, May 13, 1962, p. 5.*

THE GLASSMAKERS (1964)

This is the first in a new series on outstanding craftsmen in Colonial America. It is so well done that its brevity is a disappointment. The history and technique of glassmaking are described and illustrated in a manner that should delight all children and develop pride in their forebears.

> *Robert C. Bergenheim, "Kibitzing on Men at Work," in* The Christian Science Monitor, *November 5, 1964, p. B9.*

Illustrated in Mr. Fisher's distinctive style, a book that describes very briefly the beginnings of glassmaking in this country. The details of the glassmaking processes are adequately explained, the emphasis in the text being on the techniques rather than on the products. One of a series of books about craftsmen of colonial America, the book is not meant to be comprehensive; the information given is also found in Buehr's *The Marvel of Glass* (1963) which is more extensive in coverage. *The Glassmakers* is, however, a very handsome book and a good introductory presentation of the topic.

> *Zena Sutherland, in a review of "The Glassmakers," in* Bulletin of the Center for Children's Books, *Vol. XVIII, No. 9, May, 1965, p. 128.*

From The Glassmakers, *written and illustrated by Leonard Everett Fisher.*

THE PRINTERS; THE PAPERMAKERS   (1965)

In these little books for children of fifth grade level and up, a fine illustrator, who is also a concise, clear writer, describes the crafts of Colonial America. There will be 13 titles in the series. **The Printers** and **The Papermakers** are of bookmaking interest both because of their handsome illustrations—which emphatically *illustrate*—and for their brief, simple and illuminating accounts of the industries they describe.

Each book has two sections—historical and technical. For instance, the first part of **The Printers** notes the role of printers in the struggle for freedom of expression, and the second part explains what the printers did and the equipment they used in setting type, making up forms and operating their presses. Illustrations, besides showing the materials and tools, include legible reproductions of Colonial newsletters and book pages.

Similarly, **The Papermakers** sketches the history of American papermaking until the Revolution was under way, and then explains the process of making paper before automatic equipment was invented.

Each book has a good glossary and an index and other extra information.

> *A review of "The Printers" and "The Papermakers," in* Publishers Weekly, *Vol. 187, No. 18, May 3, 1965, p. 116.*

[**The Printers** is another] an excellent series of books on craftsmen in Colonial America. It shows the first printers in America were just as courageous as the minutemen in the fight for freedom. They fought censorship under the threat of imprisonment and stirred their countrymen to the common cause. An inspiration to children of all ages.

> *Robert C. Bergenheim, in a review of "The Printers," in* The Christian Science Monitor, *September 16, 1965, p. 7.*

As in the preceding volumes in this useful series, the text [of **The Papermakers**] is divided into a brief review of the first craftsmen in the trade and a longer section on the manufacturing procedures. The technique of papermaking in colonial times is described in considerable detail, occupational terms being italicized. The writing is brisk and dry, the illustrations handsome and, in the second part of the book, informative. A list of papermaking terms, an index, and some samples of colonial watermarks are appended.

> *Zena Sutherland, in a review of "The Papermakers," in* Bulletin of the Center for Children's Books, *Vol. 19, No. 3, November, 1965, p. 43.*

THE HATTERS; THE WIGMAKERS   (1965)

Fortunate indeed are those fifth graders who have any of Mr. Fisher's books on Colonial American craftsmen. His latest two, making a total of six with seven more to come, continue the same high quality of fact and ingenuity to capture the imaginations of youngsters and even their parents as well.

> *Robert C. Bergenheim, "Yankee Doodling," in* The Christian Science Monitor, *November 4, 1965, p. B7.*

[**The Hatters** is a] good book in the series, with a much more extensive historical section than is in most of the previous volumes about colonial industries: an emphasis due to the importance of the beaver pelts in colonial economy and to the legislative restrictions imposed by England. The section on the industry itself is detailed and interesting, although there are some instances of writing (or captioning of the handsome illustrations) that seem not quite clear.

> *Zena Sutherland, in a review of "The Hatters," in* Bulletin of the Center for Children's Books, *Vol. 19, No. 6, February, 1966, p. 97.*

As in the other books in this series, the text [of **The Wigmakers**] is divided into a section on the historical background for the industry and one on the techniques of manufacture. The illustrations are nicely detailed and quite informative, although in this volume there are, in the section on technique, a few pages in which both illustrative detail and textual explanation seem inadequate.

> *Zena Sutherland, in a review of "The Wigmakers," in* Bulletin of the Center for Children's Books, *Vol. 19, No. 6, February, 1966, p. 97.*

THE SCHOOLMASTERS   (1967)

Because of the intrinsic interest of the subject matter and the paucity of information thereon, we took a longer look at this than at some earlier entries in the series. Expectedly, it fits the role of the Colonial schoolmaster into the framework of education in general, from the European backgrounds to Independence, from the ABC's to college. The result is an enlightened essay with particular attention to the social and intellectual clime: the hornbook is here, and the hard benches, but also the established church, the established classes. And schoolmasters varied. Ichabod was one, Nathan Hale was another—here's why.

> *A review of "The Schoolmasters," in* Kirkus Service, *Vol. XXXV, No. 13, July 1, 1967, p. 742.*

Written in sober, expository style, this is an account of the development of schools and teaching in colonial America. Unfortunately, the telling is so dull that only a child bent upon fulfilling a school assignment will plod through the book. His imagination and interest will hardly be fired, despite the fine format and illustrations.

> *Gertrude B. Herman, in a review of "The Schoolmasters," in* School Library Journal, *Vol. 14, No. 1, September 15, 1967, p. 118.*

Another in a distinguished series on Colonial America by Leonard Fisher is out—*The Schoolmasters.* Youngsters in the fourth grade and up certainly will find this an eye-opener. If they think school is tough now, wait until they read how primitive and rough it was in colonial America. Teachers in those days qualified if they were sober, and big enough to beat the class bully. Often the schoolmaster could barely read or write himself. Again Mr. Fisher has shown his talent of entwining history with good conversation and vivid black and white drawings.

> *Robert C. Bergenheim, "Shape Up, Ship Out, Tune In," in* The Christian Science Monitor, *November 2, 1967, p. B10.*

THE PEDDLERS (1968)

The format of this series—half words, half pictures—makes some sense when a skilled trade, its processes and products, are involved, but this one can be read without a glance at the facing page. As a brief essay on Colonial peddlers, starting with Massachusetts, this throws a little light on early trade, a little less on trade routes and the routes of the Revolution. If you're not committed to the series per se, you'll find it easy to pass up.

> *A review of "The Peddlers," in* Kirkus Service, *Vol. XXXV, No. 23, December 1, 1967, p. 1421.*

A clear and vigorous text which, in describing the colonial peddlers, leads to an understanding of simple business and economics in terms children can comprehend. Admitting that some "damnyankee" peddlers were greedy, the author stresses their general honesty, adventurous spirit, and individualism. Even more than the text, the strong scratchboard illustrations convey the struggles and strivings of colonial America and the importance of trade to a frontier society.

> *Patricia Alice McKenzie, in a review of "The Peddlers," in* School Library Journal, *Vol. 14, No. 5, January 15, 1968, p. 70.*

THE DOCTORS (1968)

In a clear style touched with humor, the author discusses the outstanding doctors of the pre-Revolutionary era, their medical training, the early use of plants as medicines, Indian remedies, and the epidemics of the time. This book can be read for pleasure as well as information and, of course, will supple-

ment the history curriculum well. The black-and-white scratchboard illustrations are, as usual, excellent.

> *Linda Lawson Clark, in a review of "The Doctors," in* School Library Journal, *Vol. 15, No. 2, October, 1968, p. 154.*

THE ARCHITECTS (1970)

Like the other titles in Fisher's Colonial Americans series, this is a clearly organized presentation of a trade; attractive, even though some of the workmen depicted in the strong, black-and-white scratchboard illustrations are unpleasant-looking characters. Architecture in the Southern, New England and Middle Atlantic colonies is treated with regard to heritage, history, the skills and materials that produced it, and development. Devlin's *To Grandfather's House We Go* (1967) and *What Kind of a House Is That?* (1969), and Downer's *Roots Over America* (1967) offer broader historical coverage less systematically. Tunis' *Colonial Craftsmen and the Beginnings of American Industry* (1965) and *Frontier Living* (1961) treat building and designing along with all other phases of American life, with special attention to tools and techniques of construction. Langdon's *Everyday Things in American Life,* 1607-1776 (1937) discusses architecture in several chapters, covering much of Fisher's material in a conversational manner which, while dated, expresses more understanding of, for example, the Palladian style in Europe and America, or Jefferson as an architect. Fisher's book, though brief, most clearly integrates architectural styles and historical facts.

> *Merritt Donaghy, in a review of "The Architects," in* School Library Journal, *Vol. 17, No. 1, September, 1970, p. 101.*

The first colonists in the New World included no architects; the builders were craftsmen, often assisted by untrained laborers, and the designs of the buildings were based on books brought from Europe or on adaptations conceived by gentlemen amateurs. As in Europe, some outstanding architectural design was translated into handsome buildings by gifted amateurs like Thomas Jefferson. In separate sections, the author discussed architectural developments in the southern, eastern, and middle Atlantic colonies. The book is illustrated with drawings and with photographs of colonial buildings, concluding with pictures of Carpenters' Hall in Philadelphia, the home of the first organization of carpenter-builders in the colonies. The patterns described in the three sections of the country are somewhat repetitive, and the book gives less information about techniques and skills than do most of the preceding books in the series, but it is useful, if not very substantial.

> *Zena Sutherland, in a review of "The Architects," in* Bulletin of the Center for Children's Books, *Vol. 24, No. 10, June, 1971, p. 157.*

TWO IF BY SEA (1970)

Mary Kay Phelan's *Midnight Alarm: The Story of Paul Revere's Ride* (1968) accomplished more with equal authenticity and made a better story of it; this recreation of the great event, which focuses on the signalling per se not the subsequent ride, combines fictionalized reconstruction with backing and filling, in a disjunctive fashion. Emphatically so when what's filled in is an unwelcome interruption and less than germane: Revere has just been summoned to Dr. Warren's for a late, unexpected meeting—"Revere's mother, creaking back and forth in a rocking chair, had watched the quick scene at the doorway but had heard nothing of the whispered conversation. Rachel, Revere's second wife, was upstairs with her baby son. So were Revere's five daughters by his first wife, who had died two years earlier." Then, too, the flat format and the dramatic design (Mr. Fisher's familiar scratchboard specters bestride the pages) suggest something quite different from what's proffered, and for a considerably younger child. The shift from Warren to Revere to British General Gage does give the latter a chance to fuss about the colonists' ingratitude—didn't he protect their children against the pricks of the Redcoats' bayonets?—and the final trailing of Sexton Robert Newman to the belfry of Christ Church fosters suspense. But the epilogue is not a substitute for finishing the story, and anyhow there's Phelan, consonant externally and internally.

> *A review of "Two If by Sea," in* Kirkus Reviews, *Vol. XXXVIII, No. 20, October 15, 1970, p. 1152.*

[**Two If by Sea**] is a dramatic recounting of Paul Revere's Ride and an excellent example of how to build upon and retain the essential nature of a widely known folk tale while sneaking up on the young reader with a variety of "true facts." The heroes remain heroes but far more real for having worries and foibles of their own; and the text, integrated nicely with pictures and a map, is a model of accuracy. . . . The format is not particularly attractive; but **Two If by Sea** will please most readers.

> *Robin W. Winks, "How America Got Started," in* The New York Times Book Review, *Part II, November 8, 1970, p. 3.*

The strong lines and dramatic contrast of dark blue and white illustrations are an attractive complement to the tension of the minutely-described events of the evening of April 18, 1775. The book is in four sections, each giving an exact account, historically-based and with some background information, of the actions of four men during two eventful hours of that night: Joseph Warren, who sent the message to Revere; Paul Revere; the young man who lit the signal lanterns, Robert Newman; and the commanding general of the British forces, Thomas Gage. The shift of viewpoint adds to the suspense, the writing style is adequate, and the book is an attractive variant on the many books about aspects of the American Revolution. Its weakness is minor: there is, in some sections of the book, a noticeable drawing-out of material when the immediate action of the hours between nine and eleven is slight.

> *Zena Sutherland, in a review of "Two If by Sea," in* Bulletin of the Center for Children's Books, *Vol. 25, No. 1, September, 1971, p. 5.*

PICTURE BOOK OF REVOLUTIONARY WAR HEROES (1970)

Brief accounts of 50 people "who actively opposed the presence of British rule in the colonies." A page is devoted to each: it includes a descriptive paragraph along with one of Mr. Fisher's familiar scratchboard drawings; both type and drawings are blue. The subjects are arranged alphabetically within four sections (New England, middle colonies, South-

ern colonies and foreign allies), and many—e.g., Hale, Revere, Washington, Lafayette—are better covered in other sources. However, lesser known figures (including black soldiers Hector and Sisson) are difficult to locate elsewhere. In his discussion of Deborah (Sampson) Gannett, the author repeats the errors other writers have made—Deborah was most likely *not* black, and her male masquerade (as a soldier) was discovered while she was in the army, not nine years later. Nevertheless, this title is of acceptable quality as a supplement to history collections.

> *Elizabeth Gillis, in a review of "Picture Book of Revolutionary War Heroes," in* School Library Journal, *Vol. 17, No. 6, February, 1971, p. 56.*

Leonard Everett Fisher's **Picture Book of Revolutionary War Heroes** is well illustrated, but contains what seems an excess of chauvinistic comment. The etchings give a new dimension to the average youthful conceptions of some leading characters. Properly included are Negroes who participated in the war. If the selection of leaders is meant to be representative, there are important omissions.

> *North Callahan, "1776—Before Broadway," in* The New York Times Book Review, *Part II, May 2, 1971, p. 16.*

THE DEATH OF EVENING STAR: THE DIARY OF A YOUNG NEW ENGLAND WHALER (1972)

[**The Death of Evening Star**] deals with legends of the whaling ships out of New England. It is a dark tale of murder most foul in which a water-soaked diary tells us what happened to Jeremiah Poole, cabin boy on the Evening Star. Caught between a bucko mate, a mutinous crew and a corrupt captain Jeremiah's lot is awful. Pretty awful too is Fisher's unrelieved account of the slaughter of the whales. Somewhere behind it all is the ghostly presence of dead men who may or may not have existed, and ships that foundered with no trace appear mysteriously out of the night. The author's illustrations are as clean as his text is confusing.

> *Basil Heatter, "All at Sea," in* The New York Times Book Review, *November 26, 1972, p. 10.*

Subtitle notwithstanding, to classify the tale of the ill-fated *Evening Star* as merely a story of the whaling industry would be oversimplification—comparable to dismissing *Moby Dick* as a fish story. True, the whaling jargon is accurate; the handsome black-and-white scratchboard illustrations are detailed and graphic; but the author's research has produced more than an historical documentary of the days " 'when the greatest struggle on the boiling sea was the battle of man and whale—New England man and whale.' " Rather, by judicious use of the story-within-a-story technique, he adds further dimension to his tale by suggesting a sense of the past, the possible influence of supernatural forces, and the conflict between good and evil. A secret diary kept by novice seaman Jeremiah Poole in 1841 is mysteriously rediscovered in the twentieth century. When the contents of that diary are disclosed, the reader—together with the narrator—is carried back to the mid-nineteenth century and given an ingenuous, first-person account of an intriguing way of life. Much of the story's impact rests upon the style and tone of the diary which develops the characterization of Jeremiah, a preacher's son forced by circumstance into a way-of-life alien to his personality and upbringing. Indeed, the contrast between Jeremiah's youthful innocence and the varying degrees of moral indifference exhibited by his shipmates is as precisely and artistically balanced as are the meticulous illustrations. And, as in all good stories of suspense, there are hints of problems never solved. An engrossing combination of social history and the occult.

> *Mary M. Burns, in a review of "The Death of 'Evening Star': The Diary of a Young New England Whaler," in* The Horn Book Magazine, *Vol. XLVIII, No. 6, December, 1972, p. 595.*

While [this] gloomy tale is full of action, the action is all at one level, and the real author's achievement in incorporating period material and authentic details of shipping and whaling is almost obscured by the relentless aura of doom and plethora of violence. (pp. 153-54)

> *Zena Sutherland, in a review of "The Death of 'Evening Star': The Diary of a Young New England Whaler," in* Bulletin of the Center for Children's Books, *Vol. 26, No. 10, June, 1973, pp. 153-54.*

THE ART EXPERIENCE: OIL PAINTING, 15th-19th CENTURIES   (1973)

An unbelievably interesting book on art. Teachers and art students will pay particular attention to this discussion of the craft, rather than technique or interpretation, of fine art. Full-color reproductions are accompanied by photographs and black/white sketches that guide the reader to "underpaintings and other processes" that led to the finished work of art. Five other books are in preparation covering various painting techniques, and if as well done, should be valuable additions to libraries—and a thoughtful idea for gift-giving.

> *Mrs. John Gray, in a review of "The Art Experience," in* Best Sellers, *Vol. 33, No. 18, December 15, 1973, p. 428.*

In the first volume of a projected Art Experiences series, the author (a painter himself) explains the various ways in which paint—in this case, oil paint—has been applied to different surfaces. Assuming an historical viewpoint, the book unfolds the evolution of oil painting: how painters moved from a waterbased egg tempera to the warmer, softer oil medium, and how the changing application of oil paint itself created dynamic possibilities. Details about periods of art, methods of painting, and techniques of painting underlie the artist's creation, but the explanations lack sufficient depth, for the author has not clarified and highlighted the minutiae. Since the book was intended for a junior high audience, the truncation of the material and the poor placement of the illustrations limit its usefulness. But the information is interesting, the historical-technical approach unusual; and the full-color illustrations and format are attractive.

> *Anita Silvey, in a review of "The Art Experience: Oil Painting 15th-19th Centuries," in* The Horn Book Magazine, *Vol. L, No. 1, February, 1974, p. 61.*

THE WARLOCK OF WESTFALL   (1974)

Imagine a now vanished colonial village called Westfall, near Salem, Mass., where it is cocky, blustery boys rather than high-strung girls who raise the specter of witchcraft, rousing a self-righteous populace (and a self-interested preacher) to the hysterical hanging of a crusty, slightly addled, old recluse whose crime was inventing a dead wife and children in his loneliness and marking their "graves" with crosses. Fisher tells it as it might have happened, in an almost surrealistically heightened atmosphere of oppression and terror. Striking and evocative.

> *A review of "The Warlock of Westfall," in* Kirkus Reviews, *Vol. XLII, No. 3, February 1, 1974, p. 110.*

Somber yet dramatic, the stark black and white illustrations in Fisher's distinctive style are particularly well suited to the taut and brooding atmosphere evoked in this tale of witch-hunting in colonial America. The setting is the small village of Westfall, where an old, crotchety man is accused by a group of boys and hanged by the villagers, easily aroused in those hysterical times. The tense conclusion, in which the same credulous hysteria brings about the abandonment of the village, is conceived with a fine sense of theater. Both the mood of the times and the physical atmosphere are skillfully evoked in a stirring and convincing story.

> *Zena Sutherland, in a review of "The Warlock of Westfall," in* Bulletin of the Center for Children's Books, *Vol. 27, No. 11, July-August, 1974, p. 176.*

SWEENEY'S GHOST   (1975)

Well, ducks, here we have the Framer family from Aspetuck, Connecticut—sounding for all the world like they've just popped out of a sociological tract on suburbia. The Framers just want to get away from it all and spend a quiet week at their rental villa in Jamaica but end up saddled with the rambunctious though invisible haunting of pirate Thomas Sweeney whose cockney squawking and feeble tricks keep them and us in a state of purposeless agitation. Sweeney's mischief isn't confined to the villa's bar—under which his hanged remains are buried; he rides on top of the car when the family goes out and even stows away with them on the plane back to JFK. Yet his presence never seems to be more than a minor irritation to the minimally differentiated family members. And this reads more like an outline for a projected story than a finished product; only Sweeney's outrageous diatribes ("Oi'm going to be loike a ruddy angel. . .") have been filled out.

> *A review of "Sweeney's Ghost," in* Kirkus Reviews, *Vol. XLIII, No. 10, May 15, 1975, p. 567.*

The story line consists of Sweeney's persecution of the family, and it is heavily padded and interrupted by long monologues by the ghost; much of this is used to give information about Sweeney and other pirates, as is a rather large portion of the dialogue between young Jo-Jo Framer and others in his family. The portions of the text describing the ghost's activities or giving his remarks are in italics, and the whole text is printed in paragraphs that are widely spaced so that the pages look as though they carry a series of separate topics. Add to the physical fragmentation a number of instances of careless writing ("Les . . . creeped forward," "No sooner had Coraleen arrived, she removed her shoes . . .") and the limitations of the book's appeal are clear. Each part of the story obtrudes on the other and each is thereby weakened; it seems probable that only the inveterate admirer of ghost or pirate stories would enjoy the book.

> *Zena Sutherland, in a review of "Sweeney's Ghost,"*

From The Death of *Evening Star*: The Diary of a Young New England Whaler, *written and illustrated by Leonard Everett Fisher.*

in Bulletin of the Center for Children's Books, *Vol. 29, No. 1, September, 1975, p. 8.*

ACROSS THE SEA FROM GALWAY (1975)

Fisher's tale begins with the wreck of the *St. John* on Grampus Rock off the Massachusetts coast in 1849, and with a glimpse of mute, stunned Patrick Donovan, one of the few to be saved from the boatload of Irish refugees. Then it's back to Ballingarry, County Tipperary, where wandering bard Liam Donovan—"My mother was the sweet dirt of Kilfenora; my father—a potato"—settled down to marry, have children and fend off starvation. Strayed away from their land, the family wanders to Galway where Liam earns pennies singing after the speeches of nationalist Donal O'Dell and scrapes together the money to send Patrick, his brother and his sister to America where they will be "safe." We've already seen the mournfully ironic ending to Liam's dream, and that's just what it is, for Fisher keeps a good distance away from his characters and has little interest in Patrick except as a symbol of survival. Once again, the fickle, awesome ocean is Fisher's real subject—with an equally fickle land thrown in for good measure. But he tells and illustrates the story with some grace, and if the story is at times self-

consciously monumental, it does have a kind of biblical austerity to it.

A review of "Across the Sea from Galway," in Kirkus Reviews, *Vol. XLIII, No. 15, August 1, 1975, p. 848.*

The struggle for physical and spiritual survival dominates this story of the Donovan family. . . . Liam Donovan is portrayed in depth—using flashbacks, Fisher relates Liam's life from early childhood to the time of Patrick's departure in 1849—but the other characters are sketchy. The author's style is direct and cohesive; the poetry of Thomas Moore is effectively used to introduce several sections of the four-part novel; and, black-and-white illustrations realistically capture the mood and character of the Irish. A deft treatment of a survival theme as well as an accurate depiction of Irish life during the great famine. (pp. 52-3)

Cynthia Adams, in a review of "Across the Sea from Galway," in School Library Journal, *Vol. 22, No. 5, January, 1976, pp. 52-3.*

LEONARD EVERETT FISHER'S LIBERTY BOOK (1976)

This elegant pictorial celebration of liberty is a handsome

album, a kind of coffeetable children's book. Fisher has collected clips of documents, speeches, and poems that reiterate colonial aspirations for liberty and has set many of them against dramatic royal blue or deep rust-red backgrounds. Some stand alone, looking vibrantly old and distinguished with their eighteenth-century printing or writing styles; others are embellished with Fisher's exquisite scratch-line etchings. Among the selections are Patrick Henry's volatile remarks before the Virginia Provincial Assembly, an excerpt from John Adams' diary describing colonists' actions against the Stamp Act, and facsimiles of colonial works of art and design that honor liberty. For those who cast a cynical eye on what could be called glorifying a myth, Fisher maintains in his preface that though American freedom is for many an unfulfilled promise, the essential integrity of purpose remains.

> *Denise M. Wilms, in a review of "Leonard Everett Fisher's Liberty Book," in* The Booklist, *Vol. 72, No. 12, February 15, 1976, p. 855.*

A disappointing compilation of songs, slogans, and quotations from the Revolutionary period, all containing the word "liberty." Fisher's bold red, white, and blue illustrations are powerful as usual, aptly reflect the Bicentennial spirit, but too many of the scant 47 pages contain only bold type print or filler designs. The appended notes identify the contents, yet do little to explain their significance. A Bicentennial extravaganza suitable for the coffee table, perhaps, but of little practical or inspirational use.

> *Gale K. Shonkwiler, in a review of "Leonard Everett Fisher's Liberty Book," in* School Library Journal, *Vol. 22, No. 7, March, 1976, p. 102.*

LETTERS FROM ITALY (1977)

An unfocused novella revolving around the reminiscences of Angelo Cappelo, a retired Italian-American restaurant owner. The four-part story abruptly shifts back and forth in time between Angelo's musings about his son Vinny who is in Italy fighting in World War II; the profound effect his grandfather, a revolutionary who fought with Garibaldi, had on his youth; his family's immigration from Italy in 1883; and his bereavement over Vinny's death. Angelo's personality never comes across in the sober and slow-moving third-person narrative which doesn't focus long enough on any event to explore its repercussions or connection with other incidents.

> *Leah Deland Stenson, in a review of "Letters from Italy," in* School Library Journal, *Vol. 23, No. 7, March, 1977, p. 151.*

The story of four generations of the Capello family, from Garibaldi's reunification of the Italian city-states in 1870 to World War II. In trying to depict the passionate patriotism of the family, the author uses a confusing series of flashbacks which place his characters in the midst of Italian historical scenes. The information could have been transmitted more effectively as true historical narrative rather than superimposing poorly developed characters to attempt a fictional approach. It's hard to predict who would read this—or why. Not Fisher at his best.

> *Barbara Baker, in a review of "Letters from Italy," in* Children's Book Review Service, *Vol. 5, No. 10,*

May, 1977, p. 99.

NOONAN: A NOVEL ABOUT BASEBALL, ESP, AND TIME WARPS (1978)

Chock-full of baseball action and team shenanigans, this humorous story languidly unfolds like an old postgame yarn told to a bunch of cronies. In 1896, the unsuccessful Brooklyn Dutchmen Baseball Club, under the management of Charlie O'Brien, is pinning its hopes on the pitching of 15-year-old Johnny Noonan. Hit by a foul ball, Johnny is transported to 1996, where he finds he has psychokinetic powers—including the ability to think a baseball where he wants it to go. The world of 1996 is changed, mainly due to the depletion of oil, but Johnny's abilities cause a national sensation, and he wins the perfect game—pitching 81 strikes. The reaction is overwhelming and Johnny is put into a hospital for protection. There, he wakes up back in his own time, only to find that he suddenly has amazing control over a baseball. As a fantasy this has some serious shortcomings (why and from where does he get and lose the power), but as a baseball spoof and tall tale, sports style, it's fun. Comical illustrations, black line on white for the present reality, white line on black for the future, spruce up the format.

> *Barbara Elleman, in a review of "Noonan: A Novel about Baseball, ESP, and Time Warps," in* Booklist, *Vol. 74, No. 22, July 15, 1978, p. 1733.*

Unfortunately, some readers may find this story which deftly combines the topics of baseball, ESP, and time warps just a little confusing. . . . For those readers who forge ahead, a joyful experience awaits them. Fisher has a sense of fun that is rarely found. He plays with his topics, his story, and his hero the way a child plays with a beloved toy. Some readers will get into the game with great ease, others will need a little nudge. Buy the book and push hard. Noonan deserves a chance.

> *Barbara L. M. Stiber, in a review of "Noonan: A Novel about Baseball, ESP, and Time Warps," in* Kliatt Young Adult Paperback Book Guide, *Vol. XV, No. 6, September, 1981, p. 9.*

ALPHABET ART: THIRTEEN ABCs FROM AROUND THE WORLD (1978)

Whatever may be gained here by introducing children to "the look of different alphabets of some non-English-speaking people in use around the modern world" is offset by the page of ostensible information that accompanies each set of letters (or signs). In the Arabic alphabet, we're told, "there is a flow of purpose and continuity that reflects the reach of an ancient but still vigorous Semitic people who are descended from the dim Biblical past. . . ," while the German "Gothic" alphabet is said to symbolize "man's parallel natures, his ignorance and enlightenment, so sharply delineated during the Gothic period"—claptrap in both cases. The "Five Civilized Tribes" of the American Southeast—discussed apropos of the Cherokee syllabary—allegedly "knew about civilization [because] their chiefs had been to London, met with royalty, and walked the city's streets"; and on Southerners, "chiefly Georgians," is put the onus of driving the Cherokee out. In the small area of hard, modern fact, we're led to believe that the Japanese, not the Chinese, are taking steps to Romanize their writing system, whereas the opposite is the case. And even granting the attractiveness, in the abstract, of Fisher's pages of letter forms, one may wonder if it isn't more instructive to see the various alphabets side by side—especially those with common Roman and Phoenician roots—as one can in an encyclopedic entry. Otherwise, it's the encyclopedia by a mile.

A review of "Alphabet Art: Thirteen ABCs from Around the World," in Kirkus Reviews, *Vol. XLVII, No. 2, January 15, 1979, p. 68.*

Nothing would appear to be a more mundane subject than an alphabet, yet its historical importance marking the "transition from prehistory to history—from no writing to writing" is immeasurable. How people first devised a visual means of recording spoken sounds and how they conceived those representations should look are the subject of this book. To set the stage for this exposition, the evolution of modern English letter forms from the semitic constructions of the people of the Sinai through Phoenician, Greek, and Roman representations is charted. Fisher examines thirteen alphabets from the non-English-speaking world, looking at their historical significance, their creation or evolution, and their relationship to the spoken language. As the Arabic, Cherokee, Chinese, Cyrillic, Eskimo, Gaelic, German, Greek, Hebrew, Japanese, Sanskrit, Thai, and Tibetan alphabets or syllabaries are successively presented, the various approaches to written language with their structural similarities and differences are made available for inspection. Each alphabet is introduced by an illustration symbolic of those peoples, which contains a word or phrase within its frame. This is followed by a brief history of the populace, the development of its language, and some comments on the contemporary status of the language. These accounts are followed by a chart of the alphabet, which contains individual letters, their English equivalents, a phonetic transliteration, and such special functional features as influence on adjacent letters or positional restriction; for example, a particular letter might be used only at the end of a word. Two functional features that most commonly show variations are the treatment of vowels and the fine distinctions some alphabets make in closely related sounds that other languages fail to make.

Each writing system uses either true alphabets or syllabaries. The latter form Fisher defines as "a set of letter combinations, symbols, or characters representing the full range of sounds of a particular language." Some writing systems are shown to have evolved naturally through intrinsic growth or cultural borrowing; others were the products of individual efforts by such people as Cyril, Peck, or Sequoyah, who designed, respectively, the Cyrillic, Eskimo, and Cherokee scripts.

Fisher's artistry is displayed in his handsome, wine-colored scratchboard illustrations and in the book's impressive calligraphy, which shows that writing is not only a means of communication but an elegant art form as well. *Alphabet Art* effectively draws attention to a device so commonplace that it goes all but unnoticed. The various alphabets are seen as means to providing a visible representation of auditory phenomena. As divergent responses to the ubiquitous problem of formulating sounds in print are displayed, young readers can make comparisons and draw inferences. The data from which to make deductions are available, but the reader is not spoon-fed or specifically directed as to how to treat this information. Extracting the inferences latent in the book is rightfully the obligation of the reader; the intellectually aggressive

child will find here a rich source of linguistic stimulation. (pp. 130-31)

Barbara H. Baskin and Karen H. Harris, in a review of "Alphabet Art: Thirteen ABCs from Around the World," in their Books for the Gifted Child, *R. R. Bowker Company, 1980, pp. 130-31.*

THE FACTORIES; THE RAILROADS (1979)

The first titles in a new series on 19th-Century America are characterized by excellent design, well-spaced, readable type, and Fisher's dramatic black-and-white scratchboard illustrations. The thrust, in both books, is the human side of history. Industry, labor, transportation, technology are seen as the product of human inventiveness and important to the lives of people.

The Factories starts in 1789 with Sam Slater, who came from England "with a few possessions in his hands and the Industrial Revolution in his head." He set up the first mechanized textile mill in New England. For a brief period, such mills were model industrial plants, staffed by carefully chaperoned "factory girls," until Southern slavery, cheap immigrant labor, and financial panics worsened conditions. New factories supplied the Gold Rush migration, provided weapons for the Civil War, and produced consumer goods for a rapidly expanding population. By the end of the century, labor disputes had begun and reform was in the air.

The Railroads lacks the simple chronological organization of *The Factories* and, without table of contents or page headings, it suffers from confusion of purpose, though human interest stories abound. Casey Jones, General Custer, Jesse James and Buffalo Bill were all heroes or villains of the westward expansion of the railroads. The locomotives themselves expanded from the early "Tom Thumb" engine to giant powerhouses capable of traveling 100 mph. In every American town, the "wrong side of the tracks" was determined by the direction of windblown soot and smoke.

Lively writing, startling facts and striking illustrations make these books excellent supplements to standard historical coverage of industrial growth in America.

Shirley Wilton, in a review of "The Factories; The Railroads," in School Library Journal, *Vol. 26, No. 3, November, 1979, p. 76.*

Fisher is a talented artist . . . , who does strong illustrations in the style of Rockwell Kent. His publisher has produced handsome books, well bound, on high grade paper. But Fisher's texts for his books are abstract overviews, encyclopedia articles really, on the subjects he has chosen, U.S. factories and railroads in the nineteenth century. There is no individual human story, and when one briefly turns up—like the story of how the Englishman Samuel Slater stole the secret of the water loom and brought it to America in the 1790s—it is over in a page and the text moves back to generalizations like "By midcentury the marvelous hum of confidence that had been the hallmark of young America had become a raspy noise".

That is the sort of abstraction that made history schoolbooks such bummers when I was a boy. I can't imagine that there are many preteens, the audience Fisher is aiming for, who will be interested in his books. What is needed to bring history alive—that awful phrase—for children and most grown-ups, too, is particularization: individual human stories, articles, photographs, paintings, buildings of the time under study. (p. 535)

William Stott, in a review of "The Factories" and "The Railroads," in Business History Review, *Vol. LIV, No. 4, Winter, 1980, pp. 534-35.*

THE HOSPITALS (1980)

Continuing his social history of nineteenth-century America, begun with *The Railroads* and *The Factories,* Fisher explores the growth of hospitals, dividing his coverage into half centuries. Section one focuses on the few health-care institutions available in the early 1800s, speaking of them as dark, disease-ridden places and recalling the horrific conditions that patients endured (or succumbed to). The introduction of ether in the mid-1850s improved the course of events, and part two relates the upward trend in medicine that followed. The work of men and women such as Bloodgood, Blackwell, and Sims; the beginning of ambulance and emergency room service; the opening of nurses' training programs; and the start of specialized clinics were contributing factors. Clear writing and startling facts invigorate this noteworthy discussion, while dramatic and eye-riveting woodcuts accentuate the bleak and depressing conditions of early hospitals.

Barbara Elleman, in a review of "The Hospitals," in Booklist, *Vol. 76, No. 18, May 15, 1980, p. 1363.*

In addition to factual but occasionally dull accounts of the founding of hospitals, Fisher also interjects descriptions of certain events or aspects which catch readers' interest. In describing medical care in the wild West, he writes of doctors "who dug out bullets from gunshot wounds with unwashed, ungloved fingers, (and) amputated limbs without the benefit of anything more antiseptic than a bottle of whiskey." Accounts of "hospital gangrene" and the inhumane treatment of the insane characterize the first half, up to 1850, whereas the second half covering the latter part of the 19th Century is drier fare. Black-and-white woodcuts emphasize the more dismal aspects of medical care. The vocabulary and sentence structure can be difficult at times, although terms are explained in context. A lack of table of contents and a limited index may impede access to the book. However, it adequately covers a neglected subject and is a utilitarian purchase for school and public libraries to supplement standard history and sociology texts.

Paula M. Davis, in a review of "The Hospitals," in School Library Journal, *Vol. 27, No. 6, February, 1981, p. 74.*

THE SPORTS (1980)

Upholding the standards set in previous volumes of his Nineteenth Century America series, Fisher writes briskly and authoritatively about competitive games and their social implications during America's early days. The text is illustrated by the award winner's masterful etchings, depicting horse racing, sailing, gymnastics, Olympic events, etc. An illuminating view of females playing tennis tells more than words why their participation in sports was limited to "genteel" games. With their voluminous clothes, it must have been hard to get the ball over the net. In addition to reporting on the sporting events, Fisher describes the feats of legendary figures like John L. Sullivan, Chief Sitting Bull, Bob Fitzsim-

mons and others, creating an exemplary document on an energetic age.

A review of "The Sports," in Publishers Weekly, *Vol. 218, No. 25, December 19, 1980, p. 51.*

The vigorous discussion of the development of athletic competition in nineteenth-century America is certainly in a lighter vein than the companion books in the "Nineteenth Century America" series—*The Hospitals, The Railroads,* and *The Factories.* You'll find competitive athletic games requiring skill, strength and stamina "in" and bloodier amusements involving animals "out." Colorful figures and events personalize a fast-paced history. Chapter divisions are called for where the author switches topics, such as going from sports with horses to "the gentler sports" of croquet, tennis, and golf. Fisher's familiar art work follows the text, reinforcing impressions of a vigorous, self-confident society. (pp. 344-45)

Ruth M. Stein, in a review of "The Sports," in Language Arts, *Vol. 58, No. 3, March, 1981, pp. 344-45.*

A RUSSIAN FAREWELL (1980)

Minus the songs and some of the schmalz, this story of Jewish merchant Benjamin Shapiro's large family (11 children and one on the way) in pre-Revolutionary Russia (1904) borrows heavily from *Fiddler on the Roof* in theme and spirit. As Fisher mentions in a preface, the Shapiro family's exodus is broadly representative of the experiences of thousands of Russian Jews fleeing to the U.S. More effective than Fisher's other ethnic historical novels (*Across the Sea From Galway,* about the Irish, and *Letters From Italy*), the story is given added force by the author's bleak and stark black-and-white sketches. However, the characters are not as developed or memorable as Fiddler's Tevye and his family. Also, young readers will be confused by the poorly drawn and misleading map entitled "Western Imperial Russia and Her Neighbors" at the beginning of the book.

Jack Forman, in a review of "A Russian Farewell," in School Library Journal, *Vol. 27, No. 5, January, 1981, p. 60.*

You can tell a great deal about this book by its cover, which features one of the author-illustrator's stark, imposing scratchboard etchings. A man and woman pause in the foreground; children crowd behind; steam chuffs from a distant locomotive.

There's more of the same inside: sharp but stylized moments; adults dominating the picture; children we're curious to know better. . . .

The book earns higher marks as history than as a novel. Illustrations and text present a series of striking black-and-white pictures that help bring a chaotic epoch into focus. But the Shapiros' story rarely breaks into living, moving color. Many of the most compelling moments are related in flashbacks or third-hand, keeping their adventures long ago and far away. The language is stiff, the dialogue so wooden it leaves splinters on the tongue.

It's no easy task to bring a family of 13 to life, much less make them represent five million other people. Unfortunately, the author never fulfills the promise of differentiating his characters from the rest of the huddled masses yearning to breathe free.

*Ellen Schecter, in a review of "A Russian Farewell,"
in* The New York Times Book Review, *January 18,
1981, p. 31.*

STORM AT THE JETTY (1981)

This effective mood piece relies on intense blue gray paintings to convey the drama of a summer storm that engulfs the jetty where a young boy often sits watching the sea. The text tells no story; rather, it describes the moods and sensory details of the jetty where Levi waits until the storm is upon him before retreating up a seawall ladder to escape the rolling waves. The scenes, initially well lit, grow progressively darker as the storm intensifies and then light again as calm returns. For a private, pensive viewing experience.

*Denise M. Wilms, in a review of "Storm at the
Jetty," in* Booklist, *Vol. 77, No. 20, June 15, 1981,
p. 1345.*

This beautifully illustrated vignette of a summer storm is an ode to the sea. Through the masterful use of shades of white, blue-gray and blue-black, Fisher's powerful illustrations move beyond reality into symbols of the magnificent power of the natural world. With the boy Levi Farber, one witnesses the change of a bright August day from calm sea and clear sky through wild sea and violent thunderstorm and back to quiet summer day. After the sea quieted, "Levi climbed onto the rocks. Now he could sit on the jetty's point, in the cockpit of the rocks, once again." Recommended for those few children who choose to savor the majesty of our world from their private cockpits.

*Barbra Hawkins, in a review of "Storm at the Jetty,"
in* School Library Journal, *Vol. 28, No. 2, October,
1981, p. 128.*

THE NEWSPAPERS (1981)

The 19th-century American newspaper, a subject with limited potential for ten-year-olds, doesn't in any case get its due here. Writing of the early Republic, Fisher makes no point of the exceptional number of local papers or the unusual freedom they enjoyed—or the extent to which most of the major ones (not just the one cited) were the creatures of political parties. In due course, we do hear about the spread of readership with the advent of the penny press, when papers were also sold singly and not by subscription; about the speed-up in reporting with the advent of the telegraph; and about the improvement in news-gathering with the founding of the wire-services. And of course we hear about the hard life of the newsboys. But much of the text is simply a hodgepodge of tenuously-linked, incidental information—as when Fisher shifts from a New York newspaper price-rise to Jenny Lind's New York debut ("at Castle Garden, once a fort and soon to become an immigration station, an aquarium, and finally the site of a national monument at Battery Park in lower Manhattan") to P. T. Barnum's early, fractious newspapering to the "salute from a cannon" that greeted his release from jail . . . to the slavery crisis (via "Any salute from a cannon would have seemed ominous in hindsight") to civil war in China! All this, moreover, in less than two pages. And Fisher's characteristic emblematic illustrations are a very poor

substitute for a chance to see what the papers actually looked like.

A review of "The Newspapers," in Kirkus Reviews,
Vol. XLIX, No. 14, July 15, 1981, pp. 873-74.

Like other books in this series, the material here is not merely descriptive, but also relates sociologically to the society in which it existed. Fisher points out, for example, that because local news traveled quickly and published news was late, the earliest newspapers focused on political events of national or international interest, and that because subscriptions were expensive and few people could afford them (or even read them) the slant was toward the interests of the educated, the wealthy, and the owners of businesses rather than toward the concerns of the private citizen. The text describes the changes (universal education, machines that set type, improved gathering of news) that made the newspapers available and popular; it discusses freedom of the press and the obligations (not always observed, early on) to tell the truth. Fisher describes the growth of some of the great newspapers and chains in a serious, information-packed, and intelligent overview of the newspaper industry, an account enlivened by some of the dramatic events in which its representatives were involved. Indexed, the book is illustrated by Fisher's distinctive, dramatic scratchboard pictures.

*Zena Sutherland, in a review of "The Newspapers,"
in* Bulletin of the Center for Children's Books, *Vol.
35, No. 2, October, 1981, p. 28.*

Fisher continues his "Nineteenth Century America" series with another vivid high quality addition. His four chapters divide the period into well defined thirds, except for the decade devoted to the Civil War—the Lincoln-Johnson years. The wealth of information not only depicts the growth of newspapers and their effects, but also the social and political changes that accompanied and were related to the development of the press. Fisher's typical scratchboard drawings illustrate events of the times. He validates a strong theme of the importance of a free press, and the balance it must maintain with people's rights. The book is chock full of momentous issues, events at home and abroad, names—all thrown out to the rhythm of the presses at a break-neck speed. There is almost too much to absorb in the allotted pages. The book is a fine summary of the nineteenth-century, zeroing in on the role of the newspapers, but you'll need to draw breath at the end of each chapter if the information and concepts are new.

Ruth M. Stein, in a review of "The Newspapers," in
Language Arts, *Vol. 59, No. 2, February, 1982, p.
158.*

THE SEVEN DAYS OF CREATION (1981)

Oversize pages are used for the stunning paintings that show the creation of light and darkness, land and sea, of birds and beasts and fish and people, of the sun and moon and stars. Fisher's colors are rich, his composition bold, his adaptation simple without deviating from the spirit of the Biblical version. "Once there was a watery vastness without life or light. Only the spirit of God moved across the darkness," the book begins, the letters printed in electric blue against the black/blue/green stippling of the first page. Very handsome indeed.

Zena Sutherland, in a review of "The Seven Days of

From The Seven Days of Creation, *adapted from the Bible and illustrated by Leonard Everett Fisher.*

Creation," *in* Bulletin of the Center for Children's Books, *Vol. 35, No. 1, September, 1981, p. 5.*

Fisher remains true to the creation account found in Genesis while simplifying the language for his intended audience. Despite the fact that he condenses the account, he maintains the essential story. Rich full-color illustrations reinforce the majestic quality of Fisher's adaptation. The brush strokes in his paintings provide texture even for the illustrations depicting the formless nature of the universe. Later, a red-orange sun blazes against the pink sky. A white-turquoise moon shimmers against deep violet. The book's large pictures and sparse text make it ideal for reading aloud to a group. (pp. 66-7)

Kathy Piehl, in a review of "The Seven Days of Creation," in School Library Journal, *Vol. 28, No. 6, February, 1982, pp. 66-7.*

For "evolutionists," "creationists," and all those in-between who see the Bible as a rich literary source and inspiration for artists, Fisher's vision can only stun. Impressionistic, acrylic, pointillist paintings go from "a watery vastness without life or light" to the seventh day of rest—from darkness to light. Only the doublespreads of pineapple-like flowers on the third day jar. Striking color and configuration with little text.

Ruth M. Stein, in a review of "The Seven Days of Creation," in Language Arts, *Vol. 59, No. 4, April,*

1982, p. 369.

THE UNIONS (1982)

Strong and effective scratchboard illustrations (a medium in which Fisher has no peer) extend a text that focuses, as do others in the author's excellent series of books about the United States in the nineteenth century, on the period under examination but that gives some background of labor disputes and organizations in colonial times. One of the crucial decisions that shaped the movement and public opinion was the 1806 court decision that a society of shoemakers was a criminal conspiracy: their crime was organizing themselves into a union, trying to force their employers into giving them pay raises. The text, well-organized and thoroughly researched, describes the many groups and legislative measures of the century, culminating in the founding of the Knights of Labor, the American Federation of Labor, labor-backed political action, and the series of famous strikes that included Homestead and Pullman. The book ends with an account of the establishment of Labor Day as a national holiday and, in 1898, of the Erdman Act, which established the policy of government mediation.

Zena Sutherland, in a review of "The Unions," in

Bulletin of the Center for Children's Books, *Vol. 35, No. 11, July-August, 1982, p. 205.*

Noting unions' roots in the 1700s, Fisher painstakingly describes each subsequent effort at collective bargaining. He includes biographical sketches of all the early greats, ending with Eugene Debs. Fisher encompasses all, far more than other similar works, demonstrating how the industrial revolution and the recurring economic cycles of boom and bust made unions necessary. He could have included more detail about child labor, of interest to young readers; and certainly the optimism he assigns leaders at the end of the century, if in fact so, was premature to say the least; for many setbacks and bloody battles lay ahead. But for the time covered, chiefly the 19th Century, the book is splendid. Fisher's newest in this attractive and useful series is illustrated by 21 of his characteristic black-and-white drawings. While the Haymarket hangings drawing is a bit gruesome, it and others clearly convey the idea that these were troubled times for the working man. (pp. 74-5)

Ann MacLeod, in a review of "The Unions," in School Library Journal, *Vol. 29, No. 5, January, 1983, pp. 74-5.*

A CIRCLE OF SEASONS (1982)

[A Circle of Seasons *was written by Myra Cohn Livingston.*]

It's saying a great deal to say that neither the poet nor the painter has ever done better—although each has done equally distinctive work—than in this lovely book. . . . The paintings are stunning, bold and stylized but with delicate details; there is variety in the brushwork and use of color, uniformity in the excellent use of space and shape to achieve effective compositions.

Zena Sutherland, in a review of "A Circle of Seasons," in Bulletin of the Center for Children's Books, *Vol. 35, No. 11, July-August, 1982, p. 211.*

Generically, this beautiful joint production by the painter Leonard Everett Fisher and the poet Myra Cohn Livingston is in the happy company of Ted Hughes and Leonard Baskin's *Season Songs* (1975)—the perfect blending of poetry and painting. . . . [The] line, color and music of the shaped stanzas are translated metaphorically (in the literal sense) into the geometries and the coloristic patterns of the paintings.

Peter Neumeyer, in a review of "A Circle of Seasons," in School Library Journal, *Vol. 28, No. 10, August, 1982, p. 118.*

Personifying the seasons and specifying their activities metaphorically, the poet has employed both description and invocation to give her stanzas a dynamic pattern. . . . The full-color illustrations are abstractions rather than naturalistic equivalents for the verses, created from purely coloristic or geometrical elements sensitively and ingeniously generated by the phraseology of the poetry. As in the imagery of the verses, the carefully disciplined use of color and form is intense rather than startling; words and pictures taken together create a surprising combination of exaltation and serenity. (pp. 526-27)

Paul Heins, in a review of "A Circle of Seasons," in

The Horn Book Magazine, *Vol. LVIII, No. 5, October, 1982, pp. 526-27.*

NUMBER ART: THIRTEEN 123s FROM AROUND THE WORLD (1982)

A lovely, esoteric volume that is almost a "coffee-table book" for children. It has real problems—overwriting and limited use among them—but its strong points should not be overlooked. Fisher traces the development of numbers from their inception to their variety of forms throughout the world. He begins with an introduction that is so convoluted that few children will have patience with it. But the majority of the book is taken up with one-page discussions of various cultures (Arabic, Greek, Thai, Mayan) and how they discovered and used their numbering systems. These pages are faced with glorious royal blue-and-white woodcuts depicting scenes from the ancient cultures. Following are two-page spreads that reproduce the numbers in bold blue with the name of the number and its Arabic sign. The book's use is probably limited to those with a special interest or to gifted children. But everyone can enjoy the riveting artwork and the careful attention to design that makes this a pleasure to look at.

Ilene Cooper, in a review of "Number Art: Thirteen 123s from Around the World," in Booklist, *Vol. 79, No. 9, January 1, 1983, p. 617.*

In a format similar to *Alphabet Art* the author-artist traces the history of numbers from primitive attempts at record-keeping to the development of the present-day notation system based on the one first expressed in ancient Brahmi. Thirteen numerical systems—Arabic, Armenian, Brahmi, Chinese, Egyptian, Gothic, Greek, Mayan, Roman, Runes, Sanskrit, Thai, and Tibetan—are reproduced in a strong blue on white backgrounds. Each system is preceded by a succinct commentary setting it in the context of the culture from which it came and indicating, where appropriate, significant individual contributors to its development. Handsome full-page illustrations, also printed in blue, illuminate the texts. And while the layout is consistent, the artist has achieved diversity by exploring the possibilities of line, perspective, and composition to evoke a variety of effects: pyramids dwarfed by a night sky, flame-lit arches framing invading Goths, a massive slab etched with enigmatic runes. The treatment of numerical notation as symbol and as art is an interdisciplinary approach investing a familiar subject with new vigor. A thoughtful, informative, and beautiful book. (pp. 60-1)

Mary M. Burns, in a review of "Number Art: Thirteen 123s from Around the World," in The Horn Book Magazine, *Vol. LIX, No. 1, February, 1983, pp. 60-1.*

THE SCHOOLS (1983)

After a brief summary of colonial education, Fisher outlines the changes in American schools in the 19th Century, concentrating on the development of types of schools and the slow growth of public supported education. He places these changes in the context of political and economic life of the time and especially mentions the work of Mann and Barnard. Unfortunately, only a brief part of the text deals with curriculum and textbooks, except to list some titles and give a few brief quotes. School buildings are briefly described but a typical school day is not. Fine woodcuts accompany but do not clarify the text; only one shows the inside of a school building. This book is a succinct survey of the development of education but much the same information could be found in an encyclopedia.

> *Margaret C. Howell, in a review of "The Schools,"*
> *in* School Library Journal, *Vol. 29, No. 10, August,*
> *1983, p. 64.*

Fisher's 60-page synthesis can scarcely do justice to the themes he introduces: industrialization, the separation of church and state, the growth of cities, Jacksonian democracy, slavery, and trade unionism all played a part in the formation of our educational system. Though a less ambitious treatment would have better served young readers of history, those looking for a broad overview will find this helpful. As in other books in the series, distinguished scratchboard drawings are both decorative and informative, with portrayals of period schoolhouses and famous educators. (p. 84)

> *Karen Stang Hanley, in a review of "The Schools,"*
> *in* Booklist, *Vol. 80, No. 1, September 1, 1983, pp.*
> *83-4.*

Drawings and diagrams of typical schoolhouses add visual reinforcement to statements about the desolate and dreary environments provided for the young scholars. The author provides a useful survey of nineteenth-century schooling at all levels—kindergarten to university. Attractive in design, straightforward in tone, the book offers an opportunity to review the past and compare it with the present, noting that while advances have been made, many of today's debates about education are far from new.

> *Mary M. Burns, in a review of "The Schools," in*
> The Horn Book Magazine, *Vol. LIX, No. 5, October, 1983, p. 590.*

STAR SIGNS (1983)

Fisher, an author-illustrator who is as gifted as he is prolific, creates delights for the eyes and an education in myth vs. science in his stunning new book. The opening chapter describes lucidly the genesis of astrology (from the Greek *astro* and *logos,* "star" and "talk") over 4000 years ago. Ancient peoples believed mistakenly that the sun moved around Earth; Sumerians, Egyptians and others believed in deities they could see in the heavens, bodies we know as planets. In the 16th century, Copernicus established astronomy as a science (named for the Greek *nomos,* "law"). Terrific, boldly colored portraits of Taurus, Gemini, Cancer and the other zodiac signs illustrate Fisher's accounts about how their legends were born and the supposed traits of humans under their influences.

> *A review of "Star Signs," in* Publishers Weekly, *Vol. 224, No. 8, August 19, 1983, p. 78.*

As an astrological coffee-table browsing book for the junior crowd, this is superior. The cautious and open-ended historical introduction to astrology is accurate and brief, leaving readers the option of independent decision on the topic. Each sign of the zodiac is given a two-page treatment, with a full-page picture facing the text. Along with each sign and its symbol, the dates, planetary ruler and body part emphasized are stated. Fisher then gives a condensation of the myth of

each sign and the traits of those born under the sign. A sizable illustration of the constellation rounds out the discussion. In all, an excellent summary of the zodiac. The complex, vibrantly colored illustrations on the recto pages resemble Wildsmith's in brilliance of tone, but are far more realistic. The hard-edged detailed precision typical of other Fisher works has softened. Lavishly pleasing foreground designs spill over the borders, intensifying the subjects. This has more of a visual impact than Creative Education's 12-part "Sun Sign" series, which offers individual titles for each sign. For older children interested in links between astrology and mythology, Jagendorf's *Stories and Lore of the Zodiac* (1977) is the next level up. (pp. 74-5)

> *Leslie Chamberlin, in a review of "Star Signs," in*
> School Library Journal, *Vol. 30, No. 5, January, 1984, pp. 74-5.*

BOXES! BOXES! (1984)

Children will enjoy the variety of boxes shown, and they may infer concepts of size and shape, but the chief attraction of the book will surely be the beauty of the innovative selection of objects Fisher has chosen. The text is minimal and rhyming: "A box can be small. A box can be tall. Narrow and slim/Or filled to the rim." The illustrations, acrylic paintings, for these four are two small boxes, a case in which there's a toy soldier, a case of colored pencils, and a delectable box of chocolates. The bright, clean colors and the deft use of shadows add to the effectiveness of the artist's compositions.

> *Zena Sutherland, in a review of "Boxes! Boxes!" in*
> Bulletin of the Center for Children's Books, *Vol. 37, No. 8, April, 1984, p. 146.*

Each line of the pleasantly simple rhymes is accompanied by boldly placed shapes of familiar objects glowing with strong bright colors. . . . Boxes of all sizes bulge with puppies, geraniums, the author's paints, and even a pop-up clown. The brief, unpretentious text neatly avoids monotony by welcome changes in rhythm and is enhanced by the large, easy-to-read print. A cheerful book, it achieves a satisfying harmony and cumulative effect throughout as the illustrations grow ever larger, livelier, and more complex.

> *Ethel R. Twichell, in a review of "Boxes! Boxes!" in*
> The Horn Book Magazine, *Vol. LX, No. 3, June, 1984, p. 319.*

SKY SONGS (1984)

[Sky Songs *was written by Myra Cohn Livingston.*]

Beautiful illustrations and image-filled poetry are integrated to create a challenging book of quality. Fourteen brief poems about the sky encompass apt descriptions of heavenly bodies and weather conditions. Each poem is placed on an exceptional two-page acrylic painting. Fisher's colorful illustrations will raise children's sensitivity about the beauty inherent in the Earth's sky. The design of each picture is attention grabbing: it is as if the illustrator is looking at the Earth's atmosphere from the air and capturing its essence in all its moods. Unfortunately, the dark ground of one illustration obscures the text. Both Fisher and Livingston reveal a scientific knowledge of astronomy and atmospheric weather conditions, tempered by their artistic imaginations. They picture nature as beautiful and magnificent ("Shooting Stars") but also capable of menace and danger ("Storm"). *Sky Songs* can be appreciated by many ages: the very young will like the illustrations and older children will have a greater understanding of the relationship between poems and illustrations.

> *Hope Bridgewater, in a review of "Sky Songs," in*
> School Library Journal, *Vol. 30, No. 10, August,*
> *1984, p. 62.*

THE OLYMPIANS: GREAT GODS AND GODDESSES OF ANCIENT GREECE   (1984)

Twelve deities of ancient Greece are profiled in a handsomely designed volume ideally suited for introducing the characters of Greek mythology. The stage is set with a concise description of ancient beliefs about the gods and their battle with the Titans for control of the world. The dozen spreads that follow focus on each of seven gods and five goddesses in turn. Head-and-shoulders portraits rendered in Fisher's signature layered oils dominate the layouts, while an accompanying paragraph characterizes each god's traits and attributes; occasionally, references are made to important myths. The masterful, stylized paintings are trenchant summaries of the gods' distinctive personalities, but they lack vitality; Fisher's gods are iconic images, not the timeless, vital characters who move through the myths, mirroring humankind's strengths and failings. Although the brevity of the information provided about each deity is sometimes unsatisfying, the presentation will likely spur viewers to delve deeper on their own. A bibliography, a chart juxtaposing Greek and Roman names for the gods, and a family tree depicting the relationships between these most eminent Olympians further amplify the book's usefulness for the beginning student of mythology.

> *Karen Stang Hanley, in a review of "The Olympians: Great Gods and Goddesses of Ancient Greece,"*
> *in* Booklist, *Vol. 81, No. 3, October 1, 1984, p. 246.*

Textured head-and-shoulder portraits of 12 Olympians, looking every inch of their godheads—sculpturally stylized, with remote gazes and slight archaic smiles—grace the large-format pages and dominate the brief factual entries. The big question is: for what age range or use is this book intended? There are no more than a dozen lines of simple background information per divinity: no stories about the divine exploits. A family tree at the back makes clear the Olympian predilection for incest and philandering (and the text informs us that Aphrodite, wife of Hephaestus, "betrayed him with a string of lovers"). As an introduction for younger children, this doesn't compete with the d'Aulaires' *Book of Greek Myths* (1962) or Gibson's *Gods & Heroes from Greek Mythology* (1977)—and it looks too much like a picture book (and offers too little information) for older students. A note claims "most scholars agree" that the 12 divinities chosen are "the most important", but Hestia has also got to be the dullest goddess ever (a role model for Doris Day: "she never disagreed with anyone, and she never took sides in an argument") and Demeter, a strong, loving and pertinacious woman, is excluded from the collection. (pp. 123-24)

> *Patricia Dooley, in a review of "The Olympians: Great Gods and Goddesses of Ancient Greece," in*
> School Library Journal, *Vol. 31, No. 3, November, 1984, pp. 123-24.*

THE STATUE OF LIBERTY   (1985)

Leonard Everett Fisher offers one of the more eye-catching books on the subject because of its attractive layout and high-quality photographs and drawings. Most of the illustrations occupy a full page or a two-page spread. In addition to dramatic views of the statue, there are reproductions of newspaper stories and documents, historical photographs and several exceptional prints by Fisher. The text, covering Bartholdi's biography and struggle to make the statue a reality, is satisfactory. A fine complement to Mary Shapiro's *The Statue of Liberty.* (p. 86)

> *Deborah Vose, in a review of "The Statue of Liberty," in* School Library Journal, *Vol. 32, No. 4, December, 1985, pp. 86-7.*

A good new book on a timely topic is always welcome. Fisher begins this one with a full description of the dedication ceremony for Bartholdi's "Liberty Enlightening the World," one hundred years ago. The shiny copper statue's face was covered with a huge French Flag, but the "crushing, high-spirited mass of people" who had gathered could barely see, for "driving rain and gloomy clouds all but erased the view." Among the ironies of the day was that only two women were invited to Bedloe's Island to watch the unveiling of the huge female figure, and neither of them was an American. The author skips backward from this point to trace the ideas that led to the statue's existence. There is a detailed account of its construction and of the fund-raising efforts for building the pedestal, with an emphasis on the personalities involved. Brief information about Liberty's maintenance and recent refurbishing efforts tie this comprehensive history of the statue's creation to the present day. The text is long to be presented as it is without subheads, but the many photos and prints (they occupy more than half the space) serve as guides to the content. An index of proper names is another help. A few of Fisher's original scratchboard drawings are included among the well-chosen illustrations. This is a good looking book that will give children a glimpse of lifestyles and attitudes of the late nineteenth century as well as an understanding of the featured events.

> *Janet Hickman, in a review of "The Statue of Liberty," in* Language Arts, *Vol. 63, No. 1, January, 1986, p. 91.*

THE GREAT WALL OF CHINA   (1986)

Using a brief text and imposing pictures, Fisher relates the story behind the building of the Great Wall of China. He describes how 2,200 years ago King Cheng of Ch'in conquered surrounding provinces and became the first Supreme Emperor of China. Besides trying to bring order and uniformity to his country, the emperor had to do something about the fierce Mongol tribes that threatened to invade. Out of this necessity came the building of a long wall across the north of China—but not without great cost. More than a million people—peasants, artisans, prisoners, and soldiers—were forced to work on the wall, where many lost their lives. Some librarians may object to the fictionalized dialogue in the text, but it does personalize the narrative. Central to the book's appeal are Fisher's striking black-and-white acrylic paintings that spread over the pages and surround the text. Figures, buildings, and animals seem three-dimensional, as though molded from clay. Both the cruelty of the enforcers, as well as the anguish of the workers, is etched on the peoples' faces. The book has been thoughtfully designed; Chinese characters (carefully translated at the book's end) run down the sides of the pages, and a map of China and the provinces during the First Empire opens the book. Impressive—Fisher offers history in a way that is sure to intrigue.

> *Ilene Cooper, in a review of "The Great Wall of China," in* Booklist, *Vol. 82, No. 14, March 15, 1986, p. 1082.*

Awe-inspiring, impressive, black and gray illustrations set the tone for this history of the building of the Great Wall of China. These large, detailed double-spreads of the building of the Wall and of the people have a rough look entirely suitable to the subject. The story is simply told and will interest children. . . . An outstanding example of nonfiction for young children.

> *Gerri Young, in a review of "The Great Wall of China," in* School Library Journal, *Vol. 32, No. 9, May, 1986, p. 90.*

SEA SONGS (1986)

[Sea Songs *was written by Myra Cohn Livingston.*]

Livingston's **Sea Songs** are songs of praise, cast a bit precariously in the heroic cadences of the verse epics of old . . . .

A number of Leonard Everett Fisher's acrylic paintings are deeply evocative. His fishermen are monumental, timeless-looking; his sailboats, moving figures of solitude and grace. About half the paintings, though, are statically composed. **Sea Songs** is an ambitious work of parts that don't come together.

> *Leonard S. Marcus, "Songs of Moonfish, Sand Castles, and Mother's Slide Trombone," in* The Christian Science Monitor, *June 6, 1986, p. B4.*

Art and poetry are so closely melded in this celebration of the sea by two distinct talents that it is virtually impossible to discern which might have inspired the other: is this an artist's interpretation of the poetry or are the poems commentaries on the paintings? Crisp, haunting, economical, the poems create marvelous, often eerie images, each ending with an apostrophe to the moon or to the sun. The initial double-page spread sets the tone. The text reads, "Crashing on dark shores, drowning, pounding/ breaker swallows breaker. Tide follows/ tide. Lost in her midnight witchery/ moon watches, cresting tall waves, pushing/ through mist and blackness the cold waters." The accompanying dramatic, full-color illustration, executed in acrylic paints, uses a multitoned and darkened blue-green palette to suggest the awesome power of the sea, lit only by a luminous moon. In succeeding pages, as day dawns, the poetry becomes lighter in tone, the paintings less ominous; yet always there are suggestions of mystery and frontiers still to be explored. A helpful publisher's note on the copyright page not only describes the artist's medium but also the technique which he has used to achieve depth, tex-

Crashing on dark shores, drowning, pounding
breaker swallows breaker. Tide follows
tide. Lost in her midnight witchery
moon watches, cresting tall waves, pushing
through mist and blackness the cold waters.

*Moon, you have worked long.
Now rest . . .*

From Sea Songs, *written by Myra Cohn Livingston. Illustrated by Leonard Everett Fisher.*

ture, and richness in the illustrations. The combination of robust yet sensitive artwork and precise yet vibrant words results in a handsome interpretation of natural phenomena, stimulating to look at and to read. (pp. 462-63)

> *Mary M. Burns, in a review of "Sea Songs," in* The Horn Book Magazine, *Vol. LXII, No. 4, July-August, 1986, pp. 462-63.*

SYMBOL ART: THIRTEEN SQUARES, CIRCLES, TRIANGLES FROM AROUND THE WORLD (1986)

After a brief introduction to the use of symbols in the past and present, Fisher organizes the book into 13 four-page sections by subject, from astrology to weather. Each section opens with a one-page precis of the symbols used for that subject; facing this page of text is a full-page illustration relating to the subject. There follows a double-page spread of large, captioned symbols important in that area or field—the signs of the zodiac, for instance, or various business logos, proofreader's marks (printing), musical notations, etc. The book's cream-and-brown color scheme is handsome, and once the rhythm is established for a browsing reader, the organization becomes clear. However, the level of information is superficial, and the format varied enough to seem almost fragmented. This is more successful artistically than it is informationally. (pp. 24-5)

> *Betsy Hearne, in a review of "Symbol Art," in* Bulletin of the Center for Children's Books, *Vol. 40, No. 2, October, 1986, pp. 24-5.*

The subtitle of **Symbol Art,** incorporating three geometric figures—square, circle, and triangle—is more than an indication of content; it is, in effect, a visual statement of the unifying concept around which the content is structured. The preface is an exemplary and economical introduction to the meaning of the term *symbol,* the use and history of symbols, and the design elements common to all symbols. What follows is a handsomely designed presentation of symbols associated with various disciplines or vocations. Each grouping is preceded by an explanatory double-page spread in which a handsome, finely detailed, full-page illustration complements a single page of text that highlights significant aspects of the culture or environment which produces a particular set of symbols. The arrangement allows for quick reference, but potential utility is not the sole reason for recommending this book as a particularly fascinating example of the illustrator's art. Rather, it is the communication of an essential unity among seemingly disparate elements which is significant, for it offers insight into the oneness of human nature as well as human ingenuity. The book also underscores the aesthetics of symbols as decorative elements by presenting them with precision and passion. Through separation of these nonverbal means of communication from their usual contexts in manuscripts, the glossy pages of magazine ads, and television commercials and by using a standard mode of execution—sepia-toned scratch-board illustrations—Fisher has added another dimension to appreciating the familiar as well as to understanding that which may seem strange.

> *Mary M. Burns, in a review of "Symbol Art: Thirteen Squares, Circles, Triangles from Around the World," in* The Horn Book Magazine, *Vol. LXIII, No. 1, January-February, 1987, p. 71.*

EARTH SONGS (1986)

[Earth Songs *was written by Myra Cohn Livingston.*]

Poet Livingston and painter Fisher have teamed up again to create an inspiring look at a part of nature—this time, the planet Earth. As in their two previous books, **Sea Songs** and **Sky Songs,** their combined effort captures the beauty and dynamism of our planet. The poetry is first-person: the Earth tells of her mountains, her forests, her deserts, and her waters, and each page reminds readers of the power and grandeur of our often taken-for-granted surroundings. Fisher's double-page paintings are a perfect match to the poetry—indeed, one cannot imagine a better combination since the bold, haunting oil paintings on a textured surface evoke the same feeling the poet so aptly creates. (p. 91)

> *Barbara McGinn, in a review of "Earth Songs," in* School Library Journal, *Vol. 33, No. 3, November, 1986, pp. 91-2.*

Quite simply, this book is a superb example of artistic collaboration. It is visually exciting because of majestic, full-color paintings, which do not so much suggest a specific locale as convey an impression of the earth's magnificence. Each is a composition which effectively exploits the basic shapes found in nature, arranging them in stunning and haunting combinations: a triangular thrust of snow-clad peaks against a midnight blue sky is framed by the darker blue shapes of the notch through which the viewer is looking. The text is equally as exciting, for the poet has selected a challenging design with which to frame her imagery—*rime annexée* or run-over rhyme. . . . The poetry, because of this particular scheme, matches the audacity of the paintings in adding excitement and an unusual perspective to what might otherwise have been good but not extraordinary; this combination is extraordinary, a fitting addition to **Sky Songs** and **Sea Songs.** (pp. 63-4)

> *Mary M. Burns, in a review of "Earth Songs," in* The Horn Book Magazine, *Vol. LXIII, No. 1, January-February, 1987, pp. 63-4.*

ELLIS ISLAND: GATEWAY TO THE NEW WORLD (1986)

Profusely illustrated with photographs and with the author-artist's handsome scratchboard drawings, this is a detailed history of the island in Upper New York Bay that eventually came to be called Ellis Island. It served for many years as the entry point for immigrants, and it is this aspect that Fisher stresses, describing the laws that affected immigrants and the procedures that were used to screen and process them. Always a fine artist and a dependably accurate writer, Fisher serves here, as he has done in many of the earlier books about facets of American life, as a social historian. (pp. 65-6)

> *Zena Sutherland, in a review of "Ellis Island: Gateway to the New World," in* Bulletin of the Center for Children's Books, *Vol. 40, No. 4, December, 1986, pp. 65-6.*

A book that gives far broader coverage than its title implies. The focus is on the common experiences of all steerage class immigrants as they passed originally through Castle Garden and later through the Ellis Island facility. Fisher relates the experiences of the immigrants in a straightforward manner, but his choice of illustrative incidents often shows the callousness with which these people were treated. Included is a graphic description of the required eye check during which unsanitary buttonhook tools were used to lift eyelids to check for trachoma. Quotations from oral histories also demonstrate how many of the immigrants had negative feelings about their treatment during the immigration process. The black-and-white reproductions and Fisher's scratchboard drawings are excellent and enhance understanding of the clear, descriptive text. This is one of the few books for this age level that describes the immigration process without focusing on one particular nationality group. There is so much information in the photographs and the text that this is a perfect book for those who have little or no general background on this subject. Fisher's latest work deserves consideration in all libraries serving middle graders. (pp. 101-02)

> *Janet E. Gelfand, in a review of "Ellis Island: Gateway to the New World," in* School Library Journal, *Vol. 33, No. 4, December, 1986, pp. 101-02.*

LOOK AROUND! A BOOK ABOUT SHAPES (1987)

A page-filling, purple sphere cheerily greets readers opposite the eloquently simple definition of a circle. A flip of the page reveals an orbiting globe, a bright sun, a red-swirled peppermint candy, and a cascade of gaily colored balloons: circles applied. A visual puzzle follows, challenging readers to find the red, orange, and green circles in a luscious fresh fruit arrangement. The same inviting format of example and definition, applications, and visual game continues for a square, a rectangle, and a triangle. A rebus, exchanging the basic shapes and familiar images for words, and a concluding page, introducing a crescent, pentagon, parallelogram, and other forms to further expand youngsters' geometric horizons, complete the presentation. Shimmering in the vibrant acrylics Fisher also aptly used in **Boxes! Boxes!**, the uncluttered, dazzling paintings and the large, clear print will lure children to this precisely honed, imaginatively instructive presentation.

> *Ellen Mandel, in a review of "Look Around! A Book about Shapes," in* Booklist, *Vol. 83, No. 14, March 15, 1987, p. 1126.*

Circles, squares, rectangles, and triangles are all tightly and succinctly defined in Fisher's **Look Around!** This is one of the most visually pleasing concept books to come along: the text is bold in size, color, and layout; and the overall effect is electrifying. Following the definition of the shape and a large picture of the shape in a bright, flat color, Fisher provides a colorful spread that shows different objects in that shape. He then offers another spread in which that shape is abundant but which also includes other shapes so that youngsters can practice differentiating shapes. The only failing is the use of cone shapes to illustrate the concept of triangles; however, this will probably make little or no difference to the preschoolers who will undoubtedly be delighted by this book. (pp. 67-8)

> *Laura McCutcheon, in a review of "Look Around! A Book about Shapes," in* School Library Journal, *Vol. 33, No. 11, August, 1987, pp. 67-8.*

THE ALAMO (1987)

Fisher tells us that the Alamo is famous not so much for the battle that pitted Texan insurgents against a much larger Mexican army as for the "courage it took to stand up and die for . . . freedom." Yet we learn little about those heroic men, including the eloquent colonels Travis and Bowie. The fort's early role as a Catholic mission, and later efforts to preserve it, is given disproportionate treatment, obscuring more significant facts. It isn't clear, for example, why Davy Crockett and a band of volunteers from Tennessee were at the Alamo in 1836, or why the beleaguered Texans received so little help. On-site research, however, yielded photographs, maps and paintings that greatly increase the book's appeal. Powerful scratch board portraits of Santa Anna and Stephen Austin suggest a story of human endeavor that is missing from the text.

> *A review of "The Alamo," in* Publishers Weekly, *Vol. 231, No. 18, May 8, 1987, p. 74.*

An exposition of the Alamo—the building itself—telling its history prior to the battle that made it famous and describing what became of it afterward. Fisher describes in simple terms the chaotic political conditions in Mexico at the time of the Texas Revolution. He has managed, while certainly espousing the American view of the issues, to skirt the pitfall of an over-reverence for the events of March and April, 1836. He avoids over-dramatizing, mostly letting circumstances speak for themselves. The struggle of Texans to withstand the violence of Mexican politics has been sentimentalized so often in the past that Fisher's efforts seem refreshingly matter-of-fact by comparison. . . . Richards' *The Story of the Alamo* (1970) is aimed at a lower grade level, and, like Robert Penn Warren's florid *Remember the Alamo* (1958), lacks adequate illustration, while Tinkle's *The Valiant Few* (1964) is scholarly. The illustrative material and Fisher's focus on the building itself make this a unique work and altogether a commendable effort.

> *Ruth Semrau, in a review of "The Alamo," in* School Library Journal, *Vol. 33, No. 10, June-July, 1987, p. 94.*

CALENDAR ART: THIRTEEN DAYS, WEEKS, MONTHS, AND YEARS FROM AROUND THE WORLD (1987)

The effort to understand and measure the passage of time over the last 5,000 years is chronicled in this stunningly illustrated companion volume to the author's **Alphabet Art, Number Art,** and **Symbol Art.** After a short introduction to the history of calendar making, Fisher presents 13 calendars, from the ancient Sumerian to the projected World Calendar, through concise text and scratchboard drawings in vivid blue and white. These are followed by renditions of each calendar and its associated symbols, all in the same striking blue. Some confusion may result from the arrangement, which is not wholly chronological. For some not easily discernible reason, the French Revolutionary calendar is placed in the middle of the book before others much earlier in time, and the Gregorian calendar precedes the Julian effort that it is aimed to amend. A page of calendar symbols (blue again) can be found at the beginning and end of the text, and although visually impressive, some interpretation would have been helpful. Students studying various cultures will find the calendar information useful when their attention is called to this source, but above all, this handsome volume is a joy to dip into for its distinguished artwork.

> *Mary Lathrope, in a review of "Calendar Art: Thir-*

teen *Days, Weeks, Months, and Years from Around the World,"* in Booklist, *Vol. 83, No. 21, July, 1987, p. 1678.*

Using his typically well-designed and executed scratch-board illustrations . . ., Fisher explains the origins of the calendar and the human need to divide the solar year into months, weeks, and days. He describes 13 such calendars, ranging through history from the Aztecs, Babylonians, and Egyptians to the calendar devised by the druids at Stonehenge, the Romans, the Hebrews, and those in more recent history, including the one formed during the French Revolution and the 1930 World Calendar. The arrangement may be confusing to some children, as these 13 calendar systems are presented in alphabetical rather than chronological order, and it is necessary to flip back and forth to the various calendars which are related. The focus is unclear, and because of the very brief information, many will wonder whether this is an art book or a science book. However, while other books have explored this subject (Irving and Ruth Adler's *The Calendar* [1967]; Ruth Brindze's *The Story of Our Calendar* [1949]; and Marilyn Burns' *This Book Is About Time* [1978]), none has attempted to explain so many different calendars in such an attractive way in terms of graphics.

> *Patricia Homer, in a review of "Calendar Art: Thirteen Days, Weeks, Months, and Years from Around the World,"* in School Library Journal, *Vol. 33, No. 11, August, 1987, p. 82.*

THE TOWER OF LONDON (1987)

Many a rebel head has rolled since the Tower of London was built in the 11th century. This liberally illustrated book highlights the little-known aspects as well as the legendary tales about the dark tower, symbol of power for the royal line. Thirteen episodic sketches move in easy style, without excess detail: the story of Anne Boleyn; how a bishop once escaped prison by getting the guards drunk and climbing down a rope; how Henry III turned the tower into a zoo; how Wat Tyler stormed the tower with a group of overtaxed farmers; and how Richard II lost the throne. Today the Tower is a landmark museum, where axes and racks still stand, and ravens are still tended there, for legends say that when the last one leaves the Tower, the nation will fall. Fisher's moody black-and-white art—full of shadowy gray tones—well suit the book's somber subject. For dramatic nonfiction, this book sets a high standard in the genre.

> *A review of "The Tower of London,"* in Publishers Weekly, *Vol. 232, No. 14, September 25, 1987, p. 109.*

Fisher introduces the history-laden Tower of London and recounts 13 episodes from its bloody history. . . . The tellings are succinct while capturing the essence of the famous structure. Kids will be enticed by the gory goings-on ("an axman wacked off [Raleigh's] head") but will also learn a good deal about British history. Fisher provides bold black-and-white artwork throughout in double-page spreads; impressive and dramatic, they add strong flavor to the narrative.

> *Ilene Cooper, in a review of "The Tower of London,"* in Booklist, *Vol. 84, No. 4, October 15, 1987, p. 393.*

SPACE SONGS (1988)

[Space Songs *was written by Myra Cohn Livingston.*]

On pages black as the night sky, Fisher and Livingston explore the meteors, satellites, messages and planets, of that "other world, an otherwhere" that is called space. As in their past collaborations . . . the poems and paintings in this volume shimmer and dance. . . . These poems and paintings are extraordinary, not only because of their depth of vision and beauty, but because they entreat the reader to explore the secrets that space keeps hidden . . . . (pp. 93–4)

> *A review of "Space Songs,"* in Publishers Weekly, *Vol. 233, No. 14, April 8, 1988, pp. 93-4.*

With **Space Songs,** Livingston and Fisher complete the quartet they began with **Sky Songs, Sea Songs,** and **Earth Songs.** As in the others, Fisher's paintings are incredibly powerful. Each of Livingston's 13 poems is set in a painting that perfectly captures the essence of the subject, but the pairing does not create perfect harmony. The poems fail to illumine space as well as the illustrations do. Fisher's abstract milky way is paired with the rather pedestrian image of "Two hundred billion stars move here in teeming crowds/Here is the Milky Way, our galaxy, our dusky road in sky." "Meteorites" takes the form of a concrete poem but, once again, the words "Earthlings may watch a meteor's blazing trail of light" are weaker than the acryllic depiction of falling stars. Livingston's scientific facts are sound, but her space does not sing. All of the lyrics are in the illustrations.

> *Kathleen Whalin, in a review of "Space Songs,"* in School Library Journal, *Vol. 35, No. 8, May, 1988, p. 106.*

MONTICELLO (1988)

A handsomely produced history of the house that Jefferson spent a lifetime working on in his spare time, with current and historical black-and-white photos augmented by Fisher's scratchboard diagrams of some of Jefferson's unique inventions.

Most interesting here is the way this unique structure fits into architectural history: Fisher explains that Jefferson had access to the designs of Palladio, Inigo Jones, and Wren and yet (as was usual in 18th-century America) created his own design; and comments on Monticello's architectural influence on later public buildings. Unfortunately, Fisher doesn't give many of the details of building, either of construction or of the laborers and craftsmen employed over the years—who they were, either specifically or in society; it almost seems as though he is evading the question of slave labor. Instead, he outlines Jefferson's life (information easily obtained elsewhere), interpolating the progress of the building, and concludes with a summary of the years of neglect after Jefferson's death and the restoration during the last 60 years.

An uneven effort, of value for its photos and as a chronology.

> *A review of "Monticello,"* in Kirkus Reviews, *Vol. LVI, No. 10, May 15, 1988, p. 760.*

The photographs, reproductions, diagrams, and drawings are a masterly mix of graphic information, including Jefferson's sketches and drawing tools, interior and exterior pictures of the building in states of disrepair and restoration, a photo of one of Jefferson's slaves who managed his nailery, and an 1828 land-sale notice. A prerequisite for any young reader's visit to Monticello, and an armchair tour for students who can't make the trip. (pp. 203-04)

Betsy Hearne, in a review of "Monticello," in Bulletin of the Center for Children's Books, *Vol. 41, No. 10, June, 1988, pp. 203-04.*

Jack Gantos

1951-

(Born John Bryan Gantos, Jr.) American author of picture books.

Gantos has written books for preschool and early primary grade readers in which he often shows an admiration for the playfulness of childhood and commends the virtuousness of his characters. In *Greedy Greeny* (1979), for example, a young monster behaves selfishly and then faces the guilt and uneasiness that comes from lack of consideration of others, while in *Willy's Raiders* (1980) a group of unscrupulous ballplayers find that cheating never brings true success. Yet Gantos is best known for his "Rotten Ralph" books, in which he depicts a mischievous feline protagonist whose complete disregard for decorum leads to outrageous, ill-mannered behavior. Although Ralph is often ostracized as a result, this is counterbalanced by the caring attitude of his owner, Sarah, who demonstrates an unconditional acceptance of him. Most critics feel that Ralph's unrepentant demeanor, Sarah's reluctance to punish him, and her unwavering fondness for him are very appealing to young children, who have embraced Ralph with great eagerness. In all of Gantos's titles, even the most subdued, he has shown a penchant toward humor and an appreciation of the spontaneity and enthusiasm of young children. His works have been illustrated exclusively by Nicole Rubel, and it has been noted that her vibrant palette and use of exaggerated expressions and poses perfectly complement Gantos's buoyant style. Together they have offered young readers stories of sheer delight, many of which accentuate the importance of loving relationships with delectable exuberance.

(See also *Something about the Author,* Vol. 20 and *Contemporary Authors,* Vols. 65-68.)

Ruth M. Stein, in a review of "Rotten Ralph," in Language Arts, *Vol. 54, No. 5, May, 1977, p. 581.*

ROTTEN RALPH (1976)

Ralph is a cat; he's red and he's as large as Sarah, to whom he belongs; and he's nasty. He saws at a limb on which Sarah's swing is hung, he wears father's slippers, he runs his bicycle into the dining room table—and he is so disruptive when taken to a circus that the family leaves him there. Ralph is forced to work, underfed, and caged; he escapes and becomes ill, is rescued by Sarah, and comes home to be more appreciative and less rotten. There's some humor in the situation, but it seems overworked, and the story, despite the slam-bang action and [Nicole Rubel's] violent pop pictures to match—has echoes of the old minatory theme of being punished if you don't appreciate your lot in life.

Zena Sutherland, in a review of "Rotten Ralph," in Bulletin of the Center for Children's Books, *Vol. 29, No. 11, July-August, 1976, p. 174.*

Ralph, who is really a very nasty character, finally sees the error of his ways. Or does he? All seems to end well, to the satisfaction of pre-schoolers and primary graders. . . . A successful first book by both author and illustrator.

SLEEPY RONALD (1976)

[Nicole] Rubel's splashy, tutti-frutti backgrounds were a natural environment for **Rotten Ralph.** Here they just about swamp Ronald, the rabbit protagonist who nods off in school, on roller skates, at the swimming hole, and in his own bathroom, and then misses his opera rehearsal (!) altogether. Finally his buddy Priscilla discovers the trouble: "your ears. . . keep drooping over your eyes and make everything so dark you think it's bedtime." A limp ending if we ever heard one, especially since Rubel's electric turquoise, yellow, orange, and red palette is bright enough to wake the dead. But since the pictures have narrative punch to go with their visual zap, they just might carry this sleeper along.

A review of "Sleepy Ronald," in Kirkus Reviews, *Vol. XLIV, No. 16, August 15, 1976, p. 903.*

Ronald, with his striped pajamas and roller skates and his tendency to sleep on diving boards and through Wagnerian opera rehearsals, is the funniest rabbit to appear in some time. . . . [The story] is lightly told and imaginatively illustrated in amusing, vividly-colored pop-art tableaux which, though too cluttered for the tastes of the very young, will entertain most children.

> *Allene Stuart Phy, in a review of "Sleepy Ronald," in* School Library Journal, *Vol. 23, No. 2, October, 1976, p. 97.*

FAIR-WEATHER FRIENDS (1977)

Maggie and Chester are best friends, but because he hates the freezing North, where they live, and she is miserable in the sizzling tropics, where they row for a vacation, they decide to split—keeping in touch via postcards and visiting "just as often as they can." It's a contemporary solution to be sure, but a flat one as stories go. And though [illustrator Nicole] Rubel's grimacing, pop-ugly animals put on a strenuous performance (Maggie turns green in rough waters, bright red in the sun) and her backgrounds range from agitated to overwrought, it's all merely strident without any narrative zap to back it up. After their happy pairing in last year's *Rotten Ralph,* Gantos and Rubel seem as ill-matched here as Maggie and Chester.

> *A review of "Fair-Weather Friends," in* Kirkus Reviews, *Vol. XLV, No. 4, February 15, 1977, p. 161.*

The inspired team which gave us *Rotten Ralph* have another winner, an amusing story with pictures blazing with life and humor and the implicit message that you don't have to love the same things to love each other.

> *A review of "Fair-Weather Friends," in* Publishers Weekly, *Vol. 211, No. 13, March 28, 1977, p. 79.*

AUNT BERNICE (1978)

When Ida's parents leave for vacation, she welcomes her temporary guardian, Aunt Bernice, with slightly more enthusiasm than she would Attila the Hun. Aunt Bernice brings another disaster, her dog Rex, as untamed as his mistress. During the long summer, the antics of dog and aunt embarrass Ida, lose her friends and generally wreak havoc in her young life. The worst of the problem is that Ida, the innocent, somehow gets the blame for all the troubles. As the days pass, the child finds that her resentments of Aunt Bernice are gradually changing into fondness until, at last, she's sorry to see her leave. The spiffy nonsense of Gantos is perfectly complemented, once more, by [Nicole] Rubel's nutty, brashly colored cartoons. Like *Rotten Ralph* and their other books, their new one is a comic masterpiece.

> *A review of "Aunt Bernice," in* Publishers Weekly, *Vol. 215, No. 6, February 6, 1978, p. 101.*

If neither Aunt Bernice nor her wonderful (if Booth-like) dog Rex can yet face up to Gantos and Rubel's inspired red cat, still for the first time since *Rotten Ralph* Gantos' story provides a suitable outlet for Rubel's manic energy. . . . Happily, what wins the little girl over is not reform on her aunt's part but more indecorous behavior: Aunt Bernice laughs at a mushy movie (getting the two of them kicked out of the theater) and dresses as a gorilla to scare the guests at Ida's slumber party. Aunt Bernice's consistent coltish spirits could indeed be trying; but with her splashy patterns, outrageous per-

spective, exhuberant asides, and even a loving, Matisse-y hug at the end, Rubel does her to a frazzle. (pp. 173-74)

> *A review of "Aunt Bernice," in* Kirkus Reviews, *Vol. XLVI, No. 4, February 15, 1978, pp. 173-74.*

A flair for the grotesque pervades this droll, childlike picture book. . . . A sense of excitement and humor which emanates from animate and inanimate objects alike enhances the stark, brightly colored, full-page illustrations. These illustrations, juxtaposed with a carefully executed text, are designed to tempt young readers and thoroughly amuse all ages.

> *J. C., in a review of "Aunt Bernice," in* Children's Book Review Service, *Vol. 6, No. 12, Spring, 1978, p. 111.*

WORSE THAN ROTTEN, RALPH (1978)

Forget your troubles, get happy and have a good laugh with really rotten Ralph. When we left him at the end of the first book by Gantos and Rubel, the wicked cat had reformed. Here he's on his best behavior until a trio of alley cats show up and call him a softy. Sarah, Ralph's owner, is out on an errand so he has no bulwark against temptation. To show just how evil he can be, the cat leads the pack into more mischief than they have ever dreamed of. The gleefully naughty story is matched by [Nicole Rubel's] antic pictures, so brashly colored that they glow in the dark. It's hard to say whether reading about Ralph and the outlaws or studying the illustrations is more fun.

> *A review of "Worse Than Rotten, Ralph," in* Publishers Weekly, *Vol. 214, No. 3, July 17, 1978, p. 169.*

The unrelieved, gratuitous mayhem is, depending on one's age, either boring or threatening. (There is even a symbolic threat of castration when a dandified poodles' hairdresser says he'll clip off the cats' tails when he catches them.) The illustrations, however, done in intense flat colors, are fresh, lively, original, and exciting. They deserve a more imaginative story.

> *Mary B. Nickerson, in a review of "Worse Than Rotten, Ralph," in* School Library Journal, *Vol. 25, No. 2, October, 1978, p. 132.*

A do-it-yourself guide to mayhem which can be summed up in a few phrases—ridiculous, garish, and makes no sense. What happened to charm and the idea that a book for a child should reflect sensitivity and some gentleness?

> *B. W., in a review of "Worse Than Rotten, Ralph," in* Children's Book Review Service, *Vol. 7, No. 3, November, 1978, p. 22.*

THE PERFECT PAL (1979)

Vanessa decides she needs a pal and confides her requirements to Wendell, the pet store sales assistant. Guided by Wendell, Vanessa acquires, one by one, a menagerie of creatures who all quickly display serious defects—a pig proves unmannerly, a sloth, boring. With happy inevitability it is Wendell himself who turns out to be *The Perfect Pal.* A classic set-up like this is always a good bet, especially when it is told with brisk directness.

Mary B. Nickerson, in a review of "The Perfect Pal," in School Library Journal, *Vol. 26, No. 2, October, 1979, p. 139.*

Simple, colorful illustrations [by Nicole Rubel] bring to life this imaginative story about finding a friend. Written for a beginning reader, the book would also be an enjoyable read-aloud selection. With all its humor, the story might well lead to discussions about the qualities of friendship.

Sharon Spredemann Dreyer, in a review of "The Perfect Pal" in her The Bookfinder: When Kids Need Books, Annotations of Books Published 1979 through 1982, Vol. 3, *American Guidance Service, 1985, p. 113.*

GREEDY GREENY (1979)

The author and illustrator of **Rotten Ralph** and other uproarious comedies have concocted a mirthful cautionary tale, the frightful retribution of Greeny, scion of a respectable monster family. His kind mother allows Greeny a snack before bedtime, but says he's not to eat the watermelon. That's for the family dessert the next day. But greedy Greeny gobbles up everything in the refrigerator, including the huge watermelon and what a horrible nightmare he suffers. Greeny dreams that he has become a big watermelon and is about to be served to his kith and kin. Gantos keeps the story going with his brisk telling and [Nicole] Rubel's fantastic paintings make the reader laugh out loud.

A review of "Greedy Greeny," in Publishers Weekly, *Vol. 216, No. 12, September 17, 1979, p. 146.*

The author/artist team of the Rotten Ralph stories and the very fine **Perfect Pal,** Gantos and Rubel have upholstered a standard cautionary tale with a simple narration and the hot-colored, high-energy illustrations that are Rubel's signature.

Mary B. Nickerson, in a review of "Greedy Greeny," in School Library Journal, *Vol. 26, No. 3, November, 1979, p. 65.*

SWAMPY ALLIGATOR (1980)

Once again Jack Gantos has wowed us with his humor. Swampy Alligator looks just like his name when he steps out of the swamp on his birthday. He doesn't understand why his friends aren't coming to his birthday, but when he is invited to a secret party, he is thrilled. His friends' surprise for him is a bath. After his bath he realizes that it is just as much fun to get clean as it is to get "dirty," and his friends are greatly relieved.

P. P. K., in a review of "Swampy Alligator," in Children's Book Review Service, *Vol. 8, No. 10, May, 1980, p. 92.*

[Nicole] Rubel's big, boldly colored pictures boast all the life and fun one expects of them, and Gantos tells the story of a dirty alligator with his familiar laconic wit. But the new collaboration by the gifted humorists lacks the sassy charm of their earlier books, especially those about that cat, "Rotten Ralph." Basically a one-joke story, it telegraphs every turn and sinks into anticlimax.

A review of "Swampy Alligator," in Publishers Weekly, *Vol. 218, No. 3, July 18, 1980, p. 62.*

WILLY'S RAIDERS (1980)

When **Willy's Raiders** come up against the Weasels baseball team for the championship, the Weasels expand their usual repertoire of dirty tricks to include kidnapping Willy. Willy somehow escapes and the Raiders go on to triumph, "because the good guys always win." Neither Jack Gantos nor illustrator Nicole Rubel raise the book above the level of its simplistic moralizing. Next to Leo Durocher's famous observation on the fate of good guys, this looks very weak indeed. (pp. 87-8)

A review of "Willy's Raiders," in School Library Journal, *Vol. 26, No. 9, May, 1980, pp. 87-8.*

Willy Raccoon is the best player and captain of his baseball team, made up of diligent good sports who almost always win. In the other corner we have the Weasels, who "were too lazy to practice and had to win by cheating." On the morning of a scheduled match between the two teams, the weasels capture Willie and leave him locked in a trash can at the top of a hill—from which, through a hole in the can, he observes the weasels' nasty tricks on the diamond. Yet this is a world where "the good guys always win," as Willy says smugly at the end, and so we're not surprised to see the trash can barrelling down the hill in the middle of the game, and crashing smack into weasel captain Sneaky. Meanwhile the bad guys' cheating (greasing bats, bicycling around the bases) has been sufficiently outrageous to keep readers following Gantos and Rubel along the undisguised dotted line. (pp. 641-42)

A review of "Willy's Raiders," in Kirkus Reviews, *Vol. XLVIII, No. 10, May 15, 1980, pp. 641-42.*

THE WEREWOLF FAMILY (1980)

Normally the Werewolf family—Mr., Mrs., and young Harry and Mary—look properly Edwardian. But there's a full moon on the night of their family reunion, and we see the prim, stiff family growing fangs, claws, and paw hair before our eyes. "Whose side of the family are they on?" "Not mine," remark the other relatives as the Werewolfs arrive at the party, dispense snakes and spiders to the babies, select Aunt Charlotte's and Uncle Igo's pets for their dinner, and finally, in the basement rec room ("It's been in the family for centuries"), secure all their kin in racks, chains, and hanging manacles before taking off for home. The next day, posed with tea, books, hoop, and flowers in their garden, the Werewolf family is again the picture of decorum. If you can accept a sort of Rocky Horror Show equivalent for the picture-book set, Gantos and [illustrator Nicole] Rubel are the pair to give it punch. They've got more of their hearts in this one than in some of their previous, sweeter items. And kids in the Halloween mood will pounce on this where paler spooks will leave them cold.

A review of "The Werewolf Family," in Kirkus Reviews, *Vol. XLVIII, No. 19, October 1, 1980, p. 1293.*

Aside from being dull, this story about a werewolf family attending an ordinary family reunion is also distasteful and possibly offensive. . . . Medieval tortures in the "recreation room," boiling little kids in pots of water, and eating live cats hardly seem like fitting fare for storytime, except perhaps for children who like their humor on the sick side.

G. B., in a review of "The Werewolf Family," in Children's Book Review Service, *Vol. 9, No. 4, December, 1980, p. 24.*

ROTTEN RALPH'S ROTTEN CHRISTMAS (1984)

Gantos and [illustrator Nicole] Rubel present another feast of mirth, the sequel to **Rotten Ralph** and **Worse than Rotten, Ralph**. . . . At Christmastime, Sarah brings home a docile, well-mannered cat named Percy and Ralph's jealousy stretches his mean streak to the limit. He plays low tricks on patient Sarah and on timid Percy, but underneath his rottenness, Ralph fears he has lost the little girl's love to the sissy cat. In the twist that Gantos and Rubel save for the end, Ralph relaxes with the assurance he shares with his fond fans. The rotten cat knows, "Nobody can take my place."

A review of "Rotten Ralph's Rotten Christmas," in Publishers Weekly, *Vol. 226, No. 6, August 10, 1984, p. 82.*

Bright but awkward pictures of a devilish red cat, as stiffly drawn as his long-suffering owner Sarah, show the malicious excesses to which Ralph goes. It is this very excess that has made earlier books about Rotten Ralph popular, the exaggeration that appeals to the preschool audience. . . . Whatever Rotten Ralph does receives no more than a mild reprimand from Sarah, and this ability to behave atrociously and get away with it may be another appealing element in what is actually a thin story.

Zena Sutherland, in a review of "Rotten Ralph's Rotten Christmas," in Bulletin of the Center for Children's Books, *Vol. 38, No. 1, September, 1984, p. 5.*

In Jack Gantos's **Rotten Ralph's Rotten Christmas,** the cat-protagonist revels in tricks that represent playtime for him, but anguish for someone else (e.g., he unravels a sweater as it is being knitted). He demands attention (prancing along the piano keys as his friend, Sarah, tries to play), and he has a fit of vengeful jealousy when another cat pays a visit. But nothing this obnoxious "Garfield"-type does can move Sarah to a stronger reprimand than "Stop that." Rotten Ralph may be satirizing the arrested development of the spoiled child, but the characterization of Sarah serves as a wry comment upon overindulgent parents.

Donnarae MacCann and Olga Richard, in a review of "Rotten Ralph's Rotten Christmas," in Wilson Library Bulletin, *Vol. 59, No. 6, February, 1985, p. 404.*

ROTTEN RALPH'S TRICK OR TREAT (1986)

This Halloween story, one of a series of Rotten Ralph books, continues the exploits of the truly terrible cat belonging to a little girl, Sarah, who has the patience of a saint. Dressed as each other, the pair go to a costume party where everyone is convinced that it is Sarah, not Ralph, who pours the goldfish into the punch bowl and takes the lid off the popcorn popper. Sarah is humiliated, but Ralph is delighted when their hostess asks Sarah (and that nice cat of hers) to leave. Though Ralph does almost nothing to redeem himself, Sarah forgives him, saying, "Oh, Ralph, you're still my best friend." Ralph's unpenitent devilry has great appeal for children, and this story's use of role reversal provides a thought-provoking twist.

A review of "Rotten Ralph's Trick or Treat," in Publishers Weekly, *Vol. 230, No. 8, August 22, 1986, p. 95.*

Since the two main characters are in disguise, readers will enjoy paying close attention to figure out who's who at any given moment. However, Ralph's nastiness used to have minor entertainment value, and in previous stories he has shown at least a hint of remorse. Not so this time; the humor has worn too thin, and Ralph has no redeeming qualities.

John Peters, in a review of "Rotten Ralph's Trick or Treat," in School Library Journal, *Vol. 33, No. 2, October, 1986, p. 160.*

Helme Heine
1941-

German author and illustrator of picture books and reteller.

Heine is the creator of numerous picture books for preschool and early elementary grade readers which demonstrate a sense of purpose linked with pure merriment. He has stated that he attempts to entertain and, simultaneously, to create thought-provoking books with an underlying moral: for example, accepting friends as they are, the importance of accomplishments rather than beauty, and how greed can destroy good fortune. Although some reviewers find Heine's texts somewhat lifeless, they do not often complain of didacticism. Most observers note that the buoyancy of Heine's works is related to his gift for joyful expression through illustration. Often using watercolor as his medium, Heine imbues his pictures with a playful aura that lightens the solemn texts. Heine has shown a remarkable sense of humor in skillful, unconventional pictures that depict such amusing situations and characters as pigs with painted-on clothes, God as an artist doing preliminary sketches for Adam and Eve, and a man and dog who gradually change identities. Through the combination of the penetrating messages of his texts and the exuberance of his illustrations, Heine offers young readers the opportunity to learn in an an exhilarating, carefree fashion. *Freunde* (1982; *Friends*) won the *Boston Globe-Horn Book Award* in 1983.

AUTHOR'S COMMENTARY

[The following excerpt is from an interview by Margaret Carter.]

> I was looking at the Guinness Book of Records. . . . . all about the biggest or the longest or the best—and I thought what nonsense it is that we value superlatives when the biggest or the best is quite simply relative—and of no merit on their own. . . .

The result of that thought was **The Most Wonderful Egg In The World** a story of three hens quarreling as to which is the most beautiful. (Shades there of the god's choice to whom he should give the golden apple as the most beautiful woman?) Called in as referee, the King decides it isn't what the hens look like that matters but what they can do. The test is to be an amazing contest to decide which can produce the best egg. No, I will not divulge the ending: I don't want to deprive you of the delight of the illustrations: the rows of astonished hens' faces as yet another amazing egg makes its appearance: the witty endpapers and the delicious, watery paintings.

Helme Heine lives in Bavaria, a district of lakes, and perhaps it is not too fanciful to notice how often water—fountains, rivers, lakes—appear in his books, which for preference he both writes and illustrates.

> Language and illustrations are after all two sides of the same coin. Language creates pictures but an illustrator shouldn't follow the author—it is his job to create between the lines—what the author has *not* written. Art is instantaneous: when you see the

picture you know the mood. Language is the opposite—the picture builds up gradually word by word so that sometimes it isn't until the end of the story that you recognise the landscape.

His aim in his books is to

> give children a good time. I'm not a teacher but I like to put in something that continues to grow when the book is closed—a moral, or a different way of thinking about something. There are different layers in a book and it ought to grow with the child. I think it was C. S. Lewis who said that if a book for a child hasn't a higher value for an adult then it shouldn't be printed. That's why it's nonsense to try to put a specific age for a book's suitability.

Does he try out his ideas for books on children?

> I'm often asked that but the answer is no. I think doing that might limit its scope to one child's reaction whereas a book is for hundreds and hundreds of children, each of whom may have different visions. Children ought not be straightlaced into uniform response.

His desire to free rather than regiment the imagination shows in the genesis of **Imagine If.** . . . Asked to write a playlet for children (writing film scripts is yet another of his occupations) he was reluctant to direct or specify. So his text—and his illustrations—throw the onus on the child. "Imagine you're a table leg. . . ." it says and there's a picture with a boy for one of its legs. "Imagine you're a dog," he says. . . . and there's a boy-dog with a bone in its mouth. "Ask a child to imagine himself a tree," he says, "and he can feel the roots growing out of his feet."

Even the endpapers continue the same theme . . . look carefully and you'll see that same boy tucked up between two sardines in a tin, emerging, amazed and covered in prickles, from a cactus pot or standing with a bewildered expression and clock hands spread over his face.

Much of the art of illustration is knowing what to leave out. In *The Pearl . . .* his limpid pictures with their reflections in water, their hints of scenery through mist are small miracles of understatement. They tell the story of Beaver who thinks he has found a pearl but comes to realise his friends are his greatest treasures.

And so of course are books, particularly those such as these which open for a child windows on a world of gentle fun, wonder, sanity and beauty.

> *Margaret Carter, "Helme Heine," in* Books for Your Children, *Vol. 20, No. 1, Spring, 1985, p. 9.*

GENERAL COMMENTARY

DONNARAE MacCANN AND OLGA RICHARD

[Heine's] illustrations have changed from the deep, wide-ranged watercolor in *The Pigs' Wedding* to the richly varied layers of warm and cool colors in *Friends* to the light, airy, sketchy look in *The Most Wonderful Egg in the World. . . .*

Heine plays with scale changes not only by making a chicken taller than a man, but by making miniscule chickens, elephantine chickens, chickens in great masses. The zaniness of the plot is reinforced by a light pictorial tone—fresh pastel colors, loose spontaneous patterns, simple brush strokes to suggest forms.

As a storyteller, Heine holds description and dialogue to a minimum. *The Pigs' Wedding* contains big dramatic scenes with deep, luminous colors, while the narration provides just enough detail to inform us about Pig's bright ideas: painted-on party clothes for the guests, glorious mud coats after rain removes the first "garments," an elaborate bed for himself and his bride—a bed that is all whimsy and image because we see Pig paint it with a sweep of his brush. Whether the subject is a celebration or a variation on the friendship theme (as seen in *Friends*) or a comment on vain chickens, Heine makes good use of humor, suspense, and strong design.

> *Donnarae MacCann and Olga Richard, in a review of "The Most Wonderful Egg in the World," in* Wilson Library Bulletin, *Vol. 58, No. 6, February, 1984, p. 436.*

THE PIGS' WEDDING (1978)

When Porker Pig and Curlytail decide to get married they feel that their wedding guests need a good wash and brush up. To complete the picture all the pigs have new clothes painted on, but these burst after all the food at the reception. A shower of rain washes off the remainder and the wedding guests delight in wallowing in the mud once again, while the newly-weds fall asleep in a painted four-poster bed. This whimsical story certainly comes nowhere near the mark of Oxenbury's *Pig tale* in originality, and the overall effect is rather twee.

> *Elizabeth Weir, in a review of "The Pigs' Wedding," in* The School Librarian, *Vol. 27, No. 1, March, 1979, p. 29.*

Usually pigs in picture books are comic and cheerful figures. Here they are unattractive and gross because their characteristics—obesity, their snouts and even their smell (to which the bridegroom, himself a pig, takes exception)—are exaggerated to the point of vulgarity. The story is thin and the preparation for the wedding, the wedding feast and the ending when 'Cuddled close together they fell asleep, dreaming happy pig dreams', have no particular appeal for children of picture book age.

Some of the pictures are confused because of the array of piggish snouts and in places the text has been printed over colour, thus making it difficult to read.

> *E. Colwell, in a review of "The Pigs' Wedding," in* The Junior Bookshelf, *Vol. 43, No. 2, April, 1979, p. 96.*

Though the text is a drag—heavy whimsy, longwinded, almost superfluous—the exuberant watercolor pictures of pigs painting one another into wedding dresses and suits (complete with hats, cigars, glasses and watches), of pigs feasting and dancing, of pigs after a rainstorm leaping across the page into a glorious muddy bog, are great fun, witty and brilliantly executed. Despite the awkward text, the pictures had the kids in my house snorting with glee.

> *Harold C. K. Rice, in a review of "The Pigs' Wedding," in* The New York Times Book Review, *April 29, 1979, p. 29.*

DER HUND HERR MÜLLER [MR. MILLER THE DOG] (1979)

It has often been observed that a man and his dog sometimes come to resemble each other, but Heine carries the notion a step farther. In the beginning, Mr. Miller, a night watchman, lives with his dog Murphy, who fetches Mr. Miller's slippers, eats with him at the table (but chews on a bone instead of sharing the man's dinner), and generally shares his life. Gradually they come to look alike and then to envy each other's lives, until Mr. Miller finally gives in to Murphy's suggestion that they "change places." And so we see Murphy in coat and hat, lunchbox handle between his teeth, going off to the watchman's job on all fours—and returning in the morning on two. For a while both man and dog are upright and equal, but gradually Mr. Miller becomes more and more like the old Murphy, gnawing on bones and, in the last picture, curling up in the dog basket as Murphy goes to sleep in the bed. Heine's casual sketches—line drawings with a touch of Thurber, highlighted by watercolor washes—include some very funny views of the transition. The book is suitably small, the offbeat idea properly proportioned, the performance by Mr. Miller and Murphy never overstated, always on cue.

> *A review of "Mr. Miller the Dog," in* Kirkus Re-

He dreamed that his friends were looking at him in astonishment. "Beaver has found the greatest treasure in the forest," they said to themselves, and they were filled with envy.

From The Pearl, *written and illustrated by Helme Heine.*

views, *Vol. XLVIII, No. 21, November 1, 1980, p. 1392.*

Helme Heine wrote and illustrated the marvelously ebullient *The Pigs' Wedding* last year, a work that should have been on anyone's list of best picture books. The theme of this new one is role reversal, not between man and woman but man and dog.

The double transmogrification here is accomplished dexterously in Mr. Heine's line drawings and watercolors showing lolling tongues and a tuft of tail. There is a mild crudity as Mr. Miller—or is it Murphy—relieves himself on two legs. At any rate the book is best appreciated by adults for there is something faintly unpleasant, even chilling, beneath the playful intent. *The Pigs' Wedding* is still top dog.

George A. Woods, in a review of "Mr. Miller the Dog," in The New York Times Book Review, *December 7, 1980, p. 42.*

Breezy color-washed sketches—somewhat akin to James Stevenson's—not only picture but elaborate on the brief understated story until the absurdly logical conclusion is reached: Man and dog, suffering no identity crises, accomplish a successful turnabout and complete their transformations. To an adult the book might seem like a Kafkaesque spoof; to a child, pure fun. (p. 43)

Ethel L. Heins, in a review of "Mr. Miller the Dog,"

in The Horn Book Magazine, *Vol. LVII, No. 1, February, 1981, pp. 42-3.*

SUPERHARE (1979)

[Harry Nibbler] fakes the ability to swim and fly in order to win praise as a superhare. When the other rabbits try to ape him, they are killed. But when, in a final bid for fame, he ties knots in his ears, he is unable to hear the fox—who finds he tastes "just like any other hare." The satire is directed to an audience beyond the picture book years, but the German artist-author of *The Pigs' Wedding* makes it a vehicle for lively watercolor cartoons and clever designs. The endpapers almost overshadow the rest, as Harry Nibbler's ears are twisted into unicorn shape, used as a shark fin, yak's horns, etc. (He that hath hares to ear. . . .) Fun for older readers and for libraries that have everything.

Ruth M. McConnell, in a review of "Superhare," in School Library Journal, *Vol. 26, No. 8, April, 1980, p. 94.*

IMAGINE IF . . . (1979)

In this entertaining book from Germany, relaxed ink-and-wash pictures depict a series of scenes in which a small boy explores the possibility of turning into a table-leg, a fountain, a fish, a small footbridge and, finally, eight children in one (when he comforts himself with the thought that if he has to wash and clean his teeth eight times, he will also have eight ice-creams at a time and 'lots of friends'). A direct, amusing comment on childhood.

> *Margery Fisher, in a review of "Imagine If . . . ,"*
> *in* Growing Point, *Vol. 18, No. 5, January, 1980, p. 3640.*

The notions put forward—being a tree, being a fountain, being eight children—have a pleasing originality, though as a cautious mother I am not entirely happy about urging a small child to fancy it is a fish, then showing the chubby, smiling hero of the book entirely submerged in water.

Well produced on good quality paper this is an agreeable book which should fulfil the claim so many publishers make for their output and actually stimulate the imagination of very young readers.

> *R. Baines, in a review of "Imagine If . . . ," in* The
> Junior Bookshelf, *Vol. 44, No. 3, June, 1980, p. 118.*

MERRY-GO-ROUND (1980)

A good point—gently made, with humor and an intriguing, sequential plot—will hit its mark with the picture-book audience. Heine leaps right into an apparent dilemma that gets solved with ease. Katie, summering by the sea, has three compartmentalized adults for company. Her request to Auntie Dumpling to play is met with shock, for who will cook! Mr. Brainey, who only reads books, is persuaded and comes up with dinner while Katie and Auntie have a good time. The next day, it is Mr. Brainey's turn to play, and Uncle Plod, who only guards the house, reads. After Auntie Dumpling learns how to guard so Uncle Plod can play, the three grown-ups work in rotation, which benefits Katie, who has company all the time. The message of role flexibility is buoyed joyfully by large, comical, full-color pictures and a text that keeps matters simple, fanciful, and direct.

> *Judith Goldberger, in a review of "Merry-Go-*
> *Round," in* Booklist, *Vol. 77, No. 3, October 1,*
> *1980, p. 252.*

The illustrations are whimsical, the glowing watercolors conveying the feel of summer outdoors. Kate is exaggeratedly tiny, and children will like spotting her teddy bear on the pages. Humorous stereotypical characteristics suited to their jobs underscore the point that the adults can break out of their molds, and Katie's faith in her three companions' abilities is well-founded.

> *Eva-Maria Lusk, in a review of "Merry-Go-Round,"*
> *in* School Library Journal, *Vol. 27, No. 3, November, 1980, p. 63.*

KÖNIG HUPF DER 1 [KING BOUNCE THE 1st] (1982)

The plea for tolerance is a well-worn theme in children's books, but the variations seem endless. In **King Bounce the 1st,** Helme Heine has ingeniously mixed a common childhood pleasure and a common adult affliction. The heavy responsibilities of King Bounce make him so weary that he needs a way to unwind before bedtime. A few leaps on to a bouncy mattress serve this purpose admirably. But as in the lives of children, a higher authority makes the rules. When a cabinet officer discovers the unkingly therapy, he persuades his fellow ministers to pass an anti-bounce law. Now the king collapses with fatigue, and only his deathbed wish—one final bounce—averts a tragic ending. The bounce not only resuscitates him, it proves contagious and everyone is gleefully leaping up and down on the last page.

The parable exposes an all too prevalent human failing—the notion that anything unfamiliar had best be suppressed. The point is easily made with just one or two lines of narrative per page. This high compression makes the text unobtrusive and yet playfully melodramatic.

Heine's strong collage patterns may remind the viewer of illustrations by Ezra Jack Keats or Eric Carle. However, there is a serious zaniness in Heine's work which has no close antecedent—a zaniness of concept plus an unusually high standard of execution. Most pages are organized on a straight horizontal baseline. The king's outsized bed frequently serves as this foundational line, and despite the repetition of this bed image, the artist manages to vary its treatment. He plays with scale: the bed is three times longer than necessary for the small, frumpy king. He alters perspective (structures tilt and serve as flat pattern), and he revels in both realistic and abstract surface ornamentation—the floral bedspread is related to bedspreads generally, but the grapelike bas-relief shades are remarkably inventive. Value contrasts in the color and ingenious shape arrangements make the static cut-outs look animated. (pp. 58-9)

> *Donnarae MacCann and Olga Richard, in a review*
> *of "King Bounce the 1st," in* Wilson Library Bulletin, *Vol. 57, No. 1, September, 1982, pp. 58-9.*

[This] is a charmingly simple idea—unfortunately, the charm does not extend to the text which is unimaginative and flat. There is a strained feeling to the style, as if the vocabulary is deliberately being limited to simple words and phrases. It's a double shame, because the illustrations are attractively and ingeniously handled. Helme Heine uses a torn paper collage technique in double-paged spreads. Splashes of bright colors and textures on a stark white background, the characters and their accouterments roll across the pages. The illustrations promise, but the text doesn't deliver.

> *Janice M. Del Negro, in a review of "King Bounce*
> *the 1st," in* School Library Journal, *Vol. 29, No. 5,*
> *January, 1983, p. 60.*

FREUNDE [FRIENDS] (1982)

Heine, who made a splash of sorts with the waggish watercolors for the whimsical **Pigs' Wedding,** shapes this flighty outing along a string of friendship adages: "Good friends always stick together," as demonstrated when Charlie the rooster performs his morning chore and his friends Johnny Mouse and Fat Percy, a pig, go along. "Good friends always decide things together," in this case to play pirates in an abandoned rowboat. "Good friends are always fair," spoken a little ironically when wild cherries are divided, Percy gets twice as many, and Charlie, who complains, gets the pits as compensation. Finally, when it's time to go to bed, "Sometimes good friends can't be together." If the pictures amplified these turns on friendship, humorously or otherwise, it might be enough; but Heine's cartoons, however deftly painted, are vacant—without ideas, expression, or flow.

A review of "Friends," in Kirkus Reviews, *Vol. L, No. 20, October 15, 1982, p. 1151.*

Largely because of Helme Heine's watercolor illustrations, **Friends** is one of the better picture books this season. He shows special care—creates the illusion of movement by making the spokes of the bicycle shimmer as it moves past a wheat field; depicts the passage of time by lengthening the shadows of late afternoon; marks the age of farmhouse walls by mottling his colors. But what he gives us most is a sense of joy, of irrepressible glee, of fellowship and delight. The final two-page illustration says it all: The dreaming trio is walking on clouds across a star-studded sky and looking for all the world like vaudevillians making their exit into the wings, secure in the knowledge that they have been a smash. And indeed they have.

George A. Woods, in a review of "Friends," in The New York Times Book Review, *November 28, 1982, p. 24.*

With an illustration of three friends riding one bicycle through a wheat field—Charlie Rooster leaning into the wind from his handlebar perch, Johnny Mouse and fat Percy (pig) each on a pedal—all of them having a ball as they zip along—you just know you're in for a fine story. And from the title page until the final dream scene in which the chums strut around the night clouds, we are treated to a sequence of fun and games that create a sense of lighthearted warmth. None of these experiences are outlandish or even out of the ordinary. But Heine's visual imagination makes the images extraordinary. Children like to fish, but not many use a mouse's tail for the line. And to gather cherries, would you put the pig on top of the rooster on top of the mouse to reach the branches? There is such genuine affection expressed among the three: trying to sleep on a henhouse perch, Percy's arm around Charlie's shoulder while Johnny holds onto Percy's other arm. Watercolors take full advantage of the white page. The double-page scene at dusk with silhouetted cottage and tree is a fine restful transition from the frenetic daytime fun to the final funny efforts to bed down. Unasked, I've turned that trio into a quartet, so that I may join their sport.

Kenneth Marantz, in a review of "Friends," in School Library Journal, *Vol. 29, No. 6, February, 1983, p. 66.*

DAS SCHÖNSTE EI DER WELT [*THE MOST WONDERFUL EGG IN THE WORLD*] (1983)

Helme Heine has a number of successful picture books to his credit. His hallmark is a brisk text, married to eccentric illustrations. In **The Most Wonderful Egg in the World,** three hens compete to see who can lay the best egg. The King, who sets up the competition, decides that the eggs are all wonderful in their different ways, and makes all three hens princesses by ceremoniously painting their crests with gold. One of the eggs is cubic and multicoloured, and the back cover shows the three hens admiring their chicks, one of them cubic and multicoloured. . . . Heine's approach is always refreshingly uncompromising. One has the feeling that he writes and paints for the child in himself, and so his books seem never to strike a false note. With picture books one is often conscious of the author trying hard to produce what will appeal to children, whereas the best authors (Sendak, for example) write only what appeals to themselves.

Kicki Moxon Browne, "The Child Within: Picture Books 1," in The Times Literary Supplement, *No. 4200, September 30, 1983, p. 1050.*

Beautiful painting, expert design, tongue-in-cheek humour with jokes subtle and obvious on every page, on the endpapers and on the back cover. . . . Heine's books are always worth having (his ideas for books fit his talent and the form), this one being among the best.

Nancy Chambers, in a review of "The Most Wonderful Egg in the World," in The Signal Review of Children's Books, 2, *1983, p. 13.*

The message here—"What you can do is more important than what you look like"—is conveyed simply but effectively, with the theme of uniqueness and individuality nicely underplayed. The watercolor illustrations, mostly in pale tones with much open white space, are full of fun, as when the king appears amidst all the kingdom's hens, when he paints the birds' crests gold in lieu of giving them crowns or when, on the back jacket, the award-winning eggs have hatched. Children will be rewarded with new, humorous details on each rereading.

Kathleen Brachmann, in a review of "The Most Wonderful Egg in the World," in School Library Journal, *Vol. 30, No. 5, January, 1984, p. 65.*

THE PEARL (1985)

The exquisite watercolor that opens the book, showing Beaver on an island in the middle of the marsh, is lovely and serene and not at all indicative of the activity and playfulness to follow. Beaver has found a treasure—a mussel, which he hugs to his heart—and begins to dream. In his dream he finds that keeping the treasure for himself is not worth the ire it causes in relationships with his friends. Like some of Leo Leonni's picture books, **The Pearl** can be read as a political statement, but what really distinguishes it are the glorious watercolor illustrations. Helme Heine, who is a master at creating funny, endearing creatures, has "animaled" this book with a grand array of beasts—a moose with magnificent antlers, a shy Unicorn, a furious bear, a stork, a fearsome bat. The drama and action in the pictures and the expressions and poses of the characters create a picture book of great vitality.

Anita Silvey, in a review of "The Pearl," in The Horn Book Magazine, *Vol. LXI, No. 4, July-August, 1985, p. 439.*

The Pearl is fool's gold in that its eye-catching, comic watercolors coax young viewers to a story in which the heavy message is of dubious worth. Beaver finds a mussel that may hold a pearl. He falls asleep. He dreams a nightmare of jealousy, greed and hostility that his good fortune induces among his forest friends. He awakens. He throws away the mussel that may contain a pearl. He swims to meet his unwitting, playful friends. It's one of those don't-dare-to-be-different stories that reinforces the worst aspects of peer pressure for prereaders not yet aware that withstanding peer group social injustice will be their next big problem after learning how to read.

Lillian N. Gerhardt, in a review of "The Pearl," in School Library Journal, *Vol. 32, No. 1, September, 1985, p. 118.*

From One Day in Paradise, *retold and illustrated by Helme Heine.*

Helme Heine's **The Pearl** is an enchanting parable about greed . . .

With his excellent eye for color and subtle detail, Mr. Heine depicts both the most amusing and the most frightening moments imaginatively. In the dream, when Beaver lies to his friends about where to find mussels a pink unicorn peers quizzically around a tree. A bear's anger turns his nose a bright red. As the animals become greedier and greedier their eyes glow yellow.

The illustrations move the simple text along at a lyrical pace. Watercolor washes, in gradations of blues, grays, browns, pinks and greens, resemble a cartoonlike series of stained-glass windows. Mr. Heine's use of slapstick heightens the frenzy—a pig's derrière with corkscrew tail bobs out of the lake, a moose comes up from a dive with bits of seaweed dangling on his antlers. There's a wildcat's tail curled tightly, a mouse clutching a shell as he hides behind a rock, a crayfish about to pinch a frog. The dream sequence ends with Beaver holding his eyes shut to avoid a detonation of reds, yellows and oranges. . . .

In **The Pearl** the popular West German author and artist seems to have achieved a new ease of expression—the illustrations seem at once more spontaneous and sophisticated.

> *Rosalie R. Radomsky, in a review of "The Pearl,"*
> *in* The New York Times Book Review, *September*

22, 1985, p. 32.

DER RENNWAGEN [THE RACING CART] **(British edition as** *The Friends' Racing Cart;* **Canadian edition as** *The Wagon Race***);** *DER WECKER [THE ALARM CLOCK]; DER BESUCH [THE VISITOR]* **(British edition as** *The Friends Have a Visitor***)** **(***DREI KLEINE FREUNDE [THREE LITTLE FRIENDS SERIES]***) (1985)**

Friendship is . . . the subject of the Three Little Friends Series including **The Wagon Race, The Alarm Clock,** and **The Visitor,** all by West Germany's Helme Heine. An unlikely triumvirate, Johnny Mouser, Franz von Rooster, and fat Wiggle, live on a muddy farm. The mouse, pig, and rooster are a lot like real-life best friends in that they bicker among themselves and measure their own strengths and weaknesses against those of their friends. And when misfortune falls on any of them, the other two will instantly rush to the rescue. That's what friends are for.

The three pastel picture-books in the series establish their friendship to all the world. They are cheerful, colourful, and as cute as one of Wiggle's ears. Delicate water-colour illustrations are full of sly touches that will tickle adults reading the stories aloud: crossed bones fastened over the doghouse door like a family crest; the rooster making a stab (literally) at eating an ice cream cone; the pig tricked into the waiting bathtub by a trail of tempting candies.

The language of these little charmers, translated from the

original German, is a bit stiff, but somehow that doesn't hurt at all. Once you've met friends as appealing as the ones in this threesome, you'll be eager for a return visit.

Joan McGrath, "A Full Menu of Fall Reading for Youngsters of Every Taste," in Quill and Quire, *Vol. 50, No. 11, November, 1984, p. 10.*

Charlie Rooster, Johnny Mouse and fat Percy, a pig, who were so endearing in *Friends,* are back in not-so-top form as they share some mild adventures. In *The Alarm Clock,* they borrow a clock so that they can stay up until midnight. They cavort around the farm until midnight, then set the clock for sunrise. Charlie is kept awake by the ticking, so he muffles the sound and oversleeps. The other two wake him; he decides that friends are more reliable than mechanical devices. In *The Racing Cart,* Johnny Mouse finds an old cart and insists on trying it first. The cart crashes, and he realizes that everything is better when friends do things together. Johnny and Charlie become jealous when Percy pays a lot of attention to *The Visitor,* a lamb, but they get to know her and seem to decide that she is their friend too. The books are attractive, with appealing watercolors, but they lack excitement. The vocabulary is too difficult for the younger children who might read them alone, but the stories are too boring to read aloud. The books are didactic and condescending; the lessons about the value of friendship are too obviously stated. Lobel's "Frog and Toad" series (and James Marshall's "George and Martha" books have more wit and less preachiness.

Jean Hammond Zimmerman, in a review of "The Alarm Clock" and others, in School Library Journal, *Vol. 32, No. 7, March, 1986, p. 148.*

SAMSTAG IM PARADIES [*ONE DAY IN PARADISE*] (1986; British edition as *Saturday in Paradise*)

In this original interpretation of the biblical creation story, Heine casts God as a human male artist. Singlehandedly, he takes on the task of creating the universe, dons a white beard and white suit, and uses modern equipment and techniques. On the sixth day, he sits at his easel sketching human forms in his own image. Finally, he molds Adam and Eve, his boy and girl children, from clay; he gives them life, immortal souls and paradise as a gift, then watches over them like a proud father. Happy with his work, he rests. Heine handles the story with dignity and imagination, and the final spreads of the children playing in their lush tropical paradise are evocative. But the subtle humor and the human-centered interpretation of creation may be more suited for discerning adults than for literal-minded children, grappling with the wondrous mysteries of the universe.

A review of "One Day in Paradise," in Publishers Weekly, *Vol. 229, No. 17, April 25, 1986, p. 78.*

Helme Heine presents a simple, human, warm, and loving interpretation of the Creation story from Genesis for very young children. . . . The view is traditional in the sequence of Creation and in the portrayal of God as a man; it is nontraditional in depicting Adam and Eve as children and in showing God actually laboring. Heine includes gentle humor in his illustrations—such as showing three woolly mammoths tusk to tail, as in a circus parade, with Adam and Eve asleep on the furry backs. The water-color paintings vary, including a delicate landscape, a picture of God's workshop full of details and models, the lushness of Paradise, and an inky, dark night

when, "content with what He made, He looked forward to the seventh day, the day of rest." The design of the book is unusual, with the first five days of Creation summed up in a preface inserted between the title and half-title pages. The jacket and title page feature a simplified tree of life topped by Adam and Eve in a blossom, with a creature at the end of each leaf—snail, butterfly, starfish, monkey, and others. The book is carefully rendered with little details that make the reader smile: for example, the tiny devil on the back jacket, God watering the tree of life, and God's faithful companion—a tail-wagging puppy. Children will pore over the various diagrams that show the early stages of God's design. Simpler than most earlier titles, such as Daughtery's *In the Beginning* and Reed's *Adam & Eve*, the book is a lovely addition to the stories of Creation. (pp. 317-18)

Elizabeth S. Watson, in a review of "One Day in Paradise," in The Horn Book Magazine, *Vol. LXII, No. 3, May–June, 1986, pp. 317-18.*

Through delicate and soft watercolors and a simple declarative text, Heine shows God's work in forming his children, Adam and Eve. . . . Heine's perspective on the Creation story is reminiscent of M. B. Goffstein's viewpoint in *An Artist* (1980). Both author/illustrators see God as the ultimate artist, and the main figure (God in *One Day in Paradise* and the painter in *An Artist*) is depicted as a diminutive bearded man who resembles Claude Monet. Heine's unorthodox and lighthearted approach to the retelling is a celebration of Creation and is similar to Aileen Fisher's *I Stood Upon a Mountain* (1979; o.p.), as both are written in a readable style and focus on making the Creation story accessible to young children. Those looking for a more traditional telling will find Molly Cox' *The Creation* (1977; o.p.) suitable for a slightly older audience than the one intended for the Heine or Fisher books.

Lorraine Douglas, in a review of "One Day in Paradise," in School Library Journal, *Vol. 32, No. 10, August, 1986, p. 82.*

SEVEN WILD PIGS: ELEVEN PICTURE BOOK FANTASIES (1988)

Heine's watercolors in this picture book are among the finest and most masterful to be found in children's books, while the stories seem incomplete, incoherent, crazed, illogical—even hallucinatory. **"The Crazy Farm"** best indicates this style: the mouse attacks the cat, the bee collects rocks, the cow produces beer, and the pig, sleeping late, is on strike. In another story, **"Seven Wild Pigs,"** the artist himself is introduced within the painting and participates in the action. The other stories are also relatively unconventional but will appeal to children who love nonsense.

A review of "Seven Wild Pigs: 11 Picture Book Fantasies," in Publishers Weekly, *Vol. 233, No. 6, February 12, 1988, p. 86.*

A gifted German illustrator (*The Pigs' Wedding*) assembles fey vignettes, fantastic notions, and some fleeting jokes to make a very long picture book. Heine's deft watercolors are full of unexpected humor and beautifully painted images; unfortunately, appealing as they are, they can't carry this miscellany alone. The awkwardly rhymed text (satisfactory translation of whimsical doggerel is almost impossible) is a major problem; the offbeat, slight "fantasies" range from silly to gruesome. In the title story, an artist adds a hunter to his painted landscape; the hunter shoots the obstreperous pigs and feeds one to the artist, who has entered the picture; later, he emerges to find his canvas full of holes.

A review of "Seven Wild Pigs: Eleven Picture Book Fantasies," in Kirkus Reviews, *Vol. LVI, No. 5, March 1, 1988, p. 362.*

Chihiro Iwasaki (Matsumoto)

1918-1974

Japanese author and illustrator of picture books.

Associated with approximately seventy books in her native land as author or artist or both, Iwasaki is considered one of Japan's most prominent contributors to the field of children's literature. The creator of pictures for works by many notable international children's writers as well as for adaptations of fairy tales, she is recognized for writing and illustrating distinctive works for preschoolers and early primary grade readers which demonstrate her understanding of and respect for the often underrated concerns of the small child. Iwasaki presents her audience with subtle, affectionate stories composed of typical incidents from the lives of the very young; both the apprehension about and the sensuous enjoyment of such events as the arrival of a new baby brother, being home alone, and making a birthday wish are given credence in Iwasaki's quiet, gentle prose. Her illustrations, most often impressionistic watercolor paintings, are often applauded for perfectly extending the subdued tones of her texts. Through her use of delicate, translucent colors and muted outlines, Iwasaki gives a tender quality to the world as her young protagonists view it. In 1977 the Iwasaki Chihiro Art Museum of Picture Books, which exhibits Iwasaki's works as well as those by other significant artists for children, was established in Tokyo in homage to Iwasaki's noteworthy contributions to the art of the picture book. It is a legacy to an eminent illustrator who, as an author, gave her readers comforting stories which she invests with her serious and sympathetic attitude toward childhood.

GENERAL COMMENTARY

JAMES FRASER

The translucent watercolor illustrations of Chihiro Iwasaki have been familiar to collectors and readers of children's picture books in eastern and western countries for two decades now. Her first book to be published in the West was **Tears of the Dragon** (1967). It was Selma Lanes of Parents Magazine Press who saw the importance of this illustrator whose first book had appeared in 1960 but was never translated. **Tears of the Dragon** was followed by **The Crane Maiden, The Fisherman under the Sea** and **Staying Home Alone on a Rainy Day.**

Among the post World War II illustrators of children's books in Japan, Chihiro Iwasaki is certainly one of several who deservedly enjoys an international reputation. Her *Momoko* books in the early 1970s brought her wide international attention and a following that continues to this day. Of her seventy-one books, seventeen have appeared in translation; some in as many as eight, e.g. **Momoko's Birthday.**

Although her life is over, her books remain as popular, as in her lifetime, if not more so, as reception of her concern for children and peace seems to be increasing, in some quarters, at least.

In an unusual demonstration of commitment to her work and her ideals, a museum was established in 1977 as a memorial to her accomplishment. The museum, the Iwasaki Chihiro Art Museum of Picture Books, was built on the site where she lived for twenty-two years until her death. The great majority of her original art, some 7,000 pieces, is maintained in the museum under sound curatorial conditions. Changing bimonthly exhibitions give the general public an opportunity to view the development of her style. . . .

Approximately 100 pieces are shown at a time at these bimonthly exhibitions, with a special exhibition being held once a year of work related in some way to the art of children's books. In 1986, for example, an exhibition of the post World War II Japanese picture book was mounted and a catalog published.

It is the concern of the director, Tadasu Iizawa and the deputy director, Takeshi Matsumoto, that this museum be a force for encouragement of the study of the Japanese picture book as well as keeping Chihiro's legacy alive. (p. 63)

James Fraser, "The Iwasake Chihiro Art Museum of Picture Books in Tokyo," in Phaedrus: An International Annual of Children's Literature Research, *Vol. 12, 1986-87, pp. 63-4.*

STAYING HOME ALONE ON A RAINY DAY   (1969)

Staying home alone on a rainy day is a frightening experience for a little girl whose mother had promised "she'd be back soon"; it's also a very concrete title for a very vaporous book. On pages that simulate the texture of canvas are watercolors that are sometimes deft sketches of Allison cringing ("Please stop ringing," she says to the telephone) or absorbed in drawing pictures on the window panes, sometimes wet wash impressions of how she feels or of what she sees transfigured. It's a risky technique, sublimating subject matter to subjectivity, and in a few cases it fails to communicate: while Allison is watching two fish in a fishbowl, what appears to be an upended, particolored umbrella thrusts into a sea of green from which two shadowy white fish-like forms emerge. The allusiveness becomes complete abdication on the last page when Allison finally sees "Mother, her arms full of packages . . . running" and we see a blank gray page. Some of it is quite lovely to look at, all of it (except the telephone) is rather remote.

A review of "Staying Home Alone on a Rainy Day," in Kirkus Reviews, *Vol. XXXVII, No. 7, April 1, 1969, p. 370.*

A biblio-security blanket for the very young, who might be afraid to stay home alone while Mother goes shopping. The comforting message: Mommy will soon come running home; the medium: a 9¾" square picture book, with lush watercolor illustrations enhancing a minimal, explicit text that details Allison's attempts to reassure and amuse herself in the empty house during a rainstorm. Mrs. Iwasaki's paintings have in the past gracefully extended such tales as **The Crane Maiden;**

with this slighter text, her compositions frequently move toward abstraction that is not always successful, though her vibrant, translucent colors are as eye-catching as ever and the format (featuring heavy linen-textured paper) is pleasing. On balance, a useful message and an example of beautiful bookmaking.

> *Margaret A. Dorsey, in a review of "Staying Home Alone on a Rainy Day," in* School Library Journal, *Vol. 16, No. 2, October, 1969, p. 130.*

MOMOKO'S LOVELY DAY (1969)

Momoko's Lovely Day is essentially for the grown ups. This small-child's-eye view of a single day is most beautifully and sensitively done. If, as I believe, it is enough to give a memorable experience to one child in a thousand, then the book is fully justified. For the others it will, I suspect, be quite meaningless.

> *A review of "Momoko's Lovely Day," in* The Junior Bookshelf, *Vol. 33, No. 5, October, 1969, p. 292.*

Japanese artists have gone further than we have in offering children a specifically artistic experience in picture-books; we should be ready to help our children to enjoy this kind of experience, which they are often ready for before we realise it; we could benefit from books like this one, following in pictures the events of a little girl's day as she looks out of the window at flowers blurred by rain, hides behind the curtain when the telephone rings, plays with her kitten. The objects she sees emerge in wash-colour from pale backgrounds, their texture and composition suggesting all the time a child's-eye view of the external world.

> *Margery Fisher, in a review of "Momoko's Lovely Day," in* Growing Point, *Vol. 8, No. 6, December, 1969, p. 1445.*

A BROTHER FOR MOMOKO (1970)

Misty water-colours like those in *Momoko's lovely day* again illustrate important events in the life of this little girl. As she waits for the new baby to be brought home she looks at the pram, wonders about a present, shows the cradle to her teddy bear; her anticipation, fearful and happy, is reflected subtly in words and pictures. With grace and delicacy the Japanese author-artist states, but never over-states, a universal truth of childhood. (pp. 1606-07)

> *Margery Fisher, in a review of "A Brother for Momoko," in* Growing Point, *Vol. 9, No. 4, October, 1970, pp. 1606-07.*

A Brother for Momoko has one of those jackets that publishers dream of. It would sell anything. Unfortunately it is so far superior to the rest of the book as to be positively misleading. In a tiny thread of text Momoko awaits the arrival of her baby brother. It is cleverly done but, to English tastes, just a shade embarrassing. The pictures are in this artist's characteristic manner; that is, they are delicate smudgy washes which are sometimes so elusive as almost to defeat their object. This clever, sensitive and sincere book fails in one important particular; it cannot communicate fully.

> *A review of "A Brother for Momoko," in* The Junior Bookshelf, *Vol. 34, No. 5, October, 1970, p. 285.*

Most people interested in the development of books will be aware of the fact that artists and authors are turning more and more attention to the very youngest children . . . . I think that the most successful and certainly the most beautiful of this genre was Chihiro Iwasaki's *Momoko's Lovely Day* with its exquisite water-colour pictures of a small child's experiences on one day; so it was with eager apprehension—apprehension caused by the fact that it seemed to me an impossibility to equal the beauty of the first—that I turned to its sequel *A Brother for Momoko.*

Imagine my joy to discover a book of equal delight. Each page is quite lovely; every turn reveals the same thunder colouring and the story—Momoko waiting for the arrival of her new small brother—has a perfect simplicity precisely matching the artistry of the pictures.

I beg you—steal it, borrow it, buy it.

> *Gabrielle Maunder, in a review of "A Brother for Momoko," in* The School Librarian, *Vol. 18, No. 4, December, 1970, p. 500.*

A NEW BABY IS COMING TO MY HOUSE (1972)

Iwasaki's approach to the ambivalent feelings of a child waiting to meet the new baby is to ignore their existence, so that the child who might be relieved to find his own conflicts reflected is faced instead with the vapidly untroubled musings ("I would like to give my brother a present . . . I can't wait to see him . . . I want to hold him. He is my very own brother") of a moppet who floats through the pages in collagey water colors that resemble toilet paper ads. Fortunately for expectant siblings, Viki Holland offers a more recognizable view of a new arrival in her photo-illustrated *We Are Having a Baby* (1972).

> *A review of "A New Baby Is Coming to My House," in* Kirkus Reviews, *Vol. XL, No. 19, October 1, 1972, p. 1140.*

A New Baby Is Coming to My House, a little girl proudly announces, as she awaits her baby brother's imminent arrival, wondering whether he'll like the teddy and when they'll be able to play together. Sensitively illustrated in water-color by Chihiro Iwasaki, this low-key Japanese import is probably the best book of its genre this season. It isn't thoroughly informative, nor even subtly psychological; rather, it creates a mood and is awash with sincerity and love.

> *Michael J. Bandler, in a review of "A New Baby Is Coming to My House," in* Book World—The Washington Post, *November 5, 1972, p. 3.*

Delicately told and illustrated, this story of a little girl awaiting her baby brother's arrival from the hospital honestly conveys her mixed feelings. She knows that John will be using her carriage and cradle and wonders whether he will be Mommie's "very special boy" as she is her "very special girl." She wants to give him her teddy bear but decides not to because ". . . Teddy loves me." Trying on the baby's bonnet, she realizes that he must be very small and, when she finally sees him, he is so tiny that she wants to hold him. She is last seen wheeling him—and Teddy, too—in the carriage. The author-artist's impressionistic watercolor illustrations (similar to those in her *Staying Home Alone on a Rainy Day)* sensitively blend with the simple, child-like text to make a successful whole.

> *Melinda Schroeder, in a review of "A New Baby Is Coming to My House," in* School Library Journal, *Vol. 19, February, 1973, p. 61.*

MOMOKO AND THE PRETTY BIRD (1972)

Momoko and the pretty bird is executed in pale wash, but there is no lack of precision in the exquisite sequence of scenes which show a little girl in moods of longing, excitement, thoughtfulness. "I wish I had a bird of my very own, a pretty bird to sing all day" Momoko says, but when after a mad chase in the garden with her friend Fumio she has the little bird safely in a cage, she realises it can only be happy if she sets it free again. The text is brief, just enough to carry a story which unfolds clearly in the subtle, beautiful pictures.

> *Margery Fisher, in a review of "Momoko and the Pretty Bird," in* Growing Point, *Vol. 11, No. 2, July, 1972, p. 1967.*

Mrs. Iwasaki is a modern impressionist for her simple colour wash illustrations, without definite outline and drawn with the brush, convey, in their delicate colourings, feelings, moods and ideas. The third in her series about Momoko, tells how she would like a bird for her very own. . . . The story is told with the minimum of text so that all the accent is on the visual impressions given by the paintings providing an excellent experience for infant children.

> *Edward Hudson, in a review of "Momoko and the Pretty Bird," in* Children's Book Review, *Vol. II, No. 5, October, 1972, p. 145.*

MOMOKO'S BIRTHDAY (1973)

Mixture as before. The fourth in the Momoko series of nursery picture books by Japanese artist Chihiro Iwasaki who again uses delicate watercolour illustrations drawn with the brush to portray a short, inconsequential episode in the life of Momoko. Tomorrow she is five but today she shares in her friend's all too brief birthday. When her own fifth birthday finally arrives, the countryside is covered in snow in celebration, and her Mummy's present of a woolly hat and mittens is put to instant use. Mrs. Iwasaki attempts, always, to present a true-to-life experience for the young child to share in and does so with a traditional Japanese sense of tranquility which in her latest book creates a sense of irritation. The events are all too brief and fleeting and one feels that her concentration on simplicity and aesthetically pleasing illustration may have the adverse effect of creating no impression whatsoever on the mind of the young 'reader'. If Momoko (now five years old) is to survive, then more content will be needed for the story line of future books. (pp. 170-71)

> *Edward Hudson, in a review of "Momoko's Birthday," in* Children's Book Review, *Vol. III, No. 6, December, 1973, pp. 170-71.*

Mrs. Iwasaki explores again the mind of a wondering little Japanese girl as she discovers the everyday marvels of a snow-covered world. She is surely among the most original artists in this field, with an unmistakable style and an undemonstrative mastery of her theme and her medium. The very small

children who enjoy this lovely book will experience a dual experience; they will meet a sensitive and understanding mind and discover that Momoko's home is both like and unlike their own. (pp. 375-76)

> *M. Crouch, in a review of "Momoko's Birthday," in* The Junior Bookshelf, *Vol. 37, No. 6, December, 1973, pp. 375-76.*

WILL YOU BE MY FRIEND (1974)

The delicately graceful paintings of the Japanese artist make her book a rare treat for the eye as well as an appealing story. Allison is playing in front of her house when she sees a moving van coming down the street. How she prays for a child in the new family arriving next door and how crushed she is when the child turns out to be a boy who snubs her. "That boy is trouble," Allison is sure when she sees that his dog is bigger than hers and chases her pet. A meeting of minds, however, plus propinquity and shared experiences make for a happy ending, and friends the boy and girl do become. Parents who are left cold by some children's books should be enchanted with this one, especially if they appreciate superior artwork.

> *A review of "Will You Be My Friend," in* Publishers Weekly, *Vol. 205, No. 8, February 25, 1974, p. 113.*

Allison is eager to meet her new neighbor—a boy of three or four like herself. It is touch and go, however, until he decides he wants to make friends with her. The story line is slim, but the appealing, ethereal charcoal sketches, filled in with pastel watercolors, are similar to those in Iwasaki's earlier books—*Staying Home Alone on a Rainy Day* and *A New Baby Is Coming to My House.* However there is noticeably less color used here: double pages of several colors alternate with double spreads of olive green lightly daubed with pink. Nevertheless, the mood is quietly engaging, and young children will empathize as Allison struggles to master the vital art of making friends.

> *Melinda Schroeder, in a review of "Will You Be My Friend," in* School Library Journal, *Vol. 21, September, 1974, p. 63.*

THE BIRTHDAY WISH (1974)

"Oh stars, how will I ever get my birthday wish when I took Judy's," Allison wails at bedtime, for in her excitement over her own impending fifth birthday she has blown out the candles on her friend's cake. But Allison's wish for snow comes true anyway ("Oh, Mommie, look, this is my white birthday!") and she redeems herself by letting Judy blow out her candles—for "After all, I got my wish." To match the insipid story Iwasaki's pretty watercolor world of childhood is a wishy wash of pastel colored clothes and houses, shimmering candles and soft tissuey settings.

> *A review of "The Birthday Wish," in* Kirkus Reviews, *Vol. XLII, No. 12, June 15, 1974, p. 631.*

Ms. Iwasaki has again succeeded in capturing the innermost thoughts and feelings of a very young child. . . . The text is brief and the plot uncomplicated, appealing to the very young child. The soft wash illustrations by the author provide a quiet framework for the narrative. For this reason the book would be a pleasant selection for lap-reading, as it is the young listener, rather than the independent reader, who will enjoy this story most. (pp. 84-5)

Barbara Dill, in a review of "The Birthday Wish," in Wilson Library Bulletin, *Vol. 49, No. 1, September, 1974, pp. 84-5.*

WHAT'S FUN WITHOUT A FRIEND? (1975)

The artist's delicate paintings, all soft, sensuous curves and pastel tones, should make a best seller of her latest book. These are pictures which can be gazed upon for hours—a skillful blend of lovely images and endearing sentiment which never cloys. The story, simplicity itself, is about Allison who has to leave her best friend, Tippy (a dog), at home when she goes to spend the summer at grandmother's house at the seashore. In spite of exciting surroundings, a new red bathing suit, grandma's good cooking and other delights, Allison is lonely and unhappy without her friend. Fortunately for all concerned, understanding parents solve the problem.

A review of "What's Fun without a Friend?" in Publishers Weekly, *Vol. 207, No. 26, June 30, 1975, p. 57.*

As usual Iwasaki's misty slabs of water color exactly match her drippy story of Allison, vacationing at the seashore with Mommie but lonely for her dog Tippy until Daddy shows up and surprises her by bringing Tippy along. It's like that pastel colored, artificially flavored sugar candy that doesn't even look tempting.

A review of "What's Fun without a Friend?" in Kirkus Reviews, *Vol. XLIII, No. 13, July 1, 1975, p. 709.*

The illustrations are admirable: soft, bright watercolors are used with restraint; there are no edges or outlines, the composition is spare, the scale large. The story is slight, and there seems inadequate explanation of the reversal of parental decision, since the story begins with the child explaining to her dog that "Mommie says you can't come with us."

Zena Sutherland, in a review of "What's Fun without a Friend?" in Bulletin of the Center for Children's Books, *Vol. 29, No. 4, December, 1975, p. 64.*

Janet (Louise Swoboda) Lunn

1928-

American-born Canadian author of fiction and nonfiction, critic, and editor.

Recognized as one of Canada's most notable authors as well as one of its best-known reviewers and editors, Lunn is applauded for characteristically welding enchanting fantasy with intriguing mystery and authentic historical fiction while offering young readers powerful themes: the search for a national and individual identity, the awareness of an affinity with the past, and the undeniable importance of close family relationships. In her fiction for middle and upper grade readers, time travel and psychic occurences provide Lunn's resourceful young protagonists with experiences which lead to self-realization. Her first book for young people, *Double Spell* (1968, published in the United States as *Twin Spell*), describes how a pair of twin girls unlock their family history and come to a better understanding of the inevitable effects of the past on the present. Critics observe that Lunn places significant emphasis on the plight of the displaced person and accurately depicts the quest for emotional ties to a homeland. Born and raised in America but living in Canada as a naturalized citizen, Lunn often found herself in turmoil, a topic she addresses in her novel *The Root Cellar* (1981). The story relates how Rose, an unhappy, introverted orphan, finds the means to travel from present-day Ontario to the Civil War era; *The Root Cellar* also focuses on Will, a young Canadian whom Rose meets in the past who decides to join the Union Army. Just as Rose learns to accept and to love her new home, the devastation of the war brings Will to recognize his true loyalty to Canada. Often praised for the accuracy of her facts and settings, Lunn created a fictitious place in her novel *Shadow in Hawthorn Bay* (1986), in which fifteen-year-old Mary journeys from her home in Scotland to an island community in upper Canada in response to her cousin's telepathic message. Lunn has also written a collection of true stories about Canadian heroes and an adaptation of a classic European fairy tale. She has won several major Canadian awards for her books, including the Canada Council Children's Literature Prize for *Shadow in Hawthorn Bay* in 1986, the Canadian Library Association Book of the Year for Children Award for *The Root Cellar* in 1982 and for *Shadow in Hawthorn Bay* in 1987, and the Vicky Metcalf Award for her body of work in 1982.

(See also *Something about the Author,* Vol. 4; *Contemporary Authors,* Vol. 33-36, rev. ed.; and *Contemporary Authors New Revision Series,* Vol. 22.)

GENERAL COMMENTARY

JAMES HARRISON

Each of Janet Lunn's three novels for children is very precisely located in space. The first, *Double spell,* takes place in Toronto, and more specifically in a house which dates from the early nineteenth century but has benefitted or suffered from sundry additions and accretions since then. The action of *The root cellar* centres upon a tumbledown old farmhouse in

Prince Edward County, Ontario, while that of *Shadow in Hawthorn Bay* occurs in the same small corner of the same small island. What is more, Lunn lives in the very house (no longer tumbledown) of which she writes in *The root cellar,* and I should be surprised if she did not have an equally specific house in mind when writing *Double spell.* One can sense this personal knowledge of and attachment to a locality just from reading the books. But the care with which Lunn recreates the settings of all three books is more than mere self-indulgent nostalgia. For it is necessary that the houses in the first two books be recognizable when seen as they appeared a century or more ago, since in both cases characters find themselves time-travelling to the past. By contrast, the protagonist of *Shadow in Hawthorn Bay* does all her travelling in space. But it is equally important, though for different reasons, that the new community and environment she finds herself in be presented convincingly.

Double spell is the story of a whole family, and more particularly of twins with that family and the ups and downs and rich complexities of their relationship. These are intensified when they buy an antique doll and find themselves becoming involved, through shared dreams, mysterious coincidences, and finally a frightening overlap of past and present, with the lives of twins who owned the doll and its twin back in the

1830s. For the most part the story is one of mystery, suspense, and detection, with a heartstopping climax, followed by too many details left to be unravelled by hurried historical research in the epilogue. But what may well remain in the reader's mind longest is the fate of Hester — Hester the first of Lunn's misfits, a spoiled, rich, nineteenth-century misfit who resents being excluded from the special world of the country-cousin twins she visits, and whose malevolence brings tragedy to them, and hence brings trouble to their twentieth-century counterparts. Neither Hester's failure to fit in nor her guilt is resolved in her lifetime, however. She remains a shadowy minor character. What matters to us, the readers, is the understanding of her plight shown by the twins who stumble backward in time into her story, and the way the generosity of their response enables her troubled spirit to find its eventual rest.

Rose, on the other hand, the twentieth-century protagonist of *The root cellar,* is both time-traveller and misfit. She is a much more thoroughgoing time-traveller than the twins, moreover. An orphan reared in an exclusively adult world by a rich, New York grandmother, who bitterly resents having suddenly to begin a new life in Ontario with an aunt and uncle and their four sons. Her discovery of a doorway into the past provides what seems to be an escape from an intolerable present. Her adventures within that past, however, in the aftermath of the American Civil War, involve her in far more gruesome realities than those of her new home in the present, and lead to her assuming responsibilities she continues to fulfil long after she has recognized that where she truly belongs is in twentieth-century Ontario. What seemed an escape becomes her proving ground. In the end, of course, she returns to the present — in a storm and the nick of time. For the root cellar route to her discovery of where her own true roots lie has been washed out in a flash flood. However therapeutic fantasy may sometimes be, we remain there too long at our peril.

In each of these stories, though more clearly in *The root cellar,* a journey in time provides the protagonist(s) and the reader with a learning experience. In her latest novel Lunn abandons the device of linking past and present through time-travel, and substitutes a spatial journey within a purely historical narrative. The journey, moreover, is one-way, though the learning is two-way, both the traveller and those she learns to live among having something to teach each other.

In *Shadow in Hawthorn Bay,* Mary (or Mairi), a highland girl, journeys from Scotland to loyalist Upper Canada in answer to a psychic summons from her cousin, Duncan, the two of them having been inseparable until, four years earlier, his family emigrated. She arrives to find that Duncan has died while she was still in mid-Atlantic, and that his family are on their way back to Scotland. So she sets to work to earn her return passage. In spite of herself, however, she becomes more and more involved in and useful to the lives of her new neighbours. Yet still she clings to her goal and to her loyalty to the memory of Duncan, refusing to consider the possibility of marrying and settling in Canada. Her sense of not belonging is kept alive — nurtured almost — by her pathological fear of the forest and by her persistent belief in the "old ones" — spirits, ghosts, fairies — as well as her own frightening powers of prophetic second sight. And it is over such matters that much of the reciprocal learning (and therefore reader learning) takes place. As readers, we are privy to Mary's

flashes of prophetic vision, and are consequently impatient with Canadian scepticism as to the possibility of any such gift, and in more general terms with a similar undervaluing of the more imaginative side to Mary's nature. She in turn, when for instance she discovers to her horror that it is human friends rather than fairies who have been leaving her gifts of food (and therefore that she is not under special supernatural protection), must acknowledge that she has been downplaying the importance of human neighbourliness and affection.

The climax of the book comes when her neighbours are forced to admit that the charges of witchcraft to which Mary's stubborn persistence in keeping to herself and holding fast to her beliefs has led are groundless, and when Mary for her part recognizes that whatever summons she received and has continued to receive from Duncan's unhappy spirit is a selfish one to join him in death. Symbolically she forces herself to walk deep into the forest. And there she discovers such silence as tells her that in this new land, as yet scarcely inhabited even by the Indians, there are no "old ones," no guardian spirits from the past. They themselves, she and her neighbours, are the new "old ones," and it is on each other they must rely. When finally she agrees to marry her patient, loving suitor, and admits in so doing that she never felt as much a part of the community in the old country as she does now, it is on the understanding that both she and her husband will remain true to what each has always been as well as welcoming what the other will bring to the partnership.

I refer above to the book's climax. There is much less of a sense in this story than in its predecessors, however, that a climax has been deliberately contrived, just as there is no need of the device of time-travel to establish a link between past and present. The ending is the natural outcome of all that has gone before; the book's relevance to the lives its readers lead is clear throughout. Perhaps the crucial difference is that the shape of the narrative is no longer circular, ending where it began. Mary is not a misfit from the start, like Rose (or Hester). She becomes a misfit by making her journey — a journey in space rather than in time. She is therefore able to achieve her reconciliation, and it is appropriate that she should do so, in and with her new environment rather than her old one — in and with what she comes to recognize as her new home.

The message that people must often return to what they are running away from in order to be able to accept themselves is an important one. But so is the message that they can move on, can find new aspects to themselves by adjusting to a new and initially daunting environment. This lesson is implicit in *The root cellar,* since Rose's escape into the past is also an attempt to return to New York — to the familiar — and her eventual return to Ontario is an acceptance of the new as well as of the known. But this theme of adjustment to the new is altogether more up front in *Shadow in Hawthorn Bay,* even though there is again a submerged countertheme — that in adjusting one must retain an essential core of the old self. And it is the centrality of both these themes to the Canadian consciousness, far more than the truly detailed, authentic, and very engaging picture we are given of early pioneer life, which for me constitutes the Canadian content of this book. They are like opposite sides of the same coin, as when in *The diviners* Morag must return to Scotland in order to discover that her real roots are in Manawaka. But it is a pleasure to find a book — especially one for the young — in which the coin falls so unequivocally heads up (and forward looking) rather than tails. (pp. 60-3)

James Harrison, "Janet Lunn's Time/Space Travellers," in Canadian Children's Literature, *No. 46, 1987, pp. 60-3.*

DOUBLE SPELL   (1968; U.S. edition as *Twin Spell*)

[Sheila Egoff has made the] observation that the Canadian environment seems, for some reason, inhospitable to fantasy. Not only have there been comparatively few fantasies written in Canada, but the authors of those few have for the most part avoided making the Canadian landscape a significant element in their fantasies. . . . A survey of the genre shows our fantasists experimenting with interestingly varied uses of landscape, but only a few managing to make a significant use of Canadian settings. Too often, the fantasy seems to become a means of escape from an empty, mundane or intimidating environment rather than a transformation of such an environment by the revelation of spiritual powers within it. (p. 15)

The gateway between past and present in Janet Lunn's *Twin Spell* . . . is an old house in Toronto, for many generations the family home of the protagonists. Coming to live in the house, the girls first glimpse, then partially re-enact, a family tragedy which had occurred there 130 years earlier. The crucial events all take place in the house and its garden, as past and present begin to merge for the terrified girls. The house is more than just a device to get the children from one time to another; in a sense, understanding and coming to terms with the history of the house is the central purpose of the action. By providing a fixed point of reference and a rationale for the time journeys, the image of the old house helps to make the fantasy coherent and convincing.

The action of the novel is a process of discovery whereby the protagonists gradually learn to understand the connection between their present lives and the uncanny experiences they have of flashing back into nineteenth century Toronto. As part of this process of discovery the girls learn something of the development of their own city: their family house began as a lakeside farm, but had long been incorporated into the suburbs of the city. Seeking the house of their visions, the girls journey through the city streets, and only after much searching and speculation do they discover that the visionary house is their own home. Structural alterations, the growth of ivy, and the growth of the city around the house have transformed the one into the other. . . . The gradual process of coming to understand the history and nature of the house accompanies the girls' growing understanding of the past of their own family, and the tragic incident (a half-intentional murder) which took place in the house over a century before. As they discover and partially relive the past of their home and family, the girls come to a better understanding of themselves and of the value of compassion. The action and concerns of the book are admirably integrated, with the old Toronto house as their central image. (pp. 18-19)

Only, but significantly, in the works of Janet Lunn, Ruth Nichols and C.A. Clark has an imaginative use of setting brought about that transformation of the commonplace world into an extraordinary one which is the essence of fantasy. Lunn and Nichols write within traditions which have been mastered within recent years by others such as Pearce, Gar-

ner and Mayne; what the Canadian writers do is well done, but has been even better done elsewhere. (p. 28)

Gwyneth Evans, " 'Nothing Odd Ever Happens Here': Landscape in Canadian Fantasy," in Canadian Children's Literature, *Nos. 15-16, 1980, pp. 15-30.*

Tales about hauntings need to have enough of reality to enable today's young readers, feet on the ground and educated in technology, to relate them to the familiar world. Yet they also need to have the power to engender a genuine thrill of horror and apprehension. *Double spell* succeeds well in combining these qualities. . . . The build-up of tension and unease is steady and becomes gripping with a climax of real dramatic quality. Period detail is well worked in and heightens the colour. . . . The author is an American living in Canada, and this gives rise to the occasional Americanism which might confuse young British readers; but they will soon be strongly under Janet Lunn's own spell.

Jane Woodley, in a review of, "Double Spell," in The School Librarian, *Vol. 34, No. 2, June, 1986, p. 170.*

LARGER THAN LIFE   (1979)

This collection of short fictionalized stories about characters and events of Canadian historical interest, brings together such noteworthy people as Alexander Mackenzie, John A. Macdonald, Madeleine de Vercheres, Paul Kane and Crowfoot, as well as lesser known characters whose courage in the face of adversity has added depth and character to the face of Canadian history. Each story is very brief and can only deal fleetingly with one incident. The author tries to create the setting and atmosphere of the times about which she is writing, to describe the action and suspense involved in the incident, and to give an appreciation of the main character concerned. Often the events described concern the heroism of the main characters when only children. Modern young readers will easily identify with these.

The author's intention of providing Canadian children with stories of Canadian heroes can well be appreciated. The brevity and ephemeral nature of the stories is, however, regrettable. More historical research into the lives and backgrounds of the lesser known characters would give the reader a broader perspective of the events and a deeper appreciation. Although it is important to present Canadian history as a subject for enjoyment and recreational reading, it should not, in the process, be reduced to the level of popular culture.

Eva Martin, in a review of "Larger than Life," in In Review: Canadian Books for Young People, *Vol. 14, No. 2, April, 1980, p. 50.*

My earliest recollection of Canadian history is of having been compelled, in the fourth grade, to memorize the routes followed by various explorers. I never could remember them because I didn't care where they went. History provoked only yawns, and figures from history were dusty, boring and above all, not real.

Fortunately for her readers, Janet Lunn's *Larger Than Life* is a different kind of history, one that should have enormous appeal to children in the middle elementary grades. This is storytelling at its best, combining historical facts with adventure, humour, suspense and vivid characterization.

The book tells the true stories of ten Canadian "heroes" . . . . Some of these people are much better known than others and their contribution to Canadian history more obvious. What they share is the quality of courage, which may be said to be the unifying theme of the book, and every one of them becomes real to the reader.

In one story, the author comments that "people still tell stories about him as though it were only last week or last month when he lived there." That is exactly how Ms. Lunn tells her own stories, and her characters are real because they are at once "larger than life" and very ordinary. Mrs. Roblin recounts her remarkable experiences while shelling peas. John A. Macdonald takes off his socks in public. Gabriel Dumont, as a child, is sensitive about his short stature. The author's heroes are all appealing, but they aren't perfect and they are never ponderous. Madeleine de Verchères is no martyr, but an impatient girl who seizes her first chance to have a real adventure, and Cornelia de Grassi has, frankly, more than her fair share of vanity. It is these mundane details and familiar feelings that give the reader a sense of immediacy about the lives of Ms. Lunn's heroes. These are figures that don't need dusting off.

This book is beautifully written by a woman who clearly loves words and is extraordinarily skillful at using them to portray children's perceptions. Every young reader will recognize instantly "her grandfather's crackly old voice" and "small cruel eyes in a big red face". The author's language is lively and her descriptive passages evocative. We can see a summer day that is "soft and hazy and peaceful" or a spring day "smelling of melting snow and early spring plants".

Ms. Lunn has a good ear for the way real people talk. There is nothing awkward or contrived about her dialogue, so often a problem in children's books. Conversations occur naturally in these stories, and they invariably ring true.

There are nice touches too, in the author's portrayal of animals. Children will enjoy the big dog that sits in the stern of the boat "for ballast", and the cat that watches birds "with his one good eye". (pp. 77-8)

Eleanor Swainson, "Quality and Quantity in Canadian History," in Canadian Children's Literature, *No. 20, 1980, pp. 76-9.*

THE TWELVE DANCING PRINCESSES: A FAIRY STORY (1979)

In Lunn's revision of Grimms' "The Shoes Danced to Pieces," the old soldier has become a young farm boy, his suit received by the king with scorn; the vanity of the 12 sisters has blighted the royal rose gardens; the boy quickens the plants as well as the heart of the youngest princess, whom he weds. Other embellishments are all in keeping with stock fairytale conventions, but in the borrowing this particular tale loses some of its character (though the spirit is not much affected). Traditional versions are often full of inconsistencies: retellings should not be, but this one is. Discerning readers might question whether a poor farmboy returning from market would have a hawk, hound, and sword with him. Nor should the jacket copy identify the source of the tale as "French" when the Opies note in *Classic Fairy Tales* that it

is scarcely known in France! The verses given to the hero to aid him do not scan; the text asserts that the eldest princess is the most beautiful, and repeatedly states that the hand of "the fairest" is to be the reward—then without waiver gives the youngest to the hero. We are no doubt meant to think the hero kind when he gives his cake and wine to the mice, saying "There's a party for you, little friends"; but as these items are drugged, his generosity is questionable. Although the youngest princess has been alarmed by the slightest hints of the hero's presence, on the last night he actually snatches a goblet from her hand without, apparently, attracting her notice or eliciting any reaction.

Patricia Dooley, in a review of "The Twelve Dancing Princesses," in School Library Journal, *Vol. 26, No. 7, March, 1980, p. 131.*

Fairy tale magic and enchantment are an integral part of this beautiful well-designed book. Its delicately patterned end papers, elegantly illustrated title page, attractively-set text and stunning double-page paintings combine to provide a delightful format for one of the most romantic of tales.

Janet Lunn's retelling which appears to be based partially on the Grimm version and partially on the old French version, has all the story elements essential to a traditional fairy tale. The reader is instantly drawn into the plot with the poor farm boy's visionary search for the far-off golden palace and the twelve lovely princesses. Suspense builds as on three successive nights, the hero dons his invisible cloak and accompanies the princesses to an enchanted underground castle, each night becoming more daring in order to solve the mystery and thereby gain the hand of the fairest princess and inherit the kingdom. The romantic surprise ending culminates, needless to say, with happiness reigning "all the years of their lives."

Lunn relates all this in the direct, matter-of-fact style of conventional fairy tales. But rather than allowing the reader's imagination to take flight from a few well-chosen words and phrases, she tends to use description and detail, to the detriment of the flow of the text, whose stilted style fails to convey the beauty and romance inherent in the story itself.

Ann Braden, in a review of "The Twelve Dancing Princesses," in In Review: Canadian Books for Young People, *Vol. 14, No. 2, April, 1980, p. 51.*

A handful of books produced in Canada are world class. This is one, a tribute to the collaboration of author, artist, editor, and publisher. (p. 140)

Lunn retells a version from the French about a poor lad who, aided by magic gifts, solves the mystery of shoes that nightly get worn through. The shoes belong to twelve princesses who secretly slip away to dance with twelve princes in an underground palace. As reward, this gardener's boy marries the youngest princess and inherits the kingdom.

It has been truly remarked that *contes de fées* after Perreault are "perfumed, powdered and prolix". French versions are literary creations, synthesizing elements and explaining actions but also embroidering extra bits. Lunn excises some French prolixity but expands other areas in keeping with her re-creation. For example, she presents the three warnings in rhyme. The French version differs from the much more familiar, more frequently found German version collected by the Brothers Grimm. Lunn's literary version appears to be based on the French with German incursions.

Lunn as a young girl.

Certain elements have bothered all re-shapers of the story. To begin with, there is the acceptability of the protagonist to a young audience. The German version features a wounded soldier, too old and useless to continue a military life. He solves the riddle and asks to marry the eldest princess, a lady of rather scornful temperament. Some author/artists (Le Cain) intuitively or unconsciously falsify their text by showing the tattered, short, old soldier as younger, taller, thinner and entirely more prince-like on his wedding day. The French, more romantic than the Germans, preferred (as Lunn does) to feature a handsome young man who claims the beautiful youngest princess.

Second, in times conscious of violence in fairy tales, there is the question of death as penalty for failure to solve the riddle. Traditionally French versions have not chosen death for the penalty. Unsuccessful candidates disappear, or may even be added to the ghostly collection of dancing partners. Death, usually by beheading, occurs in the German, and it occurs in Lunn. Lunn probably reflects an opinion that fairy-tale deaths do not adversely affect children. She makes the statement and passes on to more important plot development.

Third, there is the unexplained intervention of an old woman who provides the magic gift(s) that enable the hero to gain his kingdom. Lunn, like other retellers, has the hero perform

a kind deed for which he is repaid. Lunn largely but not completely, dismisses the French embroidery about dreams and the golden-haired visions who act as 'fairy godmother'.

A fourth niggle arises from considering too closely the character of the princesses as revealed in various versions. These girls could be read as sly pusses, haughty types, or as nice but muddled. The oldest and the youngest are not totally likeable, while the ten between are sheep-like spacers. Lunn gives the youngest a gentle if obstinate nature, perfectly captured in the illustration where the youngest speaks with her father. Lunn also gives the girl the gumption to act at the last minute to change an unfortunate circumstance into a desired and happy outcome.

Finally, there is the peripheral but nonetheless implicit question of what happened to the princes who danced the night away. Most German versions have the princes continue in their enchanted state (the princesses having failed as spell-breakers) for a number of days equal to the number of nights the princesses danced with them (the princesses' attempt at spell-breaking either didn't matter or else even actively added to another's punishment). Other versions release the princes to marry the princesses. In that case, there is one prince left over. Some versions do not explain, and Lunn does not. She concentrates on hero, heroine and happy ending.

To focus further a child's personal identification with the hero and heroine, Lunn drops the French device of naming people and place. (pp. 141-42)

> *Claire England, in a review of "The Twelve Dancing Princesses: A Fairy Story Re-told," in* Canadian Children's Literature, *Nos. 15-16, 1980, pp. 140-43.*

THE ROOT CELLAR (1981)

AUTHOR'S COMMENTARY

[The following excerpt is from a speech Lunn delivered at the presentation of the Canadian Library Association Book of the Year Award in 1982.]

About a month ago when I was in a school in Scarborough, Ont., talking to the children about writing, a boy asked me, "why do you always write in doubles?"

I'd never thought about that before but I've thought about it a lot since. It's true and I've decided that that's what I'd like to talk to you about this evening.

Before I do, I want to thank you for giving *The Root Cellar* this award. I have strong feelings about this book. I've struggled with some of my own dilemmas through the writing of it and I've become very close to the people I've written about. So it's a joy for me to know that my story seems important to you.

As well, I want to thank publicly three people who have had almost as much to do with making the story as I have. First my husband, Richard Lunn. For one thing it was his idea that we move to the old house in Prince Edward County, Ont., where the story takes place. For another, he listened to me read aloud every page of every chapter of this book in all its many incarnations and never once admitted to being bored. Not only that, he told me it was wonderful even in those moments when I was sure it was good for nothing but resting coffee cups on. And, when the manuscript was finally ready to go to the publisher he went over its details with that kind of eye only born copy–editors have. (p. 329)

And thanks to my son John. All my children listened to me read chapters and I'm grateful to them all but it was from John I learned that boys with flutes sometimes talk with birds. John wrote Will's song for him and, in the end, although I don't remember planning it that way he was my model for Will.

And so many thanks to my editor, Louise Dennys, who is the kindest, most severe critic I have ever known. I am deeply grateful for that and for the one question she asked that opened a door in my mind, a door to ideas and sensibilities that had, all unconsciously, been clamouring to be written about. She asked me why my heroine came from Vancouver when I was from the United States. That door opened on memories, conflicts and a life-long fascination for that duality the small boy asked me about in Scarborough.

And so *The Root Cellar* is about duality and reconciliation. Very briefly the story is about Rose Larkin, an orphan, who is sent from New York City to live with an aunt and uncle and their four sons in an old farmhouse on the north shore of Lake Ontario. She hates the house, the aunt, uncle and the boys — and they don't think much of her either.

One dreary autumn day Rose finds her way into the past through an old root cellar. The year is 1862, spring, and the world is in bloom. She meets Will and Susan, the two young farm people who live in the house. She is enchanted by the whole magic world and means to stay for ever but, when a strange woman frightens her, she runs down into the root cellar and comes up the steps into her own time.

It takes her a week to find how the time switch works and, when she goes back to Will and Susan two years have passed for them. Hiding behind a tree in the apple orchard she overhears Will, now 15, tell Susan he's off to fight in the American Civil War. Rose is heartsick. She retreats again to her own world.

The next evening when she goes back to find Susan another year has passed, the war is over, but Will has not come home. Rose and Susan decide to go into the United States to look for him. The rest of the story is about their journey.

It's a story of friendship across and through time, of growing up and belonging. It's a story of opposites — of civil war, of here and there, of then and now and young and old, of one reality and another — and it's a story of where those opposites touch and are sometimes reconciled, that precarious, elusive place where writers live, in and out and at the edge of two worlds. And that is what makes life sometimes frightening, always exciting for us.

At this moment I am here in this reality, this world, talking to you about that other one, that world I invented, or maybe it invented me, or maybe its existence is separate, a reality I stumbled on in my search for a way to write about what happens to people who are pulled in two directions. Sometimes I am not quite sure.

Now, I know the world of Rose and Will and Susan occupies no place in time or space. As well, I'm aware of where most of the ideas for this story came from. Much of my sense of duality comes from my own experience. I am not an orphan as Rose was but I'm something of a displaced person. I've moved so much from place to place that belonging and not belonging have become an almost existential dilemma for me.

And I have always known about time shifting. As a small child I lived in an 18th century farmhouse outside a pre-Revolutionary War village in Vermont. The old men marching in our memorial day parades were veterans from the Civil War. My great-grandmother used to tell us about the time she saw Abraham Lincoln and sometimes when I played dress–up with my friends we dressed in hoopskirts we found in our attics. So time was not as neatly separated out for us as it is apt to be for people who live where settlement is not so old.

Alan Garner, the English writer for children, writes of time shift. He lives in what was once an Anglo-Saxon meeting hall by the Alderly Edge where he found a 4,000 year old axehead and not many hundreds of yards behind his house are the radio telescopes of the Jodrell Bank. My surroundings are not as dramatic as those but I live in United Empire Loyalist country where the names on my neighbors' mail boxes are the same as those on the 1783 land grants. Time shifts.

But, for me, it's that other duality, that living on the edge between this world and the other that has affected my life most deeply. The other world, the one where stories happen, exists out of time and in imagination to illuminate this world. It has such power, such attraction for me that I am sometimes afraid of being caught there forever so I am watchful. But I cannot stay away so I shift between this world and that and I perch nervously on the edge and I sometimes think that this is what makes a writer's life most painful.

For other writers live in the same way. Virginia Woolf talks in her diaries of the difficulties of having to be two people, herself and the character in her novel. And there's a wonderful story told about Carl Sandburg and the time he was working on the Abraham Lincoln biography.

Apparently he used to pace the beach every morning while he thought out his day's writing. A friend, aware of his habit, hired a tall, thin, actor to dress as Lincoln and walk that same beach. On a particular morning the actor passed Sandburg several times. Sandburg paced on, head lowered as he pondered. Finally, noticing the shadow, I suppose, he looked up absently. "Good morning, Mr. President," he said and went on with his pacing and his pondering.

I know the intensity of that preoccupation. Sandburg was living with Lincoln. If Rose and Will and Susan had appeared in my study while I was writing *The Root Cellar* I might easily have looked up, said an absent, "Hi, kids," and gone on working. They were as real to me as my own children.

They were so real, in fact, that, the night before I was to leave on a research trip across Lake Ontario and down the Hudson River Valley, I was terribly excited about it. "What's so wonderful," I told my husband, "is that I'll be on the same train or at least going along the same track Rose and Susan were on."

Richard pulled on my sleeve very gently, "try to remember," he said, "Rose and Susan didn't really make that journey. You did."

"Of course I know that," I said but I felt a twinge of irritation that Richard wasn't able to quite grasp the reality.

I was. I knew that reality. Unlike Virginia Woolf I never became any of the characters but they were my friends. I loved them dearly. Will's struggle to find out which country he belonged to, Rose's to find which world was hers were the struggles of people truly dear to me and I longed for their story to end happily, though I was never sure until the end. And when the book was finished — really finished, in print, neatly stored between its covers — I cried, not just a few quiet tears. I wept. I wept because I knew that my friends had gone away forever.

Of course I can remember them. I can even re-read their story, visit them now and then, but we will never live together again as we did for those wonderful, painful, sometimes insane four years. Their ghosts haunt my house as it's their house too, but they have gone away and taken with them the world I had come to know so well.

That is not to say that the duality of two worlds has gone away. Another story, another world has begun to intrude on my consciousness and, soon, I will be perched, once more, on the edge, being pulled this way and that. But the writing of this book has gone a long way toward settling one dilemma. Like Will, I have made an emotional choice. It began when Louise Dennys asked me why Rose came from Vancouver when I was from the United States and it ended when Will came to the end of his war and realized that he'd made a terrible mistake. (pp. 329-30)

With Will I found that I knew myself to be a Canadian and it is for that reason I'm especially joyful to be accepting this award from The Canadian Library Association for my friends and their book. (p. 330)

Janet Lunn, "Book of the Year for Children Award," in Canadian Library Journal, *Vol. 39, No. 5, October, 1982, pp. 329-30.*

Rose Larkin, the protagonist in Janet Lunn's **The root cellar,** is the best kind of heroine. She is old enough to think and feel, grieve, rejoice and grow, but she has not begun to do any of these before the story opens. She has never been encouraged or even allowed to explore the world of human relationships. She is as untouched by life as a fairytale princess shut up in a tower. Thus, when she is catapulted into the real world at the beginning of the story, the reader can be part of her awakening, share her false starts and grow with her as she becomes a person with all the vulnerability, pain, joy and wonder which come with being fully human. This is one of the oldest themes in children's literature, met with over and over again from *Pinocchio* to *The secret garden.* The latter is, appropriately, Rose's favourite book. It is a theme to which all of us respond with deep recognition since the journey, from the self-centred and limited realm of childhood toward the wider, more frightening and hurtful but infinitely richer world of approaching maturity, is one we are all required to make. One of the chief uses children make of the books they read is to study what routes are open to them, which signposts can be trusted, what dangers and delights lie in wait and whether or not the trip is, in fact, worth taking. Although all such stories have a built-in appeal, few prove as rewarding as *The root cellar.*

This issue of *CCL* focusses on immigrant literature, stories of or by children who move, or are moved, from a familiar environment to a strange new one and who must learn how to find a sense of belonging there. Although one would not immediately place **The root cellar** in this body of stories, it does fit in there for several reasons. Looked at from this viewpoint, it is a veritable *Pilgrim's progress.* Rose is a child who has never had a home. Her aloof and busy grandmother travels widely because of her work and the orphaned Rose is taken along, willy nilly, never staying anywhere long enough to put down roots. When her grandmother dies suddenly, the child is left to find her way into the world of real people, a world of which she is almost unaware. She is handicapped not only by ignorance but also by her own instinctive distrust of the unfamiliar and by her two responses, resentment and withdrawal.

Nobody really wants Rose and she knows it. Here is another well-known situation experienced by children in books with which readers can readily identify. Children so often fall short of what is expected of them, so seldom manage to act out their fantasies and play the hero's part, that they frequently see themselves as unlovable and, therefore, unloved. Rose's predicament has an added charm in that she manages to be both the lonely only child and the unappreciated member of a large family.

Rose is taken in by her father's sister, who has a husband and four sons, is untidy and volatile and prepared to do her best for her niece. Fastidious Rose, who has never seen outbursts of anger or been part of any family, behaves badly, knows herself unwelcome, has no idea of how to remedy this and solves things in the way children have used since time immemorial. She runs away. And in so doing, she eventually finds her way home.

Rose has technically immigrated to Hawthorne Bay in Prince Edward County, Ontario, emigrating from Nowhere Special. Her second move comes before she has discovered anything positive in her new environment. She feels alien and hard-done-by and misunderstood and so leaves for "the magic of another day." Her location on the map doesn't change but everything else does. She finds she can go through the root cellar of her aunt's house and emerge in 1865. There everything is simpler. To Susan and Will, with whom she begins to be friendly, she is an interesting stranger, not a threatening, sulky cousin. Nothing is expected of her so she can be comfortable observing and need only enter into the action when she can offer a strength. For the first time in her life she basks in a sense of belonging.

She is wrong, of course. She doesn't belong there either because it is not her relations who are causing her not to fit in but her own ungraciousness and insensitivity. Luckily for her, these attributes are not immediately apparent to Susan and Will. Wrapped up in their own troubles, they are touched by her sympathy and intrigued by the mystery surrounding her. When Will goes to the States and joins the Union army and Susan fails to hear from him and fears he has been killed, Rose, with her one positive legacy from her grandmother's casual approach to travel, sweeps Susan off on a quest to find him. Then the inevitable day dawns when Rose's daring plans do not allow for human frailty and Susan mucks things up. Rose's sympathy, easily won in the glamour of beginning, is not founded on real understanding of Susan's pain and bewilderment. Furious at the older girl for ruining everything, Rose takes the last bit of money they have, money which, in point of fact, belongs to Susan, and spends it on food for herself. When Susan discovers this betrayal, her shock and disappointment reveal Rose to herself. Earlier in the story, her behaviour had roused the wrath of her relations and she had even dimly glimpsed her own culpability but she had not learned to love them the way she now cares for Susan. She knows the other girl has respected her independence, admired her daring, been in awe of her ability to plan and given her gratitude and even affection. Only now, when she realizes she may have forfeited all of these gifts, does Rose understand how much they matter to her. In similar moments with Aunt Nan's family, Rose has justified her own actions and made no effort to redeem herself. But this time, she knows what she'll be giving up, if she runs, and the price is finally too high. She has no choice but to go to work to win back Susan's trust and liking. The test she meets is gruelling, leaving the reader as well as Rose exhausted, but she does endure to the end and proves herself worthy of friendship. She also, of course, gradually and credibly, becomes a much nicer Rose Larkin.

As she and Susan resume their search for Will, the reader begins to want this new Rose to go home to today. She herself finds New York, the one place on earth which came closest to being her home in the past, an alien and frightening place in 1865. Will, Rose's double in his search for where he belongs, is found at last in moving scenes of the Civil War's devastation, but he, like Rose and the reader, longs to return to Canada. Tension builds as the united three make their way back. They arrive literally in "the nick of time" for as Rose goes through the root cellar, it is destroyed behind her and she loses forever her gateway to the past.

Rose's reunion with her family is appropriately anticlimactic. Understandably, they fail instantly to perceive that she is now a real and perceptive person with much to offer. She has to live down her own bad reputation. She has to contend with their suspicion and also with her loneliness for Susan whom she has learned to love. She does win through however and, in her hour of homecoming, Susan visits the present to help her. This is less credible than Rose's time travel but children will be enchanted by what happens and, in a symbolic sense, an immigrant child comes "home" most satisfyingly when her or his past world fuses with the new one into the magic of today.

Janet Lunn, in earlier books, has written history, mystery, fantasy and fairytales. In *The root cellar,* she has combined her previous genres and discovered an even more exciting writing experience. Those children who travel with Rose from today to yesterday and back again are grateful. It is a wonderfully rich reading experience, too. (pp. 153-55)

Jean Little, "The Magic of Another Day," in Canadian Children's Literature, *Nos. 35 & 36, 1984, pp. 153-55.*

One of the more celebrated of recent Canadian children's books should be of especial interest to American readers. Written by Janet Lunn, who moved from the United States to Canada in 1946, *The Root Cellar* uses nineteenth and twentieth-century American and Canadian settings to explore some international themes. In particular, it combines questions to adolescent and national identity. (The treatment should appeal even to those cynics who consider the two indistinguishable in Canada.) In doing so, it relies on the quest pattern—a long journey filled with tests—that is so familiar in fantasies. It also sets up deliberate parallels to *The Secret Garden.* Nevertheless, *The Root Cellar* is not just another formulaic fantasy or an updated classic. More like *Tom's Midnight Garden* than *The Secret Garden,* *The Root Cellar* is fresh and entertaining, displaying the merits of strong char-

acterization, interesting events, and an intelligent treatment of an enduring theme.

The novel focuses on Rose Larkin, a girl somewhat like Burnett's Mary Lennox. . . . Like Mary, Rose does find solace in a "secret garden" a glade with a hawthorn tree and an abandoned root cellar. Nevertheless, she remains so alienated that she persists in a belief that she doesn't belong in this world, that she must be a creature from elsewhere. As a result, Rose's most pressing desire is to escape from the Henry household.

In spite of surface similarities, Rose is not just another protagonist in a typical adolescent problem novel. Although she does not realize it, she must establish her identity and thereby resolve her personal problems in the way of true heroines, by accomplishing difficult tasks. Rose's situation is particularly complex because the novel presents her with two apparently incompatible tasks. One requires that she stay with the Henrys and the other that she flee. Naturally, the former, which is also mundane by comparison, does not appeal to Rose, who fails to see its full significance. The latter is so dramatic and emotionally fulfilling that she willingly undertakes it. The performance of the second task, however, teaches Rose about her own identity and impels her to do something about the neglected first task. Through heroic adventure, then, Rose comes to an appreciation of domestic and personal relationships.

Rose's first task comes from an appeal by an old lady, Mrs. Morrissay, who suddenly appears before Rose and just as mysteriously vanishes. Mrs. Morrissay explains her presence by saying that she "shifts" uncontrollably. She knows Rose and begs her "to make things right in my house for me". This task is something like that in *The Secret Garden,* in which Mary puts back into order a long-neglected garden and thereby restores a loving homelife. Here, however, Rose makes no attempt to fix up the house: she is too intent on fleeing a place that makes her miserable.

The second task does not come from outside appeals. Rose imposes it on herself because of what she experiences when she discovers a way to escape the Henry household. She does so when she enters the abandoned root cellar and, upon emerging, finds that she has shifted from a twentieth-century November to June, 1862. Befriended by two kind adolescents, Will Morrissay and Susan Anderson, she undergoes the profound changes necessary before she can impose the task on herself. First, she no longer feels alienated. Looking at the beauty of the place, so startlingly opposite of its run-down condition in the twentieth century, she comes to believe that she may belong here. Second, she feels a desire to marry Will some day, a significant feeling because she had never previously even thought about loving another person.

Rose makes four trips into the past; the final time she is determined to remain, because her problems have convinced her that she doesn't belong in the Henrys' world. She knows, however, that her new world is not entirely idyllic either. During her second trip, Will—both he and Susan age in their world, but Rose remains twelve—had run away to fight in the American Civil War on the Union side. Rose goes back "determined to set her world to rights" by bringing Will back to Canada and Susan. The language here subtly suggests that this second task, even though Rose does not recognize it as such, is a more grandiose version of the first one.

The task is intimately connected with the novel's theme of

Lunn in an Eskimo suit.

I don't belong here. . .any more than you belong in the United States. . . . A funny man on the road from Albany asked me where I came from. I said Canada, and I do now. Same as you. . . . I belong in that other time and I have to go back there.

Together with demonstrations of love for him, these arguments convince Will that his place is with the living in Canada, not with his dead comrade, whom he had once promised not to leave. Like Rose, then, he has had to run away in order to discover himself and the meaning of home. For both, the journey away has been one of personal discovery, one that compels a return. . . .

[Rose's] experiences [in the past] enable her . . . to appreciate and get along in the very place that previously caused her so much misery. Rose expresses her internal change overtly by turning her attention to the first task, the setting in order of Mrs. Morrissay's house. Her initial step is also one in which she tries to reach out to express appreciation to the Henry family. She decides to show some of the quality of the house by staging an old-fashioned Christmas for the Henrys. She decorates the kitchen and tries to cook Christmas dinner, but she burns the goose. Her failure is shattering: "all Rose's longing to be a part of the family had centred on it. . .". Before any of the family can witness her humiliation, however, she receives magical recompense for her efforts to right the world of the past. Mrs. Morrissay appears with an old-fashioned dinner and decorations, and Rose learns that Mrs. Morrissay is not Will's mother but Will's wife and her old companion, Susan Anderson. Both share in the love of the house, and this love prompts Rose to the silent promise that she will work to restore it. Thus, Rose demonstrates that she bears a suitable name. The novel doesn't say so, but it is evident that her secret garden is within and that it has grown to be full of love. The child who wanted to run away is at last lovingly at home.

While *The Root Cellar* is not perfect, its flaws are relatively trivial. The allusions to *The Secret Garden* are not entirely satisfying. The adventures in the nineteenth century could have been more obviously revelatory of stages of Rose's development. Will's motives for staying away definitely should have been better—they seem much too contrived—and his resistance to returning should have been much stronger. The novel could have provided some explanation for the magic of the root cellar. As it is now, Lunn takes great pains to emphasize that the magic works when the shadow of the hawthorn tree is exactly in the centre of the cellar doors. She does not, however, give either the tree or the cellar any special emotional or symbolic meaning. Of course we do not, always demand explanations of magic; we accept unquestioningly that a wardrobe leads to Narnia. But when an author stresses particular conditions for magic, we have a right to feel that the conditions are logical, given the reality of magic. Finally, Lunn probably should have avoided the magical intrusion of the past into the present in the Christmas dinner scene. As thematically important as the scene is, it seems out of character with the more "realistic" quality of events in the rest of the novel.

Such criticisms must not, however, obscure the genuine literary merits of this rich novel. In addition to the strong development of theme outlined above, *The Root Cellar* gives a convincing presentation of Rose's alienation in the modern world and her gradual development of meaningful relationships with the members of her new family. It also presents a

identity. Will has run away because he is, in his own way, just as alienated as Rose. Like Rose, he is unhappy living in the house and believes that he doesn't belong there. He believes that the Civil War is at least partly his war, because his mother came from the States. Ironically, Rose, herself a runaway, must find him and convince him that he really does belong in Canada. . . .

The majority of episodes . . . test and develop Rose's character. Rose discovers that, although she is younger than Susan, she must take charge if their quest is to be successful. (p. 43)

Rose's growing confidence in herself leads to an ironic recognition of her own identity. She believes that when she and Susan arrive in New York, things will be easy because she will be in a place she knows. When the train arrives and Rose discovers that it is not the New York she knows, she faints. Her special sense of belonging gone, a new sense of her identity emerges: "She was just Rose, as ill-fitting in this world as she was in the one she had grown up in". . . .

When Rose and Susan find Will after a long search, their efforts to convince him to return to Canada bring to a climax questions of national and personal identity. . . .

The thematic import of the journey pattern becomes evident in Rose's persuasive appeal to Will's sense of belonging. When they had first met, Will had told her that it didn't matter where she came from. What mattered, he said, is where she belonged. Now she draws a parallel between their situations when she announces her discovery of her own sense of belonging:

I want to go home. . . . I want to be myself. . . .

vivid portrait of nineteenth-century life. Except for the presence of Rose, no magic is at work in the world of the past. Consequently, sections of *The Root Cellar* are as good historical children's fiction as one will find anywhere.

The Root Cellar is unique among children's books in using settings that cross both the international border between Canada and the United States and the usually impenetrable border between past and present. In doing so, it is convincing, intelligent, and moving. *The Root Cellar* deserves to cross the border once more: it is just too good to be confined to Canadian readers. (p. 44)

Raymond E. Jones, "Border Crossing: Janet Lunn's 'The Root Cellar'," in Children's Literature Association Quarterly, *Vol. 10, No. 1, Spring, 1985, pp. 43-4.*

An unusual aspect of the American Civil War is opened up in *The Root Cellar,* when a part-Yankee son of a Canadian farm, on an island in Lake Ontario, crosses the border with a friend to fight for the Northern army, and two girls boldly travel as far south as Richmond in search of him. . . . It is in the quiet accumulation of detail that this story makes its strong appeal; besides, the immediate, affectionate alliance of the two girls, transcending differences of period and outlook, forges a link between past and present so firm that even a few extraneous passages of historical fact pass readily in the totality of the warmly emotional, strongly pictorial narrative. (pp. 4432-33)

Margery Fisher, in a review of "The Root Cellar," in Growing Point, *Vol. 24, No. 1, May, 1985, pp. 4432-33.*

SHADOW IN HAWTHORN BAY (1986)

The territory of Janet Lunn's fiction is a corner of south-central Ontario called Prince Edward County. It is a peninsula of flat, reasonably productive farmland protruding into Lake Ontario from just west of Trenton. Loyalists who fled the U.S. after the American Revolutionary War established the first permanent white settlement there in 1784. These people and their descendants are the characters Janet Lunn writes about in her fictional world of Hawthorn Bay, which she has placed on an island off the north shore of Lake Ontario.

As in her 1981 novel *The Root Cellar,* in *Shadow in Hawthorn Bay* Lunn has built up the layers of her invented world in much the same way Margaret Laurence did in her Manawaka quartet. There are differences, of course: Laurence used childhood experiences absorbed while growing up in Neepawa, Manitoba; Lunn is writing about an adopted home, an area she had probably never seen before moving to Canada in 1946. Laurence drew on her own visual and verbal memories, while Lunn has created a world based largely on historical research. More important, however, are the similarities: a shared fascination with roots, lineage, and families, and an uncanny talent for making characters real. . . .

In *Shadow in Hawthorn Bay,* we go back . . . to 1815, and join . . . 15-year-old Mary Urquhart, who travels alone from her home in the Scottish Highlands to Hawthorn Bay in answer to the telepathic pleas of her cousin Duncan. When she finally arrives in Upper Canada after a desperate and perilous journey, Mary learns that Duncan is dead and his family has

returned to Scotland. Alone and destitute, Mary must stay in what to her is a fearsome and alien land until she can earn her passage home.

Hardest of all for Mary is acclimatizing herself to the stolid ways of her neighbours, a community of United Empire Loyalists. For the most part they are proud, thrifty, industrious people, doggedly building a new community in the wilderness. They are charitable and welcoming, but they can't accept Mary's Celtic customs, her talk of ghosts and spirits and, most of all, her talent as a seer. But Mary is too stubborn and unyielding, clinging to a past she can't reclaim and the wraith of a lover already mouldering in his grave.

In *The Root Cellar* Rose Larkin travelled back in time to learn how to appreciate the past and to find her own place in the contemporary world. For Mary Urquhart in *Shadow in Hawthorn Bay,* the task is somewhat different. She must learn to surrender the past and accept her new destiny in Upper Canada. She achieves this ultimately, but not without a great deal of heartache.

There are many riches to savour in Janet Lunn's novels — not the least of which is the engrossing narrative drive — but the quality I appreciate most is their completeness. The facts are accurate, the settings authentic, and the characters so plausible that one slides effortlessly into her world.

Sandra Martin, "Janet Lunn's Uncanny Talent for Making History Sing," in Books for Young People, *Vol. 1, No. 1, February, 1987, p. 5.*

Like her fine time-travel fantasy, *The Root Cellar,* Lunn's new book has a richly detailed historical setting. . . . The major part of the story is Mary's establishment of relationships within a pioneer community, her adjustment to different customs, her pursuit of independence and reconciliation with the gift of "second sight," and finally, her marriage to a neighboring lad. This is an ambitious number of elements to incorporate into one novel, and the realistic aspects are most convincing, although the ghostly ones have an eerie ambiguity. Readers are never sure whether Mary is intensely superstitious or supernaturally intense. Whatever the case, she is a strong protagonist and her story a satisfying one.

Betsy Hearne, in a review of "Shadow in Hawthorn Bay," in Bulletin of the Center for Children's Books, *Vol. 40, No. 10, June, 1987, p. 192.*

Janet Lunn has brought vividly to life the harsh details of a past age. The poor possessed so very little. Mary counts herself lucky to have a sound blanket. She journeys to Canada with the clothes she wears. When she looks for a rag to clean a new born baby there are none to be found in the damp, draughty cabin. She tears her clean shift in half to fold part tenderly around the baby.

Mary may be only fifteen but lives in an adult world and contends with all the difficulties and decisions that are part of that world. She is sheltered neither by her station in life nor her upbringing. No helping hands are stretched out to her in her abject poverty and yet she and her companions triumph over hardship in a way that brings a lump to the throat of the sensitive reader.

Janet Lunn writes in a consistent lilting style of the Celtic literary tradition which sometimes, almost but never quite, seems to verge on self-parody. The illustrations by Emma Chichester-Clark, recent winner of the Mother Goose

Award, capture the spirit of place so finely wrought in the text.

This is a wonderful book of great power for the adult reader. Whether its riches will be available to the younger will depend upon a leap of the imagination into a totally different lifestyle. It may go to the top of the list of Good Books for Children but prove too strong a meat to be enjoyed by them.

> *D. A. Young, in a review of "Shadow in Hawthorn Bay," in* The Junior Bookshelf, *Vol. 52, No. 3, June, 1988, p. 159.*

(Catherine) Pat(ricia Shiels) O'Shea

1931-

Irish author of fiction and reteller.

O'Shea is recognized as one of children's literature's most promising contributors to the fantasy genre as well as an especially spellbinding storyteller. Her works, which are based on Irish mythology, are noted for O'Shea's distinctive use of traditional material as well as for the richness of their language and their successful interweaving of magic and humor. Often called a masterpiece, her epic fantasy *The Hounds of the Morrigan* (1985) describes how a young brother and sister search for a stone containing a drop of blood from the Morrigan, the Irish goddess of war, in order to save the world from destruction. Pursued by the Morrigan and her unrelenting pack of canine slaves, the children travel from contemporary Ireland to the mystical land of Tir-Na-Nog and are assisted in their quest by a variety of human and animal characters, many of which are drawn from Irish folklore. O'Shea continues her fascination with Irish legends with *Finn MacCool and the Small Men of Deeds* (1987), an adaptation of a classic tale about Ireland's greatest folk hero.

THE HOUNDS OF THE MORRIGAN (1985)

The Hounds of the Morrigan is a first novel by an unknown writer. It is over 450 pages long, and it falls into no comfortable category. It is a quirky, wayward book that tries to fuse high fantasy and low comedy. In these cautious, conventional days, OUP [Oxford University Press] deserves three cheers for taking a risk on it.

It would be nice to leave matters there, but it would be scarcely fair not to admit that I found it virtually unreadable.

There may be ideal readers out there who will fall on *The Hounds of the Morrigan* as a delicious morsel prepared specially for them, but most will find it tedious going. The book is set in Ireland, and takes two present-day children on a "journey of wonder and fear" through the Celtic twilight, pursued by the hounds of the Irish triple war-goddess, the Morrigan. There are echoes of other writers, notably the Masefield of *The Box of Delights,* but the book has a strong individual flavour, because the wonder and fear are shot through with farce. On the page, especially in Pat O'Shea's rather leaden prose, this makes an uneasy mixture. One can imagine it working well as a comic-fantastic television serial, with its larger than life self-defeating villains, its dreamlike intermingling of the real and the magical, and its bewildered child heroes. The Morrigan in one of her human guises, straddling a Harley Davidson with her blue hair streaming and a dagger in her garter, might be fleshed into a figure of real menace and amusement by a good actress: in a book, the joke soon palls, and the terror never grips.

> Neil Philip, "Two Worlds Mix," in The Times Educational Supplement, No. 3620, November 15, 1985, p. 46.

[In *The Hounds of the Morrigan,*] Pat O'Shea contrives, with abundant fun and humour, to appeal to both adult and child readers. She allows one of her modern-day Morrigans to describe *War and Peace* as "Too much peace; not enough war", and creates a talking fox who inquires, with some bewilderment, what kind of creature a sausage might be and whether, when it is alive, it has hair, fur or feathers.

There is an established tradition of talking animals in children's books; but the range of verbal inventiveness contributing to their portrayal in *The Hounds* is particularly rich, especially the brogue of Puddeneen the frog, the Frenchified language of the militaristic earwigs . . ., and the style of the child-spider who insists on performing the "Fly Land Hing".

Pidge himself is ten years old, and the book should appeal to readers of that age and above. It is, however, very long for a ten-year-old and it would be a pity to classify it too rigidly. Clearly aware of the problems of length, Pat O'Shea has structured the book so that sections can be read as self-contained episodes and this should make it satisfying to read aloud. In addition, O'Shea unobtrusively recapitulates key events in the children's adventures, as they lose their sense of time and need to remember recent events, or as they re-tell these events to other characters whom they meet. Such techniques ensure that the reader does not lose sight of the central narrative.

In recent years, fantasy has come out of its somewhat murky, anomalous place on the edges of children's literature; *The Hounds of the Morrigan,* an original amalgam of classic features and qualities and a contemporary recasting of traditional elements, should take its place alongside such established nineteenth-century works as George MacDonald's fairytales for adults and contemporary fantasies such as Ursula Le Guin's *Earthsea Trilogy.*

Emma Letley, "Three Drops of Blood," in The Times Literary Supplement, No. 4313, November 29, 1985, p. 1358.

At 469 pages without a leavening of illustrations this must surely be the biggest book of 1985. Is it also the best? I am not sure. It lacks the supreme professionalism of, say, Margaret Mahy, but it has great creative energy; it surges with life.

Pat O'Shea has written an Irish fantasy, fundamentally original even if it awakens echoes of Patricia Lynch and James Stephens, perhaps because she, as they did, draws upon a national storehouse of legend, folk-lore and language. The main theme comes from the very heart of Irish legend. The Morrigan, an evil trinity of goddesses dedicated to war and death, comes to earth to renew the strength lost in far-distant times. Ranged against her (or them) is the power for good of the Dagda, a god who, perhaps because in legend he has rather a comic aspect, is not represented in physical form although his voice is heard and his name appears picked out in stars in the night sky. The Dagda chooses as his human allies and agents two small children, Pidge and Brigit. It is their quest for a blood-stained stone . . . which occupies the action-filled pages of an always exciting and often very funny narrative. (pp. 44-5)

[The story] is highly complicated and packed with serio-comic episodes. At a first reading I was tempted to question the relevance of some of these, entertaining though they were. However, when I reached page 469 I went straight back to the beginning (some indication of the book's hypnotic power) and a second reading confirmed that there were no loose ends. Everything dove-tails beautifully. A lesser writer, or perhaps a more experienced one, might have trimmed the quest of some of its stages, but only to the detriment of the overall story.

The difficulty in books of this kind, as we know from C.S. Lewis and Susan Cooper among others, is that of accepting children as agents of destiny. Miss O'Shea overcomes the reader's initial disbelief by making her two principals not superkids but tough, dogged and nicely contrasted country children. Pidge—his age is not given but presumably he is about nine or ten—is quiet and self-contained. Brigit—'five years old and five years daft' as Pidge thinks of her — is extrovert, outspoken, bubbling over with self-confidence. When the hounds of the Morrigan are hot on their trail Brigit says 'If they come near *me* they'll get a swipe on the gob', and we believe her. As forthright in her affections as her hates Brigit is entirely believable and lovable, one of the most complete and credible of child fictional portraits. 'It's too much for one boy and one little girl,' thinks Pidge at the beginning of their adventure, but, given these children, it is not.

Miss O'Shea has her share of the old Irish word-magic. Memorable phrases and passages abound. There is some very fine scene-painting as the children travel through a land that hovers between modern Ireland and Tir-na-n'Og, and tiny vivid phrases stand out from the page: a swan settles on the water 'like a cat on a cushion.' But it is in invective that Miss O'Shea, like James Stephens, excels. The Morrigan 'would make Nero look like a bit of fried bread.' And the Garda Sergeant's Horrible Auntie Hanorah — a lady whom, happily, we do not meet in the flesh, — is 'a woman constructed on a frame of sharp bones, with a thin nose that could slice cheese, a tongue like a leather strap, and a heart that wore corsets of steel or was coated in concrete.' . . .

I have not mentioned the many talking animals which are among the principal delights of the story. These include spiders, earwigs, frogs and a talking rat who is worthy of Russell Hoban. These are not introduced for fun or light relief but as essential elements in the action. The natural world is mobilized against the Morrigan, and she partly brings about her ultimate defeat by a contempt for the rights of others. (p. 45)

[This] is a most remarkable book. It is the author's first, and there are small indications of immaturity, a failure in selectivity, some weakness in narrative, minor eccentricities of punctuation. These are as nothing compared with the breadth of vision, the imaginative force, the mastery of dialogue, which mark this book indelibly as a major contribution to the literature of fantasy, as a great 'read' and as a very big bundle of fun! (pp. 45-6)

M. Crouch, in a review of "The Hounds of the Morrigan," in The Junior Bookshelf, Vol. 50, No. 1, February, 1986, pp. 44-6.

[*The Hounds of the Morrigan*] tells one of the best stories I've read for many years. . . . Above all it is in every way a book designed and written with children in mind, it addresses them as readers in an unashamed and unhesitating fashion. . . .

Several things make it a very special book. First, the characterisation. A whole host of strange and interesting characters inhabit the book. Some, like the Morrigan and her associates, move from being merely playful and deliciously wicked through to demonstrating their true evil nature. Others, like the host of friends the children meet on their travels, demonstrate a more benign attitude: the cowardly, comic frog, the excitable weather-vane man and the haunting, philosophical fox. The language is also constantly challenging, drawing at one moment from the great Welsh and Irish epic poems and at another from the Irish Comic Tradition—Flann O'Brien, Spike Milligan and James Joyce. I don't think I've ever read a fantasy novel which was both magical and funny; Garner and Cooper were never like this.

But it's the story line which most of all keep the reader glued to the pages, the threading together of memorable incidents; a carefully written journey into the past which is both eerie and subtle, the endless journey through Tir-Na-Nog followed at all times by the unshakeable hounds, a flight on the tail end of a magical kite. The influences are plain to see, especially C.S. Lewis and Susan Cooper. But there's something unique and exciting about the book considering the age range it's meant for (8-14).

What a pleasure also to find a real book again with plenty of development and detail; not the standard 30,000 words of thin plot and poor characterisation. And although it's long it's never daunting—a real object lesson to those would be fantasy writers who work in America. This is a book based in a long tradition which reflects the landscape and culture which it springs.

Undoubtedly it has flaws—the ages of the children are far too young for the intended reading audience. It also has a slight tendency to repetition, though this is not excessive. However I have no hesitation in calling it a masterpiece of children's literature, a book to treasure and read over and over again.

> *George English, in a review of "The Hounds of the Morrigan," in* Books for Your Children, *Vol. 21, No. 1, Spring, 1986, p. 22.*

As the cosmic battle between good and evil is fought in Ireland and the fantasyland of Faerie, a cast of characters from Irish mythology struggles over two small, determined children on an all-important quest. The concept is grandiose, but O'Shea carries it out flawlessly, with humor, compassion, and finally, power. . . . Throughout there is a wonderful, mad mixture of time and place, characters that appear in various forms, and an abundance of humor. . . . O'Shea is most inventive in her choice of speech patterns for various characters—the frogs, for instance, converse in a deliciously funny dialect of their own. The book is lengthy to be sure, but the brilliant tapestry that this first-time author has woven will delight and enrich those who pursue its multilayered threads. A useful glossary of Gaelic words is appended. (pp. 1144-45)

> *Mary Lathrope, in a review of "The Hounds of the Morrigan," in* Booklist *Vol. 82, No. 15, April 1, 1986, pp. 1144-45.*

[*The Hounds of the Morrigan* is] a lengthy but splendid fantasy. . . . The story takes the usual form of a conflict between the forces of dark and light and is worked out by means of the customary quest. But the protagonists are so charming, the humor and the drama so compelling, and the twists of the plot so ingenious that the reader forgets how well worn the theme is. . . . Pidge is a fine, stalwart hero, frequently worried but always willing, and Brigit is a cocky, spunky, amusing child who acts considerably older than her years. The author's style is beautiful, doing justice to the glorious countryside, and can be compared with that of Kenneth Grahame. Indeed, the episode in the underground home of a spider and his friends has some of the warm coziness of *The Wind in the Willows*. The plot is very tightly woven, with almost every incident taking on eventual importance. Although the book seems too long for the intended audience, there does not appear to be any place to stop the story to create another volume. A remarkable book, rich and satisfying, reflecting the work of the great English fantasists, yet with an ambiance of its own.

> *Ann A. Flowers, in a review of "The Hounds of the Morrigan," in* The Horn Book Magazine, *Vol. LXII, No. 4, July-August, 1986, p. 451.*

FINN MacCOOL AND THE SMALL MEN OF DEEDS (1987)

Compared with that blockbuster of hers *The Hounds of the Morrigan,* Pat O'Shea's new book is — like the men of deeds — small, but by no means unimportant. It is a small masterpiece.

Miss O'Shea has taken one of the classic legends of Ireland and retold it at some length, fleshing out the bare bones of the traditional tale with colour and humour, all this without slowing down the narrative or losing its powerful impact. Finn, the archetypal Irish hero, reluctantly answers the call for help from the king of the giants—at the time Finn was suffering from a headache and feeling sorry for himself. On his way he encounters eight little men, each of whom has a unique talent which could be useful on a dangerous enterprise. They sail in a boat made by Three Sticks, and in the giants' castle are feasted only too well. Then the testing time comes. The Giant King's newborn son is threatened, as two previous princes had been, by kidnapping. Even the combined talents of the small men cannot prevent another disaster, but Finn and his company pursue the thief, recover the little princes, and destroy the witch who has done these wicked deeds.

It is a great story, however told. Filled in with rich and funny detail, with beautifully detailed portraits of all the principals (and there are many of them), it acquires a new dimension.

The book is attractive in design and has admirable line drawings by Stephen Lavis which pick up Miss O'Shea's points as she makes them. There is also one full-page colour plate which seems to have been dropped into the text at random; it anticipates one of the high spots of the story by more than half the book! Otherwise this is just about as perfect a small book as one could hope for. (pp. 51-2)

> *M. Crouch, in a review of "Finn MacCool and the Small Men of Deeds," in* The Junior Bookshelf, *Vol. 52, No. 1, February, 1988, pp. 51-2.*

With a lilting text, honed with Irish wit and shaped in the grand tradition by a true teller of tales, this book should not be missed. . . . A magician with words, Pat O'Shea weaves a spell through her use of traditional material, giving Finn a definite personality without diminishing his stature among Irish folk heroes. Elegantly designed as well as magnificently told. (pp. 219-20)

> *Mary M. Burns, in a review of "Finn MacCool and the Small Men of Deeds," in* The Horn Book Magazine, *Vol. LXIV, No. 2, March-April, 1988, pp. 219-20.*

[*Finn MacCool and the Small Men of Deeds* is] a story that could be read in chunks (there are no chapter breaks) to older primary children. . . . There are good moments of shivery suspense, some of sympathy for the bereft giants, and plenty of humor. The telling is the best part, for O'Shea's style ranges from colloquial to lyrical with the same attention to embellishment and timing that one imagines of the early bards. (pp. 417-18)

> *Janet Hickman, in a review of "Finn MacCool and the Small Men of Deeds," in* Language Arts, *Vol. 65, No. 4, April, 1988, pp. 417-18.*

Among the most popular of the folklore tales of Ireland are those dealing with the exploits of the Fianna, a warrior band, and their leader Finn MacCool. These are hero-tales, usually involving challenges, battles, and journeys abroad to deal with villains which the local population — whether they are giants or not — are helpless against. The Fianna's fame is international. The stories are characterized by ingenious twists of plot, often involving magic or the outwitting of magic. . . .

Each story exists in many versions and the author has added individual touches which make her version fresh and distinctive. The tone is humorous throughout. We begin with the cheerfully anachronistic detail that the Fianna are often visited by the Vikings, whom they find hilarious in their funny hats with the cows' horns, and whose arrivals are looked forward to as an antidote for boredom. When we meet Finn, the great warrior is overreacting to a headache (which one of the small men later steals). The giants—or "big men" of tradition—are here described as a race of crybabies, with their King the most sentimental of all (though they are unusually handsome for giants: "The ones he had encountered up until this were ugly enough to frighten warthogs and come last, and well last, in any beauty competition").

There are good set-pieces, such as the banquet the King organizes for the visitors (where a giant child asks if they are "gobbelings"), which is a tearful washout. The one disappointing feature is that the villain is a clichéd, evil witch who had once been handsome, but "hatred, jealousy, and the sinister thoughts of the dark arts that she practised had written themselves on her face and turned her ugly; malice had almost consumed her body away."

By contrast, the depiction of the speech of the toddler princes in her captivity is wholly original: "Stoled, I was . . .", "Us ones gets lots of clumps . . .". Indeed, the dialogue is always lively and witty, and very Irish. "She'll come as sure as a dead goat can't skip" is answered by "You're a great man for the late word." Like the best narrators in the oral tradition, Pat O'Shea is . . . great . . . for telling a story and making it her own.

Matthew Sweeney, "Down among the Gobelings," in The Times Literary Supplement, *No. 4432, March 11-17, 1988, p. 289.*

J(erome) D(avid) Salinger

1919-

American author of fiction.

The following entry presents criticism of *The Catcher in the Rye*.

Considered a preeminent writer of post-World War II fiction for his accurate portrayal of the disillusionment and moral confusion of that era, Salinger is respected by the children's literature community as the creator of *The Catcher in the Rye* (1951). In his only novel, Salinger describes the personal crisis of a sensitive teenager, Holden Caulfield, in an energetic, colloquial style. *Catcher* has been heralded by critics as a classic and is often compared to such works as *The Personal History of David Copperfield* and *The Adventures of Huckleberry Finn*. Although it was not written for them, *Catcher* was soon discovered by adolescent readers, who identified with its protagonist and advocated Salinger's condemnation of phoniness and materialism. *Catcher* is now regarded as the precursor of the modern problem novel for young adults for its candor and subtly humorous depiction of the eye-opening process of maturation. Using some incidents from his own childhood and adolescence, Salinger outlines the adventures of his sixteen-year-old narrator, an upper middle-class boy who has just been expelled from his third prep school. Afraid to face his unsympathetic, somewhat uncaring parents, Holden procrastinates by spending two days in New York City, where he first experiences the seamy world of violence and perversion. Holden is an indefatigable proponent of innocence and pure love, attributes which he finds only in memories of his dead brother, Allie, and in his relationship with his ten-year-old sister, Phoebe, with whom he discovers his only refuge from the atrocities of life. Holden passionately professes his determination to protect Phoebe, and all children, from evil. Misquoting Robert Burns's poem as "If a body catch a body comin' through the rye," he tells Phoebe that his only real ambition is to be a catcher in a field of rye near "some crazy cliff," protecting young children from running headlong over the cliff. At the end of the novel, Holden awakens to a full awareness of the inevitability of the loss of innocence. He watches Phoebe ride a carousel and knows that he must let her grab for the ring and risk dangers, claiming that this realization makes him "so damn happy." But Holden has already been irreparably damaged by the decadence around him; earlier, he suspects that a trusted teacher, Mr. Antolini, has tried to seduce him. Disheartened by the corruption and indifference of the world, Holden suffers a nervous breakdown and is committed to the care of a psychiatrist; apparently, for Salinger, it is the price Holden pays for his tender, artistic nature.

In the years following its publication, *The Catcher in the Rye* grew in critical status. It was, in fact, the subject of such an immense outpouring of commentary that by the end of the 1950s critic George Steiner denounced the "Salinger Industry" for its adulation of the author. Most critics emphatically praised Salinger's perceptive depiction of the vicissitudes of life, intriguing characterizations, and extraordinary insight into the mind of his protagonist. Calling his experiences a realistic documentary of the postwar world of his contempo-

raries, admirers deem Holden the quintessential questing adolescent, one who speaks accurately in the rambling, blunt diction of his generation. Ironically, Salinger's detractors have also focused on these same elements in their disparagement of the novel. Horrified by the obscenity and profanity which they felt Salinger utilized in the story, these critics vehemently oppose *Catcher* for its expletive language and scenes of decadence. *Catcher* has faced unparalleled problems of censorship; it has been the subject of more lawsuits regarding book banning than any other American novel. This fact was undoubtedly exacerbated by the fact that *Catcher* has been consistently popular with both young people and teachers, who find it the perfect book for high school English coursework: interesting, relevant, and well crafted. Reviewers acknowledge that Holden's voice, profane and forthright, speaks to adolescents as few characters have, and that his plea for love has been understood universally by young adults through the decades since *Catcher* was published. Despite—or perhaps in part because of—the objections of censors, *The Catcher in the Rye* has continued to be a favorite among adolescent readers, who react with enthusiasm and loyalty to Salinger's expression of their feelings.

(See also *Contemporary Literary Criticism*, Vols., 1, 3, 8, 12; *Short Story Criticism*, Vol. 2; *Contemporary Authors*, Vols.

5-8, rev. ed.; and *Dictionary of Literary Biography,* Vol. 2: *American Novelists Since World War II.*)

HAROLD L. ROTH

Largely told in the first person, this is the story of a 16-year-old New York boy who has been drummed out of prep school and spends a few days on the town before going home. A successful attempt is made by the author to picture a boy's analysis of himself, developing his likes and dislikes and pointing out the problems of a highly developed imagination that has as yet not been trained to work in other than the most egoistic way. This may be a shock to many parents who wonder about a young man's thoughts and actions, but its effect can be a salutary one. An *adult* book (very frank) and highly recommended. (pp. 1125-26)

> Harold L. Roth, in a review of "The Catcher in the Rye," in Library Journal, Vol. 76, No. 13, July, 1951, pp. 1125-26.

VIRGILIA PETERSON

This first novel by J. D. Salinger, whose short stories in *The New Yorker* and other magazines have caused considerable comment, should provoke a tempest of reactions. Those who have read Mr. Salinger's stories will remember his special concern for youth and, for its despairs, a kind of crazy tenderness. In *The Catcher in the Rye,* these feelings of the author reach their apex. . . . In it lies the implication that our youth today has no moorings, no criterion beyond instinct, no railing to grasp along the steep ascent to maturity. This is the importance of *The Catcher in the Rye,* and it is upon the integrity of his portrait of a so-called privileged American youth that Mr. Salinger's novel stands or falls. . . .

Like most of his literary predecessors—that host of sad twigs being arbitrarily bent to make twisted trees—Holden Caulfield is on the side of the angels. Contaminated he is, of course, by vulgarity, lust, lies, temptations, recklessness, and cynicism. But these are merely the devils that try him externally; inside, his spirit is intact. Unlike so many of his literary predecessors, however, he does not oversimplify his troubles. He is not tilting against the whole adult world (there are some decent adults); nor does he altogether loathe his worst contemporaries (he hates to leave them). He sees the mixtures, the inextricably mingled good and bad, as it is, but the very knowledge of reality is what almost breaks his heart. For Holden Caulfield, despite all the realism with which he is supposedly depicted, is nevertheless a skinless perfectionist.

Had Ring Lardner and Ernest Hemingway never existed, Mr. Salinger might have had to invent the manner of his tale, if not the matter. *The Catcher in the Rye* repeats and repeats, like an incantation, the pseudo-natural cadences of a flat, colloquial prose which at best, banked down and understated, has a truly moving impact, and at worst is casually obscene. Recent war novels have accustomed us all to ugly words and images, but from the mouths of the very young and protected they sound peculiarly offensive. There is probably not one phrase in the whole book that Holden Caulfield would not have used upon occasion, but when they are piled upon each other in cumulative monotony, the ear refuses to believe.

Mr. Salinger speaks, no doubt, for himself as well as for his hero, when he has Holden say to little Phoebe:

> I keep picturing all these little kids playing some game in this big field of rye and all. Thousands of

little kids, and nobody's around—nobody big I mean—except me. And I'm standing on the edge of some crazy cliff. What I have to do, I have to catch everybody if they start to go over the cliff— I mean if they're running and they don't look where they're going I have to come out from somewhere and catch them . . . I'd just be the catcher in the rye and all . . .

But before it is possible to nominate Mr. Salinger as the top-flight catcher in the rye for the year or the day, it would be interesting and highly enlightening to know what Holden Caulfield's contemporaries, male and female, think of him. Their opinion would constitute the real test of Mr. Salinger's validity. The question of authenticity is one to which no parent can really guess the reply.

> Virgilia Peterson, "Three Days in the Bewildering World of an Adolescent," in New York Herald Tribune Book Review, July 15, 1951, p. 3.

ARTHUR HEISERMAN AND JAMES E. MILLER, JR.

It is clear that J. D. Salinger's *The Catcher in the Rye* belongs to an ancient and honorable narrative tradition, perhaps the most profound in western fiction. The tradition is the central pattern of the epic and has been enriched by every tongue; for not only is it in itself exciting but also it provides the artist a framework upon which he may hang almost any fabric of events and characters.

It is, of course, the tradition of the Quest. (p. 129)

There are at least two sorts of quests, depending upon the object sought. Stephen Dedalus sought a reality uncontaminated by home, country, church; for like Eugene Gant and Natty Bumppo he knew that social institutions tend to force what is ingenious in a man into their own channels. He sought the opposite of security, for security was a cataract of the eye. Bloom, on the other hand, was already an outcast and sought acceptance by an Ithaca and a Penelope which despised him. And, tragically enough, he also sought an Icarian son who had fled the very maze which he, Bloom, desired to enter. So the two kinds of quests, the one seeking acceptance and stability, the other precisely the opposite, differ significantly, and can cross only briefly to the drunken wonder of both heroes. (pp. 129-30)

American literature seems fascinated with the outcast, the person who defies traditions in order to arrive at some pristine knowledge, some personal integrity. (p. 130)

All the virtues of these American heroes are personal ones: they most often, as a matter of fact, are in conflict with home, family, church. The typical American hero must flee these institutions, become a tramp in the earth, cut himself off from Chicago, Winesburg, Hannibal, Cooperstown, New York, Asheville, Minneapolis. For only by flight can he find knowledge of what is real. And if he does not flee, he at least defies.

The protagonist of *The Catcher in the Rye,* Holden Caulfield, is one of these American heroes, but with a significant difference. He seems to be engaged in both sorts of quests at once; he needs to go home and he needs to leave it. Unlike the other American knight errants, Holden seeks Virtue second to Love. He wants to be good. When the little children are playing in the rye-field on the clifftop, Holden wants to be the one who catches them before they fall off the cliff. He is not driven toward honor or courage. He is not driven toward love of woman. Holden is driven toward love of his fellow-man, charity — virtues which were perhaps not quite virile enough for Natty Bumppo, Ishmael, Huck Finn, or Nick Adams. Holden is actually frightened by a frontier code of masculinity — a code which sometimes requires its adherents to behave in sentimental and bumptious fashions. But like these American heroes, Holden is a wanderer, for in order to be good he has to be more of a bad boy than the puritanical Huck could have imagined. Holden has had enough of both Hannibal, Missouri, *and* the Mississippi; and his tragedy is that when he starts back up the river, he has no place to go — save, of course, a California psychiatrist's couch.

So Salinger translates the old tradition into contemporary terms. The phoniness of society forces Holden Caulfield to leave it, but he is seeking nothing less than stability and love. He would like nothing better than a home, a life embosomed upon what is known and can be trusted; he is a very wise sheep forced into lone wolf's clothing; he is Stephen Dedalus and Leopold Bloom rolled into one crazy kid. And here is the point; for poor Holden, there is no Ithaca. Ithaca has not merely been defiled by a horde of suitors: it has sunk beneath waves of phoniness. He does, of course, have a Penelope who is still intact. She is his little sister Phoebe whom he must protect at all costs from the phantoms of lust, hypocrisy, conceit and fear — all of the attributes which Holden sees in society and which Huck Finn saw on the banks of the Mississippi and Dedalus saw in Dublin. So at the end, like the hero of *Antic Hay,* Holden delights in circles — a comforting, bounded figure which yet connotes hopelessness. He breaks down as he watches his beloved little Phoebe going round and round on a carousel; she is so *damned* happy. From that lunatic delight in a circle, he is shipped off to the psychiatrist. For Holden loves the world more than the world can bear.

Holden's Quest takes him outside society; yet the grail he seeks is the world and the grail is full of love. To be a catcher in the rye in this world is possible only at the price of leaving it. To be good is to be a "case," a "bad boy" who confounds the society of men. So Holden seeks the one role which would allow him to be a catcher, and that role is the role of the child. As a child, he would be condoned, for a child is a sort of savage and a pariah because he is innocent and good. But it is Holden's tragedy that he is sixteen, and like Wordsworth he can never be less. In childhood he had what he is now seeking — non-phoniness, truth, innocence. He can find it now only in Phoebe and in his dead brother Allie's baseball mitt, in a red hunting cap and the tender little nuns. Still, unlike all of us, Holden refuses to compromise with adulthood and its necessary adulteries; and his heroism drives him berserk. Huck Finn had the Mississippi and at the end of the Mississippi he had the wild west beyond Arkansas. The hero of *The Waste Land* had Shantih, the peace which passes human understanding. Bloom had Molly and his own ignorance; Dedalus had Paris and Zurich. But for Holden, there is no place to go.

The central theme of Salinger's work is stated explicitly in one of his best short stories, **"For Esme — with Love and Squalor."** Salinger quotes a passage from Dostoevski: "Fathers and teachers, I ponder 'What is Hell?' I maintain that it is the suffering of being unable to love."

The hero of **"For Esme"** is an American soldier who, driven too near psychosis by five campaigns of World War II and a moronic jeepmate, is saved in an act of childish love by two remarkable English children. (pp. 130-32)

If we could return to childhood, or to noble savagery; or if we could retain the spontaneity of childhood, our social and personal problems would disappear. (p. 132)

The flight out of the world, out of the ordinary, and into an Eden of innocence or childhood is a common flight indeed, and it is one which Salinger's heroes are constantly attempting. But Salinger's childism is consubstantial with his concern for love and neurosis. Adultism is precisely "the suffering of being unable to love," and it is that which produces neurosis. Everyone able to love in Salinger's stories is either a child or a man influenced by a child. All the adults not informed by love and innocence are by definition phonies and prostitutes. (p. 133)

Holden is the kind of person who feels sorry for the teachers who have to flunk him. He fears for the ducks when the lagoon freezes over, for he is a duck himself with no place to go. He must enter his own home like a crook, lying to elevator boys and tip-toeing past bedrooms. His dad "will kill" him and his mother will weep for his incorrigible "laziness." He wants only to pretend he is a deaf mute and live as a hermit filling-station operator, in Colorado, but he winds up where the frontier ends, California, in an institution for sick rich kids. And we can see, on the final note of irony in the book, that that frontier west which represented escape from "sivilization" for Huck Finn has ended by becoming the symbol for depravity and phoniness in our national shrine at Hollywood. (pp. 133-34)

Holden Caulfield, like Huckleberry Finn, tells his own story and it is in the language of the telling in both books that a great part of the humor lies. In the nineteenth century, Huck began, "You don't know about me without you have read a book by the name of *The Adventures of Tom Sawyer:* but that ain't no matter." The English of Huck's twentieth century counterpart, Holden Caulfield, is perhaps more correct but none-the-less distinctive: "If you really want to hear about it, the first thing you'll probably want to know is where I was born, and what my lousy childhood was like, and how my parents were occupied and all before they had me, and all that David Copperfield kind of crap, but I don't feel like going into it, if you want to know the truth."

The skepticism inherent in that casual phrase, "if you want to know the truth," suggesting that as a matter of fact in the world of Holden Caulfield very few people do, characterizes this sixteen-year-old "crazy mixed up kid" more sharply and vividly than pages of character "analysis" possibly could. In a similar manner Huck's "that ain't no matter" speaks volumes for his relationship to the alien adult world in which he finds himself a sojourner. But if these two boys lay their souls bare by their own voices, in doing so they provoke smiles at their mishandling and sometimes downright mangling of the English language. (p. 135)

Both boys are fugitives from education, but Holden has suffered more of the evil than Huck. Holden's best subject in the several schools he has tolerated briefly is English. And, too, Holden is a child of the twentieth century. Mark Twain himself would probably be startled not at the frankness of Holden's language but at the daring of J. D. Salinger in copying it so faithfully.

But of course neither J. D. Salinger nor Mark Twain really "copied" anything. Their books would be unreadable had they merely recorded intact the language of a real-life Huck and a real-life Holden. Their genius lies in their mastery of the technique of first person narration which, through meticulous selection, creates vividly the illusion of life: gradually and subtly their narrators emerge and stand revealed, stripped to their innermost beings. It is a mark of their creators' mastery that Huck and Holden appear to reveal themselves.

It is not the least surprising aspect of *The Catcher in the Rye* that trite expressions and metaphors with which we are all familiar and even bored turn out, when emerging from the mouth of a sixteen-year-old, to be funny. The unimaginative repetition of identical expressions in countless situations intensifies the humor. The things in Holden's world are always jumping up and down or bouncing or scattering "like madmen." Holden always lets us know when he has insight into the absurdity of the endless absurd situations which make up the life of a sixteen-year-old by exclaiming, "It killed me." In a phony world Holden feels compelled to reenforce his sincerity and truthfulness constantly with, "It really is" or "It really did." Incongruously the adjective "old" serves as a term of endearment, from "old" Thomas Hardy to "old" Phoebe. And many of the things Holden does, he does, ambiguously, "like a bastard."

Holden is a master of the ludicrous irrelevancy. Indeed, a large part of *The Catcher in the Rye* consists of the relevantly irrelevant. On the opening page, Holden says, "I'm not going to tell you my whole goddam autobiography or anything. I'll just tell you about this madman stuff that happened to me around last Christmas. . . ." By the time we have finished *Catcher* we feel that we know Holden as thoroughly as any biography could reveal him, and one of the reasons is that he has not hesitated to follow in his tale wherever whim and fancy lead him. (pp. 135-36)

Holden does not suffer from the inability to love, but he does despair of finding a place to bestow his love. The depth of Holden's capacity for love is revealed in his final words, as he sits in the psychiatric ward musing over his nightmarish adventures:

> If you want to know the truth, I don't *know* what I think about it. I'm sorry I told so many people about it. About all I know is, I sort of miss everybody I told about. Even old Stradlater and Ackley, for instance. I think I even miss that goddam Maurice. It's funny. Don't ever tell anybody anything. If you do, you start missing everybody.

We agree with Holden that it is funny, but it is funny in a pathetic kind of way. As we leave Holden alone in his room in the psychiatric ward, we are aware of the book's last ironic incongruity. It is not Holden who should be examined for a sickness of the mind, but the world in which he has sojourned and found himself an alien. To "cure" Holden, he must be given the contagious, almost universal disease of phony adultism; he must be pushed over that "crazy cliff." (p. 137)

> *Arthur Heiserman and James E. Miller, Jr., "J. D. Salinger: Some Crazy Cliff," in* Western Humanities Review, *Vol. X, No. 1, Winter, 1955-56, pp. 129-37.*

WILLIAM FAULKNER

I have not read all the work of this present generation of writing; I have not had time yet. So I must speak only of the ones I do know. I am thinking now of what I rate the best one: Salinger's *Catcher in the Rye,* perhaps because this one express-

es so completely what I have tried to say: a youth, father to what will, must someday be a man, more intelligent than some and more sensitive than most, who (he would not even have called it by instinct because he did not know he possessed it) because God perhaps had put it there, loved man and wished to be a part of mankind, humanity, who tried to join the human race and failed. To me, his tragedy was not that he was, as he perhaps thought, not tough enough or brave enough or deserving enough to be accepted into humanity. His tragedy was that when he attempted to enter the human race, there was no human race there. There was nothing for him to do save buzz, frantic and inviolate, inside the glass walls of his tumbler until he either gave up or was himself by himself, by his own frantic buzzing, destroyed. One thinks of course immediately of Huck Finn, another youth already father to what will some day soon now be a man. But in Huck's case all he had to combat was his small size, which time would cure for him; in time he would be as big as any man he had to cope with; and even as it was, all the adult world could do to harm him was to skin his nose a little; humanity, the human race, would and was accepting him already; all he needed to do was just to grow up in it.

That is the young writer's dilemma as I see it. Not just his, but all our problems, is to save mankind from being desouled as the stallion or boar or bull is gelded; to save the individual from anonymity before it is too late and humanity has vanished from the animal called man. And who better to save man's humanity than the writer, the poet, the artist, since who should fear the loss of it more since the humanity of man is the artist's life's blood. (pp. 244-45)

> *William Faulkner, in an extract from a lecture delivered at the University of Virginia on April 24, 1958, in his* Faulkner in the University: Class Conferences at the University of Virginia 1957-1958, *edited by Frederick L. Gwynn and Joseph L. Blotner, The University of Virginia Press, 1959, pp. 241-48.*

MAXWELL GEISMAR

The Catcher in the Rye is eminently readable and quotable in its tragicomic narrative of preadolescent revolt. Compact, taut, and colorful, the first half of the novel presents in brief compass all the petty horrors, the banalities, the final mediocrity of the typical American prep school. Very fine—and not sustained or fulfilled, as fiction. For the later sections of the narrative are simply an episodic account of Holden Caulfield's "lost week end" in New York City which manages to sustain our interest but hardly deepens our understanding.

There are very ambiguous elements, moreover, in the portrait of this sad little screwed-up hero. His urban background is curiously shadowy, like the parents who never quite appear in the story, like the one pure adolescent love affair which is now "ruined" in his memory. The locale of the New York sections is obviously that of a comfortable middle-class urban Jewish society where, however, all the leading figures have become beautifully Anglicized. Holden and Phoebe Caulfield: what perfect American social register names which are presented to us in both a social and a psychological void! Just as the hero's interest in the ancient Egyptians extends only to the fact that they created mummies, so Salinger's own view of his hero's environment omits any reference to its real nature and dynamics.

Though the book is dedicated to Salinger's mother, the fictional mother in the narrative appears only as a voice through the wall. The touching note of affection between the brother and sister is partly a substitute for the missing child-parent relationships (which might indeed clarify the nature of the neurotic hero), and perhaps even a sentimental evasion of the true emotions in a sibling love. The only real creation (or half-creation) in this world is Holden Caulfield himself. And that "compassion," so much praised in the story, and always expressed in the key phrase, "You had to feel sorry"—for him, for her, for them—also implies the same sense of superiority. If this hero really represents the nonconformist rebellion of the Fifties, he is a rebel without a past, apparently, and without a cause.

The Catcher in the Rye protests, to be sure, against both the academic and social conformity of its period. But what does it argue *for?* When Holden mopes about the New York museum which is almost the true home of his discredited childhood, he remembers the Indian war-canoes "about as long as three goddam Cadillacs in a row." He refuses any longer to participate in the wealthy private boys' schools where "you have to keep making believe you give a damn if the football team loses, and all you do is talk about girls and liquor and sex all day, and everybody sticks together in these dirty little goddam cliques." Fair enough; while he also rejects the notion of a conventional future in which he would work in an office, make a lot of dough, ride in cabs, play bridge, or go to the movies. But in his own private vision of a better life, this little catcher in the rye sees only those "thousands of little children" all playing near the dangerous cliff, "and nobody's around—nobody big, I mean—except me" to rescue them from their morbid fate.

This is surely the differential revolt of the lonesome rich child, the conspicuous display of leisure-class emotions, the wounded affections, never quite faced, of the upper-class orphan. This is the *New Yorker* school of ambiguous finality at its best. But Holden Caulfield's real trouble, as he is told by the equally precocious Phoebe is that he doesn't like *anything* that is happening. "You don't like any schools. You don't like a million things. You *don't.*" This is also the peak of well-to-do and neurotic anarchism—the one world of cultivated negation in which all those thousands of innocent, pure little children are surely as doomed as their would-be and somewhat paranoid savior. "I have a feeling that you're riding for some kind of a terrible, terrible fall," says the last and best teacher in Holden's tormented academic career. But even this prophetic insight is vitiated by the fact that Mr. Antolini, too, is one of those flits and perverty guys from whom the adolescent hero escapes in shame and fear.

He is still, and forever, the innocent child in the evil and hostile universe, the child who can never grow up. And no wonder that he hears, in the final pages of the narrative, only a chorus of obscene sexual epithets which seem to surround the little moment of lyric happiness with his childlike sister. The real achievement of *The Catcher in the Rye* is that it manages so gracefully to evade just those central questions which it raises, and to preserve both its verbal brilliance and the charm of its emotions within the scope of its own dubious literary form. It is still Salinger's best work, if a highly artificial one, and the caesuras, the absences, the ambiguities at the base of this writer's work became more obvious in his subsequent books. (pp. 197-99)

> Maxwell Geismar, *"J. D. Salinger: The Wise Child and the 'New Yorker' School of Fiction,"* in his

American Moderns: From Rebellion to Conformity, *Hill and Wang, 1958, pp. 195-209.*

DONALD P. COSTELLO

[The following excerpt is from an essay originally published in 1959.]

In coming decades, *The Catcher in the Rye* will be studied, I feel, not only as a literary work, but also as an example of teenage vernacular in the 1950s. As such, the book will be a significant historical linguistic record of a type of speech rarely made available in permanent form. Its linguistic importance will increase as the American speech it records becomes less current. (p. 87)

In addition to commenting on its authenticity, critics have often remarked—uneasily—the 'daring,' 'obscene,' 'blasphemous' features of Holden's language. Another commonly noted feature of the book's language has been its comic effect. And yet there has never been an extensive investigation of the language itself. That is what this paper proposes to do.

Even though Holden's language is authentic teenage speech, recording it was certainly not the major intention of Salinger. He was faced with the artistic task of creating an individual character, not with the linguistic task of reproducing the exact speech of teenagers in general. Yet Holden had to speak a recognizable teenage language, and at the same time had to be identifiable as an individual. This difficult task Salinger achieved by giving Holden an extremely trite and typical teenage speech, overlaid with strong personal idiosyncrasies. There are two major speech habits which are Holden's own, which are endlessly repeated throughout the book, and which are, nevertheless, typical enough of teenage speech so that Holden can be both typical and individual in his use of them. It is certainly common for teenagers to end thoughts with a loosely dangling 'and all,' just as it is common for them to add an insistent 'I really did,' 'It really was.' But Holden uses these phrases to such an overpowering degree that they become a clear part of the flavor of the book; they become, more, a part of Holden himself, and actually help to characterize him.

Holden's 'and all' and its twins, 'or something,' 'or anything,' serve no real, consistent linguistic function. They simply give a sense of looseness of expression and looseness of thought. Often they signify that Holden knows there is more that could be said about the issue at hand, but he is not going to bother going into it. . . . (p. 88)

Heiserman and Miller, in the *Western Humanities Review,* [see excerpt dated Winter 1955-56], comment specifically upon Holden's second most obvious idiosyncrasy: "In a phony world Holden feels compelled to reenforce his sincerity and truthfulness constantly with, 'It really is' or 'It really did.' " [sic] . . . Holden uses this idiosyncrasy of insistence almost every time that he makes an affirmation.

Allied to Holden's habit of insistence is his 'if you want to know the truth.' . . . Holden uses this phrase only after affirmations, just as he uses 'It really does,' but usually after the personal ones, where he is consciously being frank. . . . (p. 89)

Although always in character, the rest of Holden's speech is more typical than individual. The special quality of this language comes from its triteness, its lack of distinctive qualities.

Holden's informal, schoolboy vernacular is particularly typical in its 'vulgarity' and 'obscenity.' No one familiar with prep-school speech could seriously contend that Salinger overplayed his hand in this respect. On the contrary, Holden's restraints help to characterize him as a sensitive youth who avoids the most strongly forbidden terms, and who never uses vulgarity in a self-conscious or phony way to help him be 'one of the boys.' *Fuck,* for example, is never used as a part of Holden's speech. The word appears in the novel four times, but only when Holden disapprovingly discusses its wide appearance on walls. The Divine name is used habitually by Holden only in the comparatively weak *for God's sake, God,* and *goddam.* The stronger and usually more offense [*sic*] *for Chrissake* or *Jesus* or *Jesus Christ* are used habitually by Ackley and Stradlater; but Holden uses them only when he feels the need for a strong expression. He almost never uses *for Chrissake* in an unemotional situation. (p. 90)

The use of crude language in **The Catcher in the Rye** increases, as we should expect, when Holden is reporting schoolboy dialogue. When he is directly addressing the reader, Holden's use of such language drops off almost entirely. There is also an increase in this language when any of the characters are excited or angry. Thus, when Holden is apprehensive over Stradlater's treatment of Jane, his *goddams* increase suddenly to seven on a single page.

Holden's speech is also typical in his use of slang. I have catalogued over a hundred slang terms used by Holden, and every one of these is in widespread use. Although Holden's slang is rich and colorful, it, of course, being slang, often fails at precise communication. . . .

Holden's slang use of *crazy* is both trite and imprecise. 'That drives me crazy' means that he violently dislikes something; yet 'to be crazy about' something means just the opposite. In the same way, to be 'killed' by something can mean that he was emotionally affected either favorably ('That story just about killed me.') or unfavorably ('Then she turned her back on me again. It nearly killed me.'). This use of *killed* is one of Holden's favorite slang expressions. . . . Holden often uses this expression with no connection to the absurd; he even uses it for his beloved Phoebe. The expression simply indicates a high degree of emotion—any kind. It is hazardous to conclude that any of Holden's slang has a precise and consistent meaning or function. (p. 91)

[If] Holden's slang shows the typically 'lousy vocabulary' of even the educated American teenager, this failing becomes even more obvious when we narrow our view to Holden's choice of adjectives and adverbs. The choice is indeed narrow, with a constant repetition of a few favorite words: *lousy, pretty, crumby, terrific, quite, old, stupid*—all used, as is the habit of teenage vernacular, with little regard to specific meaning. . . .

Repetitious and trite as Holden's vocabulary may be, it can, nevertheless, become highly effective. For example, when Holden piles one trite adjective upon another, a strong power of invective is often the result:

> He was a goddam stupid moron.
> Get your dirty stinking moron knees off my chest.
> You're a dirty stupid sonuvabitch of a moron.

And his limited vocabulary can also be used for good comic effect. Holden's constant repetition of identical expressions in countless widely different situations is often hilariously funny. (p. 92)

Another aspect in which Holden's language is typical is that it shows the general American characteristic of adaptability—apparently strengthened by his teenage lack of restraint. It is very easy for Holden to turn nouns into adjectives, with the simple addition of a *-y:* 'perverty,' 'Christmasy,' 'vomity-looking,' 'whory-looking,' 'hoodlumy-looking,' 'show-offy,' 'flitty-looking,' 'dumpy-looking,' 'pimpy,' 'snobby,' 'fisty.' Like all of English, Holden's language shows a versatile combining ability: 'They gave Sally this little blue butt-twitcher of a dress to wear' and 'That magazine was some little cheerer upper'. Perhaps the most interesting aspect of the adaptability of Holden's language is his ability to use nouns as adverbs: 'She sings it very Dixieland and whorehouse, and it doesn't sound at all mushy'.

As we have seen, Holden shares, in general, the trite repetitive vocabulary which is the typical lot of his age group. But as there are exceptions in his figures of speech, so are there exceptions in his vocabulary itself, in his word stock. An intelligent, well-read ('I'm quite illiterate, but I read a lot'), and educated boy, Holden possesses, and can use when he wants to, many words which are many a cut above Basic English, including 'ostracized,' 'exhibitionist,' 'unscrupulous,' 'conversationalist,' 'psychic,' 'bourgeois.' Often Holden seems to choose his words consciously, in an effort to communicate to his adult reader clearly and properly, as in such terms as 'lose my virginity,' 'relieve himself,' 'an alcoholic'; for upon occasion, he also uses the more vulgar terms 'to give someone the time,' 'to take a leak,' 'booze hound.' Much of the humor arises, in fact, from Holden's habit of writing on more than one level at the same time. Thus, we have such phrases as 'They give guys the ax quite frequently at Pency' and 'It has a very good academic rating, Pency'. Both sentences show a colloquial idiom with an overlay of consciously selected words.

Such a conscious choice of words seems to indicate that Salinger, in his attempt to create a realistic character in Holden, wanted to make him aware of his speech, as, indeed, a real teenager would be when communicating to the outside world. (p. 93)

The structure of Holden's sentences indicates that Salinger thinks of the book more in terms of spoken speech than written speech. Holden's faulty structure is quite common and typical in vocal expression; I doubt if a student who is 'good in English' would ever create such sentence structure in writing. A student who showed the self-consciousness of Holden would not *write* so many fragments, such afterthoughts (e.g., 'It has a very good academic rating, Pency', or such repetitions (e.g., 'Where I lived at Pency, I lived in the Ossenburger Memorial Wing of the new dorms'. (p. 94)

The language of **The Catcher in the Rye** is, as we have seen, an authentic artistic rendering of a type of informal, colloquial, teenage American spoken speech. It is strongly typical and trite, yet often somewhat individual; it is crude and slangy and imprecise, imitative yet occasionally imaginative, and affected toward standardization by the strong efforts of schools. But authentic and interesting as this language may be, it must be remembered that it exists, in **The Catcher in the Rye,** as only one part of an artistic achievement. The language was not written for itself, but as a part of a greater whole. Like the great Twain work with which it is often compared, a study of *The Catcher in the Rye* repays both the linguist and the literary critic; for as one critic has said, "In them, 1884 and 1951 speak to us in the idiom and accent of two youthful travelers who have earned their passports to literary immortality." (p. 95)

> Donald P. Costello, "The Language of 'The Catcher in the Rye'," *in* If You Really Want to Know: A "Catcher" Casebook, edited by Malcolm M. Marsden, *Scott, Foresman and Company, 1963, pp. 87-95.*

EDWARD P. J. CORBETT

Adult attempts to keep *The Catcher in the Rye* out of the hands of young people will undoubtedly increase, for it is the one novel that young people of the postwar generation have been reading and discussing avidly. . . .

To the many people who have come to love the book and its hero, Holden Caulfield, all this controversy is puzzling and disturbing. They regard even the suggestion that the book needs defending as sacrilegious—almost as though they were being asked to vindicate the Constitution. Although their feelings of outrage are understandable, I feel that in view of the vast and continuing popularity of the book the objections should be confronted and appraised. My arguments in defense of *The Catcher in the Rye* are the common ones, quite familiar to those acquainted with other controversies about "forbidden" books.

The language of the book is crude, profane, obscene. This is the objection most frequently cited when the book has been banned. From one point of view, this objection is the easiest to answer; from another point of view, it is the hardest to answer.

Considered in isolation, the language *is* crude and profane. It would be difficult to argue, however, that such language is unfamiliar to our young people or that it is rougher than the language they are accustomed to hear in the streets among their acquaintances. But there is no question about it, a vulgar expression seen in print is much more shocking than one that is spoken. Lewd scribblings on sidewalks or on the walls of rest-rooms catch our attention and unsettle our sensibilities; and they become most shocking when they are seen in the sanctity of the printed page. (p. 441)

Granting the shock potential of such language, especially to youngsters, must we also grant it a corrupting influence? To deny that words can shape our attitudes and influence our actions would be to deny the rhetorical power of language. But to maintain that four-letter words of themselves are obscene and can corrupt is another matter. Interestingly enough, most reports about the banning of this novel have told that some principal or librarian or parent hastily paged through the book and spotted several four-letter words. That was evidence enough; the book must go. It is natural, although not always prudent, for adults to want to protect the young from shock. And this concern may be sufficient justification for adults wanting to keep the book out of the hands of grade-school children or the more immature high school students. But one of the unfortunate results of banning the book for this reason is that the very action of banning creates the impression that the book is nasty and highly corrosive of morals.

As has happened in many censorship actions in the past, parts are judged in isolation from the whole. The soundest defense that can be advanced for the language of this novel is a defense based on the art of the novel. Such a defense could be stated like this: Given the point of view from which the novel is told, and given the kind of character that figures as the hero, no other language was possible. The integrity of the novel demanded such language.

But even when readers have been willing to concede that the bold language is a necessary part of the novel, they have expressed doubts about the authenticity of Holden's language. Teen-age girls, I find, are especially skeptical about the authenticity of the language. "Prep-school boys just don't talk like that," they say. It is a tribute, perhaps, to the gentlemanliness of adolescent boys that when they are in the company of girls they temper their language. But, whatever the girls may think, prep-school boys do on occasion talk as Holden talks. As a matter of fact, Holden's patois is remarkably restrained in comparison with the blue-streak vernacular of his real-life counterparts. Holden's profanity becomes most pronounced in moments of emotional tension; at other times his language is notably tempered—slangy, ungrammatical, rambling, yes, but almost boyishly pure. (pp. 441-42)

Holden's swearing is so habitual, so unintentional, so ritualistic that it takes on a quality of innocence. Holden is characterized by a desperate bravado; he is constantly seeking to appear older than he really is. Despite that trait, however, Holden's profanity does not stem from the same motivation that prompts other adolescents to swear—the urge to seem "one of the boys." His profanity is so much ingrained by habit into the fabric of his speech that he is wholly unaware of how rough his language is. . . . And it is not because he has become callous, for this is the same boy who flew into a rage when he saw the obscenity scribbled on a wall where it might be seen by little children.

Some of the episodes in the book are scandalous. The episode commonly cited as being unfit for adolescents to read is the one about the prostitute in the hotel room. A case could be made out for the view that young people should not be exposed to such descriptions. It would be much the same case that one makes out in support of the view that children of a certain age should not be allowed to play with matches. But a convincing case cannot be, and never has been, made out for the view that vice should never be portrayed in a novel.

One shouldn't have to remind readers of what Cardinal Newman once said, that we cannot have a sinless literature about a sinful people. That reminder, however, has to be made whenever a censorship controversy comes up. The proper distinction in this matter is that no novel is immoral merely because vice is represented in it. Immorality creeps in as a result of the author's attitude toward the vice he is portraying and his manner of rendering the scene.

Let us consider the scene in question according to this norm in order to test the validity of the charge that it is scandalous. First of all, neither the novelist nor his character regards the assignation with the prostitute as proper or even as morally indifferent. The word *sin* is not part of Holden's vocabulary, but throughout the episode Holden is acutely aware that the situation in which he finds himself is producing an uncomfortable tension, a tormenting conflict, within him. And that vague awareness of disturbance, of something being "wrong" even if the character doesn't assign the label "sin" to it is enough to preserve the moral tone of the scene in question.

Some readers seem to forget, too, that Holden didn't seek this encounter with the prostitute. He was trapped into it; he was a victim, again, of his own bravado. "It was against my principles and all," he says, "but I was feeling so depressed I didn't even *think.*" Nor does he go through with the act. Embarrassment, nervousness inexperience—all play a part in his rejection of the girl. But what influences his decision most, without his being aware of it, is his pity for the girl. That emotion is triggered by the sight of her green dress. It is that pity which introduces a moral note into Holden's choice. Nor does Salinger render this scene with the kind of explicit, erotic detail that satisfies the pruriency of readers who take a lickerish delight in pornography. All of the scenes about sexual matters are tastefully, even beautifully, treated. It is any wonder that devotees of the novel are shocked by the suggestion that some of the scenes are scandalous?

Holden, constantly protesting against phoniness, is a phony himself. With this objection we move close to a charge against the novel that is damaging because it is based on sounder premises than the other two objections. No doubt about it, Salinger likes this boy, and he wants his readers to like the boy, too. If it could be shown that Salinger, despite his intentions, failed to create a sympathetic character, all the current fuss about the novel would be rendered superfluous, because the novel would eventually fall of its own dead weight.

Holden uses the word *phony* or some derivative of it at least 44 times. *Phoniness* is the generic term that Holden uses to cover all manifestations of cant, hypocrisy and speciosity. He is genuinely disturbed by such manifestations, so much so that, to use his own forthright term, he wants to "puke." The reason why he finds the nuns, his sister Phoebe and children in general so refreshing is that they are free of this phoniness.

But, as a number of people charge, Holden is himself a phony. He is an inveterate liar; he frequently masquerades as someone he is not; he fulminates against foibles of which he himself is guilty; he frequently vents his spleen about his friends, despite the fact that he seems to be advocating the need for charity. Maxwell Geismar puts this objection most pointedly when he says: *"The Catcher in the Rye* protests, to be sure, against both the academic and social conformity of its period. But what does it argue *for?*" [see excerpt dated 1958]. Because of this inconsistency between what Holden wants other people to be and what he is himself, many readers find the boy a far from sympathetic character and declare that he is no model for our young people to emulate.

These readers have accurately described what Holden *does,* but they miss the point about what he *is.* Holden is the classic portrait of "the crazy, mixed-up kid," but with this significant difference: there is about him a solid substratum of goodness, genuineness and sensitivity. It is just this conflict between the surface and the substratum that makes the reading of the novel such a fascinating, pathetic and intensely moral experience. Because Holden is more intelligent and more sensitive than his confreres, he has arrived prematurely at the agonizing transition between adolescence and adulthood. He is precocious but badly seasoned. An affectionate boy, yearning for love and moorings, he has been cut off during most of his teen-age years from the haven of his family. Whatever religious training he has been exposed to has failed to touch him or served to confuse him. Accordingly, he is a young man adrift in an adult world that buffets and bewilders him.

The most salient mark of Holden's immaturity is his inability to discriminate. His values are sound enough, but he views

everything out of proportion. Most of the manners and mores that Holden observes and scorns are not as monstrous as Holden makes them out to be. His very style of speech, with its extraordinary propensity for hyperbole, is evidence of this lack of a sense of proportion. Because he will not discriminate, he is moving dangerously close to that most tragic of all states, negation. His sister Phoebe tells him: "You don't like *anything* that's happening." Holden's reaction to this charge gives the first glimmer of hope that he may seek the self-knowledge which can save him.

Holden must get to know himself. As Mr. Antolini, his former teacher, tells him: "You're going to have to find out where you want to go." But Holden needs most of all to develop a sense of humor. One of the most startling paradoxes about this book is that although it is immensely funny, there is not an ounce of humor in Holden himself. With the development of a sense of humor will come the maturity that can straighten him out. He will begin to see himself as others see him.

The lovely little scene near the end of the book in which Phoebe is going around and around on the carrousel can be regarded as an objective correlative of Holden's condition at the end of his ordeal by disillusionment. Up to this point, Holden has pursued his odyssey in a more or less straight line; but in the end, in his confusion and heartsickness, he is swirling around in a dizzying maelstrom. In the final chapter, however, it would appear that Holden has had his salutary epiphany. "I sort of *miss* everybody I told about," he says. Here is the beginning of wisdom. The reader is left with the feeling that Holden, because his values are fundamentally sound, will turn out all right.

I suspect that adults who object to Holden on the grounds of his apparent phoniness are betraying their own uneasiness. Holden is not like the adolescents in the magazine ads—the smiling, crew-cut, loafer-shod teenagers wrapped up in the cocoon of suburban togetherness. He makes the adults of my generation uncomfortable because he exposes so much of what is meretricious in our way of life. (pp. 442-43)

Future controversy will probably center on just what age an adolescent must be before he is ready for this book. That may prove to be a futile dispute. But I would hope that any decisions about the book would be influenced by the consideration, not that this is an immoral, corrupting book—for it is certainly not—but that it is a subtle, sophisticated novel that requires an experienced, mature reader. Above all, let the self-appointed censors *read* the novel before they raise the barriers. (p. 443)

Edward P. J. Corbett, "Raise High the Barriers, Censors," in America, *Vol. 104, No. 14, January 7, 1961, pp. 441-43.*

PETER J. SENG

A recent article in the New York *Times Book Review* pointed out that J. D. Salinger's *The Catcher in the Rye,* first published in 1951, was still selling about 250,000 copies a year in its paperback edition. A report like this is news about any novel ten years after its first appearance. While *Marjorie Morningstar, The Adventures of Augie March,* and *By Love Possessed* have almost faded from sight, Salinger's novel seems to go on and on and on. In fact it regularly attracts attention to itself on the *front* pages of newspapers, usually when an irate school superintendent, parent, or local PTA discovers what the children have been reading in the classrooms and decides that something must be done to keep English courses moral.

The prominence of Salinger's novel in book supplements and news columns is significant evidence that *The Catcher in the Rye* is no longer merely a trade book but has become a college and high school text as well. Further evidence is provided by the articles that the "little magazines" and scholarly journals have been printing for the past six years: essays written by instructors who have apparently been teaching the novel to their classes. If it is possible to guess a pedagogical viewpoint from a critical article, then it seems likely that the school superintendents, parents, and PTAs who want to censor the book may sometimes be doing the right thing for the wrong reason. Perhaps the teacher ought to be banned and not the book. The extant academic criticism on *The Catcher in the Rye* for the most part deposes, openly or covertly, an assessment of the book which reflects a romantic view of life. I think such an interpretation represents a wholly unfair view of a novel which is in fact realistic, sensible, moral, and very hardheaded.

To talk about morality in connection with a modern novel is a distinctly unfashionable enterprise, just as unfashionable as William Dean Howells' efforts to talk about realism in the novel in the 80's and 90's. The parallel is, I think, a valid one. At the end of the last century Howells was deeply concerned with the effects of "novel-reading" on young people, especially on the protected young ladies of his era. From the romantic novels of his time Howells felt that a young lady might come to believe

> that Love, or the passion or fancy she mistook for it, was the chief interest of a life, which is really concerned with a great many other things; that it was lasting in the way she knew it; that it was worthy of every sacrifice, and was altogether a finer thing than prudence, obedience, reason; that love alone was glorious and beautiful. . . . More lately she has begun to idolize and illustrate Duty, and she is hardly less mischievous in this new role. . . .

It is melancholy to reflect now, seventy years after Howells' warnings, that perhaps our concern ought to be directed to the effects of a romantic misreading of a contemporary novel on the moral attitudes of young men.

Howells defined realism in the novel as "nothing more and nothing less than the truthful treatment of material," and he defined morality in the same terms. What he asked of a novel was:

> Is it true?—true to the motives, the impulses, the principles that shape the life of actual men and women? This truth, which necessarily includes the highest morality and the highest artistry—this truth given, the book cannot be wicked and cannot be weak.

Judged by this criterion *The Catcher in the Rye* is certainly not an immoral book. On the contrary the great appeal this book has for young people is due, I think, to the fact that it is a valid, "realistic" representation of the adolescent world. Some parents and teachers may object to Holden's thoughts, language, and activities as "immoral"; but I doubt that modern adolescents are as innocent of these things as those parents and teachers suppose. The adults would do better to mount their moral attack not against the novel but against

the interpretation that it may be given (or allowed) in the classroom. If that interpretation is not a "truthful treatment of material"—that is, a truthful treatment of the realities of life—then adults ought to be exercised far more than they are. If Holden Caulfield is being held up to students as the ideal youth, as a Galahad who carries his pure white banner undefiled through a world of sordid adults, only to fall at the novel's end as a pathetic victim of their machinations against him, then *The Catcher in the Rye* becomes an immoral novel—precisely in Howells' terms. Howells' objection to romantic novels in the nineteenth century was not an objection to wicked passages in them; rather his objections were grounded on the fact that those novels were

> idle lies about human nature and the social fabric, which it behooves us to know and to understand, that we may deal justly with ourselves and with one another.

The moral issue here is not negligible. If, as the *Times* reports, a million and a half copies of Salinger's book have been distributed in the past ten years, most of them in paperback, then *The Catcher in the Rye* is more solidly entrenched in a number of schools than the classics are. I have no objection to the entrenchment; it could be a good thing; but I think there is some reason for fear about what goes on in the trenches. Therefore I would like to suggest an interpretation of the novel which is, I think, realistic in Howells' terms.

The plot of *The Catcher in the Rye* concerns the three-day odyssey of Holden Caulfield after he has been expelled from Pencey Prep for bad grades and general irresponsibility. At the beginning of the story Holden is in a sanitarium in California recovering from a mental breakdown. He says that he is not going to tell his life-story but just the story of "this madman stuff that happened to me around last Christmas just before I got pretty run-down and had to come out here and take it easy". In the final chapter he speculates about what he is going to do when he is released and reflects on "all this stuff I just finished telling you about. . . . If you want to know the truth, I don't *know* what I think about it". Between these important framing limits the story proper is contained. It reads like an edited psychoanalysis, an illusion which is sustained by the rambling first-person narrative.

Sensitive and perceptive as Holden is, he is still an adolescent and so an immature judge of adult life. His viewpoint is as limited as that of Hazlitt's young man who thinks that he will never die. Like many young people Holden is intolerant of sickness and the debility of old age. Recalling his visit to "Old Spencer" he says,

> there were pills and medicine all over the place, and everything smelled like Vicks Nose Drops. It was pretty depressing. I'm not too crazy about sick people, anyway. What made it even more depressing, old Spencer had on this very sad, ratty old bathrobe that he was probably born in or something. I don't much like to see old guys in their pajamas and bathrobes anyway.

Nor can he bear the old history teacher's garrulity and physical habits. While Holden is quick to pass severe judgments on others he is not so quick to see the faults in himself. A number of the picayune traits he hates Ackley for in Chapter 3 are traits he reveals in himself in Chapter 4 when he talks to Stradlater. A comparison of these two chapters reveals interesting things both about Holden's character and about Salinger's narrative technique. It might be said that Holden's chief fault is his failure "to connect" (to use Forster's phrase); he hates lies, phoniness, pretense, yet these are often his own sins.

He is enraged at the thought that Stradlater may have "made time" with Jane Gallagher. His rage springs partly from the fact that he regards Jane as his own property, partly from his suspicion that Stradlater is a heel; yet there are further implications in this episode that he most deeply resents Stradlater's apparent self-possession in an area where he himself is ill-at-ease. Stradlater may have "made time" with Jane (though the reader of the novel tends to see his testimony as an adolescent's boast); but the moment Holden arrives in New York he attempts to "make time" first with a burlesque stripper and then with a hotel call-girl. There is, to be sure, a difference in the objects of each boy's affections, but the difference is not so great as Holden, not "connecting," might think. His failure in both attempts is probably adequately explained by his confession:

> Sex is something I really don't understand too hot. You never know *where* the hell you are. I keep making up these sex rules for myself, and then I break them right away. Last year I made a rule that I was going to quit horsing around with girls that, deep down, gave me a pain in the ass. I broke it, though, the same week I made it. . . . Sex is something I just don't understand.

While Holden responds to the common chord to which all fleshly creatures vibrate, he is nonetheless contemptuous of its varied—and sometimes perverse—manifestations in others.

In a similar fashion he passes harsh verdicts on people who do not measure up to his standards of taste and urban sophistication. When the tourists from Seattle—Bernice, Marty, and Laverne (the very names spell out a whole aesthetic)—plan to see the first show at Radio City Music Hall their taste depresses him; yet the following day he goes there himself. Buying drinks for the girls from Seattle he puts on a pretense of New Yorkish world-weary sophistication. On the other hand he cannot bear that sort of pretense in others, and has only contempt for the kind of people who say that something is "grand," or affect a fashionable critical attitude about Lunt and Fontanne, or who make polite social noises at each other (social noises that have to be made if society is going to endure).

What disturbs Holden about the world in which he finds himself is adults and adult values. He sees that the world belongs to adults, and it seems to him that they have filled it with phoniness, pretense, social compromise. He would prefer a world that is honest, sincere, simple. He is looking, as one critic notes, for the "simple truth" [see excerpt by Ihab Hassan dated 1961]. Such a quest is doomed from the start: *there are no simple truths.* In a complex modern society truth, too, is complex, and a certain amount of social compromise is necessary.

This kind of civilizing compromise Holden is unwilling to make. The world he wants is a world of children or children-surrogates like the nuns. He would people it with little girls whose skates need tightening, little girls like his adored sister Phoebe; with little boys like the ones at the Museum of Natural History, filled with exquisite terror at the prospect of seeing the mummies. It would include small boys with poems on their baseball gloves like his brother Allie who died some

years ago from leukemia and so has been arrested in permanent youth by death. The chief citizens of Holden's world would be the little boys who walk along the curbstone and sing,

> If a body catch a body
> Coming through the rye.

Holden's chief fantasy is built on this memory: he sees himself as the "catcher in the rye," the only adult in a world of children:

> I keep picturing all these little kids playing some game in this big field of rye and all. Thousands of little kids, and nobody's around—nobody big, I mean—except me. And I'm standing on the edge of some crazy cliff. What I have to do, I have to catch everybody if they start to go over the cliff—I mean if they're running and they don't look where they're going I have to come out from somewhere and *catch* them. That's all I'd do all day. I'd just be the catcher in the rye and all.

Holden has other fantasies as well, and these are less healthy. He imagines himself living all alone in a cabin in the far west pretending to be a deaf-mute. If anyone wanted to communicate with him, he says, that person would have to write him a note (a prescription that would also include his wife who would be deaf and dumb, too). "They'd get bored as hell doing that after a while, and then I'd be through with having conversations for the rest of my life." Both the "catcher" and the "deaf-mute" fantasies are rooted in a single desire: a wish to escape from an adult world with which Holden feels that he cannot cope.

His mental breakdown is a direct result of his inability to come to terms with adult reality. Consequently he invents other fantasies, tinged with paranoia, in which he sees himself as a martyr-victim. In front of Ackley he play-acts at going blind: " 'Mother darling, give me your *hand.* Why won't you give me your hand?' " Roughed up by a pimp-bellhop he imagines that he has been shot, and fancies himself walking down the stairs of the hotel bleeding to death. In a third fantasy he imagines his own death and funeral in great detail. Finally, in his recollections of previous events he seems to identify with a schoolmate, James Castle, who jumped from a high window rather than submit to the brutality of prep school bullies.

The crucial chapter in *The Catcher in the Rye* seems to me to be the one in which Holden calls on his former English teacher Mr. Antolini. For all his own weaknesses Antolini sees to the heart of the matter and gives saving advice to Holden; the advice is rejected because Holden measures it against impossibly absolute standards. If this view of the novel is correct then Holden's interview with Antolini is also the high point of irony in *The Catcher in the Rye:* the proffered offer of salvation comes from a teacher whom Holden enormously admires, but the counsel is nullified when Holden discovers that Antolini, like all adults, has feet of clay. From the moment the boy leaves Antolini's apartment his mental breakdown commences. This sequence of events seems to be Salinger's intention.

If the Antolini episode is crucial, as I think it is, it deserves examination in some detail. The relationship between Mr. and Mrs. Antolini is immediately clear to the reader, if not to Holden. Mrs. Antolini is older than her husband and rich. They have an elegant apartment on Sutton Place, belong to the West Side Tennis Club in Forest Hills, and are ostentatiously affectionate in public. Yet in Holden's uncomprehending phrase, they are "never in the same room at the same time".

Holden's attachment to this teacher is in sharp contrast to his antipathy for "old Spencer" at the beginning of the novel. There is ease and *rapport* between the older man and the younger one. As Mrs. Antolini retires for the night to leave "the boys" alone, her husband has a stiff highball, obviously not his first. As he drinks [Antolini] gives advice to Holden, all of it very much to the point:

> I have a feeling that you're riding for some kind of a terrible, terrible fall. But I don't honestly know what kind. . . . It may be the kind where, at the age of thirty, you sit in some bar hating everybody who comes in looking as if he might have played football in college. Then again, you may pick up just enough education to hate people who say, 'It's a secret between he and I.' Or you may end up in some business office, throwing paper clips at the nearest stenographer.

It is instructive to re-examine the previous episodes of the novel in the light of this assessment of Holden's character. What Antolini predicts for the future already, in part, exists in the present. After another drink he goes on:

> This fall I think you're riding for—it's a special kind of fall, a horrible kind. The man falling isn't permitted to feel or hear himself hit bottom. He just keeps falling and falling. The whole arrangement's designed for men who, at some time or other in their lives, were looking for something their own environment couldn't supply them with. . . . So they gave up looking. They gave it up before they ever really even got started.

Antolini writes out for Holden an epigram from the works of the psychoanalyst Wilhelm Stekel: " 'The mark of the immature man is that he wants to die nobly for a cause, while the mark of the mature man is that he wants to live humbly for one.' " This epigram is a penetrating insight into the personality of an adolescent who continually views himself as a martyr or savior, but never sees himself as modestly attempting to cope with a humdrum and very imperfect world. In effect what Antolini is saying is, "You are not alone; we have all been through this." You are not the first one, he tells Holden,

> who was ever confused and frightened and even sickened by human behavior. You're by no means alone on that score, you'll be excited and *stimulated* to know. Many, many men have been just as troubled morally and spiritually as you are right now. Happily, some of them kept records of their troubles. You'll learn from them—if you want to.

He makes up a bed for the boy on the couch and then retires to the kitchen, presumably for another drink. Holden lies awake for a few seconds

> thinking about all that stuff Mr. Antolini'd told me. . . . He was really a pretty smart guy. But I couldn't keep my goddam eyes open, and I fell asleep.

That sleep is symbolic as well as literal. Suddenly waking during the night Holden finds Antolini sitting on the floor next to his couch-bed patting him on the head. Panicked by what

he regards as something "perverty" he flees from the apartment.

The irony built into this denouement is clear: the saving advice that Antolini has given Holden has been rendered useless because the idol who gave it has fallen. Antolini is a shabby adult like all the others. In his reactions Holden is like the man in the Stephen Crane poem who climbed to the top of the mountain only to cry out:

> Woe to my knowledge!
> I intended to see good white lands
> And bad black lands,
> But the scene is grey.

It is worth noting that Salinger takes pains to keep the end of the Antolini episode ambiguous: that is to say, while there can be little doubt in a reader's mind about Antolini's propensities, his gesture toward Holden is considerably short of explicit. In fact Salinger raises this very doubt in Holden's mind:

> I wondered if just maybe I was wrong about thinking he was making a flitty pass at me. I wondered if maybe he just liked to pat guys on the head when they're asleep. I mean how can you tell about that stuff for sure? You can't.

Whatever doubts he may have about Antolini's motives, there can be no doubts about the meaning of his own feelings as he walks up Fifth Avenue the next day:

> Then all of a sudden, something very spooky started happening. . . . Every time I came to the end of a block and stepped off the goddam curb, I had this feeling that I'd never get to the other side of the street. I thought I'd just go down, down, down, and nobody'd ever see me again.

This, of course, is the beginning of the fall which Antolini had predicted.

So much for the edited psychoanalysis of Holden Caulfield. It seems to me that if *The Catcher in the Rye* is viewed along the lines suggested above it is a moral novel in the fullest sense of that word. According to this interpretation Holden is not a mere victim of modern society, but is in some sense a tragic figure. His temporary mental defeat is brought about by a flaw in his own character: a naive refusal to come to terms with the world in which he lives. To regard him, on the other hand, as a pure young man who is martyred in his unavailing struggle against a sordid world of adult phoniness, is to strip him of any real dignity. Such an interpretation makes the novel guilty of idle romanticism. Howells would have called it immoral romanticism because he would have seen it as filled with "idle lies about human nature and the social fabric," areas where we must know the truth if we are to deal "justly with ourselves and with one another."

Salinger himself is reported to have said that he regretted that his novel might be kept out of the reach of children. It is hard to guess at the motives behind his remark, but one of them may have been that he was trying to tell young people how difficult it was to move from their world into the world of adults. He may have been trying to warn them against the pitfalls of the transition.

To my mind one of the most penetrating reviews of *The*

Catcher in the Rye was the one which appeared in *The Nation* in 1951 when the novel first came out:

> It reflects something not at all rich and strange but what every sensitive sixteen-year-old since Rousseau has felt, and of course what each one of us is certain he has felt. . . . *The Catcher in the Rye* [is] a case history of all of us.

The reviewer was Dr. Ernest Jones, and for the sickness he diagnosed he also prescribed a remedy. His prescription was a line from Auden: "We must love one another or die."

Holden will survive; but first he must learn to love other human beings as well as he loves children. He must acquire a sense of proportion, a sense of humor. He must learn compassion for the human, the pompous, the phoney, the perverse; such people are the fellow inhabitants of his world, and behind their pitiful masks are the faces of the children in the rye. In Stekel's phrase, he must learn to live humbly for a cause. (pp. 203-09)

> *Peter J. Seng, "The Fallen Idol: The Immature World of Holden Caulfield," in* College English, *Vol. 23, No. 3, December, 1961, pp. 203-09.*

IHAB HASSAN

The dramatic conflict which so many of Salinger's stories present obviously does not lend itself to sociological classification. It is more loving and particular, and it partakes of situations that have been traditionally available to literature. The conflict, however, suggests a certain polarity between what might be called, with all due exaggeration, the Assertive Vulgarian and the Responsive Outsider. Both types recur with sufficient frequency to warrant the distinction, and their interplay defines much that is most central to Salinger's fiction. The Vulgarian, who carries the burden of squalor, stands for all that is crude, venal, self-absorbed, and sequacious in our culture. He has no access to knowledge or feeling or beauty, which makes him all the more invulnerable, and his relationship to the world is largely predicated by Buber's I-It dyad. . . . The Outsider, on the other hand, carries the burden of love. The burden makes of him sometimes a victim, and sometimes a scapegoat saint. His life is like "a great inverted forest/with all foliage underground." It is a quick, generous, and responsive life, somehow preserved against hardness and corruption, and always attempting to reach out from its isolation in accordance with Buber's I-Thou dyad. Often there is something in the situation of the Outsider to isolate him, to set him off, however slightly, from the rest of mankind. He might be a child or an adolescent, might wear glasses or appear disfigured, might be Jewish, though seldom is he as crippled or exotic as the characters of Capote and McCullers often are. (pp. 261-62)

The response of these outsiders and victims to the dull or angry world about them is not simply one of withdrawal: it often takes the form of a strange, quixotic gesture. The gesture, one feels sure, is the bright metaphor of Salinger's sensibility, the center from which meaning drives, and ultimately the reach of his commitment to past innocence and current guilt. It is a gesture at once of pure expression and of expectation, of protest and prayer, of aesthetic form and spiritual content—as Blackmur would say, it is behavior that sings. There is often something prodigal and spontaneous about it, something humorous or whimsical, something that disrupts our habits of gray acquiescence and revives our faith in the willingness of the human spirit. But above all, it gives of itself

as only a *religious* gesture can. In another age, Cervantes endowed Don Quixote with the capacity to perform it, and so did Twain and Fitzgerald endow their best creations. For the gesture, after all, has an unmistakably American flourish. The quest of American adolescents . . . has always been for an idea of truth. It is this very idea of truth that the quixotic gesture is constantly seeking to embody. The embodiment is style in action: the twist and tang, the stammering and improvisations, the glint and humor of Salinger's language. (pp. 262-63)

As a "neo-picaresque," [*The Catcher in the Rye*] shows itself to be concerned far less with the education or initiation of an adolescent than with a dramatic exposure of the manner in which ideals are denied access to our lives and of the modes which mendacity assumes in our urban culture. The moving, even stabbing, qualities of the novel derive, to some extent, from Salinger's refusal to adopt a satirical stance. The work, instead, confirms the saving grace of vulnerability; its protest, debunking, and indictments presuppose a willing responsiveness on the part of its hero.

On the surface, Holden Caulfield is Salinger's typical quixotic hero in search, once again, of the simple truth. Actually, Holden is in flight from mendacity rather than in search of truth, and his sensitivity to the failures of the world is compounded with his self-disgust. In comparison with his dear, dead brother, Allie, a kind of redheaded saint who united intelligence and compassion as no other member of the family could, setting for all a standard of performance which they try to recapture, Holden seems intolerant, perhaps even harsh. The controlling mood of the novel—and it is so consistent as to be a principle of unity—is one of acute depression always on the point of breaking loose. But despair and depression are kept, throughout, in check by Holden's remarkable lack of self-interest, a quality of self-heedlessness which is nearly saintly, and by his capacity to invoke his adolescent imagination, to "horse around," when he is most likely to go to pot. These contrary pressures keep the actions of the novel in tension and keep the theme of sentimental disenchantment on the stretch; and they are sustained by a style of versatile humor. (p. 272)

Holden is motivated by a compelling desire to commune and communicate, a desire constantly thwarted by the phoniness, indifference, and vulgarity that surround him. He resents the conditions which force upon him the burden of rejection. In protest against these conditions, he has devised a curious game of play-acting, of harmless and gratuitous lying, which is his way of coming to terms with a blistered sensibility, and of affirming his values of truth and imagination. But above all, he is continually performing the quixotic gesture. Thus he socks Stradlater, who is twice his weight, because he suspects the latter of having seduced Jane Gallagher, without any consideration of the fact that she is the kind of girl to keep all her kings, at checkers, in the back row. He gives money away to nuns. He can read a child's notebook all day and night. He furiously rubs out obscenities from the walls of schools. And when Phoebe asks him very seriously what he would like to be, he muses on Robert Burns's song, "If a body meet a body coming through the rye," which he had heard a kid hum in the street, and answers back:

> I keep picturing all these kids playing some game in this big field of rye and all. Thousands of little kids, and nobody's around—nobody big, I mean—except me. And I'm standing on the edge of some

crazy cliff. . . . That's all I'd do all day. I'd just be the catcher in the rye and all. I know it's crazy. . . .

A closer look at *The Catcher in the Rye* might allow us to separate its real from imaginary failings. Mr. Aldridge, for instance, taking his cue perhaps from Phoebe's comment to her brother, "You don't like *any*thing that's happening," has recently observed—Maxwell Geismar makes exactly the same point [see essay dated 1958]—that Holden "has objects for his contempt but no objects other than his sister for his love." It is true that Holden has *more* objects for his contempt than his love—this is the expense of his idealism and the price of his rebellion. But it is impossible to overlook his various degrees of affection for Allie, his dead brother, for James Castle, the boy who was killed because he wouldn't retract a statement he thought true, for the kettle drummer at Radio City, the nuns at the lunch counter, the kid humming the title song, or even the ducks in the park, without missing something of Holden's principal commitments. And his answer to Phoebe, "People never think anything is anything *really*. I'm getting goddam sick of it," may do for those who find these commitments rather slim. Nor can we disallow the feeling of pity which often modifies Holden's scorn, his pity for Ackley and the girls in the Lavender Room, or his confession to Antolini that he can hate people only part of the time, and that he quickly misses those whom he may have once hated. Holden, of course, is not in the least cynical; nor is he blind except to part of the truth which he can otherwise entertain so steadily. Still, there are those who feel that the novel accords no recognition to its hero, and that it fails to enlist our sense of tragedy. The lack of recognition, the avoidance of conversion and initiation, is almost as inherent in the structure of the novel as it is consonant with the bias of the American novel of adolescence. The action of the book is recollected by Holden who is out West recuperating from his illness, and Holden only chooses to tell us "about this madman stuff that happened to me around last Christmas"—nothing more. He refuses to relate incidents to his past or to his character, and he refuses to draw any conclusions from his experience: "If you want to know the truth, I don't *know* what I think about it. . . . About all I know is, I sort of *miss* everybody I told about. Even old Stradlater and Ackley, for instance. . . . Don't ever tell anybody anything. If you do, you start missing everybody." This is an embarrassed testament of love, full of unresolved ambiguities, the only lyrical and undramatic recognition the novel can afford. The partial blindness of Holden, which has been correctly attributed to Holden's juvenile impatience with the reality of compromise, is made more serious by Salinger's failure to modify Holden's point of view by any other. In *Joseph Andrews,* for instance, the innocence of Adams is constantly criticized by the tone of the book and the nature of its comic incidents. There is also some danger that we may be too easily disarmed by the confessional candor of Salinger's novel. When Holden says time and time again, "I swear to God I'm crazy," the danger is equally great in taking Holden at his word as in totally discounting his claim. Holden does succeed in making us perceive that the world is crazy, but his vision is also a function of his own adolescent instability, and the vision, we must admit, is more narrow and biased than that of Huck Finn, Parson Adams, or Don Quixote. It is this narrowness that limits the comic effects of the work. Funny it is without any doubt, and in a fashion that has been long absent from American fiction. But we must recall that true comedy is informed by the spirit of compromise, not intransigence. Huck Finn and Augie March are both, in this sense, closer to the assumptions of comedy than Holden Caulfield. This once understood, we can see how *The Catcher in the Rye* is *both* a funny and terrifying work—traditional distinctions of modes have broken down in our time—a work full of pathos in the original sense of the word. But suffering is a subjective thing, and the novel's sly insistence on suffering makes it a more subjective work than the two novels which relate the adventures of Huck Finn and Augie March. Adventure is precisely what Holden does not endure; his sallies into the world are feigned; his sacrificial burden, carried with whimsey and sardonic defiance, determines his fate. The fate is that of the American rebel-victim. (pp. 273-76)

Ihab Hassan, "J. D. Salinger: Rare Quixotic Gesture," in his Radical Innocence: Studies in the Contemporary American Novel, *Princeton University Press, 1961, pp. 259-89.*

ROBERT O. BOWEN

When a well-to-do college student was gathered in recently for bank robbery, he confessed to understanding himself better for the experience, and several journalists praised his humble candor. J. D. Salinger's characters demonstrate the same caustic humility which slashes as sentimentalists those who attempt virtue while relieving the slob of any onus of failure: no strain, no pain, as the saying runs.

Cast in a jargon promulgated from the shoddier prep schools of the East, the Salinger philosophy parallels the sick-sick line transmitted by Mort Sahl and related cosmopolitan think people. A sneer at a physical defect here, a cutting remark at an ideal there, and the audience falls into line rather than risk a turn at the whipping post. From the first wild ballyhoo at the publication of *The Catcher in the Rye* to Salinger's canonization through the presentation of his peaked visage on a *Time* magazine cover, his work has been relentlessly pushed by social science teachers, editors, and "Garment District" critics of the Lionel Trilling cut. Salinger, they staunchly agree, holds the mirror up to a degenerate American culture. . . .

Sick or not, Salinger's fiction attracts many young people, a symptom which ought not be blinked. He militates against traditional strictures, and because they are rebellious, many youths develop a Salinger syndrome temporarily. Perhaps Salinger's strongest appeal—being that usually aped by students—is his aggressiveness against language taboos. Unlike Henry Miller, Salinger rarely violates the statute, but his tone and diction violate good taste. . . . Such gaucheries amuse as "twenty-three skiddoo" or "Oh you kid!" once did, but with the difference that the Salinger fan repeats them in mockery, often boasting that he is tearing down established standards. Grandfather's gaucheries differed in kind since they aimed at elevating the boy rather than reducing the surroundings. (p. 52)

Probably Salinger is not basically any more anti-Christian than he is basically antagonistic to any undefended group, say hydrocephalics or basket cases. Still, in *Catcher in the Rye* as other-where, his victims regularly belong to unmilitant minorities or disorganized social elements. The headmaster's daughter bites her nails to the quick; the old history teacher is a nose-picker; Ackley, the Catholic, picks pimples on other people's beds; Stradlater, the handsome Ivy League type, uses a filthy razor; and on through the nauseous world.

Usually instead of being ethnically partisan, Salinger holds to bourgeois manners as taught in prep schools. He trails a victim until he catches him picking his nose; then he hollers "Shame!" and lights out after the next victim. Nose-picking falls under manners rather than the more profound value judgments of philosophy; and the foibles of Salinger's characters are specified by the advertisers of the magazines which publish his fiction: halitosis, dermatitis, and similar cosmetic derelictions. Ironically Salinger has borrowed a value system, superficial as it is, from the merchandising field of consumer consumption goods his un-heroes so passionately despise.

A cautious reader may ask whether Salinger is being accused of the snobberies his characters demonstrate but which he intended with fully conscious irony as snobberies. If the stories and the one thin novel offered alternatives, this might be the case. If Holden, for instance, said that cheap luggage was a contemptible thing, and then Salinger paraded an admirable person with cheap luggage, the irony would be evident. In *Catcher in the Rye,* Ackley has cheap luggage. Another bad guy has cheap luggage. The nuns have cheap luggage. In each case the persons involved are inferior, and their inferiority is reported partly in terms of luggage. . . .

No critic has yet pointed out the heavy vein of caste snobbery in Salinger. . . . Salinger's elevator operator is looked down on as old and a failure, and two cab drivers react to Holden's importunities in exactly the same stupidly unsympathetic fashion. The sum of this is that cab drivers are surly and stupid people and office girls from Seattle are gawking and contemptible natives. Teachers, if not old nose-pickers in shoddy bathrobes, are homosexuals as with Mr. Antolini. All in all, the Salinger tone echoes with remarkable precision the essential meanness of the notorious 19th century English expression: "The natives begin at Calais." (p. 55)

In Salinger's world only physical things in their most mundane sensory nature are discussed or offered up for silent meditation. By definition such a system is logical positivist and is limited to passions. Neither prime causes, universal moral law, nor other concepts of abstract principle are available to the logical positivist. Naturally, then, Salinger reverts to the tribal totems of the *New Yorker* advertisers and Manhattan provincials. He has no other where to turn.

Even as a logical positivist, though, Salinger is inconsistent. His cast of characters suffers a steady attrition through suicide. If valid extra-personal values are denied, a character need feel no qualms about anything. Why weep? In truth, why smile? A man could simply ignore as utterly inconsequential the phony utterances of square teachers and related duds, but suicide he would not because death would lack point. Still Salinger wants a deep anti-Existential sympathy for his little league Existentialists although ambiguously he will not acknowledge the value system upon which sympathy is predicated, for such an acknowledgment would require responsibility, which Salinger denies.

Salinger's failure as a philosopher or moralist comes through worst in his skirting the central moral dilemma posed by *Catcher in the Rye,* for evidently the author did not realize the significance of the climactic scene of his novel. The reference is to Mr. Antolini's pass at Holden and the bearing of this scene on the rest of the narrative. In Holden's wanderings, everyone he met was a slob. Only one character, Mr. Antolini, has shown the milk of human kindness. This man is truly concerned for Holden, not merely as a sexual target

but as a human being. In simple, Mr. Antolini is the only one in the book capable of constructive, virtuous action. Mr. Antolini does have a social flaw, though: he is homosexual.

The dramatic complication Mr. Antolini raises must be distinctively resolved in order for the book to depict the character development which defines a novel. Holden had been kicked out of school and was afraid to go home. Mr. Antolini took him in, and during the night Holden awoke to find Mr. Antolini stroking his head in the dark. Any doubt of Mr. Antolini's intention is checked by the man's vague, embarrassed refrain: "You're a strange boy," hardly the comment of nocturnal innocence.

However Holden resolves the complication, his action will express the judgment of the novel itself since this complication has clewed up the major cords of the narrative. As noted above, Mr. Antolini is a last resort. He is virtuous in being kind, loyal, hospitable, and affectionate; and if good should be nurtured, surely his charity should be done so, for there is little enough of it in the world of this novel. He also is the only youth counselor the book offers above the level of farce. Holden's reaction must reflect judgment on these issues. Furthermore, if he has reached any maturity at all, he will understand the issues and act consciously about them. He need not be sophisticated, but he must be cognizant.

A glance at a moral problem in the purported model for *Catcher in the Rye* will demonstrate the distinction intended here as to consciousness but not necessarily sophistication. In *Huckleberry Finn,* the hero is ashamed to help a poor old widow's property escape, namely his companion Jim, a slave seeking his free family in Yankeeland. Huck accepts that if he helps Jim, he'll never be able to hold his head up to a white person again and that he will go to Hell. He does decide to help Jim, though. His judgment is unsophisticated but extremely moral. He saw the issues clearly. Jim was kind, loyal, brave, loving, and so on; and Huck helped him because of these virtues, despite his social faults. No matter what partisan feeling caste demanded, Huck knew his basis for judgment though he did not have a name for that. The modern Huckleberry Finn, as Holden Caulfield is known, hardly offers such a moral solution to Mr. Antolini's stealthy approach.

What can Holden do? He can beat Mr. Antolini's brains out as an argument for his own virtue. The action would be definite and would set Holden as a cruel person, a selfish person, possibly a perverse person. Or he could allow Mr. Antolini to have his way, thus encouraging his corruption. Or he could take the mature and morally rich position of remaining in the apartment so as to encourage Mr. Antolini's real virtues while protecting him from the weakness of perversion. The need for the last alternative is great because Mr. Antolini is apparently the *only* adult of any known virtue at all and so should be helped lest virtue fail entirely for lack of seed. Thus Holden's choice is of paramount importance to the dramatic statement of the book at large.

As a matter of fact, Holden does not elect any of the alternatives offered here. Instead he grabs his shoes and with a flourish of his casual wit lights out downtown. Holden dodged the issue. More to the point, nothing in the passage or otherwise indicates that Salinger himself perceived the moral nature of the problem. Salinger didn't dodge the issue; he just didn't know it had passed by. (pp. 57-9)

Salinger's nearest brush with profundity is a quotation cited by the homosexual teacher in *Catcher in the Rye* from a psychoanalyst. "The mark of the immature man is that he wants to die nobly for a cause, while the mark of the mature man is that he wants to live humbly for one." In the Caulfield-Antolini context the speech signifies the failure of sacrifice, or trying, of faith ultimately. Taken as offered, as the sole truth, the statement casts an inference across the patronizing tone toward Jesus earlier; and outside of Salinger, from our long and ancient literary past it undercuts our vision of heroes and their motives from Beowulf and Roland to the nobility of those Welsh Guards who in our own time lay behind at Dunkirk to stall the German armour and save a British army. Like so much of Salinger, the citation turns all values upside down. The martyr is a fool; the coward a hero.

Aggressive attacks of this sort against our culture have been made by many with Salinger as ammunition. Other propagandists include Nabokov, inventor of the nymphette in *Lolita;* Tennessee Williams, notorious for the queer passions of his drama figures; Henry Miller, the Paris-Big Sur sexmonger; and a legion of others. Such partisan views are held with sufficient vehemence not to be ignored. However, the fervor of the opposition should not mislead us from the statistical conclusion that neither Salinger nor his cohorts have drawn a picture of the average or typical twentieth century American youth. Even taking into account students corrupted by Freudian psychology teachers and beatnik humanities lecturers, the Holden Caulfield type is relatively rare and remains a grotesque, an aberrant.

When our culture was more consciously Christian, aberrants were considered wrong; in mediaeval carvings artists pointedly depicted grotesques as evil monsters. In Salinger we find the grotesque not designed to hold our pity because it is a poor soul lost to order, to virtue, but rather designed for our admiration *because it is grotesque*. We do not see Holden across the chasm, lost from our humanity; instead he is offered as a model which our youth is asked to ape.

Quite clearly Salinger draws a picture of evil, and his apologists use that picture as propaganda in an effort to draw us into evil.

Far from being a kind and gentle and mature and objective and above all wise book, *The Catcher in the Rye,* like all of Salinger's fiction, is catty and snide and bigotted in the most thorough sense. It is crassly caste-conscious as the treatment of cabbies and elevator operators witnesses; it is religiously bigotted as the treatment of Catholics and the Salvation Army witnesses; it is caste-conscious as the Negro chauvinism witnesses; it is vehemently anti-Army and even anti-American in equating the American military with the Nazi military. All of these things are the reasons for the book's success, for its success lies in its utility as propaganda.

Let those of us who are Christian and who love life lay this book aside as the weapon of an enemy and let those who wish it so read it. But let us be honest in this and charge bigotry where it stands. Feeding spite is no charity simply because the spite is against the faith and hope of a Christian vision of life. (pp. 59-60)

> *Robert O. Bowen, "The Salinger Syndrome: Charity against Whom?" in* Ramparts, *Vol. 1, No. 1, May, 1962, pp. 52-60.*

WAYNE C. BOOTH

[*The author of* The Rhetoric of Fiction, *Booth was professor of English at the University of Chicago when this essay was first published in 1964.*]

I have a frequently recurring fantasy in which I am called before a censorship committee and asked to justify my teaching of such-and-such a book. As hero of my own dream, I see myself starting on page one of whatever book is attacked and reading aloud, with commentary and discussion, page by page, day by day, until the censors either lynch me or confess to a conversion.

A pipedream, clearly. And the one I use for substitute is not much less fantastic. An irate committeeman comes to me (I am a very young instructor in a highly vulnerable school district), and he threatens to have me fired for teaching *The Catcher in the Rye* (or *Huckleberry Finn,* or *Catch-22*—one can of course mold one's daydreams to suit current events). I look him boldly in the eye and I ask him one question: "Will you, before you fire me, do me one last favor? Will you read carefully a little statement I have made about the teaching of this book, and then reread the book?" And since it is fantasy, he says, "Well, I don't see why not. I want to be reasonable." And away he goes, bearing my neatly-typed manuscript and my marked copy of *Catcher.* Some hours later he comes back, offers his humble apologies for what he calls his "foolish mistake," and returns my manuscript [which is titled "What to Do With a Literary Work Before Deciding to Censor It"]. Here it is. (pp. 157-58)

Let us begin by assuming that we ought to censor all books that we think are immoral. . . . What should determine whether a book is among those we want to censor?

The question will not arise, of course, unless you have found, as in *Catcher,* something objectionable. There you have found such things as teenagers speaking profanities, the phrase "Fuck you"—repeated!—and a schoolboy visit to a prostitute. It must seem to you that I am being merely perverse when I say that such a book is really highly moral, when "read properly." . . .

The big job is to relate the seemingly offensive passages to the context provided by the whole work. (p. 158)

[Here is] what the good censor will want to do before carrying out his job.

(1) He will refuse to draw any conclusions whatever from any element of a work taken out of its context. This means that he will read the whole work.

(2) He will not be satisfied with one reading. When a work is assigned and discussed in class, it receives several "readings," sometimes quite literally and always in the sense that first impressions are modified by sustained reflection. . . . What the censor should be interested in is what the student will get after such reflective rereading, not the errors he might fall into if he read the work without the teacher's encouragement to thoughtful rereading. . . .

(3) The true values of a work—the real moral center which we may or may not want to rule out of our children's experience—cannot usually be identified with the expressed values of any one character. What we might call the *author's* values, the *norms* according to which he *places* his characters' values, are always more complex than those of any one of the characters he invents. . . . [It is] absurd to censor any book for ex-

pressed values which are, for the proper reader, repudiated by the author's implied criticism. (p. 160)

With all of this as background, suppose we turn now to your objections to *The Catcher in the Rye.* You said that you objected to the printing of the obscene phrase that Holden tries to erase. But in the light of your objections to the book, it is surely strange to find that you and Holden have the same feelings about this phrase: you would both like to get rid of it.

> It drove me damn near crazy. I thought how Phoebe and all the other little kids would see it, and how they'd wonder what the hell it meant, and then finally some dirty kid would tell them—all cockeyed, naturally—what it meant, and how they'd all *think* about it and maybe even *worry* about it for a couple of days. I kept wanting to kill whoever'd written it.

Holden could hardly be more strongly opposed to the phrase; it is significant, surely, that throughout the scene from which this passage is taken, the tone is entirely serious—there is none of the clowning that marks Holden's behavior in many other passages. (p. 161)

Clearly we are driven to thinking about what kind of character the author has created for us, in his lost wild boy. What kind of person is it who, a moment later, concludes that his effort to wipe out the obscenities of the world is "hopeless, anyway," because they are unlimited.

You said this afternoon that you found him to be a terrible person. But supposing we begin from the other direction and ask ourselves why young readers find him, as they do (I have yet to find an exception), so entirely sympathetic. When I ask my adolescent students why they like Holden so much, they usually say, "Because he is so real" or "Because he is so honest." But it takes no very deep reading to find many additional virtues that win them to him, virtues that even you and I must admire. It is true that his honesty, or rather his generally unsuccessful but valiant attempt at honesty, is striking. But a far stronger magnet for the reader's affections is his tremendous capacity for love, expressed in deeds that would do credit to a saint. The book opens, for example, with his visit, extremely distasteful to him, to the sick and aging history teacher. Holden knows that the old man loves him and needs him, just as he needs the love of the old man; it is out of real feeling that he subjects himself to the sights and smells of age and illness. The moral sensitivity revealed in this scene is maintained through the book. Again and again Holden reveals himself—often in direct contradiction of his own claims—to be far more sensitive than most of us to the feelings of others. (pp. 161-62)

A full catalog of his virtues and good works would be unfair to the book, because it would suggest a solemn kind of sermonizing very different from the special *Catcher* brand of affectionate comedy. But it is important to us in talking about possible censorship of the book to see its seeming immoralities in the context of Holden's deep morality.

The virtue most pertinent to the obscene phrase is of course Holden's struggle for purity. The soiled realities of the "phony" world that surrounds him in his school and in the city are constantly contrasted in his mind with the possible ideal world that has not been plastered with obscenities. His worrying about what Stradlater has done to Jane, his fight with Stradlater, his inability to carry through with the prostitute because he "feels sorry" for her, his lecture to himself

about the crudities he watches through the hotel windows, his effort to explain to Luce that promiscuity destroys love—these are all, like his effort to erase the obscenity, part of his struggle to find "a place that's nice and peaceful," a world that is "nice and white." Though he himself soils, with his fevered imagination, the pure gesture of Antolini, revealing how helplessly embedded he is in another kind of world altogether, his ideal remains something like the world of the nuns, or the world of a Christ who will not condemn even Judas to eternal damnation. He is troubled, you will remember, when one of the nuns talks about *Romeo and Juliet,* because that play "gets pretty sexy in some parts, and she was a nun and all." Nuns ought to live in the pure, sexless, sinless, trouble-free world of his ideal, just as his sister ought to live in a world unsullied by nasty scrawlings on stairway walls.

All of this—the deep Christian charity and the search for an ideal purity—is symbolized in his own mind by the desire to be a catcher in the rye. He wants to save little children from falling, even though he himself, as he comes to realize, is a child who needs to be saved. The effort to erase the words is thus an ultimate, desperate manifestation of his central motive. Though it is a futile gesture, since the world will never in this respect or any other conform fully to Holden's ideal of purity, it is produced by the very qualities in his character which make it possible for him to accept his sister's love at the end, give up his mad scheme of going west, and allow himself to be saved by love. It is clear that he is, for his sister, what she has become for him: a kind of catcher in the rye. Though he cannot protect her from knowledge of the world, though he cannot, as he would like, put her under a glass museum case and save her from the ravages of the sordid, time-bound world, he can at least offer her the love that comes naturally to him. He does so and he is saved. Which is of course why he is ecstatically happy at the end.

Now none of this is buried very deep in the novel. I've not had to probe any mystical world of symbols or literary trickery to find it out; it is all evident in the actions and words of Holden himself, and it is grasped intuitively, I have found, by most teen-age readers. Their misreadings are caused, in fact, by carrying this line too far: they often overlook Holden's deficiencies. So strong is the persuasive power of his obvious virtues (obvious to them) that they overlook his limitations of understanding and his destructive weaknesses: they take him at his word. They tend to overlook the strong and unanswerable criticism offered by his sister ("You don't like *any*thing that's happening") and by Antolini, who tries to teach him how to grow up ("The mark of the immature man is that he wants to die nobly for a cause, while the mark of the mature man is that he wants to live humbly for one"). They also overlook the author's many subtle contrasts between what Holden says and what he does. In learning to read these and other built-in criticisms, students can learn to criticize their own immaturities. They learn that such a book has been read only when they have seen Holden's almost saint-like capacity for love and compassion in the light of his urge to destroy the world, and even himself, because it cannot live up to his dreams.

I am aware that what I have said does not "prove" that *Catcher* is harmless. I'm sure there are some young people who might be harmed by it, just as reading the Bible has been known to work great harm on young idealists given to fanaticism. I have not even "proved" that the book can be beneficial. Only your own reading can convince you of that; . . .

[Perhaps] you will return to it now and try once more, moving from page 1 to page 277, thinking about Holden's moral life as you go. (pp. 162-63)

Wayne C. Booth, "Censorship and the Values of Fiction," in English Journal, *Vol. LIII, No. 3, March, 1964, pp. 155-64.*

JAMES E. MILLER, JR.

Holden Caulfield, the fumbling adolescent nauseated by the grossness of the world's body, may be the characteristic hero of contemporary fiction and the modern world. There can be no doubt that for today's American youth, Holden is an embodiment of their secret terrors and their accumulated hostilities, their slender joys and their magnified agonies. In his persistent innocence and his blundering virtue, he may represent to the rest of the world an adolescent America uncertainly searching for the lost garden, suspicious of alien or intimate entanglements, reluctant to encounter the horrors of reality.

No other writer since World War II has achieved the heights of popularity of J. D. (for Jerome David) Salinger. And his popularity has rested primarily on one hero, Holden Caulfield, and on one book, *The Catcher in the Rye.* (p. 5)

The Catcher in the Rye is a deceptively simple, enormously rich book whose sources of appeal run in deep and complexly varied veins. The very young are likely to identify with Holden and to see the adult world in which he sojourns as completely phony and worthless; the book thus becomes a handbook for rebels and a guide to identification of squares. The older generation is likely to identify with some part of the society that is satirized, and to see Holden as a bright but sick boy whose psyche needs adjustment before he can, as he will, find his niche and settle down. Holden as ideal rebel or Holden as neurotic misfit—the evidence for either interpretation lies loosely on the surface of the novel. Beneath the surface lies the evidence for a more complicated as well as more convincing Holden than some of his admirers are willing to recognize. (p. 8)

[A] skeleton of events in *Catcher* distorts the book considerably, and demonstrates how dependent it is on incidental detail, what might even be called plot irrelevancies, for its most moving and profound meanings. Such detail and such crucially relevant irrelevancies are woven into the book's very texture. Salinger is able to achieve this loose-seeming yet tightly woven structure through ingenious exploitation of his chosen point of view. Like Mark Twain in *Huckleberry Finn,* Salinger appears to have hit upon the perfect way of telling the tale—or of letting the tale tell itself. Holden speaks out in his own idiom, and although his clichés belong to us all, the intonation and gesture are his own—and they strike home. Moreover, Salinger carefully places Holden on the psychiatrist's couch in California, apparently on the way to some kind of recovery from his spiritual collapse (we learn on the opening page of the novel that D. B. may be driving him home the next month). This allows Holden a free play of mind around the events he recounts, enabling him to see them from a more objective perspective than he could possibly have had during their actual happening, and enabling him also to move back beyond those three critical days into his past in recollection of more distant excursions, encounters, and collisions that seem somehow to have a bearing on his predicament. This point of view results in the novel's marvelous richness of texture.

As the Holden on his journey is re-created for us by the Holden on the psychiatrist's couch, we recognize that the journey is more than movement through space—it is a movement, also, from innocence to knowledge, from self-ignorance to self-awareness, from isolation to involvement. . . . [Holden] penetrates to his own deception and his own phoniness, and is one more step on the way to the kind of involved awareness that will enable him at the end, after he has finished reconstructing his tale, to say: "About all I know is, I sort of *miss* everybody I told about." This knowledge, though it is casually presented in the closing lines of the book, is a difficult, profound, and mature knowledge that lies at the novel's center of gravity. It involves both a recognition that there can be no self-monopoly of innocence and a discovery that there can be no shield from complicity.

Holden's quest, then, may be stated in a number of ways. In one sense, his quest is a quest to preserve an innocence that is in peril of vanishing—the innocence of childhood, the spotless innocence of a self horrified at contamination in the ordinary and inevitable involvements of life. In another sense, the quest is a quest for an ideal but un-human love that will meet all demands but make none; a relationship so sensitively attuned that all means of communication, however subtle, will remain alertly open, and all the messages, in whatever language, will get through. Perhaps in its profoundest sense Holden's quest is a quest for identity, a search for the self—he does, for example, go through a number of guises, such as Rudolf Schmidt when he talks with his classmate's mother or Jim Steele when he is visited by the prostitute Sunny. But he remains, however he might wish to the contrary, Holden Caulfield, and the self he is led to discover is Holden's and none other. And that self he discovers is a human self and an involved self that cannot, finally, break what Hawthorne once called the "magnetic chain of humanity"; he cannot deny the love within him when he begins to miss all the people, "bastards" included, he has told about.

Holden vacillates throughout *Catcher* between the imperative of involvement and revulsion at involvement, and the result is a dual series of compelling images that act as magnets that both attract and repel. He is driven first to make some connection; like Whitman's "Noiseless Patient Spider," Holden launches forth filament after filament, but his "gossamer thread" never catches anywhere—until at the end it catches Phoebe in an entangled web from which Holden is obligated to release her. At the same time that he is casting forth, out of the agony of his loneliness, the filaments spun from his soul, Holden is repelled to the point of nausea (he is frequently about to puke or vomit) by the fundamental physicality of the human predicament. This inescapable physicality is a phenomenon of all human relationships, all human situations, by their very nature of being human. It is this terrible knowledge to which Holden must reconcile himself. Even a casual relationship with a schoolmate is heavily colored and shaped by the individual's imprisonment in his physical identity. . . . It is in a context of this kind that Holden's attitude toward sex, that most intense form of all human involvement, must be placed in order to comprehend both the fascination and the fear that he feels at its invocation. This ambivalence is portrayed vividly in the episode in which Holden looks out of his New York hotel window and is confronted by a series of scenes of sexual tragicomedy . . .

, and comments: "The trouble was, that kind of junk is sort of fascinating to watch, even if you don't want it to be. . . . Sometimes I can think of *very* crumby stuff I wouldn't mind doing if the opportunity came up." The insight is penetrating, and the understanding is a step beyond wisdom.

Just as one part of Holden drives him forward in his painful quest for some responsive relationship with people, in spite of the terror of the physical, another and deeper part urges his withdrawal and flight, and even the ultimate disengagement of death—the utter abandonment of physicality. A controlling image in this sequence is that of the abandoned ducks on the frozen lagoon in Central Park. Obviously Holden repeatedly sees his own plight symbolized by the forlorn and freezing ducks. Another image that recurs is Holden's dead brother Allie's baseball mitt, in which are inscribed the poems of Emily Dickinson (a poet whose dominant subject was death). Again and again, Holden (like Emily Dickinson) imagines his own death, as, for example, after the degrading incident with the hotel pimp and the prostitute:

> What I really felt like, though, was committing suicide. I felt like jumping out the window. I probably would've done it, too, if I'd been sure somebody'd cover me up as soon as I landed.

The tone of levity betrays just how deep the suicidal impulse is lodged—to surge again on later occasions dangerously near to the surface. Holden's fascinated interest in the Museum of Natural History, particularly in those human scenes (a squaw, an Eskimo) statically preserved behind glass, where nobody moves and nothing changes, no matter how many times you come back—this intense interest is clearly related in some subterranean way to his deepest instincts. (pp. 11-15)

On one level, **The Catcher in the Rye** may be read as a story of death and rebirth. It is symbolically relevant that the time of year is deep winter: it is the time of Christmas, a season of expiration and parturition. Holden is fated, at the critical age of sixteen years, to fall from innocence, to experience the death of the old self and to arise a new Holden to confront the world afresh—much like Ishmael and his symbolic immersion and resurrection at the end of *Moby Dick*. The metaphor of the fall is sounded again and again in the closing pages of the novel. Holden himself introduces it, when talking with Phoebe, in his vision of himself as the catcher in the rye. His own stance at the edge of the cliff, is, in fact, precarious; ironically he is unable to prevent his own imminent fall. Mr. Antolini sounds the warning for Holden, directly and fervently, when he tells him that he is heading for "a terrible, terrible fall". . . . It is only a short while after this warning that Holden awakens to find Mr. Antolini patting him on the head, abandons in panic this last refuge open to him, and starts to run—or fall—again. The precise motives behind Mr. Antolini's odd, but very human, gesture are obscure, as Holden himself comes shortly to realize: his patting Holden's head is, in its context, certainly a suggestive physical act; but it is also, surely, an act of profound, human, non-sexual affection, a gesture of the spirit as much as of the hand. Mr. Antolini's motives (he has been drinking) are no doubt muddled in his own mind. But Holden's shrinking back in horror from this physical touch, his immediate assumption that Mr. Antolini is a "flit" on the make, betrays his revulsion at the inevitable mixture of the dark and the light in any human act—a mixture inevitable because of the inescapable *physicality* of the

human condition. It is from this level of lofty innocence that Holden is doomed to fall. (pp. 15-16)

At Phoebe's school, he rubs out one obscenity only to be confronted with another, scratched deeply into the wall. He decides, "If you had a million years to do it in, you couldn't rub out even *half* the 'Fuck You' signs in the world. It's impossible." Holden is thus close to realizing the futility of any attempt to be a catcher in the rye: the kids cannot, in the world as it is, be shielded from the crazy cliff. While waiting at the Metropolitan Museum for Phoebe, Holden descends into the Egyptian tomb, where he finds it "nice and peaceful"—until he notices the obscenity once more, scrawled in red crayon, "under the glass part of the wall." He then imagines his own tombstone, displaying under his own name the revolting words of the obscenity.

At this point, Holden's horror and his dream, his revulsion at the world and his fantasy of death, come together in the image of his tombstone and he finds himself confronting the critical moment of decision—life or death; the world with all its obscenities or suicide with all its denials. The image of the tombstone bearing the obscenity suggests that suicide itself would be a kind of ultimate capitulation to the terrible physicality of life, an ironic involvement of the flesh at the very moment of abdication of the flesh. Death thus becomes not a gesture of defiance but of surrender. Holden feels both nausea and faintness, and he actually passes out momentarily, and falls to the floor, a final fall that marks the end of the descent. When he arises, he feels better; the crisis is past, the choice for life symbolically made, the slow ascent begun. Phoebe's spontaneous generosity expressed in her willingness to run away with him confirms his decision to stay, to become involved, and to rejoin the human race! In the closing pages of the novel, as he watches Phoebe, in her blue coat, go around and around on the carrousel, Holden becomes afraid that as she grabs for the gold ring, she will fall, but he restrains himself:

> The thing with kids is, if they want to grab for the gold ring, you have to let them do it, and not say anything. If they fall off, they fall off, but it's bad if you say anything to them.

Gone now is the dream of being the catcher in the rye. Whether in the fields of rye, or on the circular carrousel, children must eventually fall, as Holden has fallen. Holden can be happy—"so damn happy"—now in the knowledge that Phoebe is held by the magic and endless circle of the carrousel in a suspended state of perfect and impenetrable innocence; and his happiness can be intensified and rendered poignant in the mature awareness that the state is momentary, that the music will stop and the magic circle break, that the fall, finally, cannot be stayed. (pp. 16-18)

For all its seriousness, **Catcher in the Rye** is one of the funniest books in American literature, and much has been said relating its humor to the native American tradition, and particularly to Mark Twain's *Huckleberry Finn*. Perhaps of equal importance with its connections to the past is the role of **Catcher** in the development of the post-World War II "black" humor, the humor that has occasional elements of irresponsibility, cruelty, despair, and insanity. Examples are Wright Morris' *Ceremony in Lone Tree* (1960), Joseph Heller's *Catch-22* (1961), and Ken Kesey's *One Flew over the Cuckoo's Nest* (1962). One small episode in **Catcher** will suggest its place in this new direction of contemporary American humor. After leaving the Antolini apartment, as Holden is wandering in a daze about the streets, he comes upon a small vignette that seems to sum up the weird incongruities of modern life as he has encountered it:

> I passed these two guys that were unloading this big Christmas tree off a truck. One guy kept saying to the other guy, 'Hold the sonuvabitch *up!* Hold it *up,* for Chrissake!' It certainly was a gorgeous way to talk about a Christmas tree. It was sort of funny, though, in an awful way, and I started to sort of laugh. It was about the *worst* thing I could've done, because the minute I started to laugh I thought I was going to vomit. I really did, I even started to, but it went away. I don't know why.

It is, of course, *for the sake of Christ* that the tree has been reaped and hauled and now put into place. But the mover's remark, "Hold it *up,* for Chrissake," is only ironically and absurdly an invocation of this now lost original meaning, embedded like a fossil in language—the language not of a blessing but of a curse.

Absurdity, nausea—these terms seem recurrently relevant to Holden's predicament as he hangs suspended between laughter and sickness. And is not Holden's predicament in some sense the modern predicament? At one point he remarks:

> I'm sort of glad they've got the atomic bomb invented. If there's ever another war, I'm going to sit right the hell on top of it. I'll volunteer for it, I swear to God I will.

Perhaps the post-World War II comedy of blackness points the way of endurance in an insanely reeling world: if we do not at times feel nausea at contemporary horrors, we are, in a way, already dead; if we cannot occasionally laugh at contemporary absurdities, we shall in the darkness of our despair soon die. (pp. 18-19)

James E. Miller, Jr., in his J. D. Salinger, *University of Minnesota Press, Minneapolis, 1965, 48 p.*

WARREN FRENCH

Unquestionably the novelist who dominated the 50s was J. D. Salinger, whose generally available writings are contained in four rather slender volumes—***The Catcher in the Rye, Nine Stories*** (1953), ***Franny and Zooey*** (1961), and ***"Raise High the Roof Beam, Carpenters"*** and ***"Seymour: An Introduction"*** (1963), all composed of material originally published between 1948 and 1959. Despite his limited production Salinger with his complementary creations of Holden Caulfield and Seymour Glass (both surrounded by siblings) so captivated the fancies of the Americans of this intellectually and emotionally arid era that the decade of the 50s can justly be called from more than a literary point of view "The Age of Salinger." (pp. 12-13)

Certainly no writer has won a remotely similar place in American affections during the 60s; nor did any single writer so largely monopolize readers during any earlier decade. Because of the singular relationship between Salinger and the years of the "silent generation," it would seem that we might learn something about the feelings of the inarticulate youth of the period by examining the assumptions underlying the fiction of the writer that most attracted them.

First, though, we must bear in mind that Salinger was not universally acclaimed during the 50s. His works have always

polarized opinion. ***The Catcher in the Rye*** was widely denounced and rejected. Older critics dismissed it impatiently; school boards and self-appointed professional moralists objected to its colloquial style and obscene language. Although some older readers had the perceptiveness to admire Salinger, his novel appealed principally to high school and college students; and he is important — among other things — as one of the earliest chroniclers of the now formidable "generation gap." (pp. 24-5)

Holden surely spoke for many of his contemporaries even if they didn't always recognize his message. The 50s were a period of supreme disillusionment. Men had fought for years and millions had died in the hope of defeating the forces of evil and madness and creating a better world; but by 1949 it was painfully apparent that the Western Allies had enjoyed a material triumph, but a spiritual defeat. Sheer physical power and technical know-how had brought the fanatical Germans and Japanese to their knees; but with the slicing up of Germany and Korea, the collapse of China, the erection of an iron curtain, suspicion drove out love. People, it was demonstrated, could band together to die, but could not learn to live together. The naive idealism of American and British wartime leaders was directly or indirectly discredited, while obsessively vindictive men like Stalin and smiling hollow men like Eisenhower flourished.

Most people of the 50s resembled Holden Caulfield. When he says, "If you want to stay alive, you have to say that stuff," he speaks for his readers. Extraordinarily for a book that has been so frequently and intensively read, ***The Catcher in the Rye*** has often been completely misinterpreted. Both youthful partisans and older fault-finders have viewed the novel as an account of a callow rebellion against pompous propriety. On the contrary, the book preaches not rebellion, but resignation. More than that, it is not even romantic in its approach. Jacques Barzun in *Classic, Romantic, and Modern* explains the difference between the first two of these views of life as they are exemplified by works of Descartes and Goethe:

> In the romantic view, the lesson of Faust has to be relearned individually through experience. The lesson of Descartes can presumably be learned from reading the remainder of the *Discourse on Method.* Descartes has alone done the perilous work; he has taken the risks and wrested the true answers from his experiences. The lesson that Faust learns can only be found in the undergoing of experience itself.

The clearest indication of the intention of ***The Catcher in the Rye*** is found in Holden's remark after spending a night in the waiting room at Grand Central Station, "It wasn't too nice. Don't ever try it. I mean it. It'll depress you." Even at the climax of the novel, though Holden realizes that kids can't be protected from falling over "some crazy cliff," he continues to tell *the reader* what to do, "The thing with kids is, if they want to grab for the gold ring, you have to let them do it, and not say anything." Holden is not a Romantic urging his readers — like the later Beatniks — to go "on the road" and discover life for themselves. Barzun's remark about Descartes applies exactly to Holden as Salinger presents him, he "has alone done the perilous work; he has taken the risks and wrested the true answers from his experiences." The reader can learn his lesson by reading the book. Far from encouraging rebellion and flight, Salinger attempts to make ***The Catcher in the Rye*** a surrogate for them, so that the reader by vicariously sharing Holden's depressing experiences need not himself undergo a parallel ordeal.

Although few young readers could probably have articulated their response to the book and although few of them probably even tried to analyze this response (as Holden said of Jesus, "He didn't have time to go around analyzing everybody"), many of them probably were provided by the novel with the vicarious experience that enabled them to compromise with their own private, impractical dreams — the aesthetic resolution of their frustrations. In the many battles that have raged over *The Catcher in the Rye,* few have noted that the novel is a virtually flawless fictional embodiment of the traumatic experience of accepting the destruction of one's illusions as the price for moving from childhood to manhood. One of my students, Greg Naganuma, expresses the concept behind the book memorably when he writes that the "responsibility" of education is to help one "to learn to compromise with his surroundings." The book depicts the moral growth that is the necessary complement to Holden's rapid physical growth if he is not to remain — like so many Americans — a child in an adult's body. The picture that the novel offers of this painful process of maturation is likely to be the quality that will insure its survival when its fascinating portrayal of a particular era becomes of only historical interest.

Something else that the horde glossing *The Catcher in the Rye* has failed to notice is that Holden Caulfield is a masochist. He discloses an irrational aspect of his personality when he comments after looking out the window of a hotel of the "perverts" in the other rooms, "The trouble was, that kind of junk is sort of fascinating to watch, even if you don't want it to be." On other occasions, he observes, "I hate the movies like poison, but I get a bang imitating them" and, after a fight with a pimp who is attempting to cheat him, "I had blood all over my mouth and chin and even on my pajamas and bathrobe. It partly scared me and it partly fascinated me." Most significantly, at the end of the book he climaxes his recital of his new feelings of communality with the statement, "I think I even miss that goddam Maurice." Maurice, the pimp, is the man who has hurt Holden most both physically and ethically (by taking deliberate advantage of his naivete). Holden recognizes that an acceptance of the world involves an acceptance of suffering. Reflecting on the "perverty bum" who he imagines wrote the obscene phrase on the wall of Phoebe's school, Holden writes,

> I kept wanting to kill whoever'd written it. . . . I kept picturing myself catching him at it, and how I'd smash his head on the stone steps till he was good and goddam dead and bloody. But I knew, too, I wouldn't have the guts to do it. I knew that. That made me even more depressed. I hardly even had the guts to rub it off the wall with my *hand,* if you want to know the truth. I was afraid some teacher would catch me rubbing it off and would think *I'd* written it.

Again Holden serves as a perfect reflector of his time. He not only knows that he is incapable of initiating any risky positive action to benefit others because he feels his motives may be misconstrued by the authorities. He is in precisely the position of the conscientious but timid people of the 50s who were intimidated by the irresponsible persecution of the Joseph McCarthys. Everyone could envision himself as the kind of victim of "guilt-by-association" that Dr. J. Robert Oppenheimer became. As a result a significant portion of our society was morally immobilized at a time when constructive action

was desperately needed to avert a racial crisis at home and to support dynamic rather than decadent regimes abroad (like those in China and Viet Nam). *The Catcher in the Rye* gratified its audience not only by providing it with an aesthetic resolution of its frustrations in a colloquial language that it could understand, but also by providing it with the consolation of an understanding portrayal of its irresolute and irrational behavior. Salinger imposed upon a tacky age the style that it lacked. (pp. 27-30)

Holden's old teacher Antolini urges upon Holden a quotation from Wilhelm Stekel, " 'The mark of the immature man is that he wants to die nobly for a cause, while the mark of the mature man is that he wants to live humbly for one.' " Whether Antolini is good angel or devil's advocate (and I doubt that Salinger accepts the idea that to die nobly for a cause is a mark of immaturity), the statement that he treasures does express what Salinger conceives to be the only alternatives open to people. Either one lives humbly (as Holden will if he continues to accept suffering) for a cause or one dies nobly for it. Salinger seems to reject the Socratic possibility of leading the truly "examined life" (like Jesus, one doesn't have time to go around "analyzing everybody"), but so probably did most of his contemporaries, too caught up in the "rat race" to have the leisure or even the inclination to scrutinize their own and other's behavior. (p. 31)

Since the end of the 50s Salinger's works — though still widely read and admired — have declined in popularity. Sensitive youth has turned activist in the 60s, and Salinger does not speak as clearly to a dynamic generation as he did to a passive one. The shortcoming of the quite justified attitude of withdrawal from the world held by sensitive people of the 50s is that it is self-indulgent. By assuming that any effort to improve conditions is going to be defeated and will probably simply get one into trouble, one can rationalize a failure even to make any effort. Celebrity is undoubtedly accompanied by formidable problems; but Salinger's characters — and Salinger himself — never tried to surmount these problems. Instead he withdrew into his own "inverted forest" in New Hampshire. While it is undeniable that too many public demands may be destructive of one's career, so also may too much isolation from the world. Brooding in his retreat over the history of the Glass family, Salinger lost touch with a changing world.

His behavior is, of course, his own business; but our concern is not with Salinger the man so much as with Salinger the spokesman for the 50s. His resigned refusal to try to make the world come around to his terms is characteristic of his audience's. The result is that an entire generation of Americans lacked either any constructive ideas or the will to implement them. (pp. 37-8)

"The Age of Salinger" provides compelling reasons for describing as sentimental and decadent an "either/or" vision which perceives defeat or death as the only alternatives in the struggle between the affectionate individual and squalid society. None of Salinger's characters ever expresses the attitude championed by Marlow in Conrad's *Heart of Darkness* that "for good or evil mine is the speech that cannot be silenced."

What a writer has his characters say is, of course, as much his own business as his attitude toward the world. What matters is not that a defeatist attitude underlies Salinger's work, but that works embodying such an attitude were extremely popular during the 50s. Salinger's writings have sometimes been called "decadent" for the wrong reasons by unthinking people reacting automatically to words or incidents in the stories. Perhaps in the long run the most important contribution made by *The Catcher in the Rye* to the development of American literature was the novel's providing the perennially necessary refurbishing of the colloquial idiom; and Salinger needed to "invent" very few of the things that happen to Holden. As the poet in "The Inverted Forest" insisted one should, the novelist "found" his material by observing the world around him.

The Catcher in the Rye is, however, like most of Salinger's work, decadent from one point of view because it expresses a hopeless acquiescence in squalor. "It didn't seem at all like Christmas was coming soon. It didn't seem like *any* thing was coming," Holden Caulfield says at one point as he surveys Central Park. Christmas had become a commercial orgy, not the mystical celebration of a promised rejuvenation of the world. It did look to the people of the 50s indeed as if "nothing was coming." It was a black-and-white decade — the white of horrified faces slashed with the black of willful violence. It was not one of those eras whose features we necessarily crave to see fixed in art; but the era found in J. D. Salinger the artist who fixed those features. Through his work those of us who endured the 50s can re-experience them (from an aesthetic distance, happily) and those who did not can grasp the feeling of living in that age of decadent apathy as they cannot such periods as the campy 60s, which seem not to have found their artistic match, or the fearful 40s, which were too much for any one man to contain. (pp. 38-9)

> *Warren French, "The Age of Salinger," in* the Fifties: Fiction, Poetry, Drama, *edited by Warren French, Everett/Edwards, Inc., 1970, pp. 1-39.*

MYRA POLLACK SADKER AND DAVID MILLER SADKER

The problems confronting characters . . . [in literature for young adults], problems related to self-understanding and the quest for acceptance, are typical and sometimes critical issues during early adolescence. The older teenager also faces a difficult and demanding period of maturation. On the verge of adulthood, the adolescent must deal with a growing awareness of sexuality, decisions about future adult roles, and perhaps friction with parents and other adults. Although portraying these problems with sensitivity and humor presents a great challenge, it is a challenge that several authors have successfully met. Certainly one of the earliest and most influential of these books is J. D. Salinger's *The Catcher in the Rye*.

In many ways *The Catcher in the Rye* set a precedent for the humorous adolescent novel. Holden Caulfield's interaction with society uncovers artificial and phony adults holding empty values. The book is written in the first person, with candor and humor, and although it was not originally written for adolescents, they have taken it as their own. The penetrating honesty, the unmasking of societal pretense, and the first-person narrative of a teenager are characteristics that have made *The Catcher in the Rye* immensely popular with teenagers, the object of widespread censorship, and an influential precedent for other authors.

> *Myra Pollack Sadker and David Miller Sadker, in a review of "The Catcher in the Rye," in their* Now Upon a Time: A Contemporary View of Children's Literature, *Harper & Row, Publishers, 1977, p. 346.*

KENNETH L. DONELSON AND ALLEEN PACE NILSEN

Intrigued and concerned as many young adults were about social issues and dilemmas, something far more immediate constantly pressed in upon them [during the years 1940 to 1966]—their own personal need to survive in an often unfriendly world. . . .

Survival was hardly the theme of many popular writers for girls. The watchword for Janet Lambert was acceptance. . . .

After Lambert there was a deluge of girls' books detailing their emotional traumas, but almost entirely ignoring their physical concerns. (p. 163)

Superior to the earlier authors, Anne Emery certainly preached acceptance of the status quo, especially acceptance of parental rules, but she offered better books that proved popular with young adult women. . . .

At the same time conventional girls' books appeared, Mina Lewiton dealt with far more suspect, even controversial, topics. . . . Later, Zoa Sherburne proved more enduring with her portrait of alcohol's effect in *Jennifer*. . . .

But something far more significant and enduring appeared during the same years that the personal problem novel seemed supreme. The *Bildungsroman,* a novel about the initiation, maturation, and education of a young adult, began to grow in appeal. The number of such books, most of them originally published for adults but soon read by young adults, appearing from 1940 onward was prodigious. (p. 164)

But no book won the young adult favor or the adult opposition that J. D. Salinger's *The Catcher in the Rye* did. Still the most widely censored book in American schools, and still hated by people who assume that a disliked word (*that* word) corrupts an entire book, *Catcher* has been avidly read ever since it became a selection of the Book-of-the-Month Club. Holden Caulfield may indeed be what so many have accused him of being, vulgar and cynical and capable of seeing only the phonies around him, but he is also loyal and loving to those he sees as good or innocent. His struggle to preserve innocence leads him to the brink and a mental breakdown. *Catcher* is many things, literary, profane, sensitive, cynical. For many young adults it is the most honest and human story they know about someone they recognize—even in themselves—a young man caught between childhood and maturity and unsure which way to go. Whether *Catcher* is a masterpiece like James Joyce's *Portrait of an Artist as a Young Man* depends on subjective judgment, but there is no question that Salinger's book captured—and continues to capture—the hearts and minds of countless young adults as no other book has. (pp. 164-65)

> *Kenneth L. Donelson and Alleen Pace Nilsen, in a review of "The Catcher in the Rye," in their* Literature for Today's Young Adults, *Scott, Foresman and Company, 1980, pp. 163-65.*

LAWRENCE JAY DESSNER

J. D. Salinger's *The Catcher in the Rye* has long since been accused of several million counts of impairing the morals of a minor. He has doled out candy which rots more than the victim's teeth; he has thrown us apples in which fragments of razor blades were embedded. And as we became dizzy, as our lips bled, he smiled down at us—a smile that said, Yes, Yes, minds are made to go soft, lips to bleed; blood *is* sweet, and so is the taste and smell of our soul's surrender. So while a few have found Salinger a pernicious influence, the many have gratefully applauded what he did to them. He gave them Holden Caulfield, an idealization of their worst selves, to cherish. While they were doing so, their best selves, their potential to be, in whatever way, better, was ignored, despised, unexercised, indefinitely postponed. (p. 91)

Beware of the novelists bearing gifts. The more delicious and enthralling the gifts, the more wary we must be. Best of the sweets Salinger has Holden giftwrap and deliver to us is the idea that to the degree that we like Holden Caulfield we were better than anyone who doesn't. The method of Salinger's flamboyant and insidious flattery goes like this: Line up all the people in the world who we, in our weakness, our failures of sympathy, our ignorance, our narrow-mindedness, have ever allowed ourselves to hate. Include in this line-up caricatures of people we know we should not have hated. (Once having hated them, we have a vested interest in seeing them worthy of hatred.) Include persons we hated because we knew they were better than we were. (There is nothing like jealousy to prompt and sustain hate.) Now introduce before that line-up a tortured, bleeding and sublimely "cute" victim of all the insults and injuries all of us have ever imagined ourselves to have suffered. Let this victim be on the edge of insanity, the result, of course, of what others have done to him. Let him ooze the sentimental notion that the doctrine of Original Sin, and all its modern parallels, have been revoked. This is crucial. Not only does it let our victim be perfect, it removes any excuse the evil-doers might otherwise offer on their behalf. Let our victim believe that what the world needs now is not love, not even Coca-Cola, but that fool's gold, Sincerity. He himself has it of course, and some of it rubs off on his admirers, but no one else has it at all. Now the scene is set and the action commences. Blood in his eyes and trickling from his battered little nose, our victim raises a machine-gun and shoots everyone lined up before him. And he cries, weeps, as he does so. You see, utterly guilty as his tormentors are, he forgives them, he likes them! (p. 93)

We have no reason to assume that Salinger's attitudes differ from those of Holden Caulfield. It is the author's obligation to unmistakably untangle himself from his hero, or at least to give the reader the means to discover their relationship. But Salinger does neither. It seems absurd that a grown man, and a literate man at that, should hold the jejune opinions of Holden Caulfield. But he does and he lacks the grace or courage to say so outright, in or out of the novel. There isn't a whisper of any other view of life emanating from either quarter. We must take Salinger's silence in the novel to give consent. He is evidently angry that with the exception of himself—and his Holden—sincerity is in very short supply. . . . Perfect sincerity requires and implies perfect spontaneity. And of course this utterly denies all the arts of life as well as the arts of Art. How does one know, Holden inquires, if the lawyer who has saved his client's life did so because "he really *wanted* to save guys' lives, or because . . . what [he] *really* wanted to do was to be a terrific lawyer, with everybody slapping [him] on the back and congratulating [him] in court when the goddam trial was over". This is the question Holden asks of everyone. Its force is rhetorical. Holden wants a guarantee of the purity of human motive. He has been given everything else he wanted, but this complete absolution, of himself and his world, he cannot have. He cries "phoney," and takes up his bat and ball and leaves the game. We are to play by his rules or His Holiness will not play with us.

There is little point in using Salinger's text to show that Holden himself behaves with less than perfect kindness, less than Saintly sincerity. And to take that line against this novel is to accept its premise. *The Catcher in the Rye* urges the young to destroy their own, their only world, and to take refuge in their own soft dream-world peopled by themselves and by shadows of their perfected selves. No adolescent has ever entirely avoided this temptation. All of us had what used to be called "growing pains," fell into what used to be called a "brown study." Among the very rich, in our very rich country, all pleasures, no matter how self-deluding and self-defeating, no matter how selfish, are seized upon, and sold, and admired. Holden is a child of wealth, and most children wish they were too. The richer one is, the longer one may prolong one's adolescence. That is what Holden Caulfield is doing, and what Salinger and his admirers, are praising. (p. 95)

Those of us of a "certain age," brought up in the same streets and schools as Holden Caulfield, may be especially susceptible to Salinger's siren song. The present writer, along with a goodly percentage of our country's literati, shared Holden Caulfield's environment. We wondered about the ducks in Central Park lakes. We enjoyed a good cry about the sadness of life, the disappointments, the rain falling on our tennis courts. We too, in Salinger's most un-mean streets, discovered puberty, the painful way. But we managed to grow up, more or less; to see that it was not true, ever, that everybody was out of step but ourselves, to see that the words "compromise," "compassion," "tact," even "hypocrisy," were not obscenities which desecrated God's creation, but marks of the fact that none of us was, himself, God.

Holden's youthful idealism, his bitterness toward the world he never made might have, had a Holden himself come before us, made for a successful novel. What could be funnier than the confessions of such a one as he? And while we would laugh at Holden, he would be laughing at us. How young we were, how charmingly silly. We could have had some good laughs, shed a tear for auld lang syne, shaken hands all round, and been on our way. But Salinger's Holden Caulfield is made of soggy cardboard. The death of his younger brother Allie hangs over his story forbidding anyone in it more than a momentary laugh. That death, utterly unrelated to the vapid social criticism which is Holden's prime activity, should have made Holden atypical, a special case whose opinions may be regarded only as pointers to his private distress. But Salinger ignores this; evidently he wants Holden's opinions on the general condition of society to be highly regarded, and he wants no one involved, character, author, reader, critic, to see his story as a comedy. We must, out of courtesy, courtesy that has been uncourteously forced upon us, take it all with high seriousness. Salinger needs the dead Allie in his novel so that we may not laugh. Yet the story itself is the quintessential comedy, the story of maturity looking back, with a wince and a smile and a guffaw at its own immaturity.

No character of Holden Caulfield is the only certifiable "phoney" in the novel. No youth, no matter how emotionally shaken, goes so long, so seriously single-mindedly after his real and imagined enemies. When the real Holden Caulfields encounter the terrors, such as they are, of their gilded ghettoes, they stumble every now and then on those insights which will add up to their definition of being grown-up. Not Holden. His larger considerations are bogus. He meanders about as if he were free to find out about things for himself, free to stumble on the other sides of the "phoney" question, to learn why people behave the way they do. But Salinger has put blinders around the boy. He never learns anything; never considers anything antagonistic to his sustaining faith that everything and everybody is wrong. It is as if Holden grew up at the knee of Abbie Hoffman—but even that is more funny than true. No matter how doctrinaire the upbringing, bright boys have a way of seeing around the blinders their elders set in place. But then Holden is not a real boy at all; he is Salinger's dream-boy, the boy who will not grow up. He is immaturity's best defense, a non-stop assault on maturity.

But after all this we really should petition the court to reduce the charge brought against Mr. Salinger. Boys being what we know them to be, despite the example of Holden, the crime is not impairment of the morals of a minor, but only attempted impairment. No real harm will be done by this book, unless professors succeed in making it a classic. *The Catcher in the Rye* is no more than an insult to all boys, to us who have been boys, and to the girls and ex-girls too. It is an insult to childhood and to adulthood. It is an insult to our ideas of civilization, to our ideal land in which ladies and gentlemen try to grow up, try to find and save their dignity. (pp. 95-7)

> Lawrence Jay Dessner, *"The Salinger Story, or, Have It Your Way,"* in Seasoned "Authors" for a New Season: The Search for Standards in Popular Writing, *edited by Louis Filler, Bowling Green University Popular Press, 1980, pp. 91-7.*

JUNE EDWARDS

Still heading the list of favorite books to be censored . . . is the classic story of a teenager's quest for maturity, J.D. Salinger's *The Catcher in the Rye.* "Obscene" is the usual cry, based on the four-letter words. "Blasphemous" claim the protestors over the boy's caustic comments about religious hypocrisy. *Catcher* has become a symbol for critics of what they perceive to be a vile, ungodly plot on the part of schools to undermine the morals of American school children.

Book selectors, of course, do not agree. They choose *Catcher* for the library or classroom on a number of important bases—literary quality, interest, readability, and relevance as well as moral worth. Protestors censor the book on only one—"immorality." When a book has been thus labeled, educators must confront the charge directly if they wish to protect their right to choose worthwhile books. English teachers are prone to defend a controversial book on the basis of literary merit rather than moral worth. That is like defending a prisoner on the basis of his achievements when he has been charged with murder. He may be an outstanding engineer, but it won't convince a jury he did not murder his wife. Likewise, though a book may have many character witnesses as to its literary quality, unless we address the issue of morality, we will not convince critics, judges, or the public that it should remain in the classroom.

Is *The Catcher in the Rye* immoral as censors claim? It depends on how one defines immorality. Certainly if one sees it as any work that contains "dirty" words, refers to a sexual act, or questions religious dogma, no matter what the content, then *Catcher* fits the description. One does not have to read the book. Just flip a few pages and the offending words and passages can be easily spotted.

But there are other ways to define *morality.* . . . First, schools in a democratic society can claim the early docu-

ments of our nation as a legitimate authority for determining society's definition of morality. The Constitution, for instance, states that "all men are created equal." If one uses "men" in its generic sense, the moral tenet is that each person has the right to be treated with equal respect and dignity. . . .

Second, over the centuries, philosophers have espoused numerous ways of evaluating moral behavior. (p. 39)

Third, philosophers in recent years have developed theories about morality as a result of empirical research into human behavior. Most notable is Lawrence Kohlberg's work on moral reasoning. Basing his studies on the work of Dewey and Piaget, Kohlberg redefined their concepts through longitudinal and cross-cultural means until he developed his six stages. The most advanced stage contains such universal, abstract principles as justice, human rights, and respect for individuals. . . .

The New Testament is not the only available source for moral reasoning, but it is a strong one. Since it is used by critics to attack books, it can be used by educators to defend them. . . .

What, then, is moral about *The Catcher in the Rye?* Let us look at some examples from the story that show the New Testament definition of morality in action. One of the most endearing qualities of the teenage protagonist is his empathy for other people, especially those whom others reject. The story opens with Holden Caulfield skipping a football game at his elite boys' school to visit an infirm, elderly history teacher. Thanksgiving vacation is near and Holden has heard he must leave school after Christmas because of failing grades. The boy realizes "Old Spencer" will lecture him about not fulfilling his potential, and he doesn't like seeing old men in their pajamas with "their bumpy old chests" and their legs "so white and unhairy." But he goes anyway out of respect for a teacher who cares about his subject and his students. On the last test Holden wrote an apology to Spencer for doing poorly, "so he wouldn't feel so bad about flunking me." For a sixteen-year-old to worry about an elderly teacher's feelings is moral behavior. To visit the sick man is even more so.

Other people in Holden's life also benefit from his caring attitude. Everybody hates Ackley. Besides snoring loudly, he has "sinus trouble, pimples, lousy teeth, halitosis, crumby fingernails." But, says Holden, "You had to feel a little sorry for the crazy sonuvabitch." Holden is the only one who does. Though Ackley irritates him, he never turns him away. (p. 40)

Family unity is a moral value espoused by the New Testament and by critics of *The Catcher in the Rye.* No teenager could demonstrate more love and respect for his family than Holden Caulfield. He admires his father's abilities as a corporation lawyer, his mother's taste in clothes and decorating (typical reactions for the 50s), and his older brother's skill as a writer in Hollywood. He shows special affection for his ten-year-old sister, Phoebe. . . .

Catcher's leading character is not rebelling against parental values. He is roaming the streets of New York because he wants to protect his family from the hurt he thinks his failure will bring. In the end, it is his love for Phoebe, and her love for him, that ends his escapades, keeps him in the family circle, and restores his self-respect.

Holden is a virgin. He tells us that right off. Despite all the thoughts typical of an adolescent, and "quite a few opportunities," he has set a limit. . . . When a girl tells him to stop, he says, he stops. He never wants to hurt or offend. . . .

The poignant scene [with the prostitute] dispels any belief that Holden is anything but a mixed-up adolescent with a strong sense of values.

Like Jesus who became incensed over the behavior of the scribes and pharisees, *Catcher*'s main character rails against those who behave one way in public and another in private. (p. 41)

He sees the school as manufacturing a public image that belies reality—a type of hypocrisy not uncommon in educational institutions.

Religious phoniness upsets him even more. Holden considers himself an atheist, but he "likes Jesus and all." The disciples, however, are another matter. They were all right after Jesus died, he says, but while he was alive "they were as much use to Him as a hole in the head. All they did was keep letting him down." Loyalty is a very strong value for Holden. His own predicament stems from the belief that he himself is letting down his family and is thus unworthy of their love.

While still in New York, the boy invites an old girlfriend to see the Christmas program at Radio City Hall. It is supposed to be a religious theme, but Holden cannot "see anything religious or pretty, for God's sake, about a bunch of actors carrying crucifixes all over the stage. When they finished . . . you could tell they could hardly wait to get a cigarette or something." Religion, in his mind, should be simple, not gawdy and profit-making. (pp. 41-2)

In contrast to the show-biz religion at Radio City Hall, Holden meets two nuns in the lunchroom at the train station carrying cheap suitcases. . . . Their humility and gentleness epitomize for Holden what religion ought to be.

Jesus stated that one must become like a little child before one can enter the Kingdom of God. The innocence and simplicity of children holds an especial appeal for Holden as well. He demonstrates repeatedly his love for his sister. He empathizes with a little boy in a movie whose mother will not take him to the bathroom. He shows two young brothers how to find the mummies in the public museum. . . .

Toward the end of the book, Holden goes to Phoebe's school to send her a note. He sees the words "Fuck You" scrawled on the wall and goes crazy. He thinks of how Phoebe and the other children will wonder what it means. He wants to kill whoever wrote the words, to smash his head against the stone steps. Finally, he rubs them off with his hands, afraid somebody will think *he* wrote them. The scene illustrates Holden's main wish, to protect children from getting a "cockeyed" version of sex from "some dirty kid." Obviously, sex for him is not an obscenity but an act of love between two people who respect each other.

In this sometimes funny, sometimes painful, novel of a teenager's search for self-worth and values, the protagonist uses

words typical of an insecure young man trying to appear grown-up. He tries out sexual ventures, only to retreat when he oversteps his moral limits. He drinks to escape the fear of hurting his family and falls into depression. None of this is painted as glamorous. None is likely to entice other teenagers to go and do likewise.

Contrary to the claims of the censors, *The Catcher in the Rye* is a moral book. Whether one takes as a basis for morality the teachings of Jesus, the documents of our democracy, Kohlberg's levels of moral reasoning, or some other source, Holden Caulfield emerges as a confused but moral person. He befriends the friendless. He respects those who are humble, loyal, and kind. He demonstrates a strong love for his family. He abhors hypocrisy. He values sex that comes from caring for another person and rejects its sordidness. And, finally, he wants to be a responsible member of society, to guide and protect those younger than he. What greater morality can one want from a novel? (p. 42)

June Edwards, "Censorship in the Schools: What's Moral about 'The Catcher in the Rye'?" in English Journal, *Vol. 72, No. 4, April, 1983, pp. 39-42.*

HUMPHREY CARPENTER

In the mid-1950s there began in England what has often been described as a second Golden Age of children's literature. (p. 214)

Up to this point America, with only a few notable exceptions, had produced three general types of children's fiction: the family story, the historical novel, and the animal story. . . . But abruptly in 1951 all that changed. J. D. Salinger's *The Catcher in the Rye,* published that year, was not a children's book, but was seminal in altering American writers' attitudes to children and their relationship to the adult world and adult morality. Holden Caulfield, the novel's hero, has an aggressive, detached, ultra-critical view of adult society which appealed instantly to American teenage readers of the 1950s. Some of those readers themselves became, in following years, children's authors, and wrote fiction for the young dealing (often in a style closely resembling Salinger's) with adversity, the acceptance of responsibility, and the child or adolescent's awareness of the foibles and fallibility of adults. These subjects could scarcely have been admitted into the canon of American children's writing before 1945, except in the hands of such subtly subversive authors as Louisa Alcott and Frank Baum. In recent decades, with novels on these subjects by such accomplished 'realist' American children's writers as E. L. Konigsburg, Paula Fox, Vera and Bill Cleaver, and Robert Cormier, the children's book in America would appear, in every sense, to have 'grown up'. (pp. 214-15)

Humphrey Carpenter, "Epilogue: The Garden Revisited," in his Secret Gardens: A Study of the Golden Age of Children's Literature, *Houghton Mifflin Company, 1985, pp. 210-23.*

Sonia Sanchez

1934-

(Born Wilsonia Driver) Black American poet, author of picture books and fiction, and editor.

As a writer for children, Sanchez has vowed to impress black youngsters, as leaders and parents of the future, with the importance of maintaining a distinct racial identity. In *It's a New Day: Poems for Young Brothas and Sistuhs* (1971), she couples this theme with Islamic ideology to form verse in which she strives to instruct her audience to learn about their African heritage and to reject the damaging influences of drugs and prostitution. Sanchez is also a well-respected poet and playwright for adults, for whom she holds forth the same forceful message: it is essential for blacks to be proud of their race and to earn self-love. For Sanchez, this is the means by which the black community will grow strong and will attain freedom from oppression. A writer who consciously repudiates standard conventions, Sanchez speaks eloquently in emotionally-charged vernacular in her poetry, employing black idiom and vigorously emphasizing the genre's oral tradition as signs of the significance of racial identity. She writes her verse to be read aloud, with cadence carefully dictated by her use of punctuation and caesuras. Sanchez does, in fact, give frequent poetry readings in which she touches young audiences with her fervor and unfailing confidence in her race. In addition to her poetry for children, Sanchez has written a fable, *The Adventures of Fathead, Smallhead, and Squarehead* (1973), its sequel *The Afternoon of Fathead, Smallhead, and Squarehead* (1974), and a collection of short stories, *A Sound Investment* (1980), as well as a volume of poetry for adults, *We a BaddDDD People* (1969), which has been used in classroom curricula.

(See also *Something about the Author*, Vol. 22; *Contemporary Authors*, Vols. 33-36, rev. ed.; and *Dictionary of Literary Biography*, Vol. 41: *Afro-American Poets Since 1955*.)

AUTHOR'S COMMENTARY

[*The following excerpt is from an interview by Herbert Leibowitz.*]

HL: How does black dialect and the vitality and humor of street talk get into your poems?

SS: That happens from listening and talking and speaking, not just as an adult but as a little girl. Not, interestingly enough, as an Alabamian, not those eight years in Alabama. My memory is very quick on that because when we came to New York City I remember we didn't have a southern accent—you know how people expect you to have a southern accent? Well, we didn't—and we had not even eaten chitterlings. We spoke very tactfully, very properly, no street talk. My father was a schoolteacher in Alabama. But we learned street talk because everyone else outside the house spoke it. I learned it consciously. (p. 358)

HL: You have a very good ear for street talk.

SS: My stepmother, who was a very interesting woman, spoke what I call black English. I remember coming home from school and carrying on dual conversations with her. In school, they were pulling us to get beyond ourselves, beyond our "defects." But I used to listen to the students who would not conform in class, the hip kids. I would walk with them sometimes and think, "that's really a great way of saying it." But above all, I remember my grandmother, who also spoke in black English. She was not an educated woman but I remember listening to her imagery. . . . I remember taking her words sometimes and repeating them. "Why?" she would ask. "Because I like to float into words," I answered. Now that was a child's way of saying that her words were beautiful and couched in interesting similes and images. I could really see them floating. And she was so permissive and loving that she allowed the imitations. She knew I wasn't mocking her. She gave me that language. Now I hear some little kid out in the street acting tough and sassy and speaking black English, and I'll stop and talk to him and say, "isn't that pretty?"

HL: Black kids invent metaphors with ease?

SS: Their metaphors are unbelievable. I taught one of the first courses in black English at San Francisco State. The English Department was wondering what in the hell I was going to do. I shrugged. "I know how the students will greet me, how nervous they'll be in the classroom. I'm going to let them understand that black English exists alongside standard English and that it's fascinating." I didn't know how to teach it initially. I had to fight through it, to come home and even battle myself, but that was a very exciting class. My students were able to release a part of themselves without shame or guilt.

HL: When did you write your first poem?

SS: In Alabama, after Momma died. I must have been seven. I was sitting in the corner and I had a real "Live" stepmother—I had three of them—who was really classic, mean like in the fairy tales. She came over and grabbed what I was doing and read it to someone (I believe it was her sister) who said, "that's a poem!" My first real poem as such, if you can call a ten-year-old's scribblings poems, was about my grandmother, memories of her that began to come back in a very sharp fashion in New York. We were not accustomed to living in a small apartment, or to a bedroom window that faced a blank wall. I began to suffer from claustrophobia. The poem was about Mama and how she let me run; I ran with the boys instead of playing with dolls. She allowed that. I could come home with my dresses torn and she'd say, "Don't put those on her, she's not a fancy girl." I've never worn frilly things; I've kept my style to this day. If I see little girls dressed in pinafores, I collapse. So the first piece I wrote was about that. I don't have it anymore. You get older, and see that it's terrible and throw it out. But the Schomburg—I'm giving my papers to the Schomburg Collection—they get upset about things like that. The first poem I ever published, in the *New England Review,* was again about the South. Once an aunt and I were on a segregated bus on which blacks could only sit at the back and whites up front. When it got very crowded, blacks had to move to the last seat and when it got jammed, they had to stand up. That day the driver stopped it and said, "Get the hell off." Well, she wouldn't get off. You know how tall I am now, you can imagine at that age how little I was. I was also very thin. I was holding on to her. This bus driver came towards her and she spit on him. There was an uproar and so she was rushed out of town under cover of darkness.

HL: Why did you choose poetry instead of prose?

SS: I don't know. Perhaps because of the fun with words I had with Momma. I've always been trying to recreate that. I did it in a streetwise manner in New York City where I spent all my years from nine on. We spent time playing dozens, and tripping people out. The poems were my way of protesting: how could you let me grow up in this country and not tell me about black history? How could you make me feel so inferior? Playing with words, as I used to, was like going outside and running and jumping over walls and getting cuts that are still with me. I was running into words because I thought they were so inventive and beautiful. My grandmother was a deaconness, and the Sisters would have meetings on Saturdays at our house. I'd go behind the couch or sit under a table and listen. That's where I learned how to watch people. My grandmother would become very emphatic about a particular kind of woman she respected or despised and to this day I identify people from what she said to me. (pp. 358-61)

HL: Which writers were the important influences on your work?

SS: When I first started to write in school I had to read the usual people—Longfellow, Whittier, Scott—and I knew I didn't write poetry like them. I never read any real modern poets until I was in college. And then I found a black woman

in the library on 145th St. who gave me Langston Hughes and Pushkin, which was fascinating. I'd come in and she'd say, "you're always in the poetry section. You should read this man because he was a black man." And then she said, "Have you read Robert Browning?" She began to redirect me, handing me, interestingly enough, some of the Latin poets I'd never touched, and though I didn't quite understand some of their imagery, I still read the poems. I didn't understand Pushkin completely but I read him.

Louise Bogan was a very important influence. I studied with her at NYU. One of the first things she said was: If you're going to write poetry, you must read it aloud. None of us believed that. I was one of the first people who had to read aloud in that class, and as I read the damn poem, Bogan, in her droll, distant fashion, remarked, "Did you read that poem aloud, Miss Sanchez?" The rest of the students looked at me as if to say: I'm glad it's you. I was literally caught, and I started to fake it. Bogan just looked away and commented, "Well, I hear some problems in the poems." But she never rewrote any of the content, and I felt safe on that point.

At that time of course I didn't write anything that really said anything about being black or being a woman because no one wanted to bring her face or sex to anyone's attention; that was naughty, especially if you were a woman who declared "I'm a woman." People would say, "Please, you shouldn't be writing poetry if you're a woman. Or if you're black, by god, you shouldn't be writing poetry at all." So I never referred to it. But every now and then something would creep in. Usually I'd write a mild little poem about something that was happening in the south; the civil rights struggle was intense. And a poet in the workshop said: "We don't want to hear that at all." It was really rough.

HL: How did Bogan respond to your poems?

SS: I never came out and asked: "Do you think I can write?" She remarked drily, "There are some people who can write and others who can't. I would say that you can write if you work and study form." Then I began to read her work and I saw her structures. This classical woman poet was shaping a lot of us. Though some resisted form as too rigorous, I did not because I thought that my sprawling work needed form. To this day, I teach my students the villanelle, the sonnet: I preach all the exercises and discipline that Bogan gave to me. I began to move, to see how form can work, can demand a certain kind of response. That was very important for me. I realize now that she was not necessarily interested in her students. She was not a woman who'd open up to you, but she was honest and fair. That was what I needed.

HL: It sounds fortunate to have had so rigorous a mentor at the foundation of your career rather than somebody who was permissive. What other poets exerted an influence on you?

SS: Neruda and Lorca for their imagery, their showing that you could pile image on image and still make people understand. Langston Hughes, Gwendolyn Brooks, Margaret Walker. At the Schomburg Collection, I met Jean Hutson, the curator, who told me that the library was devoted to books about black folk. My reaction was, "You must be kidding." I had just gotten out of Hunter College and hadn't read anything by blacks. She gave me an entire library; that's where I first read W.E.B. Dubois, Claude McKay, and Zora Neale Hurston. One day I turned to Jean Hutson and said: "I'm going to have my books in here," and she looked at me as though thinking that I was a rash young woman, but now she tells my students, "This is the young woman who vowed that one day she'd have her books in here," and she hugged me. After I read these black writers, I knew I was on the right track. They nurtured me. Later on I greedily read a lot of women poets: Atwood and Piercy, Brooks and Walker, Dickinson and Bogan. Then I began to buy books of poetry—that's the one thing I would spend money on—and write in the margin, to indicate the things I liked and disliked. I also read aloud. Bogan really insisted that a poet must read her work aloud. She said, "You will not always have people with you who will tell you whether something's good or bad, but your ear will."

HL: Could you talk about Neruda's importance to your writing of political poems?

SS: My early poetry was introspective, poetry that probably denied or ignored I was black. I wrote about trees, and birds, and whatever, and that was hard, living in Harlem, since we didn't see too many trees, though I did draw on my residual memories of the South. People kept saying to me, if you write a political poem, it will be considered propaganda—an ineffective and poor poem—but I read Neruda and saw that he didn't deny the personal. In the early Sixties I became aware that the personal was the political. Even my loneliness was never just my own but a much larger loneliness that came out of a society that did not encourage blacks to learn for the sheer joy of it, to expand beyond drinking a bottle of beer at the end of the day and watching the idiot box. I may show you a picture of an alienated and hostile person, but there are reasons for it, and lessons to learn, too.

HL: You call your latest book **Homegirls and Handgrenades.** A hand grenade is very explosive, destructive. Do you intend us to think that poetry is in some way like a grenade?

SS: The hand grenade can also explode myths. Take the poem about the Amtrak ride. It really happened. A young/old/black man bopped on at Newark; he had a mobster's look. I immediately put my shopping bag on the seat, warning him that I didn't want to be bothered. He looked away but sure enough, he sat right behind me and began to talk to a middle-class white man. I heard this man inhale, from unease, you know, and I felt that the young old man heard it also. They had a conversation that I had to record because myths exploded there. It finally ended with the man not taking in those uneasy breaths and the black man saying simply, "I've been trying to deal with the problem of how non-work makes you less of a man in this country" and then they said goodbye and smiled at each other. That's what I mean: hand grenades are the words I use to explode myths about people, about ourselves, about how we live and what we think, because this is really the last chance we have in this country.

HL: Were you stereotyped as a political poet?

SS: Writing has been a long, tense road of saying what I wanted and needed to say. When I gave my book **Love Poems** to a friend, she said, "god, I didn't know you wrote love poems." But in every book of mine there's been a section of lyrical pieces. If you describe me, as some critics do, as a lyrical poet, I say yes, I am, but I'm also a hard-hitting poet and a political poet because this is a lyrical world and a terrible world, too, and I have to talk about that.

I have also been deeply involved in Philadelphia with what they call the literacy campaign. I go to older men and women who are learning how to read and read the poems aloud and discuss them. Once someone said to me, "I read that because it was about me, and I read it well." This person actually said good, I read it good, and I felt that she did read it good. "If this is poetry," they say, "I like poetry." And the whole point is to bring poetry to a larger audience, something I've tried to do for a long, long time.

HL: Are you conscious of writing for a particular audience?

SS: No—but I know my audience, if that makes sense. From the beginning I've had a black audience, women, and students, black and white. Now because of what's happening in this country, that audience has widened. I get letters from people saying "I understand what you're doing because I feel the same thing." What I felt as a woman, as a black woman, had to get translated to other women, too. (pp. 362-65)

My work, really, has always been motivated by love. In the Sixties, the country had to be shocked with the horror of how it had raised Negroes who hated themselves, who were bent on wiping themselves out, intent on not seeing themselves, on being invisible. So I have a poem about Norma, who had a genius for language. I saw her on 145th St years later, with tracks on her damn legs. What in the hell could she have done? Can you imagine what her four little girls, involved in that drug scene, see and know? She said they're going to be different, but of course I knew they weren't going to be different. This is what, finally, I'm talking about in my poems.

HL: What is your argument when somebody, not only a conservative, says that poetry transcends gender, that ultimately a poet has to be judged on the variety and brilliance of the language rather than on the question of being male or female, black or white?

SS: That time has not arrived. So the poet must educate people, which is what a lot of us are doing. If someone says, I am this, because my hair curls when it gets in water, there can still be beauty in the work. There can still be brilliance in the language that informs. Exhorts. (p. 366)

HL: What are your criteria for deciding whether poems are good?

SS: Is it well structured? Is the imagery vivid? Is there beauty in it? I might say something smartly, but the poem must have another leap and another bound to it so that style and content can walk together, can become fused. When a poet relies only on the crutch of "I'm this or I'm that" and does not bring us the sharpened tools of craft, we have to look up and protest. Some people think that the poem should not have a race or gender; it should be weightless. Whether you're Wallace Stevens or Audre Lorde, you bring what you are to the poem. (p. 367)

HL: When did the African influence enter your poetry? I take it you're fascinated by African religions.

SS: There were some phenomena I could not explain, like the collective unconscious, but I wanted to. When I read *Flash of the Spirit,* the Egyptian Book of the Dead, I laughed. That's the person I talked to, that was Yémaya. I was born on the ninth month and the ninth day and one of the numbers for Yémaya is nine. I was bringing into the arena of poetry the sense of another sensibility, another way of looking at the world, another life force. If I touch you, I give you a life force, also. To those who record desolation and say you can't do anything about it, I'm affirming that a person can do something, I'm saying yes. In other words, I'm taking what might be considered a metaphysical concept, this collective unconscious, and using my relationship to it to change real things. (p. 368)

Sonia Sanchez, in an interview with Herbert Leibowitz, in Parnassus: Poetry in Review, *Vol. 12 & 13, Nos. 2 & 1, 1985, pp. 357-68.*

GENERAL COMMENTARY

R. RODERICK PALMER

Sonia Sanchez . . . is concerned with black identity. Within this framework, however, she manages to achieve an amazingly wide variety of treatments. [She] feels that the return to black identity is a "home-coming" (the title, by the way, of her first published volume of verse) after a sojourn in a white-oriented society geared to UN-black the Black man—to mold him to a white standard of values. (p. 31)

It is Sonia Sanchez's belief that the orientation to blackness should start early. School children need redefinitions. They have been brainwashed to stereotypes by white teachers. What is a policeman? she asked one little black girl. The child's answer was typical: "He is a man who protects you." This is not the answer the poet gives. In her poem, **"in definition for blk / children,"** she says that to the ghetto child, a policeman is

> a pig
> and he shd be in
> a zoo . . .
> and
> until he stops
> killing blk / people
> cracking open their heads
> remember
> the policeman
> is a pig

To her eighth grade class in New York City—with children, many of whom had never before been taught by a black person—she says in **"poem for dsc 8th graders—1966-1967"**:

> look at me 8th
> grade
> i am black
> beautiful. i have a
> man who looks at
> my face and smiles.

Sonia Sanchez can be tender and warm as these words from her **"personal letter no. 2"** attest:

> if i were young
> i wd stretch you
> with my wild words.

She can be mystical and introspective as exemplified in her **"poem at thirty"** . . . . As her mood changes, some of her poems display a peculiar humor; others reveal a disdainful spirit; and still others show that she can be mean and angry, at times. In her poem **"for unborn malcolms,"** she is indignant and belligerent . . . . (pp. 32-3)

As a protest poet, like Don L. Lee, Sonia Sanchez chooses themes from a wide range of the so-called "black experience." Her poems, however, are more personalized. She uses the first person "i" more frequently, and equates the black experi-

ence within the realm of her own identity as a black woman. Nevertheless, she is never maudlin. "A poet must never succumb to self-pity," she says. Self-pity spells the death of poetry. Her poems are strong, direct, and forcefully articulate in the free verse idiom of contemporary verse. (pp. 33-4)

R. Roderick Palmer, "The Poetry of Three Revolutionists: Don L. Lee, Sonia Sanchez, and Nikki Giovanni," in CLA Journal, *Vol. XV, No. 1, September, 1971, pp. 25-36.*

JANET LEMBKE

They had requested the company of the author of **We a BaddDDD People,** the 8th and 9th graders at predominantly white Coleytown Junior High in Westport, Connecticut, and they found it gooddDDD. Poet Sonia Sanchez was invited to give a reading as part of a recent three-day "Happening," when the academic schedule was suspended to allow for a series of special mini-courses. Most of the 9th grade English classes and one 8th grade class had devoted a quarter of the school year to the study of black writing. . . .

The students had learned that black poetry was to be felt and understood by the emotions rather than decoded by the brain. And Ms. Sanchez agreed with that. Describing the oral tradition in the works of black poets, she explained that it had its roots in music and street speech. "I write song-poems," she added.

It became apparent, once she was into her readings, that she writes mostly about love—love between man and woman, mother and children and, most of all, about love for oneself because, ". . . without that, it is impossible to love anyone else."

Sonia, a tiny woman, stood very straight as she faced her audience. Although her voice was soft, it filled the room; no one rustled or coughed or clacked pencil on teeth. She told of black people being taught self-hate for centuries and how, starting in the 1960s, they had to begin to learn to love themselves.

The close connection of her work to oral art was apparent as she read from **We a BaddDDD People,** first "a poem for nina simone to put some music to and blow our nigguh/minds." Its chanted "yeh yeh yeh" refrain seemed to pull the listeners bodily into the echoing rhythm. . . .

She has a fierce concern for the problems of the young, especially those on drugs: "I grew up in Harlem where the important people were pimps and numbers runners and junkies. This poem is for junior high school students telling them not to be like that." Then she read "don't wanna be no pimp cuz pimps hate me and you. . . ."

Besides the creations based entirely on street language and black music, Sonia has published works in other forms. She appreciates the haiku, for instance, and her **Love Poems** has many examples of the short, Oriental expressions. . . .

She also said that she had just published her first story-prose book for young children, **The Afternoon of Smallhead, Fathead and Squarehead.** When the twins were about five, they asked their mother for a bedtime story and so she made one up and is now working on her second children's book.

Janet Lembke, "Black Poet, White Schoolchil-

dren," in Publishers Weekly, *Vol. 206, No. 3, July 15, 1974, p. 77.*

JOYCE ANN JOYCE

The diversity of Sanchez' subject matter reflects the depth and progression of her thought with each new volume of poetry exemplifying a mind in transition. Two of the more dominant concerns that take shape throughout her canon are her interest in the relationship between Black men and Black women and her interest in Black children. Two volumes of her work are written specifically for the young: the 1971 collection of poetry *It's a New Day (poems for young brothas and sistuhs)* and the more recent 1980 collection of short stories, *A Sound Investment.* The message in these works coincides with Sanchez' consistent purpose from *Home Coming* and *We a BaddDDD People* to *Blues Book* and *I've Been a Woman:* to teach Black people to know themselves, to be themselves, and to love themselves. Only her style and the influence on her thought differ in these works written for young Blacks. By the publication of *It's a New Day* in 1971, Sanchez had become a member of Elijah Muhammad's Muslim community. Her Islamic ideology infuses *It's a New Day* and *Blues Book,* her important fifth book of poetry. The introduction of Islam into her poetry is much like, yet smoother, than Richard Wright's use of existential doctrine in his fiction. Just as the early Bigger Thomas is no less an existential figure than Cross Damon, Wright's existential outsider, Sanchez espouses much the same philosophy in *It's a New Day* as she did in the works that precede her obvious conversion to Islam. And interestingly enough, by the time she gets to *I've Been a Woman* (1978) and *A Sound Investment,* her Islamic doctrine becomes suffused by a broader Pan-African worldview.

It seems natural to suppose that Sanchez' readings in Islamic doctrine and her own search for the history of Black peoples led the way to her Pan-African ideology. In both the Islamic and African communities the family is an essential element of the larger community. And, of course, children form the basis of the family. *It's a New Day* addresses the problems in the Black community that impede the psychological development of the children who make up the core of the Black family and who will become the Black mothers, fathers, and political leaders of the future. Sanchez realizes that reinforcement is the most effective method of teaching. Thus if young Blacks learn to love themselves and respect their African heritage and if they are taught early to recognize and shun the psychologically crippling elements of the American culture, they will be strong, adult Black men and women. In **"Safari,"** a representative poem from this collection, the poet uses metaphors from an African landscape to emphasize the young adults' African heritage and to sustain the attention of young minds:

> C mon yall
>   on a safari
> into our plantation/jungle/minds
> and let us catch the nigger
> roamen inside of us.
>   let us hang
>   our white aping
>   actions
>   on walls
>   with signs that
>   announce the last
>   of our nigger thoughts

is dead.
only blackness
runs in our veins.
Cmon yall
     follow me on a new african safari
     and Live!

Like many of Sanchez' poems, this poem progresses through a sustained metaphor. The African safari becomes a psychological, mind-opening journey for the Black youth. Through learning of his African heritage, the Black youth will be able to catch the "nigger" inside of him made by slavery and racism and destroy him.

A part of this process requires that the Black man annihilates the image of God given to him by a Euro-American Christian tradition. In the middle section of the poem the poet calls to mind the picture of the last supper that hangs on the walls of many Black American homes. Instead of hanging the picture of a white Christ on the walls of his home, the Black man must slough off his mocking (aping) of the attitude, beliefs, and actions of the American hegemony. Ironically, he must replace the picture of Christ with his "white aping actions" and with signs that announce the death of a Black man who sees himself only through the eyes of white society. Just as the last supper marked the impending death of Christ who died to redeem mankind (in the Euro-American Christian tradition), so will the "new african safari" awaken a consciousness in the Black man that will give him new life, self-respect and self-knowledge.

"Safari" is not typical of other poems in this volume. Its metaphysical conceit is perhaps too subtle for the very young. Nevertheless, their imaginations will capture the African landscape and in turn reinforce their affinity with Africa, fulfilling Sanchez' goal of making young adults curious of their history. She also lures the attention of her young readers by using repetition and rhyme in poems like **"Don't Wanna Be"** and the title poem **"It's a New Day."** **"Don't Wanna Be"** uses a refrain which introduces the poet's repudiation of pimps, numbers runners, and junkies respectively, all debilitating figures for the young to emulate. The "new day" will have arrived when the youth of today become the Farrakhans, Elijahs, Nyereres, Kings, Gwendolyns, Sojourners, and Muslim women of tomorrow. Sometimes the poet's references to Islam or Islamic figures are sparse and at other times as in **"We're not learnen to be paper boys (for the young brothas who sell Muhammad Speaks),"** the ideology of the Black Muslims forms the basis of the poem.

Stylistically *It's a New Day* marks a change in Sanchez' poetry. Beginning with this third volume, the poet removes the obscenity from her poetry. In an interview conducted in 1977 by poet E. Ethelbert Miller for WHUR Radio at Howard University, she explained that she wrote *It's a New Day* for a group of students in New York who told her that they were not allowed to read her poetry because of its obscenity indigenous to Black speech, adding that she "curses" in her poetry to achieve emphasis and to get people interested in poetry, to pull them in. Although she stresses her desire to "hurl obscenities at the obscene," she changes her tactics in her later works. (pp. 49-51)

Joyce Ann Joyce, "The Development of Sonia Sanchez: A Continuing Journey," in Indian Journal of American Studies, *Vol. 13, No. 2, July, 1983, pp.*

37-71.

IT'S A NEW DAY: POEMS FOR YOUNG BROTHAS AND SISTUHS (1971)

Who is Sonia Sanchez?

She is an upfront woman, witty, bright, black, and utterly devoted to those revolutionary ideals she sees as the best hope for Black people. Her poems are raps, good ones, aimed like guns at whatever obstacles she detects standing in the way of Black progress . . . . (pp. 44-5)

Her praises are as generous as her criticisms are severe, both coming from loyalties that are fierce, invulnerable, and knowing. Whether she's addressing her praises to Gwendolyn Brooks or to the late Malcolm X, to her husband or to a stranger's child, always they emerge from and feed back into the shared experience of being Black. One concern she always comes back to is the real education of Black children:

> who's gonna give our young
> blk/people new heroes
>   (instead of catch/phrases)
>   (instead of cad/ill/acs)
>   (instead of pimps)

and the dozens of other pacifiers she knows are there to tempt Black youths to stall and self-destruct . . . .

So *It's a New Day* (**poems for young brothas and sistuhs**) comes as a pleasure, not a surprise. Like each of her others, this book comes in an attractive, cheap, paperback edition out of Dudley Randall's Broadside Press in Detroit. . . . Sonia Sanchez's poems include songs and chants, all, of course, firing kids' pride in their Blackness. Addressing a "high/yellow/black girl", she says,

> Those who
> laugh at yo/color
>   have not moved
> to the blackness we be about
> cuz as Curtis Mayfield be sayen
> we people be darker than blue
>   . . . .
>
> yeah. high/yellow/black/girl
> walk/yo black/song
>   cuz some of us
>   be hearen yo/sweet/music.

In another she concludes,

> if i cud ever write a poem as beautiful
> as u, little 2/yr/old/brotha,
> poetry wud go out of bizness.

Sonia Sanchez spends little time arguing her points. She as-

sumes them, then works at putting them across straight as she can, not the least hesitant about being overtly instructive:

> don't wanna be
> no pimp
>
>   cuz pimps hate me and you
>   they mommas, women, sistuhs too
>
>   **"Don't wanna be"**
>
> we gon be
>   outa sight black/men
>   gon be part/
>   panther
>   . . . .
>
>   gon rap like RAP
>   . . . .
>
>   gon believe like King believed
>   gonna be TCB/ing black men
>
>   **"It's a New Day"**

When she says "our talk is new. it be/original talk . . ." the seeming paradox comes to life and walks off on its own feet, piping a tune I suspect is reaching the ears it is meant for. I just hope it's a long looooong time before Sonia Sanchez goes out of bizness. (pp. 46-8)

William Pitt Root, in a review of "It's a New Day," in Poetry, *Vol. CXXIII, No. 1, October, 1973, pp. 44-8.*

THE ADVENTURES OF FATHEAD, SMALLHEAD, AND SQUAREHEAD (1973)

From bedtime stories for her two children, author and playwright Sanchez has fashioned this fable of three friends who set out for Mecca. As they travel through the jungles of the Sudan, Smallhead and Squarehead decide to build something without telling Fathead, who is "so slow." They make a lion which comes to life when they put on its head. It gobbles them up, but Fathead, who has climbed a tree, continues his journey to Mecca. Two morals conclude the story: "Slow is not always dumb and fast is not always smart," and "Just as a lion is never dangerous without a head so a people never progress without a leader." A strange but interesting double allegory.

A review of "The Adventures of Fathead, Smallhead and Squarehead," in Publishers Weekly, *Vol. 205, No. 22, June 3, 1974, p. 158.*

Sir John Tenniel

1820-1914

English illustrator and cartoonist.

Tenniel is best known as the illustrator of Lewis Carroll's *Alice's Adventures in Wonderland* (1865) and its sequel *Through the Looking-Glass* (1872), a collaboration which is generally regarded as the most perfect marriage of text and pictures in children's literature. [See entry on Carroll beginning on page 38 of this volume.] Acclaimed as a genius whose interpretation of Carroll's words are superior to the more than one hundred illustrators who have attempted to define them pictorially, Tenniel is lauded for capturing the essence of the texts while investing them with his distinctive artistic vision. Tenniel illustrated over thirty books and produced two thousand cartoons as the political cartoonist for *Punch* magazine, a position he held for fifty years. As a cartoonist, Tenniel is credited with changing the direction of the English political caricature. Before Tenniel, cartoons on political and social issues were thought to be largely sketchy works which reflected the partisan attitude of their artists. Tenniel is acknowledged for bringing artistic skill, impartiality, and wit to his cartoons, qualities which most observers note as characteristics of his drawings for the *Alice* books.

Essentially a self-taught artist, Tenniel became an illustrator and cartoonist after working in mosaics and watercolor. Influenced by the Pre-Raphaelites as well as by continental artists such as the French illustrator J. J. Grandville, he began providing black-and-white pictures for such works as Thomas James's *Aesop's Fables* (1848) and R. H. Barham's *The Ingoldsby Legends* (1864). Usually engraved in wood by the Brothers Dalziel and Joseph Swain, England's most popular engravers, Tenniel's illustrations—which he drew strictly from memory or from photographs—caught the attention of Lewis Carroll, who especially admired his pictures of animals. When Tenniel agreed to do the drawings for *Alice's Adventures in Wonderland*, Carroll insisted on instructing him on their subjects, sizes, and positions on the page as well as commanding that he draw his animals from life rather than from memory, a dictate which Tenniel chose to ignore. Despite the storminess of their relationship, Carroll and Tenniel later collaborated on *Looking-Glass*, a work on which their personalities clashed once again; *Looking-Glass* was, in fact, the last book illustrated by Tenniel. For the *Alice* tales, Tenniel created works which are usally celebrated as exquisite depictions of the beauty, humor, and fantastic qualities of the stories. His strong, straightforward style is generally regarded as the perfect complement to Carroll's solid, literal prose. Tenniel's rendition of Alice is often considered anatomically incorrect and too mature for her textual descriptions, and some observers are convinced that Carroll's more primitive illustrations for *Alice's Adventures Under Ground* express the spirit and subtleties of Alice's experiences more effectively. However, most commentators concur that Tenniel is the definitive illustrator of the *Alice* books, and agree with critic John Rowe Townsend that "Alice is Tenniel's Alice as well as Carroll's." Tenniel was knighted in 1893 in recognition of his artistic achievements.

(See also *Something about the Author,* Vol. 27, and *Contemporary Authors,* Vol. 111.)

AUTHOR'S COMMENTARY

[The following excerpt is from an interview by M. H. Spielmann.]

I never learned to draw, except in so far as attending a school and being allowed to teach myself. I attended the Royal Academy Schools after becoming a probationer, but soon left in utter disgust of there being no teaching. I had a great idea of High Art; in fact, in 1845, I sent in a 16-foot-high cartoon for Westminster Palace. In the Upper Waiting Hall, or 'Hall of Poets,' of the House of Lords I made a fresco, but my subject was changed after my work had been decided on and worked out. At Christmas, 1850, I was invited by Mark Lemon to fill the place suddenly left by [Richard] Doyle, who, with very good reason for himself—that of objection to the so-called 'Papal Aggression' campaign—suddenly severed his connection with *Punch.* . . . I was applied to by Lemon, on the initiative of [Douglas] Jerrold, to fill the breach. This was on the strength of my illustrations to

Aesop's Fables, which had recently been published by Murray. (pp. 201-02)

As for political opinions, . . . if I have my own little politics I keep them to myself, and profess only those of my paper. If I have infused any dignity into cartoon designing, it comes from no particular effort on my part, but solely from the high feeling I have for art. In any case, if I am a 'cartoonist'—the accepted term—I am not a 'caricaturist' in any sense of the word. My drawings are sometimes grotesque, but that is from a sense of fun and humour. Some people declare that I am no humourist, that I have no sense of fun at all; they deny me everything but severity, 'classicality,' and dignity. Now, *I* believe that I have a very keen sense of humour, and that my drawings are sometimes really funny. (p. 202)

As to my work, I never use models or nature for the figure, drapery, or anything else. But I have a wonderful memory: a memory of *observation*—not for dates, for instance (for the only date I remember is that of the Great Fire)—but anything I see I remember. Well, I get my subject on Wednesday night; I think it out carefully on Thursday, and make my rough sketch. On Friday morning I begin, and I stick to it all day, with my nose well down on the block. By means of tracing paper—on which I make such alterations of composition and action I may consider necessary—I transfer my design to the wood and draw on that. The first sketch I may, and often do, complete later on as a commission; indeed, at the present time I have a huge undertaking on hand in which I take great delight—the finishing of scores of my sketches, of which I have many hundreds. They are for a friend, an 'enthusiastic admirer,' if you won't mind my expressing it so. Well, the block being finished, it is handed over to Swain's boy at about 6:30 to 7 o'clock, who has been waiting for it for an hour or so, and at 7:30 it is put in hand for engraving. That is completed on the following night, and on Monday night I receive by post the copy of next Wednesday's paper. Although casehardened in a sense, I never have the courage to open the packet. I always leave it to my sister, who opens it and hands it across to me, when I just take a glance at it and receive my weekly pang. They are not so well engraved now—so different to what they were in 1870, at the time of the Franco-Prussian war; but with Furniss and Sambourne both doing political work, it is hardly surprising if it should have to be somewhat scamped. My work would be difficult to photograph on to the wood, as it is all drawn in pencil; the only pen-and-ink work I have done so far being for the almanack and pocket-book.

As I never use a model I never draw from life, but always from a photograph, though not in quite the same spirit as Sambourne does. I get a photograph only of the man whom I want to draw, and seek to get his character. Then, if the photograph is in profile, I have to 'fudge' the full face and *vice versa;* but if I only succeed in getting the character I seldom go far wrong—a due appreciation being an almost infallible guide. (pp. 202-03)

> M. H. Spielmann, "Our Graphic Humourists: Sir John Tenniel," in The Magazine of Art, *Vol. 18, May, 1895, pp. 201-07.*

THE ATHENAEUM

Mr. Carroll has laboured hard [in *Alice's Adventures in Wonderland*] to heap together strange adventures, and heterogeneous combinations; and we acknowledge the hard labour. Mr. Tenniel, again, is square, and grim, and uncouth in his illustrations, howbeit clever, even sometimes to the verge of grandeur, as is the artist's habit. We fancy that any real child might be more puzzled than enchanted by this stiff, over-wrought story.

> A review of "Alice's Adventures in Wonderland," in The Athenaeum, *No. 1990, December 16, 1865, p. 844.*

THE TIMES, LONDON

[Mr. Tenniel] has illustrated a little work—*Alice's Adventures in Wonderland,* with extraordinary grace. Look at the first chapter of this volume, and note the rabbit at the head of it. His umbrella is tucked under his arm and he is taking the watch out of his pocket to see what o'clock it is. The neatness of touch with which he is set living before us may be seen in a dozen other vignettes throughout the volume, the letterpress of which is by Mr. Lewis Carroll, and may best be described as an excellent piece of nonsense. (p. 5)

> A review of "Alice's Adventures in Wonderland," in The Times, *London, December 26, 1865, pp. 4-5.*

MARGARET GATTY

[*The following excerpt is from an essay originally published in the first number of* Aunt Judy's Magazine for Young People, *1866.*]

[*Alice's Adventures in Wonderland* has an] exquisitely wild, fantastic, impossible, yet most natural history . . . . [Mr. Lewis Carroll] has a secret, and he has managed his secret so much better than any author who ever "tried on" a secret of the same sort before, that we would not for the world let it out. No; the young folks for whom this charming account is written must go on and on and on till they find out the secret for themselves; and then they will agree with us that never was the mystery made to feel so beautifully natural before. . . .

Of Mr. Tenniel's illustrations we need only say that he has entered equally into the fun and graceful sentiment of his author, and that we are as much in love with little Alice's face in all its changes as we are amused by the elegant get up of the white rabbit in ball costume, the lobster quadrille on the sands, or the concourse of animals fresh from the "Pool of Tears" drying themselves in the mouse's most dry historical memories. . . . The above hints will probably make "parents and guardians" aware that they must not look to *Alice's Adventures* for knowledge in disguise.

> Margaret Gatty, in a review of "Alice's Adventures in Wonderland," in Children and Literature: Views and Reviews, *edited by Virginia Haviland, Scott, Foresman and Company, 1973, p. 20.*

THE ATHENAEUM

It is with no mere book that we have to deal here [in *Through the Looking-Glass, and What Alice Found There*] . . . , but with the potentiality of happiness for countless thousands of children of all ages; for it would be difficult to over-estimate the value of the store of hearty and healthy fun laid up for whole generations of young people by Mr. Lewis Carroll and Mr. John Tenniel in the two books which they have united to produce. In the first volume, Alice won the affections of a whole child-world as she wandered through Wonderland;

in the second, that now before us, she will be sure to add fresh troops to the number of her unknown friends, besides retaining her place in the hearts of her old admirers. . . .

Many of Mr. Tenniel's designs are masterpieces of wise absurdity. We may refer, for instance, to that in which the Oysters, incarnations of old-womanishness, are listening to the dulcet speech of the Walrus and the Carpenter, or those of Humpty Dumpty shouting into "Someone's" ear, of the White Knight shaking the aged man who sat upon the gate, and of the Messenger expiating in prison the crime he was going to commit; not to speak of some drawings which deserve still higher and more serious praise, such as that in which Alice is rowing the boat along the stream which is half river and half grocer's shop. The skill with which the dreamlike blending of the one with the other is rendered is worthy of Wonderland itself. . . .

[Bands] of children will deservedly feel personally grateful to both author and illustrator . . . .

> *A review of "Through the Looking-Glass, and What Alice Found There," in The Athenaeum, No. 2303, December 16, 1871, pp. 787-88.*

THE SPECTATOR

People have from time immemorial found their way into fairyland in some odd unexpected fashion: nobody was ever known to succeed in going there on purpose. In this respect Alice is as orthodox as any of her elders. Last time, it came of following a white rabbit, this time [in *Through the Looking-glass*] of talking to a black kitten. Mr. Tenniel has given us two portraits of that kitten at the beginning and end of the book. There is a certain uncanny look about it which would make us anxious if it belonged to us. On this occasion it only turned into a Red Queen, but it might some day go behind the stove and swell to the size of a hippopotamus. On the whole we are contented that it exists only in woodcut. (pp. 1607-08)

[When Alice goes through the looking-glass, the] first thing she sees is that the chessmen are all alive and walking about amongst the cinders on the hearth. Mr. Tenniel has made us see them too. His King and Queen are oddities that run all through the book; but there is one figure, neither mentioned in the text, nor ever seen again, which is more droll than anything else in all the fifty woodcuts. There is a white bishop sitting on a big cinder with his back to us, the round stool which serves him for feet tucked up on a smaller cinder, reading his newspaper with exquisite gravity. It looks quite natural—for the other side of the Looking-glass—that there is no head in his mitre. (p. 1608)

Mr. Tenniel has added to [The White Knight's] interest by throwing in reminiscences of Albert Dürer's Knight and Don Quixote. . . . And there is a mysterious railway passenger dressed in white paper whose picture makes us much desire his further acquaintance. (p. 1609)

> *A review of "Through the Looking-Glass, and What Alice Found There," in The Spectator, Vol. 44, No. 2270, December 30, 1871, pp. 1607-09.*

EDWARD SALMON

[*The following excerpt is from Salmon's book* Juvenile Literature As It Is, *which was originally published in 1888.*]

Though *Alice's Adventures in Wonderland* and *Through the*

Looking-Glass are, of course, undeniably clever, and possess many charms exclusively their own, there is nothing extraordinarily original about either, and certainly the former cannot fairly be called, as it once was, the most remarkable book for children of recent times. John Tenniel's illustrations did much to make these records of Alice's adventures attractive. The ingenious developments and the humorous conceptions of the writer would seem less ingenious and less humorous if merely written about than they do under the exquisite interpretation of Mr Tenniel's sketches. (p. 55)

> *Edward Salmon, "Literature for the Little Ones," in* A Peculiar Gift: Nineteenth Century Writings on Books for Children, *edited by Lance Salway, Kestrel Books, 1976, pp. 46-61.*

GLEESON WHITE

Sir John Tenniel . . . more than any other of the *Punch* staff, seems never thoroughly at home outside its pages. The very idea of a Tenniel drawing has become a synonym for a political cartoon; so that now you cannot avoid feeling that all his illustrations to poetry, fiction, and fairy-tale must have some satirical motive underlying their apparent purpose. (p. 22)

> *Gleeson White, "Some Illustrated Magazines of the Sixties: 'Once a Week'," in his* English Illustration: 'The Sixties', 1855-70, *Archibald Constable and Co., 1897, pp. 16-37.*

STUART DODGSON COLLINGWOOD

When [Mr. Dodgson] promised to write out **Alice** for Miss Liddell he had no idea of publication; but his friend, Mr. George MacDonald, to whom he had shown the story, persuaded him to submit it to a publisher. Messrs. Macmillan agreed to produce it, and as Mr. Dodgson had not sufficient faith in his own artistic powers to venture to allow his illustrations to appear, it was necessary to find some artist who would undertake the work. By the advice of Tom Taylor he approached Mr. Tenniel, who was fortunately well disposed, and on April 5, 1864, the final arrangements were made. (pp. 97-9)

The first edition, which consisted of two thousand copies, was condemned by both author and illustrator, for the pictures did not come out well. All purchasers were accordingly asked to return their copies, and to send their names and addresses; a new edition was prepared, and distributed to those who had sent back their old copies, which the author gave away to various homes and hospitals. The substituted edition was a complete success, "a perfect piece of artistic printing," as Mr. Dodgson called it. He hardly dared to hope that more than two thousand copies would be sold, and anticipated a considerable loss over the book. His surprise was great when edition after edition was demanded, and when he found that **Alice,** far from being a monetary failure, was bringing him in a very considerable income every year. (p. 104)

The success of **Alice in Wonderland** tempted Mr. Dodgson to make another essay in the same field of literature [with **Through the Looking-glass**]. (p. 129)

One question which exercised Mr. Dodgson very much was whether the picture of the Jabberwock would do as a frontispiece, or whether it would be too frightening for little children. On this point he sought the advice of about thirty of his married lady friends, whose experiences with their own children would make them trustworthy advisers; and in the end he chose the picture of the White Knight on horseback. In 1871 the book appeared, and was an instantaneous success. (p. 142)

The story, as originally written, contained thirteen chapters, but the published book consisted of twelve only. The omitted chapter introduced a wasp, in the character of a judge or barrister, I suppose, since Mr. Tenniel wrote that "a *wasp* in a *wig* is altogether beyond the appliances of art." Apart from difficulties of illustration, the "wasp" chapter was not considered to be up to the level of the rest of the book, and this was probably the principal reason of its being left out.

"It is a curious fact," wrote Mr. Tenniel some years later, when replying to a request of Lewis Carroll's that he would illustrate another of his books, "that with *Through the Looking-Glass* the faculty of making drawings for book illustration departed from me, and, notwithstanding all sorts of tempting inducements, I have done nothing in that direction since." (p. 146)

> *Stuart Dodgson Collingwood, in his* The Life and Letters of Lewis Carroll, *The Century Co., 1899, 448 p.*

MAX BEERBOHM

[*The following excerpt is from an essay originally published in 1900.*]

I conceive the illustrator of books as an active fiend, who clips with long sharp shears the tender wings of illusion. I hate him. Especially do I hate him when he illustrates a work of fantasy. It is bad enough to be robbed of my own vision of a realistic scene, even when the illustrator's vision happens, by some rare chance, to strike me as better than my own. It is far worse to see materialised a scene of sheer fantasy, even if, by another rare chance, the illustrator's vision of it has coincided with my own. But, though I deplore all illustrations, I do discriminate. Though I should prefer that *Alice in Wonderland* and *Through the Looking-Glass* had never been illustrated at all, by Sir John Tenniel or any other artist, I do admit readily that Sir John's illustrations are the best imaginable. I rejoice in the goodness of them, if only because they are so good, so sure, that they have permanently benumbed the hundred-and-one hands which would otherwise have been itching to illustrate *Alice.* It is a good thing, also, that there never was an edition of *Alice* unillustrated. We have never read the book save under Sir John's auspices. He, mercifully, clipped our wings before they had fluttered ever so little, and so his ingenious flying-machine has never really chafed us. The true fiend of illustration suffers us to soar alone ere he swoops with his shears. We ought, also, to thank Sir John for this mercy: that he has so paved the way that the inevitable dramatic version of *Alice* need not be painful to us. Imagine what would have happened if *Alice* had never been illustrated at all, or had been illustrated badly by various ladies and gentlemen! However well-inspired the conceiver and the costumier of the play, how we should have shuddered! As it is, we have but one common vision of all the characters and monsters whom Alice met—Sir John's vision. And we are perfectly content if these characters and monsters realise that vision. In the present production at the Vaudeville Theatre, they do realise it, obediently and fully. One and all, they are as we know them in the book. Poor Alice herself is the sole disturber of our preconception. . . . Her whole appearance is a defiance, rather than a compromise. However, for the others, I have nothing but praise to offer. The Mad Hatter

and the Knave of Hearts, the Mock Turtle and the Duchess, and all the other creatures, are precisely as Sir John gave them to us, only with the added graces of colour, mobility, voices, and three dimensions. These added graces would, of course, be mere aggravations, were not Sir John's forms copied faithfully, or had not these forms existed at all. Wherefore, once and away, I may be entirely grateful to an illustrator. I beg leave to withdraw my wish that *Alice* had never been illustrated at all. (pp. 109-10)

> *Max Beerbohm, " 'Alice' Again Awakened," in his* Around Theatres, *revised edition, Rupert Hart-Davis, 1953, pp. 109-12.*

RUFUS ROCKWELL WILSON

Long holding first place in his chosen calling, Sir John Tenniel has just retired, after half a century of brilliant service, from the staff of London *Punch.* . . . For the better part of four decades his pencil has been a force which sagacious statesmen have been compelled to take into account in every forecast of public opinion. (p. 141)

Nor does his fame rest alone upon his drawings for *Punch.* His water-color paintings have gained him a reputation amply sufficient to have handed him down to posterity as one of the leading British artists of his period; and in the pauses

Mary Hilton Babcock, whom Carroll introduced to Tenniel in 1865 as an excellent model for Alice. Although controversy exists regarding the extent of Babcock's influence, most of his biographers agree that Tenniel was largely inspired by his own preconception of an ideal maiden.

of his regular labors he has found time to illustrate a number of books that owe no small part of their popularity to his pencil. *Alice in Wonderland* and *Through the Looking-Glass* would lose much of their charm without the delightful pictures which accompany them, and the best illustrations in the *Ingoldsby Legends* are signed with the initials J. T.

Yet, when due praise has been given to Tenniel's fugitive efforts, the fact remains that it is through his drawings for *Punch* that he must take definitive place in the art history of the past century. (pp. 147-48)

> *Rufus Rockwell Wilson, "Sir John Tenniel and His Work," in* The Critic, *New York, Vol. XXXVIII, No. 2, February, 1901, pp. 141-48.*

COSMO MONKHOUSE

[*The following excerpt is from an essay originally published in the Easter number of the* Art Journal, *1901.*]

[Tenniel's pictures for the *Alice* books] combine the merits of two kinds of illustrations: they are as faithful as possible to the text, and at the same time are fresh expressions of an individual, artistic genius. They are divided from his other illustrations and from nearly all those of other men by their exquisite, gentle, and ingenious humor. . . . Fortunately there are few who do not love Alice and have not an intimate acquaintance with the White Rabbit, the March Hare, the White Queen and the rest of that delightful but bewildering company met by Alice in her adventures. Tenniel has drawn them for us so that we could not believe in them one little bit if they were redrawn by any one else. He has drawn for us Wonderland itself, and above all, Alice, that perfect ideal of an English girl; innocent, brave, kind, and full of faith and spirit. Even her face as drawn by Tenniel has a sweet look of wonder and expectation but never one of confusion or fear, whether she finds herself swimming with a mouse or playing croquet with a flamingo for a mallet. (pp. 107-08)

> *Cosmo Monkhouse, in an excerpt in* Contemporary Illustrators of Children's Books, *edited by Bertha E. Mahony and Elinor Whitney, The Bookshop for Boys and Girls, 1930, pp. 107-08.*

PETER NEWELL

[*An American artist whom Michael Patrick Hearn has called "one of the most original of the country's designers," Newell was especially well known for the novelty picture books which he wrote and illustrated. He was chosen by Harper and Brothers to illustrate three of Lewis Carroll's works:* Alice's Adventures in Wonderland (*1901*), Through the Looking-Glass (*1902*), *and* The Hunting of the Snark (*1903*).]

The dominant note in the character of Alice is childish purity and sweetness, and this characteristic Sir John Tenniel has caught and fixed in a way none may rival. His appreciation of the many grotesque personages peopling this wonderland is broad and sympathetic, and his work will live as long as Alice. (p. 713)

> *Peter Newell, "Alice's Adventures in Wonderland: From an Artist's Stand-Point," in* Harper's Monthly Magazine, *Vol. CIII, No. DCXVII, October, 1901, pp. 713-17.*

THE TIMES, LONDON

[What] a great deal of the humour of Lewis Carroll's delightful characters we should have missed if they had not been drawn for us in Tenniel's inimitable style! Alice herself, the Red Queen, the Hatter, the Cheshire Cat, the White Knight, Bill the Lizard—how they all come back to one, and what genuine enjoyment they gave! It seems appropriate enough that the illustrator of *Alice in Wonderland* and *Through the Looking-glass* should provide pictures for *Aesop's Fables* and the *Ingoldsby Legends*. . . . As an illustrator on the wood-block he stood very high; his drawings for *Lalla Rookh* were perhaps the finest of all his work in power and technical excellence. Sir John Tenniel was the author of one of the mosaics, **"Leonardo da Vinci,"** in the Victoria and Albert Museum, and his highly-stippled water-colour drawings were sometimes seen in the exhibitions of the Royal Institute, which elected him a member in 1874. Still, it was by his work for *Punch* that John Tenniel became known to the mass of the English people; by it he will be remembered. His memory will live, not only because his level of achievement was so uniformly high, but also because he had the courage to revolutionize political caricature—a revolution for which we cannot be too grateful when we look at even the best comic periodicals and the best political skills of 50 or 60 years ago.

> *"Death of Sir John Tenniel: The Art of Caricature," in* The Times, *London, February 27, 1914, p. 11.*

PUNCH

It was in 1864 that Tenniel accepted the commission for . . . the series of drawings upon which, with his 2,000 and more cartoons, his fame will rest—the illustrations to *Alice's Adventures in Wonderland*. Mr. Balfour, in his speech at the Tenniel banquet in 1901, said what ought to be said about those joyous pictures. "We must not," he remarked, "forget, in drinking his health, that it is not only as a man who has contributed that immortal series of cartoons to English history that he is known to fame, but he has other claims upon the gratitude of the world. I do not mean to dwell upon that subject, yet I cannot forget that he is in some respects one of the most successful illustrators of books that I think we have ever seen.

There are books in which the text is a mere otiose and almost unnecessary appendage to the illustrations. There are other books, still larger in number, in which the illustration is an impertinent intrusion upon the attention of the reader, distracting his mind from the literary masterpiece with which he is concerned, and intruding alien and unsympathetic ideas to disturb the current of his thoughts. Those books are numerous. But there is a third class of book, in which the illustration and the text are so intimately connected, in which the marriage between the two is so happy and so complete that you cannot conceive the text adequately without the illustrations any more than you could conceive the illustrations unelucidated by the text. Our guest of this evening is one of the happy creators of this kind of illustration. There are books known to all of us in which it would be as impossible to forget the illustrator as it is impossible—and as I hope it will be long impossible—to forget the author." (pp. 4-5)

Before he had been invited to join the staff of *Punch* he had attracted considerable attention by his black-and-white illustrations, among which will be remembered his *Aesop's Fables* and *Lalla Rookh*. Later on he gave us some delicious *Ingoldsby Legends,* and, almost recently as it seems, so fresh are the pictures in everyone's memory, so frequently are they adapted, quoted and apologetically imitated, he delighted everyone with his immortal illustrations to **Alice in Wonderland** and **Through the Looking-glass.** (p. 10)

"Sir John Tenniel," in Punch, Vol. CXLVI, March 4, 1914, pp. 1-16.

THE OUTLOOK

If Sir John Tenniel's cartoons were not enough to insure him fame, his illustration to Lewis Carroll's masterpieces, **Alice in Wonderland** and **Through the Looking-glass,** would have brought it to him. Not even Cruikshank's illustrations to *Pickwick Papers* and other Dickens novels more adequately carry out the Dickens text than do these in their illustration of the Carroll text. Indeed, one hardly conceives the text without them.

This is not all. What illustrations have ever more successfully satirized the characters and tendencies of public men? In this they have given an especially sharp reality to Lewis Carroll's pages. Not only was there plenty of humor in the pictures of the Cheshire Cat, the Mad Hatter, and the Red Queen, there was in the Dodo, the Jabberwock, the March Hare, and the Mock Turtle reference to a universal humanity, and especially to that humanity when found in a parliamentary chamber. As Mr. Choate, one of the speakers at the dinner given to Tenniel some years ago, asked, What statesman, scholar, poet, or soldier of England has had a fame equal to the White Rabbit's?—would it be possible to go through the British House of Lords or the American Senate without finding some reflection of that great character? Thus the illustrator who had already appealed to a large audience by his *Punch* cartoons now appealed, through his Lewis Carroll pictures, to an even larger audience. (pp. 513-14)

"The Illustrator of 'Alice'," in The Outlook, Vol. CVI, March 7, 1914, pp. 513-14.

ARCHIBALD MacMECHAN

Apt as [Carroll's words are in **Alice in Wonderland**], and cunningly as they are joined together, they would miss something of their effect without the pictures. As Alice thought, "What *is* the use of a book without pictures and conversations?" Indeed, it is almost impossible to imagine **Alice,** without the illustrations. Pictures are not always an aid to the understanding of books; very often, they only spoil one's ideas; the illustrated books which are unqualified successes are very rare. But in this case the talent of the artist has been so happily inspired by the talent of the writer that each heightens the effect produced by the other.

The artist is the second, not the first, but he has entered so thoroughly into the spirit of the text that his interpretation is well-nigh perfect. Without him, we should never have realized to the full the delightful fatuity of the King of Hearts, or the ferocity of his terrible consort with the *penchant* for beheading all who offended her, or the fussiness of "Brer Rabbit," or the immense dignity of the Caterpillar. His skilful pencil has created a whole gallery of portraits. There is the March Hare with the wisp of hay about his ears, and the Hatter with the advertising ticket on his "topper": the wild light in their eyes tells the tale of their insanity. In striking contrast to their eccentric demeanour is the reposeful manner of the Dormouse, whose ideal of life has been so admirably summed up as "Nuts ready cracked, and between nuts, sleep." Here are many ingenious turns in the plates. The most original conception of all is the melancholy Mock-Turtle who was once a real turtle. For this the artist found no hint in the text;

so he grafted the head, tail, and hind legs of a calf on the carapace and fore-flippers of a tortoise; and a more woe-begone beast it would be hard to find in fact or fable. I have always wanted to know Ruskin's opinion of the Gryphon, having in mind his famous criticism of the Lombardic and Renaissance griffins in *Modern Painters.* Are the lion and eagle natures perfectly fused in it? Would the motion of this creature's wings give it the earache? In my humble judgment, it seems a most satisfactory result of the constructive imagination. As he lies asleep, in the way of Alice and the Duchess, he looks like a coiled steel spring. When his hand is perfectly free, our artist is perhaps even more amusing. The humours of the trial scene are almost wholly original and admirable, the finest, perhaps, being the portraits of the counsel,—an eagle, a crow, and a parrot, all in barrister's robes and wigs. In the second part of the trial, where the King-Judge is explaining so lucidly to the jury the verses imputed to the Knave, all the lawyers are sound asleep. Most of all are we grateful for the pictures of Alice. She is not a perfect heroine. She has her little tempers, is not exactly philosophical in distress; nor is she altogether free from certain affectations and a desire to show off. But this is the worst that can be said of her. She is a capital representative of the finest race of children in the world, a substantial, graceful, well-groomed, innocent, fresh-faced little English lass, "And sweet as English air could make her." There is a certain national primness in all her attitudes, suggestive of nursery governesses and extremely well-regulated families. She is a little gentlewoman, never forgetting her manners. The finest grotesque, to my mind, is the picture in which she appears with the baby in her arms that turned, dream-fashion, into a pig. The contrast between the sweet, shy, wondering face of the lovely child and the smug vulgarity of the little porker's phiz is simply delightful. It is Titania, Queen of the Fairies, caressing Nick Bottom the weaver, over again. (pp. 263-66)

And who is the artist? Some young lady, with a talent for draughtsmanship? Some student in the Academy schools? Not at all. The illustrator of this child's story-book is the veteran artist, Sir John Tenniel, who for forty years probably did as much as any one man to form English opinion on political and social questions. . . . It seems like condescension for an artist of this importance to make pictures for children; but Tenniel did not think it beneath him. The opinion of Mr. Pennell, who is well qualified to judge, is that, from the artist's point of view, Tenniel's **Alice** drawings are his very best work. (pp. 266-67)

Archibald MacMechan, "Everybody's Alice," in his The Life of a Little College and Other Papers, Houghton Mifflin Company, 1914, pp. 233-72.

FORREST REID

The work of John Tenniel . . . never exercised the slightest influence on his contemporaries . . . . He is said by the Dalziels to have studied in Germany, and to have been 'strongly impressed with German Art'. Be that as it may, his style is his own, and, once formed, he never deviated from it. One may add that, though admirably adapted to his work as *Punch* cartoonist, for serious illustration, and above all for the illustration of tales of modern life, it was an unsympathetic and unsuitable style.

Tenniel drew in pencil on the wood, leaving Swain, his usual engraver, to interpret the delicate greys of the drawing as best he might. Sometimes he drew from photographs; to the end of his life he refused to draw from the living model. Lewis Carroll, in a letter to Miss [Emily Gertrude] Thompson on the subject, says, 'I want you to do my fairy drawings from *life*. Mr. Tenniel is the only artist, who has drawn for me, who resolutely refused to use a model, and declared he no more needed one than I should need a multiplication-table to work a mathematical problem!'—after which there is no more to be said; and it is not, of course, the absence of the living model that gives to Tenniel's line its coldness or to his drawings their hardness. (p. 26)

Tenniel, who could put so much beauty into a horse's head, never found it easy to give beauty to his human figures. For female beauty especially, he relied entirely on regular features and unnaturally long eyelashes. . . . [*Lalla Rookh* (1861)] was at one time regarded as his masterpiece. *The Times* actually went so far as to declare *Lalla Rookh* to be 'the greatest illustrated achievement of any single hand'. It does contain several notable designs—those on pages 46 and 149 in particular—but *Lalla Rookh* was hardly the kind of poem likely to inspire Tenniel's best work, and did not in fact do so. Where his talent found its most lively expression was in what we may call grotesque comedy, or farce. We have only to turn to the very early volumes of *Punch,* while Leech was still doing the cartoons, to discover scores of instances of this. There, in initial letters, in head-pieces, tail-pieces and vignettes, in the *Illustrations to Shakespeare,* and other whimsical drawings, we find just the qualities which have made the designs for the two *Alices* famous. And except for the *Alices,* and *The Ingoldsby Legends* (1864), in which he collaborates with Cruikshank and Leech, Tenniel never got a text that suited him. He was essentially a humorous draughtsman: that is to say, taken by themselves, without any printed joke attached to them, his drawings are funny enough to make us laugh. Also he could draw animals with great skill and understanding. There is more charm in the picture of the black kitten at the end of *Through the Looking Glass* than in any of the pictures of Alice herself, pleasant little girl as she is. One has an idea that the black kitten actually sat for its portrait, but the portraits of Alice seem now and then slightly out of drawing, the head just a shade too large for the trim little body. (pp. 26-7)

It is on his designs for the two *Alices* . . . that Tenniel's fame as an illustrator rests. Never was a text more completely grasped, expanded, and illuminated. Picture and text are indeed so entirely in harmony that one marvels and resents that any later artist should have attempted a re-illustration. (p. 28)

Lewis Carroll was never again to find such an illustrator. The choice of Harry Furniss for *Sylvie and Bruno* hardly strikes us as the happiest alternative he might have hit upon, though Furniss certainly took a lot of trouble over the drawings, and they pleased the author. A. B. Frost's designs for *Rhyme and Reason* are infinitely better, and Henry Holiday's for *The Hunting of the Snark* in their decorative beauty carry on the true Pre-Raphaelite tradition, bringing it into the world of grotesque. Nevertheless, neither Frost nor Holiday was inspired in the way Tenniel was inspired. They had not the same chance, it might be urged, and this is true. Still, the Tenniel designs remain supreme, and looking over the proofs in the Dalziel albums we see what pains he took with them. There are two entirely different versions of the picture of the King's Messenger (our old friend the Hatter) in prison, for instance. The first is good, but the second, which is the one used in the book, is better. And some of her admirers may not know that the incomparable Duchess is more or less a portrait of a real lady and a real duchess. The lady lived a good many years ago, and has the remarkable reputation of being the ugliest woman in history. She was the Duchess Margaret of Carinthia and Tyrol, and her portrait was painted by Quentin Matsys, the great Flemish master, in the fifteenth century. She is distinctly more simian than Alice's friend, and has an even longer upper lip; but there she is, head-dress and all, the latter hardly a whit exaggerated, in Quentin Matsys's picture. Where that picture was when Tenniel drew his Duchess from it I do not know, but comparatively recently it passed into the possession of Mr. Hugh Blaker, who bought it when it was put up for sale at Christie's a few years ago. (pp. 28-9)

> *Forrest Reid, "Some Precursors," in his* Illustrators of the Sixties, *Faber & Gwyer Limited, 1928, pp. 20-9.*

F. J. HARVEY DARTON

> [*Children's Books in England was originally published in 1932.*]

None of [Dodgson's] later works is on a par with the two *Alice* books, which themselves are an almost unique example of a precedent and sequel inseparably linked and absolutely equal in excellence. Every reader has his preferences for particular chapters. But those who think the Mad Hatter's tea-party the supreme joy of the first volume will be quite ready to put the Tweedledum and Tweedledee chapter in the second on a level with it. Those who agree with the Cheshire Cat that 'we're all mad here', or with the unanswerable truths of the tea-party nonsense, will accept with equal joy the version of Bishop Berkeley furnished by Tweedledum and Tweedledee at 'the *lovely* sight' of the Red King asleep. It is sometimes only by remembering that the one tale is about a pack of cards, and the other about a chess-problem, that a devoutly familiar reader can separate the different scenes and persons into their appropriate books. The whole twofold work is Wonderland, one and indivisible.

And the same criticism or argument for the foolishness of criticism—applies to the illustrations. They were not only the happiest achievement of John Tenniel in his long and honoured career, containing his freest draughtsmanship (never his strong point) and his most universal humour, but they were never unequal, and they cannot ever be dissociated from the text. Carroll and Tenniel, though not one name to the extent that Gilbert and Sullivan became fifteen years or so later, make one complete work of art—and the *Alices* are each a work of art, with a climax, a beginning, a middle and an end, as inevitable as in any greater fabric of the literary imagination, but entire and indivisible in the imagination of all affectionate readers.

The drawings do not 'date', except for the Victorian figure of Alice herself, and she only wears the wrong costume for today. The fact that Tenniel's work remained in copyright while Dodgson's text ran out of it has shown that clearly enough. The admirable living or recent artists who have re-illustrated the stories prove it. The best of them have made a charming modern flesh-and-blood Alice. But—as they would doubtless admit generously enough—they have not invented a new Gryphon, or a new Mock Turtle, White Rabbit, March Hare, Hatter, Caterpillar, Cheshire Cat, Red Queen, White Knight. These are essentially, and must always so remain, the creation of the first artist and of the author whose fantasy provided the vivid details. A twentieth-century heroine merely accentuates that fact.

The collaboration was curious. Dodgson was not an easy man to work with: both Holiday and Harry Furniss were made aware that he believed in verbal rather than imaginative inspiration for an artist. He actually drew for Alice Liddell the picture of Wonderland Alice with the extensible neck, the White Rabbit, the animals in the pool of tears, Bill the Lizard, the Caterpillar, Father William, the Court Hearts (though they are very like those in Lamb's *King and Queen of Hearts*), the flamingo, the Gryphon and Mock Turtle, and some other details. Tenniel . . . took these models and translated them from amateur homeliness into riper, more workmanlike copies so individual as to be almost fresh imaginings. The rest—and the ***Looking-Glass*** pictures—he seems to have more or less invented, but on the basis of the strict text and verbal conference.

The strange thing is that in spite of this joint originality some of the drawings look as if they had been based on other illustrations or things of the day, or even upon older sources. The Duchess is neither more nor less than Margaretta of Carinthia, the 'ugly Duchess' of Matsys. And if a forgotten picture-book of 1864, an anonymous *Rummical Rhymes,* be exhumed, it will be found to contain much the same Duchess, and several other figures oddly like Tenniel's. There is here no suggestion of plagiarism. The artists of the day had much technique in common, as well as a slight general identity of conception. If less personally characteristic minor work by Tenniel, Linley Sambourne, C. H. Bennett, Stacy Marks, and even Dick Doyle, were assembled without identification, it would sometimes be hard to name the artist correctly. Sambourne, in the *New Sandford and Merton,* often uses Tenniel's rather rigid line with more of his own fluidity. And for comic characters they all had a certain repertory in the pantomime-stage of that Planché era. It remains true that the Duchess for all English children is the work of John Tenniel, not of Matsys, Old Father William a credible absurdity in a poem by Lewis Carroll, not a bore in Southey's *Old Man's Comforts:* just as Portia is from a play by Shakespeare and not from a tale in *Gesta Romanorum.* Tenniel, at least, never did better drawings. Indeed, he did not do much other book illustration in the narrow sense. When the decoration of *Sylvie and Bruno* was suggested to him, he declined it: he had somehow lost the faculty for such work; which, considering the completely different temper of the later book, is something to be thankful for. There is not a word in the ***Alices,*** nor a line of drawing, to be explained or regretted. (pp. 257-59)

F. J. Harvey Darton, "The Sixties: 'Alice' and After," in his Children's Books in England: Five Centuries of Social Life, *edited by Brian Alderson, third edition, Cambridge University Press, 1982, pp. 252-92.*

HAROLD HARTLEY

In 1865, when the imperishable tale of ***Alice in Wonderland*** charmed its readers for the first time, English book illustration, as distinguished from book decoration, was in its golden period, a happy and versatile adventurer; and among its best friends were Lewis Carroll and his heroine. 'What is the use of a book', thought Alice, 'without pictures or conversations?'

It was the survival of the child in Dodgson that invaded Wonderland as Carroll, and invested so much time and money in illustrative drawings and engraved prints. Dodgson was thirty-three in 1865, and not at all well-to-do; so he was often alarmed by the costs of Carroll's fondness for illustrations. His chosen artist, John Tenniel, forty-five years old, went into Wonderland as Alice's companion, and his forty-two drawings had rare good luck, for they were engraved on wood by two artists who enjoyed and retained their inimitable wit and spirit. I refer to the Dalziel brothers. The author and his tale, the illustrator and his engravers, worked together in precisely the right way, so the woodcuts looked as necessary to Alice as Alice and her adventures were to them. Happily, too, in ***Through the Looking-Glass,*** the art of loyal illustration was equally good, thanks to Tenniel and the same engravers.

In some books, you will remember, the text is almost an unnecessary appendage to the illustrations; and there are other books, perhaps more numerous, in which the illustrations are intrusive and annoying, because they distract a reader's attention by introducing alien and unsympathetic ideas. What Carroll needed, and he got it as a rule, was a perfect marriage between his own work and the engraved pictures.

As Tenniel had a style of his own, exceedingly vital and distinctive, he might have become assertive as Tenniel, and thus apart from Carroll's Wonderland. As he suffered no such mishap, we have no more desire to separate his drawings from Carroll's genius than we have to separate Alice's adventures from Tenniel's right companionship. Every picture grows out of the story as if by magic; and when one considers the humanity in the animals that Carroll created with his pen and that Tenniel charmed into portraiture, one is inclined to think that here, in these illustrated animals, are the real missing links. It has been said, indeed, that most persons could find their own selves if they looked for them in Tenniel's Alician humour. No statesman of the 1860's, and no soldier, achieved a fame equal to the White Rabbit's; and then, as now, symptoms of the March Hare abounded everywhere, and among all classes. (pp. 109-10)

Let us try to be quite fair when we think of Tenniel in relation to the rest of Carroll's artists. He was the best of them all, no doubt, but the others had not equal opportunities. He gained his great success from Carroll's most enjoyable achievements. That is why he renewed his youth in middle age, with a right enthusiasm that went gaily into improved work. The other artists were handicapped by Carroll himself, and yet we think of them all with pleasure. (p. 111)

Harold Hartley, "Lewis Carroll and His Artists and Engravers," in Lewis Carroll Centenary Exhibition: Catalogue, *edited by Falconer Madan, J. & E. Bumpus, Ltd., 1932, pp. 109-16.*

MONTAGU FRANK MODDER

Wherever the ***Adventures of Alice in Wonderland*** is read—and that means almost *everywhere*—the charming drawings by Sir John Tenniel that illustrate that popular favorite are admired and enjoyed by both young and old. The drawings of Alice, the Duchess, the Rabbit, the Mad Hatter, Tweedledum and Tweedledee, and the numerous other entertaining characters that flit through the pages of the great nonsense classic are as much a part of the story as the writing itself. If ever two men were made by nature to work together, they were Lewis Carroll and John Tenniel. The irrepressible humor of Tenniel's grotesque figures and humanized animals

Illustration from Alice's Adventures in Wonderland. *Tenniel's Duchess is thought to be inspired by Margaret of Carinthia and Tyrol, who has the reputation of being the ugliest woman in history and served as the model for the painting* The Ugly Duchess *by Flemish artist Quinten Massys.*

were exactly in the spirit of the ingenious and fanciful Carroll. . . .

If Carroll . . . had continued to work with Tenniel, perhaps all his books would have been as successful as the two in which they worked together. Who, alas, remembers Carroll's *Sylvie and Bruno,* which was *not* illustrated by J. T.?

Montagu Frank Modder, "Sir John Tenniel: The Famous Cartoonist Who Illustrated 'Alice in Wonderland'," in Scholastic, Vol. 30, No. 3, February 20, 1937, p. 12.

GEORGE SHELTON HUBBELL

A child's character is desperately complex, as students of childhood all know, and as all discriminating parents agree. In fact, Carroll fails to do justice to this complexity, at least to the extent of his Victorian reticences. And other people may complain that as they remember Alice of Wonderland from their early reading, she seemed a very simple child, colorless, with little or no character of her own, moving among a phantasmagoria of sharply defined individuals. (p. 192)

Any such attribution of colorlessness to the character of Alice is probably due to: (1) the influence of Tenniel's illus-

trations; (2) the failure of some readers, as children, lost in a gorgeous story, to appreciate or even notice character at all; (3) the natural tendency of a fairly realistic personality to seem unremarkable among vigorous caricatures; (4) the too common assumption that any child, by virtue of being a child, can as a matter of course have no significant traits, no general interest. Most of these obstacles to an appreciation of Alice vanish as soon as one recognizes their existence. But the effect of the Tenniel drawings will require some explanation.

Harry Furniss, who illustrated *Sylvie and Bruno,* wrote that Carroll did not, in general, like Tenniel's drawings. While this statement may be colored by professional jealousy (Carroll asked Tenniel to illustrate another of his books), there is evidence that the illustrations, which have rivaled the popularity of the stories themselves, were less satisfactory to the author than to the general public. He complained, for one thing, that Tenniel would not work from models, and that artists who drew from their own imagination made their characters monotonously alike, or without significant individualizing traits. Though this lack of individuality can hardly be urged against most of Tenniel's Wonderland creatures, it is true that his Alice has rather blank, regular features, generally suggesting too much maturity, and almost never revealing the inward appreciativeness suggested by the text. One suspects that Tenniel interpreted the various situations of Alice as if she were a grown woman, and then accommodated the postures and expressions as best he could to the scale of the child. But the worst of it is that he always presents Alice with an apparent extravert interest in her surroundings, whereas the text reveals her as busy with her own speculations, often very skeptical of her specious companions. Carroll's photographs of Alice Liddell show a child with an air of being spiritually remote from the present physical scene. Probably Tenniel, with his gift for sharp perception of those conspicuous signs which feed the cartoonist's craft, had not the temperament, the perception, or the art to draw Alice subtly with the knowing abstraction of a Mona Lisa beneath a child's simplicity. Most children, probably, would fail to appreciate such illustrations, just as they overlook the deeper implications of the story itself. Children seldom complain of a blank pretty face in a picture; they enjoy the dimpled insipidity of their dolls. They may deplore Alice's old-fashioned clothes or her long straight hair, but they hardly notice the frequent mature sophistication of her features. If she seems rather old, they attribute the impression to the length of her dress, but for most children her diminutive size is sufficient evidence of her youth. Lewis Carroll, however, may well have deplored in Tenniel's work the almost total absence of Alice Liddell's genuine child nature with its piquant individual air of abstraction; and the absence or misinterpretation of his idealized Alice's inner poise and naïve, uncynical skepticism. The main trouble is that Alice is no subject for caricature. The story puts a caricatured society in very unflattering comparison with the candid intelligence of a wise but realistic child. The author was able to do both the satiric sketch and the subtly significant portrait. But Tenniel's great gift sufficed only for the sketch. His attempt at a sympathetic portrait of Alice resulted in a somewhat too graceful doll, with the expression and most of the features of an adult sophisticate. Tenniel was wise in declining to undertake illustrations for *Sylvie and Bruno,* a story that stressed the seriousness of Lewis Carroll, and diminished the satire.

Children often gaze intently at Tenniel's pictures while some one reads aloud the story of the *Alice* books. At all events, the pictures are likely to make the deeper, more immediate impression upon them, and suggest an easy, unsubtle interpretation of Alice's character. Child readers hardly heed or easily forget the heroine's revealing reveries, but remember the doll-like figure from the drawings, quaint, not very impressive, and somewhat irrelevant to the astonishing creatures of wonder and satire. When these child readers become adults, they recall Alice as the admirable but unimportant little spectator who won immortality by happening upon a gorgeous pageant of marvels, thanks to the unique genius of Lewis Carroll.

But Alice was a real child without whose unique qualities Carroll himself would never have discovered Wonderland. And she was also a creature of his own imagination, embodying many of his best qualities and standing for that which he found best in life. As such, she was simple, candid, shrewd, a child of good will, not to be stultified by all the bluster of imposing stupidity, immortal in her forthright and beautiful integrity. (pp. 192-95)

George Shelton Hubbell, "Triple Alice," in The Sewanee Review, *Vol. XLVIII, No. 2, Spring, 1940, pp. 174-96.*

FLORENCE BECKER LENNON

Tenniel was a mild and gentle man who knew his own mind. In illustrating, he put himself in the author's place and used all his imagination and artistry to recreate the latter's ideas. He was, like Carroll himself, incorruptible and original. These two incompatibles in double harness won the race—and cut the traces. "With *Through the Looking-Glass,"* said Tenniel tactfully, "the faculty of making book illustrations departed from me." (p. 110)

Carroll's own drawings always expressed two principal aspects of his nature—the humorously horrible and the "sweet." The latter gradually encroached on the former, but without quite replacing it. Tenniel's work, of course, was infinitely more vigorous, without much of either the "sweet" or the horrible . . . . (p. 111)

For the *Alice* books [their] collaboration was ideal. In their first form, the books are as finished as the Parthenon was before the Turks thought of storing munitions in it. The futile attempts to make new illustrations to the *Alice* books resemble the further finishing of the Parthenon when the munitions exploded. An explosion that harmed neither Carroll nor Tenniel, however, is Marguerite Mespoulet's book, *Creators of Wonderland.* With text and illustration she shows that Tenniel, at least, and Carroll very probably, was influenced by the work of J. J. Grandville. In the picture of the two footmen in *Wonderland* Tenniel definitely used a frog footman of Grandville's. The Paris *Charivari,* founded in 1832, that used Grandville's pictures, circulated quite freely in England. *Punch,* of course, is the London *Charivari,* and Thackeray, one of its founders, shuttled back and forth between Paris and London, and knew Grandville's work well, as indeed many art lovers in England did. (p. 113)

Tenniel . . . made his own whatever he touched. His personal style, unmodified by Grandville, would have been too harsh and uncompromising for the dream books. His taste told him what to use, as in the case of the Ugly Duchess, whom he handled much more mercifully than her original Creator did. (p. 114)

Florence Becker Lennon, "Escape into the Garden," in her Victoria through the Looking-Glass: The Life of Lewis Carroll, *Simon and Schuster, 1945, pp. 107-20.*

MAY HILL ARBUTHNOT

[There] has never been a happier combination of author and artist than Tenniel and Carroll—both satirists and scholars, both properly serious about children's innate good taste, and both meeting children's demands for the best. (p. 24)

Sir John Tenniel in his illustrations for *Alice* has fixed forever the face, figure, and dress of this beloved little girl. Long straight hair, a grave, prim face, a neat, perky dress covered with a pinafore, and the straight, slim legs clad in horizontally striped stockings make an appealing little figure which no one ever forgets. This is Alice, the Alice who remains impeccably Alice even when her neck has grown as long as a giraffe's. The Tenniel rabbit is an equally unforgettable figure with his sporty tweed coat, his massive gold watch and chain, his swagger walking stick, just the kind of fellow who *would* keep the Duchess waiting. For Tenniel does not merely illustrate. He interprets, giving the mood and the manner of the creature as well as his outer appearance. The Duchess and the Red Queen wear the habiliments of nobility, but they are ferocious looking. The Mock Turtle is shedding tears all right, but you don't trust him; and the funny daftness of the Mad Hatter's appearance puts you in the mood for his conversation.

You also have to admire the remarkable technique of these pictures. Tenniel draws Alice stepping through the looking glass, with curious and plausible ease, half of her on one side, half on the other. The Cheshire Cat disappearing, leaving only his grin behind, and the playing-card and chess people are only a few of his pen-and-ink wonders. These sketches are so alive, so profoundly interpretative that no one has ever wished for colored illustrations of Alice. They have been made from time to time, and some of them are pleasing, but no other artist has been able to illustrate Alice with the nonchalant magic of Tenniel. If possible, let the children's first experience with Alice be accompanied by the drawings of her first illustrator, Sir John Tenniel, most excellent interpreter of Wonderland. (p. 293)

> *May Hill Arbuthnot, "Children's Books: History and Trends" and "New Magic," in her* Children and Books, *Scott, Foresman and Company, 1947, pp. 11-31, 276-359.*

FRANCES SARZANO

When Sir John Tenniel died in 1914, at the age of ninety-three, he left by his industry ten thousand pounds for his relatives and friends, two thousand *Punch* cartoons for future historians, thirty-eight books for the collectors of Victoriana, and two small volumes for successive generations—*Alice's Adventures in Wonderland* and *Through the Looking-Glass.* His work had spanned the finest period of nineteenth-century book illustration; English satire had changed countenance in his cartoons; half a century of British history had been recorded with a six-H pencil on the wood-block. (p. 9)

Tenniel was a conscientious illustrator who studied his texts carefully. His authors could be comfortably certain that he would not (as Leech in one illustration to Dickens's *Christmas Books*) slip in a character who had no right to be there, or produce a picture entirely independent of the printed word, as the indomitable Rossetti did for Tennyson.

Viewed as a whole, his illustrative work shows that in spite of occasional lapses he was a careful and capable draughtsman, with a strong sense of composition and an agreeable eye for pattern. The play of light interested him; in Bryant's *Poems* (1858) and *Lays of the Holy Land* (1858) night scenes of battlefields are lit with the chill, ineluctable quality of moonlight. A formula of strong light and shadow occurs also in the *Aesop*—the goat looking down the well and the bull at the mouth of the cave follow the same pattern. In this book, the artist seems to probe delicately into his medium and the drawings suggest an interest in experiment which compensates for the slight immaturities of the technique. Tenniel loved animals: he drew them sympathetically, with faintly humanized expressions, and their charm for him touches every illustration in the book. In spite of hours spent watching them in their cages, however, he was guilty of a few zoological inaccuracies, and for the second edition some of the illustrations were drawn by Josef Wolf, while Tenniel himself redrew others.

Aesop gave the first hint of Tenniel's powers of drollery, which reappear, unexpectedly, in *The Grave* (1858), as well

as in *Puck on Pegasus* (1861) and in some of the drawings for the *Ingoldsby Legends.*

As distinct from his drollery, Tenniel's humour must be enjoyed as part of the Victorian manner. It is humour that is consciously funny, like a comedy over-acted by an amateur dramatic society. Even when Tenniel's people express serious emotion, they do so with ripe Victorian over-emphasis; at times he seems positively to be drawing in italics. His characters hop from one emotional cliché to another: their teeth 'chatter with rage'; their faces are 'radiant with joy'; they 'weep uncontrollably' when they are 'harrowed by grief', and doubtless they ultimately die, like the era that bred them, with their features 'nobly composed'. Nevertheless, Tenniel's illustrations to Shirley Brooks's two novels, *The Silver Cord* (serialized in *Once a Week*, 1860-1) and *The Gordian Knot* (1860), include some very pleasing drawings—attractive enough to make one regret that he illustrated so few novels and so many ballads and Norse legends.

Two major faults appear in Tenniel's illustrative work.

He had not a craftsman's understanding of the possibilities and limitations of the wood-block (as, for example, Boyd Houghton had), consequently his work suffered badly in reproduction. It is useless to blame the engraver for the artist's fault: the Dalziels, notably, achieved superhuman results, but they could not overcome the nature of boxwood and printer's ink. Inevitably, Tenniel's thin, grey, thistledown lines printed thin, black and hard. When his work is etched on steel (as in *The Gordian Knot*), the difference is startling. The line becomes fluent and the drawings take on a persuasive charm that is wholly absent on wood.

Secondly, Tenniel relied too much on an excellent memory. Partly from the impact of the pre-Raphaelite doctrine of 'Truth to Nature', illustrators had begun to use models, yet Tenniel, apart from his time at Clipstone Street, never drew from life. But a memory, however good, is apt to play visual tricks: occasionally it may become two-dimensional when three dimensions are needed. Some of Tenniel's drawings seem pictures drawn from other pictures, as if there were no first-hand intimacy between the draughtsman and his subject. Again, it is fatally easy to record what is remembered without suspecting what has been forgotten, and often Tenniel draws, as it were, the features of things without their personality. The essential quality eludes him. He remembers how a wall is built or how a sleeve falls, but the stoniness of stone and the silkiness of silk have slipped unnoticed from his mind.

Certainly one cannot demand, indiscriminately and from all draughtsmen equally, some specific quality such as appreciation of form or texture: it is for the draughtsman to express himself in his own terms, laying what emphasis he chooses on this or that aspect of drawing. Yet, considering Tenniel's work in its own terms, it may be that its quality would have been more sympathetic if the artist had not had, as he put it, 'a wonderful memory of observation'.

For *Alice's Adventures in Wonderland* and *Through the Looking-Glass,* Tenniel produced ninety-two drawings, of which Lewis Carroll liked one. Author and artist agreed on Humpty Dumpty, and with Humpty Dumpty agreement ended.

Carroll . . . was condemned by nature to be an irritating patron. Saddled with a strong visual imagination, he lacked sufficient manual skill to transfer his images to paper. He was forced to rely on other people's hands for the expression of his own vision; he felt profound distress if they failed in an exact appreciation of what was clear to his inner eye, and mortification if they interposed an alien vision of their own. . . .

After his *Alice* experiences, Tenniel tried hard to avoid illustrating *Through the Looking-Glass,* but he was pressed into accepting the commission. Relations did not improve, and contentious correspondence passed between the two eminently obstinate Victorians. But it was all completely courteous: like the Red and the White Knights, Carroll and Tenniel 'observed the Rules of Battle'. (pp. 13-17)

The body-blow came . . . when the author advised the artist to draw from life. 'Mr Tenniel is the only artist who has drawn for me,' Carroll sadly informed Miss Thompson, 'who resolutely refused to use a model and declared he no more needed one than I should need a multiplication table to work a mathematical problem!' Carroll was the last man to refute an argument that could be expressed in mathematical terms, so presumably Tenniel was left to draw the Jabberwock unhampered by life.

The fractious relations of author and illustrator resolved into a perfect companionship in print.

There have been many better drawings for books than those done by Tenniel in the *Alices,* but better illustrations do not exist. Carroll's two books not only exact from the artist every ability he possesses, they turn his limitations equally to account. Elsewhere, Tenniel's precise, matter-of-fact line seems sometimes insensitive; as a container for Carroll's explicit imagination, it is this very quality of flat statement which makes the drawing ideal. *Alice* could not be illustrated with fairy-tale gossamers; its characters are too trenchant with reality—though it is reality encountered on uncustomary planes. From Tenniel's exact pencil the creatures of Wonderland spring into definition: one after another, they are seen with the dreamer's precise vision and overwhelming certitude.

The *Alices* harvest the work of early days on *Punch,* the plump humour of the little initial letters and the *Pocket Book* burlesque. In *Alice* the expressive animals of *Aesop* reappear, drawn with a tenderness that the human subjects lack. Alice herself lacks this sympathetic sense: hers is the least realized character in Wonderland. But, once again, Tenniel is well served by a fault. As if by mistake, he strikes the perfect Wonderland unbalance: it is the small human presence which lacks conviction in the land where normality somersaults.

There has been a suggestion that, through his work in the *Alices,* Tenniel might be counted among the lesser precursors of surrealist art. Lewis Carroll, certainly, is near the boundaries of surrealist writing: all his ideas, he said, 'came of themselves', some, apparently, as hypnagogic illusions at night. (pp. 18-19)

Tenniel's contribution to *Alice* 'surrealism', however, was no more than the technique of precise delineation and sharp detail which he, in common with the pre-Raphaelites, had learned from Cornelius and his school. Among notable surrealists, Dali acknowledges the pre-Raphaelites' influence, and their technique has reappeared in his work. Tenniel's style is related thus to one of the techniques used in present-day surrealism, but there the association ends. His brilliant *Alice*

work is not creative but interpretative: the decisive mental impulse is that of Lewis Carroll.

With the possible exception of Henry Holiday, who drew nine illustrations to *The Hunting of the Snark,* none of Carroll's other illustrators had Tenniel's opportunities. Certainly none produced work that equalled his. Holiday goes two-thirds of the way to good illustrations, but his drawings are not a co-ordinated series; neither characterization nor technique is evenly maintained. Carroll's own sketched illustrations to *Alice* are weak and inept drawings, but occasionally they have an almost Lear-like charm, hybrid of sophistication and innocence. His drawings for 'Father William' are admirable burlesque. But so complete is the tyranny of Tenniel that Lewis Carroll, as illustrator, seems an intruder in his own book.

Equally, one finds it impossible to do justice to the later illustrators of *Alice.* For most people, Tenniel's drawings have the inviolability peculiar to things seen and accepted in youth. To alter them is to tamper with childhood's *credo,* when no article can be sacrificed with out imperilling the whole. The child believed equally in the sepia photograph of its grandmother and the Mad Hatter as drawn by Tenniel; on these are piled a toy-brick structure of visual experiences and acceptances, and the adult, try as he will, cannot welcome the artist who pulls out the bottom brick by re-illustrating *Alice.* (pp. 19-20)

> *Frances Sarzano, in her* Sir John Tenniel, *Pellegrini & Cudahy, 1948, 96 p.*

JANET ADAM SMITH

[Other illustrated *Alices*] have one merit: to remind us, by contrast, of Tenniel's capacity to take *Alice* seriously. Where later illustrators snigger and exaggerate, make everything absurd and grotesque, where even Carroll in his original sketches tended to caricature, Tenniel takes the story at its face value. The drawings in themselves are not funny, as Lear's are funny; they are serious illustrations of funny situations: just as in dreams, though we may be doing the most absurd things, we keep our everyday appearance. The White Knight blundering through the wood on his horse is just as realistic as Undine riding through the forest with her knight beside her in the frontispiece to the first book Tenniel illustrated (*Undine,* 1846). Without raising an eyebrow Tenniel could set down the Rocking-horse fly, the weeping Walrus, the Rabbit consulting his watch, the spectacled Sheep at her knitting—so that it comes as a surprise to find him roundly stating in a letter to Carroll that "a wasp in a wig is altogether beyond the appliances of art." . . . There is a great deal of queerness in *Alice,* but there is never anything silly, and Tenniel's grave drawings have all the logic as well as the fantasy of Carroll's invention. (pp. 23-4)

> *Janet Adam Smith, "Illustrated Story-Books," in her* Children's Illustrated Books, *Collins, 1948, pp. 21-9.*

ALEXANDER L. TAYLOR

[*Through the Looking-Glass*] is unlike anything else, a separate and distinct form of art. (p. 145)

For such a book, Tenniel was the ideal illustrator. His method, too, was a form of metaphor, of which the famous '**Dropping the Pilot**' cartoon to mark the dismissal of Bismarck is a good example. Nevertheless, Tenniel was not a great and original artist like Dodgson. He was an illustrator, and few of the ideas even in his *Punch* cartoons were his own. On the contrary, he was given his ideas to illustrate at the Wednesday *Punch* conferences in which he took little part, his political opinions being mildly Conservative, whereas the policy of *Punch* at that time was mildly Liberal.

Altogether, Tenniel did ninety-two illustrations for Dodgson, and Harry Furniss's story that the only one Dodgson liked was Humpty Dumpty is quite incredible. According to Furniss, Tenniel could not tolerate 'that conceited old don' any more, and he quotes Sir John as giving him a week in which to reach the same opinion as himself. There was undoubtedly constant well-bred friction between Dodgson and Tenniel. The latter tried hard to avoid illustrating *Through the Looking-glass,* and when Dodgson wrote to him about a later book *(The Hunting of the Snark?)* declined on the grounds that *Through the Looking-glass* had exhausted his interest in book illustration. This he regarded as 'a curious fact'.

Dodgson himself had a pictorial mind and never gave up the practice of making preliminary sketches for his illustrator to copy. He had pictures in his mind which his own hand had not the skill to capture on paper. Tenniel was to do that and the sketches were intended to assist Tenniel. The trouble was that Tenniel brought an alien intelligence to bear on the problem. Of Dodgson's real purposes he had not the smallest inkling, but he saw wonderful opportunities of a quite different kind in Dodgson's queer dream-characters, and, from his point of view, rightly and properly imparted to them his own style of drollery, which he had developed in his work for *Punch,* his illustrations for *Aesop's Fables* and other books. The details of the story were less important to him than the artist's duty to make a good picture at all costs, and the pictures he produced were so good in themselves that Dodgson often had to compromise. (pp. 145-46)

Perhaps if Dodgson had taken Tenniel into his confidence there would have been less friction. As it was, Dodgson had no reason to be dissatisfied. Tenniel tried his best to reconcile the demands of his author with those of his medium, and it must be remembered that to him many of Dodgson's requirements must have seemed capricious and unreasonable. Only very occasionally did he kick over the traces, as in the case of the 'wasp in a wig', which he declared was 'beyond the appliances of art'.

There have been, as Frances Sarzano declares in her study of Sir John Tenniel, better drawings but no better illustrations [see excerpt above]. In fact, they are simply the illustrations to the *Alice* books and nobody else need try. (pp. 146-47)

> *Alexander L. Taylor, "—And What Alice Found There," in his* The White Knight: A Study of C. L. Dodgson (Lewis Carroll), *Oliver & Boyd, 1952, pp. 117-47.*

DEREK HUDSON

Lewis Carroll finished writing *Alice's Adventures Under Ground* some time before February 10th, 1863, and soon afterwards sent it to his friend George MacDonald for his opinion. Mrs MacDonald read the manuscript to her assembled family with such success that the verdict was not in doubt. On May 9th, 1863, the author noted that they wished him to publish it.

So much is clear from the diary. But [Canon Robinson]

Illustration from Alice's Adventures in Wonderland.

Duckworth maintained that Henry Kingsley saw the manuscript at the Deanery, and that it was Kingsley's advocacy—to which Duckworth added his own (coupled with a warm recommendation of John Tenniel as the illustrator)—that induced Dodgson to decide on publication. Both Kingsley and Duckworth presumably gave advice at some point, but as it stands, this account is open to doubt; for Dodgson himself embarked on the slow process of illustrating his original manuscript for Alice's benefit, and this took him such a long time that he did not get it done until the autumn of 1864, so that he only sent the manuscript book to Alice at the Deanery on November 26th, 1864.

By that time—and after much consultation with many people—several things had happened. Dodgson had enlarged the 18,000 words of *Alice's Adventures Under Ground* into the 35,000 words of his famous book; and John Tenniel had read it, had consented to draw and was well advanced on the illustrations.

Two distinct undertakings were therefore in progress, and were overlapping. Mr Dodgson was painstakingly decorating the shorter manuscript as his private present for Alice Liddell—the *"Ur-Alice",* as the Germans would call it—and John Tenniel, working on the enlarged version, was making the professional illustrations which all the world knows and which will never be bettered. . . . Though increasingly busy with his work for *Punch,* Tenniel was still not averse to undertaking the occasional illustration of books, especially when he could introduce plenty of animals, which he was particularly good at.

Tenniel had made his name with his drawings for the Rev. Thomas James's version of *Aesop's Fables.* These had conditioned his style in such later commissions as the illustration of Tupper's *Proverbial Philosophy* and Barham's *Ingoldsby Legends.* By the time he came to *Alice,* a dignified and somewhat archaic formalism was ripe for blending with the lighter touch of the *Punch* artist. It is interesting to notice, on looking back, that the girl who is having a letter read to her in Tupper's chapter "Of Writing" is almost a prototype of Alice herself; while the solemn trial scene illustrating Tupper's reflections "Of Estimating Character" is parodied in the comic trial of the Knave of Hearts.

Tom Taylor's recommendation would naturally have predisposed Tenniel in Dodgson's favour, and after reading the text (or parts of it, though one must assume it was virtually complete by now) he announced his willingness to collaborate in April, 1864. Dodgson promptly got into touch with the Clarendon Press at Oxford—whom he had decided should print the book at his expense—and was able to send Tenniel the first "slip proofs" (galley-proofs, they would now be called) as early as May 2nd. It was not until the following year, when many of the drawings were already done, that Dodgson introduced Tenniel to a photograph of Mary Hilton Badcock, daughter of Canon Badcock of Ripon, whom he recommended as an excellent model for Alice. But Tenniel did not like using models. The resemblance to Mary Badcock, not striking in *Alice in Wonderland,* is only slightly more suggestive in *Through the Looking-Glass;* and it is probable that Miss Badcock provided only a small part of Tenniel's inspiration and that he was not less influenced by Lewis Carroll's drawings and by his own preconception of an ideal maiden. (pp. 133-35)

The author went to Macmillan's on [15 July 1865] and "wrote in twenty or more copies of *Alice* to go as presents to various friends"; but on July 20 he was compelled to call again on a less pleasant errand, in order to show Macmillan "Tenniel's letter about the fairy-tale—he is entirely dissatisfied with the printing of the pictures, and I suppose we shall have to do it all again". This drastic decision was, in fact, taken on August 2nd. The first edition was recalled after only forty-eight copies had been sold or (as was largely the case) given away. (p. 137)

Probably only someone as meticulous about the production of his books as Lewis Carroll would have bothered to have the whole work reprinted, though we must remember that the initial complaint came from Tenniel. However, it is gratifying to know that the author was entirely satisfied with the second edition when he received a copy of it on November 9th, 1865, considering it "very *far* superior to the old, and in fact a perfect piece of artistic printing". (pp. 138-39)

In the original manuscript [*Alice's Adventures Under Ground*], we must first grow accustomed to the unfamiliar idea of seeing Lewis Carroll's own illustrations in the place of Tenniel's. As the earnestness of the amateur draughtsman occasionally rises in them to a weird frenzy that is almost Blake-like in its intensity, this is an exciting rather than a disappointing experience; Carroll's drawings, lacking Tenniel's professional accomplishment, could never have assisted *Alice* to a popular success, but, unlike Tenniel's, they are the work

of a poet and have a private anguish which is more moving than it is amusing. They represent a genuine artistic achievement which has never been properly appreciated. (p. 141)

> It will probably be some time before I again indulge in paper and print. I have, however, a floating idea of writing a sort of sequel to *Alice,* and if it ever comes to anything, I intend to consult you at the very outset, so as to have the thing properly managed from the beginning.

Thus Lewis Carroll to Macmillan's on August 24th, 1866, nine months after the successful launching of *Alice in Wonderland.* But he did not propose to start writing his new story until he had obtained a satisfactory illustrator, and he found this difficult. Tenniel was the obvious choice, but Tenniel had thought Dodgson very fussy over *Alice in Wonderland,* and (though that book had vastly increased his reputation) he declared at first that he could not afford the time to illustrate its sequel. . . . By April, 1868, Dodgson was getting anxious, and in that month he made another approach to Tenniel, who still remained adamant and saw no chance of being able to do the drawings till 1870, "if then". Dodgson thereupon enquired of Sir Noel Paton, whose work he greatly admired, to see whether he could illustrate the book—which he was now calling *Looking-Glass House.* Paton pleaded ill-health, and urged, very properly, that "Tenniel is *the* man". W. S. Gilbert was momentarily considered; then a final desperate plea to Tenniel at last brought his consent, and on June 18th, 1868, Dodgson wrote gratefully to him "accepting his kind offer to do the pictures (at such spare times as he can find) for the second volume of *Alice.*

It was not until now that Dodgson systematically embarked on the writing of the book. (pp. 173-74)

> *Derek Hudson, in his* Lewis Carroll, *Constable, 1954, 354 p.*

THE JUNIOR BOOKSHELF

In a letter published in *The Junior Bookshelf,* some time ago, Mr. M. S. Crouch asked, "Must it be Tenniel?" and suggested that new illustrations might shed new light on the two *Alice* books. Mr. Malcolm Muggeridge has said much the same thing in his introduction to the double edition recently illustrated by Mervyn Peake, and indeed, it is a question asked quite often, perhaps because it seems quite logical and is easier to defend than it is to deny. For anyone who can defend such a position is obviously not much personally involved, whereas the Tenniel advocates are invariably involved in a rather emotional way, and therefore too much excited to be logical, let alone convincing. But the very affection that keeps them from putting up a rational argument is a sort of proof of Tenniel's irreplaceability, for few illustrators could rouse that degree of feeling. Certainly none of his successors could . . . . (p. 207)

The text and Tenniel are so closely associated that this is not surprising, nor is it altogether surprising, in the absence of similar cases, that someone should support their separation on what would appear to be undeniably logical grounds. But who has shown better than the author of *Alice* that logic is not all? And what other author has taken such pains to insure that his illustrator should make every creation tally with his own? Not only did Carroll supervise the drawings with unusual vigilance; he also decided upon their place in the text, and the whole format of the book in which they were to appear, making the present standard edition literally the authorised version. Besides this authority, Tenniel had another which is no longer obtainable—that of being a Victorian and a gentleman of the old school. Alice's appeal is timeless, but she is an essentially Victorian child, and like her literary and pictorial creators, saw things from a point of view it would seem impossible to recapture, serene, courteous and un-self-conscious. The pictures show us a real person—the very person who would think and behave like the child in the text; everything is all of a piece.

And Tenniel was a great artist in black-and-white work at a time when such work was seen at its best. His drawings might be championed just to insure that children might still have access to at least one representative of a memorable period, though it has plenty of other qualities to recommend it, strength, sureness, accuracy and humour, all giving the impression he knew just what he wanted to show and how to show it, and that he took great delight in the process. His appeal is always direct, leaving his details to be relished after the central idea is assured, while his style is unmistakable, both in *Alice* and in his cartoons for *Punch,* and eminently "quotable" as has been shown by their frequent use, with telling effect, in many cartoons since his day.

Alice is like a literary Mt. Everest—other illustrators may attempt it, but they must remember that Sir John's flag was there first, and *his* name enduringly linked with her creator's. (pp. 207-08)

> *"Yes, It Must Be Tenniel," in* The Junior Bookshelf, *Vol. 19, No. 4, October, 1955, pp. 207-08.*

BETTINA HÜRLIMANN

[Three Centuries of Children's Books in Europe *was originally published in 1959.*]

The original manuscript [of *Alice in Wonderland*] was illustrated by the author himself and from our present view of the subject we may find it difficult to understand why these illustrations were not used as originals for the finished book (even though Carroll himself referred to them as rough drawings which sinned against every law of anatomy). Perhaps they do, in fact, express a feeling which is too close to that of the text, while John Tenniel, whom Carroll commissioned, brought a fresh approach to the book which served to enrich it even more. He worked exactly to the author's instructions, accepting the crazy story with an objective seriousness as though it were all very normal, and seeking out a little girl to act as his model for Alice just as Carroll had done. In this way he devoted all his sympathies not to building up the nonsensical or grotesque elements of the story but rather its immediately understandable ones. (p. 71)

> *Bettina Hürlimann, "Jabberwocky," in her* Three Centuries of Children's Books in Europe, *edited and translated by Brian W. Alderson, Oxford University Press, London, 1967, pp. 64-75.*

HENRY C. PITZ

Victorian humor had many practitioners but two had a touch of genius: Edward Lear and Lewis Carroll. (p. 36)

Like Lear, Carroll could draw, but not as successfully. He did make pictures for his books, but aware of his limitations, looked for a better artist and found the ideal one. John Tenniel was a good workmanlike illustrator, above average but scarcely inspired. . . . Carroll's texts proved to be an ideal vehicle for his talent. They brought out his best and resulted

in a definitive collaboration. Tenniel's Alice pictures have none of the usual artifices of humorous drawings. Faithfully presenting the situations of Carroll's text in a straightforward technique, they have about them a disarming enchantment that few have been able to resist. Carroll's and Tenniel's Alice is a monument to the neglected side of Victorianism, the deep well of laughter behind the portentous facade. (p. 38)

> *Henry C. Pitz, "England after 1800," in his* Illustrating Children's Books: History—Technique—Production, *Watson-Guptill Publications, 1963, pp. 31-50.*

BRIAN ROBB

At first sight the *Alice* books seem to stand as far outside time as the pyramids or a Gothic cathedral, and to be just as anonymous. Partly this is because of the reticence of Victorian biographers and diarists, and partly because Carroll and Tenniel seem to have shared a faculty for disappearing into the grey middle-class Victorian background. Which leads one to think that it was in fact perhaps only because they were both completely submerged in the pattern of their age that they were able to give such vivid expression to its fantasy life; to represent the innermost thoughts of the Prince Consort's era as accurately as Rowlandson had done the outer life of the Prince Regent's; or to complement Frith, the Pre-Raphaelites, the Great Exhibition, and the photographs of Octavius Hill, rather in the same way as the Brighton Pavilion had complemented the Battle of Waterloo. (p. 310)

After a few months' study at the R. A. Schools and some more on his own, [Tenniel] had, while still in his teens, begun life as a painter of the historical romantic pictures then in vogue. His first illustrations proper were made when he was twenty-one years old, but he continued to work both as painter and illustrator until nine years later he joined *Punch,* in place of Dicky Doyle. His first two formative influences seem to have been the art of the German painter Cornelius, which he saw during a trip to Munich to study fresco technique for a mural painting commissioned for the new House of Lords; and that of the first phase of the Pre-Raphaelite Brotherhood, itself a German derivative, which formed in 1848 when Tenniel was approaching thirty.

When he joined *Punch,* which was about nine years old and still under the editorship of Mark Lemon, these influences were reinforced by the infusion of lighter elements borrowed from Dicky Doyle and John Leech. Combined they form the bold, honest, literal, thorough, solid style we find in the *Alice* pictures. And if the results sometimes seem rather wooden, this is no doubt partly due to the transmutation of his pencil drawings by the Dalziel brothers, skilful engravers though they were. . . .

He is thus in effect a kind of Pre-Raphaelite comic illustrator, though he failed to follow Pre-Raphaelite precept by working directly from nature. 'Mr Tenniel', says Carroll, 'is the only artist who has drawn for me who resolutely refused to use models, and declared he no more needed one than I should a multiplication table to work a mathematical problem'. Tenniel's procedure was, whatever Carroll may have thought, time-honoured for artists working in his particular genre. It presents however the danger of leading to clichés in drawing, and these Tenniel failed sometimes to avoid. But with animals, prodigies, or monsters he is a master. They have rather the same charm, the same freshness and simplicity, and the same surprising ability to believe in themselves, as Carpaccio's lions, dogs, and dragons; though more robust, and in form perhaps more redolent of the inventions of Hieronymus Bosch.

For Carroll's text quite translated Tenniel, and his illustrations to the *Alice* books raise him to a creative height he never approached on his own. From this it might seem logical to suppose that a more imaginative artist might in his shoes have achieved even more remarkable results. But the failures of the many other talented illustrators who have tried their hands with *Alice* have in my opinion proved this theory to be fallacious. Tenniel's unique qualification lay, it seems, in his detachment as a recorder; in a dispassionate attitude to the irrational that triumphantly brings out the demonic logic of his author. It is for this reason that I feel that, taken as a whole, the marriage was uniquely successful; and that better illustrations in the strict sense than Tenniel's to the *Alice* books do not exist.

Nor can I agree with those who maintain that he ought to have portrayed Alice herself with more sympathy, or as Carroll would have liked, more prettily. She is, as she so clearly ought to be, a serious little girl, as intent as we are on what goes on around her, from which she never, like so many illustrators' heroines, distracts our attention with irrelevant charm, fluffiness, or egocentric mannerism. Anxiously we follow her through the mirror in the overmantel; share her amazement as she talks to a leg of mutton, listens to a tiger-lily, or looks at the faces of roses which seem to be prim cousins of flowers by Chagall, Odilon Rédon, or Dicky Doyle. Practical and sensible, she is in fact the ideal travelling companion throughout two hazardous but rewarding journeys; and which of us would not welcome the opportunity to accompany her on a third? (p. 311)

> Brian Robb, "Tenniel's Illustrations to the 'Alice' Books," in The Listener, *Vol. LXXIV, No. 1900, August 26, 1965, pp. 310-11.*

JOHN DAVIS

Tenniel's illustrations for *Alice's Adventures in Wonderland* are a perfect example of the combination between artist and author and to many they are inseparable. Perhaps Tenniel's weakness, if any be admitted, is in his drawings of Alice herself who frequently appears overly serious and expressionless. But he must be placed unequivocally as one if not the greatest of the many illustrators of Alice. (p. 8)

[With *Through the Looking-glass;* once] again Tenniel had excelled himself with fifty illustrations compared with the forty-two in *Wonderland.* Again his mastery of animals and humans was apparent and in this book, his drawings of Alice seem softer and less wooden; his interpretation and technique both superb, his Jabberwock is suitably fearsome whilst the original frontispiece of the White Knight seems to have an echo of Durer in both composition and print quality. It is interesting, too, that the pictures of Alice entering and emerging from the looking-glass appear on subsequent pages, as if her entry into wonderland was happening in the book, itself. The combination of artist and writer seems more satisfying in this, than in the preceding work, and is perhaps best described in the words of one of Tenniel's biographers who said that there may be better drawings but no better illustrations. (p. 9)

[Lewis Carroll] should be regarded as the first illustrator of *Alice in Wonderland* as his original manuscript for Alice Lid-dell included many of his own sketches. . . . It is understandable that these drawings lacked appeal to the upper middle class children's readership of the nineteenth century whose taste was largely dictated by their parents. However, Carroll's drawings warrant reassessment now that technical accuracy in presentation is no longer held in such high esteem. In their way they have a soul which is lacking in those of Tenniel and are much more moving. (p. 10)

> John Davis, in an introduction to The Illustrators of Alice in Wonderland and Through the Looking Glass, *edited by Graham Ovenden, Academy Editions, 1972, pp. 7-14.*

WELLERAN POLTARNEES

I want to like Tenniel's illustrations for *Alice in Wonderland.* I want to succumb to the general fondness in which they are held. Choosing carefully, I look at the Cheshire Cat—wonderful, diabolical two-faced catness. The White Rabbit and the Dormouse sleeping with his head tucked down do not offend, but the March Hare is wooden, hardly capable of knocking over a milk jug. The misshapen forms of the Duchess, and the various natural and unnatural creatures are well drawn, but stiff. Look at Alice herself. She is the dreamer. Our first thought is that she deserved every nasty moment of that nightmare and none of the fun. A permanent frown relaxes occasionally into petulant dissatisfaction. Her eyes are hard, not truly fearing because they do not believe, and she does not appear to wonder at wonderland, but only to disapprove in varying degrees. Alice's eyes rarely look at what they are supposed to be looking at. She actually looks under the Mock Turtle's paw and into the distance. She looks not at the bottle that says "Drink Me", but at a point on the floor somewhere to the left, behind the table. Hers is not the face of a little girl, but the face of a young woman forced to this ignominious role by a domineering and somewhat pathological parent. Lewis Carroll himself complained that Tenniel's Alice was out of proportion and attributed it to Tenniel's refusal to use a model. This failure to picture the central character, the character whose innocence and vulnerability should balance the madness of the story, is disastrous to the sum of Tenniel's effort. The illustrations, with their failures of draughtsmanship, and, more importantly, lack of proper spirit, do not serve well a story which by its audacity and inventiveness forces itself into the vanguard of children's literature.

> Welleran Poltarnees, in an excerpt in his All Mirrors Are Magic Mirrors, *The Green Tiger Press, 1972, p. 17.*

ERIC S. RABKIN

Today, of course, we view Tenniel's drawings as strongly related to his political satire, which they certainly are. But in his own day, other aspects of his work would have been immediately noticeable. Carroll is [a] most thoroughgoing fantasist . . . . Just as satire implies a move to the right on the continuum of the fantastic when examining works within a single super-genre, so the use of satire is one of the qualities that makes the *Alice* books Fantasies. Tenniel, of course, creates a fairy tale world, or something even a bit more fantastic than that, with such pictures as those of the Cheshire cat disappearing into his own grin. But Tenniel, like Carroll, goes further. The Pre-Raphaelites, by reversing qualities of lighting, for example, created fantastic pictorial worlds. A glance at Millais' *Sir Isumbras at the Ford* (1857) will remind us of this. A glance at the White Knight in the frontispiece to *Through the Looking Glass* will reveal immediately that Tenniel, by further exaggerating Pre-Raphaelite conventions, was not only creating a fantastic world, but like Carroll, directly satirizing such contemporaries as Millais.

As in fiction, so in painting, we see that a consideration of the uses of the fantastic gives us insights that complement those resulting from normal analytic methods. More important than that, however, since these insights are based on micro-contextual structural variation, they can be translated from one medium to another and we can with justice decide, for instance, whether Tenniel is more or less successful than Carroll, although they did not work in the same materials. [Author's footnote: In my own estimation, Carroll is the more successful. The conventions of political cartoon satire were clear in Tenniel's day, and he works within them, reversing, exaggerating, and inventing when he can. Carroll takes foregiven conventions, reminds us of them, and reverses them, only to reverse again the results. Tenniel's illustrations work wonderfully with Carroll's text, but would be of decidedly less interest alone; Alice is alive in the very words. Hers is the primary fantastic world.] And perhaps most important, the pervasive utility of the fantastic in approaching so many realms of art strengthens our hypothesis that the fantastic represents a basic mode of human knowing, something much broader than the disciplines of criticism, literary history, or art history alone. (pp. 203-05)

> Eric S. Rabkin, "The Scope of the Fantastic," in his
> The Fantastic in Literature, *Princeton University*
> *Press, 1976, pp. 189-228.*

MICHAEL PATRICK HEARN

[With his illustrations for the 1907 Heinemann edition of *Alice's Adventures in Wonderland,* Arthur Rackham] did not intend to replace Tenniel. He had great respect for the celebrated *Punch* cartoonist and admitted that he found the art for the original *Alice in Wonderland* "work which I take to be as nearly ideal in the way of children's picture-books as anything ever achieved." In his own drawings Rackham paid homage to Tenniel's contribution. In a Christmas issue of the pictorial weekly *Black and White,* Rackham drew a cartoon in which adaptations of Tenniel's depictions of Alice and the Wonderland and Looking-Glass characters dominate a book party celebrating favorite childhood illustrations. . . . And among the figures dancing around a calendar drawn by Rackham for *Punch's Almanac for 1907* are Alice and the White Knight, who bears a striking resemblance to Tenniel himself.

Rackham clearly recognized the historical importance of Tenniel's mid-Victorian woodcuts. The new Heinemann edition proposed in part to provide in color what Tenniel could only have done in black and white. . . . Certainly Rackham's edition was designed not to knock Tenniel's off the nursery shelf but to give a new dress to an old favorite.

The public's response was mixed. Although acknowledged as "*the* gift book of the season," Rackham's *Alice in Wonderland* was among the more controversial offerings of the year. Some reviewers found the new work an uninvited invasion of their private nurseries; one noted that to reillustrate Carroll in a contemporary style one might likewise rewrite the text. Not everyone was offended, however. One correspondent assured Rackham, "Your delightful Alice is alive and makes Tenniel's Alice look like a stiff puppet." The most damaging comment came from *Punch,* the humor weekly that had published so much of Tenniel's original work. In a cartoon, "Tenniel's 'Alice' Reigns Supreme" by E. T. Reed, the many new conceptions of Alice are paraded before the original, and at the appearance of parodies of Rackham's characterizations, Tenniel's cries, "Curiouser and curiouser!". (pp. 32-5)

Rackham admittedly was not completely divorced from Tenniel's work. Every illustrator who has attempted to picture *Alice in Wonderland* has had in part derived some inspiration from the original depictions. So closely did Carroll work with Tenniel (at times to the point of bullying him) that his pictorial conceptions developed from conversations and correspondence with the author. Carroll in his text gives little to help the artist. His narrative is strikingly free of descriptive passages; unlike that of his many contemporaries, Carroll's style is surprisingly bare of adjectives. The most detailed description of a figure is that of "a large blue caterpillar, that was sitting on top with his arms folded, quietly smoking a hookah." For the more unusual characters (the Mad Hatter, the March Hare, the Mock Turtle) Carroll tells nothing of their physical appearance; the reader is completely dependent on the artist's renditions.

Carroll recognized the value of illustration in a child's book and consciously used them to supplement his prose. For example, in referring to the way the King of Hearts wears his crown upon his wig while in court, he suggests that the reader "look at the frontispiece if you want to see how he did it." He advises at another point in the story, "If you don't know what a Gryphon is, look at the picture." This suggestion is obviously his answer to anyone who wishes to know what a Mad Hatter or a March Hare or a Mock Turtle might be.

The reader learns what each is, not through Carroll's text, but through Tenniel's drawings. Rackham's Hatter and Hare are actually Tenniel's conceptions transformed into characteristically Rackham grotesques; they remain basically the same as the originals, down to a notation on the Hatter's hat. (p. 36)

What crucially differentiates the two artists is that each figure in the Rackham drawings is individually depicted, each with his own expression, while Tenniel's are not. Rackham's characters react. This distinction is nowhere more apparent than in the pictures of Alice herself. Tenniel's child is indeed a stiff puppet. In the drawing of Alice and the pig, for example, the figure stands expressionless as if to deliver a speech and holds the animal as if it were a prize ham. Rackham's Alice must struggle to keep a grip on the squirming creature. Rackham has instilled a rather conventional scene with his own drama. (p. 37)

The result of Rackham's labors is a remarkable interpretation of the Carroll classic. He lovingly embellished the volume with an understanding expressed by no other artist—no other artist except Tenniel. Rackham was certainly restricted in illustrating a story conceived in both word and picture as a unit. Carroll and Tenniel together kept in mind Alice's question, "What was the use of a book without pictures or conversations?"

Tenniel must remain the perfect artist of *Alice in Wonderland,* because he was the first. By being the author's choice, he received inspiration and encouragement not always evident in the actual text. No matter how fine Rackham's art is, it cannot replace the original illustrations. Rackham's edition is a magnificent contribution to the illustration of children's books, but it must remain supplementary to the original. (p. 38)

Michael Patrick Hearn, "Arthur Rackham's Adventures in Wonderland," in Lewis Carroll Observed: A Collection of Unpublished Photographs, Drawings, Poetry, and New Essays, *edited by Edward Guiliano, Clarkson N. Potter, Inc., 1976, pp. 31-44.*

DONALD RACKIN

Some may argue that . . . a grim interpretation of **Alice in Wonderland** and the book's undeniably funny atmosphere do not square. But laughter is by no means reserved for optimistic, sunny views of the world. Indeed, there is considerable evidence that nineteenth-century critics and taste-makers were keenly aware that laughter often arose from a perception of the world's disorder, discontinuity, disunity. Thus many of them stressed the view that laughter was not essential to humor, only to wit. For they saw humor as "natural, emotional, vital, organic, and in touch with the universal, and wit as artificial, impersonal, mechanical, and presumably imprisoned within finitude. . . ." This dichotomy suggests another comic tension in **Alice in Wonderland:** the tension between humor and wit, between the essentially warm, sympathetic amusement of the narrator, a humor that dissolves and merges apparent incongruities, and the rather cold, unsympathetic wit of the adventures themselves, full of inhuman and never-ending incongruities. (p. 7)

Twentieth-century black humorists have created a whole body of comic work based on grim underground visions of mankind's absurd condition. . . . Indeed, contemporary comedy is sometimes directly indebted to **Alice in Wonderland:** an excellent example is Chapter 36 of Joseph Heller's **Catch-22,** a clearly deliberate adaptation of the trial scene at the end of **Wonderland.** That these post-Freudian writers are usually fully conscious of what they are doing with comedy and that the Victorian Carroll probably was not is of little concern here.

This is not to say, however, that Carroll was completely unaware of the sort of comedy he was producing. Examination of his original illustrations for *Alice's Adventures Under Ground* indicates that at some imaginative level he certainly sensed the true quality of that comedy. Unfortunately, most modern readers picture only Tenniel's illustrations when they summon up graphic memories of the **Alice** books. And those delightful illustrations have become so integral a part of the literary experience we call "Alice," that Tenniel's rendition of the adventures has become for many the "official" one. This is a pity because Carroll's illustrations—spontaneously naïve as they are—offer a far better companion for both the original and the published text. They do so mainly because they better reflect the Wonderland horror-comedy that I have been outlining, a horror-comedy that genuinely resides in those texts. Thus Tenniel's illustrations, good as they are, might well be considered a kind of sugaring over of the threatening implications of the text, the way many daytime reconstructions of nightmares sugar over the nightmares' worst episodes. Like the shift in titles from "Under Ground" to the rather innocuous "Wonderland," this shift from Carroll's often horrifying illustrations to Tenniel's more comfortable ones fails, of course, to dispel the permanent horrors that reside in the very depths of Carroll's comic fantasy. (pp. 7-8)

Carroll's drawing [of the Queen of Hearts] (the last in *Under Ground*) possesses an eerie disquieting power not at all present in the rather tame, gentle, contained comedy of Tenniel's [drawing of the King and Queen of Hearts]. Although Carroll is obviously no accomplished draftsman, his picture displays something of a natural poetic talent (reminiscent of D. H. Lawrence's pictures). Here is a case of a very competent professional illustrator in contrast to the true amateur. Moreover, Carroll's illustration gains in intensity from its intimate physical relationship to its text; Tenniel's, on the other hand, stands in a formal separated relation to the text (as do all of Tenniel's other illustrations in the first edition). One might say that Carroll's pictures (like Blake illuminations) often grow out of the adventures; Tenniel's merely illustrate them. (pp. 8-11)

[To contrast] *Under Ground's* Mock Turtle and Gryphon with their Wonderland counterparts: In Wonderland they are thoroughly ridiculous, while underground they seem possibly menacing. In any case, Tenniel, quite famous for his animal cartoons, deftly reveals the patently *artificial* (and therefore unthreatening) nature of these mythical creatures: the oxtail and bovine head reveal the true mock nature of the imitation soup—and the false sentiment of the turtle himself, large as he is. [The illustration] from *Under Ground,* with Alice so small in comparison to the creatures, contrasts sharply with the *pas de trois* of Wonderland in [Tenniel's picture]. Again, Tenniel sugars over the inherent horrors, emphasizing only the joys.

Of course, it is not so simple: some of Tenniel's illustrations could be viewed as a bit disturbing, and one or two might even be considered more disturbing than Carroll's counterparts. But by and large the issue, I think, is clear. Carroll's powerful, spontaneous illustrations fit perfectly the spirit and meaning of his comic nightmare. (p. 12)

Donald Rackin, "Laughing and Grief: What's So Funny about 'Alice in Wonderland'?" in Lewis Carroll Observed: A Collection of Unpublished Photographs, Drawings, Poetry, and New Essays, *edited by Edward Guiliano, Clarkson N. Potter, Inc., 1976, pp. 1-18.*

RODERICK F. McGILLIS

In Sir John Tenniel's illustration of the meeting between Alice and the Queen of Hearts in Chapter eight of **Alice's Adventures in Wonderland,** the Queen pointing an accusing finger at Alice, and Alice standing resolute with folded arms, occupy the centre of the composition. The King of Hearts, other kings and queens, and an array of lesser courtiers stand behind the Queen and Alice. To the right and holding a crown on an enormous cushion is the Knave of Hearts, while tucked behind him and only partially visible is the White Rabbit. We see the Rabbit's torso and legs from the rear; he is turned away from the action and the court. Why does Tenniel draw the White Rabbit with his back to the King and Queen? The Rabbit is superfluous to the scene; he does not appear in Carroll's own illustration of this incident. Why does Tenniel choose to depict the White Rabbit turning away from his superiors, and why does he place him in conjunction with the Knave of Hearts who appears here as the self confident court playboy? At least three answers are possible: 1) Tenniel is merely mystifying, teasing the reader with unexpected detail; 2) he is drawing attention to the Rabbit's excessive diffidence; or 3) he is providing not only another joke, but also a searching and possibly subversive comment on the social and sexual concerns of Carroll's story for children. The

A letter from Tenniel to Carroll about Through the Looking-Glass.

third possibility is the most interesting and reasonable, including, as it does, the first two.

The illustration examines all the ambiguities in the book. In it Tenniel faithfully visualizes Carroll's scene while commenting on it, and what he reveals is a complex of social, sexual, and solipsistic themes that run throughout the book. Social hierarchy is implicit in the court, sexual matters lurk in the nursery rhyme that speaks of a knave stealing tarts, and the dangers of solipsism are ever apparent in a land where everyone talks to himself. The turned rabbit implies all three: he is a hanger on at court, he is a rabbit, and he turns away from everyone at a moment of drama. This illustration is the most striking example of Tenniel's interpretive ability.

The Tenniel-Carroll relationship is well known, and it is clear that the artist often chafed under the determined direction of the author who "so far as possible, used the artist as if he were a piece of machinery hired for the purpose" [in the words of Roger Lancelyn Green]. But Tenniel too was a perfectionist, as his demand for the withdrawal of the first issue of *Alice's Adventures in Wonderland* indicates. Considering Carroll's fussy inspection of the illustrations, I find it difficult to believe with Alexander Taylor that Tenniel "had not the smallest inkling" of Carroll's "real purposes." Tenniel faithfully refashioned twenty of Carroll's original drawings and added twenty-two of his own. His success derives from his ability to preserve his artistic independence while at the same time to adhere meticulously to Carroll's instructions. A set of illustrations which perfectly complement the text is the result.

Tenniel's eye for Wonderland detail is sure: he puts a handkerchief in Alice's pocket, a simian among the creatures that come out of the pool of tears, a bite in the Hatter's teacup, and bootjack by the Lobster's dressing table. He also follows the spirit of the book by providing visual jokes: his court clerks are a parrot, an eagle and a raven, and each of them sleeps in the second last illustration in the book. He reverses

the size of the trumpet and scroll in his depiction of the White Rabbit in Chapter eleven, and he gives the Duchess a huge v-shaped headdress. It may be that Tenniel also followed Carroll in parody: his Duchess and baby are a grotesque mother and child, and his Alice with her unkempt hair and pouting lips is a witty rendering of the Pre-Raphaelite beauty. Stylistically, Tenniel's illustrations are similar to Carroll's prose, literal and solid. The clarity of outline counterparts the dream atmosphere and is the pictorial version of the matter-of-fact manner in which Alice reacts to Wonderland. Alice may be puzzled at what she sees, but of what she sees there can be no mistake. Tenniel's depiction of flowers and foliage, his depiction of characters, and his depiction of Alice are Pre-Raphaelite in tone, although his details and characters are without the moral and spiritual significance of much Pre-Raphaelite work. Tenniel's wit is to dispassionately and meticulously record Carroll's nonsense.

Both writer and illustrator are Pre-Raphaelite in another sense: they surprise our conventional expectations. *Alice in Wonderland* is a miniature epic in structure: Alice's journey occupies twelve chapters and takes her, in Chapter six, to the underworld of the Duchess's kitchen where she meets this book's Tiresias, the Cheshire Cat, who tells her how to get "somewhere or nowhere." Carroll overturns the conventions: his garden is anything but Paradisal; his Phaeacians, the Hatter and the Hare, are anything but hospitable; his Victorian innocent is anything but innocent; and his heroine cannot order her environment. Tenniel's illustrations also play with convention: the organization of his compositions is classic, controlled by geometric lines—triangles, ovals, horizontals—but his subject is absurd rather than grand. The elegant eighteenth-century facade to his illustration of the Frog Footman and Fish Footman is rendered ridiculous by the visual comedy of the subject. Form and content are not so much one as they are mediations, the one counterpointing the other. Tenniel transcends classical limits, just as Carroll transcends those writers he parodies or adapts. Tenniel also transcends Carroll's strictures and creates a focus for the reader.

Tenniel's illustrations provide a structure of meaning for the reader largely through his depiction of Alice. He clearly perceives the ambiguous innocence of Carroll's Victorian child. Critics have criticized Tenniel for depicting an "overly serious" Alice, an "expressionless" Alice, or better yet, an "adult" Alice, but none have considered Tenniel's motive. Depicting children as adults is, in part, Victorian convention, as a look at Thackeray's little Betsinda dancing before the king and queen of Paflagonia (she even has a cleavage) or at some of John Leech's children will show, but Tenniel also strikes just the right note. His Alice is not an adult, but she often tries to look like one precisely because an adult is what she wants to be. This, in large part, accounts for the melancholy and the humour of Carroll's narrative: we see a little girl willing away her childhood. Tenniel's illustrations show Alice for what she is, a young girl aggressively asserting her social identity. She can be polite and deferential as in her meeting with the caterpillar; she can also be rude and malicious as in her treatment of the mouse. (Tenniel draws Alice and the mouse pulling away from each other in the pool of tears.) Tenniel subtly draws our attention to Alice's brutality in his illustration of Alice and the enormous puppy in Chapter four. The text tells us Alice "dodged behind a great thistle", but Tenniel by aligning Alice's outstretched hand grasping the "little bit of stick" with protruding spikes of thistle and by drawing Alice in extreme profile so that her face is hidden has given us a figure who could as easily be enticing the unsuspecting puppy into the thistle as warding him off. Tenniel's Alice squeezed into the Rabbit's house looks an angry giantess; Alice at the March Hare's table is a graceless intruder; and Alice knocking over the juror's bench in the trial scene is a nonchalant disturber. Tenniel's illustrations show us a self-assured little girl with a strong sense of self-importance. Just as there is a realm of chaos lurking beneath our waking obeisance to the reality principle, so there is a dark side to this prim Victorian ingénue. Tenniel is clear about this; what he is less forthright about is Alice's fear of sexuality.

I do not wish to overstate Alice's savagery, nor her sexual fears, but I cannot agree with Donald Rackin who attempts to desexualize the *Alice* books. I do agree that the Freudian and Jungian approaches are often dubious and ludicrous, and my own concern is not to see Alice as penis or vagina, animus or anima, mother or father, but to consider her as a little girl trying to grow up. Unavoidably linked with growing up is a concern for social and sexual identity, and these two concerns are on Alice's young mind, which we see turned inside out as she sleeps beside her sister. The White Rabbit is central to Alice's social desires and sexual fears. Rackin argues that the White Rabbit is a potential sexual symbol whose potential remains buried beneath "his waistcoat and watch and his debilitating fear." This is what Carroll would like us to believe.

To the child eye a rabbit is harmless and attractively soft . . . . Carroll's White Rabbit is also meek. He is, in Carroll's own estimation, "nervously shilly-shallying," "timid," and "feeble." Representing gentility and class, the White Rabbit demonstrates the insecurity of social status. He fears the instability of his position at court, and neurosis follows. His voice quavers and his knees quiver with fear that he may upset the Queen of Hearts. In the trial scene near the end of the book the White Rabbit reminds us of an unsure Osric obsequiously "smiling at everything that was said".

The White Rabbit is sensitive to the problem of social identity. Smartly dressed in waistcoat, collar, and tie, he is a Victorian gentleman complete with country estate and aristocratic associations. This gentlemanly White Rabbit arouses Alice's curiosity. In Tenniel's depiction of him at the beginning of chapter one he presents both reader and Alice with an invitation to descend; the diagonal line of the Rabbit's ears and umbrella counters the horizontal of his watch and the flower on the right and leads the eye downward. The details that Tenniel emphasizes and that Alice notices are the accoutrements of wealth. Tenniel's Rabbit here is a portly well-to-do gentleman, the ideal of mid-Victorian England. And it is this, Carroll stresses, that arouses Alice's curiosity; the fact that the Rabbit talks is not "*very*" remarkable," but the watch and the waistcoat, emblems of wealth and status, lead her down the rabbit hole. She burns with curiosity!

Alice's main interests in life include social status and material wealth. She is a little girl with grown-up pretensions. Anxious to show off her learning and her breeding, she recalls her lessons in Latitude and Longitude and she ludicrously tries to curtsey to an imaginary lady while she is falling in mid air. This "curious child," Carroll tells us, is fond "of pretending to be two people": both child and adult. From adults she has learned to give herself good advice and to box her own ears, but the natural child in her often disobeys. Her child-self cries in despair at her inability to enter the garden, and her adult-self scolds her child-self for being so silly. The sight of the finely dressed Rabbit, who reappears at this moment, touches at the same time her child and her adult sensibility. The Rabbit is an animal a child can relate to; it offers no obvious threat. The Rabbit also represents all Alice seeks socially in her desire to leave the innocence of childhood. Unfortunately, he unconsciously represents something she fears: sexuality. Alice impulsively associates herself with the White Rabbit; she literally chases him, later picking up his fan and kid gloves only to ruminate on her social status. She certainly does not wish to be Mabel who lives in a "poky little house" and who has no toys.

Later, the White Rabbit has the temerity to mistake Alice for his housemaid, Mary Ann, but Alice slyly remarks: "How surprised he'll be when he finds out who I am!" After entering the White Rabbit's house to fetch his fan and gloves, Alice proves herself a true Victorian; she fills the house, only not with plaster fruit and antimacassars, but with herself. She literally takes over and refuses to allow the man of the house entry. She wants to grow up since she is "quite tired of being such a tiny little thing", but she does not want the vulgarity of sex to intrude into her world of things. But the Rabbit, like the rabbit in the fairy tale "The Rabbit's Bride," expects obedience from the woman in his house, and he sends Bill the Lizard down the chimney in the hope of getting Alice under control. Alice kicks poor Bill up the chimney. She ejects Bill and rejects the sexual responsibility of adult life. Her quest moves not only toward adulthood, but also toward what she believes is an eternal garden, a place of refreshment and repose. Her garden is in her head and is sexually Victorian, a place in which adults are children, at least in sexual matters. She shrinks from adult responsibility and leaves the house.

Alice's changes in size are manifestations of her desires and anxieties; they reflect her quest for identity and they express her wish to grow up. When she is large she is either lonely or she faces aggressive antipathy from "adult" figures, a screaming bird or a squire rabbit. Alice's growth magically expresses her desire to grow up. After falling down the rabbit hole, Alice first looks through a tiny door and sees the loveliest garden imaginable, but the door is locked. The key, presumably that golden key that opens the door of eternity, is within reach and Alice manages to use it. However, she is too large and the door is too small. She drinks the shrinking potion and finds herself in front of the door, but she has forgotten the key. Only if she grows up again can she retrieve it.

The key's association with maturity and sexuality is evident here . . . . (pp. 326-30)

Alice can only grasp the key while grown up and the garden remains inaccessible to her. She may have the key while big, but while small she loses it. Alice cannot enter the garden of her childish imagination since it does not exist; she embarks on a quest to find some means of entry. She tries to grow up. She takes over the Rabbit's house, but rejects that. Then she becomes governess (more likely than mother) when she takes the baby/pig from the Duchess. Tenniel's illustration of Alice holding the pig makes no attempt to depict the ludicrous posture that Carroll describes. Instead, Tenniel pictures her in the attitude of an adult, or of a young girl playing at being an adult. After this incident Alice takes her place at the Mad Tea Party and graduates from this to the Court. She enters the garden not of her childhood fancy, but the garden of what she conceives to be adulthood.

There is ample warning for the reader that she will not like what she finds. The paradox is that Alice can accept neither the adult aspects of the court life (its gamesmanship, its sexual antics, its sentimentalism, its injustice), nor its spirit of play, its liveliness, what the Cheshire Cat calls madness. Her sense of self, which is based on the etiquette of mid-Victorian gentile society, is all important to her. What is pathetic about Alice is not her desire to grow up, but her desire to be proper; she is restrained, polite, and pleased with her grasp of rules of any kind. . . . Alice cannot abandon herself to a place in which the one rule is absence of rules. She is unable to cope with such imaginative freedom since it demands a discipline from within rather than from without. Alice is lost inside her imagination and she finds stability only in the platitudes of leisured upper class life: expensive clothes, fine food, afternoon teas, and hypocritical social niceties. Alice's deepseated conventionality is clear in her recitation of Watt's "The Sluggard" . . . . That such slavish service to social identity is self-concern almost to the point of solipsism is reinforced by Tenniel's illustration of the Lobster in which the Lobster's filaments form an oval with the mirror. This sense of self enclosure occurs in several illustrations, but there are two which strikingly depict the sense of self that isolates: the Caterpillar encircled by the hookah tube, and the book's final illustration in which Alice beats off the pack of cards as they rise up around her and enclose her in a circle of her own making. Solipsism becomes more prominent in *Through the Looking Glass,* but it is not absent from *Wonderland.* Besides the Caterpillar there is the Mock Turtle, whose shell is a concrete manifestation of his self-concern, and the dormouse, who spends much of his time in that most inward of activities, sleep. Tenniel draws attention to the lack of communication between the Wonderland inhabitants. The cook in the Duchess's kitchen (where Wordsworthian domestic ideals stand on their heads) wears a bonnet which hides her eyes and strengthens not only her mean nature, but also her separation

from the others. She grasps her ladle in a clenched fist and turns directly away from the Duchess, baby, and Alice. The gigantic v of the Duchess's head-dress is repeated in the feet and arms of the squealing baby and in the knees and feet of the Duchess, forming a self-contained block. Alice, whose skirt is cut off by the right edge of the illustration, is an intruder who appears to look at the cook (once again she is in extreme profile). Each character group is separate and no two characters look at each other. To the left, the smiling Cheshire Cat knowingly regards this scene of nightmare separation and isolation. Questions of identity, as usual, abound. The baby looks like a baby to Alice, but he turns out to be a pig; the mother is no mother; and Alice is an interloper who assumes the role of nurse. Alice's changes in attitude and her changes in size highlight the difficulty of presenting a stable identity.

The problem the book raises is that of fashioning an identity that is individual and yet communicable and accessible to others. Alice's dream quest leads her to a confrontation between her social vision of herself and her unconscious anarchic vision of human potential. Those critics who see in all this Carroll's tap root to the High Romantics are surely correct, but what Carroll has done in *Alice's Adventures in Wonderland* is to invert the Romantic quest for transcendence of self. The Romantic poet attempts to overcome the pressures of reality, to find gardens within, and consequently he faces the spectre of self-consciousness. His antagonist, once the social self has been overcome, is this very self-absorption which blocks imaginative creativity. The Romantics struggled with social consciousness and self-consciousness . . . . But Alice wishes to avoid the struggle. The "antagonists" of her quest present her, in a richly ambiguous way, with the possibility of imaginative freedom. Rather than submit to the liberating madness of Wonderland, Alice attempts to socialize the zany creatures of her imagination. The Romantic poet escapes from self through a creative outgoing of the self; he seeks to slough off identity. Alice, on the other hand, seeks identity. She is self-concerned and her self-concern is linked with social values. Alice does not try to overcome the reality principle by controlling it; rather she embraces it. Externals control her.

The kernel of pessimism is here, and the curious ending to the story is Carroll's way of disguising the gloom. Alice wakes and runs dutifully in to her tea. The final paragraphs shift the point of view to Alice's older sister and also explain away the terror of Alice's dream by naturalizing (in Wordsworthian fashion) much of the Wonderland adventures. Alice's sister then has a vision of Alice as a "grown woman" who has kept "through all her riper years the simple and loving heart of her childhood". This is a valiant though vain attempt to reinstate Alice into the tradition of the Romantic child. The child becomes poet and the poet carries on [in the words of S. T. Coleridge] "the feelings of childhood into the power of manhood." But the Alice we have seen is no sage or seer blessed. Tenniel's last illustration shows an angry Alice beating at the card people, who return to their inorganic form. The picture shows the disintegration of the dream. Tenniel leaves it there. The return to nature, the vision of the sister are unimportant. They merely confirm that nothing has changed, that the Victorian clichés remain intact.

The Tenniel illustration that we started with brings all of this together and reunites Alice and the White Rabbit in a curious kinship. Both the White Rabbit and Alice stand apart from

Page 12 from the first edition of Through the Looking-Glass.

the others, and Tenniel draws them, one on each side of the Knave of Hearts, to the right of centre and ranged against the King, Queen, and court. Neither Alice's face nor the White Rabbit's is completely visible, but standing back to back they mirror each other, and both turn away from the Knave. Alice's stance, feet set, arms folded decisively, and head turned, suggests defiance. Instinctively, the White Rabbit feels drawn to Alice, confiding to her news that the Duchess is under sentence of execution. Admittedly, action is swift in this dream world and the two are never long together, but Carroll has indicated a point of contact. And later, as the trial of the Knave of Hearts proceeds, the White Rabbit clearly shows contempt for the King of Hearts by politely contradicting him while "frowning and making faces at him as he spoke". Tenniel's illustration indicates the White Rabbit's underlying detachment, his disrespect for the absurdity of court proceedings. His detachment does not compare with the Cheshire Cat's since the Cat has a self-awareness none of the others possess. He has a wholeness enabling him to withdraw completely into himself, and an awareness of his own as well as everyone's absurdity. Such madness frightens. The adult cannot match it and the child cannot understand it. The Cheshire Cat disturbs; the White Rabbit entertains.

But the White Rabbit's Victorian primness amuses everyone except himself. He can dissociate himself from the fury and inanity of the court, from its false front which both Tenniel and Carroll emphasise in their respective illustrations of the Queen above the three prostrate gardeners, but not from his own concern for social position. The White Rabbit is at once a conforming and an anarchic character. Like Alice, the White Rabbit strives to maintain his social identity, and this

endeavour brings him (and Alice) face to face with the falsity of social distinctions and social ritual. The White Rabbit is immersed in the legal chaos and corruption of the trial, with its implications about the profligacy of members of the court, and Alice faces the silly social ritual of the Mad Tea Party from which the Hatter and Hare try to exclude her.

The obvious lie to social pretension, however, is Carroll's use of the deck of cards: from the back all numbers are equal. Tenniel's brilliant use of the features and perspective of the faces on a conventional deck of cards subtly reveals the speciousness of social hierarchy. The flatness of the King, Queen, and Knave along with the rows of cards behind the King and the limbless and headless cards face down in the foreground, remind us, and should remind Alice and the Rabbit, that behind surfaces appearances are all the same. It is a lesson ignored by the two outsiders. Significantly, Tenniel draws the White Rabbit from behind, demonstrating the Rabbit's individuality. But by leaving his pastoral country seat and submitting to court life, the Rabbit compromises his independence. The same is true of Alice, who eagerly desires entrance to the stratified pastoral of the Queen's garden.

Tenniel depicts the garden in this illustration by sketching a few trees behind the rigid row of card courtiers. (These suggest the formality and also the lack of individuality of the courtiers, including the King of Hearts, who is barely distinguishable from the kings behind him.) A fountain rises on the left above the Queen, and a tall hedge which is cut through with a series of inviting arches. The sexual aspects are subtly, but firmly suggested. And that there is a trap for Alice (the little girl) in this garden is implied by the several encircling objects, the dome of the conservatory, the oval hedge, and the small iron fence around the flower bed at the lower left corner of the illustration. This latter object is in a direct line with Alice.

Latent in this illustration is the sexual threat of the adult world. When Alice reaches the garden with its "beds of bright flowers" and "cool fountains" she finds herself in a nightmare of sexual activity where a raging Queen of Hearts continually yells for the decapitation of her male subjects and female rivals, and where a croquet game, as Carroll's own illustration suggests, barely masks free-for-all sexual antics. The Knave of Hearts offends the most; he is an inveterate tart snatcher. Tenniel, by drawing the White Rabbit as a kind of reflection of the Knave, reminds us of the Knave's sexuality, and by drawing him in an ambiguous position he also suggests the vulgarity behind the smarmy, conceited front the Knave presents with his pompous lift of the head and his Errol Flynn moustache.

The organizing lines of the illustration also draw our attention to the *doppelganger* motif Carroll uses. The diagonal formed by the three cards in the lower right corner (which reflect in their facelessness the blank similarity of the court) connects Alice, the Knave, and the White Rabbit. Horizontal lines connect the Queen with Alice. She stands between the outstretched arm of the Queen and the outstretched arm of the Knave; she comes between them. Alice confronts her possible future, a female tyrant and bellicose wife. The King as husband is almost without identity, his hat blending with those of other courtiers behind him. He looks his part: ineffectual. He stands opposite the Knave, but actually between the Knave and the Rabbit. Again, the Knave's sexuality is contrasted with the King's. All the characters stand aside from a centre of sexual images. In the centre of the composition are the blank folds of the King's fur robes, his heart shaped sceptre, and, more emphatically, the Queen's extended finger which is the centre point of the whole illustration. Alice stands resolutely with her back to the Knave as the Queen, guarding her heart, accusingly demands that the Knave of Hearts tell her who the intruder is. He replies with an ambiguous smile. (pp. 330-34)

Roderick F. McGillis, "Tenniel's Turned Rabbit: A Reading of 'Alice' with Tenniel's Help," in English Studies in Canada, *Vol. III, No. 3, Fall, 1977, pp. 326-35.*

EDWARD HODNETT

It is universally agreed that Carroll's books [*Alice in Wonderland* and *Through the Looking-Glass*] are among the special achievements of the English imagination, and Tenniel's drawings come close to illustrating them perfectly. Such agreement is almost unique in the history of English book illustration and is fortified by the fact that it is the vote of both critics and millions of ordinary readers. (p. 167)

Sir John Tenniel is one of the best known of all English book illustrators solely because his drawings are inseparable from Lewis Carroll's immortal *Alice's Adventures in Wonderland* and *Through the Looking-Glass.*

By the time the first *Alice* book appeared, Tenniel's work as a book illustrator was almost over. Except for the second *Alice* book, he was to produce only one more substantial series of illustrations. (pp. 167-69)

Tenniel's best serious illustrations are twenty-two in Shirley Brooks' long-forgotten novel *The Gordian Knot* (1860). They are steel-etchings and realize with a sensitivity foreign to his wood-engravings a diversity of scenes . . . . (p. 169)

If Tenniel had illustrated more books of literary consequence on his own, he would surely have established himself as one of the leaders among book illustrators of his time. But excellent as some of his general work is, except for the etched *Gordian Knot* series, it fails to stand out in the forest of mid-Victorian illustrated books. He remains the *Punch* political cartoonist who illustrated *Alice in Wonderland.* (p. 170)

The tendency to think of John Tenniel's ninety-two illustrations and Lewis Carroll's two *Alice* books as an entity and the illustrations as uniformly excellent makes it difficult to judge them objectively. Let us try to disentangle our impressions.

Alice's Adventures in Wonderland seems more spontaneous, more playful, and more comprehensible to children than *Through the Looking-Glass.* Wonderland contains small and endearing creatures. Strange as the happenings may be, children can understand them. They know what playing-cards look like and can enjoy the make-believe of the cards coming to life without necessarily knowing how to play any card game. With the possible exception of the trial scenes, all the illustrations can be 'read' by any child who understands what in general is supposed to be going on—and to a considerable extent they can still be enjoyed by children too young to follow the events.

Through the Looking-Glass, and What Alice Found There is a more adult, more contrived work with a good deal of Mr Dodgson in it. Relatively few children, or adults, are sufficiently familiar with chess to be able to see the incidents of the dream as moves in a chess game. The *Looking-Glass* material is more verbal than that in *Alice's Adventures* and consists to a great extent of sophisticated word-play. The characters tend to be a contrary, negative lot often bent on belittling Alice. *Through the Looking-Glass* is a study in frustration and inadequacy. Even Alice is dissatisfied when she reaches her goal and becomes a queen. She has not had 'such a nice time' as she says she has had by any means.

The reason for the difference in the two books seems clear. *Alice's Adventures in Wonderland* was spoken extempore on a sunny boat ride to an adoring audience of three children. Though that first version was extended and worked over, the Wonderland narrative retains the flow of free association and oral composition and keeps within the limits of childhood entertainment. The success of *Alice's Adventures* turned Carroll into an author, writing 'another *Alice* book' for a huge heterogeneous market. 'Alice', the seven-and-a-half-year-old child character in the first book, became a convenient unifying device; the real Alice had grown into a remote young lady. The dedicatory verse to Alice at the beginning of *Through the Looking-Glass* and the acrostic verse to her at the end are positively elegiac. Carroll himself is several years older and a celebrity outside Oxford, even as far as America. Though possibly he did not acknowledge it to himself, Carroll's effort had turned into an intellectual exercise with the expectation of an audience of adult readers, very like Mr Dodgson's friends, to savour the deeper meanings.

If we accept this analysis, Tenniel's two series of illustrations fulfil their functions at different levels. The first series was conceived for young children. They can enjoy the designs in *Alice's Adventures in Wonderland*—and so can anyone else—whether or not they have read or understood the book. With only two or three exceptions, every one of the illustrations of the events on the other side of the looking-glass requires some knowledge of the text. At this level Tenniel composed designs of greater substance and complexity, both in subject matter and draughtsmanship, although perforce he dealt with the surface narrative.

The success of Tenniel's illustrations . . . is uneven—the absolutely right designs, such as those of Father William and the White Knight, tend to fill our memories and crowd out the more ordinary ones. But the latter have their usefulness. They answer questions, especially those of young listeners. What does Alice look like? the Dodo? a hookah? the Gryphon? the Red Queen? the Unicorn? The list is long and almost as urgent for adults as for children. But a wide assortment of familiar birds and animals also fills the pages, and children must see them, too. In addition, the strange encounters of the dream sequences introduce fantastic characters and incidents into a scenario that changes so fast it generates a need for visual realization to aid adjustment. Tenniel's precise, literal style was just right for bestowing believability on Carroll's fantasies. Carroll said absurd things with a straight face, and Tenniel supported him without comic exaggeration, just as he illustrated jokes in *Punch*. The illustrations have permanently fused with the dream-tales, which have become one classic, endlessly enchanting to generation after generation of readers, young and old, wandering in the Alicean fields. (pp. 194-95)

Edward Hodnett, "Tenniel in Wonderland," in his Image and Text: Studies in the Illustration of English Literature, *Scolar Press, 1982, pp. 167-95.*

JOSEPH H. SCHWARCZ

[It] must surely be one of the main objectives, and also one of the vexing problems for the artist who takes on Alice, to convey the uncanniness and surreality of her adventures and at the same time communicate the humor inherent in these frightfully delightful experiences. It seems that in order to succeed in this, the artist has first of all to create a gripping Alice, one that the reader will be able to identify with because her appearance will allow him to believe that she was strong enough, and willing, to pass through all these surprising realms. Is not this the secret of Tenniel's achievement? (pp. 96-7)

> Joseph H. Schwarcz, "Modes, Moods, and Attitudes," in his Ways of the Illustrator: Visual Communication in Children's Literature, American Library Association, 1982, pp. 93-105.

MICHAEL HANCHER

The *Times,* the chief newspaper of Victorian England, first reported the existence of *Alice's Adventures in Wonderland* toward the end of an unsigned omnibus review that appeared the day after Christmas 1865. . . .

For the *Times* reviewer, as for other contemporary readers of *Alice's Adventures,* it was not Carroll's text but the set of illustrations by John Tenniel that made the book worth noticing. . . .

In the last century, Carroll's fame as the author of the two *Alice* books has eclipsed that of his artist-collaborator. For a mix of reasons, Lewis Carroll, like Alice herself, has become a creature of popular legend. And yet Tenniel's own contribution to the books is probably as well known as Carroll's—perhaps more widely known, for there must be thousands of persons (children and adults alike) who are familiar with reproductions of some of the drawings, despite never having actually read the text. In a ghostly way, Tenniel retains something of his original precedence over Carroll. (p. xv)

[Tenniel's illustrations for the *Alice* books are] the most famous illustrations in English literature. (p. xvii)

By now Tenniel's illustrations have become perfect mirror images of the world that Alice discovered down the rabbit hole and through the looking-glass. They make up the other half of the text, and readers are wise to accept no substitutes, not even those drawn by Arthur Rackham, certainly not those by Salvador Dali. This parity of word and image, unmatched in any other work of literature, fulfills the rules of symmetry set out in the second of Carroll's two *Alice* books, which is itself a reflection on the first. It also satisfies our modern and Romantic need to see in literature a hall of mirrors that gives no outlook on the world.

Nonetheless, like Alice herself, I can't help wondering if there isn't something of interest to be found on the other side of the mirror, behind (or before) the impassive surface of Tenniel's realistic fantasies. And so, like her, I will venture back and through.

The first discovery to be made on the other side is that things look much the same: Tenniel shared a world of imagery with Alice. In this respect, as in others, the *Punch* career was crucial. It was through a friend on the *Punch* staff, the dramatist and humorist Tom Taylor, that Carroll first approached Tenniel to do the *Alice* illustrations. More importantly, Tenniel's

growing success as the chief cartoonist of *Punch* guaranteed his work the esteem of thousands of middle-class readers.

Like us, Victorian readers would find much of Alice's strange world to be reassuringly familiar. For them, however, the familiarity would not come from having read the books and studied the pictures at age six, or from having been overexposed to the reproduction of Tenniel's images in novel contexts (such as IBM advertisements), but from having been granted frequent previews of Wonderland in images drawn for *Punch* by Tenniel and his colleagues on the staff. (p. 3)

What place does [Alice] have in *Punch*'s England? She plays essentially the same role there as her usual role in the *Alice* books, that of a pacifist and noninterventionist, patient and polite, slow to return the aggressions of others. At the end of June 1864, when he had read Carroll's manuscript but probably had not yet begun drawing the illustrations for *Alice's Adventures,* Tenniel put Alice in the center of a patriotic *Punch* title page (January–June 1864). Only a few days had passed since Palmerston's cabinet had decided, in a narrow but momentous vote, not to intervene against Bismarck in the deteriorating Schleswig-Holstein affair, which had become a war between the German states and Denmark. The decision, which Parliament quickly confirmed, proved Palmerston's earlier vague threats to be empty, but the English public in general greeted it with "relief at having escaped the horrors of war." In this cartoon Tenniel fittingly images that relief in domestic terms. The English cannon stands at the ready, but only to protect the domestic scene; and the British lion is changed from a ferocious agent of war to a noble household pet, suitable to amuse boys or girls.

In decorating that militant animal with the garlands of peace, Alice is much more at her ease than she is later in *Alice's Adventures,* when she confronts the officious Do-Do-Dodgson. But though her demeanor is thus subtly different in the two images, the figure and the posture are essentially the same. Of course no reader in the middle of 1864, when this *Punch* frontispiece appeared, could have recognized Alice in this her first appearance. And by the time, a year and a half later, she finally appeared as herself in *Alice's Adventures,* the old image from *Punch* would have slipped from memory. Yet, like the absent-minded White Rabbit, the Victorian reader might well suppose that he already knew who Alice was. (p. 20)

The established view has been that Carroll's illustrations to *Alice's Adventures under Ground* were not an important influence on Tenniel's drawings for *Alice's Adventures in Wonderland.* The opinion of one of Carroll's early bibliographers, Falconer Madan, has proven influential: "In spite of some inevitable similarities, it may be doubted whether Tenniel derived any ideas directly from this book, though he may have seen it." But it is very likely that Tenniel did indeed see the Carroll illustrations, and, furthermore, that they helped shape his drawings for the book. (p. 28)

[It] is clear that Tenniel was respectful of his pictorial source as well as of the text that he was illustrating. He departs selectively from Carroll's prototype, usually in the interests of greater realism. For a century readers have approved the way that Tenniel creates a realistic counterpart to the fantastic world that Carroll describes. In a few instances, . . . the primitivism of Carroll's drawings hints at subtleties and sophistications more interesting for the modern reader than anything that Tenniel's literalism can express. And Tenniel, needing the space to illustrate the additions that Carroll made to the text of the published version, ignored some of Carroll's drawings, quite possibly on Carroll's own recommendation. One or two of these may be regretted, such as the poignant scene of Alice being left behind by the frightened creatures. But these are exceptional cases. By and large Tenniel improved, as he was supposed to do, upon the model presented by Carroll's illustrations for *Alice's Adventures under Ground.* (p. 34)

Alice's dual requirements for a useful book—"pictures" and "conversations"—are remarkable not only for putting pictures first but also for not mentioning descriptions. Young readers are easily bored by scenic descriptions; Carroll wisely let the pictures that he commissioned from Tenniel do much of his descriptive work for him. Twice in *Alice's Adventures* Carroll refers the reader to an illustration for some descriptive detail—and thereby implies a kind of priority for the illustrations over the text. (In *The Nursery Alice,* outfitted with enlarged and colored pictures to make up for a greatly reduced text, Carroll often interrupts his story to discuss the pictures.) Furthermore, as Richard Kelly has pointed out in a recent essay, the physical appearances of the major characters of *Alice's Adventures* can hardly be guessed from what Carroll says in the text: to visualize clearly how most of them look, the reader must first look at the pictures. Much the same is true of *Through the Looking-Glass.* And of course the text of *Through the Looking-Glass* was written under the influence of the earlier illustrations to *Alice's Adventures,* especially as regards the continuing character and image of Alice.

Granting that Carroll's text and Tenniel's pictures are virtually simultaneous and "about" each other, and also that such mutual reference presupposes not identity but difference, in what general ways does the basic difference reveal itself? And what is the reader to make of any particular difference?

Most generally, and least subtly, illustrations will differ from the text in the matter of narrative emphasis. Even when the scene of the illustration corresponds directly to a specific scene in the narrative—which is usually the case for both Carroll's own illustrations to *Alice* and Tenniel's—the illustration, as an illustration, is foregrounded, and therefore more emphatic than the corresponding passage by itself. By italicizing the passage, so to speak, the illustration heightens it, and distinguishes the whole narrative from what it would be without the illustration. That is why what Hodnett calls "the moment of choice" is so important. Carroll, who knew this, probably chose *which* narrative moments Tenniel was to illustrate, so as to control, himself, the novelties of emphasis that illustrations inevitably bring about.

At the same time, he saw to it that the "point of view" of the illustrations faithfully matched the corresponding point of view of the narration. The omniscient third-person narrator who tells the story of Alice in each book varies his attention from scenes in which Alice is an important protagonist and the main object of our observation, to scenes in which she figures mainly as an observer, and in which the narration foregrounds the things that Alice sees. Tenniel varies his pictorial point of view in a similar way. The contrast of the trial scene and the garden scene—otherwise alike in many details— shows the use of such rhetorical variation. The trial scene is a remarkable scene in itself, something that holds Alice's attention and ours, without Alice's participation. But the power of the garden scene, as narrated and as shown in the illustration, lies in the threat that it poses to Alice—who

properly plays a leading role in the narration and in the picture. (Alice appears and disappears like this in Carroll's own illustrations.) In this respect Tenniel's illustrations "differ" from the text less than do those that Barry Moser produced for the recent and remarkable Pennyroyal Edition of *Alice's Adventures,* where all the illustrations between Alice's falling asleep and her waking leave Alice herself literally out of the picture. (pp. 113-14)

[The] most general aspect of the "style" of the Tenniel illustrations has less to do with Tenniel than with the medium in which he worked, black-and-white wood engraving. The general impression made by the *Alice* illustrations would be quite different if they were chromolithographs, or even hand-colored black-and-white engravings—two other Victorian options. Economics and the sixties vogue for "black-and-white" together determined Carroll's choice of technology, which had its consequences.

As a series of visions in black and white, the Tenniel illustrations inevitably differ from the sometimes colorful details of Alice's dreams. The red chessmen, the red paint on the white roses, the green hedges of the checkerboard landscape, the golden key and the golden crown: Tenniel reduces all of these to combinations of black and white.

And yet the reduction is not a major loss, for color does not saturate Alice's dreams. Scenes are more likely to be "bright" or "dark" than specifically colored. Alice sees "the bright flower-beds and the cool fountains"; or, finding herself in "a little dark shop," she is attracted to "a large bright thing, that looked sometimes like a doll and sometimes like a work-box." In *Alice's Adventures* the Caterpillar may be "blue," the King's crown may rest on "a crimson velvet cushion," and the Queen may turn "crimson with fury," but there are not many other striking details of color in either book. Even "the little golden key"—a much-repeated phrase—is more a nominal formula than a vivid perception; and the red chessmen are easily imagined as their conventional black equivalents— significant because not white. (The Red Queen herself is a transformation of a black kitten.) Carroll's hobby as a photographer may have something to do with the understatement of color in the two books.

If Tenniel's illustrations were brightly colored they would differ more than they now do from Carroll's narrative style, which usually avoids particularizing, and is more conceptual than visual. (pp. 114-15)

The straightforward sobriety of the Tenniel illustrations befits Carroll's deadpan narration of Alice's adventures. What is wonderful about Wonderland is not that the dream is fantastic but that it feels real; and the pictures convey this matter-of-fact actuality as effectively as the text. By contrast, Carroll's own illustrations show the quirkiness of an incredible homemade world.

The Tenniel illustrations differ in content from Carroll's narrative as modestly as they differ in style. Hardly any of the differences involve positive *contradiction* of the text. Most involve either *supplementation* (the addition of details not specified in the text), or *neglect* (the omission of textual details that might be expected to appear within the picture frame), or *selection* (the omission of some textual details by leaving them outside the picture frame).

Tenniel's Duchess exemplifies both contradiction and supplementation. It is a contradiction of the text (noticed by Richard Kelly) for Tenniel to show the Duchess as having a broad and bulky chin: Carroll three times describes it as a "sharp little chin"—one that Alice doesn't want to have pressed onto her shoulder. But Tenniel's rendering of the Duchess's headdress goes beyond or supplements what the text specifies. Indeed, no matter how Tenniel had shown the top of the Duchess's head, he could not have avoided going beyond the description in the text—which is nil. . . . Tenniel had to picture the Duchess's head in *some* way not specifically authorized by the text.

Nonetheless, though supplementation is necessary to illustration, it will be more or less remarkable depending upon how well it jibes with the reader's expectations. Tenniel's basic image of Alice supplements what the text specifies, but it would not have been remarkable for Victorian readers, because it conformed so much to the expected type. . . . The supplementary image of the Duchess, however, is quite remarkable: the reader would have had no reason to expect such grotesquely disproportionate features in a Duchess, even an "ugly" one, nor any outsized headdress, nor indeed any medieval headdress at all. By being unexpected the supplementary image calls attention to itself and raises the question of motivation. Perhaps . . . the image of the Duchess refers to the iconographic tradition of the supposedly hideous duchess Margaret Maultasche. The reference may have been Carroll's idea; or possibly Tenniel was allegorizing on his own hook, greatly elaborating the sole mention of the Duchess as "ugly." (p. 115)

The work of this image as a supplement to the text is more typical than is its work as a contradiction. For aside from the blunt chin that Tenniel gave the Duchess, there are virtually no contradictory images in the *Alice* books. There is, however, another kind of contradiction to acknowledge, not contradiction of the text, but contradiction of another illustration as regards some aspect not mentioned in the text: iconic inconsistency. For example, the White Rabbit, on his first appearance, wears a solid-colored waistcoat; but two chapters later, as he crashes into the cucumber-frame, the waistcoat matches his checked jacket. There are several ways to explain this: the Rabbit changed his waistcoat; Alice changed her dream; Tenniel or Dalziel forgot what the Rabbit was wearing. Similar accounts might explain why the Mad Hatter's bow tie points to the left in three illustrations but to the right in one—or there may just have been some mixup in imposing Tenniel's drawing onto the woodblock, which reverses left/right relationships. Tweedledum's tie even changes style . . . . (pp. 115-16)

The frontispiece to *Alice's Adventures* diverges from the text in a way that might seem contradictory of the text but that is in fact more a matter of selection than of contradiction. Carroll sets the scene for the trial by mentioning "a great crowd assembled about" the King and Queen—"all sorts of little birds and beasts, as well as the whole pack of cards." Tenniel omits most of this from his frontispiece, selecting only the central details; but the reader can imagine the crowd as extending beyond the picture frame.

In fact, Tenniel will often be extremely selective, deemphasizing background and setting altogether, focusing instead on one or two characters. Anne Clark has suggested that this close visual focus matches Carroll's narrative interest: "Both author and illustrator were concerned primarily with characters, and very little with setting. Tenniel's background is rarely more than a little cross-hatching." It is true that many of

Tenniel's illustration of the Jabberwock was originally the frontispiece for Through the Looking-Glass. *After personally conducting an audience-reaction test, which determined that the picture was too frightening, Carroll replaced it with Tenniel's drawing of the White Knight.*

the vignettes are like that: what we see is a character or two at a significant moment of action, with most other details omitted. But Tenniel also drew some fully developed backgrounds—which usually show a good deal more than the narrative specifies. He was likely to enlarge his focus to take into account a distinctive landscape setting, but he could also provide fully detailed genre interiors (for example, the two interiors in the "Father William" series; the scene of Alice and the Sheep in the shop). Most of the illustrations have a moderately close focus, showing enough background detail to anchor the scene.

Not all omissions can be explained as a matter of selective close focus; some result from mere neglect. For example, the jug of milk that the March Hare upsets at the tea-party doesn't show in [the illustration]: it should be there, close to the March Hare and the Dormouse (while moving to take the Dormouse's place, the March Hare "upset the milk-jug into his plate")—not offstage, at the imaginable other end of the table. In most cases, like this one, the detail (usually a minor detail) gets mentioned only several pages away from the narrative moment that the picture illustrates; no wonder that Tenniel and Carroll overlooked it. Even Homer nods.

The frontispiece to *Looking-Glass* is harder to "place" in its narrative than the frontispiece to *Alice's Adventures,* so its fidelity is harder to judge. There is a passage of high sentiment in chapter 8, which frames the moment when the White Knight sings "A-sitting On A Gate," to a tune of his own invention:

> Years afterwards she could bring the whole scene back again, as if it had been only yesterday—the mild blue eyes and kindly smile of the Knight—the setting sun gleaming through his hair, and shining on his armour in a blaze of light that quite dazzled her—the horse quietly moving about, with the reins hanging loose on his neck, cropping the grass at her feet—and the black shadows of the forest behind— all this she took in like a picture, as, with one hand shading her eyes, she leant against a tree, watching the strange pair, and listening, in a half dream, to the melancholy music of the song.

"Like a picture," but not quite like *this* picture; for though the sunlight and shadows are there, Alice is not shading her eyes, not leaning against any tree, and the White Knight is not singing, and the horse is not free to crop grass.

But there is no contradiction if the picture shows a different moment in the story, one close to the moment described above but not explicitly mentioned in the text; this would be a fairly ordinary supplementation. Or the picture may show a later moment that *is* mentioned in the text, the important moment when Alice and the Knight part, soon after the end of his song:

> As the Knight sang the last words of the ballad, he gathered up the reins, and turned his horse's head along the road by which they had come. "You've only a few yards to go," he said, "down the hill and over that little brook, and then you'll be a Queen— But you'll stay and see me off first?" he added as Alice turned with an eager look in the direction to which he pointed. "I shan't be long. You'll wait and wave your handkerchief when I get to that turn in the road? I think it'll encourage me, you see."
> "Of course I'll wait," said Alice: "and thank you very much for coming so far—and for the song—I liked it very much."
> "I hope so," the Knight said doubtfully: "but you didn't cry so much as I thought you would."
> So they shook hands, *and then the Knight rode slowly away into the forest.* [Emphasis added.]

On this reading, what the frontispiece shows at the start of *Looking-Glass* is the end of the relationship between Alice and the White Knight—that is, between Alice and Lewis Carroll—just before Alice grows up and becomes a Queen. Carroll thought this image less threatening than Tenniel's drawing of the Jabberwock, which it displaced from the front of the book, but it represents an equivalent crisis.

There is . . . one strikingly contradictory aspect of the frontispiece: the White Knight's advanced age. However, what that detail contradicts is not what the text says but rather Carroll's conception of the story, communicated privately to Tenniel, which is something else again.

Although in the last analysis neither frontispiece really con-

tradicts the text, both do contain supplementary imagery that is remarkable . . . . (pp. 116-17)

The *Looking-Glass* frontispiece, that is, is a synoptic mirror of the whole book, an emblem of the looking-glass world. And the supplementary details that Tenniel has added to this scene refer to the text just as much as do the images that the passage calls for. Carroll presumably intended the accessories that he does mention to function synoptically. It is hard to say whether the additional details, equally significant, were Tenniel's idea (his elaborating on Carroll's basic conceit) or details that Carroll called for outside the text. (pp. 117-18)

The normal metaphor for the process of illustration, which is the mimetic metaphor of the mirror, may seem especially appropriate for the *Alice* books in all their many symmetries; but the metaphor is flawed, like the mirror itself. Imitation always drifts and differs—a truism as old as Plato. It follows that no illustration can simply "reflect" a text. But it does not follow that text and illustration are fundamentally at odds. Though an illustration cannot copy a text, it can—indeed, as an illustration it must—recreate part of the same world that the text creates.

It has been said that Lewis Carroll liked only a single one of Tenniel's illustrations, the well-known picture of Humpty Dumpty. The story is not convincing; why, if he was so disappointed, did Carroll ask Tenniel to illustrate the second book? But Tenniel's image of Humpty Dumpty, implausibly steadying himself between the impossible backward fall into mere copy and the inevitable forward fall into mere difference, is a happy emblem for the dangerous poise of his creator. (p. 119)

> *Michael Hancher, in his* The Tenniel Illustrations to the "Alice" Books, *Ohio State University Press, 1985, 152 p.*

CHARLES FREY AND JOHN GRIFFITH

Alice offers to readers who are relatively new at the serious study of literature a splendid opportunity to learn respect instead of suspicion for one of the great modes of literature, satire. Satire seems duplicitous and overly sophisticated to some readers who are easily put off by it. But *Alice* provides such genuine delight as well as mystification that such readers may be willing to work with their distrust and modify it. Tenniel's illustrations may be studied in this connection to underline the sense of grotesque vivacity that animates the creatures. We need to ponder why Tenniel drew Alice as he did, making her look somewhat mature and severe. How does Tenniel's version of Wonderland compare to Disney's? Why would Carroll want a political cartoonist to illustrate the book? What qualities in the text are emphasized by Tenniel? Certainly Tenniel's drawings belie the cuteness and sentimentality sometimes associated with Alice and even promoted to some extent by Carroll's own framing commentary. (p. 121)

> *Charles Frey and John Griffith, "Lewis Carroll: Alice's Adventures in Wonderland," in their* The Literary Heritage of Childhood: An Appraisal of Children's Classics in the Western Tradition, *Greenwood Press, 1987, pp. 115-22.*

JOHN ROWE TOWNSEND

Of all Victorian illustrations, those of John Tenniel . . . for the *Alice* books are by far the best known. . . . Many artists have now illustrated the *Alice* books in many styles, but (with the exception perhaps of Arthur Rackham) their efforts seem little more than curiosities. The Carroll texts and Tenniel illustrations are inextricably woven together in the public mind. Alice is Tenniel's Alice as well as Carroll's. (p. 128)

> *John Rowe Townsend, "Pictures That Tell a Story," in his* Written for Children: An Outline of English-Language Children's Literature, *third revised edition, J. B. Lippincott, 1987, pp. 125-42.*

CUMULATIVE INDEX TO AUTHORS

This index lists all author entries in *Children's Literature Review* and includes cross-references to them in other Gale sources. References in the index are identified as follows:

CA: *Contemporary Authors* (original series), Volumes 1-125
CANR: *Contemporary Authors New Revision Series,* Volumes 1-25
CAP: *Contemporary Authors Permanent Series,* Volumes 1-2
CA-R: *Contemporary Authors* (revised editions), Volumes 1-44
CDALB: *Concise Dictionary of American Literary Biography,* Volumes 1-3
CLC: *Contemporary Literary Criticism,* Volumes 1-52
CLR: *Children's Literature Review,* Volumes 1-18
DLB: *Dictionary of Literary Biography,* Volumes 1-78
DLB-DS: *Dictionary of Literary Biography Documentary Series,* Volumes 1-6
DLB-Y: *Dictionary of Literary Biography Yearbook,* Volumes 1980-1987
LC: *Literature Criticism from 1400 to 1800,* Volumes 1-10
NCLC: *Nineteenth-Century Literature Criticism,* Volumes 1-20
SAAS: *Somthing About the Author Autobiography Series,* Volumes 1-7
SATA: *Something about the Author,* Volumes 1-54
TCLC: *Twentieth-Century Literary Criticism,* Volumes 1-31
YABC: *Yesterday's Authors of Books for Children,* Volumes 1-2

Author Index

CUMULATIVE INDEX TO NATIONALITIES

Nationality Index

CUMULATIVE INDEX TO TITLES

Title Index

Title Index

Title Index

Title Index

Title Index

Title Index